Finance
in Canada

Public Finance in Canada

Harvey S. Rosen
Department of Economics
Princeton University

Paul Boothe
Department of Economics
University of Alberta

Bev Dahlby
Department of Economics
University of Alberta

Roger S. Smith
Faculty of Business
University of Alberta

McGraw-Hill Ryerson

Toronto New York Burr Ridge Bangkok Auckland Bogotá Caracas
Lisbon London Madrid Mexico City Milan New Delhi
Seoul Singapore Sydney Taipei

McGraw-Hill
Ryerson Limited

A Subsidiary of The McGraw-Hill Companies

PUBLIC FINANCE IN CANADA

ISBN: 0-07-560417-5

1 2 3 4 5 6 7 8 9 10   GTC   8 7 6 5 4 3 2 1 0 9

Printed and bound in Canada

Care has been taken to trace ownership of copyright material contained in this text. The publishers will gladly take any information that will enable them to rectify any reference or credit in subsequent editions.

Statistics Canada information is used with the permission of the Ministry of Industry, as Minister responsible for Statistics Canada. Information on the availability of the wide range of data from Statistics Canada can be obtained from Statistics Canada's Regional Offices, its World Wide Web site at http://www.statcan.ca and its toll-free access number 1-800-263-1136.

Sponsoring Editor: Gord Muschett
Senior Supervising Editor: Margaret Henderson
Production Editor: Wayne Herrington
Developmental Editor: Daphne Scriabin
Production Co-ordinator: Nicla Dattolico
Cover and Interior Design: Dianna Little
Cover Photo: Canali Photobank, Italy
Typesetter: Bookman Typesetting Co. Inc.
Typeface: Sabon
Printer: Transcontinental Printing

Canadian Cataloguing in Publication Data

Main entry under title:

Public finance in Canada

Includes bibliographical references and index.

ISBN 0-07-560417-5

1. Finance, Public – Canada.   I. Rosen, Harvey S.

HJ793.P82 1998   336.71   C98-931220-8

Contents

PART 3: A FRAMEWORK FOR THE ANALYSIS OF PUBLIC EXPENDITURE   129

Chapter 7: Public Goods   131

Chapter 8: Externalities   152

Preface

A NOTE FROM HARVEY S. ROSEN

The field of public finance has been changing rapidly in recent years. On the theoretical side, one of the main achievements has been to integrate the analysis of government spending and taxing more closely with basic economic theory. A prime example is the literature on optimal taxation, which has attempted to derive prescriptions for government fiscal behavior using standard economic tools, rather than to annunciate a set of ad hoc "principles" for tax design. On the empirical side, the most exciting development has been the widespread application of the tools of econometrics to understanding how expenditure and tax policies affect individual behavior and how the government itself sets its policies.

The results of modern research have been slow in entering traditional texts. This book takes its readers to many of the frontiers of current research. The approach to the material, while accessible to undergraduates, is the same as the approach shared by most economists who are now active in the field.

The development of public finance has not proceeded free of controversy. In this book, disputes concerning both methodological and substantive issues are discussed at length. One reviewer of an early draft of the manuscript warned against displaying too much of the profession's dirty laundry in public. My feeling, however, is that "full disclosure" should apply not only in the market for securities, but also in the market for ideas.

There is some tendency for economic analysis to lose touch with the reality it is supposed to describe. I have tried to avoid this tendency. The relevant institutional and legal settings are described in ample detail. Moreover, the links between economic analysis and current political issues are constantly emphasized.

This book is designed for use in undergraduate curricula as well as graduate programs in public administration. It is assumed readers are familiar with microeconomic theory at the level of the standard introductory course. Because some use is made of indifference curve analysis, a topic that is not covered in all introductory courses, indifference curves are carefully explained in an appendix, which is available on the McGraw-Hill Ryerson Web site. In addition, this appendix provides a brief review of other topics in basic microeconomics, including the supply and demand model and marginal analysis. This review should be adequate to refresh the memories of readers who have been away from microeconomics for a while.

It is hoped that this book will whet readers' appetites to learn more about public finance. To this end, a large number of articles and books are cited within the chapters. A typical citation consists of the author's name followed by the date of publication in brackets. The full reference can then be found by consulting the References section that appears at the end of each chapter. These references vary considerably in technical difficulty; those who wish to pursue specialized topics further will have to pick and choose. Finally, a glossary of key terms appears at the end of the book.

Harvey S. Rosen

ABOUT THIS CANADIAN EDITION

In preparing the Canadian edition of Harvey Rosen's *Public Finance*, our goal was to build on that text's strengths—its modern treatment of the theory of public finance and its thorough discussion of empirical issues. However, in addition to describing Canadian institutions and policy issues, we wanted to extend Rosen's text in three ways.

First, we wanted to provide an integrated introduction to tax and expenditure decisions because we believe that even in a course devoted to public spending students should know something about taxation issues, and vice versa. To this end, we have written a new chapter on spending and taxation decisions (Chapter 5), which could be included in one-semester courses on either taxation or public expenditures. We have also devoted more attention to the financing of expenditures in the chapters on public goods, education, and unemployment insurance. Second, we wanted to provide a detailed treatment of the federal–provincial dimension of the public sector in Canada. The need for greater emphasis on federalism in a Canadian public finance textbook arises because provincial and local governments in Canada play a more important role in taxation and spending than do their counterparts in the United States. To this end, we have moved the chapter on fiscal federalism (Chapter 6) toward the beginning of the book and provided a more detailed treatment of some of the distinctively Canadian aspects of federalism such as equalization grants. We also discuss provincial policies on social welfare, health care, education, personal and corporate income taxes, and sales taxes in the various chapters of the text. Finally, we wanted to provide a detailed treatment of asymmetric information as a source of market failure and of the issues that arise in the provision of social insurance programs because these programs—such as unemployment insurance, medicare, and public pensions—represent a very high proportion of total public spending. To this end, we have written a new chapter on asymmetric information, market failure, and social insurance (Chapter 9) and have incorporated it in Part 3.

While we have worked on the Canadian edition as a team and have provided extensive comments on each other's chapters, Roger Smith was primarily responsible for Chapters 1, 2, and 16 to 24. Bev Dahlby was primarily responsible for Chapters 3, 4, 5, and 7 to 14. Paul Boothe was primarily responsible for Chapters 6 and 15.

The structure of the book reflects the way undergraduate public finance courses are organized at the University of Alberta, where we have one-semester courses on public expenditures, taxation, project evaluation, and welfare economics (at the fourth-year level). The text can be used either in a one-semester course on public expenditures (Parts 1, 2, 3, and 4), or in a taxation course (Parts 1, 2, 5, and 6). It could also be used in a one-semester course covering both taxation and expenditures if the focus is on policy issues (Parts 1, 2 [Chapters 5 and 6], 4, and 6).

Because of the addition of two new chapters and the more extensive treatment that we have given to some topics, such as unemployment insurance and public pensions, we have decided not to include chapters on cost–benefit analysis and government deficits in this text. The former is often covered in other courses specifically on cost–benefit analysis or project evaluation, and the latter is covered in all intermediate macroeconomics courses. There are also a number of other books and texts that deal with these topics. However, for those instructors who want to include these topics in their public finance course, fully revised chapters on cost–benefit analysis and deficit finance are available on the McGraw-Hill Ryerson Web site.

ACKNOWLEDGMENTS

We would like to thank the students in our tax policy courses; colleagues Stuart Landon and Stuart McFadyen, University of Alberta; Ken Battle, Caledon Institute of Social Policy; George Marshall, Department of Finance; Glenn Jenkins, Harvard University; and Bob Young, University of Western Ontario. We are also grateful to Janine Robbins for her research assistance.

Also, we would like to thank the reviewers who offered helpful suggestions on various drafts of the manuscript. Special thanks in this regard go to John

Allan, University of Regina; Richard Bird, University of Toronto; James Davies, University of Western Ontario; Livio Di Matteo, Lakehead University; Diane Dupont, Brock University; Ted Horbulyk, University of Calgary; Hasan Imam, Brock University; Taejong Kim, York University; Doug May, Memorial University of Newfoundland; Kenneth McKenzie, University of Calgary; Tracy Snoddon, Wilfrid Laurier University; Marianne Vigneault, Bishop's University; Terry Wu, University of Regina.

Paul Boothe
Bev Dahlby
Roger Smith

Part 1

Introduction

*P*eople's views on how the government should conduct its financial operations are heavily influenced by their political philosophies. Some people care most about individual freedom, others care more about promoting the well-being of the community as a whole. Philosophical differences can and do lead to disagreements as to the appropriate scope for government economic activity.

However, forming intelligent opinions about governmental activity requires not only a political philosophy, but also an understanding of what the government actually does. Where does the legal power to conduct economic policy reside? What does government spend money on, and how does it raise revenue?

Chapter 1 discusses how political views affect attitudes toward public finance, and Chapter 2 outlines the operation of the Canadian system of public finance. Together these two chapters provide a broad perspective that is useful to remember as we discuss various details in the rest of the book.

Chapter 1

Public Finance and Attitudes toward Government

It shall be lawful for the Queen, by and with the Advice and Consent of the Senate and House of Commons, to make Laws for the Peace, Order, and good Government of Canada, in relation to all Matters not coming within the Classes of Subjects by this Act assigned exclusively to the Legislatures of the Provinces.

–1867 Constitution Act as amended (to 1991)

The year is 1030 BC. For decades, the Israelite tribes have been living without a central government. The Bible records that the people have asked the prophet Samuel to "make us a king to judge us like all the nations" (1 Sam. 8:5). Samuel tries to discourage the Israelites by describing what life will be like under a monarchy:

> This will be the manner of the king that shall reign over you; he will take your sons, and appoint them unto him, for his chariots, and to be his horsemen; and they shall run before his chariots.... And he will take your daughters to be perfumers, and to be cooks, and to be bakers. And he will take your fields, and your vineyards, and your oliveyards, even the best of them, and give them to his servants.... He will take the tenth of your flocks; and ye shall be his servants. And ye shall cry out in that day because of your king whom ye shall have chosen. (1 Sam. 8:11–18)

The Israelites are not deterred by this depressing scenario: "The people refused to hearken unto the voice of Samuel; and they said: 'Nay; but there

3

shall be a king over us; that we also may be like all the nations; and that our king may judge us, and go out before us, and fight our battles'" (1 Sam. 8:19–20).

This biblical episode illustrates an age-old ambivalence about government. Government is a necessity—"all the nations" have it, after all—but at the same time it has undesirable aspects. These mixed feelings toward government are inextricably bound up with its taxing and spending activities. The king will provide things that the people want (in this case, an army), but only at a cost. The resources for all government expenditures ultimately must come from the private sector. As Samuel so graphically explains, taxes can become burdensome.

Centuries have passed, mixed feelings about government remain, and much of the controversy still centres around its financial behaviour. This book is about the taxing and spending activities of government, a subject usually called **public finance**, but sometimes referred to as **public sector economics** or simply **public economics**. Our focus is on the microeconomic functions of government, the way government affects the allocation of resources and the distribution of income. Nowadays, the macroeconomic functions of government—the use of taxing, spending, and monetary policies to affect the overall level of unemployment and the price level—are usually taught in separate courses.

It is not always exactly clear whether certain subjects belong in public finance. Governmental regulatory policies have important effects on resource allocation. Such policies have goals that sometimes can also be achieved by government spending or taxing measures. For example, if the government wishes to limit the size of corporations, one possible policy is to impose large taxes on big corporations. Another policy is to issue regulations making firms that exceed a particular size illegal. However, while corporate taxation is a subject of intense study in public finance, anticombine issues are generally treated only tangentially in public finance texts and are covered instead in courses on industrial organization and government and business. Such a practice seems arbitrary, but it is necessary to limit the scope of the field. This book follows tradition by focusing on governmental spending and revenue-raising activities.

ALTERNATIVE VIEWS OF GOVERNMENT

Public finance economists analyze not only the effects of actual government taxing and spending activities, but also what these activities ought to be. Views of how government should function in the economic sphere are influenced by general attitudes concerning the relationship between the individual and the state. Political philosophers have distinguished two major approaches.

Organic View

Society is conceived of as a natural organism. Each individual is a part of this organism, and the government can be thought of as its heart. Yang Chang-chi, Mao Tse-tung's ethics teacher in Beijing, held that, "A country is an organic whole, just as the human body is an organic whole. It is not like a machine which can be taken apart and put together again" (quoted in Johnson, 1983: 197). The individual has significance only as part of the community, and the good of the individual is defined with respect to the good of the whole. Thus, the community is stressed above the individual. For example, in the *Republic* of Plato, an activity of a citizen is desirable only if it leads to a just society. Perhaps the most infamous instance of an organic conception of government is provided by Nazism: "National Socialism does not recognize a separate individual sphere which, apart from the community, is to be painstakingly protected from any interference by the State.... Every activity of daily life has meaning and value only as a service to the whole."[1]

The goals of the society are set by the state, which leads society toward their realization. Of course, the choice of goals differs considerably. Plato conceived of a state whose goal was the achievement of a golden age in which human activities would be guided by perfect rationality. On the other hand, Adolf Hitler (1971/1925: 393) viewed the state's purpose to be the achievement of racial purity: "The state is a means to an end. Its end lies in the preservation and advancement of a community of physically and psychically homogeneous creatures." According to Lenin (1968/1917: 198), the proletarian state has the purpose of "*leading the whole people* to socialism, ... of being the teacher, the guide, the leader of all the working and exploited people."

Because societal goals can differ, a crucial question is how they are to be selected. Proponents of the organic view usually argue that certain goals are *natural* for the societal organism to pursue. Pursuit of sovereignty over some geographical area is an example of such a natural goal. (Think of the Nazi drive for domination over Europe.) However, despite the fact that philosophers have struggled for centuries to explain what natural means, the answer is far from clear.

Mechanistic View

In this view, government is not an organic part of society. Rather, it is a contrivance created by individuals to better achieve their individual goals. As the

---

[1] Stuckart and Globke (1968: 330). Wilhelm Stuckart and Hans Globke were ranking members of the Nazi Ministry of the Interior.

American statesman Henry Clay (Bartlett, 1968: 538) suggested in 1829, "Government is a trust, and the officers of the government are trustees; and both the trust and the trustees are created for the benefit of the people." The individual rather than the group is at centre stage.

Accepting that government exists for the good of the people, we are still left with the problem of defining just what *good* is and how the government should act to promote it. There is virtually universal agreement that it is good for individuals when government protects them from violence. To do so, government must have a monopoly on coercive power. Otherwise, anarchy develops, and as the seventeenth-century philosopher Thomas Hobbes (1963/1651: 143) noted, "The life of man [becomes] solitary, poor, nasty, brutish and short." Recent events in countries such as Somalia, Bosnia, and Northern Ireland, where private armies are common, confirm Hobbes's observation. Similarly, in *The Wealth of Nations*, Adam Smith argues that government should protect "the society from the violence and invasion of other independent societies," and protect "as far as possible every member of the society from the injustice or oppression of every other member of it" (1977/1776, Book V: 182, 198).

The most limited government, then, has but one function—to prevent its members from being subjected to physical coercion. Beyond that, Smith argued that government should have responsibility for "creating and maintaining certain public works and certain public institutions, which it can never be for the interest of any individual, or small number of individuals, to erect and maintain" (1977/1776, Book V: 210–11). Here one thinks of items such as roads, bridges, and sewers—the infrastructure required for society to function.[2]

At this point, opinions within the mechanistic tradition diverge. Libertarians, who believe in a very limited government, argue against any further economic role for the government. In Smith's words, "Every man, as long as he does not violate the laws of justice, is left perfectly free to pursue his own interest his own way" (1977/1776, Book V: 180). In contrast, those whom we might call social democrats believe that substantial government intervention is required for the good of individuals. These interventions can take such diverse forms as safety regulations for the workplace, laws banning racial and sexual discrimination in housing, health care for the sick and elderly, or welfare payments to the poor. When social democrats are confronted with the objection that such interventions are likely to impinge on individual freedom, they are apt to

---

[2] Some argue that even these items should be provided by private entrepreneurs. Problems that might arise in doing so are discussed in Chapter 7 under "Efficient Provision of Public Goods."

respond that freedom refers to more than the absence of physical coercion. An individual with a very low income may be free to spend that income as he or she pleases, but the scope of that freedom is quite limited. Of course, between the libertarian and social democratic positions there is a continuum of views with respect to the amount of government intervention that is appropriate.

VIEWPOINT OF THIS BOOK

The notion that the individual rather than the group is paramount is relatively new and is stronger in some countries, such as the United States, than in others such as Canada or Sweden. Historian Lawrence Stone (1977: 4–5) notes that before the modern period,

> it was generally agreed that the interests of the group, whether that of kin, the village, or later the state, took priority over the wishes of the individual and the achievement of his particular ends. "Life, liberty and the pursuit of happiness" were personal ideals which the average, educated 16th-century man would certainly have rejected as the prime goals of a good society.

Since then, however, the mechanistic view of government has come to dominate Anglo-American political thought. However, its dominance is not total—as reflected in the Canadian commitment to "peace, order, and good government." Anyone who claims that something must be done in the "national interest," without reference to the welfare of some individual or group of individuals, is implicitly taking an organic point of view. More generally, even in highly individualistic societies, people sometimes feel it necessary to act on behalf of, or even sacrifice their lives for, the nation. As Kenneth Arrow (1974: 15) observes, "The tension between society and the individual is inevitable. Their claims compete within the individual conscience as well as in the arena of social conflict."

Not surprisingly, Anglo-American economic thought has also developed along individualistic lines, although less so in Canada than in the United States. Individuals and their wants are the main focus in mainstream economics, a view reflected in this text. However, as stressed earlier, within the individualistic tradition there is much controversy with respect to how active a role government should take. In contrast to the United States, Canada has long embraced a major role for government in the provision of health care; and federal equalization payments, embedded in the Canadian Constitution, ensure "sufficient revenues to provide reasonably comparable levels of public services at reasonably comparable levels of taxation" regardless of the province of residence. Adopting a mechanistic point of view does not by itself provide us with

an ideology that tells us whether any particular economic intervention should be undertaken.[3]

This point is important because economic policy is not based on economic analysis alone. The desirability of a given course of government action (or inaction) inevitably depends in part on ethical and political judgments. As Canada's ongoing public debate over government tax and expenditure policies illustrates, reasonable people can disagree on these matters. We attempt to reflect different points of view as fairly as possible.

SUMMARY

- Public finance, also known as public sector economics or public economics, focuses on the taxing and spending activities of government and their influence on the allocation of resources and distribution of income.

- Public finance economists both analyze actual policies and develop guidelines for government activities. In the latter role, economists are influenced by their attitudes toward the role of government in society.

- In an organic view of society, individuals are valuable only in their contribution to the realization of social goals. These goals are determined by the government.

- In a mechanistic view of society, government is a contrivance erected to further individual goals. There is considerable disagreement over how the government should promote sometimes conflicting individual goals.

- Individual decision making is the focus of much economics and is consistent with the mechanistic view of society adopted in this book. This does not eliminate much controversy over the appropriate role of the government in our economy.

DISCUSSION QUESTIONS

1. In *The End of Liberalism*, Theodore Lowi (1979: xii) offers the following article as part of a present-day constitution: "The public interest shall be defined by the satisfaction of the voters in their constituencies. The test of the public

---

[3] Note that this question really makes no sense in the context of an organic view of government in which the government is above the people, and there is an assumption that it should guide every aspect of life.

interest is reelection." What does this imply about the role of government in society? Do you agree or disagree? Why?

2. In *The Closing of the American Mind*, Allan Bloom (1987) writes:

> In the tightest communities, at least since the days of Odysseus, there is something in man that wants out and senses that his development is stunted by being just a part of a whole, rather than a whole itself. And in the freest and most independent situations men long for unconditional attachments. The tension between freedom and attachment, and attempts to achieve the impossible union of the two, are the permanent condition of man. But in modern political regimes, where rights precede duties, freedom definitely has primacy over community, family and even nature.

    a. Does Bloom identify modern society with a dominance of individuals' rights? Does such a correspondence seem appropriate to Western cultures? What about non-Western societies?

    b. Areas of public debate that have highlighted the tension between individual rights and social control include gun control and the required registration of guns; abortion; reproductive technologies; and health care. Can you think of other areas of debate that reflect this tension?

REFERENCES

Arrow, Kenneth J. *The Limits of Organization*. New York: W.W. Norton, 1974.

Bartlett, John. *Bartlett's Familiar Quotations*, 14th ed. Boston: Little, Brown, 1968.

Bloom, Allan. *The Closing of the American Mind*. New York: Simon and Schuster, 1987.

Hitler, Adolf. *Mein Kampf*. Translated by Rolph Manheim. Boston: Houghton Mifflin, 1971 (1925).

Hobbes, Thomas. *Leviathan*. New York: Meridian Books, 1963 (1651).

Johnson, Paul. *Modern Times*. New York: Harper and Row, 1983.

Lenin, Vladimir. "The Marxist Theory of the State and the Tasks of the Proletariat in the Revolution," in *Lenin on Politics and Revolution*, ed. James E. Connor. Indianapolis: Bobbs-Merrill, 1968, pp. 184–232.

Lowi, Theodore J. *The End of Liberalism*. New York: W.W. Norton, 1979.

Smith, Adam. *The Wealth of Nations*. London: J.M. Dent and Sons, 1977 (1776).

Stone, Lawrence. *The Family, Sex, and Marriage in England, 1500–1800*. New York: Harper and Row, 1977.

Stuckart, Wilhelm, and Hans Globke. "Civil Rights and the Natural Inequality of Man," in *Nazi Culture*, ed. George L. Morse. New York: Universal Library, 1968.

APPENDIX

Doing Research in Public Finance

Throughout the text, we cite many books and articles. These references are useful for those who want to delve into the various subjects in more detail. Students interested in writing term papers or theses on subjects in public finance should also consult the following journals that specialize in the field:

- *Journal of Public Economics*
- *Canadian Tax Journal*
- *National Tax Journal*
- *Public Finance*
- *Public Finance Quarterly*
- *International Tax and Public Finance*

The *Journal of Public Economics* is relatively technical compared to the others and is most useful to those who have taken a course in microeconomic theory at the intermediate level and have a working knowledge of calculus.

In addition, all the major general-interest economics journals frequently publish articles that deal with public finance issues. These include, but are not limited to:

- *Canadian Journal of Economics*
- *American Economic Review*
- *Canadian Public Policy*
- *Journal of Economic Perspectives*
- *Journal of Political Economy*
- *Review of Economics and Statistics*
- *Canadian Business Economics*

Articles on public finance in most of these and many other journals are indexed in the *Journal of Economic Literature.*

Vast amounts of data are available on government spending and taxing activities. Publications of the Canadian Tax Foundation are a particularly useful source. These include:

- *The National Finances* (annually until 1994)
- *Provincial and Municipal Finances* (biannually to 1993)
- *Finances of the Nation* (beginning in 1995)

In addition, the research monographs published by the Canadian Tax Foundation and the proceedings of the Foundation's annual conferences are valuable references. The Web site for the Canadian Tax Foundation is <http://www.ctf.ca>. A number of other Canadian research institutes interested in public finance issues have Web sites. These include the Canadian Centre for Policy Alternatives at <http://www.policyalternatives.ca>, the C.D. Howe Institute at <http://www.cdhowe.org/eng>, the Fraser Institute at <http://www.fraserinstitute.ca>, and the Institute for Research on Public Policy at <http://www.irpp.org/index.html>. These institutes provide alternative views and analysis by public finance scholars.

Budget papers prepared annually by the federal minister of finance, and counterparts at the provincial level, provide additional data, and the Department of Finance publishes occasional papers on various topics. The Web site for the Department of Finance is <http://www.fin.gc.ca/fin-eng.html>. Statistics Canada regularly publishes detailed federal and provincial public finance data in *Public Sector Finance*, and in 1992 published *Public Finance Historical Data, 1965–66 to 1991–92*. *Historical Statistics of Canada*, 2nd ed., by M.C. Urquhart and K.A.H. Buckley (Ottawa: Supply and Services, 1983) provides early Canadian public finance data. Revenue Canada's *Taxation Statistics* is the best published source of detailed information on the personal income tax.

Research monographs commissioned by the Economic Council of Canada (until 1993) made major contributions to the Canadian public finance literature. Reports by three royal commissions—the Royal Commission on Dominion–Provincial Relations, 1940 (Rowell–Sirois), the Royal Commission on Taxation, 1966 (Carter), and the Royal Commission on the Economic Union and Development Prospects for Canada, 1985 (Macdonald)—and research papers prepared for these commissions, are an additional valuable source.

Canadian tax and expenditure policies are much influenced by U.S. policies. The student of public finance in Canada is well advised to be acquainted with the U.S. situation. In particular, students should consult the volumes included in the Brookings Institution's series *Studies of Government Finance*. These books include careful and up-to-date discussions of important public finance issues using relatively nontechnical language. The working paper series of the National Bureau of Economic Research, available in many Canadian libraries, is another good source of recent research on public finance. The technical difficulty of these papers is sometimes considerable, however.

Chapter 2

Government at a Glance

'What government does with scarce resources shows what its values are.
—The Honourable Paul Martin, Budget Speech, February 18, 1997, p. 28

It is useful to have a broad description of the Canadian system of public finance before delving into its details. We begin with a brief discussion of the legal framework within which government conducts its economic activities. Then we consider problems that arise in attempts to quantify the role of government in the economy.

THE LEGAL FRAMEWORK

According to Perry (1990: 17), "the first recorded taxes under the French regime were export taxes on furs—half of the beaver and one-tenth of the moose, first levied about 1650." As trade increased, taxes on imports (referred to as customs duties or tariffs) and excise taxes on items such as tobacco supplanted export taxes as the main source of government revenues. By 1847 taxes set by the colonies on imported goods had replaced the Imperial tariffs, and the colonies were in control of their taxes. Revenues from the taxes were being used to finance roads, canals, ports, bridges, and other public infrastructure.

Canada's initial Constitution, the 1867 British North America Act (now the Constitution Act, 1867) specifies taxing and spending powers of the federal and provincial governments. We first look at the provisions relating to the taxing and spending powers of the federal government and then turn to the provinces.

Federal Government

Section 91 of the 1867 Constitution Act gives the federal government the power "to make laws for the peace, order, and good government of Canada." This includes the power to raise money by any system or mode of taxation, although Section 125 prevents the federal government from levying taxes on provincial lands and property.

The main sources of tax revenues in Canada at the time of Confederation were taxes on imports and excise taxes. Although the provinces raised 99 percent of their tax revenues (77 percent of total revenues) from these two sources in 1866, the Constitution excluded provinces from future use of these and other "indirect" taxes; customs duties, excise duties and taxes, and other indirect taxes were reserved for the federal government. The Fathers of Confederation planned for a strong federal government and for most of the taxing power to reside at the federal level. Direct taxes—income taxes, taxes on estates and inheritances at time of death, and property taxes—which could also be used by provincial governments were unpopular and little used in the 1860s.

With the federal taxing power went major responsibilities that had previously resided with the provinces. What were these?

The first half of the nineteenth century in North America saw growing appreciation for government's role. According to Donald Creighton (1939: 67), "the philosophy of 'public improvements' made very rapid progress among colonial populations which were otherwise still addicted to negative views of the state." Infrastructure was needed to move people and goods. Adequate private capital was unavailable. Nova Scotia, New Brunswick, Ontario, and Quebec had, prior to 1867, incurred debt to build ports, railways, roads, canals, wharfs, lighthouses, and bridges; in 1866, 29 percent of provincial expenditures were for debt servicing. With Confederation, the federal government assumed the existing debts of the provinces and the responsibility for servicing and repaying these debts. The federal government was also given responsibility for defence, navigation and shipping, regulation of trade and commerce, the criminal justice system, and money and banking, among others areas.

The intent was to balance responsibilities with revenues, and to achieve this the federal government provided statutory subsidies to provinces for general government, justice, education, welfare, and internal transport services. These subsidies were specified at the time of Confederation, and any future growth in sub-sidies was to be strictly limited. The Fathers of Confederation did not foresee the extent to which federal grants to provinces would grow and change.

Revenues from customs and excise duties effectively met federal government needs for the first fifty years following Confederation. Today's major taxes remained unused. World War I brought the introduction of an excess profits tax and taxes on corporate (1916) and personal incomes (1917). It was not until 1920 that the federal government introduced a general sales tax. As late as 1919, excise and customs duties accounted for 78 percent of federal tax revenues. Given the prominence of the GST (Goods and Services Tax) and the personal income tax in today's tax discussions, it may seem surprising that income taxes and a broad-based sales tax had no role in federal government finance for more than half a century.

Although there was no change to the Constitution Act, the federal government managed to extend its spending powers into areas of provincial responsibility through the use of conditional grants, first in 1912 in the area of agricultural education—education being an area of exclusive provincial jurisdiction. By 1928 conditional grants were being made for employment services, highway construction, technical education, and disease prevention, all areas for which the provinces had major responsibility. And in 1927 the federal government provided conditional grants for old age pensions. The Great Depression of the 1930s created the need to greatly expand federal conditional grants to provinces for social assistance. The terms of the social assistance grants varied by the needs of individual provinces. By 1936–37 conditional grants accounted for $69 million of the $90 million transferred by the federal government to the provinces. By providing support for provincial action in specified areas, the federal government encouraged provincial governments to use their own limited resources in certain ways. So long as provinces are free to choose whether to participate through their own legislation, and the federal government does not become involved in providing services that are a provincial responsibility, the conditional grants do not appear to violate the Constitution.

A 1940 amendment (Section 91(2A)) to the 1867 Constitution Act gave the federal government responsibility for unemployment insurance, and another amendment in 1951 (Section 94A) provided for shared jurisdiction with provinces in the area of old age pensions. One result flowing from these two measures has been rapid growth in payroll tax rates and revenues over the past several decades.[1]

---

[1] Di Matteo and Shannon (1995) provide a useful overview of payroll tax evolution in Canada over the past several decades.

The expansion of federal powers into areas reserved to the provinces has been protested by many of the provinces, and most strongly by Quebec, over the years. This has led to "opting out" arrangements whereby provinces that choose not to participate in a conditional grant program have obtained increased tax room, or taxing power, in order to finance a similar program of their own.

Income taxes, payroll taxes, and the federal sales tax, all unknown at the time of Confederation, grew from 37 percent of federal revenues in 1934 to 83 percent by 1994. Customs and excise tax revenues pale in comparison. The federal government has used the flexibility provided by the Fathers of Confederation to meet the demand for growing revenues.

Government bills to tax and to spend must originate in the House of Commons (Section 53 of the 1867 Constitution Act), and such actions must be introduced to the House by a minister of the government. A clear distinction between the powers held by the elected House and by the appointed Senate is that tax and spending bills cannot originate in the Senate.

Expenditure estimates for the broad range of federal programs must be prepared and approved annually for new and old programs. Tax measures, in contrast, continue to generate revenues without yearly action. The government introduces budgets that include changes in tax legislation more or less as often as economic and political conditions dictate.

As Canada's large and growing federal debt so emphatically demonstrates, the federal government is not required to finance all its expenditures by taxation. If expenditures exceed revenues, it is empowered to "the borrowing of Money on the Public Credit" (Section 91(4)). In 1873 the gross public debt that had been assumed by the Dominion at Confederation stood at $93.7 million ($27 per capita). Although this had risen to over $622 billion ($21,000 per capita) by 1996, about the same share (30 percent) of federal government spending was required to service the debt as was true 120 years earlier (27 percent).

Provincial and Local Governments

The 1867 Constitution Act limited provinces to the use of direct taxation within the province in order to raise revenue for provincial purposes.[2] The

---

[2] A "direct tax" is one that is imposed on the individual who is expected to bear the tax. Thus, the personal income tax is a direct tax. Sales taxes and excise are generally classified by economists as "indirect" taxes; although the person selling or producing the good or service has the statutory obligation to pay the tax, the tax is expected to be borne by the final consumer of the good or service.

provinces were not to have the power to inhibit interprovincial trade through the use of indirect taxes. Statutory subsidies to the provinces compensated for the prohibition on indirect taxes. Per capita subsidies, federal grants to operate government and legislatures, licences and fees, the sale of goods and services, and revenues from provincial lands and natural resources were to fund the necessary provincial services. Property taxes, income taxes, and succession duties, little used at the time, were also available to provinces.

Federal subsidies, which accounted for about 60 percent of provincial revenues in 1867, fell to 10 percent by 1930. Increased demand for welfare, health, and education services and for intraprovincial transport accompanied economic development and urbanization and led provinces to seek new sources of revenue. British Columbia (1876) and Prince Edward Island (1894) enacted taxes on personal incomes. Ontario, following the example of New York and Pennsylvania, introduced a succession duty in 1892 in order to increase revenues. By 1896 all provinces had succession duties. Taxes on gasoline and motor vehicle licences were introduced by the 1920s as a way to finance the needed road systems that accompanied increasing use of automobiles and trucks.

Provinces held primary responsibility for social welfare, and the Great Depression placed enormous strain on provincial finances. Federal transfers rose from 10 percent in 1930 to 25 percent of provincial revenues by 1937 (Eggleston and Kraft, 1939) due to increasing welfare needs. By 1940, financial pressures had forced all provinces to introduce taxes on personal and corporate incomes, with Saskatchewan and Quebec also using retail sales taxes.[3] Thus, by the time of World War II, both the federal and provincial governments were using corporate and personal income taxes as well as a general sales tax.

Growing disparity between provincial financial needs and resources and an overlap in major revenue sources led the Royal Commission on Dominion–Provincial Relations (1940) to recommend that the federal government be the sole user of taxes on personal and corporate income and of successions duties, that it assume responsibility for provincial debts, and that it provide adequate transfers to provincial governments. World War II rather than the royal commission's recommendations led the provinces to relinquish their use of the personal and corporate income taxes. Following the war a series of federal–

---

[3] In contrast to the generally accepted classification of retail sales taxes and excise taxes on gasoline or tobacco products as "indirect taxes," courts in Canada have classified these taxes as "direct" taxes in interpreting the 1867 Constitution Act. The seller of the good is deemed as the agent designated to collect the tax from the consumer who pays, and bears, the tax in proportion to the amount of the good consumed.

provincial agreements provided for federal transfers to provinces based on a combination of per capita grants and a share of the revenues from the income taxes. Per capita grants and statutory subsidies provided an element of equalization among provinces prior to 1957, and the 1957–62 agreement included unconditional (equalization) grants based on the per capita yield of the personal and corporate income taxes and succession duties in the two wealthiest provinces—Ontario and British Columbia. The purpose was to guarantee that per capita provincial revenue would reach a certain standard for all Canadians. Subsequent agreements expanded the basis for equalization payments, and by 1994 they included thirty-seven provincial revenue sources. Section 36(2) of the 1982 Constitution Act, which entrenches the concept of equalization payments in the Canadian Constitution, states:

> Parliament and the government of Canada are committed to the principle of making equalization payments to ensure that provincial governments have sufficient revenues to provide reasonably comparable levels of public services at reasonably comparable levels of taxation.

The 1982 Constitution Act also amended the Constitution to give provinces greater control over their natural resources, explicitly allowing them to levy indirect taxes on natural resources. Provinces may now raise money by "any mode or system of taxation in respect of ... non-renewable resources and forestry resources in the province and the primary production therefrom ..." (Section 92A).

This brief review makes clear that federal transfers to provinces have been important since Canada was founded. They accounted for 60 percent of provincial revenues at that time. They fell to 10 percent by 1930, sixty-three years later, but then rose rapidly due to the Great Depression. The share of provincial revenues that came from federal transfers in fiscal 1997 ranged from 9.2 percent in British Columbia to 43 percent in Newfoundland (see Table 2.1).

In the past half century the public finance role of provinces has grown rapidly relative to that of the federal government. In 1946 the ratio of federal to provincial government expenditures (excluding grants made to provinces) equalled 4.33 to 1. Following the war effort this fell to 1.72 to 1 in 1950, and continued to fall to 0.8 to 1 by 1993. The ratio of federal government revenue to provincial revenue (net of federal grants) also fell sharply, from 4.86 to 1 in 1946 to 3.13 to 1 in 1950 and 1.13 to 1 by 1993.

Provincial revenue sources were restricted and federal spending was several times that of all the provinces in the 1860s and 1870s. Although the Fathers of

Table 2.1

Federal Transfers to Provinces as a Percentage of Provincial
Revenues, 1997

PROVINCE	GRANTS AS PERCENT OF PROVINCIAL REVENUES
Newfoundland	43.0
Prince Edward Island	36.4
Nova Scotia	40.3
New Brunswick	38.3
Quebec	17.6
Ontario	12.9
Manitoba	31.7
Saskatchewan	17.3
Alberta	10.1
British Columbia	9.2

SOURCE: Karin Treff and David Perry, *Finances of the Nation, 1996* (Toronto: Canadian Tax Foundation, 1997), 8:4, table 8.3.

Confederation may have intended for the federal government to dominate the provinces, in the last quarter of the twentieth century provincial annual spending has exceeded federal spending (net of grants to provinces), and provincial own-source revenues nearly equalled federal revenue. Areas of provincial responsibility—health, education, welfare—have grown particularly rapidly during the past half century. The federal and provincial governments jointly occupy all major tax fields. The distribution of taxing and spending among levels of government is very different than at the time of Confederation.

The 1867 Constitution Act does not refer to local governments. Local authorities have only those taxing and spending powers that provincial governments choose to delegate to them. One result is substantial variation across provinces in local taxing and spending decisions. The dominant revenue source for local authorities was, and is, the property tax. Local government own-source revenues, which were more than double provincial own-source revenues in 1926, were only 30 percent of provincial own-source revenues in 1993. As provincial reliance on sales and income tax revenues grew rapidly, local governments increasingly relied on transfers from provincial governments. Grants from provincial governments, which accounted for 6.7 percent of local revenues in 1926, accounted for 43.9 percent in 1993. In sum, since the time of Confederation the role of provincial governments has increased sharply relative to that of local governments and the federal government.

THE SIZE OF GOVERNMENT

What has been the result of these legal prescriptions and trends for government taxing and spending activities? The first item that belongs in any such description is a measure of their magnitude. Just how big is government? The whole public debate concerning the government's size presupposes there is some way of measuring it.

One measure often used by politicians and journalists is the number of workers in the public sector. However, inferences about the size of government drawn from the number of workers it employs can be misleading. Imagine a country where a few public servants operate a powerful computer that guides all economic decisions. In this country, the number of individuals on the government payroll certainly underestimates the importance of government. Similarly, it would be easy to construct a scenario in which a large number of workers is associated with a relatively weak public sector. Although for many purposes it is useful to know the number of public sector employees, it does not cast light on the central issue—the extent to which society's resources are subject to the control of government.

A more sensible (and common) approach is to measure the size of government by the volume of its annual expenditures, of which there are basically three types:

1. *Purchases of goods and services.* The government buys a wide variety of items, everything from fighter planes to services provided by forest rangers.
2. *Transfers of income to people, businesses, or other governments.* The government takes income from some individuals or organizations and gives it to others. Examples are welfare programs such as the Guaranteed Income Supplements under the Old Age Security Act and farm programs that guarantee prices for certain commodities.
3. *Interest payments.* The government often borrows to finance its activities and, like any borrower, must pay interest for the privilege of doing so.

The federal minister of finance presents the budget each year, traditionally in the month of February. This budget outlines anticipated changes in tax and spending programs and sets forth the anticipated revenues and expenditures for the coming fiscal year. The federal budget for fiscal year 1998 anticipates spending of $151.8 billion, and revenues of $137.8 billion, resulting in a deficit of $14 billion. Each provincial finance minister goes through a similar process. Local authorities also approve their tax and spending programs set forth in an annual budget. The latest available (fiscal 1995) consolidated financial data for

federal, provincial, and local governments show $303 billion in revenues, and $357.6 billion in spending. This is $12,200 per capita in spending with a per capita deficit of more than $1,850.

Unfortunately, conventional budget expenditures can convey a misleading impression of the extent to which society's resources are under government control. There are at least two reasons for this: the methods of accounting for off-budget items and hidden costs of government.

Accounting Issues

Several complications arise in the computation of government expenditures. Some of these are due to the government's role in lending programs. The government provides **loan guarantees** for individuals, crown corporations and other businesses, and nonprofit institutions. Because of the government guarantee, the loans are at lower rates than otherwise. In the case of default, the government is on the hook. Such explicit guarantees by the federal government totalled $23 billion in 1993, of which $3.7 billion was for student loans and $18.6 billion for loans to crown corporations. In order to attract investments, provincial governments also provide loan guarantees, and make direct loans in some cases. These too lead to future draws on the public purse at time of default.

How should these credit programs be treated for budgetary purposes? One possibility would be to recognize payments and receipts associated with these programs only in the year they are made or arrive. To see the problems with this approach, suppose the government guarantees some student loans this year, and the loans do not come due for four years. The loan guarantees would not show up on this year's budget. However, there will be defaults on at least some of these loans in the future, so by making the loan guarantees now, the government is committing itself to some expenditures in the future. A sensible approach, then, would be so-called accrual accounting, which takes into account the future liabilities created by present decisions. Public accounts normally make provision for such liabilities, but high levels of uncertainty may accompany the size of any such provision.[4]

---

[4] Similar issues arise in the context of government insurance activities, which are also sizable. The Canada Deposit Insurance Corporation (CDIC) protects hundreds of billions of dollars in individual deposits in banks and trust and loan companies. Up to $60,000 is protected in each deposit, and individuals may have more than one account that is protected. Bank failures in the early 1980s resulted in a CDIC loss of $650 million in 1983 on insured deposits of about $150 billion. Losses could have been larger in this tumultuous period, although in the sixteen years from 1967 to 1982 there had been virtually no losses (Working Committee on Canada Deposit Insurance Corporation, *Final Report*, Ottawa, 1985).

Government pension plans, including the Canada and Quebec Pension Plans (CPP and QPP), also result in contingent liabilities. Governments have an obligation to pay pensions to individuals who have been paying into the pension plans, and the government's net liability changes from year to year depending on the number and age of the contributors. Through accrual accounting an increase in liability would be reflected as an expenditure commitment, which increases the deficit. If, on the other hand, the increased pension payments only show up on the government accounts at the time they are paid, the public accounts show a lower level of expenditure, and a lower level of accumulated debt. Canada's Financial Management System (FMS) maintains accounts that annually include the accrued liabilities due to employee pension plans, while the System of National Accounts (SNA) considers government employee pension plans and the CPP and QPP to be pay-as-you-go programs with the revenues and expenditures for each program shown on an annual basis. As a result, the December 31, 1990 SNA balance sheet showed liabilities for public pensions to be $77 billion less than the FMS accounts.

We conclude, then, that the size of the official government budget depends on some rather arbitrary accounting decisions concerning whether and how certain items are to be included. Hence, considerable caution is required in interpreting budgetary figures.

Hidden Costs of Government

Some government activities have substantial effects on resource allocation even if they involve minimal explicit outlays. For example, issuing regulations per se is not very expensive, but compliance with the rules can be costly. Seat-belt and other safety requirements raise the cost of cars. Regulations ensuring sanitary conditions in slaughterhouses, dairies, and bakeries were among Canada's early health regulations that raised costs for businesses. Regulations to control the spread of plant, animal, or human diseases also may raise business costs. Permit and inspection fees increase the price of housing. Banks, insurance companies, brokerage firms, stock markets, and other financial institutions are subject to extensive regulation. Health and safety regulations for workers increase the cost of labour, and expensive testing required of the drug industry slows the pace and increases the price at which new drugs become accessible to consumers.

Unfortunately, it is exceedingly difficult to compute the total costs of regulation. For example, we can easily imagine even pharmaceutical experts disagreeing on what new cures would have been developed in the absence of drug regulation. Similarly, it is hard to estimate how much government-mandated safety procedures in the workplace increase production costs. As with other

government activity, the benefits may far outweigh the costs. Nonetheless, through regulatory activity the government sector has a major impact on society and the economy; private costs of compliance may, in some cases, add as much to total costs as do tax liabilities.

Two other "hidden" aspects that deserve mention are (a) **tax expenditures**, and (b) the flow of current services from capital investments. Tax expenditures refer to the value of incentives and preferences given through the tax system for purposes that could be achieved through direct expenditures. For example, a government may choose to provide a direct payment to individuals who are 65 or older, or it may allow a deduction of $1,000 from pension income that would otherwise be taxable. Similarly, the government could make a grant of $250 to a business for every $1,000 invested on Cape Breton, or it could give a tax credit of 25 percent. Although tax expenditures and direct expenditures may reflect comparable levels of government activity and involvement, in the case of direct expenditures this is reflected in the annual budget; in the case of tax expenditures it is not.[5]

The government does not distinguish between capital and current expenditures in the way the private sector does. Capital investments are usually consumed, or depleted, over several years as the capital is used to produce goods and services. A high-level capital spending by a company in a given year does not mean it is more active or productive in that year than in any other year, as it may be replacing worn-out equipment. Private accounting practices recognize this by depreciating the equipment over a period of years. In contrast, with no government capital accounts, large capital expenditures appear to reflect a high level of government activity when in fact the involvement is more accurately reflected in the services from schools, roads, canals, dams, hospitals, and water systems that occur over many years. A related problem is that of valuing the services as they are consumed. The value is assumed to be the amount spent by the government, which may or may not be a good approximation.

Some Numbers

We reluctantly conclude that there is no feasible way to summarize in a single number the magnitude of government's impact on the economy. Having made

---

[5] The Department of Finance first published estimates of tax expenditures in December 1979. Their most recent publication is *Government of Canada Tax Expenditures, 1995* (Ottawa: Department of Finance, 1996). The estimates include federal tax expenditures made through the corporate income tax and the Goods and Services Tax (GST) as well as the personal income tax. Several provinces have provided estimates of provincial tax expenditures at the time of their annual budgets.

this admission, we are still left with the practical problem of finding some reasonable indicator of government's size that can be used to estimate trends in the growth of government. Most economists are willing to accept conventionally defined government expenditure as a rough but useful measure. Like many other imperfect measures, it yields useful insights as long as its limitations are understood.

With all the appropriate caveats in mind, we present in Table 2.2 data on expenditures made by all levels of Canadian government over time. The first column indicates that annual expenditures have increased by a factor of about 500 since 1926. This figure is a misleading indicator of the growth of government for several reasons:

1. Because of inflation, the dollar has decreased in value over time. In column 2, the expenditure figures are expressed in 1986 dollars. In real terms, government expenditure in 1995 was about forty-eight times the level in 1926.

2. The population has also grown over time. An increasing population by itself creates demands for a larger public sector. (For example, more roads and sewers are required to accommodate more people.) Column 3 shows real government expenditure per capita. Now the increase from 1926 to 1995 is a factor of somewhat over fifteen.

Table 2.2

Local, Provincial, and Federal Government Expenditures, Selected Years

YEAR	TOTAL EXPENDITURES (MILLIONS)	1986 DOLLARS	IN 1986 $ PER CAPITA	PERCENT OF GDP
1926	$ 704	$ 5,770	$ 611	13.1
1930	871	7,444	729	14.5
1940	1,588	14,436	1,268	22.7
1950	3,583	19,687	1,433	18.7
1960	9,869	41,121	2,296	25.0
1970	27,928	85,146	3,993	31.3
1980	116,633	159,771	6,497	37.6
1990	300,485	253,573	9,124	44.9
1995	353,819	277,505	9,373	45.6

SOURCE: Statistics Canada, *Canadian Economic Observer: Historical Statistical Supplement, 1995/96*, Cat. no. 11-210-XPB, Vol. 10 (Ottawa, July 1996).

3. For some purposes, it is useful to examine government expenditure compared to the size of the economy. If government doubles in size but at the same time the economy triples, then, in a relative sense, government has shrunk. Column 4 shows government expenditure as a percentage of gross domestic product (GDP), the market value of goods and services produced by the economy during the year. In 1926 the figure was 13.1 percent, and in 1995 it was 45.6 percent.

In light of our previous discussion, the figures in Table 2.2 convey a false sense of precision. Still, there is no doubt that in the long run the economic role of government has grown enormously. With close to one-half of GDP going through the public sector, government is an enormous economic force.

To put the Canadian data in perspective, it helps to make some international comparisons. Table 2.3 shows figures on government expenditure relative to gross domestic product for a number of developed countries. The data indicate Canada is not alone in having an important public sector. Compared to Sweden, Canada's public sector is relatively small. Compared to the United States, Australia, and Japan, it is quite large.

EXPENDITURES

We now turn from the overall magnitude of government expenditures to their composition. It is impossible to reflect the enormous scope of government

Table 2.3

Government Expenditures as a Percentage of GDP, Selected Countries, 1994

COUNTRY	EXPENDITURES AS PERCENTAGE OF GDP
Australia	37.0
CANADA	47.1
France	54.2
Germany	49.0
Italy	54.1
Japan	34.3
Sweden	68.7
United States	33.0
United Kingdom	43.2

SOURCE: Organization for Economic Cooperation and Development, *OECD Economic Outlook, June, 1996* (Paris: Organization for Economic Cooperation and Development, 1996).

spending activity in a brief table. The major categories of government expenditure and their growth between 1933 and 1995 are illustrated in Table 2.4. The following aspects of the table are noteworthy:

1. Health and social welfare have become increasingly important areas of government activity since the 1930s, increasing from 17.7 percent to 37.2 percent of total government spending. Rising costs of health care, a publicly provided health care system, and an aging population all contribute to health care costs. Federal unemployment compensation and income security programs for the aged and provincial welfare systems for others who are unable to earn sufficient income are the major welfare programs. Growth in welfare expenditures has been particularly rapid since the 1960s.

2. The share of government spending on education increased substantially from 1933 to 1963, but decreased significantly (from approximately 16 percent to 12 percent) in the next thirty-two years. Responsibility for spending on education rests mostly with the provincial governments.

3. Debt charges absorb a large share of total government spending in the 1990s. Although the share of government spending on debt charges has been higher at times in our past, the share more than doubled from 1963 to 1995 (to 19.9 percent). The past decade has been a time of large federal and provincial deficits, each contributing to debt charges.

4. Transportation and communication have historically been important areas of government spending in Canada. The need to maintain and improve

Table 2.4

Expenditures by Function, All Levels of Government, 1933, 1963, 1995

FUNCTION	1933	1963	1995
Health	3.7	9.2	13.2
Social Welfare	14.0	15.0	24.0
Education	11.3	16.2	12.3
Transportation and Communication	9.4	12.2	4.4
Protection of Property and Persons	4.2	4.0	6.8
Debt Charges	31.5	8.5	19.9
Other	30.2	34.7	19.4
TOTAL	100.0	100.0	100.0

SOURCE: Data for 1933 and 1963 are from M.C. Urquhart and K.A.H. Buckley, *Historical Statistics of Canada*, 2nd ed. (Ottawa, 1983), p. H148-160. Data for 1995 are from Karin Treff and David Perry, *Finances of the Nation, 1996* (Toronto: Canadian Tax Foundation, 1997), A:4, table A.4.

existing infrastructure, and the need for government involvement in infra-structure related to new technologies, will require continuation of substantial government involvement.

Note that some fast-growing areas such as social welfare and interest payments are relatively fixed in the sense that they are determined by previous decisions. Indeed, much of the government budget consists of so-called *entitlement programs*—programs with cost determined not by fixed dollar amounts, but by the number of people who qualify. Laws governing the Canada Pension Plan and many public programs, such as unemployment insurance, include rules that determine who is entitled to benefits and their magnitude. Expenditures on entitlement programs are therefore out of the hands of the current government, unless it changes the rules. Similarly, debt payments are determined by interest rates and previous deficits, again mostly out of the control of current decision makers. Much of the federal budget is relatively uncontrollable. In Chapter 11, we discuss whether government spending is out of control and, if so, what can be done about it.

It is useful to break down total expenditures by level of government, as in Table 2.5. Of the $319 billion of direct expenditures made in 1993, the federal government accounted for 42.6 percent, the provincial and local governments for 39.9 and 17.4 percent, respectively. Focusing on the period 1960 to 1993, of particular note are the growing share of total expenditures due to the provinces and the significant decrease in the share of both the federal and local governments. Provincial and local governments are clearly important players, with the provincial role growing rapidly. They account for the bulk of spending on

Table 2.5

Government Revenues and Expenditures by Level of Government,* 1926, 1960, and 1993

YEAR	1926		1960		1993	
	REV.	EXP.	REV.	EXP.	REV.	EXP.
Federal	44.9	37.8	60.8	50.5	49.2	42.6
Provincial	18.0	20.2	21.8	24.8	39.0	39.9
Local	37.1	42.0	17.3	24.7	11.7	17.4
TOTAL	100.0	100.0	100.0	100.0	100.0	100.0

*Includes hospitals with provincial revenues and expenditures and CPP/QPP with federal revenues and expenditures, and excludes grants by governments to other levels of government.

SOURCE: Canadian Tax Foundation, *The National Finances, 1994* (Toronto: Canadian Tax Foundation, 1994), tables 3.11 and 3.13.

items such as police and fire protection, health, education, transportation, and environmental policy. Substantial public welfare expenditures are also made through the provinces. The complications that arise in coordinating the fiscal activities of different levels of government are discussed in Chapter 6.

Table 2.5 illustrates the imbalance between revenues and expenditures. While the federal government's share of revenues has been persistently larger than its expenditures, the reverse has been true for local governments. The imbalances are largely reflected in the federal grants to the provinces and the provincial grants to local governments.

REVENUES

The principal components of the Canadian tax system are noted in Table 2.6. For 1934, 1964, and 1994, the table shows the percentage of total revenues attributable to each of the major taxes. The personal income tax is the single most important source of revenue, accounting for about 33 percent of taxes raised by all levels of government. Note the importance of payroll taxes, predominantly for public pension plans, unemployment insurance, and provincial worker's compensation programs. They yielded $29 billion in 1994, or 13 percent of total government revenues. At the same time that social welfare expenditures have been increasing, so have the taxes raised to pay for them. The fall in the relative importance of the corporate income tax is also of some interest.

Table 2.6

Sources of Revenue, All Levels of Government, 1934, 1964, and 1994

TAX	1934	1964	1994
Personal income tax	4.3	20.7	33.2
Corporate income tax*	7.4	15.7	6.0
Payroll taxes**	2.7	5.5	13.0
Customs, excises, and sales taxes	34.9	30.8	19.4
Property taxes	30.8	12.5	9.1
Investment income	5.2	6.9	13.0
Other revenue	14.7	7.9	6.2
TOTAL	100.0	100.0	100.0

*Includes withholding taxes on nonresidents.

**Includes employer and employee contributions to public service pensions, CPP and QPP contributions, worker's compensation premiums, and unemployment insurance premiums.

SOURCE: Statistics Canada, *National Income and Expenditure Accounts, Annual Estimates 1926–1986,* Cat. no. 13-531 (occasional) (Ottawa, 1988), and *National Income and Expenditure Accounts, Annual Estimates, 1983–1994,* Cat. no. 13-201 (annual) (Ottawa, 1995).

In 1964 it accounted for 15.7 percent of all revenue collected, but by 1994 this figure was down to 6 percent.[6]

In 1993 the federal government collected 49.2 percent of all receipts, while local governments accounted for 11.7 percent (Table 2.5). In 1933 local revenues were not that much smaller than federal revenues, and at 37.1 percent of the total they were over twice provincial revenues. That picture has changed sharply, and in 1993 provincial revenues (39 percent of total revenues) were more than three times local revenues (11.7 percent of total revenues).

Changes in the Real Value of Debt

In popular discussions, taxes are usually viewed as the only source of government revenue. However, when the government is a debtor and the price level changes, changes in the real value of the debt may be an important source of revenue. To see why, suppose that at the beginning of the year you owe a creditor $1,000, which does not have to be repaid until the end of the year. Suppose further that during the year, prices rise by 10 percent. Then the dollars you use to repay your creditor are worth 10 percent less than those you borrowed from him. In effect, inflation has reduced the real value of your debt by $100 (10 percent of $1,000). Alternatively, your real income has increased by $100 as a consequence of inflation. Of course, at the same time, your creditor's real income has fallen by $100.[7]

At the end of fiscal year 1997, the federal government's net public debt was nearly $600 billion. During 1997, the inflation rate may be about 2 percent. Applying the same logic as previously, 2 percent inflation will reduce the real value of the federal debt by $12 billion ($600 billion × 0.02). In effect, this is as much a receipt for the government as any of the taxes listed in Table 2.6. However, the government's accounting procedures exclude gains due to inflationary erosion of the debt on the revenue side of the account.

AGENDA FOR STUDY

This chapter has set forth a collection of basic "facts"—facts on governmental fiscal institutions, on the size and scope of government spending, and on the

---

[6] As discussed in Chapter 24, a major force driving this change is the globalization of capital markets. The ability of capital to migrate to countries with the lowest taxes has created tax competition and downward pressure on corporate income taxes.

[7] If the inflation is anticipated by borrowers and lenders, one expects that the interest rate charged will be increased to take inflation into account. This phenomenon is discussed in Chapter 20 under "Taxes and Inflation."

methods used by government to finance itself. Parts of the rest of this book are devoted to presenting more facts—filling in the rather sketchy picture of how our fiscal system operates. Just as important, we explore the significance of these facts, asking whether the status quo has led to desirable outcomes, and if not, how it can be improved.

SUMMARY

- Legal constraints on federal and provincial government economic activity are embodied in the 1867 Constitution Act and the 1982 Constitution Act.

- The federal government may use any form of taxation and may incur debt to finance its expenditures. Although some major expenditure areas (e.g., education and health) are reserved for provincial governments, the federal government is, and has been, involved in these areas through conditional grants.

- The 1867 Constitution Act forbids provincial governments to use indirect taxes. They may levy "direct taxes within the province in order to raise revenue for provincial purposes." Courts have opened the field of sales and excise taxes to provincial governments by interpreting them as "direct" taxes. Provinces may not, however, use customs duties or other taxes that directly inhibit the flow of interprovincial trade.

- All common measures of the size of government—employees, expenditures, revenues, etc.—involve some deficiency. In particular, these items miss the impact of off-budget activities such as tax expenditures and regulatory costs. Nonetheless, there is strong evidence that the impact of the government on the allocation of national resources has increased over time.

- The level of government expenditures has increased in both nominal and real absolute terms, in per capita terms, and as a percentage of gross domestic product.

- The share of spending on public welfare, health, and payments on outstanding debt has increased in importance. The combination of entitlement programs and interest payments has resulted in reduced yearly control over the level of expenditures.

- Personal income taxes, payroll taxes, and general sales taxes are currently the largest sources of government revenue.

DISCUSSION QUESTIONS

1. In each of the following circumstances, decide whether the impact of government on the economy increases or decreases and why. In each case, how

does your answer compare to that given by standard measures of the size of government?

   a. Provincial governments mandate that employers provide day care centres for the use of their employees.

   b. The ratio of government purchases of goods and services to gross domestic product falls.

   c. The federal budget is brought into balance by reducing grants to provincial governments.

2. High and rising health care expenditures are one important element that has contributed to provincial government deficits. New, or additional, payroll taxes may be one way to finance the higher health care costs. If adopted, how would the higher payroll taxes affect the size of the provincial budgets? How would this affect the role of government in the economy?

3. Proponents argue that the government guarantees on loans to students do not result in an increase in government spending since only "loans" are involved. The same claim is heard from corporations that receive government guarantees on billions of dollars of loans by (private) banks for private sector projects. Evaluate these claims.

REFERENCES

Creighton, Donald G. *British North America at Confederation: A Study Prepared for the Royal Commission on Dominion–Provincial Relations.* Ottawa, 1939.

Department of Finance. *Government of Canada Tax Expenditures, 1995.* Ottawa: Department of Finance, 1996.

Di Matteo, Livio, and Michael Shannon. "Payroll Taxation in Canada: An Overview." *Canadian Business Economics* 3, no. 4 (1995): 5–22.

Eggleston, Wilfred, and C.T. Kraft. *Dominion–Provincial Subsidies and Grants: A Study Prepared for the Royal Commission on Dominion–Provincial Relations.* Ottawa, 1939.

Perry, J. Harvey. *Taxation in Canada,* 5th ed. Toronto: Canadian Tax Foundation, 1990.

Part 2

Basic Concepts of Public Finance

*I*n this section, we review the basic tools and concepts that economists use to analyze the provision and financing of public services in a federal state. We begin with a review of positive and normative economics. Economists seek to explain how the economy works—positive economics—and to determine whether or not it is producing good results—normative economics. Positive analysis does not require value judgments, because its purpose is descriptive. Normative analysis, on the other hand, requires an ethical framework, because without one it is impossible to say what is good. Although it is sometimes difficult to keep the positive and the normative from getting entangled, the distinction is worthwhile. Discussions of how the world is should not be coloured by a view of how it ought to be.

Chapters 3 and 4 describe the tools used by public finance economists to analyze both normative and positive issues. In Chapter 5, we provide an overview of expenditure and taxation analysis. Building on the framework of welfare economics, the first part of the chapter examines two questions: What role should government play in the economy? Under what circumstances do private markets fail to function adequately? Having identified a role for government in providing some goods and services and in redistributing income to improve distributional equity, we consider the alternative ways in which government expenditures can be financed. The important role that taxation plays in financing government expenditures is discussed, and the criteria for evaluating alternative taxes are considered.

Canada has one of the most decentralized systems of government in the world, and fiscal federalism is a key aspect of Canadian public finance. In Chapter 6, we discuss the provision of government services, intergovernmental grants, and tax policy issues in a country, such as Canada, with a federal system of government.

Chapter 3

Tools of Positive Analysis

When you can measure what you are speaking about, and express it in numbers, you know something about it; when you cannot measure it, when you cannot express it in numbers, your knowledge is of a meager and unsatisfactory kind.

−Lord Kelvin

A good subtitle for this chapter is "Why Is It So Hard to Tell What's Going On?" We constantly hear economists—and politicians—disagree vehemently about the likely consequences of various government actions. Consider the controversy over the effects of reduced income tax rates on the amount of labour that people supply. Conservatives argue that lower tax rates create incentives for people to work harder. Liberals are skeptical, arguing that no major changes can be expected. Each side has economists to testify that its opinion is correct. Is the cynicism expressed in the cartoon on the next page really surprising?

An important reason for the lack of definitive answers is that economists are generally unable to perform carefully controlled experiments with the economy. To determine the effects of a fertilizer on cabbage growth, a botanist can treat one plot of ground with the fertilizer and compare the results with an otherwise identical unfertilized cabbage patch. The unfertilized patch serves as the control group. Economists do not have such opportunities. Although the government can change the economic environment, there is no control group with which to make comparisons. Therefore, we never know for certain the extent to which changes in the economy are consequences of policy changes.

*"That's the gist of what I want to say. Now get
me some statistics to base it on."*

Lacking controlled experiments, economists use other methods to analyze the impact of various government policies on economic behaviour. One of the most exciting developments in public finance in recent decades has been the widespread use of modern statistical tools to study public policy issues. We will use the debate over the effect of taxes on labour supply to illustrate how empirical work is done in public finance. The general principles used are applicable to any number of problems.

THE ROLE OF THEORY

One often hears the assertion that "the numbers speak for themselves." What do the numbers say about income tax rates and labour supply? Table 3.1 gives information on how the proportion of the last dollar of earnings taken by the tax collector—the **marginal tax rate**—varied over the period 1950 to 1993. The table also shows how the average weekly hours per worker have changed. The figures indicate tax rates have generally increased, and the hours of work have decreased. The numbers appear to say that taxes have depressed labour supply.

Is this inference correct? At the same time that tax rates were changing, so were numerous other factors that might influence labour supply. If *unearned income*—income from dividends, interest, and so forth—rose over the period, people may have worked less because they were richer. Alternatively, changing attitudes—a decrease in the Protestant ethic, for example—might have decreased labour supply. Neither of these effects, and you can certainly think

Table 3.1

Income Tax Rates and Labour Supply in Canada

YEAR	MARGINAL TAX RATE*	HOURS**
1950	0.00	43.21
1960	17.00	40.41
1970	25.57	36.24
1980	29.36	34.06
1990	26.69	33.29
1993	26.35	32.91

*Roger S. Smith, "Personal Income Tax: Average and Marginal Rates in the Post-War Period," *Canadian Tax Journal* 43, no. 5 (1995): 1055–76, table 9, p. 1069. The marginal personal income tax rate has been calculated for an individual earning the average industrial wage with a non-earning spouse and two children between 12 and 16.

**Average hours worked per week by employed persons. The data for 1950 and 1960 are from Statistics Canada, CANSIM Matrix 613 series D240361. The data for 1970 to 1993 are from CANSIM Matrix 1112 series I191201.

of many more, is taken into account by the numbers given. Clearly, what we need to know is the *independent* effect of taxes on labour supply. This effect simply cannot be learned solely from examining the trends in the two variables over time. Here is a typical situation—when we turn to data for answers, *the numbers never speak for themselves.*

In a sense, this observation opens a Pandora's box; an unlimited number of variables change over time. How do we know which ones have to be considered to find the tax effect? One major purpose of economic theory is to help isolate a small set of variables that are important in influencing behaviour. The taxes and labour supply example illustrates how basic economic theory is useful in organizing thoughts.

The theory of labour supply posits that the work decision is based on the rational allocation of time.[1] Suppose Mr. Dressup has only a certain number of hours in the day: How many hours should he devote to work in the market, and how many hours to leisure? Dressup derives satisfaction (utility) from leisure, but to earn income he must work and thereby surrender leisure time. Dressup's problem is to find the combination of income and leisure that maximizes his utility.

---

[1] The theory of labour supply is presented here verbally. A graphical exposition appears in Chapter 21 under "Labour Supply."

Suppose Dressup's wage rate is w per hour. The wage is the cost of Dressup's time. For every hour he spends at leisure, Dressup gives up $w in wages—time is literally money. However, a "rational" individual generally will not work every possible hour, even though leisure is costly. People spend time on leisure to the extent that leisure's benefits exceed its costs.

This model may seem absurdly simple. It ignores the possibility that an individual's labour supply behaviour may depend on the work decisions of other family members. Neither does the model consider whether the individual can work as many hours as desired. Indeed, the entire notion that people make their decisions by rationally considering costs and benefits may appear unrealistic.

However, the whole point of model building is to simplify as much as possible, so that a problem is reduced to its essentials. The literary critic Lytton Strachey said, "Omission is the beginning of all art" (Lipton, 1977: 93). Omission is also the beginning of all good economic analysis. A model should not be judged on the basis of whether or not it is true, but on whether the model is plausible and informative. Most work in modern economics is based on the assumption that maximization of utility is a good working hypothesis. This point of view is taken throughout the book.

Imagine that Mr. Dressup has found his utility-maximizing combination of income and leisure based on his wage rate of w. Now the government imposes a tax on wage income of t percent. Then Dressup's after-tax or net wage is $\$(1 - t)w$. (Thus, for example, if his before-tax wage rate is $10 and his tax rate is 20 percent, his net wage is $8.) How will a rational individual react—work more, work less, or not change? In public debate, arguments for all three possibilities are made with great assurance. In fact, however, the impact of an earnings tax on hours of work *cannot* be predicted on theoretical grounds.

To see this, first observe that the wage tax lowers the effective price of leisure. Before the tax, consumption of an hour of leisure cost Dressup $w. Under the earnings tax, because Dressup's net wage is lower, an hour of leisure costs him only $\$(1 - t)w$. Since leisure has become cheaper, he will tend to consume more of it—to work less. This is called the *substitution effect*.

Another effect occurs simultaneously when the tax is imposed. Assume Dressup will work a certain number of hours regardless of all feasible changes in the net wage. After the tax, Dressup receives only $\$(1 - t)w$ for each of these hours, while before it was $w. In a real sense, Dressup has suffered a loss of income. To the extent that leisure is a *normal good*—consumption increases when income increases and vice versa—this income loss leads to less consumption of leisure. But less leisure means more work. Because the earnings tax makes Dressup poorer, it induces him to work more. This is called the *income effect*.

Thus, the tax simultaneously produces two effects: It induces substitution toward the cheaper activity (leisure), and it reduces real income. Since the substitution and income effects work in opposite directions, the impact of an earnings tax cannot be determined by theorizing alone. Consider the following two statements:

1. "With these high taxes, it's really not worth it for me to work as much as I used to."
2. "With these high taxes, I have to work more to maintain my standard of living."

For a person making the first statement, the substitution effect dominates, while in the second statement the income effect dominates. Both statements can reflect perfectly rational behaviour.

The importance of the uncertainty caused by the conflict of income and substitution effects cannot be overemphasized. Only **empirical work**—analysis based on observation and experience as opposed to theory—can answer the question of how labour force behaviour is affected by changes in the tax system. Even intense armchair speculation on this matter must be regarded with considerable skepticism.

Although we have developed the argument with a labour supply example, the lesson is more general—one major purpose of theory is to make us aware of the areas of our ignorance.

METHODS OF EMPIRICAL ANALYSIS

Theory helps to organize thoughts about how people react to changes in their economic environment. But it usually cannot tell us the magnitude of such responses. Indeed, in the labour supply case just discussed, theory alone cannot even predict the *direction* of the likely changes. Empirical work becomes necessary. The three types of empirical strategies are personal interviews, experiments, and econometric estimation. With each technique, the connections to theory are vital. Theory influences how the study is organized, which questions are asked, and how the results are interpreted.

Interviews

The most straightforward way to find out whether some government activity influences people's behaviour is simply to ask them. In a crude way, this is the kind of empirical "analysis" done by reporters. ("Tell me, are you going to delay your retirement if the government lowers your Canada Pension Plan benefit?") A number of sophisticated interview studies have been done to assess the effect of taxes on labour supply. A group of British lawyers and accountants were carefully questioned as to how they determined their hours of work, whether they were aware of the tax rates they faced, and if these tax rates created any incentives or disincentives to work. The responses suggested that relatively few people were affected by taxes (Break, 1957: 549). A later survey of a group of affluent Americans told much the same story. "Only one-eighth … said that they have actually curtailed their work effort because of the progressive income tax.… Those facing the highest marginal tax rates reported work disincentives only a little more frequently than did those facing the lower rates" (Barlow, Brazer, and Morgan, 1966: 3).

Pitfalls of interviews. However, interpretation of these survey results requires caution. After all, just because an individual cannot recite his or her tax rate does not mean the individual is unaware of the discrepancy between before- and after-tax pay.

An old Chinese proverb counsels, "Listen to what a person says and then watch what he does." The fact that people *say* something about their behaviour does not make it true. Some people are embarrassed to admit that financial considerations affect their labour supply decisions. ("I work for fulfilment.") Others complain about government just for the sheer fun of it, while in reality they are not influenced by taxes. If you want to find out what radio station a family listens to, what makes more sense: to ask them, or to see where the radio dial is set?

Experiments

At the outset, we stressed that the basic problem in doing empirical work in economics is the inability to do controlled experiments with the economy. However, the federal and provincial governments have funded several studies, such as the Mincome experiment in the 1970s and the NB Works program in the 1990s, that have applied experimental methodologies to the study of economic behaviour. For example, in the Mincome experiment over one thousand families in Manitoba were enrolled in a study that compared the labour supplies of a control group of households with other households who were offered income support programs with marginal tax rates of 35, 50, and 75 percent.

The objective of the study was to determine how alternative levels of income support and tax rates on earnings affected households' incentives to work.[2]

Pitfalls of social experiments. Although experiments are a promising way to learn about economic behaviour, technical problems tend to diminish their usefulness. One reason is that the classical methodology for experiments requires that samples be truly random—the members of the sample must be representative of the population whose behaviour is under consideration. In social experiments, it is virtually impossible to maintain a random sample, even if one is available initially. Some people leave the program to take new jobs. Others simply decide they don't want to participate. Because such people *self*-select out of the sample, the characteristics of the group left are no longer representative of the population.

In addition, unlike plants or laboratory animals, human beings are aware they are participating in an experiment. This consciousness affects their behaviour. A related point is that people within the group may react differently to a program when only a small number of participants are involved than they would when the program is universal. Or an experiment that lasts only a few months may produce different behaviour from a program expected to be permanent.

One thing is certain. Social experiments are costly. For example, the NB Works program, which provides education, training, and employment for social assistance recipients with low educational attainment, is projected to cost between $60,000 and $100,000 per participant.[3] But such costs should be kept in perspective. It may be worthwhile to spend a few million dollars to determine the efficacy of a program that would involve the expenditure of billions of dollars.

Laboratory experiments. Certain kinds of economic behaviour can also be studied in laboratory settings, an approach often used by psychologists. An investigator recruits a group of people (subjects) who perform various tasks. The investigator observes their behaviour. To study labour supply, an investigator might begin by noting from the theory of labour supply that a key variable is the net wage rate. A possible experimental strategy would be to offer subjects different rewards for completing various jobs and record how the amount of effort varies with the reward.

---

[2] Hum and Simpson (1991 and 1993) found that there were modest reductions in the labour supplied by participants in the Mincome experiment.
[3] Milne (1995: 142–43).

Laboratory experiments are subject to some of the pitfalls of social experiments. The main problem is that the environment in which behaviour is observed is artificial. Moreover, the subjects, who are often college undergraduates, are unlikely to be representative of the population as a whole. However, laboratory experiments are much cheaper than social experiments and provide more flexibility. Their popularity has been growing in recent years, and as we see in later chapters, they have provided some very interesting results.

Econometric Studies

Econometrics is the statistical analysis of economic data. While economists are unable to control historical events, econometrics makes it possible to assess the importance of events that *did* occur.

The simple labour supply model suggested that annual hours of work (L) depend on the net wage rate (w_n). (By definition, $w_n = (1 - t)w$, where t is the tax rate.) A bit of thought suggests that nonlabour income such as dividends and interest (A), age (X_1), and number of children (X_2) may also influence hours of work. The econometrician chooses a particular algebraic form to summarize the relationship between hours of work and these explanatory variables. A particularly simple form is:

$$L = \alpha_0 + \alpha_1 w_n + \alpha_2 A + \alpha_3 X_1 + \alpha_4 X_2 + \varepsilon \qquad (3.1)$$

The α's are the **parameters** of the equation and ε is a **random error**. The parameters show how a change in a given right-hand side variable affects hours of work. If $\alpha_1 = 0$, the net wage has no impact on hours of work. If α_1 is greater than 0, increases in the net wage induce people to work more—the substitution effect dominates. If α_1 is less than 0, increases in the net wage induce people to work less—the income effect dominates.

The presence of the random error ε reflects the influences on labour supply that are unobservable to the investigator. No matter how many variables are included in the study, there is always some behaviour that cannot be explained by the model.

Clearly, if we knew the α's, all debate over the effect of taxes on labour supply would be settled. The practical side of econometrics is to estimate the α's by application of various techniques. The most popular method is called **multiple regression analysis**. The heat of the debate over labour supply indicates that this technique does not always lead to conclusive results. To understand why, we consider its application to the labour supply example.

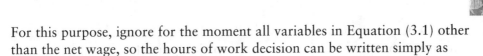

For this purpose, ignore for the moment all variables in Equation (3.1) other than the net wage, so the hours of work decision can be written simply as

$$L = \alpha_0 + \alpha_1 w_n + \varepsilon \qquad (3.2)$$

Equation (3.2) is characterized as linear because if it is graphed with L and w_n on the axes, the result is a straight line.

Suppose information is obtained on hours of work and on after-tax wages for a sample of people. Plotting those observations gives a scatter of points like that in Figure 3.1A. Obviously, no single straight line can fit through all these points. The purpose of multiple regression analysis is to find the parameters of the line that fits best.[4] Such a **regression line** is illustrated in Figure 3.1B. The regression line is a geometric representation of Equation (3.2), and its slope is an estimate of α_1. (A parameter estimate is sometimes called a *regression coefficient.*)

After α_1 is estimated, its reliability must be considered. Is it likely to be close to the "true" value of α_1? To see why this is an issue, suppose our scatter of points looked like that in Figure 3.1C. The regression line is identical to that in Figure 3.1B, but the scatter of points is more diffuse. Even though the estimates of the α's are the same as those in Figure 3.1B, one has less faith in their reliability. Econometricians calculate a measure called the standard error, which indicates how much an estimated parameter can vary from the true

Figure 3.1

Multiple Regression Analysis

A. A scatter diagram   B. A regression line   C. A regression line in a scatter diagram with increased dispersion

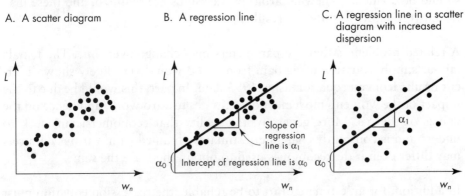

---

[4] The best line minimizes the sum of the squared vertical distances between the points on the line and the points in the scatter. See Gujarati (1978).

value. When the standard error is small in relation to the size of the estimated parameter, the coefficient is said to be **statistically significant**.

This example assumed there is only one explanatory variable, the net wage. Suppose that instead there were two variables in the equation: the net wage and nonlabour income. In analogy to fitting a regression *line* in a two-dimensional space, a regression *plane* can be fitted through a scatter of points in a three-dimensional space. For more than two variables, there is no convenient geometrical representation. Nevertheless, similar mathematical principles are applied to produce estimates of the parameters for any number of explanatory variables (provided there are fewer variables than observations). The actual calculations are done with computers.

With estimates of the α's in hand, inferences can be made about the changes in L induced by changes in the net wage. Suppose $\alpha_1 = 100$. If a tax increase lowers the wage by 50 cents, then an individual will work 50 hours (100 × $.50) less per year.

Pitfalls of econometric analysis. There are difficulties involved in doing econometrics that explain why different investigators may reach contradictory conclusions. For example, implicit in Equation (3.1) is the assumption that the same equation can describe everyone's behaviour. However, different types of people may have different hours-of-work equations. Married women may react differently than married men to change in the net wage. Similarly, the young and the old have different behavioural patterns. Grouping together people with different behaviour results in misleading parameter estimates. Investigators generally do not know beforehand along what lines their samples should be divided. Somewhat arbitrary decisions are required, and these may lead investigators to different results.

A related problem is that the parameters may change over time. The female labour supply equation using data from 1960 would very likely show different results from an equation using 1995 data. In part, this would be due to the impact of the women's movement on attitudes toward work, and hence on the values of the α's. More generally, the reality that econometricians seek to understand is constantly changing. Estimates obtained from various data sets may differ even if the techniques used to obtain them are the same.

In addition, for an estimate of α_1 to be reliable, the regression equation must include all the relevant variables. Otherwise, some effects that are actually due to an omitted variable may be attributed to the net wage. Important variables are sometimes left out of an equation because information on them is simply not available. For example, it is very difficult to obtain reliable information on people's sources of nonlabour income. Suppose:

1. As nonlabour income increases (other things being the same), people tend to work less.
2. There is a tendency for people with high wages also to have high non-labour income.

If nonlabour income is omitted from the equation, part of its effect on hours of work would be attributed to the wage, and the estimate of α_1 would be lower than its true value. In general, an estimate of α_1 is biased unless all the other variables that affect hours of work and that are also systematically related to the net wage are included.

A more severe version of this problem occurs when a potentially important variable is inherently unmeasurable. Attitudes such as aggressiveness may influence work decisions, but there are no satisfactory ways for quantifying these attitudes.

Sometimes there are controversies over which variables should be included in a regression equation. Should an individual's educational level be included? Some argue that education affects attitudes toward work and therefore should be included as an explanatory variable. Others believe education affects work decisions only to the extent that it changes the wage, and therefore should not be included. While economic theory helps give some structure to the search for explanatory variables, it is rarely definitive. Different investigators make different judgments.

Difficulties in measuring variables can also make it hard to obtain reliable estimates. Consider the problems in measuring hours of work. Superficially, this seems like a straightforward issue—merely find out how much time elapses at the workplace. But a better measure would consider coffee breaks and "goofing off" time. These factors are obviously more difficult to measure. Measuring the wage rate also presents substantial problems. Ideally, the computation should include not only what a worker receives in the paycheque at the end of the week, but also the value of fringe benefits—pension rights, insurance programs, access to a company car, and so forth.

Finally, an important assumption is that variables on the right-hand side of the equation affect the left-hand variable, but not vice versa. If this is not true, serious problems arise. Suppose that α_1 of Equation (3.1) is found to be positive. One interpretation is that when the net wage increases, people choose to

work more. Another plausible interpretation is that employers pay higher wages to people who work longer hours. Indeed, wage rates might affect hours worked, and *simultaneously* hours worked might affect wages. If so, then the estimate of α_1 generated by multiple regression analysis does not correctly measure the effect of changes in the net wage on people's work decisions.

Several statistical techniques are available for dealing with this simultaneity problem. They tend to be complicated, and different techniques can lead to different answers. This is another source of discrepancies in the results of econometric studies.

CONCLUDING REMARKS

For those who seek to describe economic behaviour, theory plays a crucial role in helping to isolate a set of potentially important variables. Empirical work is then needed to see whether the theory is consistent with real-world phenomena. Currently the most widespread method of empirical work in economics is econometric analysis, because economists tend to be most comfortable with results based on data from real-world environments. However, honest econometricians may come to very different conclusions. The data they use are imperfect, and implementation requires that assumptions be made. Reasonable people can disagree on the proper interpretation of a particular set of "facts."

This does not mean we should abandon all hope of learning about the factors that influence economic behaviour. The economist researching an empirical question will doubtless come across a number of studies, each making somewhat different assumptions, each emphasizing a somewhat different aspect of the problem, and each therefore arriving at a somewhat different conclusion. In many cases one can reconcile the different studies and construct a coherent picture of the phenomenon under discussion. Feldstein (1982: 830) has likened the economist who undertakes such a task to the maharaja in the children's fable about the five blind men who examined an elephant: The important lesson in that story is not the fact that each blind man came away with a partial and "incorrect" piece of evidence. The lesson is rather that an intelligent maharaja who studied the findings of these five men could probably piece together a good judgmental picture of an elephant, especially if he had previously seen some other four-footed animal.

On the numerous occasions throughout this book when we refer to the results of empirical studies, the caveats presented here should be kept in mind. In

cases where the profession has failed to achieve consensus, the opposing views are discussed. But more generally, it is hoped that this introduction to empirical methodology induces a healthy skepticism concerning claims about economic behaviour that occur in public debate and begin with the magic words "studies have proved."

SUMMARY

- Because economists are generally unable to perform carefully controlled experiments with the economy, the effects of economic policy are difficult to determine.

- Economic theory helps specify the factors that might affect a given kind of behaviour. Generally, however, theory alone cannot say how important any particular factor is.

- Empirical research attempts to measure both the direction and size of the effect of government policy changes on behaviour. Common types of empirical studies are interview studies, social and laboratory experiments, and econometric analysis.

- Interview studies consist of directly asking people how various policies affect their behaviour. However, people may not actually react to policies in the way they say they do.

- Social experiments subject one group of people to some policy and compare their behaviour with that of a control group. Problems can arise because the experiment itself may affect people's behaviour, because it is difficult to obtain a random sample, and because social experiments are quite costly.

- Laboratory experiments are used to study some types of economic decisions, but in the artificial atmosphere subjects may not replicate real-world behaviour.

- Econometrics is the statistical analysis of economic data. In econometrics, the effects of various policies are inferred from observed behaviour.

- Techniques such as multiple regression analysis are used to pick the "best" parameters for the model. Knowing the parameters allows one to predict the effects of policy changes.

- Econometrics is not without pitfalls. Misleading results are obtained if data from greatly dissimilar groups are combined; if important variables are omitted; if the wrong mathematical form is adopted; if variables are incorrectly measured; or if there is simultaneous causation between variables.

DISCUSSION QUESTIONS

1. Like economists, astronomers are generally unable to perform controlled experiments. Yet astronomy is considered more of an exact science than economics. Why?

2. In October 1993, the Alberta government cut welfare benefits by between 10 and 20 percent. Between October 1993 and October 1995, the total welfare case load in Alberta declined from 70,486 to 46,715.

    a. Does the theory of labour supply predict a decline in the welfare case load in response to a reduction in welfare benefits?
    b. How would you construct a survey to find out what happened to former welfare recipients?
    c. If you were to conduct an experiment to investigate the effect of welfare payments on the number of welfare recipients, would it be a social or a laboratory experiment? Why? Describe your experiment.
    d. How would you conduct an econometric investigation? Which data would you need? Which algebraic function would you choose?
    e. In any of your studies did you consider variables other than the size of welfare payments? If so, why did you choose them?

3. In 1994 the National Cancer Institute in the United States stated there was no conclusive evidence that regular mammograms reduce the rate of breast cancer deaths for women under 50. The American Medical Association disagreed, and recommended that women in their 40s have regular mammograms. Relate the problems faced by researchers trying to determine the usefulness of mammograms to the problems faced by economists trying to determine the effects of economic policy.

4. In the 1970s, researchers at the RAND Corporation conducted a social experiment to investigate the relationship between health insurance coverage and health care utilization. In this experiment, samples of individuals were induced to trade their normal insurance policies for new RAND policies that offered various coinsurance rates (i.e., different rates at which the insurance would reimburse the individual for health care expenses). In 1993, the Clinton administration used the results of the RAND experiment to predict how health care utilization would increase if insurance coverage were made universal. What problems might arise in using the social experimentation results to predict the impact of universal coverage?

REFERENCES

Barlow, Robin, Harvey E. Brazer, and James N. Morgan. *Economic Behavior of the Affluent*. Washington, DC: Brookings Institution, 1966.

Break, George F. "Income Taxes and Incentives to Work." *American Economic Review* 47 (1957): 529–49.

Feldstein, Martin S. "Inflation, Tax Rules, and Investment: Some Econometric Evidence." *Econometrica* 50, no. 4 (July 1982): 825–62.

Gujarati, D. *Basic Econometrics.* New York: McGraw-Hill, 1978.

Hum, Derek, and W. Simpson. "Economic Response to a Guaranteed Annual Income: Experience from Canada and the United States." *Journal of Labor Economics* 11, no. 1 (1993): S263–96.

Hum, Derek, and Wayne Simpson. *Income Maintenance, Work Effort, and the Canadian Mincome Experiment.* Ottawa: Economic Council of Canada, 1991.

Lipton, James. *An Exaltation of Larks.* New York: Penguin Books, 1977.

Milne, William. "Revising Social Assistance Programs in New Brunswick: A Look at the Demonstration Projects," in *Helping the Poor: A Qualified Case for "Workfare."* Toronto: C.D. Howe Institute, 1995, pp. 121–50.

Chapter 4

Tools of Normative Analysis

[The goals of government] should be to realize maximum human dignity, maximum human welfare, maximum environmental quality and minimum violence in human relationships.

—Pierre Elliott Trudeau

As citizens we are called on to evaluate a constant flow of proposals concerning government's role in the economy. Should income taxes be raised? Is it sensible to change the age at which Canada Pension Plan payments begin? Should there be stricter controls on auto emissions? The list is virtually endless. Given the enormous diversity of the government's economic activities, some kind of general framework is needed to organize thoughts about the desirability of various government actions. Without such a systematic framework, each government program ends up being evaluated on an ad hoc basis, and a coherent economic policy becomes impossible to achieve.

WELFARE ECONOMICS

The framework used by most public finance specialists is **welfare economics,** the branch of economic theory concerned with the social desirability of alternative economic states.[1] In this chapter we sketch the fundamentals of welfare economics. The theory is used to distinguish the circumstances

---

[1] Welfare economics relies heavily on certain basic economic tools, particularly indifference curves.

under which markets can be expected to perform well from those under which markets fail to produce desirable results.

Pure Exchange Economy

We begin by considering a very simple economy: only two people who consume two commodities with fixed supplies. The only economic problem here is to allocate amounts of the two goods between the two people. As simple as this model is, all the important results from the two goods–two person case hold in economies with many people and commodities.[2] The two-by-two case is analyzed because of its simplicity.

The two people are Adam and Eve, and the two commodities are apples (food) and fig leaves (clothing). An analytical device known as the **Edgeworth Box** depicts the distribution of apples and fig leaves between Adam and Eve.[3] In Figure 4.1, the length of the Edgeworth Box, *Os*, represents the total number of apples available in the economy; the height, *Or*, is the total number of fig leaves. The amounts of the goods consumed by Adam are measured by dis-

Figure 4.1

Edgeworth Box

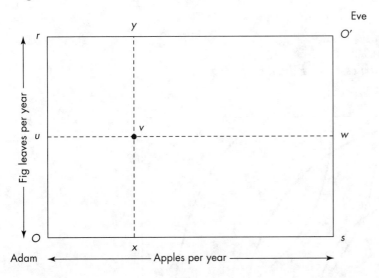

[2] See chapter 11 of Henderson and Quandt (1980) where the results are derived using calculus.
[3] Named after the great nineteenth-century economist F.Y. Edgeworth.

tances from point O; the quantities consumed by Eve are measured by distances from O'. For example, at point v, Adam consumes Ou fig leaves and Ox apples, while Eve consumes $O'y$ apples and $O'w$ fig leaves. Thus, any point within the Edgeworth Box represents some allocation of apples and fig leaves between Adam and Eve.

Now assume Adam and Eve each have a set of conventionally shaped indifference curves that represent their preferences for apples and fig leaves. In Figure 4.2, both sets of indifference curves are superimposed onto the Edgeworth Box. Adam's are labelled with A's; Eve's are labelled with E's. Indifference curves with greater numbers represent higher levels of happiness (utility). Adam is happier on indifference curve A_3 than on A_2 or A_1, and Eve is happier on indifference curve E_3 than on E_2 or E_1. In general, Eve's utility increases as her position moves toward the southwest, while Adam's utility increases as he moves toward the northeast.

Suppose some arbitrary distribution of apples and fig leaves is selected—say point g in Figure 4.3. A_gA_g is Adam's indifference curve that runs through point g, and E_gE_g is Eve's. Now pose the following question: Is it possible to reallocate apples and fig leaves between Adam and Eve in such a way that Adam is made better off, while Eve is made no worse off? A moment's thought suggests such an allocation, at point h. Adam is better off at this point because indif-

Figure 4.2

Indifference Curves in an Edgeworth Box

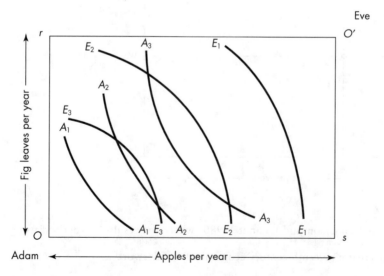

Figure 4.3

Making Adam Better Off without Eve Becoming Worse Off

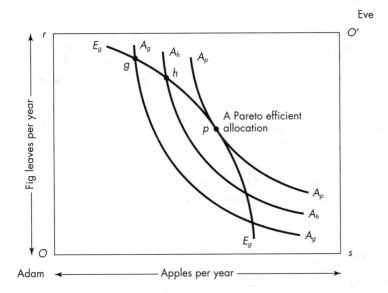

ference curve $A_h A_h$ represents a higher utility level for him than $A_g A_g$. On the other hand, Eve is no worse off at h because she is on her original indifference curve, $E_g E_g$.

Can Adam's welfare be further increased without doing any harm to Eve? As long as Adam can be moved to indifference curves further to the northeast while still remaining on $E_g E_g$ it is possible. This process can be continued until Adam's indifference curve is just touching $E_g E_g$, which occurs at point p in Figure 4.3. The only way to put Adam on a higher indifference curve than $A_p A_p$ would be to put Eve on a lower one. An allocation such as point p, at which the only way to make one person better off is to make another person worse off, is called **Pareto efficient**.[4] Pareto efficiency is often used as the standard for evaluating the desirability of an allocation of resources. If the allocation is not Pareto efficient, it is "wasteful" in the sense that it is possible to make someone better off without hurting anybody else. When economists use the word *efficient*, they usually have the notion of Pareto efficiency in mind.

---

[4] Named after the nineteenth-century economist Vilfredo Pareto.

A related notion is that of a **Pareto improvement**—a reallocation of resources that makes one person better off without making anyone else worse off.[5] In Figure 4.3, the move from g to h is a Pareto improvement, as is the move from h to p.

Point p is not the only Pareto efficient allocation that could have been reached by starting at point g. Figure 4.4 examines whether we can make Eve better off without lowering the utility of Adam. Logic similar to that surrounding Figure 4.3 suggests moving Eve to indifference curves further to the southwest, provided that the allocation remains on A_gA_g. In doing so, a point like p_1 is isolated. At p_1, the only way to improve Eve's welfare is to move Adam to a lower indifference curve. Then, by definition, p_1 is a Pareto efficient allocation.

So far, we have been looking at moves that make one person better off and leave the other at the same level of utility. In Figure 4.5 we consider reallocations from

Figure 4.4

Making Eve Better Off without Adam Becoming Worse Off

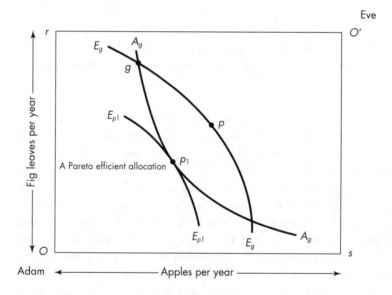

[5] A **potential Pareto improvement** is a reallocation where the gains achieved by those who are made better off exceed the losses sustained by those who are made worse off. This type of reallocation is referred to as a "potential" Pareto improvement because with appropriate lump-sum taxes on those who gain and lump-sum compensation for those who lose, a Pareto improvement could be achieved.

Figure 4.5

Making Both Adam and Eve Better Off

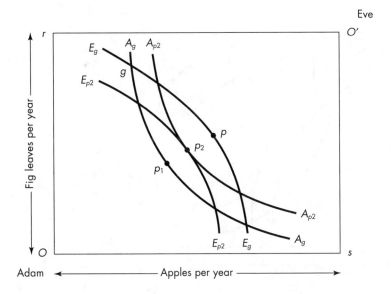

point *g* that make *both* Adam and Eve better off. At p_2, for example, Adam is better off than at point *g* ($A_{p2}A_{p2}$ is further to the northeast than A_gA_g) and so is Eve ($E_{p2}E_{p2}$ is further to the southwest than E_gE_g). Point p_2 is Pareto efficient, because at that point it is impossible to make either individual better off without making the other worse off. It should now be clear that starting at point *g*, a whole set of Pareto efficient points can be found. They differ with respect to how much each of the parties gains from the reallocation of resources.

Recall that the initial point *g* was selected arbitrarily. We can repeat the procedure for finding Pareto efficient allocations with any starting point. Had point *k* in Figure 4.6 been the original allocation, Pareto efficient allocations like p_3 and p_4 could have been isolated. This exercise reveals a whole set of Pareto efficient points in the Edgeworth Box. The locus of all the Pareto efficient points is called the **contract curve**, and is denoted *mm* in Figure 4.7. Note that for an allocation to be Pareto efficient (to be on *mm*), it must be a point at which the indifference curves of Adam and Eve are barely touching. In mathematical terms, the indifference curves are tangent—the slopes of the indifference curves are equal.

In economic terms, the absolute value of the slope of the indifference curve indicates the rate at which the individual is willing to trade one good for an

Figure 4.6

Starting from a Different Initial Point

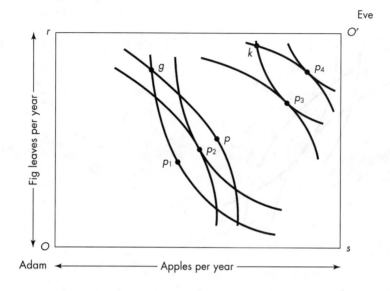

Figure 4.7

The Contract Curve

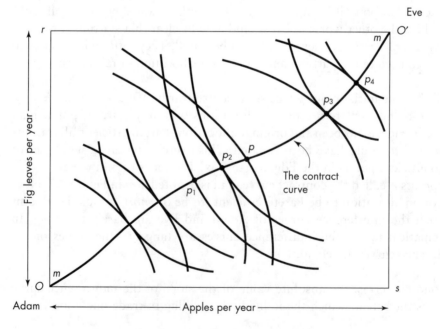

additional amount of another, called the *marginal rate of substitution* (MRS). Hence, Pareto efficiency requires that marginal rates of substitution be equal for all consumers:

$$MRS_{af}{}^{Adam} = MRS_{af}{}^{Eve} \qquad\qquad (4.1)$$

where $MRS_{af}{}^{Adam}$ is Adam's marginal rate of substitution of apples for fig leaves, and $MRS_{af}{}^{Eve}$ is Eve's.

An Economy with Production

The production possibilities curve. So far we have assumed that supplies of all the commodities are fixed. Consider what happens when productive inputs can shift between the production of apples and fig leaves, so the quantities of the two goods are alterable. Provided the inputs are efficiently used, if more apples are produced, then fig leaf production must necessarily fall and vice versa. The **production possibilities curve** shows the maximum quantity of fig leaves that can be produced along with any given quantity of apples.[6] A typical production possibilities curve is depicted as *CC* in Figure 4.8. As shown in Figure 4.8, one option available to the economy is to produce *Ow* fig leaves and

Figure 4.8

Production Possibilities Curve

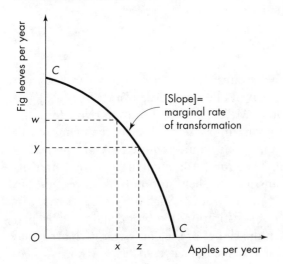

---

[6] The production possibilities curve can be derived from an Edgeworth Box whose dimensions represent the quantities of inputs available for production.

Ox apples. The economy can increase apple production from Ox to Oz, distance xz. To do this, inputs have to be removed from the production of fig leaves and devoted to apples. Fig leaf production must fall by distance wy if apple production is to increase by xz. The ratio of distance wy to distance xz is called the **marginal rate of transformation** of apples for fig leaves (MRT_{af}) because it shows the rate at which the economy can transform apples into fig leaves. Just as MRS_{af} measures the absolute value of the slope of an indifference curve, MRT_{af} measures the absolute value of the slope of the production possibilities curve.

It is useful to express the marginal rate of transformation in terms of **marginal cost** (MC)—the incremental production cost of one more unit of output. To do so, recall that society can increase apple production by xz only by giving up wy fig leaves. In effect, then, the distance wy represents the incremental cost of producing apples, which we denote MC_a. Similarly, the distance xz is the incremental cost of producing fig leaves, MC_f. By definition, the absolute value of the slope of the production possibilities curve is distance wy divided by xz, or MC_a/MC_f. But also by definition, the slope of the production possibilities curve is the marginal rate of transformation. Hence, we have shown that

$$MRT_{af} = \frac{MC_a}{MC_f} \qquad (4.2)$$

Efficiency conditions with variable production. When the supplies of apples and fig leaves are variable, the condition for Pareto efficiency in Equation (4.1) must be extended. The condition becomes

$$MRT_{af} = MRS_{af}^{Adam} = MRS_{af}^{Eve} \qquad (4.3)$$

A simple arithmetic example demonstrates why the first equality in Equation (4.3) must hold. Suppose that at a given allocation Adam's MRS_{af} is 1/3, and the MRT_{af} is 2/3. By the definition of MRT_{af}, at this allocation two additional fig leaves could be produced by giving up three apples. By the definition of MRS_{af}, if Adam lost three extra apples, he would require only one fig leaf to maintain his original utility level. Therefore, Adam could be made better off by giving up three apples and transforming them into two fig leaves, and no one else would be made worse off in the process. Such a trade is *always* possible as long as the marginal rate of substitution does not equal the marginal rate of transformation. Only when the slopes of the curves for each are equal is it impossible to make a Pareto improvement. Hence, $MRT_{af} = MRS_{af}$ is a necessary condition for Pareto efficiency. The rate at which apples can be transformed into fig leaves (MRT_{af}) must equal the rate at which consumers are willing to trade apples for fig leaves (MRS_{af}).

Using Equation (4.2), the conditions for Pareto efficiency can be reinterpreted in terms of marginal cost. Just substitute (4.2) into (4.3), which gives us

$$\frac{MC_a}{MC_f} = MRS_{af}{}^{Adam} = MRS_{af}{}^{Eve} \qquad (4.4)$$

as a necessary condition for Pareto efficiency.

THE FUNDAMENTAL THEOREM OF WELFARE ECONOMICS

Now that we have described the necessary conditions for Pareto efficiency, we may ask whether a real-world economy will achieve this apparently desirable state. The Fundamental Theorem of Welfare Economics provides an answer:

- As long as producers and consumers act as perfect competitors, that is, take prices as given, then under *certain conditions* (discussed in Chapter 5) a Pareto efficient allocation of resources emerges.

Thus, a competitive economy "automatically" allocates resources efficiently, without any need for centralized direction (shades of Adam Smith's "invisible hand"). In a way, the fundamental theorem merely formalizes an insight that has long been recognized: When it comes to providing goods and services, free enterprise systems are amazingly productive.[7]

A rigorous proof of the fundamental theorem requires fairly sophisticated mathematics, but we can provide an intuitive justification. The essence of competition is that all people face the same prices—each consumer and producer is so small relative to the market that his or her actions alone cannot affect prices. In our example, this means Adam and Eve both pay the same prices for fig leaves (P_f) and apples (P_a). A basic result from the theory of rational choice is that a necessary condition for Adam to maximize utility is

$$MRS_{af}{}^{Adam} = \frac{P_a}{P_f} \qquad (4.5)$$

---

[7] "The bourgeoisie, during its rule of scarce 100 years, has created more massive and more colossal productive forces than have all preceding generations together," according to Karl Marx and Friedrich Engels in *The Communist Manifesto*, Part I (Tucker, 1978: 477).

Similarly, Eve's utility-maximizing bundle is characterized by

$$MRS_{af}{}^{Eve} = \frac{P_a}{P_f} \qquad (4.6)$$

Equations (4.5) and (4.6) together imply that

$$MRS_{af}{}^{Adam} = MRS_{af}{}^{Eve}$$

This condition, though, is identical to Equation (4.1), one of the necessary conditions for Pareto efficiency.

However, as emphasized in the preceding section, we must consider the production side as well. A basic result from economic theory is that a profit-maximizing competitive firm produces output up to the point at which marginal cost and price are equal. In our example, this means $P_a = MC_a$ and $P_f = MC_f$, or

$$\frac{MC_a}{MC_f} = \frac{P_a}{P_f} \qquad (4.7)$$

But recall from Equation (4.2) that MC_a/MC_f is just the marginal rate of transformation. Thus, we can rewrite (4.7) as

$$MRT_{af} = \frac{P_a}{P_f} \qquad (4.8)$$

Now, consider Equations (4.5), (4.6), and (4.8), and notice that P_a/P_f appears on the right-hand side of each. Hence, these three equations together imply that $MRS_{af}{}^{Adam} = MRS_{af}{}^{Eve} = MRT_{af}$, which is the necessary condition for Pareto efficiency. Competition, along with maximizing behaviour on the part of all individuals, leads to an efficient outcome. The necessary condition for Pareto efficiency holds in a competitive economy because all consumers and producers face the same prices.

Finally, we can take advantage of Equation (4.4) to write the conditions for Pareto efficiency in terms of marginal cost. Simply substitute (4.5) or (4.6) into (4.4) to find

$$\frac{P_a}{P_f} = \frac{MC_a}{MC_f} \qquad (4.9)$$

Pareto efficiency requires that prices be in the same ratios as marginal costs, and competition guarantees this condition is met. The marginal cost of a commodity is the additional cost to society of providing it. According to Equation (4.9), efficiency requires that the additional cost of each commodity be reflected in its price.

The Role of Fairness

If properly functioning competitive markets allocate resources efficiently, what role does the government have to play in the economy? Only a very small government would appear to be appropriate. Its main function would be to establish a setting in which property rights are protected so that competition can work. Government provides law and order, a court system, and national defence. Anything more is superfluous. However, such reasoning is based on a superficial understanding of the fundamental theorem. Things are really much more complicated. For one thing, it has implicitly been assumed that efficiency is the only criterion for deciding if a given allocation of resources is good. It is not obvious, however, that Pareto efficiency by itself is desirable.

To see why, let us return to the simple model in which the total quantity of each good is fixed. Consider Figure 4.9, which reproduces the contract curve *mm* derived in Figure 4.7. Compare the two allocations p_5 (at the lower left-

Figure 4.9

Efficiency versus Equity

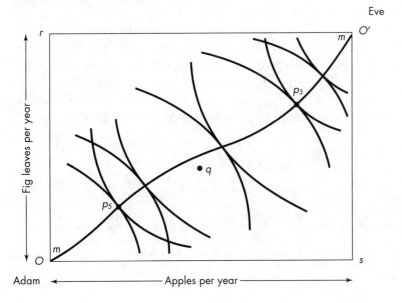

hand corner of the box) and q (located near the centre). Because p_5 lies on the contract curve, by definition it is Pareto efficient. On the other hand, q is inefficient. Is allocation p_5 therefore better? That depends on what is meant by better. To the extent that society prefers a relatively equal distribution of real income, q might be preferred to p_5, even though q is not Pareto efficient. On the other hand, society might not care about distribution at all, or perhaps care more about Eve than Adam. In this case, p_5 would be preferred to q.

The key point is that the criterion of Pareto efficiency by itself is not enough to rank alternative allocations of resources. Rather, explicit value judgments are required on the fairness of the distribution of utility. To formalize this concept, note that the contract curve implicitly defines a relationship between the maximum amount of utility that Adam can attain for each level of Eve's utility. In Figure 4.10, Eve's utility is plotted on the horizontal axis, and Adam's utility is recorded on the vertical axis. Curve *UU* is the **utility possibilities curve** derived from the contract curve.[8] It shows the maximum amount of one person's utility given the other individual's utility level. Point $\tilde{p}_5$ corresponds to point p_5 on the contract curve in Figure 4.9. Here, Eve's utility is relatively high compared to Adam's. Point $\tilde{p}_3$ in Figure 4.10, which corresponds to p_3 in Figure 4.9, is just the opposite. Point $\tilde{q}$ corresponds to point q in Figure 4.9. Because q is off the contract curve, q must be inside the utility possibilities curve, reflecting the fact that it is possible to increase one person's utility without decreasing the other's.

All points on or below the utility possibilities curve are attainable by society; all points above it are not attainable. By definition, all points on *UU* are Pareto efficient, but they represent very different distributions of real income between Adam and Eve. Which point is best? The conventional way to answer this question is to postulate a **social welfare function**, which embodies society's views on the relative deservedness of Adam and Eve. Imagine that just as an *individual's* welfare depends on the quantities of commodities he or she consumes, *society's* welfare depends on the utilities of each of its members. Algebraically, social welfare (W) is some function $F( )$ of each individual's utility:

$$W = F(U^{Adam}, U^{Eve}) \tag{4.10}$$

---

[8] The production possibilities curve in Figure 4.8 is drawn on the reasonable assumption that the absolute value of its slope continually increases as we move downward along it. The more apples produced, the more fig leaves given up to produce an apple. However, there is no reason to assume this holds for the trade-off between individuals' utilities. This is why *UU* in Figure 4.10 is wavy rather than smooth.

Figure 4.10

Utility Possibilities Curve

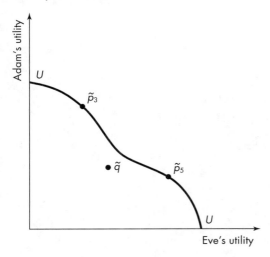

We assume the value of social welfare increases as either U^{Adam} or U^{Eve} increases—society is better off when any of its members becomes better off. Note that we have said nothing about how society manifests these preferences. Under some conditions, members of society may not be able to agree on how to rank each other's utilities, and the social welfare function does not even exist. For the moment, we simply assume it does exist.

Just as an individual's utility function for commodities leads to a set of indifference curves for those commodities, so does a social welfare function lead to a set of indifference curves between people's utilities.

Figure 4.11 depicts a typical set of social indifference curves. Their downward slope indicates that if Eve's utility decreases, the only way to maintain a given level of social welfare is to increase Adam's utility, and vice versa. The level of social welfare increases as we move toward the northeast, reflecting the fact that an increase in any individual's utility increases social welfare, other things being the same.

In Figure 4.12, the social indifference curves are superimposed on the utility possibilities curve from Figure 4.10. Point *i* is not as desirable as point *ii* (point *ii* is on a higher social indifference curve than point *i*) even though point *i* is Pareto efficient and point *ii* is not. Here, society's value judgments, embodied in the social welfare function, favour a more equal distribution of real income,

Figure 4.11

Social Indifference Curves

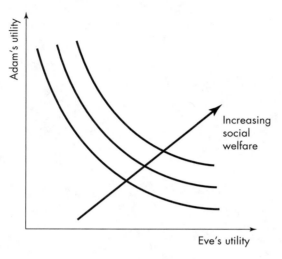

inefficient though it may be. Of course, point *iii* is preferred to either of these. It is both efficient and "fair."

Now, the Fundamental Theorem of Welfare Economics indicates that a properly working competitive system leads to some allocation on the utility possibilities

Figure 4.12

Maximizing Social Welfare

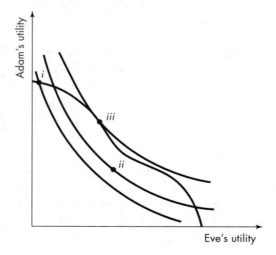

curve. There is no reason, however, that it is the particular point that maximizes social welfare. We conclude that, even if the economy generates a Pareto efficient allocation of resources, government intervention may be necessary to achieve a "fair" distribution of utility.

A second reason the fundamental theorem need not imply a minimal government has to do with the fact that the certain conditions required for its validity may not be satisfied by real-world markets. As we show in Chapter 5, an absence of these conditions may lead free markets to allocate resources inefficiently.

EVALUATION

These days, the most dramatic examples of debate over how to organize an economy are occurring in formerly Communist countries. Nevertheless, the same basic issues arise in Western nations as well: How much of national output should be devoted to the public sector, and how should public expenditures be financed? The theory of welfare economics introduced in this chapter provides the standard framework for thinking about these issues. There are, however, some controversies surrounding the theory.

First, the underlying outlook is highly individualistic, with a focus on people's utilities and how to maximize them. This is brought out starkly in the formulation of the social welfare function, Equation (4.10). The basic view expressed in that equation is that a good society is one whose members are happy. As suggested in Chapter 1, however, other societal goals are possible—to maximize the power of the state, to glorify God, and so on. Welfare economics does not have much to say to people with such goals.

Because welfare economics puts people's preferences at centre stage, it requires that these preferences be taken seriously. People know best what gives them satisfaction. If one believes that individuals' preferences are ill formed or corrupt, a theory that shows how to maximize their utility is essentially irrelevant.

Musgrave (1959) developed the concept of **merit goods** to describe commodities that ought to be provided even if the members of society do not demand them. Government support of the fine arts is often justified on this basis. Operas and concerts should be provided publicly if individuals are unwilling to pay enough to meet their costs. But as Baumol and Baumol (1981: 426–27) have noted:

> The term *merit good* merely becomes a formal designation for the unadorned value judgment that the arts are good for society and therefore

deserve financial support ... [the] merit good approach is not really a justification for support—it merely invents a bit of terminology to designate the desire to do so.

Another possible problem with the welfare economics framework is its concern with *results*. Situations are evaluated in terms of the allocation of resources, and not of *how* the allocation was determined. Perhaps a society should be judged by the *processes* used to arrive at the allocation, not the actual results. Are people free to enter contracts? Are public processes democratic? If this view is taken, welfare economics loses its normative significance.

On the other hand, the great advantage of welfare economics is that it provides a coherent framework for thinking about the appropriateness of various government interventions. Every government intervention, after all, involves a reallocation of resources, and the whole purpose of welfare economics is to evaluate alternative allocations. The framework of welfare economics impels us to ask three key questions whenever a government activity is proposed:

- Will it have desirable distributional consequences?
- Will it enhance efficiency?
- Can it be done at a reasonable cost?

If the answer to these questions is no, the market should probably be left alone. Of course, to answer these questions may require substantial research and, in the case of the first question, value judgments as well. But just asking the right questions provides an invaluable structure for the decision-making process. It forces people to make their ethical values explicit, and it facilitates the detection of frivolous or self-serving programs.

SUMMARY

- Welfare economics is the study of the desirability of alternative economic states.

- A Pareto efficient allocation occurs when no person can be made better off without making another person worse off. A necessary condition for Pareto efficiency is that each person's marginal rate of substitution between two commodities equals the marginal rate of transformation. Pareto efficiency is the economist's benchmark of efficient performance for an economy.

- The Fundamental Theorem of Welfare Economics states that, under certain conditions, competitive market mechanisms lead to Pareto efficient outcomes.

- Despite its appeal, Pareto efficiency has no obvious claim as an ethical norm. Society may prefer an inefficient allocation on the basis of equity, justice, or

some other criterion. This provides one possible reason for government intervention in the economy.

- A social welfare function summarizes society's preferences concerning the utility of each of its members. It may be used to find the allocation of resources
  that maximizes social welfare.

- Welfare economics is based on an individualistic social philosophy. It does not
  pay much attention to the processes used to achieve results. Thus, although it
  provides a coherent and useful framework for analyzing policy, welfare economics is controversial.

DISCUSSION QUESTIONS

1. Hamlet will trade two pizzas for one six-pack of beer and be equally happy.
   At the same time, Ophelia will gladly exchange two of her six-packs for six
   pizzas. Is the allocation of beer and pizza Pareto efficient? Illustrate using
   an Edgeworth Box.

2. Imagine a simple economy with only two people, Augustus and Livia.

   a. Let the social welfare function be

   $$W = U_L + U_A$$

   where U_L and U_A are the utilities of Livia and Augustus, respectively.
   Graph the social indifference curves. How would you describe the relative importance assigned to their respective well-being?

   b. Repeat (a) when

   $$W = U_L + 2U_A$$

   c. Assume that the utility possibility frontier is as follows:

   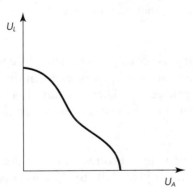

Graphically show how the optimal solution differs between the welfare functions given in parts (a) and (b).

3. In 1993, Serbian politician Zeljko Raznatovic stated, "We are fighting for our faith, the Serbian Orthodox Church. We are fighting for a united Serbian state. This party will believe in God and Serbia" (Kifner, 1993: A1). What social welfare function is consistent with this statement? Compare it to the social welfare function associated with conventional welfare economics.

REFERENCES

Baumol, William J., and Hilda Baumol. "Book Review." *Journal of Political Economy* 89, no. 2 (April 1981): 425–28.

Henderson, James M., and Richard E. Quandt. *Microeconomic Theory: A Mathematical Approach*, 3rd ed. New York: McGraw-Hill, 1980.

Kifner, John. "An Outlaw in the Balkans Is Basking in the Spotlight." *The New York Times*, November 22, 1993, p. A1.

Musgrave, Richard A. *The Theory of Public Finance*. New York: McGraw-Hill, 1959.

Tucker, Robert C., ed. *The Marx–Engels Reader*, 2nd ed. New York: W.W. Norton, 1978.

Willig, Robert. "Consumer's Surplus without Apology." *American Economic Review* (September 1976): 589–97.

APPENDIX

Consumer Surplus

This chapter emphasized that reallocations of resources affect individuals' welfare. We often want to know not only whether a certain change makes people better or worse off, but also by how much. Suppose, for example, that initially the price of apples is P_0, but then it falls to some lower price, P_1. Clearly, apple consumers are better off because of the change. But can we put a dollar figure on the improvement in their welfare? Consumer surplus is a tool for obtaining such a dollar measure.

To begin our discussion of consumer surplus, consider the demand curve for apples, D_a, depicted in Figure 4.13. Assume consumers can obtain all the apples they demand at the going market price, P_0. Then the supply curve for apples, S_a, is a horizontal line at P_0. According to the diagram, when the price is P_0, the quantity demanded is a_0.

Suppose now that more land is brought into apple production, and the supply curve shifts to S'_a. At the new equilibrium, the price falls to P_1, and apple con-

Figure 4.13

Measuring Consumer Surplus

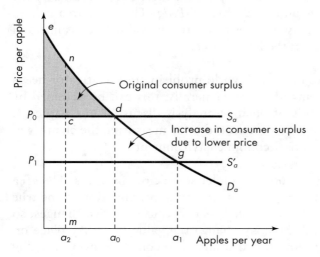

sumption increases to a_1. How much better off are consumers? Another way of stating this question is, "How much would consumers be willing to pay for the privilege of consuming a_1 apples at price P_1 rather than a_0 apples at price P_0?"

To provide an answer, begin by recalling that the demand curve shows the maximum amount that individuals would be willing to pay for each apple they consume. Consider some arbitrary quantity of apples, a_2. The most people would be willing to pay for the a apple is the vertical distance up to the demand curve, mn dollars. At the initial price, consumers in fact had to pay only mc per apple. In a sense then, on their purchase of the a apple, consumers enjoyed a surplus of nc dollars. The amount by which the sum individuals would have been willing to pay exceeds the sum they actually have to pay is called the consumer surplus.

Of course, the same exercise could be repeated at any quantity, not just at a_2. When the price is P_0 per unit, the consumer surplus at each output level equals the distance between the demand curve and the horizontal line at P_0. Summing the surpluses for each apple purchased, we find that the total consumer surplus when the price is P_0 is the area P_0ed. More generally, consumer surplus is measured by the area under the demand curve and above a horizontal line at the market price.

When the price falls to P_1, consumer surplus is still the area under the demand curve and above a horizontal line at the going price; because the price is now P_1, the relevant area is P_1eg. Consumer surplus has therefore increased by the difference between areas P_1eg and P_0ed—area P_1P_0dg. Thus, the area behind the demand curve between the two prices measures the value to consumers of being able to purchase apples at the lower price.

To implement this procedure for a real-world problem, an investigator needs to know the shape of the demand curve. Generally, this can be obtained by using one or more of the tools of positive analysis discussed in Chapter 3. Hence, consumer surplus is a very practical tool for measuring the changes in welfare induced by changes in the economic environment.

There is a caveat that may be important under some circumstances. The area under an ordinary demand curve provides only an approximation to the true value of the change in consumer welfare. This is because as price changes, so do people's real incomes, and this may change the value that they place on additions to their income (the marginal utility of income). However, Willig (1976) has shown that measuring consumer surplus by the area under the ordinary demand curve is likely to be a good approximation in most cases, and this approach is used widely in applied work.[9]

---

[9] Alternatively, one can compute welfare changes using areas under a compensated demand curve.

Chapter 5

An Overview of Expenditure and Taxation Analysis

The promises of yesterday are the taxes of today.

–William Lyon Mackenzie King

What role should government play in an economy? Economists have been grappling with this question for at least the last two hundred years. It is one of those questions that does not have a definitive answer, but in seeking answers to it economists have increased our understanding of the basic issues. In this chapter, we briefly describe the main issues concerning the governments' role in the allocation of resources, the distribution of income, and stabilization of the economy. We then discuss the alternative ways in which governments can finance their expenditures. Since taxation is by far the most important revenue source for governments, we outline the basic theory of how the tax burden is distributed across the population and how taxes affect the allocation of resources in the economy.

MARKET FAILURE AND THE RESOURCE ALLOCATION ROLE OF GOVERNMENT

In the famous film *Casablanca*, whenever something seems amiss, the police chief gives an order to "round up the usual suspects." Similarly, whenever markets appear to be failing to allocate resources efficiently, economists round up the same group of possible causes for the supposed failure. A market economy may fail to generate an efficient allocation of resources for three general reasons:

- market power
- asymmetric information
- externalities and public goods

Market Power

The Fundamental Theorem of Welfare Economics holds only if all consumers and firms are price takers. If some individuals or firms are price makers (they have the power to affect prices), then the allocation of resources will generally be inefficient. Why? A firm with market power may be able to raise price above marginal cost by supplying less output than a competitive firm would. Thus, one of the necessary conditions for Pareto efficiency—that relative prices equal relative marginal costs of production—is violated. An insufficient quantity of resources is devoted to the commodity.

Situations in which firms are price makers can arise in several different ways. An extreme case is monopoly, where there is only one firm in the market, and entry is blocked because other firms are unable to produce a similar product. A so-called natural monopoly occurs when the production of some good or service is subject to continually decreasing average costs—the greater the level of output, the lower the cost per unit. Consequently, any given output can be produced at the minimum total cost if it is produced by one firm. Examples are the provision of water, electricity, and television. In some cases, these commodities are produced by the private sector and regulated by the government (electricity in Alberta is mainly generated by TransAlta and Alberta Power, which are privately owned); and in other cases they are produced by the public sector (in Ontario, electricity is mainly generated by Ontario Hydro, a crown corporation). Thus, a natural monopoly creates a role for government either in the form of regulation or ownership of the firm.

Market power can also occur in the less extreme case of oligopoly (a few sellers) and in industries where there are many firms, but each firm has some market power because the firms produce differentiated products. For example, a lot of firms produce running shoes, yet Reeboks, Nikes, and Brooks are regarded by many consumers as distinct commodities. Governments have a role in ensuring that competitive forces prevail in markets, whether this takes the form of regulation, ownership, or anticombines activities.

Asymmetric Information

The economic model that was used in Chapter 4 to discuss the welfare properties of a market economy was based on the (implicit) assumption that the participants, Adam and Eve, had complete information about all of the variables that are important for their consumption and production decisions, such as the prices and qualities of the goods they consume, their income (or endowments), and the production technology. We know that in "real life" individuals have imperfect information about these and many other economic variables. Future income is uncertain because of potential changes in the demands for an individual's labour and capital. Wealth may be affected by natural disasters such as fire, earthquakes, or floods. Even the length of an individual's life is uncertain. Will the market allocate resources in an efficient manner in the face of imperfect information about important economic variables and uncertainty about future economic events?

Before attempting to answer this question, we note that most individuals in making major financial decisions try to avoid, or at least reduce, the impact of economic uncertainty on their lives, and private market institutions have developed to ameliorate the impact of uncertainty on individuals and their families. Thus, the Cooperators and Allstate provide collision insurance for automobiles, fire and theft insurance for homes, and life insurance to provide financial protection for dependents. Will insurance markets provide coverage for all of the risks that individuals would like to have insured at a premium that reflects the marginal cost of an insurance policy? In trying to answer this question, economists have discovered that the critical issue is whether all participants in the market have access to the same information, however imperfect. If the buyer of the insurance policy has more information about the nature of the risk than the insurance company, then the level of insurance coverage may be reduced and in some cases no insurance coverage may be provided.

Consider the following example. Most university students face the risk of getting low grades, which may reduce their future earnings potential. Students would like to buy an insurance policy against low grades—say a contract that indemnifies a student with $2,000 if he or she receives less than an A. Why don't insurance companies sell low grade insurance to students? A moment of reflection will suggest two reasons why this type of insurance is not provided in the market. First, students' grades are affected by how diligently they apply themselves to their studies. If they were fully insured against the financial loss from receiving a low grade, what incentive—aside from the thirst for knowledge—would students have to study? Because an insurance company cannot observe the number of hours that a student has spent in studying for a course, neither the insurance premium nor the payout can depend on a student's effort. Casual observation of students' behaviour leads us to predict that if grade insurance were provided, students' effort would decline, students would receive lower grades, and the insurance company providing the coverage would have to raise premiums, or reduce the coverage, in the face of large payouts. These premium and coverage adjustments would make grade insurance less attractive, perhaps to the point where no student would be willing to buy a policy. The phenomenon that we have described is called **moral hazard.** It occurs in an insurance market where the insureds' actions can affect the probability or the magnitude of a loss, and the insurance company cannot observe the individuals' actions.

Even if grade insurance did not affect students' effort, the market for grade insurance may be affected by an **adverse selection** problem. Suppose, for the sake of argument, that the probability that a student will receive an A in this course is determined by his or her innate ability. Students know their own abilities, but an insurance company cannot observe an individual's innate ability. The students with the lowest abilities would have the strongest desire to purchase grade insurance. If the premiums for grade insurance were based on the grade distribution for all students, then the students with the greatest ability will not find the policy very attractive and will not purchase it. The percentage of insured students receiving low grades would exceed the percentage based on the entire student population, and the insurance company would have to raise its premiums to cover the higher than expected payouts. The higher premiums might induce even more high-ability students to drop their insurance coverage, which would increase the insurance companies' losses, leading to further premium increases, and so on. At the end of this process, the insurance premium may either be so high (or the coverage level so low) that no student would find grade insurance attractive.

The adverse selection problem is distinct from the moral hazard problem because adverse selection is a problem of hidden information whereas moral hazard is a problem of hidden action.[1] They share the same general feature that the buyer of the insurance contract has more information about the probability of a loss or the actions taken to avoid losses than the insurance company. These phenomena have detrimental effects on the performance of private insurance markets. They cause insurance premiums to be high and insurance coverage to be low or non-existent. A high proportion of government spending in Canada has at least some aspect of insurance to it. The most obvious examples are unemployment insurance and health insurance. Whether asymmetric information is responsible for a failure of the market to allocate resources efficiently and therefore justifies public provision of this form of insurance will be discussed in more detail in Chapter 9. Even if asymmetric information does not constitute a form of market failure, publicly provided

---

[1] This way of distinguishing adverse selection and moral hazard was first suggested by Riley (1985).

insurance may be affected by adverse selection and moral hazard problems, which may affect the design and performance of these programs.

Asymmetric information has been discussed within the context of an insurance market, but these are general phenomena that affect a wide range of markets. The seminal paper on adverse selection was by George Akerlof (1970). As its title "The Market for Lemons: Quality Uncertainty and the Market Mechanism" suggests, the notion of adverse selection was used to analyze the market for used cars. He also explained how asymmetric information can be used to understand a wide range of economic institutions, from warranties to money-lending. In addition to its relevance for the social insurance programs, asymmetric information has important implications for the income redistribution programs, the market for education, and tax policy.

Externalities and Public Goods

Another type of market failure may occur if there is an **externality**, a situation in which one person's behaviour affects the welfare of another in a way that is outside existing markets. For example, suppose your roommate begins smoking large cigars, polluting the air and making you worse off. Why is this an efficiency problem? Your roommate uses up a scarce resource, clean air, when he smokes cigars. However, there is no market for clean air that forces him to pay for it. In effect, he pays a price of zero for the clean air and therefore "overuses" it. The price system is failing to provide correct signals about the opportunity cost of a commodity.

Externalities have a simple interpretation in the analytics of welfare economics. In the derivation of Equation (4.9) in Chapter 4, it was implicitly assumed marginal cost meant social marginal cost—it embodied the incremental value of all of society's resources used in production. In the example above, however, your roommate's private marginal cost of smoking is less than the social marginal cost because he does not have to pay for the clean air he uses. The price of a cigar, which reflects its private marginal cost, is not correctly reflecting its social marginal cost. Hence, Equation (4.9) is not satisfied, and the allocation of resources is inefficient. Incidentally, an externality can be positive—confer a benefit—as well as negative. Think of a molecular biologist who publishes a paper about a novel gene-splicing technique that can be used by a pharmaceutical firm. In the case of a positive externality, the amount of the beneficial activity generated by the market is inefficiently small.

Closely related to an externality is the case of a **public good,** a commodity that is nonrival in consumption—the fact that one person consumes it does not prevent anyone else from doing so as well. The classic example of a public good is a lighthouse. When the lighthouse turns on its beacon, all the ships in the vicinity benefit. The fact that one person takes advantage of the lighthouse's services does not keep anyone else from doing so simultaneously.

In using the lighthouse, people may have an incentive to hide their true preferences. Suppose it would be worthwhile to me to have the lighthouse operate. I know, however, that once the beacon is lit, I can enjoy its services, whether I pay for them or not. Therefore, I may claim the lighthouse means nothing to me, hoping that I can get a "free ride" after other people pay for it. Unfortunately, everyone has the same incentive, so the lighthouse may not get built, even though its construction could be very beneficial. The market mechanism may fail to force people to reveal their preferences for public goods, and possibly result in insufficient resources being devoted to them.

Governments can provide public goods that will not be provided by the private sector because governments can coerce payments from individuals. Through taxation and other means, governments can force individuals to contribute to the provision of public goods. Furthermore, governments can regulate, promote, or discourage private sector activities that generate externalities. A detailed discussion of the provision of public goods and the regulation of externalities is contained in Chapters 7 and 8.

Overview

The Fundamental Theorem of Welfare Economics states that a properly working competitive economy generates a Pareto efficient allocation of resources without any government intervention. However, we have just shown that in real-world economies, competition may not hold, and markets for some goods and services may not exist (or function adequately) because of asymmetric information or the presence of externalities and public goods. Hence, the market-determined allocation of resources is unlikely to be efficient. There are, then, opportunities for government to intervene and enhance economic efficiency.

It must be emphasized that while efficiency problems provide opportunities for government intervention in the economy, they do not require it. The fact that the market-generated allocation of resources is imperfect does not mean the government is capable of doing better. For example, in certain cases, the costs of setting up a government agency to deal with an externality could exceed the cost of the externality itself. Moreover, governments, like people, can make mistakes. Some argue that government is inherently incapable of acting efficiently, so while in theory it can improve on the status quo, in practice it never will. While this argument is extreme, it highlights the fact that the

Fundamental Theorem is helpful only in identifying situations in which intervention may lead to greater efficiency.

However, as was pointed out in Chapter 4, it is not obvious that an efficient allocation of resources is per se socially desirable; some argue that fairness must also be considered. The role of governments in redistributing income is considered below.

ECONOMIC JUSTICE AND THE REDISTRIBUTIVE ROLE OF GOVERNMENT

Individuals are primarily concerned with the distributional effects of government policies—the allocative effects are secondary—and they expect governments to actively intervene in the economy to produce a fairer or more equitable distribution of income, consumption, and wealth.

Why does government have to provide a social safety net? Why can't redistribution be left to private voluntary charitable activity or private insurance coverage? There are several reasons why governments should be involved in redistribution. First, it is true that private charitable activities, often undertaken by churches, service clubs, and other philanthropic organizations such as the Food Bank and the United Way, play a role in redistributing income. Altruism toward the poor is the motivation behind the private charitable activity. If well-to-do individuals are altruistic toward the poor (although they may display different degrees of altruism), then a charitable contribution by one individual makes the poor better off and it also makes other altruistic, well-to-do individuals better off. Thus, a charitable act generates a positive externality, and as argued in the preceding section, activities that generate positive externalities will, under certain conditions, not be undertaken to the point where the marginal social benefit of the activity equals its marginal social cost. This is an argument for subsidizing, in some way, charitable activity.

Income redistribution can also promote social stability and cohesion. As Charlotte Brontë observed, "Misery generates hate." Societies with high levels of poverty and extreme differences in the distribution of income may breed social conflict and strife and lack the cohesion and solidarity that are required to overcome natural disasters or foreign invasions. A social safety net provides the "glue" that holds a market-based economy together and makes democracy compatible with the private ownership of property and free markets.

Another rationale for governmental income support programs is that they provide "poverty insurance" that is unavailable privately. Why doesn't the private market provide insurance against the possibility of becoming poor? There are two reasons why a private market for poverty insurance may not exist. First, poverty for some individuals is not a temporary condition. It is a permanent condition. For these individuals there is no "risk of being poor"—it is a dead certainty—and insurance policies do not cover events that are certain to occur. Second, even for individuals who are not poor, but face the risk of low incomes in the future, asymmetric information problems would affect the provision of private poverty insurance. Individuals who purchased such insurance might decide not to work very hard or save for the future. To discourage such behaviour, the insurance firm would have to monitor their behaviour to determine whether an individual's low income was due to bad luck or to "goofing off." Such monitoring would be very costly. Furthermore, poverty insurance would be most attractive to those who faced the greatest risk of being poor, creating an adverse selection problem. Hence, there is no market for poverty insurance—it simply cannot be purchased. Income redistribution by government can be considered as social insurance. The premium on this "social insurance policy" is the taxes you pay when you are able to earn income. In the event of poverty, your benefit comes in the form of welfare payments.

While the externality and the asymmetric information arguments provide support for income redistribution by government, most people feel that income redistribution is justified because individuals have an inherent right to a reasonable standard of living. Article 25 of the United Nations Universal Declaration of Human Rights states, "Everyone has the right to a standard of living adequate for the health and well-being of himself and his family." The Canadian Constitution Act, 1982 states that:

> the government of Canada and the provincial governments, are committed to
> (a) promoting equal opportunities for the well-being of Canadians;
> (b) furthering economic development to reduce disparity in opportunities; and
> (c) providing essential public services of reasonable quality to all Canadians.

These statements imply that the ethical framework to be used in evaluating Canadian society goes beyond the notion of Pareto optimality.

Given that government has a role to play in redistributing income in a market economy, what types of transfers should be used and how much should be transferred? Let us consider these questions within the context of Figure 5.1. Suppose with the existing distribution of resources—land, labour, and capital—a market economy would achieve the point i on the utility possibility

Figure 5.1

Redistribution with Distortionary Taxation

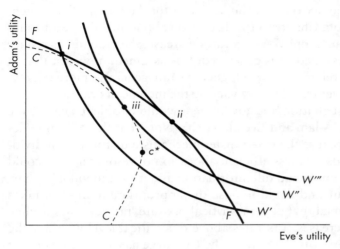

frontier *FF*. If the government could use lump-sum taxes and lump-sum transfers to reallocate resources among Adam and Eve, then any allocation on the *FF* frontier could be achieved. A lump-sum tax is a tax whose value is independent of the individual's behaviour. A lump-sum transfer is a payment whose value is independent of the individual's behaviour. If the social welfare function displays a basic preference for equality, then a social indifference curve would be tangent to the *FF* frontier at the point *ii*, and this point could be achieved with appropriate lump-sum taxes and transfers to Adam and Eve.

Asymmetric information plays an important role in determining the extent of redistribution and the types of taxes and transfers that are used. A government may not have enough information about individuals' characteristics or behaviour in order to design a complete set of lump-sum taxes and transfers that would allow it to achieve the allocations along *FF*. For example, the government may be able to observe the incomes of Adam and Eve, but not the amount of time or effort that they expended to earn that income. If the government makes taxes and transfers a function of individuals' incomes, then the taxes and transfers are no longer lump sums. Individuals can affect them by altering the amount of income that they generate by varying the time and effort expended in earning income.

Suppose that the government levied a proportional income tax and used the tax revenues to finance an equal payment to Adam and Eve. This scheme would redistribute income from the rich to the poor because if Adam's income is greater than Eve's, then Adam's taxes will exceed the payment that he receives from the government, and he will be making a net transfer to Eve.[2] Suppose that the income tax reduces the incentive for Adam and Eve to generate income. (Recall from Chapter 3 the discussion about the income and substitution effects on labour supply.) As tax rates increase, the individuals reduce their work effort and less income is generated. It is assumed, however, that at least when tax rates are relatively low, a higher tax rate generates more tax revenue, which leads to larger transfers. By varying the income tax rate and therefore the amount of redistribution, the government would be able to achieve the utility combinations for Adam and Eve along CC. Note that the CC curve lies inside the FF frontier because the tax-transfer mechanism distorts the individuals' behaviour and leads to a less efficient allocation of resources than could be achieved if the government had full information about the individuals' characteristics and behaviour and could impose the appropriate lump-sum taxes and transfers. It is assumed that at some critical tax rate, tax revenues decline with further tax rate increases. Tax rates above this critical level would make both Adam and Eve worse off. Therefore, the CC curve has a vertical slope at c^* when the revenue-maximizing tax rate is imposed, and it has a positive slope when the tax rate exceeds this critical value.

With the social welfare function shown in Figure 5.1, the optimal redistribution policy, given the use of this distortionary tax-transfer system, occurs where the social indifference curve W'' is tangent to CC at iii. Compared with the point ii, which would have been achieved with lump-sum taxes and transfers under full information, Eve attains a lower level of utility. The reason is that the CC curve has a steeper slope than the FF curve. This indicates that when governments have to use distortionary taxes and transfers to redistribute income, the rate at which Adam's utility has to decline in order to increase Eve's utility is higher. In effect, society is faced with an equity-efficiency trade-off when it uses a distortionary tax-transfer mechanism to redistribute income.

Quantifying the equity-efficiency trade-off rate for existing tax-transfer mechanisms and evaluating changes that would reduce the trade-off rate are some of the contributions that economists can make to the public debate about income redistribution. Economists cannot answer the question of where a soci-

---

[2] This is essentially a negative income tax, which will be discussed in more detail in Chapter 12.

ety should be on the *CC* curve. The answer to this question depends on the ethical values that are expressed through the political process.

In discussing the tax-transfer process depicted in Figure 5.1, it was assumed that income tax revenues were used to finance a money income transfer. Other types of transfers are possible, indeed common. For example, governments could make in-kind transfers in the form of a price subsidy for certain commodities, such as housing, or provision of a specific good, such as education or health care, free of charge. Whether governments should provide income or in-kind transfers is a frequently debated topic that will be discussed in Chapter 10.

MACROECONOMIC DISFUNCTION AND THE STABILIZATION ROLE OF GOVERNMENT

In classical economic models, relative prices adjust to equate the supply and demand for goods and services, including labour. Unemployment is either a temporary phenomenon, because it takes time for real wage rates to adjust, or it is a characteristic of a long-run equilibrium because governments or unions prevent real wage rates from declining to their market clearing values. Dissatisfaction with the classical model as an explanation of the high and persistent unemployment in the 1930s led John Maynard Keynes to develop an alternative model that, especially in the hands of his interpreters, emphasized output adjustments as the economy's equilibrating mechanism. Fluctuations in aggregate output, caused by fluctuations in private investment or exports, could be offset by a discretionary fiscal policy. Government expenditures could be increased or tax rates could be cut when private aggregate demand declined to stabilize the aggregate demand for labour and keep the economy at full employment. This Keynesian view dominated economic policy discussions in Canada and other Western countries from 1945 to around 1970. At the high-water mark of Keynesian policy, Richard Musgrave (1959), in a highly influential text book on public finance, argued that stabilizing the economy was one of the fundamental functions of government.

Whether the Keynesian economic model provides an adequate framework for understanding macroeconomic fluctuations and whether government can or should engage in discretionary fiscal policy to stabilize the economy has been intensely debated since the early 1970s. The stabilization role of government is now normally covered in undergraduate macroeconomic courses, and it is not discussed at any length in this book. However, the effects of macroeconomic fluctuations on unemployment and unemployment insurance are discussed in Chapter 13 on unemployment insurance.

FINANCING GOVERNMENT SPENDING

Government spending on goods and services and income transfers is essential in maintaining a high and equitable standard of living in a modern society. To perform its function, governments need to obtain command over resources.

Taxation: Mankind's Great Invention

Taxation is one of mankind's great inventions, ranking with the other great inventions—the wheel, nuclear power, and money—in terms of its capacity to improve mankind's standard of living. Taxation has allowed our society to harness resources for collective purposes that have vastly improved our material well-being. For example, everyone relies on the transportation facilities—the sidewalks, streets, and highways—that governments provide. Governments can provide these facilities because they are able to obtain command over resources—land, labour, and capital—through the use of the tax system. As with all of mankind's great inventions, the capacity to do good is accompanied by the capacity to do harm. Hence the aphorism, the power to tax is the power to destroy.

The Alternatives to Taxation

To appreciate why taxation is such a great invention, we have to compare it with the other instruments that governments can use to obtain command over resources:

- borrowing
- expanding the money supply
- conscripting resources
- charging for government services

Borrowing. Governments can obtain command over resources by borrowing funds from savers and using the funds to purchase goods and services and to make income transfers. Governments often use this method of finance when resources have to be mobilized quickly and for a limited period, as in the case of a war, or finance large capital expenditures. However, over the last twenty years Canadian governments have borrowed—run deficits—to finance current expenditures. Could all government expenditure be financed through borrowing? The problem with financing all government expenditures by borrowing is that lenders want interest payments on the funds that they lend to the government, and they may want the principal repaid at some future date. No lender will be confident that a government will meet its obligations if it has to borrow to meet the interest payments on its outstanding debt. In order to borrow at reasonable interest rates, a government must be able to demonstrate that it can generate enough revenues so that payments on debt can be met without recourse to further borrowing. Thus, government borrowing is a useful adjunct to the other methods of government finance—one that is especially useful in spreading the cost of financing a major expenditure, such as a war or a large capital project, over a number of years. Borrowing cannot be used to finance all government expenditures.

Expanding the money supply. National governments can also finance their expenditures by creating more money. In its simplest form, this means printing more money to pay for the goods and services that the government buys. Governments often rely on this method of finance in national emergencies, such as wars, and some Latin American countries have used it to finance their ongoing activities. Expanding the money supply inevitably leads to inflation. If a substantial amount of revenue is to be raised through the "inflation tax," the money supply must be expanded very rapidly, leading to a hyperinflation. This has undesirable consequences because the inflation tax falls disproportionately on those on fixed incomes and creditors and because in hyperinflation households and firms abandon money as a means of payment and resort to barter, which is a less efficient means of effecting market transactions. The serious problems created by hyperinflation mean that the inflation tax should only be used under extreme conditions, such as when the very existence of a society is threatened.[3]

Conscription. Governments can also obtain resources by conscripting or expropriating them. That is, a government can simply compel individuals to supply the land, labour, and capital that the government needs. In Western democratic countries, conscription has often been used in wartime, when the need to obtain resources is extremely urgent. But conscription isn't just a wartime phenomenon. Consider the following prosaic example—a by-law in Edmonton requires home-owners to shovel the snow from the sidewalk in the front of their homes. Home-owners are thereby required to provide resources for the benefit of the general public.

Conscription has the same drawbacks as the inflation tax—it is inequitable and inefficient. For example, if a government wants to provide a highway, it will need some particular tracts of land, heavy earth-moving machines, machine operators, and civil engineers. If the government relied on conscription to

---

[3] As noted in Chapter 2, even low rates of inflation result in some decrease in the real value of outstanding debt and are a form of inflation tax. See Bank of Canada (1991) on the cost of inflation.

obtain these resources, only the individuals with these particular resources or skills would "pay" for the construction of the highway. The cost of the highway would be imposed on a narrow segment of the population—those with the skills and resources that the government required and who were not able to evade conscription. Thus, the burden of providing facilities for the enjoyment of the general public would be concentrated on a narrow segment of the population and would be considered very inequitable.

If conscription were used to obtain the resources for the construction of highways, the incentives to avoid conscription would be immense because a relatively large burden would be imposed on a relatively narrow segment of society. Young people studying civil engineering would try to avoid capture when the government swooped down on the university to fill its annual quota of civil engineers. Furthermore, less care and attention might be devoted to designing and building the highway. Most importantly, it would greatly reduce the attractiveness of certain occupations and certain forms of capital equipment if they were particularly susceptible to conscription by government. Individuals would tend to invest their time and money in acquiring those skills and physical assets that the government did not require or would have difficulty in conscripting. Needless to say, this would deprive the economy of many very valuable resources and skills and would greatly reduce the overall standard of living. Conscription should therefore be used for limited purposes and in emergency situations.

Charging for government services. The fourth method that a government can use to finance its activities is to charge for the public services that the government provides. In this way, the government would operate like a privately owned firm, using the revenue generated from the sales of its services to pay for the resources that it needs. While user fees are an important and efficient way of financing certain government activity, user fees can only play a limited role in financing government. The main reasons why user fees cannot completely replace taxation are:

- Some public services, such as national defence or public health measures, are public goods. If the service is provided to one individual, others cannot be excluded from the benefits of the services. The ability to exclude is essential if the government is going to be able to charge individuals for the use of the service.
- Even if exclusion is possible, it may be very costly. For example, it would be possible to set up toll gates on all city streets, but the cost of setting up and running the toll booths at every intersection would be prohibitive. New electronic technology makes charging for the use of streets

feasible. In Singapore, "the government plans an electronic road-pricing system, with sensors at key intersections to record cars automatically as they enter certain congested zones. Using a 'smart card' installed in each dashboard, the roadside sensor will debit the car owner's bank account automatically as they enter certain congested zones" (*Globe and Mail*, June 7, 1996, p. A8).

- Even if exclusion is feasible, charging for the service is inappropriate if the service is nonrival (e.g., the city streets are not congested so that one individual's use of the street does not slow down traffic and detract from the use of the street by other motorists).

- Finally, user charges cannot be used to pay for welfare services and other government programs that are intended for the redistribution of income. We cannot make the poor pay for programs that are intended to raise the incomes of the poor.

Accordingly, user fees can play an important role in helping to finance government activity, but they cannot be relied upon to provide all of the revenues that governments need.

When we consider the alternatives—borrowing, monetary expansion, conscription, user fees—we see that taxation must play a central role in government finance. Without taxation, the ability of the government to mobilize resources for the provision of public goods and to redistribute income would be substantially impaired.

Criteria for Evaluating Taxes

To say that taxation must play a central role in financing government begs the question: Which taxes should be imposed? The four main criteria used by economists to evaluate alternative forms of taxation are: equity, efficiency, administration and compliance cost, and visibility.[4]

Equity. One of the main advantages of taxation over the other means of financing government activity is that the burden of obtaining the resources can be spread over a large segment of the population and not just the owners of the resources required by government. Through the choice of tax bases and tax rates, a more equitable distribution of the cost of government can be achieved.

---

[4] The criteria for evaluating taxes are discussed in more detail in Chapters 17, 18, and 19.

Equity in taxation can be interpreted according to[5]:

- the **benefit** principle—the tax burden should be distributed in relation to the benefit that an individual receives from public services;
- the **ability to pay** principle—the tax burden should be distributed in relation to an individual's ability to pay taxes.

The benefit principle can be applied to the financing of public sector activities where there is a clear link between an activity and the benefit that an individual receives; for example, charges for the use of recreational facilities. The benefit principle is not readily applicable in situations where the public sector provides a public good or where the redistribution of income, wealth, or consumption is desired.

In applying the ability-to-pay principle, it is necessary to define what constitutes the ability-to-pay taxes. Conventionally, income has been considered the most appropriate measure of the ability to pay taxes, but lifetime consumption and wealth are also regarded by some economists as appropriate measures of the ability to pay taxes.

There are two dimensions to equity based on ability to pay:

- **horizontal equity** or equal treatment of equals. Two individuals who have the same ability-to-pay should pay the same amount of tax.
- **vertical equity** or unequal treatment of unequals. The total tax burden should be higher for those who have a greater ability-to-pay.

The tax burden is considered to be:

- **progressive** if the ratio of an individual's tax burden to his or her income increases as the individual's income increases;
- **proportional** if the ratio of an individual's tax burden to his or her income is the same at all income levels; or
- **regressive** if the ratio of an individual's tax burden to his or her income decreases as the individual's income increases.

Determining the distribution of the tax burden is a complicated problem because tax burdens may be shifted. Taxes impose burdens by altering the prices of the commodities that consumers purchase and altering the returns that the owner of inputs—land, labour, and capital—receive when they sell or

---

[5] For a more detailed discussion of equity issues in taxation, see Boadway and Kitchen (1984).

rent these inputs. We say that the tax burden is shifted forward when a tax causes a firm to raise the price of its product so that the consumer is made worse off and bears the burden of the tax even though the firm makes the actual tax payment to the government. For example, the burden of an excise tax on cigarettes is borne by the consumers of cigarettes if the tax causes the price of cigarettes to increase. The cigarette manufacturers may not bear the tax, even though they make the tax payment to the government, because of the increase in the price of the cigarettes. The tax burden is shifted backward when the tax leads to a reduction in the price of an input, such as a reduction in the price paid to tobacco farmers.

The analysis of tax incidence is complicated because tax burdens may be shifted forward or backward. The extent of tax shifting will depend on the following:

- the responsiveness of the demand and supply for the taxed good to changes in its price. That is, the elasticities of demand and supply determine the extent of backward and forward shifting in a competitive market.
- the time-frame. The short-run incidence of tax may be quite different from the long-run incidence because demand and supply responses to price changes may be modest in the short term and massive in the long term. Hence, the distribution of the burden of a tax may change over time.
- the degree of competition in a market, which will affect the extent of tax shifting. (It may surprise you to learn that a less competitive market does not necessarily imply that more forward-shifting will occur.)
- whether or not more than one tax rate is changed at the same time.
- whether or not government expenditures are also changed.
- whether or not the tax and expenditure changes are revenue neutral.

As with most questions in economics, there is a good deal of uncertainty and debate over the incidence of individual taxes and the distribution of the burden of the tax system as a whole. The conceptual issues and the empirical studies of tax incidence in Canada will be discussed in more detail in Part 5 and Part 6.

Efficiency. Most of the public debate on taxation is concerned with equity. If the question of efficiency arises at all, it usually focuses on the administration or compliance costs of taxation. It is a commonly held view that a simple tax, with low collection costs, is an efficient tax.

For economists, efficient taxation is more than minimizing the administrative and compliance costs of collecting taxation. Indeed, taxes that have low collection costs may be very inefficient taxes. A good example of this is to be found in Adam Smith's *The Wealth of Nations* where he described a window tax that was imposed on dwellings in England. This tax was simple to collect because the tax collector merely had to stand in the street and count the number of windows in a house. The rate structure was progressive—the tax per window increased with the number of windows—and so the distribution of the burden of the tax would have been progressive if, as seems likely, the number of windows per dwelling increased with the household's income. Do economists consider the window tax, with its simplicity and low collection costs, an efficient tax? The answer is no because individuals responded to the tax by boarding up windows or building new dwellings with fewer windows. (The effects of the tax can still be seen today if one visits some of the stately homes in England, where large exterior walls contain no windows.) These alterations no doubt reduced the enjoyment that households obtained from their dwellings and may even have posed health problems. The deterioration in living standards caused by the window tax is likely to have greatly exceeded the advantages inherent in its low administrative cost.

Taxes have efficiency costs when they cause firms to produce alternative products or to use alternative methods of production and when they cause households to alter their consumption, savings, work, or investment decisions. Distortionary taxation alters the pattern of consumption and production, generating a less efficient allocation of resources. The more the tax system distorts the pattern of production and consumption, the greater the efficiency loss from taxation. The distortionary effects of taxes are generally greater the higher the tax rate. Taxes with a broad base can collect a given amount of revenue at a lower tax rate than a narrowly based tax, and therefore broadly based taxes will generally be less distortionary.

Intuitively, we can think of the total value of the goods and services and leisure consumed in an economy as the economic pie. When a government imposes taxes, it reduces the size of the economic pie that is available for private consumption. For every dollar collected, the economic pie shrinks by more than one dollar because of the distortions in consumption and production decisions caused by taxation. The excess burden (or deadweight loss) of taxation is the total reduction in economic well-being that results from using a given tax system instead of lump-sum taxes to raise the same revenue.

For many policy issues, such as determining how much tax revenue should be collected from different taxes, we would like to know the social cost of raising an additional dollar of revenue from the alternative taxes. The marginal cost of public funds (MCF) is the cost to the economy of raising an additional dollar from that revenue source. Economists try to measure the MCFs for various taxes because if one tax has a higher MCF than another tax, then the efficiency cost of taxation can be reduced by lowering the tax with the higher MCF and increasing the tax with the lower MCF. For example, Hamilton and Whalley (1989), using a general equilibrium model of the Canadian economy in 1980, calculated that the MCF for a provincial retail sales tax (RST) was 1.16. In other words, an additional dollar raised through a provincial retail sales tax cost the economy 1.16 because it increased the distortion in consumption decisions—services are taxed at relatively low rates under the RST—and production decisions—the RST is imposed on some inputs used by firms. Hamilton and Whalley also found that the MCF for the federal manufacturers' sales tax (MST) was 1.34, and the MCF for a hypothetical general sales tax was 1.07. Their research indicated that the federal MST was a relatively inefficient tax and that replacing it with a general sales tax would reduce the total excess burden of taxation.

Compliance and administration costs. These are the costs that are imposed on the private sector in complying with the tax system and the costs incurred by the public sector in administering the tax system. Compliance costs are incurred in maintaining tax records, completing tax returns, and learning new tax procedures when the tax system changes. The Goods and Services Tax (GST), which was introduced in 1991, has been criticized because of the high compliance costs that were imposed on the private sector, especially small business. A study for the Department of Finance found that the GST compliance costs equalled 16.97 percent of the tax collected for businesses with annual sales of $100,000 or less, and 2.65 percent for firms with sales over $1 million.[6]

In general, the tax system should have low compliance and administration costs, bearing in mind the potential trade-off between these costs and excess burden of the tax system that was illustrated by the example of the window tax.

Visibility. Canadians need to know how much they pay in taxes in order to make informed decisions about the level of public sector spending that they are prepared to support. Public awareness of taxation levels is essential in achieving a reasonable balance between the private and public sectors' provision of goods and services. Thus, it is generally agreed that visible taxes are preferable to hidden taxes. However, it can be argued that if the public is unaware of the

---

[6] See House of Commons, Standing Committee on Finance, *Replacing the GST: Options for Canada* (Ottawa: June 1994), 13–19.

benefits that flow from national defence policies, R&D subsidies, public health measures, and social welfare policies, then greater awareness of taxes may not lead to a better mix between public and private sector activities.

The issue of tax visibility was highlighted when the federal government replaced the MST with the GST in 1991. Many people were unaware that the MST had been imposed on some of the goods that they purchased because it was collected directly from the manufacturers and incorporated in the final price to the consumer. The GST was very visible because many firms quoted prices exclusive of the GST and added the GST at the cash register. This created the impression that the GST represented a tax increase when in fact it was (approximately) a revenue-neutral substitution for a previously hidden tax.

Other desirable characteristics for taxes. Economists often list a number of other desirable characteristics for taxes such as revenue potential, buoyancy, and certainty. The revenue potential of various taxes differs. Taxes with a broad base will generally fall on a large number of taxpayers and raise needed revenues at low tax rates. Thus, broadly based taxes will tend to be equitable and efficient. More inclusive tax bases that do not differentiate between types of sales or types of income will have relatively low administrative and compliance costs. Buoyancy refers to revenue growth relative to economic growth. Taxes that increase automatically as prices rise and incomes increase—the progressive income tax is an example—are more buoyant than excise taxes, which are imposed on the quantity sold. Buoyant tax bases that yield growing revenues without the need for new legislation have low administration and compliance costs and are efficient because they can be levied at low rates. Certainty refers to the taxpayer's ability to anticipate a tax and to plan accordingly. Taxes that lack certainty are likely to be seen as unfair to taxpayers who make decisions based on one set of rules only to find that the rules are constantly changing. Uncertainty about the tax burden can distort investment and savings decisions, and ambiguity in the interpretation or application of tax laws increases compliance costs.

SUMMARY

- A market economy may fail to generate an efficient allocation of resources because of market power, asymmetric information, or externalities and public goods.

- If a firm has the power to affect prices, it will set its price above marginal cost. Output will be restricted, and the value that consumers place on an additional

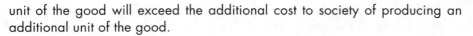

unit of the good will exceed the additional cost to society of producing an additional unit of the good.

- If the buyer of the insurance policy has more information about the nature of the risk than the insurance company, then the level of insurance coverage may be reduced and in some cases no insurance coverage may be provided.

- An externality occurs when one person's behaviour affects the welfare of another in a way that is outside existing markets. In these situations, the market price may not reflect the marginal social benefit or cost of the good. A public good is a commodity that is nonrival in consumption. One person's consumption of the good does not diminish any other person's benefit from the good.

- The fact that the market does not allocate resources perfectly does not necessarily mean the government can do better. Each case must be evaluated on its own merits.

- Government intervention in the economy can also be justified on the basis of attempting to provide a more just distribution of economic well-being than can be achieved in the market. Such intervention often leads to a trade-off between equity and economic efficiency.

- Governments can obtain resources to carry out their functions by taxing, borrowing, expanding the money supply, conscripting resources, and charging for government services.

- Taxation is the most important source of finance for government activities.

- The four main criteria used by economists to evaluate alternative forms of taxation are: equity, efficiency, administration and compliance cost, and visibility.

DISCUSSION QUESTIONS

1. In which of the following markets do you expect efficient outcomes in the absence of government intervention? Why?

   a. Personal computers
   b. Medical care
   c. Stock market
   d. Retail food

2. When several people died because of poisoned capsules of Tylenol pain reliever, strict government regulations were enacted to control the packaging of retail pharmaceuticals. Would private markets have reached the same result?

3. In each case listed below, can you rationalize the government intervention in the economy on the basis of welfare economics?

    a. Some governments set a maximum interest rate that lenders can charge to borrowers.
    b. University education is subsidized by the government.
    c. Alberta used public funds to subsidize home mortgages by middle-income families.

REFERENCES

Akerlof, G. "The Market for Lemons: Quality Uncertainty and the Market Mechanism." *Quarterly Journal of Economics* 84 (1970): 488–500.

Bank of Canada. "The Benefits of Price Stability." *Bank of Canada Review* (March 1991): 17–22.

Boadway, R.W., and H.M. Kitchen. *Canadian Tax Policy.* Toronto: Canadian Tax Foundation, 1984.

Hamilton, B., and John Whalley. "Reforming Indirect Taxes in Canada: Some General Equilibrium Estimates." *Canadian Journal of Economics* 22, no. 3 (August 1989): 561–75.

Musgrave, Richard A. *The Theory of Public Finance.* New York: McGraw-Hill, 1959.

Riley, John G. "Competition with Hidden Knowledge." *Journal of Political Economy* 93, no. 5 (October 1985): 958–76.

Smith, Adam. *The Wealth of Nations.* London: J.M. Dent and Sons, 1977 (1776).

Chapter 6

Fiscal Federalism

A community of a higher order should not interfere in the internal life of a community of a lower order. ... but rather should support it in case of need and help to coordinate its activity with the activities of the rest of society, always with a view to the common good.

– Pope John Paul II

In the spring of 1997, Glen Clark, the premier of British Columbia, declared "war" ... on the United States Navy. He announced the decision to cancel the provincial lease that allowed U.S. and Canadian navel vessels to conduct military exercises in the Georgia Strait between the mainland and Vancouver Island. Clark's announcement followed the breakdown of talks between Canada and the United States to share the salmon fishery north of Vancouver Island.

Subnational units of government function with considerable autonomy. Attempts from the outside to change their behaviour are likely to be met with active or passive resistance. Is decentralized decision making desirable?

Different types of public services are customarily provided by various levels of government. The reason the B.C. salmon wars received so much attention was the incongruity of a provincial government in effect making foreign policy. International relations "belong" to the federal government. On the other hand, decisions regarding the management of public lands "belong" to provinces. How should different functions be allocated to various levels of government?

These are important issues in Canada where, as noted earlier, there are a multitude of governmental jurisdictions. The appropriate division of power among them has been a matter of controversy since the founding of the nation. This chapter examines the normative and positive aspects of public finance in a federal system.

BACKGROUND

Oates (1972: 17) provides a useful economic definition of a federal system of government:

> A public sector with both centralized and decentralized levels of decision making in which choices made at each level concerning the provision of public services are determined largely by the demands for those services of the residents of (and perhaps others who carry on activities in) the respective jurisdictions.

One federal system is characterized as being more centralized than another when more of its decision-making powers are in the hands of authorities with a larger jurisdiction. The most common measure of the extent to which a system is centralized is the **centralization ratio**, the proportion of total direct government expenditures made by the central government. ("Direct" government expenditure comprises all expenditures except transfers made to other governmental units.) Centralization ratios vary widely across nations: in France, it is 59 percent; in Australia, 55 percent; in the United States, 50 percent; and in Canada, 42 percent.[1]

The centralization ratio is by no means a foolproof indicator. Suppose that provinces make expenditures for social assistance, but a portion of the money comes in the form of grants from the federal government. Ottawa decides that no province will receive these grants unless it mandates that there will be no residency requirement placed on social assistance recipients. Every province complies. Who is really in charge? The point is that if provincial government spending behaviour is constrained by the federal government, the centralization ratio underestimates the true extent of centralization in the system. Conversely, if provinces effectively lobby the federal government to achieve their own ends, the centralization ratio may overestimate the degree of decentralized economic power. In fact, in Canada, very little provincial spending is dictated by the federal government. Recently, reductions in federal grants that were not accompanied by reductions in federal conditions on spending have caused strains in the Canadian federal system.

Table 6.1 shows how the distribution of Canadian government expenditure by level of government has been changing. The long-run trend has been for both the federal and provincial governments to increase their share of spending at the expense of local government. However, the provincial share of spending has increased the most. While in 1930 the ratio of federal to provincial spending

---

[1] Computed from Organization for Economic Cooperation and Development, National Accounts: Detailed Tables, vol. 2 (1982–94), 1996.

Table 6.1

Distribution of all Canadian Government Expenditure
by Level of Government, Selected Years

	FEDERAL	PROVINCIAL	LOCAL
1930	32.7%	22.2%	45.1%
1935	35.3%	31.8%	32.9%
1939	34.7%	34.0%	31.3%
1945	84.1%	8.4%	7.5%
1950	56.8%	24.0%	19.2%
1955	63.8%	17.3%	18.9%
1960	55.9%	22.3%	21.8%
1965	47.8%	28.2%	24.1%
1970	40.8%	35.8%	23.4%
1975	43.7%	36.7%	19.6%
1980	41.5%	39.8%	18.7%
1985	44.3%	39.5%	16.2%
1990	43.1%	40.7%	16.2%
1995	42.1%	41.2%	16.7%

Note: 1940 represents the first year of significantly increased federal expenditure from World War II, so chose 1939 as more representative of period 1936–1940.

SOURCE: CANSIM database: Series D11157, D11164, D11165, D11180, D11185, D11198.

was approximately 3:2 and peaked during World War II at almost 8:1, the ratio has declined since its peak in 1945 to a current value of approximately 1:1.

Figure 6.1 shows the division of public spending by level of government for various government functions. The figures indicate that a number of important activities are in the hands of provincial and local governments. In the context of the current debate over health reform, it is noteworthy that more than 90 percent of public health care expenditures are made by provincial and local governments. This figure may give a somewhat exaggerated view of the degree of decentralization in the delivery of health services for two reasons: (1) a (declining) share of health expenditures by provinces are supported by grants from the federal government; and (2) the federal government attaches the five conditions described in the Canada Health Act.[2]

Figure 6.1 leaves us with a critical question: Does the division of powers as laid out in the Canadian Constitution and interpreted by the courts make sense according to some economic criteria? Before we can provide an answer, we need to discuss the special features associated with subnational government.

---

[2] See Chapter 15.

Figure 6.1

Percentage of Expenditures by Selected Functions and Levels of Government

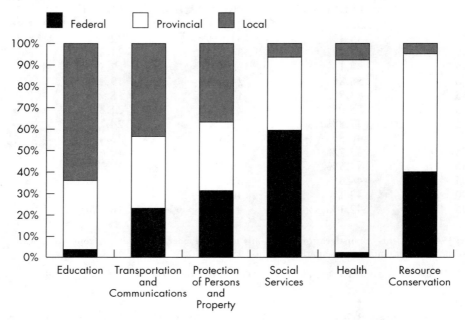

Expenditures by Type and Government
(millions of 1993/94 dollars)

| | LEVEL OF GOVERNMENT | | | |
	FEDERAL	PROVINCIAL	LOCAL	TOTAL
Education	1,617	14,407	28,314	44,338
Transportation and Communications	3,531	5,087	6,609	15,227
Protection of Persons and Property	4,926	5,009	5,750	15,685
Social Services	52,145	29,969	5,571	87,685
Health	1,035	42,029	3,578	46,642
Resource Conservation	5,695	7,817	685	14,197

COMMUNITY FORMATION

To understand the appropriate fiscal roles for local jurisdictions, we consider why communities are formed. In this context, it is useful to think of a community as a club—a voluntary association of people who band together to share some kind of benefit. This section develops a theory of clubs and uses

that theory to explain how the size of a community and its provision of public goods are determined.[3]

Consider a group of people who wish to band together to purchase land for a public park. For simplicity, assume that all members of the group have identical tastes and that they intend to share equally the use of the park and its costs. The "community" can costlessly exclude all nonmembers, and it operates with no transaction costs. Given the assumption of identical tastes, we need to consider only the desires of a representative member. Two decisions must be made: how large a park to acquire and how many members to have in the community.

Assuming that it wants to maximize the welfare of its citizens, how does the community make these decisions? Consider first the relationship between the total cost per member and the number of members, given that a certain size park is selected. Clearly, the larger the community, the more people there are to shoulder the expense of the park, and the smaller the required contribution per member. But if the per capita cost continually decreases with membership size, why not simply invite an infinite number of people to join? The problem is that as more people join the community, the park becomes congested. The marginal congestion cost measures the dollar cost of the incremental congestion created by each new member. We assume that marginal congestion cost increases with the number of members. The community should expand its membership until the marginal decrease in the membership fee just equals the per person marginal increase in congestion costs.

Now turn to the flip side of the problem: For any given number of members in the community, how big should the park be? A bigger park yields greater benefits, although like most goods, we assume it is subject to diminishing marginal utility. The per member marginal cost of increased park acreage is just the price of the extra land divided by the number of members sharing its cost. Acreage should be increased to the point where each member's marginal benefit just equals the per member marginal cost.

We can now put together these two pieces of the picture to describe an optimal community or club. The optimal community is one in which the number of members and the level of services simultaneously satisfy the condition that the marginal cost equal the corresponding marginal benefit. Although this club model is very simple, it highlights the crucial aspects of the community-

---

[3] Most club models are based on the work of Buchanan (1965). For a survey of this area, see Sandler and Tschirhart (1980). Breton and Scott's (1978) seminal work considers the optimal design of federations.

formation process. Specifically, it suggests how community size depends on the type of public goods the people want to consume, the extent to which these goods are subject to crowding, and the costs of obtaining them, among other things. However, viewing communities as clubs leaves unanswered several important questions that are relevant for understanding subnational public finance:

1. How are the public services to be financed? A country club can charge a membership fee, but a community normally levies taxes to pay for public goods.
2. A club can exclude nonmembers and so eliminate the free-rider problem. How can communities achieve this end?
3. When people throughout the country organize themselves into many different clubs (communities), will the overall allocation of public goods prove to be equitable and efficient?

These questions are taken up in the next section.

THE TIEBOUT MODEL

"Love it or leave it." When people who oppose government policy are given this advice, it is generally as constructive as telling them to "drop dead." Only in extreme cases do we expect people to leave their country because of government policy. Because of the large pecuniary and psychic costs of emigrating, a more realistic option is to stay home and to try to change the policy. On

Drawing by Lee Lorenz © 1985 from The New Yorker Collection. All rights reserved.

the other hand, most citizens are not as strongly attached to their local communities. If you dislike the policies being followed in Scarborough, Ontario, the easiest thing to do may be to move a few kilometres away to Markham. This section discusses the relationship among intercommunity mobility, voluntary community formation, and the efficient provision of public goods.

Chapter 5 examined the idea that markets generally fail to provide public goods efficiently. The root of the problem is that the market does not force individuals to reveal their true preferences for public goods. Everyone has an incentive to be a free rider. The usual conclusion is that some kind of government intervention is required.

In an important article, Tiebout (1956) (rhymes with "me too") argued that the ability of individuals to move among jurisdictions produces a market-like solution to the local public goods problem. As suggested in the cartoon, individuals vote with their feet and locate in the community that offers the bundle of public services and taxes they like best. Much as citizens satisfy their demands for private goods by purchasing them on the market, they satisfy their demands for public services by the appropriate selection of a community in which to live and pay taxes. In equilibrium, people distribute themselves across communities on the basis of their demands for public services. Each individual receives his or her desired level of public services and cannot be made better off by moving (or else he or she would). Hence, the equilibrium is Pareto efficient, and government action is not required to achieve efficiency.

TIEBOUT'S ASSUMPTIONS

Tiebout's provocative assertion that a quasi-market process can solve the public goods problem has stimulated a large amount of research. Much of that research has been directed toward finding a precise set of sufficient conditions under which the ability of citizens to vote with their feet leads to efficient public goods provision. Some of the conditions are as follows[4]:

1. No externalities arise from local government behaviour. As noted later, to the extent there are spillover effects among communities, the allocation of resources is inefficient.
2. Individuals are completely mobile. Each person can travel costlessly to a jurisdiction whose public services are best for him or her. The location of

---

[4] Mieszkowski and Zodrow (1989) provide more detail. Not all of these conditions were included in Tiebout's original article.

a place of employment puts no restriction on where individuals reside and does not affect their income.

3. People have perfect information with respect to each community's public services and taxes.

4. There are enough different communities so that each individual can find one with public services meeting his or her demands.

5. The cost per unit of public services is constant, so that if the quantity of public services doubles, the total cost also doubles. In addition, the technology of public service provision is such that if the number of residents doubles, the quantity of the public service provided must double.

   To see why these conditions are required for a Tiebout equilibrium to be efficient, imagine instead that the cost per unit of public services fell as the scale of provision increased. In that case, there would be scale economies of which independently operating communities might fail to take advantage.

   This assumption makes the public service essentially a publicly provided private good. "Pure" public goods (such as national defence) do not satisfy this assumption. However, many local public services such as education and garbage collection appear to fit this description to a reasonable extent.

6. Public services are financed by a proportional property tax. The tax rate can vary across communities.[5]

Communities can enact exclusionary zoning laws—statutes that prohibit certain uses of land. Specifically, they can require that all houses be of some minimum size. To see why this assumption is crucial, recall that in a Tiebout equilibrium, communities are segregated on the basis of their members' demands for public goods. If income is positively correlated with the demand for public services, community segregation by income results. In high-income communities, the level of property values tends to be high, and hence the community can finance a given amount of public spending with a relatively low property tax rate. Low-income families have an incentive to move into rich communities and build relatively small houses. Because of the low tax rate, low-income families have relatively small tax liabilities, but nevertheless enjoy the high level of public service provision. As more low-income families get the idea and move in, the tax base per family in the community falls. Tax rates must be increased to finance the expanded level of public services required to serve the increased population.

---

[5] Tiebout (1956) assumed finance by head taxes. The more realistic assumption of property taxation is from Hamilton (1975).

Since we assume perfect mobility, the rich have no reason to put up with this. They can just move to another community. But what stops the poor from following them? In the absence of constraints on mobility, nothing. Clearly, it is possible for a game of musical suburbs to develop in a Tiebout model. Exclusionary zoning prevents this phenomenon and thus maintains a stable Pareto efficient equilibrium.

TIEBOUT AND THE REAL WORLD

The Tiebout model is clearly not a perfect description of the real world. People are not perfectly mobile; there are probably not enough communities so that each family can find one with a bundle of services that suits it perfectly; and so on. Moreover, contrary to the model's implication, we observe many communities within which there are massive income differences and, hence, presumably different desired levels of public service provision. Just consider any major city. However, we should not dismiss the Tiebout mechanism too hastily. There is a lot of mobility in the Canadian economy. For example, in 1996 more than 360,000 people (1.2 percent of the total population) changed their province of residence.

There have also been a number of empirical tests of the Tiebout hypothesis. One type of study looks at whether the values of local public services and taxes are capitalized into local property values. The idea is that if people move in response to local packages of taxes and public services, differences in these packages should be reflected in property values.[6] A community with better public services should have higher property values, other things (including taxes) being the same. Day and Winer (1994) review the Canadian empirical studies on capitalization. Capitalization may occur because of either differences in tax rates or differences in public services provided. Overall, the evidence for capitalization within jurisdictions is mixed, with more recent studies supporting at least partial capitalization. Stronger evidence exists for capitalization between jurisdictions.

Another interesting test was done by Gramlich and Rubinfeld (1982). They analyzed responses to survey questions in which individuals were asked about their desired levels of local public expenditures. If the Tiebout mechanism is operative, we would expect to find substantial homogeneity of demands within suburbs located near many other communities, because, in such a setting, the model suggests that those who are dissatisfied with current spending levels sim-

---

[6] There are some circumstances under which the Tiebout hypothesis does not imply that capitalization necessarily will occur; see Rubinfeld (1987).

ply move elsewhere. On the other hand, in areas where there are few other communities nearby, it is harder to exit if you are unhappy. In such areas, people with very different demands for public goods may be lumped together in a single community. Gramlich and Rubinfeld found that, compared to areas where there is little scope for choice, there are indeed relatively small differences in tastes for public goods within communities located in large metropolitan areas. This result suggests that, at least in some settings, the Tiebout model is a good depiction of reality.

INTERPROVINCIAL FISCALLY INDUCED MIGRATION

In Canada, economists have paid a good deal of attention to the implications of Tiebout's theory for migration between provinces. In the absence of government, economic theory suggests that the people will move from one province when they expect to earn a higher income and thus a higher standard of living. In Figure 6.2 (adapted from Day and Winer, 1997) we consider two provinces, M (Mountainia) and A (Atlantica). Downward sloping curves MPL_M and MPL_A represent the marginal product of labour (demand) curves for each region. Thus, the vertical axes measure wage rates (dollars per hour) and the horizontal axis measures numbers of workers in the two provinces. Suppose the initial distribution of workers among the two provinces is found at point B. At this point, wages are higher in province M than in province A and we would expect some workers to migrate from A to M seeking the higher wages. The increased (reduced) supply of labour in province M (A) will cause wages to fall (rise) until equilibrium is reached at point C. At this point the supply of labour in province M is measured by the distance $0_M C$ and the supply of labour in province A is measured by the distance $0_A C$. At point C, marginal products of labour are equalized in both provinces and an efficient distribution of labour is achieved.

Tiebout's theory applies when, in addition to wage differentials, there are also higher net fiscal benefits (NFBs) in one of the two provinces. Net fiscal benefits are simply the value of publicly provided services minus their cost to the recipient of those services. According to a theory proposed by Boadway and Flatters (1982), higher NFBs in province M may provide an incentive for too many people to migrate. The parallel line above MPL_M adds the NFB that might come as a result of a greater endowment of natural resources to province M. In this case (again starting at point B) too many workers will migrate from A to M to achieve an efficient distribution of labour. The difference in migration caused by the NFB is measured by the segment DC. This migration response to differences in NFBs is called fiscally induced migration. One proposal for correcting

Figure 6.2

Analysis of the Effect of Net Fiscal Benefits on Migration

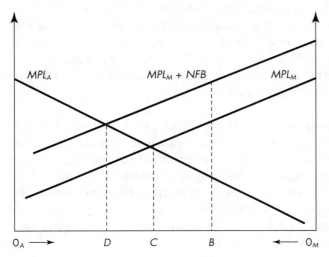

SOURCE: Adapted from Day and Winer (1997).

this inefficiency is to use intergovernmental grants to equalize NFBs across provinces. This reasoning has often been offered as the efficiency justification for the Canadian federal government's extensive equalization program.

So far the discussion has been based solely on economic theory. Before making the step to designing and implementing policy, two important practical questions must be answered. First, is there compelling evidence that migration actually responds to differences in NFBs? Second, can we calculate the "right amount" of equalization needed to restore the efficient distribution of labour across provinces, and do the benefits outweigh the costs?

Day and Winer (1994) provide an extensive review of the empirical work on this issue, beginning with the work of Courchene (1970). Overall, Day and Winer found that migration did respond to regional differences in unemployment insurance benefits.[7] There was also some evidence of migration responding to differences in the levels of expenditure, transfers, and taxation across provinces, although the magnitude of these responses would likely be empirically fairly small in the short term and would take long periods of time to have a significant effect. There is little evidence that migration responds directly to intergov-

---

[7] This conclusion is disputed in recent work by Lin (1995).

ernmental transfers such as equalization, although these programs may have an indirect impact through their effect on levels of expenditure and taxation.

Courchene and others have argued that the response of migration to regional differences in unemployment benefits actually leads to a less efficient labour market by inhibiting migration that should come about as a result of wage differentials. This leads to what Courchene has called "transfer dependency." In this case, intergovernmental transfers may make the distribution of labour across provinces worse rather than better.

Finally, Watson (1986) uses estimates from Winer and Gauthier (1982) to attempt to calculate the welfare gains that would accrue to Canada if an equalization program were able to close the gap in incomes that arise from differences in NFBs between provinces. In his simple calculation, the cost of the program far outweighed its benefits in terms of increased labour market efficiency. Watson concludes that the justification for equalization must be based on the desire to attain goals such as redistribution of income rather than improving the efficiency of the labour market.

OPTIMAL FEDERALISM

Now that we have an idea of how to characterize subnational governments, we return to our earlier question. Based on economic criteria, what is the optimal allocation of responsibilities among levels of government in a federal system? The goal of the theory of optimal federalism is to determine the proper division of activities among the levels of government. Let us first briefly consider macroeconomic functions.

While textbook treatments of fiscal policy portray governments as actively adjusting taxation and spending levels to smooth out slumps and booms in economic activity, the reality for most federations is that almost all macroeconomic stabilization comes from so-called automatic stabilizers; see Boothe and Petchey (1996). Automatic stabilizers are taxes such as income or sales taxes that rise when the economy is strong and decline when it is weak. On the spending side, automatic stabilizers include government programs such as employment insurance and social assistance that rise when the economy is weak and fall when it is strong. As long as a government's budget includes automatic stabilizers, it will contribute to macroeconomic stabilization regardless of whether it is at the national or subnational level.[8]

---

[8] While this is true for fiscal policy, it is not true for monetary policy. Federations with a common currency and integrated financial markets can only have a single interest rate or exchange rate policy, even if that policy has different impacts in different regions of the country.

With respect to the microeconomic activities of enhancing efficiency and equity, there is considerably more controversy. Posed within the framework of welfare economics, the question is whether a centralized or decentralized system is more likely to maximize social welfare.[9] For simplicity, most of our discussion assumes just two levels of government: central and "regional." No important insights are lost with this assumption.

ADVANTAGES OF A DECENTRALIZED SYSTEM

Tailoring government to local tastes. Some people want expensive computers used in the education of their children; others believe this is unnecessary. Some people enjoy parks; others do not. Some people believe government should be financed by income taxes, others think user fees are best. A central government tends to provide the same level of public services throughout the country, regardless of the fact that people's tastes differ. As de Tocqueville observed, "In great centralized nations the legislator is obliged to give a character of uniformity to the laws, which does not always suit the diversity of customs and of districts" (Oates, 1972: 31). Clearly it is inefficient to provide individuals with more or less of a public good than they desire if the quantity they receive can be more closely tailored to their preferences. Under a decentralized system, individuals with similar tastes for public goods group together, so communities provide the types and quantities of public goods desired by their inhabitants. (Remember the "club" view of communities.) A closely related notion is that regional government's greater proximity to the people makes it more responsive to citizens' preferences than central government. This is especially likely to be the case in a large country where the costs of obtaining and processing information on everybody's tastes are substantial.

In the same way, economic regulations enacted at the national level may not make sense in every community. In Canada, regulations for workplace health and safety are set by provincial governments. Should a single set of regulations be set in Ottawa if the nature of work varies greatly across provinces? Standards for student–teacher ratios are set by individual school boards. Should a single standard be set by the federal government when educational circumstances and resources vary from city to city and province to province? Finally, regulations regarding Sunday shopping are set by provinces (or municipalities). Will local wishes and needs be considered if a single rule is imposed by the federal Parliament for the entire country?

---

[9] Of course, this assumes that we can even define a consistent social welfare function and, further, that there is agreement over which population—regional or national—in which citizens wish to redistribute income. See Chapter 4.

Fostering intergovernmental competition. Many theories of government behaviour focus on the fact that government managers may lack incentives to produce at minimum feasible cost (see Chapter 11). Managers of private firms who fail to minimize costs are eventually driven out of business. In contrast, politicians and government managers can continue to muddle along. However, if citizens are aware of other jurisdictions where programs are better managed, then substantial mismanagement may cause citizens to use their vote to support political parties that promise change. This threat may create incentives for politicians and government managers to produce more efficiently and be more responsive to their citizens.

Experimentation and innovation in regionally provided goods and services. For many policy questions, no one is certain what the right answer is, or even whether there is a single solution that is best in all situations. One way to find out is to let each region choose its own way, and then compare the results. A system of diverse governments enhances the chances that new solutions to problems will be sought. As U.S. Supreme Court Justice Louis Brandeis once observed, "It is one of the happy incidents of the Federal system that a single courageous state may, if its citizens choose, serve as a laboratory, and try moral, social, and economic experiments without risk to the rest of the country."

From all appearances, Brandeis's laboratories are busily at work in Canada as well:

- *Item:* In 1962, the province of Saskatchewan instituted a program of health insurance in which the government eliminated private payment for doctors' services. Doctors were thereafter paid their fee from the provincial fund. After an initial bitter strike by Saskatchewan doctors, the program became a model that was adopted by provinces across the country.
- *Item:* Although the bulk of the cost of university education is supported by provincial taxes, universities are granted a good deal of local autonomy. Acadia University in Nova Scotia recently instituted the "Acadia Advantage," a program where all students are provided with notebook computers to be used as an integral part of their studies. The cost of the computer is included in their tuition. Universities in other provinces are closely monitoring the results of the Acadia experiment.

In the past, some programs that began as experiments at the provincial level eventually became federal policy. After the Great Depression, for example, the designers of the federal unemployment insurance program took advantage of the experience of several provinces that had earlier instituted programs for unemployment relief.

DISADVANTAGES OF A DECENTRALIZED SYSTEM

Consider a country composed of a group of small communities. Each community government makes decisions to maximize a social welfare function depending only on the utilities of its members—outsiders do not count.[10] How do the results compare to those that would emerge from maximizing a national social welfare function that attempts to take into account all citizens' utilities? We consider efficiency and then equity issues.

Efficiency Issues

There are several reasons why a system of decentralized governments might lead to an inefficient allocation of resources, outlined below.

Externalities. We define a public good with benefits that accrue only to members of a particular community as a local public good. For example, the public library in Brandon, Manitoba, has little effect on the welfare of people in Sherbrooke, Quebec. However, in many situations, the activities undertaken by one community can affect the utility levels of people in other communities. If one town provides good public education for its children and some of them eventually emigrate, then other communities may benefit from having a better-educated work force. Towns can affect each other negatively as well. If Edmonton, Alberta, does not properly clean the water it returns to the North Saskatchewan River, some of the waste makes its way to Prince Albert, Saskatchewan. In short, communities impose externalities (both positive and negative) on each other. If each community cares only about its own members, these externalities are overlooked. Hence, according to the standard argument (see Chapter 8), resources are allocated inefficiently.

Scale economies in provision of public goods. For certain public services, the cost per person may fall as the number of users increases. If several communities coordinate their use of such services, the members of all participating communities are better off because each person pays less for the service. Thus, for example, it might make sense for neighbouring communities to run

---

[10] Recall that we are ignoring, for now, the questions of how the social welfare function is determined and whether the people who run the government actually try to maximize it. See Chapter 11.

their police departments jointly and so avoid the costs of acquiring duplicate communications equipment. Communities that operate with complete independence lose such opportunities for cost savings.

Of course, various activities are subject to different scale economies. The optimal scale for library services might differ from that for fire protection. And both surely differ from the optimal scale for national defence. This observation, incidentally, helps rationalize a system of overlapping jurisdictions—each jurisdiction can handle those services with scale economies that are appropriate for the jurisdiction's size.

On the other hand, consolidation is not the only way for communities to take advantage of scale economies. A town might contract out to other governments or to the private sector for the provision of certain public goods and services. For example, Ottawa has privately provided garbage collection.

Inefficient tax systems. Roughly speaking, efficient taxation requires that inelastically demanded or supplied goods be taxed at relatively high rates and vice versa.[11] Suppose that the supply of capital to the entire country is fixed, but capital is highly mobile across subfederal jurisdictions. Each jurisdiction realizes that if it levies a substantial tax on capital, the capital will simply move elsewhere, thus making the jurisdiction worse off. In such a situation, a rational jurisdiction taxes capital very lightly, or even subsidizes it. Tax competition may lead to underprovision of public goods.

In reality, of course, the total capital stock is not fixed in supply. Nor is it known just how responsive firms' locational decisions are to differences in local tax rates, although there is some statistical evidence from the United States that the number of new businesses in a state is inversely correlated with its effective tax rate on capital (see Papke, 1991). In any case, the basic point remains: taxes levied by decentralized communities may not be efficient from a national point of view. Instead, communities may select taxes on the basis of whether they can be exported to outsiders. For example, Saskatchewan rebates a portion of the gasoline tax paid by residents, thus imposing the full tax only on visitors.[12]

An implication of tax shifting is that communities may purchase too many local public goods. Efficiency requires that local public goods be purchased up

---

[11] See Chapter 19.

[12] As usual, a precise answer to the tax incidence question requires information on market structure, elasticity of demand, and the structure of costs. See Chapters 5 and 8.

to the point where their marginal social benefit equals marginal social cost. If communities can shift some of the burden to other jurisdictions, the community's perceived marginal cost is less than marginal social cost. This induces them to purchase local public goods with marginal social benefit equal to the perceived marginal cost, but less than marginal social cost. The result is an inefficiently large amount of local public goods.

Scale economies in tax collection. Individual communities may not be able to take advantage of scale economies in the collection of taxes. Each community has to devote resources to tax administration, and savings may be obtained by having a joint taxing authority. Why not split the costs of a single computer to keep track of tax returns, rather than have each community purchase its own? Of course, some of these economies might be achieved just by cooperation among the jurisdictions, without actual consolidation taking place. In some provinces, for example, provincial sales taxes are collected by the federal revenue department.

Equity Issues

In a utilitarian philosophical framework, the maximization of social welfare may require income transfers to the poor. Suppose that the pattern of taxes and expenditures in a particular community is favourable to its low-income members. If there are no barriers to movement between communities, we might expect an in-migration of the poor from the rest of the country. As the poor population increases, so does the cost of the redistributive fiscal policy. At the same time, the town's upper-income people may decide to exit. Why should they pay high taxes for the poor when they can move to another community where the expenditure pattern is to their own benefit? Thus, the demands on the community's tax base increase while its size decreases. Eventually the redistributive program has to be abandoned.

This argument relies heavily on the notion that people's decisions to locate in a given community are influenced by the available tax-welfare package. There is some casual support for this proposition. For example, in 1992, California welfare officials asserted that about 7 percent of that state's welfare recipients were recent arrivals from out of state, and about half of them had been on welfare immediately before moving to California (Saunders, 1992: A18). As a consequence, the state government passed a law paying lower welfare benefits to the poor who moved to California from other states. The law is being challenged in the courts. In his survey of econometric research on the determinants of migration, Moffitt (1992) argues that welfare does exert a significant effect on residential location. This reinforces the notion that substantial income redistribution cannot be carried out by decentralized communities. As we saw above in our discussion of fiscally induced migration, the Canadian evidence is that migration of this type is relatively small, and will only have significant effects, if at all, over a long period of time.

IMPLICATIONS

The foregoing discussion makes it clear that a purely decentralized system cannot be expected to maximize utilitarian social welfare. Efficiency requires that those commodities with spillovers that affect the entire country—national public goods—be provided at the national level. Defence is a classic example. On the other hand, it seems appropriate for local public goods to be provided locally. This leaves us with the in-between case of community activities that create spillover effects that are not national in scope. One possible solution is to put all the communities that affect each other under a single regional government. In theory, this government would take into account the welfare of all its citizens, and so internalize the externalities. However, a larger governmental jurisdiction carries the cost of less responsiveness to local differences in tastes.

An alternative method for dealing with externalities is a system of Pigouvian taxes and subsidies. Chapter 8 shows that efficiency can be enhanced when the government taxes activities that create negative externalities and subsidizes activities that create positive externalities. We can imagine the central government using similar devices to influence the decisions of regional governments. For example, if primary and secondary education create benefits that go beyond the boundaries of a jurisdiction, the central government can provide regions with educational subsidies. Regional autonomy is maintained, yet the externality is corrected. As we will see in Chapter 16, this is exactly the rationale used in Canada for federal grants to support postsecondary education, a provincial responsibility.

Our theory suggests a fairly clean division of responsibility for public good provision—local public goods by regions, and national public goods by the central government. In practice, there is considerable interplay between levels of government. For example, although provinces have primary responsibility for environmental regulation, citizens and firms must also obey numerous federal regulations. Given that regions might ignore the externalities created by their actions in the absence of such regulations, the presence of regulations may improve welfare. However, some believe the system of federal in addition to provincial government regulation has become so complicated that it may be difficult to determine which government has responsibility for what. In 1996, provincial premiers made a number of proposals to rebalance the division of responsibilities between federal and provincial governments in an effort to improve accountability and reduce overlap and duplication.

THE ROLE OF THE CONSTITUTION

Although economic theory provides some guidance regarding the division of spending responsibilities and taxation in federal systems, generally speaking the actual division of powers is dictated by the country's constitution and its interpretation by the courts. Canada is no exception to this general rule. Canada's original Constitution of 1867 (the British North America Act, now the Constitution Act, 1867) was an agreement among four British colonies: New Brunswick, Nova Scotia, Ontario (Upper Canada), and Quebec (Lower Canada). The BNA Act laid out specific responsibilities for both the federal (Section 91) and the provincial (Section 92) governments. Federal powers include such matters as public debt, the regulation of trade and commerce, the postal service, defence, currency and coinage, and Indians and lands reserved for Indians. Provincial powers include such matters as provincial borrowing, the management and sale of public lands, hospitals and asylums, and generally all matters of a local or private nature within the province. Section 93 also gives powers over education to the provinces.

Over time, the Constitution has been interpreted by the courts, first by the Judicial Committee of the Privy Council in London, and later by the Supreme Court of Canada. These interpretations have resulted in an actual division of responsibilities that differs in some respect from the written Constitution. An important theme in judicial interpretation has been affirmation of the federal government's right to act in areas of provincial responsibility through its use of the "spending power" under the general provision of Section 91 for the federal government "to make laws for the Peace, Order and Good Government of Canada." Thus, today we observe the federal government involved in funding such activities as health care and education, which constitutionally are the exclusive responsibility of the provinces.

In 1982 the federal government and all provinces except Quebec agreed to a major revision of the Constitution (Constitution Act, 1982). Although many important, new provisions were added, one of the most interesting for students of fiscal federalism was related to regional disparities. In Section 36, the federal government and the provinces committed to reducing regional economic disparities. Further, in Section 36(2) the federal government committed to the principle of "making equalization payments to ensure that provincial governments have sufficient revenues to provide reasonably comparable levels of public services at reasonably comparable levels of taxation." This brings us to the matter of intergovernmental transfers.

INTERGOVERNMENTAL GRANTS

As already noted, federal grants are a very important source of revenue to provinces. Grants from one level of government to another are the main method for changing fiscal resources within a federal system. Table 6.2 indicates that between 1930 and 1995, grants from the federal government to provinces and local governments have ranged from 3.7 percent to 22.9 percent of total federal outlays. Grants grew rapidly in the postwar period until the mid-1970s and declined gradually thereafter to their current level of about 19 percent. Grants as a percentage of provincial and local expenditures exhibit the same pattern. The importance of grants for local public finance is particu-

Table 6.2

Relation of Federal Transfers to Federal, Provincial, and Local Expenditures

	TOTAL FEDERAL TRANSFERS NOMINAL $	TOTAL FEDERAL TRANSFERS 1986 DOLLARS	TRANSFERS AS PERCENTAGE OF	
			TOTAL FEDERAL EXPENDITURE	PROVINCIAL AND LOCAL EXPENDITURE
1930	25	439	8.0%	4.2%
1935	74	1,423	17.6%	11.7%
1939	79	1,436	17.6%	11.4%
1945	157	2,066	3.7%	20.1%
1950	251	2,485	11.0%	16.2%
1955	450	3,462	9.7%	18.9%
1960	994	6,174	15.3%	22.8%
1965	1,431	7,571	17.4%	19.3%
1970	3,397	12,819	22.9%	20.5%
1975	7,670	18,219	22.2%	22.1%
1980	12,831	19,208	21.3%	19.1%
1985	21,746	22,442	19.3%	19.1%
1990	26,681	22,478	17.8%	16.3%
1995	32,125	24,655	18.6%	16.7%

Note: Real Dollars converted by Government Goods and Services IPI. Provincial Expenditure is net of transfers to local governments to avoid double counting the expenditures as transfers for the provincial government and general expenditures by the local government.

SOURCE: CANSIM database: Series D11157, D11164, D11165, D11180, D11185, D11196.

Table 6.3

Federal and Provincial Transfers to Local Governments

	TOTAL FEDERAL & PROVINCIAL TRANSFERS NOMINAL $	TOTAL FEDERAL & PROVINCIAL TRANSFERS 1986 DOLLARS	PERCENT OF TOTAL LOCAL REVENUE
1930	36	632	9.5%
1935	22	423	6.3%
1939	32	582	8.8%
1945	63	829	14.6%
1950	172	1,703	23.2%
1955	334	2,569	26.3%
1960	746	4,634	31.1%
1965	1,514	8,011	39.9%
1970	3,180	12,000	45.6%
1975	6,699	15,912	52.3%
1980	11,325	16,954	50.4%
1985	17,539	18,100	50.8%
1990	24,837	20,924	48.4%
1995	30,361	23,301	48.3%

larly striking. Table 6.3 indicates that grants from the provincial and federal governments are now about one-half of total local revenues.

Grants help finance activities that run practically the entire gamut of government functions. More than half of federal grant outlays go for programs relating to postsecondary education, health, and social assistance. Grants are also used for general fiscal assistance, development of infrastructure, and other purposes.

Why are intergovernmental transfers such an important source of finance for provincial programs? One explanation for the importance of grants emphasizes that over the last several decades the demand for the types of services traditionally provided by provincial and local governments—health, education, and social assistance—has been growing rapidly. However, provincial and local revenue structures, which depend heavily on sales and property taxes, have not provided the means to keep pace with the growth of desired expenditures. In contrast, federal tax revenues have tended to grow automatically over time, largely due to the substantial federal share of the personal income tax. Hence, there is a "mismatch" between where tax money is collected and where it is demanded. Grants from the federal government to provinces, and from provinces to municipalities, provide a way of correcting this mismatch.

A major problem with the mismatch theory is that it fails to explain why provinces and municipalities cannot raise their tax rates to keep up with increases in the demand for local public goods and services. Inman (1985) proposes a politically oriented alternative explanation for the growth of grants in the United States. From 1945 to 1960, new coalitions emerged that had a common interest in larger state and local governments. These coalitions included public employee unions, suburban developers (who wanted increased infrastructure spending), and welfare rights organizations. Because of the mobility of their tax bases, local politicians were unable to transfer much income to these coalitions. Therefore, they organized as the intergovernmental lobby and went to Washington looking for money. The federal government responded with increased grants.

THE THEORY OF INTERGOVERNMENTAL GRANTS

A grant's structure can influence its economic impact. There are basically two types of grants, conditional and unconditional, which we discuss in turn.

Conditional Grants

Conditional grants are sometimes called categorical grants. The donor specifies, to some extent, the purposes for which the recipient can use the funds. The ways in which conditional grant money must be spent are often spelled out in minute detail. Until recently, federal grants to provinces to fund social assistance spending were accompanied by pages of regulations. Under reforms that took effect in 1995/96, the only requirement now accompanying grants intended for social assistance is the prohibition of provincial residency requirements. There are several types of conditional grants.

Matching grant. For every dollar given by the donor to support a particular activity, a certain sum must be expended by the recipient. For example, a grant might indicate that whenever a province spends a dollar on an approved infrastructure project, the federal government will contribute a dollar as well.

The standard theory of rational choice can help us understand the effects of a matching grant. In Figure 6.3, the horizontal axis measures the quantity of provincial government output, G, consumed by the residents of the Province of Atlantica. The vertical axis measures Atlantica's total consumption, c. Assume for simplicity that units of G and c are defined so the price of one unit

Figure 6.3

Analysis of a Matching Grant

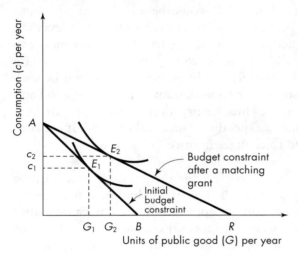

of each is $1. Hence, assuming no saving, c is equal to after-tax income. With these assumptions, Atlantica's budget constraint between c and G is a straight line whose slope in absolute value is one. The unitary slope indicates that for each dollar Atlantica is willing to spend, it can obtain one unit of public good. The budget constraint is denoted AB in Figure 6.3.

Suppose that Atlantica's preferences for G and c can be represented by a set of conventionally shaped indifference curves.[13] Then if the province seeks to maximize its utility subject to the budget constraint, it chooses point E_1, where public good consumption is G_1 and provincial after-tax income is c_1.

Now suppose that a matching grant regime of the sort just described is instituted. The federal government matches every dollar that Atlantica spends. When Atlantica gives up $1 of income, it can obtain $2 worth of G —one of its own dollars and one from the federal government. The slope (in absolute value) of Atlantica's budget line therefore becomes one-half. In effect, the matching grant halves the price of G. It is an ad valorem subsidy on consumption of the public good. The new budget line is drawn in Figure 6.3 as AR.[14]

---

[13] Of course, this supposition ignores all the problems—and perhaps the impossibility—of preference aggregation, considered in Chapter 11.

[14] It is worth noting that in this partial analysis, the budget line does not take into account the federal taxes required to finance the matching grant.

At the new equilibrium, Atlantica consumes G_2 public goods and has c_2 available for private consumption. Note that not only is G_2 greater than G_1, but c_2 is also greater than c_1. Atlantica uses part of the grant to buy more of the public good and part to reduce its tax burden. It would be possible, of course, to draw the indifference curves so that c_2 equals c_1, or even so that c_2 is less than c_1. Nevertheless, there is a distinct possibility that part of the grant meant to stimulate public consumption will be used not to buy more G, but to obtain tax relief. In an extreme case, the province's indifference curves might be such that $G_2 = G_1$—the province consumes the same amount of the public good and uses the entire grant to reduce taxes. Thus, theory alone cannot indicate how a matching grant affects a province's expenditure on a public good. It depends on the responsiveness of demand to changes in price.

A matching grant is a sensible way to correct for the presence of a positive externality. As explained in Chapter 8, when an individual or a firm generates a positive externality at the margin, an appropriate subsidy can enhance efficiency. The same logic applies to a province. Of course, all the problems that arise in implementing the subsidy scheme are still present. In particular, the federal government has to be able to measure the actual size of the externality.

Matching closed-ended grant. With a matching grant, the cost to the donor ultimately depends on the recipient's behaviour. If Atlantica's consumption of G is very stimulated by the program, the federal government's contributions will be quite large and vice versa. To put a ceiling on the cost, the donor may specify some maximum amount that it will contribute. Such a closed-ended matching grant is illustrated in Figure 6.4. As before, prior to the grant, Atlantica's budget line is AB, and the equilibrium is at point E_1. With the closed-ended matching grant, the budget constraint is the kinked line segment ADF. Segment AD has a slope of minus one-half, reflecting the one-for-one matching provision. But after some point D, the donor no longer matches dollar for dollar. Atlantica's opportunity cost of a unit of government spending again becomes \$1, which is reflected in the slope of segment DF.

The new equilibrium at E_3 involves more consumption of G than under the status quo, but less than under the open-ended matching grant. The fact that the grant runs out limits its ability to stimulate expenditure on the public good. Note, however, that in some cases the closed-endedness can be irrelevant. If desired provincial consumption of G involves an expenditure below the ceiling, the presence of the ceiling simply does not matter. In graphical terms, if the new tangency had been along segment AD of Figure 6.4, it would be irrelevant that points along DR were not available.

Figure 6.4

Analysis of a Closed-Ended Matching Grant

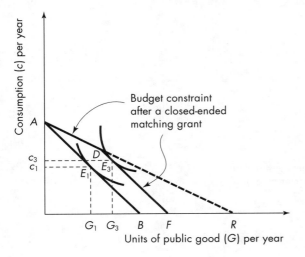

Nonmatching grant. Here the donor gives a fixed sum of money with the stipulation that it be spent on the public good. Figure 6.5 depicts a nonmatching grant to buy AH units of G. At each level of provincial income, Atlantica can now buy AH more units of the public good than it did before. Thus, the new budget constraint is found by adding a horizontal distance AH to the original budget constraint AB. The result is the kinked line AHM.

Atlantica maximizes utility at point E_4. Note that although public good consumption goes up from G_1 to G_4, the difference between the two is less than the amount of the grant, AH. Atlantica has followed the stipulation that it spend the entire grant on G, but at the same time it has reduced its own expenditures for the public good. If the donor expected expenditures to be increased by exactly AH, then Atlantica's reaction has frustrated these hopes. It turns out that the situation depicted in Figure 6.5 is a good description of reality. In the United States, there is evidence that communities often use some portion of nonmatching conditional grant money to reduce their own taxes (see Craig and Inman, 1986).

Unconditional Grants

Observe from Figure 6.5 that budget line AHM looks almost as if it were created by giving the province an unrestricted lump-sum grant of AH dollars. An

Figure 6.5

Analysis of a Nonmatching Grant

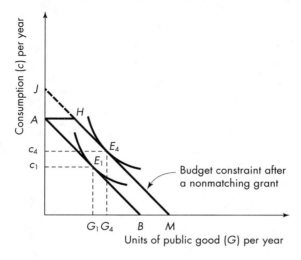

unconditional grant would have led to a budget line *JM*, which is just segment *MH* extended to the vertical axis. Atlantica happens to behave exactly the same way facing constraint *AHM* as it would have if it had faced *JM*. In this particular case, then, the conditional grant could just as well have been an unrestricted lump-sum grant. Intuitively, as long as the province wants to consume at least an amount of the public good equal to the grant, the fact that the grant is conditional is irrelevant. In contrast, if the province wanted to consume less of the public good than *AH* (if the indifference curves were such that the optimum along *JM* is to the left of *H*), then the conditional nature of the grant actually affects behaviour.

Why should the federal government be in the business of giving unconditional grants to provinces? The usual response is that such grants can equalize the income distribution. It is not clear that this argument stands up under scrutiny. Even if a goal of public policy is to help poor people, it does not follow that the best way to do so is to help poor provinces. After all, the chances are that a province with a low average income will probably have some relatively rich members and vice versa. If the goal is to help the poor, why not give them the money directly?

One possible explanation is that the federal government is particularly concerned that the poor consume a greater quantity of the publicly provided good.

An important example is education. However, as we just demonstrated, with unconditional grants we cannot know for sure that all the money will ultimately be spent on the favoured good. (Indeed, the same is generally true for conditional grants as well.)

Measuring need. In any case, an unconditional grant program requires that the donor determine which provinces "need" money and in what amounts.[15] Federal allocations are based on complicated formulas established by the federal government. The amount of grant money received by a province may depend on such factors as the size of provincial tax bases, per capita income, and unemployment relative to the national average.

An important factor in determining how much a province receives from the federal government is its tax effort, normally defined as the ratio of tax collections to tax capacity. The idea is that provinces that try hard to raise taxes but still cannot finance a very high level of public services are worthy of receiving a grant. Unfortunately, it is quite possible that this and related measures yield little or no information about a province's true effort. Suppose that Atlantica is in a position to export its tax burden in the sense that the incidence of any taxes it levies falls on outsiders. Then a high tax rate tells us nothing about how much the residents of the province are sacrificing.

More fundamentally, the tax effort approach may be rendered totally meaningless because of the phenomenon of capitalization. Consider two towns, Sodom and Gomorrah. They are identical except for the fact that Sodom has a brook providing water at essentially zero cost. In Gomorrah, on the other hand, it is necessary to dig a well and pump the water. Gomorrah levies a property tax to finance the water pump. If there is a tax in Gomorrah and none in Sodom, and the communities are otherwise identical, why should anyone live in Gomorrah? As people migrate to Sodom, property values increase there (and decrease in Gomorrah) until there is no net advantage to living in either community. In short, property values are higher in Sodom to reflect the presence of the brook.

For reasons discussed previously, we do not expect the advantage to be necessarily 100 percent capitalized into Sodom's property values. Nevertheless, capitalization compensates at least partially for the differences between the towns. Just because Gomorrah levies a tax does not mean it is "trying harder" than

---

[15] In some cases, eligibility for conditional grants is also based on need. For example, until recently, grants for social assistance were greater for provinces receiving equalization payments than for those that did not.

Sodom, because the Sodomites have already paid for their water in a higher price for living there. We conclude that conventional measures of tax effort may not be very meaningful.

INTERGOVERNMENTAL GRANTS IN CANADA

As we saw earlier in the chapter, intergovernmental transfers are an important source of revenue for both provincial and municipal governments, and an important expenditure item for the federal government. Constitutionally, both federal and provincial governments are sovereign within their spheres of influence, while municipalities have no special constitutional status and are creatures of the provincial governments. Thus, in this section we will focus on intergovernmental grants from the federal government to the provinces.

Most federal–provincial transfers come under three major transfer programs: the Canadian Health and Social Transfer (CHST), Equalization, and Territorial Formula Financing. Together, these transfers make up about 90 percent of total intergovernmental transfers by the federal government. Figure 6.6 indicates the shares of the total devoted to each of the three programs as well as all other intergovernmental transfers. In the fiscal year 1997/98, the CHST transferred about $12.5 billion to the provinces, while Equalization transferred about $8.3 billion. Territorial Formula Financing to the Yukon and Northwest Territories accounted for $1.1 billion, and the sum of all other transfers added an additional $2.5 billion.

Figure 6.6

Federal Transfers to Provinces

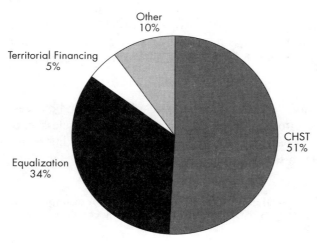

CHST. This program transfers money to support provincial programs in the areas of health, postsecondary education, and social services. The transfer is essentially a "block" grant; that is, few conditions are attached to use of the funds. Important conditions are the prohibition of residency requirements to determine eligibility for social assistance and an adherence to the five principles of the Canada Health Act (discussed in Chapter 15). The size and nature of the program, as well as whether the conditions of the program are being met, are determined solely by the federal government.

The distribution of the CHST is uneven across the provinces, with a greater per capita share going to the seven provinces receiving equalization than to the three that do not. The distribution is based on the shares of the programs that the CHST replaced. Over time, the CHST will move slowly toward equal per capita shares.[16]

Equalization. This program, to which the federal government is constitutionally committed, is the main vehicle for redistributing income among provincial governments. First formally initiated in 1957, the program has evolved substantially over the years and is renewed at five-year intervals. The current program is designed to equalize fiscal capacity across thirty-three different tax bases (called the representative tax system, RTS). Unlike other federations (e.g., Australia), no attempt is made to measure or equalize differences in fiscal need—differences in the costs of delivering services.

Initially, equalization grants were calculated using the Representative National Average Standard (RNAS) formula. The variables in the formula are defined as follows:

E_{ij} *is the equalization grant to province i for tax source j;*   (6.1)

N_i *is province i's population;*

N_c *is the population in all provinces;*

B_{ij} *is the magnitude of tax base j in province i;*

B_{cj} *is the magnitude of the total tax base j in all provinces;*

R_{cj} *is the revenue raised from taxation of j in all provinces; and*

t_{cj} *is the average tax rate on j in all provinces.*

---

[16] By 2002/03, it is estimated that Alberta's per capita share (the lowest) will be 88 percent of the national average, while Quebec's per capita share (the highest) will be roughly unchanged at 121 percent of the national average.

Note that t_{cj} is equal to the following:

$$t_{cj} = \frac{R_{cj}}{B_{cj}} \qquad (6.2)$$

The equalization grant to province i with respect to tax base j was calculated so that if the province levied the average tax rate on j, t_{cj}, on its tax base, B_{ij}, it would have the same per capita revenue that it would have had if it had levied a tax rate of t_{cj} on the average tax base B_{cj}. Thus, the E_{ij} will satisfy the following formula:

$$\frac{E_{ij}}{N_i} + t_{cj}\left(\frac{B_{ij}}{N_i}\right) = t_{cj}\left(\frac{B_{cj}}{N_c}\right) \qquad (6.3)$$

This equation could also be expressed as follows:

$$\frac{E_{ij}}{N_i} = t_{cj}\left[\frac{B_{cj}}{N_c} - \frac{B_{ij}}{N_i}\right] \qquad (6.4)$$

Alternatively, making use of the definition of t_{cj}, the equalization grant formula could be written in terms of the province's share of tax base j and its share of the population, as indicated below:

$$E_{ij} = R_{cj}\left[\frac{N_i}{N_c} - \frac{B_{ij}}{B_{cj}}\right] \qquad (6.5)$$

The tax bases are measured either in dollars or physical quantities. For example, the tax base for the sales tax is the value of retail sales. The tax base for noncommercial vehicle licencing is the number of passenger vehicle registrations. If the equalization formula applies to n tax bases, the total equalization grant received by province i is the following:

$$G_i = \sum_{j=1}^{n} E_{ij} \; if \; \sum_{j=1}^{n} E_{ij} > 0 \qquad (6.6)$$

If the sum of the E_{ij} is negative, then the equalization grant is zero. These equalization grants would be paid by the federal government out of general tax revenues.

The RNAS formula (with some modifications) was used for calculating equalization grants until 1982, when it was replaced by the "five-province standard." In that formula the standard tax base is not the Canadian average, but the average over five provinces—British Columbia, Saskatchewan, Manitoba, Ontario, and Quebec. Let B_{FPj} denote the total tax base in these five provinces and let N_{FP} denote the population of these five provinces. Then with the five-province standard for equalization, the equalization grants are calculated as follows:

$$\frac{E_{ij}}{N_i} = t_{cj}\left[\frac{B_{FPj}}{N_{FP}} - \frac{B_{ij}}{N_i}\right] \qquad (6.7)$$

In Figure 6.7 we see the estimated equalization payments to each province for the year 1997/98. These transfers range from more than $3 billion to Quebec to less than $200 thousand to Prince Edward Island. Much of the variation is related to the differences in population among the provinces. The picture changes significantly when population is taken into account. In Figure 6.8 we see that, in per capita terms, Newfoundland is the largest recipient of equalization at more than $1,600 per person, while Saskatchewan received the smallest per capita transfer at $232.

Territorial Formula Financing. The program is similar in nature to equalization and is designed to allow the two territories to provide public services comparable to those available in the provinces.

Other. This category includes federal grants in lieu of taxes (a replacement for property tax on federal buildings and lands since the Crown cannot be taxed), infrastructure grants, transportation grants, and other items.

GRANTS AND SPENDING BEHAVIOUR

Our provincial indifference curve analysis begs a fundamental question: Whose indifference curves are they? According to median voter theory (Chapter 11), the preferences are those of the province's median voter. Bureaucrats and elected officials play a passive role in implementing the median voter's wishes.

A straightforward implication of the median voter rule is that a $1 increase in individual income has exactly the same impact on public spending as receipt of a $1 unconditional grant. In terms of Figure 6.5, both events generate identical parallel outward shifts of the initial budget line. If the budget line changes are identical, the changes in public spending must also be identical.

A considerable amount of econometric work has been done on the determinants of local public spending; see Wyckoff (1991) for a survey. Contrary to

Figure 6.7

Estimated Equalization, 1997/98 (billions of dollars)

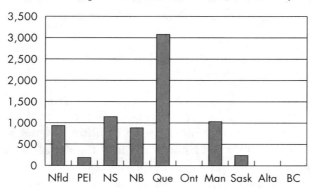

Figure 6.8

Estimated Per Capita Equalization, 1997/98 (dollars)

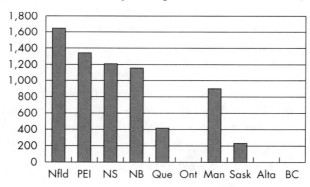

Estimated Equalization

PROVINCE	POPULATION	EQUALIZATION	PER CAPITA
NFLD	567	933	1,646
PEI	138	185	1,341
NS	946	1,144	1,209
NB	763	883	1,157
QUE	7,407	3,078	416
ONT	11,327	—	—
MAN	1,147	1,030	898
SASK	1,025	238	232
ALTA	2,815	—	—
BC	3,903	—	—

SOURCE: Federal Department of Finance and CANSIM Matrix 001. Reproduced with permission of the Minister of Public Works and Government Services Canada, 1997.

what one might expect, virtually all studies conclude that a dollar received by the community in the form of a grant results in greater public spending than a dollar increase in community income. Roughly speaking, the estimates suggest that a dollar received as a grant generates 40 cents of public spending, while an additional dollar of private income increases public spending by only 10 cents. This phenomenon has been dubbed the flypaper effect because the money seems to stick in the sector where it initially hits.

Some explanations of the flypaper effect focus on the role of bureaucrats. In the model of Filimon, Romer, and Rosenthal (1982), bureaucrats seek to maximize the sizes of their budgets. As budget maximizers, the bureaucrats have no incentive to inform citizens about the community's true level of grant funding. By concealing this information, the bureaucrats may trick citizens into voting for a higher level of funding than would otherwise have been the case. According to this view, the flypaper effect occurs because citizens are unaware of the true budget constraint. To support their theory, Filimon, Romer, and Rosenthal noted that in states with direct referendums on spending questions, ballots often contain information about the tax base, but rarely have data on grants.

An alternative explanation of the flypaper effect is provided by Locke (1990). Locke shows how the simple median-voter model can be modified to explain why optimizing politicians would respond differently to increases in grants than to increases in own-source revenue. Thus, his model of the flypaper effect is independent of the presence of budget-maximizing bureaucrats.

OVERVIEW

At the beginning of this chapter we posed some questions concerning federal systems: Is decentralized decision making desirable? How should responsibilities be allocated? How should local governments finance themselves? We have seen that economic reasoning suggests federalism is a sensible system. Allowing local communities to make their own decisions very likely enhances efficiency in the provision of local public goods. However, efficiency and equity are also likely to require a significant economic role for a federal government. In particular, a system in which only local resources are used to finance local public goods is viewed by many as inequitable.

While our focus has naturally been on economic issues, questions of power and politics are never far beneath the surface in discussions of federalism. The dispersion of economic power is generally associated with the dispersion of political power. How should power be allocated? Do you view your provincial premier as a warrior fighting for recognition of regional concerns in national decision making, or as an agent of big business, ignoring environmental concerns in favour of economic development? When you think of the federal government, do you picture an uncaring and remote bureaucrat imposing bothersome regulations, or a strong prime minister standing up for Canada's national interests? The different images coexist in our minds, creating conflicting feelings about the proper distribution of governmental power.

SUMMARY

- In a federal system, different governments provide different services to overlapping jurisdictions. The Canadian federal system includes the federal government, provinces, and municipalities.

- Community formation may be analyzed using the club model. The club model indicates that community size and the quantity of public goods depend on tastes for public goods, costs of providing public services, and the costs of crowding.

- The Tiebout model emphasizes the key roles of mobility, property tax finance, and zoning rules in local public finance. Under certain conditions, "voting with the feet"—moving to one's preferred community—results in a Pareto efficient allocation of public goods. In Canada, empirical studies suggest that the migration response to intergovernmental transfers is small or non-existent.

- The advantages of decentralization are the ability to alter the mix of public services to suit local tastes, the beneficial effects of competition among local governments, and the potential for low-cost experimentation at the subnational level.

- Disadvantages of decentralization are intercommunity externalities, forgone scale economies in the provision of public goods, inefficient taxation, and loss of scale economies in tax collection. In Canada, the Constitution and its subsequent interpretation by the courts plays an important role in the division of expenditure responsibilities between Ottawa and the provinces.

- Grants may be either conditional (categorical) or unconditional (lump sum). Each type of grant embodies different incentives for local governments. The final mix of increased expenditure versus lower local taxes depends on the preferences dictating local choices.

- Empirical studies of intergovernmental grants indicate a flypaper effect—an increase in grant money induces greater spending on public goods than does an equivalent increase in local income. One possible explanation is that bureaucrats exploit citizens' incomplete information about the community budget constraint. Another explanation relies on distortionary taxation and the median-voter model.

DISCUSSION QUESTIONS

1. For each of the following, decide whether the activity should be under the control of the federal, provincial, or municipal government, and explain why.

   a. Auto air pollution control regulations.
   b. Regulations governing whether physicians infected with the HIV virus should be allowed to perform invasive surgery.
   c. Provision of weather satellites.
   d. Public refuse collection.

2. Illustrate the following circumstances using community indifference curves and the provincial government budget constraint:

   a. An unconditional grant increases both the quantity of public goods purchased and local taxes.
   b. A matching grant leaves provision of the public good unchanged.
   c. A closed-ended matching grant has the same impact as a conditional nonmatching grant.
   d. A closed-ended matching grant leaves local taxes unchanged.

3. The federal government drastically cut transfers to provinces and replaced some conditional grants for social assistance with unconditional ones. Discuss the effects of these changes on the following:

   a. The level of spending by provincial municipal governments.
   b. The composition of spending by provincial municipal governments.
   c. The quality of social assistance programs.

REFERENCES

Boadway, Robin, and Frank Flatters. *Equalization in a Federal State: An Economic Analysis.* Ottawa: Supply and Services Canada for the Economic Council of Canada, 1982.

Boothe, Paul, and Jeffrey Petchey. "Assigning Responsibility for Regional Stablization: Evidence from Canada and Australia," in *Reforming Fiscal Federalism for Global Competition*, ed. P. Boothe. Edmonton: University of Alberta Press, 1996, pp. 141–62.

Breton, Albert, and Anthony Scott. *The Economic Constitution of Federal States.* Toronto: University of Toronto Press, 1978.

Buchanan, James M. "An Economic Theory of Clubs." *Economica* 32 (February 1965): 1–14.

Courchene, Thomas. "Interprovincial Migration and Economic Adjustment." *Canadian Journal of Economics* 3 (1970): 550–76.

Craig, Steven G., and Robert P. Inman. "Education, Welfare and the 'New' Federalism: State Budgeting in a Federalist Republic," in *Studies in State and Local Public Finance*, ed. Harvey S. Rosen. National Bureau of Economic Research Project Report Series. Chicago: University of Chicago Press, 1986, pp. 187–222.

Day, Kathleen, and Stanley Winer. "Internal Migration and Public Policy: A Research Proposal." Mimeo. February 1997.

Day, Kathleen, and Stanley Winer. "Internal Migration and Public Policy: An Introduction to the Issues and a Review of Empirical Research in Canada," in *Issues in the Taxation of Individuals*, ed. Allan Maslove. Toronto: University of Toronto Press, 1994, pp. 3–61.

Filimon, R., T. Romer, and H. Rosenthal. "Asymmetric Information and Agenda Control: The Bases of Monopoly Power and Public Spending." *Journal of Public Economics* 17 (1982): 51–70.

Gramlich, Edward M., and Daniel L. Rubinfeld. "Microestimates of Public Spending Demand Functions and Test of the Tiebout and Median-Voter Hypotheses." *Journal of Political Economy* 90 (June 1982): 536–60.

Hamilton, Bruce. "Zoning and Property Taxation in a System of Local Governments." *Urban Studies* 12 (June 1975): 205–11.

Inman, Robert P. "Fiscal Allocations in a Federalist Economy: Understanding the 'New' Federalism," in *American Domestic Priorities—An Economic Appraisal*, ed. John M. Quigley and Daniel L. Rubinfeld. Berkeley: University of California Press, 1985, pp. 3–33.

Lin, Z. "Interprovincial Labour Mobility: The Role of Unemployment Insurance and Social Assistance." Human Resources Development Canada, 1995.

Locke, Wade. "Property Tax Distortion as an Explanation of the Flypaper Effect." John Deutsch Institute Discussion Paper No. 11. October 1990.

Mieszkowski, Peter, and George R. Zodrow. "Taxation and the Tiebout Model." *Journal of Economic Literature* (September 1989): 1098–146.

Moffitt, Robert. "Incentive Effects of the U.S. Welfare System: A Review." *Journal of Economic Literature* 30, no. 1 (March 1992): 1–61.

Oates, Wallace E. *Fiscal Federalism*. New York: Harcourt Brace, 1972.

Papke, Leslie E. "Interstate Business Tax Differentials and New Firm Location: Evidence from Panel Data." *Journal of Public Economics* 45, no. 1 (June 1991): 47–68.

Rubinfeld, Daniel. "The Economics of the Local Public Sector," in *Handbook of Public Economics*, vol. 2, ed. Alan J. Auerbach and Martin Feldstein. Amsterdam: North-Holland, 1987, ch. 11.

Sandler, Todd, and John T. Tschirhart. "The Economic Theory of Clubs: An Evaluative Survey." *Journal of Economic Literature* 18, no. 4 (December 1980): 1481–521.

Saunders, Debra J. "Welfare Reform, California Style." *The Wall Street Journal*, February 25, 1992, p. A18.

Tiebout, Charles. "A Pure Theory of Local Expenditures." *Journal of Political Economy* 64 (1956): 416–24.

Watson, William. "A Estimate of the Welfare Gain from Fiscal Equalization." *Canadian Journal of Economics* 19 (1986): 298–308.

Winer, Stanley, and Denis Gauthier. *Internal Migration and Fiscal Structure: An Econometric Study of the Determinants of Interprovincial Migration in Canada.* Ottawa: Supply and Services Canada for the Economic Council of Canada, 1982.

Wyckoff, Paul G. "The Elusive Flypaper Effect." *Journal of Urban Economics* 30 (November 1991): 310–28.

Part 3

A Framework for the Analysis of Public Expenditure

$\mathcal{M}$arket outcomes need be neither efficient nor fair. This part examines how various "market failures" can be remedied by government intervention. We discuss both the normative question of how the government ought to solve a particular problem and the positive question of how government actually changes the status quo.

Chapters 4 and 5 focused our attention on market failure and economic justice as reasons for considering government intervention. The chapters in this part examine these issues in greater detail and provide the conceptual framework for analyzing the expenditure areas examined in Part 4. Chapter 7 examines public goods. Chapter 8 deals with externalities, with special emphasis on environmental issues. Chapter 9 examines market failures that occur in the context of insurance. Chapter 10 is devoted to income redistribution. In the final chapter of this part, Chapter 11, we discuss whether our political institutions are likely to respond to market failures with efficiency-enhancing policies.

Chapter 7

Public Goods

There exists an intrinsic connection between the common good on the one hand and the structure and function of public authority on the other. The moral order, which needs public authority in order to promote the common good in human society, requires also that the authority be effective in attaining that end.

—Pope John XXIII

Which goods and services should the public sector provide, and in what amounts? As the annual debate over the federal budget demonstrates, this question lies at the heart of some of the most important controversies in public policy. In this chapter, we discuss the conditions under which public provision of commodities is appropriate. Special attention is devoted to understanding why markets may fail to provide particular goods at Pareto efficient levels.

PUBLIC GOODS DEFINED

A **pure public good** is nonrival in consumption. This means that once the good is provided, the additional resource cost of another person consuming the good is zero. Consider again the lighthouse example from Chapter 5. Once the beacon is lit, no resource cost is incurred when an additional ship uses it for guidance. My consumption of the services provided by the lighthouse does not at all diminish your ability to consume the same services.

Several aspects of our definition of a public good are worth noting:

Even though everyone consumes the same quantity of the good, there is no requirement that this consumption be valued equally by all. Owners of ships with relatively valuable cargoes place a higher value on being guided safely to shore than those with inexpensive

131

cargoes, other things being the same. Indeed, people might differ over whether the value of certain public goods is positive or negative. When a new missile system is constructed, each person has no choice but to consume its services. For those who view the system as an enhancement to their safety, the value is positive. Others believe additional missiles only escalate the arms race and decrease national security. Such individuals value an additional missile negatively. They would be willing to pay not to have it around.

Classification as a public good is not an absolute; it depends on market conditions and the state of technology. The reading room of a large library is a public good when only a few people are present. But as the number of users increases, crowding and traffic problems occur that are inimical to serious scholarly research. The same "quantity" of library is being consumed by each person, but because of congestion, its quality decreases with the number of people. Hence, the nonrivalness criterion is no longer strictly satisfied. (Some research libraries deal with this problem by severely limiting access by high school students.) In many cases, then, it is useful to think of publicness as a matter of degree. A pure public good satisfies the definition exactly. Consumption of an **impure public good** is to some extent rival. It is difficult to think of many examples of really pure public goods. However, just as analysis of pure competition yields important insights into the operation of actual markets, so the analysis of pure public goods helps us to understand problems confronting public decision makers.

The notion of excludability is often linked to that of public goods. The consumption of a good is *nonexcludable* when it is either very expensive or impossible to prevent anyone from consuming the good who is not willing to pay for it. Many goods that are nonrival are also nonexcludable. For example, our lighthouse produces a nonexcludable good, because no particular vessel can be prevented from taking advantage of the signal. However, nonexcludability and nonrivalness do not have to go together. Consider the streets of a downtown urban area during rush hour. In most cases, nonexcludability holds, because it is not feasible to set up enough toll booths to monitor traffic. But consumption is certainly rival, as anyone who has ever been caught in a traffic jam can testify. On the other hand, many people can enjoy a huge seashore area without diminishing the pleasure of others. Despite the fact that individuals do not rival each other in consumption, exclusion is quite possible if there are only a few access roads. Just like nonrivalness, nonexcludability is not an absolute. It depends on the state of technology and on legal arrangements. The road congestion example is relevant here. Technologies are currently being evaluated that use radio waves to identify passing cars and automatically deduct tolls from prepaid accounts. If the technologies work, then it would be possible to charge cars as they entered congested city streets—the streets would become excludable.

A number of things that are not conventionally thought of as commodities have public good characteristics. An important example is honesty. If each citizen is honest in commercial transactions, all of society benefits due to the reduction of the costs of doing business. Such cost reductions are characterized both by nonexcludability and by nonrivalness. Similarly, Thurow (1971) argues that income distribution is a public good. If income is distributed "fairly," each person gains satisfaction from living in a good society, and no one can be excluded from having that satisfaction. Of course, because of disagreements over notions of fairness, people may differ over how a given income distribution should be valued. Nevertheless, consumption of the income distribution is nonrival, and therefore it is a public good.

Private goods are not necessarily provided exclusively by the private sector. There are many **publicly provided private goods**—rival commodities that are provided by governments. Medical services and housing are two examples of private goods sometimes provided publicly. Similarly, as we see later, public goods can be provided privately. (Think of an individual donating a park to a community.) In short, the label *private* or *public* does not by itself tell us anything about which sector provides the item.

Public provision of a good does not necessarily mean that it is also *produced* by the public sector. Consider refuse collection. Some communities produce this service themselves—public sector managers purchase garbage trucks, hire workers, and arrange schedules. In other communities, the local government hires a private firm for the job and does not organize production itself. For example, in the Regional Municipality of Ottawa–Carleton, all of the garbage collection is contracted out to private firms.

EFFICIENT PROVISION OF PUBLIC GOODS

To derive the conditions for efficient provision of a public good, it is useful to begin by re-examining private goods from a slightly different point of view from that in Chapter 4. Assume again a society populated by two people, Adam and Eve. There are two private goods, apples and fig leaves. In Figure 7.1A, the quantity of fig leaves (f) is measured on the horizontal axis, and the price per fig leaf (P_f) is on the vertical. Adam's demand curve for fig leaves is denoted by D_f^A. The demand curve shows the quantity of fig leaves that Adam would be willing to consume at each price, other things being the same. Similarly, D_f^E in Figure 7.1B is Eve's demand curve for fig leaves.

Figure 7.1

Horizontal Summation of Demand Curves

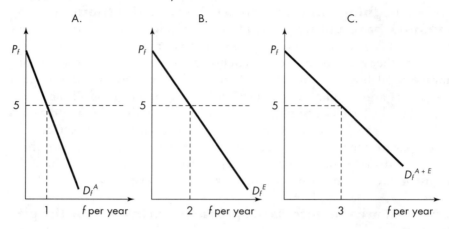

Suppose we want to derive the market demand curve for fig leaves. To do so, we simply add together the number of fig leaves each person demands at every price. In Figure 7.1A, at a price of $5, Adam demands one fig leaf, the horizontal distance between D_f^A and the vertical axis. Figure 7.1B indicates that at the same price, Eve demands two fig leaves. The total quantity demanded at a price of $5 is therefore three leaves. The market demand curve for fig leaves is labeled D_f^{A+E} in Figure 7.1C. As we have just shown, the point at which price is $5 and quantity demanded is three lies on the market demand curve. Similarly, finding the market demand at any given price involves summing the horizontal distance between each of the private demand curves and the vertical axis at that price. This process is called **horizontal summation**.

Figure 7.2 reproduces the information from Figure 7.1. Figure 7.2C then superimposes the market supply curve, labelled S_f, on the market demand curve D_f^{A+E}. Equilibrium in the market is at the price where supply and demand are equal. This occurs at a price of $4 in Figure 7.2C. At this price, Adam consumes one-and-one-half fig leaves and Eve consumes three. Note that there is no reason to expect Adam's and Eve's consumption levels to be equal. Due to different tastes, incomes, and other characteristics, Adam and Eve demand different quantities of fig leaves.

The equilibrium in Figure 7.2C has a significant property: The allocation of fig leaves is Pareto efficient. In consumer theory, a utility-maximizing individual sets the marginal rate of substitution of fig leaves for apples (MRS_{fa}) equal to

Figure 7.2

Efficient Provision of a Private Good

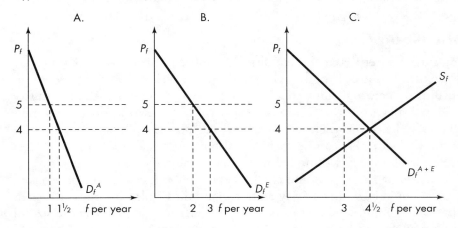

the price of fig leaves (P_f) divided by the price of apples (P_a): $MRS_{fa} = P_f/P_a$. Because only relative prices matter for rational choice, the price of apples can be arbitrarily set at any value. For convenience, set $P_a = \$1$. Thus, the condition for utility maximization reduces to $MRS_{fa} = P_f$. The price of fig leaves thus measures the rate at which an individual is willing to substitute fig leaves for apples. Now, Adam's demand curve for fig leaves ($D_f{}^A$) shows the maximum price per fig leaf that he would pay at each level of fig leaf consumption. Therefore, the demand curve also shows the MRS_{fa} at each level of fig leaf consumption. Similarly, $D_f{}^E$ can be interpreted as Eve's MRS_{fa} schedule.

In the same way, the supply curve S_f in Figure 7.2C shows how the marginal rate of transformation of fig leaves for apples (MRT_{fa}) varies with fig leaf production.[1] At the equilibrium in Figure 7.2C, Adam and Eve both set MRS_{fa} equal to four, and the producer also sets MRT_{fa} equal to four. Hence, at equilibrium

$$MRS_{fa}{}^{Adam} = MRS_{fa}{}^{Eve} = MRT_{fa} \qquad (7.1)$$

---

[1] To demonstrate this, note that under competition firms produce up to the point where price equals marginal cost. Hence, the supply curve S_f shows the marginal cost of each level of fig leaf production. As noted in Chapter 4 under "Welfare Economics," $MRT_{fa} = MC_f/MC_a$. Because $P_a = \$1$ and price equals marginal cost, then $MC_a = \$1$, and $MRT_{fa} = MC_f$. We can therefore identify the marginal rate of transformation with marginal cost, and hence with the supply curve.

Equation (7.1) is the necessary condition for Pareto efficiency derived in Chapter 4. As long as the market is competitive and functions properly, the Fundamental Theorem of Welfare Economics guarantees that this condition holds.

Public Good Case

Having now reinterpreted the condition for efficient provision of a private good, we turn to the case of a public good. Let's develop the efficiency condition intuitively before turning to a formal derivation. Suppose Adam and Eve both enjoy displays of fireworks. Eve's enjoyment of fireworks does not diminish Adam's and vice versa. Hence, a fireworks display is a public good. The size of the fireworks display can be varied, and both Adam and Eve prefer bigger to smaller displays, other things being the same. Suppose that the display currently consists of 19 rockets and can be expanded at a cost of $5 per rocket, that Adam would be willing to pay $6 to expand the display by another rocket, and that Eve would be willing to pay $4. Is it efficient to increase the size of the display by one rocket? As usual, we must compare the marginal benefit to the marginal cost. To compute the marginal benefit, note that because consumption of the display is nonrival, the 20th rocket can be consumed by *both* Adam and Eve. Hence, the marginal benefit of the 20th rocket is the *sum* of what they are willing to pay, which is $10. Because the marginal cost is only $5, it pays to acquire the 20th rocket. More generally, if the sum of individuals' willingness to pay for an additional unit of a public good exceeds its marginal cost, efficiency requires that the unit be purchased; otherwise, it should not. Hence, *efficient provision of a public good requires that the sum of each person's marginal valuation on the last unit just equal the marginal cost.*

To derive this result graphically, consider Figure 7.3A in which Adam's consumption of rockets (r) is measured on the horizontal axis, and the price per rocket (P_r) is on the vertical. Adam's demand curve for rockets is D_r^A. Similarly, Eve's demand curve for rockets is D_r^E in Figure 7.3B. How do we derive the group willingness to pay for rockets? To find the group demand curve for fig leaves—a private good—we horizontally summed the individual demand curves. That procedure allowed Adam and Eve to consume different quantities of fig leaves at the same price. For a private good, this is fine. However, the services produced by the rockets—a public good—*must* be consumed in equal amounts. If Adam consumes a 20-rocket fireworks display, Eve must also consume a 20-rocket fireworks display. It makes no sense to try to sum the quantities of a public good that the individuals would consume at a given price.

Instead, to find the group willingness to pay for rockets, we add the prices that each would be willing to pay for a given quantity. The demand curve in Figure

Figure 7.3

Vertical Summation of Demand Curves

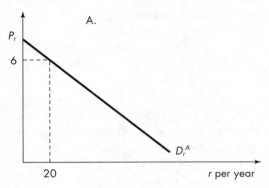

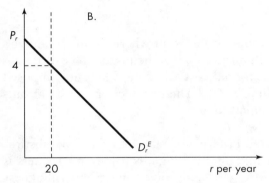

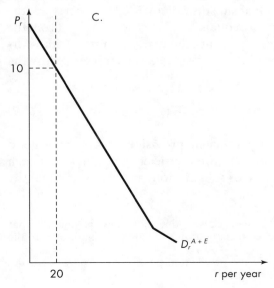

7.3A tells us that Adam is willing to pay $6 per rocket when he consumes 20 rockets. Eve is willing to pay $4 when she consumes 20 rockets. Their group willingness to pay for 20 rockets is therefore $10 per rocket. Thus, if we define D_r^{A+E} in Figure 7.3C to be the group willingness to pay schedule, the vertical distance between D_r^{A+E} and the point $r = 20$ must be 10.[2] Other points on D_r^{A+E} are determined by repeating this procedure for each output level. For a public good, then, the group willingness to pay is found by **vertical summation** of the individual demand curves.

Note the symmetry between private and public goods. With a private good, everyone has the same MRS, but people can consume different quantities. Therefore, demands are summed horizontally over the differing quantities. For public goods, everyone consumes the same quantity, but people can have different MRSs. Vertical summation is required to find the group willingness to pay.

The efficient quantity of rockets is found at the point where Adam's and Eve's willingness to pay for an additional unit just equals the marginal cost of producing a unit. In Figure 7.4C, the marginal cost schedule, S_r, is superimposed on the group willingness to pay curve D_r^{A+E}.[3] The intersection occurs at output 45, where the marginal cost is equal to $6.

Once again, prices can be interpreted in terms of marginal rates of substitution. Reasoning as before, Adam's marginal willingness to pay for rockets is his marginal rate of substitution (MRS_{ra}^{Adam}), and Eve's marginal willingness to pay for rockets is her marginal rate of substitution (MRS_{ra}^{Eve}). Therefore, the sum of the prices they are willing to pay equals $MRS_{ra}^{Adam} + MRS_{ra}^{Eve}$. From the production point of view, price still represents the marginal rate of transformation, MRT_{ra}. Hence, the equilibrium in Figure 7.4C is characterized by the condition

$$MRS_{ra}^{Adam} + MRS_{ra}^{Eve} = MRT_{ra} \qquad (7.2)$$

Contrast this with the conditions for efficient provision of a private good described in Equation (7.1). For a private good, efficiency requires that each individual have the same marginal rate of substitution, and that this equal the

---

[2] D_r^{A+E} is not a conventional demand schedule because it does not show the quantity that would be demanded at each price. However, this notation highlights the similarities to the private good case.
[3] This analysis does not consider explicitly the production possibilities frontier that lies behind this supply curve. See Samuelson (1955).

Figure 7.4

Efficient Provision of a Public Good

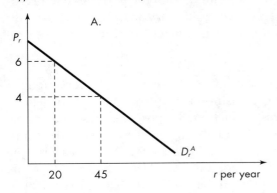

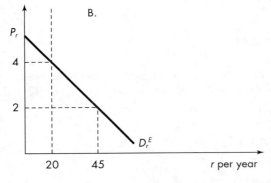

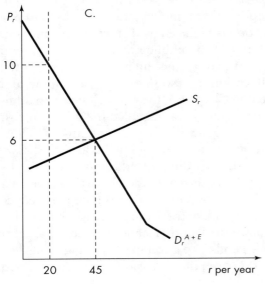

marginal rate of transformation. For a pure public good, the sum of the marginal rates of substitution must equal the marginal rate of transformation. Because everybody must consume the same amount of the public good, its efficient provision requires that the total valuation they place on the last unit provided—the sum of the MRSs—equal the incremental cost to society of providing it—the MRT.

An alternative, and perhaps more intuitive, way of expressing the condition for the optimal provision of a public good is in terms of the marginal benefit to consumers and the marginal cost of production. Suppose the price of an apple is one dollar. Then the MRS_{ra}^{Adam} can be interpreted as the marginal benefit of a unit of the public good to Adam, MB^{Adam}. Similarly, MRS_{ra}^{Eve} measures the marginal benefit of a unit of the public good to Eve, MB^{Eve}, and MRT_{ra} is the marginal cost of producing a unit of the public good, MC. Therefore the optimality condition is:

$$MB^{Adam} + MB^{Eve} = MC \qquad (7.3)$$

That is, the public good should be provided up to the point where the sum of the marginal benefits to all of the individuals in the society equals the marginal cost of producing another unit of the public good.

Provision of Public Goods Financed by Distortionary Taxation

The condition for the optimal provision of public goods, given by Equation (7.2) or (7.3), is based on the assumption that lump-sum taxes are used to pay for the public good. When a public good is financed by distortionary taxation, the cost of providing an additional unit of the public good is affected in two ways. First, increasing distortionary taxes to finance an additional unit of the public good further distorts the allocation of resources in the economy and reduces economic efficiency. As noted in Chapter 5, the cost of raising an additional dollar of revenue through a distortionary tax is called the marginal cost of public funds (MCF), and the MCF will generally be greater than one. Thus, the gross cost of providing an additional unit of the public good with distortionary taxation is $MCF \cdot MC$. Second, providing an additional unit of the public good may affect the government's tax revenues, thereby affecting the net cost of the public good. For example, the provision of a lighthouse may reduce the cost of shipping goods that might stimulate trade and increase the government's income and sales tax revenues. On the other hand, providing a lighthouse might make it easier to smuggle goods into a country, allowing smugglers to evade tariffs and excise taxes. In this case, the provision of the public good would reduce the government's tax revenues. Let MR denote the additional revenue that the government obtains when it provides an additional unit of the public good. If the public good generates more revenues for the government, MR is positive. If provision of the public good reduces tax revenues, MR is a negative number. Thus, the net amount of revenue that the government has to raise when it provides an additional unit of the public good is $(MC - MR)$. This additional net revenue has to be financed through increases in a distortionary tax, and therefore the total cost to the society of providing the additional unit of the public good is $MCF \cdot (MC - MR)$.

The direct marginal benefit of the public good is still given by $MB^{Adam} + MB^{Eve}$, and therefore the optimality provision of the public good is determined by the following condition[4]:

$$MB^{Adam} + MB^{Eve} = MCF \cdot (MC - MR) \qquad (7.4)$$

In other words, when public good provision is financed by distortionary taxation, the public good should be provided up to the point where the sum of the direct marginal benefits equals the net additional tax revenue that has to be raised times the marginal cost of public funds.

This optimality condition could be rewritten in the following form:

$$MB^{Adam} + MB^{Eve} + MCF \cdot MR = MCF \cdot MC \qquad (7.5)$$

The MR can be viewed as an indirect benefit of providing the public good, and this additional benefit should be added to the direct marginal benefit, $MB^{Adam} + MB^{Eve}$, to obtain the total benefit from additional public good provision. Each additional dollar of tax revenue allows us to reduce our reliance on distortionary taxes, and therefore the social value of the additional revenue is $MCF \cdot MR$.

Does the use of distortionary taxation imply that public good provision will be lower than under lump-sum tax financing? Not necessarily. Note that when MCF is greater than one and MR is positive, $MCF \cdot (MC - MR)$ may be either greater or smaller than MC. Thus, with distortionary taxation, the cost to the

---

[4] See Atkinson and Stern (1974) for a formal derivation of this condition. If a government only used lump-sum taxes, then the MCF would be one and the MR would be zero (because by definition lump-sum tax revenue would not vary with changes in the provision of the public good), and therefore Equation (7.3) can be viewed as a special case of Equation (7.4).

society of providing public goods may be either greater or less than it would be with lump-sum tax financing. To see this, consider the example in Figure 7.4, where the optimal provision of the public good is 45 units with lump-sum tax financing. At this level of provision, the sum of the marginal benefits, $6, is equal to the marginal cost of producing the public good.

Suppose instead that the government financed the public good with distortionary taxation, that *MCF* is 1.33 and that each additional unit of the public good generates $2 in additional tax revenues. When 45 units of the public good are provided, the cost of providing an additional unit of the public good is $1.33(6 - 2)$ or $5.33. Since the total direct marginal benefit is $6, more than 45 units should be provided when distortionary taxation is used.[5] On the other hand, if *MR* is less than $1.50, the cost of providing an additional unit of the public good is more than $6, and the optimal provision of the public good with distortionary taxation would be less than 45. Consequently, the use of distortionary taxation may either increase or reduce the optimal provision of the public good, relative to the optimal level with lump-sum taxation.

Private Provision of Public Goods

As stressed in Chapter 4, under a reasonably general set of conditions, one can expect a decentralized market system to provide goods efficiently. Thus, in the absence of imperfections, the market will provide the efficient quantity of fig leaves in Figure 7.2C. Will similar market forces lead to the efficient output level of public goods? The answer depends in part on the extent to which Adam and Eve reveal their true preferences for fireworks. When a private good is exchanged in a competitive market, an individual has no incentive to lie about how much he or she values it. If Eve is willing to pay the going price for a fig leaf, then she has nothing to gain by failing to make the purchase.

For a nonexcludable public good, however, people may have incentives to hide their true preferences. Suppose for the moment that rocket displays are nonexcludable. Adam may falsely claim that fireworks mean nothing to him. If he can get Eve to foot the entire bill, he can still enjoy the show and yet have more money to spend on apples and fig leaves. This incentive to let other people pay while you enjoy the benefits is known as the **free-rider problem.** Of course, Eve also would like to be a free rider. Where there are public goods, "any one person can hope to snatch some selfish benefit in a way not possible under the self-policing competitive pricing of private goods" (Samuelson, 1955: 389). Hence, the market may fall short of providing the efficient amount of the public good.

---

[5] The use of distortionary taxation may also affect the individuals' direct MBs from the public good.

No automatic tendency exists for markets to reach the efficient allocation in Figure 7.4.

Even if consumption is excludable, market provision of a public good is likely to be inefficient. Suppose now that the fireworks display is excludable; people cannot see the show without purchasing an admission ticket to a stadium. A profit-maximizing entrepreneur sells tickets. Recall from Chapter 4 that Pareto efficiency requires that price equal marginal cost. Because a public good is nonrival in consumption, by definition the marginal cost of providing it to another person is zero. Hence, efficiency requires a price of zero. But if the entrepreneur charges everyone a price of zero, then the entrepreneur cannot stay in business.

Is there a way out? Suppose the following two conditions hold: (1) the entrepreneur knows each person's demand curve for the public good; and (2) it is difficult or impossible to transfer the good from one person to another. Under these two conditions, the entrepreneur could charge each person an individual price based on willingness to pay, a procedure known as **perfect price discrimination**. People who valued the rocket display at only a penny would pay exactly that amount; even they would not be excluded. Thus, everyone who put any positive value on the show would attend, an efficient outcome.[6] However, because those who valued the display a lot would pay a very high price, the entrepreneur would still be able to stay in business.

Perfect price discrimination may seem to be the solution until we recall that the first condition requires knowledge of everybody's preferences. But if individuals' demand curves were known, there would be no problem in determining the optimum provision in the first place.[7] We conclude that even if the public good is excludable, private provision is likely to lead to efficiency problems.

The Free-Rider Problem

Some suggest that the free-rider problem necessarily leads to inefficient levels of nonexcludable public goods; therefore, efficiency requires government provision of such goods. The argument is that the government can somehow find out everyone's true preferences, and then, using its coercive power, force everybody to pay for public goods. If all this is possible, the government can avoid the free-rider problem and ensure that public goods are optimally provided.

---

[6] The outcome is efficient because the price paid by the marginal consumer equals marginal cost.
[7] A number of mechanisms have been designed to induce people to reveal their true preferences to a government agency.

It must be emphasized that free ridership is not a *fact*; it is an implication of the *hypothesis* that people maximize a utility function that depends only on their own consumption of goods. To be sure, one can find examples in which public goods are not provided because people fail to reveal their preferences. On the other hand, much evidence suggests that individuals can and do act collectively without government coercion. Fund drives spearheaded by volunteers have led to the establishment and maintenance of churches, music halls, libraries, scientific laboratories, art museums, hospitals, and other such facilities.[8] One prominent economist has even argued, "I do not know of many historical records or other empirical evidence which show convincingly that the problem of correct revelation of preferences has been of any practical significance" (Johansen, 1977: 147).

These observations do not prove that free ridership is irrelevant. Although some goods that appear to have public characteristics are privately provided, others that "ought" to be provided (on grounds of efficiency) may not be. Moreover, the quantity of those public goods that are privately provided may be insufficient. The key point is that the importance of the free-rider problem is an empirical question whose answer should not be taken for granted.

Marwell and Ames (1981) conducted laboratory experiments to investigate the importance of free-rider behaviour. Subjects in the experiment were given a number of tokens that they invested in an "individual exchange" or in a "group exchange." Investments in the individual exchange earned a set amount, regardless of the behaviour of other group members. The return was excludable in the sense that it neither affected nor was affected by the other members. On the other hand, "the group exchange ... paid its cash earnings to *all* members of the group by a pre-set formula, regardless of who invested.... [It] provided a joint, nonrival, nonexcludable, or *public* form of payoff" (p. 297). The incentive to free ride was provided by the fact that the group exchange could offer a substantially larger return.

> Under these circumstances, all members of the group would be better off if all the group's resources were invested in the group exchange than if all were invested in the individual exchange. On the other hand, each individual would be best off if she/he invested in the individual exchange while everyone else invested in the group exchange. (p. 297)

---

[8] There is even some evidence of successful private provision of that classic public good, the lighthouse. See Coase (1974).

What did the results show? On average, people voluntarily contributed 40 to 60 percent of their resources to the provision of the public good. Some free riding therefore was present in the sense that the subjects failed to contribute a substantial portion of their resources. On the other hand, the results flatly contradicted the notion that free riding will lead to zero or trivial amounts of a public good. People's notions of fairness and responsibility may work counter to the pursuit of narrow self-interest.

However, Isaac, McCue, and Plott (1985) criticized the structure of this study. They noted that in the Marwell/Ames experiment, the subjects played the game only once. Perhaps as people repeat the game, they begin to realize the advantages of free riding and start exhibiting that behaviour. Isaac, McCue, and Plott ran an experiment in which subjects were allowed to play several times, and they found that the level of public goods provision fell as the number of replications increased.

In another interesting experimental study, Chan, Mestelman, Moir, and Muller (1996) investigated how changes in the distribution of income affect the voluntary provision of a public good. They found that low-income individuals usually did not contribute to the provision of a public good, but higher-income individuals did contribute, and their contributions increased as their incomes increased. If income was redistributed among contributors (holding average income constant), then total group contributions were unchanged. If income was redistributed from noncontributors to contributors (again holding average income constant), then total contributions to the public good increased.

As was stressed in Chapter 3, caution must be exercised in interpreting the results of such experiments. The setting is artificial, and the sample of individuals being observed may not be representative of the population. Still, these experiments are an important tool for investigating the relevance of the free-rider problem.

Public versus Private Provision

In some cases, the services provided by publicly provided goods can be obtained privately. The commodity "protection" can be obtained from a publicly provided police force. Alternatively, to some extent, protection can also be gained by purchasing strong locks, burglar alarms, and bodyguards, which are obtained privately. A large backyard can serve many of the functions of a public park. Even substitutes for services provided by public courts of law can be obtained privately. For example, because of the enormous costs of using the government's judicial system, companies sometimes bypass the courts and instead settle their disputes before mutually agreed-upon neutral advisers or arbitrators.

Over time, the mix between public and private modes of provision has changed substantially. During the nineteenth century, there was much greater private responsibility for education, police protection, libraries, and other functions than there is now. However, there appears to be a trend back to the private sector for provision of what we have come to consider publicly provided goods and services. For example, in some U.S. cities home-owners and businesses purchase fire protection and security services from private firms.

The national debate over **privatization** concerns the question of whether society would be better off if more of the goods and services now provided or produced publicly were supplied by the private sector. To analyze the privatization issue, think of publicly and privately provided goods as inputs into the production of some output that people desire. Teachers, classrooms, textbooks, and private tutors are inputs into the production of an output we might call educational quality. Assume that what ultimately matters to people is the level of output, educational quality, not the particular inputs used to produce it. What criteria should be used to select the amount of each input? There are several considerations:

Relative wage and materials costs. If the public and private sectors pay different amounts for labour and materials, then the less expensive sector is to be preferred on efficiency grounds, *ceteris paribus*. Input costs faced by public and private sectors may differ if public sector employees are unionized while their private sector counterparts are not. We discuss other differences between public and private production in the next section.

Administrative costs. Under public provision, any fixed administrative costs can be spread over a large group of people. Instead of everyone spending time negotiating an arrangement for garbage collection, the negotiation is done by one office for everybody. The larger the community, the greater the advantage to being able to spread these costs.

Diversity of tastes. Households with and without children have very different views about the desirability of high-quality education. People who store jewels in their homes may value property protection more than people who do not. To the extent such diversity is present, private provision is more efficient because people can tailor their consumption to their own tastes. However, the benefits of allowing for diversity must be weighed against any possible increases in administrative costs.

Distributional issues. The community's notions of fairness may require that some commodities be made available to everybody, an idea sometimes referred to as **commodity egalitarianism** (Tobin, 1970). Commodity egalitarianism may help explain the wide appeal of publicly provided education—people believe everyone should have access to at least some minimum level of schooling. This notion also arises in the ongoing debate over medical care.

Public versus Private Production

In the privatization debate, conservatives want more functions provided by the private sector, while liberals prefer government provision. Moreover, even when it is agreed that certain items should be provided by the public sector, there is disagreement over whether they should be produced publicly or privately.[9] Part of the controversy stems from fundamental differences regarding the extent to which government should intervene in the economy (see Chapter 1). Part is due to differences of opinion about the relative costs of public and private production. Some argue that public sector managers, unlike their private sector counterparts, do not have to worry about making profits or becoming the victims of takeovers or bankruptcy. Hence, public sector managers have little incentive to monitor the activities of their enterprises carefully. Borins and Boothman (1985: 121) surveyed a number of studies comparing the efficiency of public and private enterprises in Canada and have concluded that:

1. There is no consistent evidence demonstrating that public enterprise is inherently less efficient than private enterprise.
2. Environment [i.e., regulation and competition] appears to be a stronger determinant of efficiency than form of ownership.

In other words, the performance of an enterprise—public or private—depends on the market environment in which it operates. A privately owned monopoly may produce very inefficient results from society's standpoint, while a publicly owned operation that has a lot of competition may produce quite efficiently. Caves and Christensen (1980: 974) came to this conclusion on the basis of a careful econometric study of CN and CP railway operations in Canada: "The oft-noted inefficiency of government enterprises stems from isolation from effective *competition* rather than public ownership *per se*." Hence, when a government is deciding whether to privatize some service, one important consideration is what kind of market structure will emerge if provision is left to private enterprise.

---

[9] See Vickers and Yarrow (1991) for an overview of the issues concerning privatization.

The privatization of liquor stores in Alberta provides an interesting example of the effect of privatization on market structure. Prior to privatization, the Alberta Liquor Control Board (ALCB) had a near monopoly in liquor retailing. (There were a few privately owned retail beer and wine stores in Alberta.) In the fall of 1993, the government of Alberta announced that it was closing its ALCB stores and turning liquor retailing over to the private sector. However, the ALCB continued to retain its monopoly control of wholesale liquor distribution. West (1996) has documented the following effects of privatization of liquor stores in Alberta:

- The number of liquor stores increased from 258 (205 ALCB stores and 53 privately owned beer and wine stores) in August 1993 to 604 privately owned liquor stores in December 1995. Most of the privately owned stores operate as individual businesses and are not part of a chain.
- Liquor prices increased by between 8.5 and 10 percent, compared to the overall rate of inflation of about 5 percent.
- Product selection in individual, privately owned stores in Edmonton and Calgary declined on average, but the range of products offered by all stores more than doubled.
- Employment in liquor stores tripled, but the average wages of liquor store employees declined by up to 50 percent as unionized workers were replaced by non-unionized workers.
- There was no evidence that privatization increased the consumption of alcohol or the commission of alcohol-related crimes.

The merits of privatizing retail liquor stores are inherently difficult to evaluate because, while retail prices increased, the total cost to the consumer, including time and transportation costs, may have decreased. Furthermore, while the product selection in individual stores decreased, the range of products that consumers can access if they visit different stores has substantially increased. Finally, the gain in overall employment in the retail sector has to be set against the decline in the wage rates received by the workers formerly employed by the ALCB.

Liquor retailing is a relatively straightforward business. Evaluating the effects of privatization in other areas, such as education, is confounded by the problem of measuring the outputs produced by the public sector. How does one quantify the amount of education produced by a school? Test scores alone won't be sufficient, because schools are also supposed to encourage creativity and to teach self-discipline and good citizenship. In any case, test scores depend on a multitude of factors outside the school's control, such as family background. Similar problems in measuring outputs arise in comparing public and private costs of producing medical services, police protection, and transportation. It is not an accident that the public sector tends to produce the services that are difficult to measure. But if outputs of many public sector activities cannot be measured properly, how can we compare costs of production in the public and private sectors? Obtaining better measures of public sector outputs is one of the most important steps needed to improve the performance of the public sector.

SUMMARY

- Public goods are characterized by nonrivalness in consumption—each person consumes the same quantity.

- Consumption of a good is nonexcludable when it is either very expensive or impossible to prevent anyone from consuming the good. Many public goods are also nonexcludable.

- With lump-sum taxation, efficient provision of public goods requires that the sum of the individuals' MRSs equal the MRT, unlike private goods where each MRS equals the MRT. Equivalently, the sum of the individuals' marginal benefits equals the marginal cost of production with the efficient provision of a public good.

- With distortionary taxation, efficient provision of public goods requires that the sum of the individuals' marginal benefits equal the marginal cost of financing the provision of an additional unit of the public good. This is equal to the marginal cost of public funds times the difference between the marginal cost of producing the public good and the additional revenue that is generated when an additional unit of the public good is provided.

- Market mechanisms are unlikely to provide public goods efficiently, even if they are excludable in consumption.

- Casual observation and laboratory studies indicate that people do not fully exploit free-riding possibilities. Nonetheless, in certain cases, free riding is likely to be a significant problem.

- Public goods can be provided privately, and private goods can be provided publicly. The choice between public and private provision should depend on relative wage and materials costs, administrative costs, diversity of tastes for the good, and distributional issues.

- Even in cases where public provision of a good is selected, a choice between public and private production must be made. A key factor in determining whether public or private production will be more efficient is the market environment.

DISCUSSION QUESTIONS

1. Which of the following do you consider public goods? Private goods? Why?

   a. Wilderness areas.
   b. Roads.
   c. Peace-keeping in Bosnia.
   d. Public television programs.
   e. Cable television programs.

2. Tarzan and Jane live alone in the jungle and have trained Cheetah both to patrol the perimeter of their clearing and to harvest tropical fruits. Cheetah can collect three pounds of fruit an hour and currently spends six hours patrolling, eight hours picking, and ten hours sleeping.

   a. What are the public and private goods in this example?
   b. If Tarzan and Jane are each currently willing to give up one hour of patrol for two pounds of fruit, is the current allocation of Cheetah's time Pareto efficient? Should he patrol more or less?

3. Should private businesses operate the highway system? Would this lead to profiteering? Can governments run the highway system as efficiently as private companies? Do you think privatizing roads is a sensible idea?

4. Thelma and Louise are neighbours. During the winter, it is impossible for a snowplow to clear the street in front of Thelma's house without clearing the front of Louise's. Thelma's marginal benefit from snowplowing services is $12 - Z$, where Z is the number of times the street is plowed. Louise's marginal benefit is $8 - 2Z$. The marginal cost of getting the street plowed is $16. Sketch the two marginal benefit schedules and the aggregate marginal benefit schedule. Draw in the marginal cost schedule, and find the efficient level of provision for snowplowing services.

REFERENCES

Atkinson, Anthony B., and Nicholas H. Stern. "Pigou, Taxation and Public Goods." *Review of Economic Studies* 41 (1974): 119–28.

Borins, Sanford, and Barry Boothman. "Crown Corporations and Economic Efficiency," in *Canadian Industrial Policy in Action*, ed. Donald McFetridge. Volume 4 of the research studies commissioned by the Royal Commission on the Economic Union and Development Prospects for Canada. Toronto: University of Toronto Press, 1985, pp. 75–129.

Caves, Douglas W., and Laurits R. Christensen. "The Relative Efficiency of Public and Private Firms in a Competitive Environment: The Case of Canadian Railroads." *Journal of Political Economy* 88, no. 5 (October 1980): 958–76.

Chan, Kenneth S., Stuart Mestelman, Rob Moir, and R. Andrew Muller. "The Voluntary Provision of Public Goods Under Varying Income Distributions." *Canadian Journal of Economics* 29, no. 1 (February 1996): 54–69.

Coase, Ronald H. "The Lighthouse in Economics." *Journal of Law and Economics* (October 1974): 357–76.

Isaac, R. Mark, Kenneth F. McCue, and Charles R. Plott. "Public Goods Provision in an Experimental Environment." *Journal of Public Economics* 26, no. 1 (February 1985): 51–74.

Johansen, Leif. "The Theory of Public Goods: Misplaced Emphasis?" *Journal of Public Economics* 7, no. 1 (February 1977): 147–52.

Marwell, Gerald, and Ruth E. Ames. "Economists Free Ride, Does Anyone Else? Experiments on the Provision of Public Goods, IV." *Journal of Public Economics* 15, no. 3 (June 1981): 295–310.

Samuelson, Paul A. "Diagrammatic Exposition of a Theory of Public Expenditure." *Review of Economics and Statistics* 37 (1955): 350–56.

Thurow, Lester C. "The Income Distribution as a Pure Public Good." *Quarterly Journal of Economics* (May 1971): 327–36.

Tobin, James. "On Limiting the Domain of Inequality." *Journal of Law and Economics* 13 (1970): 263–77.

Vickers, John, and George Yarrow. "Economic Perspectives on Privatization." *Journal of Economic Perspectives* 5 (Spring 1991): 111–32.

West, Douglas S. "The Privatization of Liquor Retailing in Alberta." WPS #13–1996. Centre for the Study of State and Market, Faculty of Law, University of Toronto, 1996.

Chapter 8

Externalities

We have always known that heedless self-interest was bad morals: we know now that it is bad economics.

—Franklin D. Roosevelt

As a by-product of their activities, pulp mills produce the chemical dioxin. It forms when the chlorine used for bleaching wood pulp combines with a substance in the pulp. Once dioxin is released into the environment, it ends up in everyone's fat tissue and in the milk of nursing mothers. According to some scientists, dioxin is responsible for birth defects and cancer, among other health problems.

The Fundamental Theorem of Welfare Economics from Chapter 4 suggests that markets allocate resources efficiently. Dioxin is the outcome of the operation of markets. Does this mean that having dioxin in the environment is efficient? To answer this question, it helps to begin by distinguishing different ways in which people can affect each other's welfare.

Suppose large numbers of suburbanites decide they want to live in an urban setting. As they move to the city, the price of urban land increases. Urban property owners are better off, but the welfare of tenants already there decreases. Merchants in the city benefit from increased demand for their products, while their suburban counterparts are worse off. By the time the economy settles into a new equilibrium, the distribution of real income has changed substantially.

In this example, all the effects are transmitted *via changes in market prices*. Suppose that before the change in tastes, the allocation of resources was Pareto efficient. The shifts in supply and demand curves change relative prices, but the Fundamental Theorem of Welfare Economics guarantees that these will be brought into equality with the relevant marginal rates of substitution. Thus, the fact that the behaviour of some people affects the welfare of others does not necessarily cause market failure. As long as the effects are transmitted via prices, markets are efficient.[1]

The dioxin case embodies a different type of interaction than does the urban land example. The decrease in welfare of the dioxin victims is not a result of price changes. Rather, the output choices of the paper mill factories directly affect the utilities of the neighbouring people. When the activity of one entity (a person or a firm) directly affects the welfare of another in a way that is not transmitted by market prices, that effect is called an **externality** (because one entity directly affects the welfare of another entity that is "external" to it). Unlike effects that are transmitted through market prices, externalities adversely affect economic efficiency.

In this chapter, we analyze these inefficiencies and possible remedies for externalities. One of the most important applications of externality theory is the debate over environmental quality, and much of the discussion focuses on this issue.

THE NATURE OF EXTERNALITIES

Suppose Bart operates a factory that dumps its garbage into a river nobody owns. Lisa makes her living by fishing from the river. Bart's activities make Lisa worse off in a direct way that is not the result of price changes. In this example, clean water is an input to Bart's production process. Clean water gets used up just like all other inputs: land, labour, capital, and materials. Clean water is also a scarce resource with alternative uses, such as fishing by Lisa and swimming. As such, efficiency requires that for the water he uses, Bart should pay a price that reflects the water's value as a scarce resource that can be used for other activities. Instead, Bart pays a zero price and, as a consequence, uses the water in inefficiently large quantities.

Posing the externality problem this way allows us to expose its source. Bart uses his other inputs efficiently because he must pay their owners prices that reflect their value for alternative uses. Otherwise, the owners of the inputs sim-

---

[1] Of course, the new pattern of prices may be more or less desirable from a distributional point of view, depending on one's ethical judgments as embodied in the social welfare function. Effects on welfare that are transmitted via prices are sometimes referred to as **pecuniary externalities**. Mishan (1971) argues convincingly that because such effects are part of the normal functioning of a market, this is a confusing appellation. It is mentioned here only for the sake of completeness and is ignored henceforth.

ply sell them elsewhere. However, if no one owns the river, everyone can use it for free. An externality, then, is a consequence of the failure or inability to establish property rights. If someone owned the river, a price would have to be paid for its use, and the externality would not materialize.

Suppose Lisa owned the stream. She could charge Bart a fee for polluting that reflected the damage done to her catch. Bart would take these charges into account when making his production decisions and no longer use the water inefficiently. On the other hand, if Bart owned the stream, he could make money by charging Lisa for the privilege of fishing in it. The amount of money that Lisa would be willing to pay Bart for the right to fish in the stream would depend on the amount of pollution present. Hence, Bart would have an incentive not to pollute too much. Otherwise, he could not make much money from Lisa.

As long as someone owns a resource, its price reflects the value for alternative uses, and the resource is therefore used efficiently (at least in the absence of any other "market failures"). In contrast, resources that are owned in common are abused because no one has an incentive to economize in their use. To expand on the subject, note the following characteristics of externalities:

Externalities can be produced by consumers as well as by firms. Just think of the person who smokes a cigar in a crowded room, lowering others' welfare by using up the common resource, fresh air.

Externalities have the characteristic that they are reciprocal in nature. In our example, it seems natural to refer to Bart as the "polluter." However, we could just as well think of Lisa as "polluting" the river with fishermen, increasing the social cost of Bart's waste disposal. As an alternative to fishing, using the river for waste disposal is not obviously worse from a social point of view. As we show later, it depends on the costs of alternatives for both activities.

Externalities can be positive or negative. If I spray my trees to kill gypsy moths, my neighbours benefit directly from my actions. If there is no way to get my neighbours to pay me for these benefits, I do not consider them when deciding how much to spray. Therefore, I do less spraying than is justified by the beneficial spillovers I create. In the case of a positive externality, an inefficiently low level of the activity is undertaken.

The distinction between public goods and externalities is a bit fuzzy. According to Mishan (1971: 2), "the essential feature of the concept of an external effect is that the effect produced is not a deliberate creation but an *unintended* or *incidental* by-product of some otherwise legitimate activity" (emphasis in original). Public goods are those activities that are *intentionally produced* to provide benefit to a community, whereas externalities are those activities where the effect on the community is the *unintended consequence* of an activity that an individual or firm undertakes for its own benefit. Thus, a lighthouse is considered a public good if it is constructed with the intention of aiding all shipping along a coastline, whereas acid rain is an externality because it is the unintended by-product of industrial activity. Although externalities and public goods are quite similar from a formal point of view, in practice it is usually useful to distinguish between them.

GRAPHICAL ANALYSIS

Figure 8.1 analyzes the Bart–Lisa example described earlier. The horizontal axis measures the amount of output, *Q*, produced by Bart's factory, and the vertical axis measures dollars. The curve labelled *MB* indicates the marginal benefit to Bart of each level of output; it is assumed to decline as output increases.[2] Also associated with each level of output is some marginal *private*

Figure 8.1

An Externality Problem

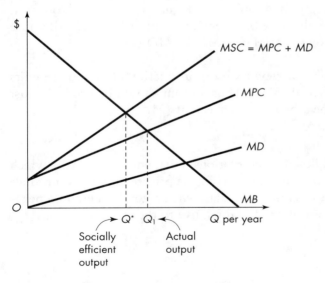

---

[2] If Bart consumes all the output of his factory, then the declining *MB* reflects the diminishing marginal utility of the output. If Bart sells his output in a competitive market, *MB* is constant at the market price.

cost, *MPC*. Marginal private cost reflects payments made by Bart for productive inputs and is assumed here to increase with output. As a by-product of its activities, the factory produces pollution that makes Lisa worse off. Assume that as the factory's output increases, so does the amount of pollution it creates. The marginal damage inflicted on Lisa by the pollution at each level of output is denoted by *MD*. *MD* is drawn sloping upward, reflecting the assumption that as Lisa is subjected to additional pollution, she becomes worse off at an increasing rate.

If Bart is interested in maximizing profits, how much output does he produce? Bart produces each unit of output for which the marginal benefit *to him* exceeds the marginal cost *to him*. In Figure 8.1, he produces all levels of output for which *MB* exceeds *MPC*, but does not produce where *MPC* exceeds *MB*. Thus, he produces up to the output at which *MPC* intersects *MB*, at output Q_1.

From society's point of view, production should occur as long as the marginal benefit *to society* exceeds the marginal cost *to society*. The marginal cost to society has two components. First are the inputs purchased by Bart. Their value is reflected in *MPC*. Second is the marginal damage done to Lisa as reflected in *MD*. Hence, marginal social cost is *MPC plus MD*. Graphically, the marginal social cost schedule is found by adding together the heights of *MPC* and *MD* at each level of output. It is depicted in Figure 8.1 as *MSC*. Note that, by construction, the vertical distance between *MSC* and *MPC* is *MD*. (Because *MSC = MPC + MD*, it follows that *MSC − MPC = MD*.)

Efficiency from a social point of view requires production of only those units of output for which *MB* exceeds *MSC*. Thus, output should be produced just up to the point at which the schedules intersect, at Q^*.

Implications

This analysis suggests the following observations. First, unlike the case in which externalities are absent, there is no reason to expect private markets to produce the socially efficient output level. In particular, when a good generates a negative externality, too much of it is produced relative to the efficient output.[3]

---

[3] This model assumes the only way to reduce pollution is to reduce output. If antipollution technology is available, it may be possible to maintain output and still reduce pollution. However, the analysis is basically the same, because the adoption of the technology requires the use of resources.

Second, the model not only shows that efficiency would be enhanced by a move from Q_1 to Q^*, but also provides a way to measure the benefits from doing so. Figure 8.2 replicates from Figure 8.1 the marginal benefit (*MB*), marginal private cost (*MPC*), marginal damage (*MD*), and marginal social cost (*MSC*) schedules. When output is cut from Q_1 to Q^*, Bart loses profits. To calculate the precise size of his loss, recall that the marginal profit associated with any unit of output is the difference between marginal benefit and marginal private cost. If the marginal private cost of the eighth unit is $10 and its marginal benefit is $12, the marginal profit is $2. Geometrically, the marginal profit on a given unit of output is the vertical distance between *MB* and *MPC*. If Bart is forced to cut back from Q_1 to Q^*, he therefore loses the difference between the *MB* and *MPC* curves for each unit of production between Q_1 and Q^*. This is area *dcg* in Figure 8.2.

At the same time, however, Lisa becomes better off because the less Bart produces, the smaller the damages done to Lisa's fishery. For each unit that Bart's output is reduced, Lisa gains an amount equal to the marginal damage associated with the unit of output. In Figure 8.2, Lisa's gain for each unit of output reduction is the vertical distance between *MD* and the horizontal axis. Therefore, Lisa's gain when output is reduced from Q_1 to Q^* is the area under the marginal damage curve between Q^* and Q_1, *abfe*. Now note that *abfe* equals area *cdhg*. This is by construction—the vertical distance between *MSC* and *MPC* is *MD*, which is the same as the vertical distance between *MD* and the horizontal axis.

Figure 8.2

Gains and Losses from Moving to an Efficient Level of Output

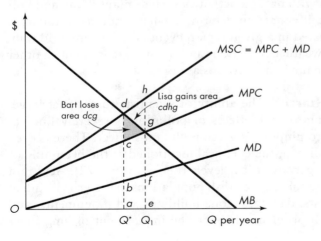

In sum, if output were reduced from Q_1 to Q^*, Bart would lose area *dcg* and Lisa would gain area *cdhg*. Provided that society views a dollar to Bart as equivalent to a dollar to Lisa, then moving from Q_1 to Q^* yields a net gain to society equal to the difference between *cdhg* and *dcg*, which is *dhg*.

Third, the analysis implies that, in general, zero pollution is not socially desirable. Finding the right amount of pollution requires trading off its benefits and costs, and this generally occurs at some positive level of pollution. Because virtually all productive activity involves some pollution, requiring pollution to be set at zero is equivalent to banning production, clearly an inefficient solution. Adopting infeasible and inefficient objectives, eliminating the discharge of all effluents, is not only silly but, as shall be argued later, may also actually hinder *any* movement away from points like Q_1.

Finally, to implement the framework of Figure 8.2, it is not enough to be able to draw some hypothetical marginal damage and benefit curves. Their actual shapes must be determined, at least approximately. However, difficult practical questions arise when it comes to identifying and valuing pollution damage.

What activities produce pollutants? The types and quantities of pollution associated with various production processes must be identified. Consider acid rain, a phenomenon of widespread concern. Scientists have shown that acid rain forms when sulfur oxides and nitrogen oxides emitted into the air react with water vapour to create acids. These acids fall to earth in rain and snow, increasing the general level of acidity with potentially harmful effects on plant and animal life.

However, it is not known just how much acid rain is associated with factory production and how much with natural activities such as plant decay and volcanic eruptions. Moreover, it is hard to determine what amounts of nitrogen and sulfur emissions generated in a given region eventually become acid rain. It depends in part on local weather conditions and on the extent to which other pollutants such as nonmethane hydrocarbons are present.

Which pollutants do harm? The ability of scientists to conduct large-scale controlled experiments on the effects of pollution is severely limited. Hence, it is often difficult to pinpoint a given pollutant's effect. There is even some doubt over whether dioxin, the chemical mentioned at the beginning of this chapter, is actually dangerous at low levels (Begley, 1992: 72). Acid rain is another case in point. Acid rain reduces fish populations in eastern Canadian lakes, lowers timber harvests, damages stone buildings and monuments, and may cause long-term health problems through the impairment of lung function. Quantifying the costs is difficult and controversial.[4] For example, a ten-year, $500-million study by the U.S. government "suggests that acid rain is having virtually no effect on agricultural output, and that its effects on forests are limited to mountain tops in the northeastern United States" (Portney, 1990: 175). This finding has led some scientists to disagree with the consensus that acid rain causes great damage in the United States. Its effects on Canada may be another matter.

The acid rain issue illustrates the transboundary aspect of many pollution problems. Sulfur dioxide emissions in the United States cause acid rain problems in Canada and vice versa.[5] Measuring the impact of emissions in only one country may cause a serious underestimation of the global impact of pollutants. International cooperation is often required to tackle air and water pollution problems. Thus, uncertainty about the long-term effects of emissions and transboundary pollution lead to serious problems in formulating environmental policy.

What is the value of the damage done? Once the physical damage a pollutant creates is determined, the value of eliminating it must be calculated. When economists think about measuring the value of something, typically they think of people's willingness to pay for it. If you are willing to pay $162 for a bicycle, that is its value to you.

Unlike bicycles, there are generally no explicit markets in which pollution is bought and sold. (Some exceptions are discussed below.) How then can people's marginal willingness to pay for pollution removal be measured? Some attempts have been made to infer it indirectly by studying housing prices. When people shop for houses, they consider both the quality of the house itself and the characteristics of the neighbourhood, such as cleanliness of the streets and quality of schools. Suppose in addition that families care about the level of air pollution in the neighbourhood. Consider two identical houses situated in two identical neighbourhoods, except that the first is in an unpolluted area, and the second is in a polluted area. We expect the house in the unpolluted area to have a higher price. This price differential measures people's willingness to pay for clean air.

These observations suggest a natural strategy for estimating people's willingness to pay for clean air. Examine houses identical in all respects except for the

[4] Government of Canada (1991: ch. 24, 15–22).
[5] See Dewees (1990) and Field and Olewiler (1995: 345–47).

surrounding air quality and compare their prices. The apparent problem is to find such houses. Luckily, the necessity of doing so can be avoided if the statistical technique of multiple regression analysis is used (see Chapter 3). The results of one careful econometric analysis by Gyourko and Tracy (1991) imply that people would be willing to pay an amount equal to 1.4 percent of their house value to obtain a 10 percent reduction in the concentration of particulates. As stressed in Chapter 3, the validity of econometric analysis depends in part on the completeness with which the model is specified. If important determinants of housing prices are omitted by Gyourko and Tracy, their estimate of the pollution effect may be unreliable. More fundamentally, the use of a willingness-to-pay measure can be questioned. People may be ignorant about the effects of air pollution on their health, and hence underestimate the value of reducing it. The econometric approach is promising, but it does not close the debate.

Conclusion

Implementing the framework of Figure 8.2 requires the skills of biologists, engineers, ecologists, and health practitioners, among others. A resolutely interdisciplinary approach to investigating the pollution problem is needed. Having said this, however, we emphasize that even with superb engineering and biological data, efficient decisions simply cannot be reached without applying the economist's tool of marginal analysis.

PRIVATE RESPONSES TO EXTERNALITIES

Our analysis has indicated that in the presence of externalities, an inefficient allocation of resources can emerge if nothing is done about it. This section discusses the circumstances under which private individuals, acting on their own, can avoid the inefficiencies of externalities.

Mergers

One way to solve the problems posed by an externality is to "internalize" it by combining the involved parties. For simplicity, imagine there is only one polluter and one pollutee, as in the Bart–Lisa scenario from earlier in the chapter. As stressed above, if Bart took into account the damages he imposed on Lisa's fishery, then a net gain would be possible. (Refer back to the discussion surrounding Figure 8.2.) In other words, if Bart and Lisa coordinated their activities, then the profit of the joint enterprise would be higher than the sum of their individual profits when they don't coordinate. In effect, by failing to act together, Bart and Lisa are just throwing away money! The market, then, provides a strong incentive for the two firms to merge—Lisa can buy the factory, Bart can buy the fishery, or some third party can buy both of them. Once the two firms merge, the externality is internalized—it is taken into account by the party that generates the externality. For instance, if Bart purchased the fishery, he would willingly produce less output than before, because at the margin doing so would increase the profits of his fishery subsidiary more than it decreased the profits from his factory subsidiary. Consequently, the existence of external effects would not lead to inefficiency. Indeed, an outside observer would not even characterize the situation as an "externality" because all decisions would be made within a single firm.

Social Conventions

Unlike firms, individuals cannot merge to internalize externalities. However, a number of social conventions can be viewed as attempts to force people to take into account the externalities they generate. Schoolchildren are taught that littering is irresponsible and not "nice." If this teaching is effective, children learn that even though they bear a small cost by holding on to a candy wrapper or a banana peel until they find a garbage can, they should incur this cost because it is less than the cost imposed on other people by having to view their unsightly garbage. Think about the golden rule, "Do unto others as you would have others do unto you." A (much) less elegant way of expressing this sentiment is, "Before you undertake some activity, take into account its external marginal benefits and costs." Some moral precepts, then, induce people to empathize with others, and hence internalize the externalities their behaviour may create. In effect, these precepts correct for the absence of missing markets.

PUBLIC RESPONSES TO EXTERNALITIES

In cases where individuals acting on their own cannot attain an efficient solution, there are several ways in which government can intervene.[6]

Taxes

Bart produces inefficiently because the prices he faces for inputs incorrectly signal social costs. Specifically, because his input prices are too low, the price of his output is too low. A natural solution, suggested by the British economist A.C. Pigou, is to levy a tax on the polluter that makes up for the fact that some of his inputs are priced too low. A **Pigouvian tax** is a tax levied on each unit of a polluter's output in an amount just equal to the marginal damage it inflicts *at the efficient level of output.* Figure 8.3 reproduces the example of Figures 8.1 and 8.2. In this case, the marginal damage done at the efficient output Q^*

---

[6] The list of possibilities considered here is by no means exhaustive. See Cropper and Oates (1992) for a careful discussion of several alternatives.

Figure 8.3

Analysis of a Pigouvian Tax

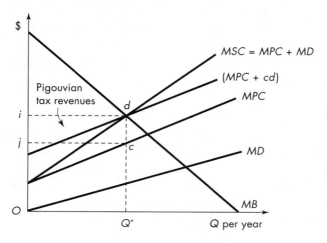

is distance *cd*. This is the Pigouvian tax. (Remember that the vertical distance between *MSC* and *MPC* is *MD*.)

How does Bart react if a tax of *cd* dollars per unit of output is imposed? The tax raises Bart's effective marginal cost. For each unit he produces, Bart has to make payments both to the suppliers of his inputs (measured by *MPC*) *and* to the tax collector (measured by *cd*). Geometrically, Bart's new marginal cost schedule is found by adding *cd* to *MPC* at each level of output. This involves shifting up *MPC* by the vertical distance *cd*.

Profit maximization requires that Bart produce up to the output at which marginal benefit equals marginal cost. This now occurs at the intersection of *MB* and *MPC* + *cd*, which is at the efficient output *Q**. In effect, the tax forces Bart to take into account the costs of the externality that he generates and induces him to produce efficiently. Note that the tax generates revenue of *cd* dollars for each of the *id* units produced (*id* = *OQ**). Hence, tax revenue is *cd* × *id*, which is equal to the area of rectangle *ijcd* in Figure 8.3. It would be tempting to use these revenues to compensate Lisa, who still is being hurt by Bart's activities, although to a lesser extent than before the tax. However, caution must be exercised. If it becomes known that anyone who fishes along the river receives some money, then some people may choose to fish there who otherwise would not have done so. The result is an inefficiently large amount of fishing done in the river. The key point is that compensation to the victim of the pollution is not necessary to achieve efficiency.

There are practical problems in implementing a Pigouvian tax system.[7] In light of the previously mentioned difficulties in estimating the marginal damage function, finding the correct tax rate is bound to be hard. Still, sensible compromises can be made. Suppose a certain type of automobile produces noxious fumes. In theory, a tax based on the number of kilometres driven enhances efficiency. But a tax based on kilometres might be so cumbersome to administer as to be infeasible. The government might instead levy a special sales tax on the car, even though it is not ownership of the car per se that determines the size of the externality, but the amount it is driven. The sales tax would not lead to the most efficient outcome, but it still might lead to a substantial improvement over the status quo.

More generally, the tax approach assumes it is known who is doing the polluting and in what quantities. In many cases, these questions are very hard to answer. However, technological changes may make it easier to monitor pollution in the future. A new technology being tested in southern California involves attaching to each major source of pollution a sensor that continually detects emissions. The information is then sent to a computer. One can imagine the computer determining the appropriate Pigouvian tax for each polluter and sending a bill.

Of course, the relevant issue is not whether Pigouvian taxes are a perfect method of dealing with externalities, but whether or not they are likely to be better than the other alternatives. In this context, it is useful to note that Sweden and Norway have levied significant taxes on the carbon content of motor fuels (15 to 20 cents per litre), and France, Germany, and the Netherlands have all imposed taxes on various types of pollution.[8] In the Netherlands, which has one of the best administered systems, there is some evidence that the taxes have substantially lowered the amounts of several pollutants (Cropper and Oates, 1992). Emission charges have not been used, to any significant extent, by Canadian governments. However, British Columbia has adopted a system of contaminant fees that are levied on the emission of certain hazardous chemicals. For example, the contaminant fees for ammonia and chlorine are $69.30 and $184 per tonne, respectively.[9]

Although we have been discussing Pigouvian taxation in the context of environmental damage, it is equally relevant for dealing with other externalities.

---

[7] See Olewiler (1990) for a discussion of the pros and cons of using taxes to minimize the distortions caused by harmful externalities.

[8] For a survey of environmental taxes in the OECD countries, see Barde and Owens (1996).

[9] Field and Olewiler (1995: Table 18–3, p. 369).

Heavy trucks, for example, create externalities by damaging highways. The marginal damage depends on the weight of the truck and the number of axles. Small and Winston (1986) estimate that if U.S. trucking firms were forced to pay a tax equal to the marginal damage caused by their vehicles, the welfare gain by the U.S. economy—area *dhg* in Figure 8.2—would be $1.2 billion per year.

Subsidies

Under the assumption that the number of polluting firms is fixed, the efficient level of production can be obtained by paying the polluter not to pollute. Although this notion may at first seem peculiar, it works much like the tax scheme. This is because a subsidy for not polluting is simply another method of raising the polluter's effective production cost.

Suppose the government announces that it will pay Bart a subsidy of *cd* for each unit of output that he does not produce. What will Bart do? In Figure 8.4, Bart's marginal benefit at output level Q_1 is measured by the distance between *MB* and the horizontal axis, *ge*. The marginal cost of producing at Q_1 is the sum of the amount Bart pays for his inputs (which we read off the *MPC* curve), and the subsidy of *cd* that he forgoes by producing. Once again, then, the perceived marginal cost schedule is *MPC + cd*. At output Q_1, this is distance *ek* (= *eg + gk*). But *ek* exceeds the marginal benefit, *ge*. As long as the marginal cost exceeds the marginal benefit, it does not make sense for Bart to produce the Q_1st unit of output. Instead, he should forgo its production and accept the subsidy. The same line of reasoning indicates that Bart will choose not to produce any output in excess of Q^*. At all output levels to the right of Q^*, the sum of the marginal private cost and the subsidy exceeds the marginal benefit. On the other hand, at all points to the left of Q^*, it is worthwhile for Bart to produce even though he has to give up the subsidy. For these output levels, the total opportunity cost, *MPC + cd*, is less than the marginal benefit. Hence, the subsidy induces Bart to produce just to Q^*, the efficient output.

The distributional consequences of the tax and subsidy schemes differ dramatically. Instead of having to pay the tax of *idcj*, Bart receives a payment equal to the number of units of forgone production, *ch*, times the subsidy per unit, *cd*, which equals rectangle *dfhc* in Figure 8.4.[10] That an efficient solution can be associated with different income distributions is no surprise. It is analogous to the result from Chapter 4—there are an infinite number of efficient allocations in the Edgeworth Box, each of which is associated with its own distribution of real income.

---

[10] In Figure 8.4, Q_1 is the baseline from which Bart's reduction in output is measured. In principle, any baseline to the right of Q^* would do.

Figure 8.4

Analysis of a Pigouvian Subsidy

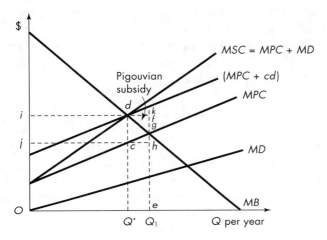

In addition to the problems associated with the Pigouvian tax scheme, the subsidy program has a few of its own. First, recall that the analysis of Figure 8.4 assumes a fixed number of firms. The subsidy leads to higher profits, so in the long run more firms may be induced to locate along the river. The subsidy may cause so many new firms to relocate on the river that total pollution actually increases.

Second, the subsidy payments have to be raised by taxes levied somewhere in the economy. In general, taxation distorts people's incentives. And it is not obvious that these distortion effects would be less costly than the externality itself. (The efficiency costs of taxation are discussed in detail in Chapter 18.)

Finally, subsidies may be ethically undesirable. As Mishan (1971: 25) notes:

> It may be argued [that] the freedom to operate noisy vehicles, or pollutive plant, does incidentally damage the welfare of others, while the freedom desired by members of the public to live in clean and quiet surroundings does not, of itself, reduce the welfare of others. If such arguments can be sustained, there is a case ... for making polluters legally liable.

Creating a Market

As we emphasized above, the inefficiencies associated with externalities can be linked to the absence of a market for the relevant resource. This suggests another way for the government to enhance efficiency—sell producers permits to pollute. By doing so, the government in effect creates a market for clean air or water that otherwise would not have emerged. Under this scheme, the government announces it will sell permits to spew Z^* of pollutants into the environment (the quantity of pollutants associated with output Q^*). Firms bid for the right to own these permissions to pollute, and the permissions go to the firms with the highest bids. The fee charged is that which clears the market, so the amount of pollution equals the level set by the government. The price paid for permission to pollute is called an **effluent fee**.

The effluent fee approach is illustrated in Figure 8.5. The horizontal axis measures the number of *rights to produce sulfur oxides*, and the vertical axis measures the price of these rights. The government announces it will auction off Z^* pollution rights. In effect, the supply of pollution rights is perfectly vertical at Z^*. The demand for pollution rights, D_z, is downward sloping. The equilibrium price per unit is P_1. Those firms that are not willing to pay P_1 for each unit of pollution they produce must either reduce their output or adopt a cleaner technology.

Incidentally, the scheme also works if, instead of auctioning off the pollution rights, the government assigns them to various firms that are then free to sell them to other firms. The market supply is still perfectly vertical at Z^*, and the price is still P_1. Nothing changes because a given firm is willing to sell its pollution rights provided the firm values these rights at less than P_1. Even though the efficiency effects are the same as those of the auction, the distributional consequences are radically different. With the auction, the money goes to the government; with the other scheme, the money goes to the firms that were lucky enough to be assigned the pollution rights.

In any case, in this simple model, the effluent fee and the Pigouvian tax both achieve the efficient level of pollution. Implementing both requires knowledge of who is polluting and in what quantities. How is one to choose between them? Cropper and Oates (1992) argue that the effluent fee has some practical advantages over the tax scheme. One of the most important is that the effluent scheme reduces uncertainty about the ultimate level of pollution. If the government is certain about the shapes of the private marginal cost and marginal benefit schedules of Figure 8.3, then it can safely predict how a Pigouvian tax will affect behaviour. But if there is poor information about these schedules, it is hard to know how much a particular tax will reduce pollution. If lack of information forces policy makers to choose the pollution standard arbitrarily, with a system of pollution permits, this level is more likely to be obtained. In addition, under the assumption that firms are profit maximizers, they will find the cost-minimizing technology to attain the standard.

Figure 8.5

Market for Pollution Rights

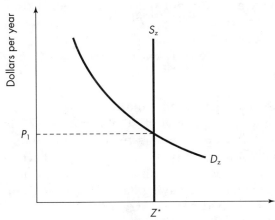

Rights to produce sulfur oxides
(parts per 100 million) per year

Moreover, when the economy is experiencing inflation, the market price of pollution rights would be expected to keep pace automatically, while changing the tax rate could require a lengthy administrative procedure. On the other hand, one possible problem with the auctioning scheme is that incumbent firms might be able to buy pollution licences in excess of the firms' cost-minimizing requirements to deter other firms from entering the market. Whether such strategic behaviour is likely to occur is hard to predict.

Establishing Property Rights

In the auctioning scheme just described, the government creates a market and, by setting the vertical supply curve, determines the amount of pollution. Under some circumstances, it may make sense for the government to create conditions in which a market can come into existence, but then stay out of the market. To understand this idea, recall our earlier argument that the root cause of an externality is the absence of property rights. Therefore, a natural way to cure the problem is to put the resource in question into private hands. Suppose property rights to the river are assigned to Bart. Assume further that it is costless for Lisa and Bart to bargain with each other. Is it possible for the two parties to strike a bargain that will result in output being reduced from Q_1?

Bart would be willing to not produce a given unit of output as long as he received a payment that exceeded his net incremental gain from producing that unit (*MB − MPC*). On the other hand, Lisa would be willing to pay Bart not to produce a given unit as long as the payment were less than the marginal damage done to her, *MD*. As long as the amount that Lisa is willing to pay Bart exceeds the cost to Bart of not producing, the opportunity for a bargain exists. Algebraically, the requirement is that *MD* > (*MB − MPC*). Figure 8.6 (which reproduces the information from Figure 8.1) indicates that at output Q_1, *MB − MPC* is zero, while *MD* is positive. Hence, *MD* exceeds *MB − MPC*, and there is scope for a bargain.

Similar reasoning indicates that the payment Lisa would be willing to make exceeds *MB − MPC* at every output level to the right of *Q**. In contrast, to the left of *Q**, the amount of money Bart would demand to reduce his output would exceed what Lisa would be willing to pay. Hence, Lisa pays Bart to reduce output just to *Q**, the efficient level. We cannot tell without more information exactly how much Lisa will end up paying Bart. This depends on the relative bargaining strengths of the two parties. Regardless of how the gains from the bargain are divided, however, production ends up at *Q**.

Now suppose the shoe is on the other foot, and Lisa is assigned the property rights to the stream. The bargaining process now consists of Bart paying for Lisa's permission to pollute. Lisa is willing to accept some pollution as long as the payment is greater than the marginal damage (*MD*) to her fishing enterprise. Bart finds it worthwhile to pay for the privilege of producing as long as the amount is less than the value of *MB − MPC* for that unit of output.

Figure 8.6

Coase Theorem

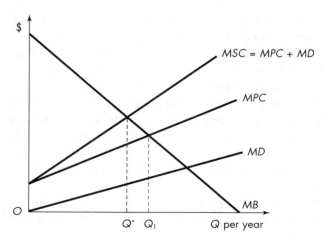

Reasoning similar to the foregoing suggests that they have every incentive to reach an agreement whereby Lisa sells Bart the right to produce at Q^*.

The conclusion is that the efficient solution will be achieved *independently* of who is assigned the property rights, as long as *someone* is assigned those rights. This result, known as the **Coase Theorem** (after Nobel laureate Ronald Coase), implies that once property rights are established, no government intervention is required to deal with externalities (Coase, 1960). However, there are at least two reasons society cannot always depend on the Coase Theorem to solve externality problems.

First, the theorem requires that the costs of bargaining do not deter the parties from finding their way to the efficient solution. However, externalities such as air pollution involve millions of people (both polluters and pollutees). It is difficult to imagine them getting together for negotiations at a sufficiently low cost.[11]

Second, the theorem assumes resource owners can identify the source of damages to their property and legally prevent the damages. Consider again the important case of air pollution. Even if property rights to air were established, it is not clear how owners would be able to identify which of thousands of potential polluters were responsible for dirtying their airspace and for what proportion of the damage each would be liable.

The Coase Theorem is most relevant for cases in which only a few parties are involved and the sources of the externality are well defined. Of course, even when these conditions hold, the assignment of property rights is relevant from the point of view of income distribution. Property rights are valuable; if Lisa owns the stream it will increase her income relative to Bart's, and vice versa.

U.S. states have recently been given greater freedom to devise market-oriented plans based on property rights. In 1993, for example, California started a plan that allowed 390 of its largest polluters to trade pollution rights. However, as Cropper and Oates (1992: 729) note, "Effluent charge and marketable permit programs are few in number and often bear only a modest resemblance to the pure programs of economic incentives supported by economists." Nonetheless, as the costs of traditional environmental programs continue to increase, the efficiency of market-oriented approaches may make them more attractive to policy makers.

---

[11] As we have emphasized earlier, there is no guarantee that the transaction costs of implementing a government solution will be less.

Regulation

Under regulation, each polluter is told to reduce pollution by a certain amount or else face legal sanctions. In our model, Bart would simply be ordered to reduce output to Q^*. Regulation is likely to be inefficient when there is more than one firm. To see this, consider two firms, X and Z, each of which emits carbon dioxide (CO_2), a chemical that is thought to contribute to global warming. In Figure 8.7, output of the firms is measured on the horizontal axis and dollars on the vertical. MB_X is the marginal benefit schedule for X and MB_Z the schedule for Z. For expositional ease only, X and Z are assumed to have identical MPC schedules and profit-maximizing outputs $X_1 = Z_1$.

Suppose it is known that the marginal damage at the efficient level of total output is d dollars. Then efficiency requires that each firm produce at the point of intersection of its marginal benefit curve with the sum of its marginal private cost curve and d. The efficient outputs are denoted X^* and Z^* in Figure 8.7. The crucial thing to observe is that efficiency does not require the firms to reduce their CO_2 emissions equally. The efficient reduction in production of Z exceeds that of X. Here this is due to different MB schedules, but in general each firm's appropriate reduction in output depends on the shapes of its marginal benefit and marginal private cost curves. Hence, a regulatory rule that mandates all firms to cut back by equal amounts (either in absolute or proportional terms) leads to some firms producing too much and others too little.

Figure 8.7

Two Polluting Firms

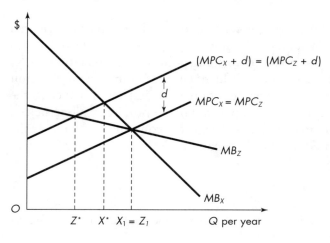

This analysis simply illustrates that the costs and benefits of pollution reduction are likely to differ from case to case. A car that operates in a relatively uninhabited area creates less damage than one that operates in a heavily populated area. What sense does it make for both cars to have exactly the same emissions standard? If all cars must meet standards that are set to improve the air quality in just a few heavily polluted metropolitan areas, such as Montreal, Toronto, and Vancouver, then the policy will be inefficient. Of course, the regulatory body could assign each polluter its specially designed production quota. But in the presence of a large number of polluters, this is administratively infeasible.

A number of empirical studies have sought to compare the costs of obtaining a given reduction in pollution using economic incentives and regulations. The particular results depend on the type of pollution being considered and the site of the pollution. In every case, though, economic incentives provide a much cheaper solution (see Cropper and Oates, 1992: 686). A good example is provided by an analysis of the costs of meeting the target, adopted at the Rio convention on climate change in 1992, of stabilizing carbon dioxide emissions at their 1990 level by the year 2000. It has been estimated that achieving this target in Canada through a mandated emissions reduction of 19 percent would reduce real GDP by 0.8 percent, whereas the target could be achieved with a carbon tax that would reduce real GDP by only 0.5 percent, a difference of over $2 billion (see Hamilton and Cameron, 1994: 388).

Evaluation

The presence of externalities often requires some kind of intervention to achieve efficiency. Implementing any environmental policy entails a host of difficult technical issues. No policy is likely to do a perfect job. However, of the options available, most economists prefer Pigouvian taxes or the sale of pollution permits. These are more likely to achieve efficient outcomes than either subsidies or direct regulation.

IMPLICATIONS FOR INCOME DISTRIBUTION

Our main focus so far has been on the efficiency aspects of externalities. Welfare economics indicates that we must take distributional as well as efficiency considerations into account. However, attempts to assess the distributional implications of environmental improvement raise a number of difficult questions.

Who Benefits?

In our simple model, the distribution of benefits is a trivial issue because there is only one type of pollution and one pollution victim. In reality, there are many different types of individuals who suffer differently from various externalities. Some evidence suggests that poor neighbourhoods tend to have more exposure to air pollution than high-income neighbourhoods (Cropper and Oates, 1992: 727). If this is true, lowering the level of air pollution might make the distribution of real income more equal, other things being the same. On the other hand, the benefits of environmental programs that enhance the quality of recreational areas such as national parks probably benefit mainly high-income families, who tend to be their main users.

Even knowledge of who is suffering from a given externality does not tell us how much it is worth to them to have it removed. Suppose a high-income family would be willing to pay more for a given improvement in air quality than a low-income family. Then even if a cleanup program reduces more of the *physical* amount of pollution for low- than for high-income families, in *dollar* terms the program can end up favouring those with high incomes.

Who Bears the Costs?

Suppose that large numbers of polluting firms are induced to reduce output by government policy. As these firms contract, the demand for the inputs they employ falls, making the owners of these inputs worse off.[12] Some of the polluters' former workers may suffer unemployment in the short run and be forced to work at lower wages in the long run. If these workers have low incomes, environmental cleanup increases income inequality.

Another consideration is that if polluting firms are forced to take into account marginal social costs, their products tend to become more expensive. From an efficiency point of view, this is totally desirable, because otherwise prices give incorrect signals concerning full resource costs. Nevertheless, buyers of these commodities will be made worse off.[13] If the commodities so affected are consumed primarily by high-income groups, the distribution of real income becomes more equal, other things being the same, and vice versa. Thus, to assess the distributional implications of reducing pollution, we also need to know the demand patterns of the goods produced by polluting companies.

It is obviously a formidable task to determine the distribution of the costs of pollution control. A study by Hamilton and Cameron (1994: Table A3, p. 398)

---

[12] More specifically, under certain conditions, those inputs used relatively intensively in the production of the polluting good suffer income losses. See Chapter 17 under "General Equilibrium Models."

[13] One cannot know a priori how high consumer prices will rise. It depends on the shapes of the supply and demand schedules. See Chapter 17 under "Tax Incidence: General Remarks."

estimated that the distributional effect of a carbon tax in Canada would be "moderately regressive." They calculated that reduction in the real incomes of the 20 percent of households with the lowest incomes would be 3.4 percent while the income reduction for the 20 percent of households with the highest incomes would be 2.7 percent. Other studies of the distributional effects of energy taxes in the United States and Europe have found that the distributional effects are regressive.[14] If these results are correct, they pose a dilemma for those who favour both a more equal income distribution and a cleaner environment.

POSITIVE EXTERNALITIES

Most of the focus in this chapter has been on negative externalities. We did observe, however, that spillover effects could just as well be positive. The analysis of this case is symmetrical. Suppose that when a firm does research and development (R&D), the marginal private benefit (MPB) and marginal cost (MC) schedules are as depicted in Figure 8.8. The firm chooses R&D level R_1, where $MC = MPB$. Assume further that the firm's R&D enables other firms to produce their outputs more cheaply, but that these firms do not have to pay for using scientific results because they become part of general knowledge.[15]

Figure 8.8

Positive Externality

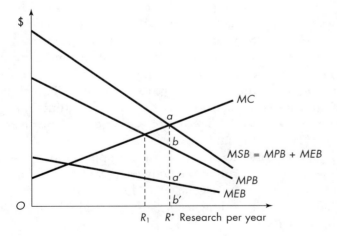

---

[14] OECD (1995: 74–76).
[15] Sometimes this type of situation can partially be avoided by patent laws. But in many cases, the results of pure research are not patentable, even though they may be used for commercial purposes.

In Figure 8.8, the marginal benefit to other firms of each quantity of research is denoted *MEB* (for marginal external benefit). The marginal social benefit of research is the sum of *MPB* and *MEB*, which is depicted as schedule *MSB*.

Efficiency requires the equality of marginal cost and marginal social benefit, which occurs at R^*. Hence, not enough R&D is done. Just as a negative externality can be corrected by a Pigouvian tax, a positive externality can be corrected by a Pigouvian subsidy. Specifically, if the R&D-conducting firm is given a subsidy equal to the marginal external benefit at the optimum—distance *ab* in Figure 8.8—it will be induced to produce efficiently.[16] The lesson is clear: When an individual or firm produces positive externalities, the market under-provides the activity or good, but an appropriate subsidy can remedy the situation. Of course, all the difficulties concerning problems in measuring the quantity and value of the externality are still relevant. In a survey of empirical work on R&D, Nadiri (1993) concluded that the private rate of return to R&D is about 20 to 30 percent, while the social rate of return is about 50 percent. If these figures are correct, then the positive externalities associated with R&D are substantial.

A Cautionary Note

Many people who have never heard the term *positive externality* nevertheless have a good intuitive grasp of the concept and its policy implications. They understand that if they can convince the government their activities create beneficial spillovers, they may be able to dip into the treasury for a subsidy. Requests for such subsidies must be viewed cautiously for two reasons. First, one way or another, the subsidy has to come from resources extracted from taxpayers. Hence, every subsidy embodies a redistribution of income from taxpayers as a whole to the recipients. Even if the subsidy has good efficiency consequences, the distributional implications may not be desirable. This depends on the value judgments embodied in the social welfare function. Second, when the presence of a beneficial externality is claimed, its precise nature must be determined. The fact that an activity is beneficial per se does *not* mean that a subsidy is required for efficiency. A subsidy is appropriate only if the market does not allow those performing the activity to capture the full marginal return. For example, a brilliant surgeon who does much good for humanity creates no positive externality as long as the surgeon's salary reflects the incremental value of his or her services.

---

[16] Note that by construction, $ab = a'b'$.

SUMMARY

- An externality occurs when the activity of one person affects another person outside the market mechanism. Externalities may generally be traced to the absence of property rights.

- Externalities cause market price to diverge from social cost, bringing about an inefficient allocation of resources.

- A Pigouvian tax is a tax levied on the polluters' output in an amount equal to the marginal social damage at the efficient output. Such a tax gives the producer a private incentive to produce the efficient output.

- A subsidy for output not produced can induce polluters to produce at the efficient level. However, subsidies can lead to too much production, are administratively difficult, and are regarded by some as ethically unappealing.

- Pollution rights may be traded in markets. This fixes the total level of pollution, an advantage when administrators are uncertain how polluters will respond to Pigouvian taxes.

- The Coase Theorem indicates that private parties may bargain toward the efficient output if property rights are established. However, bargaining costs must be low and the source of the externality easily identified.

- Regulation is likely to be inefficient because the social value of pollution reduction varies across firms, locations, and the populace. Nevertheless, this is the most widespread form of environmental policy—a source of dismay to economists.

- Positive externalities generally lead to underprovision of an activity. A subsidy can correct the problem, but care must be taken to avoid wasteful subsidies.

DISCUSSION QUESTIONS

1. Every year in December, the Smith family decorates their home with a lavish display of Christmas decorations. People come from all over Edmonton to look at the decorations. Consequently, the roads in their part of the city become congested. The Smiths' neighbours complain that at times their streets become impassable, and they are virtual prisoners in their homes. Identify the externalities in this situation. Is the allocation of resources efficient?

2. In the figure below, the number of parties that Cassanova gives per month is measured on the horizontal axis, and dollars are measured on the vertical. MC_p is the marginal cost of providing parties and MB_p is Cassanova's marginal benefit schedule from having parties.

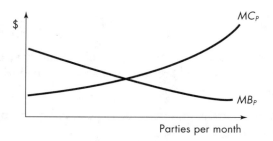

a. Graphically, show how many parties Cassanova will host.
b. Suppose there is a fixed marginal benefit, $b, per party to Cassanova's friends. Illustrate this on your graph.
c. What is the socially (no pun intended) optimal level of parties? How could the Social Committee induce Cassanova to host this number of parties?
d. On your graph, show the optimal subsidy per party and the total amount paid to Cassanova. Who gains and loses under this plan?

3. For each of the following situations, is the Coase Theorem applicable? Why or why not?

a. A group of university students in a dormitory share a communal kitchen. Some of the users of the kitchen never clean up the messes they make when cooking.
b. The heat from a copper smelter interferes with the neighbouring ice company, but aids an adjacent dry cleaner.
c. The pollution from a copper smelter drifts out over a surrounding residential area.
d. Loud gasoline-powered leaf blowers are used by some home-owners for driving leaves and other debris into piles, but also driving leaves and dust into the yards of neighbours.

4. The government of British Columbia has suggested a "cash-for-clunkers" program. Under this program, the government would buy up "clunkers" (older cars that emit a lot of pollutants and do not meet current pollution standards). Is this a sensible policy? Explain.

5. In 1983, the U.S. Environmental Protection Agency (EPA) asked the citizens of Tacoma, Washington, to decide whether they wanted "to accept some risk of cancer from arsenic in the air rather than face the probable closing of a copper smelter that provide[d] 800 jobs" (Shabecoff, 1983). Is this a good policy, or should the EPA simply make the decision on its own?

6. The private marginal benefit for commodity X is given by $10 - X$, where X is the number of units consumed. The private marginal cost of producing X is constant at $5. For each unit of X produced, an external cost of $2 is imposed on members of society. In the absence of any government intervention, how much X is produced? What is the efficient level of production of X? What is the gain to society involved in moving from the inefficient to

the efficient level of production? Suggest a Pigouvian tax that would lead to the efficient level. How much revenue would the tax raise?

REFERENCES

Barde, Jean-Phillippe, and Jeffrey Owens. "The Evolution of Eco-taxes." *The OECD Observer* no. 198 (February–March 1996): 11–16.

Begley, Sharon. "Can a Little Be Too Much?" *Newsweek*, September 21, 1992, p. 72.

Coase, Ronald H. "The Problem of Social Cost." *Journal of Law and Economics* (October 1960): 1–44.

Cropper, Maureen L., and Wallace E. Oates. "Environmental Economics: A Survey." *Journal of Economic Literature* 30 (June 1992): 675–740.

Dewees, Donald. "The Regulation of Sulphur Dioxide in Ontario," in *Getting It Green: Case Studies in Canadian Environmental Regulation*, ed. G. Bruce Doern. Policy Study No. 12. Toronto: C.D. Howe Institute, 1990, pp. 129–54.

Field, Barry C., and Nancy D. Olewiler. *Environmental Economics*, 1st Can. ed. Toronto: McGraw-Hill Ryerson, 1995.

Government of Canada. *The State of Canada's Environment*. Ottawa: Ministry of Supply and Services Canada, 1991.

Gyourko, Joseph, and Joseph Tracy. "The Structure of Local Public Finance and the Quality of Life." *Journal of Political Economy* 99, no. 4 (August 1991): 774–806.

Hamilton, Kirk, and Grant Cameron. "Simulating the Distributional Effects of a Canadian Carbon Tax." *Canadian Public Policy* 20 (December 1994): 385–99.

Mishan, E.J. "The Postwar Literature on Externalities: An Interpretative Essay." *Journal of Economic Literature* 9, no. 1 (March 1971): 1–28.

Nadiri, M. Ishaq. "Innovations and Technological Spillovers." Working Paper 4423. Cambridge, MA: National Bureau of Economic Research, August 1993.

OECD. *Taxation, Employment and Unemployment*. The OECD Jobs Study. Paris: OECD, 1995.

Olewiler, Nancy D. "The Case for Pollution Taxes," in *Getting It Green: Case Studies in Canadian Environmental Regulation*, ed. G. Bruce Doern. Policy Study No. 12. Toronto: C.D. Howe Institute, 1990, pp. 188–208.

Portney, Paul R. "Policy Watch: Economics and the Clean Air Act." *Journal of Economic Perspectives* 4, no. 4 (Fall 1990): 173–82.

Shabecoff, Philip. "Tacoma Gets Choice: Cancer Risk or Lost Jobs." *The New York Times*, July 13, 1983, p. 1.

Small, Kenneth A., and Clifford Winston. "Welfare Effects of Marginal-Cost Taxation of Motor Freight Transportation: A Study of Infrastructure Pricing," in *Studies in State and Local Public Finance*, ed. Harvey S. Rosen. Chicago: University of Chicago Press, 1986, pp. 113–28.

Chapter 9

Uncertainty, Asymmetric Information, and Market Failure

The failure of the market to insure against uncertainties has created many social institutions in which the usual assumptions of the market are to some extent contradicted.

–Kenneth Arrow (1963)

*L*ife is full of uncertainties. Unexpected events such as a fire or an illness can dramatically lower a person's well-being. One way to gain some protection against such eventualities is to purchase insurance. In return for paying premiums to an insurance company, an individual receives benefits in the event of a loss. Federal and provincial programs, such as unemployment insurance, worker's compensation, and medicare, replace lost income or cover losses that are consequences of events at least partly outside personal control. Public pensions ensure that individuals do not suffer drastic declines in their incomes when they retire and that they do not "outlive their savings." These programs, collectively referred to as social insurance, represent a large proportion of government expenditures in Canada.

Although the various programs serve different functions, they often have some of these characteristics:

- Participation is compulsory.

- Eligibility and benefit levels depend, in part, on past contributions made by the worker.
- Benefit payments begin with some identifiable occurrence such as unemployment, illness, or retirement.
- The programs are not means-tested—financial distress need not be established to receive benefits.

We begin by discussing an individual's demand for insurance and the supply of insurance by the private sector. We then examine possible causes of market failure, and whether they provide a rationale for government involvement in social insurance.

THE DEMAND FOR INSURANCE

The **expected utility model** is the most widely used framework for analyzing decision making under uncertainty, and we use this model to explain an individual's demand for insurance.[1] Suppose Jones has wealth equal to W. However, if a fire burns his home down he will face a loss of L and his wealth will be reduced to $W - L$. Let the probability of a fire be π, where π is a number between 0 and 1. Therefore his **expected loss** from fire is πL and his **expected wealth** is:

$$EW = \pi(W - L) + (1 - \pi)W = W - \pi L \qquad (9.1)$$

It is assumed that Jones evaluates his situation by calculating his **expected utility**. He does this by assigning a utility index number to the situation in which a loss occurs. It will be denoted by $U(W - L)$. The utility index number assigned to the situation where no loss occurs is denoted by $U(W)$. Since Jones is worse off if a loss occurs, $U(W - L)$ is less than $U(W)$. Figure 9.1 shows the utility indices assigned by Jones under the assumption that he uses a concave utility function to evaluate these alternative outcomes. (As will be noted later, the shape of the U curve reflects the individual's attitude toward risk.) His expected utility is defined as:

$$EU = \pi U(W - L) + (1 - \pi)U(W) \qquad (9.2)$$

Consequently, the expected utility level can be represented by a point on the vertical axis that lies between $U(W)$ and $U(W - L)$. The EU level can

---

[1] Most intermediate microeconomics textbooks contain a more detailed discussion of decision making under uncertainty. See, for example, Pindyck and Rubinfeld (1998: ch. 5) or Varian (1987: ch. 13).

Figure 9.1

The Demand for Insurance

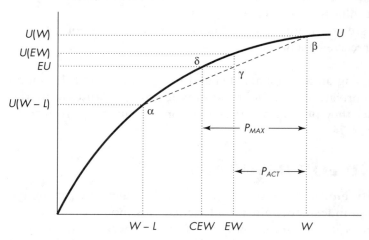

be determined by the following geometric procedure. Draw a straight line between the points α and β on the U curve. Draw a vertical line from the individual's expected wealth to the line $\alpha\beta$. The length of this vertical line is equal to EU.

The expected utility model assumes that Jones will decide whether or not to purchase a fire insurance policy by comparing the expected utility with the policy to his EU without insurance. Suppose that an insurance company offered Jones a full coverage insurance policy for a premium of P dollars. Under this contract, Jones pays the insurance company P dollars before it is known whether a fire will occur or not. If a fire occurs, the insurance company will pay Jones L dollars, and he is fully compensated for his loss. If a fire does not occur, Jones does not receive any payment from the insurance company. Thus, with the full coverage policy, Jones's wealth is $W - P$, whether or not an accident occurs, and therefore his expected utility level will be $U(W - P)$. The expected utility model predicts that Jones will purchase the policy if his expected utility level with the policy exceeds his expected utility without insurance coverage, or in other words if:

$$U(W - P) > \pi U(W - L) + (1 - \pi)U(W) \qquad (9.3)$$

Whether or not Jones will purchase the policy depends on the premium and on his attitude toward risk.

We will begin by considering whether Jones will purchase the insurance policy at what is known as an **actuarially fair premium,** P_{ACT}. For a full coverage insurance policy, the actuarially fair premium is the individual's expected loss, or:

$$P_{ACT} = \pi L \qquad (9.4)$$

If the insurance company offered Jones the full coverage policy at P_{ACT}, he would have his expected wealth level with certainty:

$$W - P_{ACT} = W - \pi L = EW \qquad (9.5)$$

Figure 9.1 shows that Jones would be willing to purchase this policy because the $U(EW)$ is greater than EU. Why? Because the U curve is concave. Any cord such as $\alpha\beta$ will always lie below the U curve, and therefore EU, the vertical distance to the $\alpha\beta$ line at EW, will always be less than $U(EW)$, the vertical distance to the U curve. Individuals, such as Jones, who use a concave U function in calculating the expected utility to evaluate risky alternatives are said to be **risk averse.** Such individuals will always be willing to purchase a full coverage insurance policy at an actuarially fair premium.

If Jones had used a utility function that was a linear function of wealth, such as $U(W) = a + bW$ where a and b are constants and b is positive, then Jones would have been indifferent about purchasing the insurance policy at the actuarially fair premium or going without insurance. (It is left to the reader to demonstrate this using a diagram.) Such individuals are said to be **risk neutral.**

On the other hand, if Jones had used a convex utility function—such that the tangent lines to the utility curve become steeper when wealth increases—then the $\alpha\beta$ line joining the points $U(W - L)$ and $U(W)$ on the U curve would lie above the U curve. In this case, the $U(EW)$ would be less than EU and Jones would not want to purchase the full coverage insurance policy at an actuarially fair premium. Such individuals are said to be **risk seekers.**

To summarize, individuals are said to be risk averse if they are willing to purchase a full coverage insurance policy at an actuarially fair premium. Such individuals use a concave utility function in evaluating alternative courses of action that result in different levels of wealth. The fundamental characteristic of the concave utility function is that the marginal utility of wealth, which is given by the slope of the tangent to the U function, decreases as wealth increases. In other words, risk-averse behaviour is implied by diminishing marginal utility of wealth. We will assume that most individuals can be characterized as risk averse because most people are willing to purchase insurance to avoid major financial losses.

The *EU* model predicts that a risk-averse individual will never purchase a lottery ticket if the price of the lottery ticket is equal to, or greater than, the expected prize. (See Discussion Question 1 at the end of this chapter.) In fact, many individuals who purchase insurance also participate in unfair gambles—they purchase lottery tickets at prices that exceed their actuarially fair value. This suggests that their behaviour is inconsistent with the simple model of risk aversion that we have outlined above. However, since the amounts that most individuals are prepared to bet on unfair gambles are very small compared to their total wealth or income, and because they generally behave in ways that are consistent with risk aversion, such as holding diversified portfolios of assets, when it comes to major financial decisions, we will treat individuals as if they are risk averse.

Having established that a risk-averse individual will always purchase full insurance coverage at an actuarially fair premium, we can ask: What is the maximum premium that a risk-averse individual would be willing to pay for a full coverage policy? The maximum premium, P_{MAX}, leaves the individual no better off than he or she would be without insurance, and it is implicitly defined by the following equation:

$$U(W - P_{MAX}) = \pi U(W - L) + (1 - \pi)U(W) \tag{9.6}$$

Figure 9.1 shows Jones's P_{MAX}. Note that for a risk-averse individual, $P_{MAX} > P_{ACT}$ and that P_{MAX} increases as π increases. The wealth level, $W - P_{MAX}$, which Jones views as equivalent to his expected utility without insurance, is called his **certainty equivalent wealth**, CEW. For a risk-averse individual, $CEW < EW$.

The consumer surplus, G, from purchasing a full coverage policy at an actuarially fair premium can be defined as the difference between the maximum premium that an individual would be willing to pay and the actuarially fair premium, or:

$$G = P_{MAX} - P_{ACT} = EW - CEW \tag{9.7}$$

In Figure 9.1, G is the horizontal distance, $\delta\gamma$, between the U function and the $\alpha\beta$ line, measured at EU.

The magnitude of G obviously depends on the individual's degree of risk aversion—the more risk averse, the greater the concavity of the U function, the

larger G will be. The expected utility model also predicts that the consumer surplus from actuarially fair insurance will be very small when the losses are very small, very rare, or very common.[2] As we will see in the next section, this has implications for the types of losses that will be covered by private insurance markets.

THE SUPPLY OF INSURANCE

Having described the demand for insurance, we will now consider under what terms and conditions private firms will provide insurance coverage. Long-run equilibrium in a perfectly competitive insurance market requires that the firms earn zero economic profit. This implies that the premium for a policy must equal the expected average cost of providing the insurance coverage. The average cost of a policy can be decomposed into three components:

average cost per policy = expected claim per policy + administration cost per policy + insurance risk per policy

$$= \pi L + A + R$$

The claims that an insurance company has to pay are a major component of its costs. The expected claim loss, πL, is what each policy adds to the firm's expected total claims. Note that this is equal to the P_{ACT}. The administration costs or "loading costs" are the costs incurred by the firm in handling claims and billing customers. This component includes the wages and salaries, rent, and other input costs of the insurance company. R is the risk premium that the shareholders of the insurance company must be paid to compensate them for the risks they are assuming in providing the insurance policy. The premium, P, charged by the insurance company, will equal $\pi L + A + R$, and therefore because resources are used up in running an insurance company and the shareholders may have to be compensated for risking their wealth by investing in the insurance company, the premium charged by the insurance company will exceed the actuarially fair premium.

Since Jones will only purchase the insurance contract if P_{MAX} exceeds P, it follows he will only purchase insurance if the following condition is satisfied:

---

[2] These predictions can be demonstrated with reference to Figure 9.1. As π goes to zero, EW approaches W, EU approaches $U(W)$, and γ approaches β. Therefore the horizontal distance $\delta\gamma$ shrinks to zero. Conversely, if π approaches 1, EW approaches $W - L$, EU approaches $U(W - L)$, γ approaches α, and therefore $\delta\gamma$ shrinks to zero. The demonstration that G goes to zero as L goes to zero is similar, except that the point α also approaches β as L goes to zero, which implies that G declines at a faster rate as L decreases than as π decreases.

$$P_{MAX} = G + P_{ACT} > P = \pi L + A + R \qquad (9.8)$$

or equivalently if:

$$G > A + R \qquad (9.9)$$

That is, Jones will only buy the insurance policy if his consumer surplus from actuarially fair insurance exceeds the administration cost per policy and the risk premium that the shareholders of the insurance company must be paid.

This presents an interesting problem. If the shareholders of the insurance company are as risk averse as the individuals who would like to buy insurance, how is it possible for insurance policies to be traded? Risk-averse shareholders need to be compensated for the risk that they incur by insuring Jones, and this compensation, R, may be so large that Jones would not be prepared to pay it. The answer to this question is that there are mechanisms by which R can be greatly reduced or eliminated entirely. These mechanisms are known as **risk pooling** and **risk spreading**, and we discuss them below.

Risk Pooling and Insurance

Consider the following story. Captain Ahab sends ships to the Levant. Over many years, he has observed that in one out of four years his ships are attacked by pirates off the Barbary Coast. The attacks are random events. When his ships are attacked, he suffers a financial loss of L. Ahab, after receiving word of an attack on this year's convoy, goes to Lloyd's Coffee House in the City of London, to console himself. Isaac Mutant also frequents the coffee house and overhears Ahab's fulminations against the pirates. He decides to plot a histogram of the probability of Ahab's annual losses, which is shown in Figure 9.2, and he calculates that Ahab's expected loss is $(1/4)L$. Captain Bligh also hears Ahab's stories and is very sympathetic. He sends ships to Jamaica, and by a remarkable coincidence, he also suffers a loss of L in one out of four years because storms sink his ships. Bligh, in an effort to cheer Ahab, tells him about his situation. Upon overhearing Bligh's story, Isaac Mutant decides to plot the histogram of probability of the average losses incurred by Ahab and Bligh. Mutant reasons that the losses of Ahab and Bligh are independent events since they occur in different parts of the world and have different causes. Therefore, the probability that both Ahab and Bligh would have a loss in the same year is $(1/4)^2$ or $1/16$. In that case the average loss is L. On the other hand, the probability that neither captain has a loss in a given year is $(3/4)^2 = 9/16$. The probability that Ahab has a loss and Bligh does not is $(1/4)(3/4) = 3/16$. Similarly, the probability that Bligh has a loss but Ahab does not is $3/16$. The average loss, when only one of the captains has a loss, is $L/2$. Mutant tells the captains that if they share the losses that are incurred, they would face the probability distribution shown in Figure 9.3. Both captains agree that the distribution of losses in Figure 9.3 is less risky than the distribution in Figure 9.2 because the probability of having to pay L drops from 1/4 to 1/16. On the other hand, there is also a lower probability of suffering no loss and a high probability of having to contribute $(1/2)L$ if one of them has a loss. They want to know what their expected contribution will be if they share in the losses. Isaac Mutant calculates that each captain's expected contribution when they share in the losses is:

$$\textit{Expected Contribution When Losses Are Shared} = \frac{9}{16} \cdot 0 + \frac{6}{16} \cdot \frac{L}{2} + \frac{1}{16} \cdot L$$

$$= \frac{L}{4} \qquad (9.10)$$

Thus, the expected contribution when the captains share their losses is exactly the same as the expected loss that each captain faces on his own. Both captains recognize that they are better off when they share their losses because their expected payment or loss is the same as when they are on their own, but by sharing in the losses they will face a situation where there is a lower probability of incurring a loss of L.

At this point all of the other captains in Lloyd's Coffee House ask to see what the probability distribution of the average loss would look like if they also

Figure 9.2

Probability Distribution for Ahab's Losses

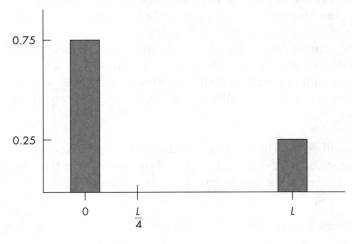

Figure 9.3

Probability Distribution of Ahab's Share of the Total Losses

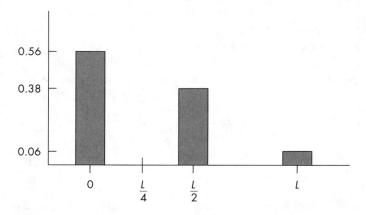

shared the losses with Ahab and Bligh. Mutant refuses to draw any more diagrams, but he agrees to derive another measure of the risk that each sea captain faces. There are n captains in Lloyd's Coffee House. Let L_i be the loss sustained by captain i where L_i is a random variable that takes on values of 0 or L. The probability of a loss of L is π. The expected loss for each captain is πL, and the variance of his loss is:

$$Var(L_i) = \pi(1 - \pi)L^2 \qquad (9.11)$$

Mutant then notes that if the n sea captains form The Sea Dogs Mutual Insurance Company, they will have to contribute S/n where S is the sum of their losses. The expected value for S is the number of captains times their expected loss, or $n\pi L$. The expected contribution that each captain will make to the insurance pool is πL. However, the contribution will vary from year to year depending on how many of the captains experience losses. If they are extremely lucky and no captains experience any losses, their contributions will be zero. However, if they are very unlucky and they all suffer losses, each will have to contribute L. Thus, their contribution will vary from year to year depending on the members' losses.

What risk would the members of The Sea Dogs Mutual face? Suppose that the members' losses are statistically independent, then Mutant shows that the variance of each member's contribution would equal the following[3]:

---

[3] See the appendix to this chapter for the derivation of this equation.

$$Var(S/n) = \frac{\pi(1 - \pi)L^2}{n} \qquad (9.12)$$

Thus, the variance of a member's contribution becomes smaller as n increases, and if the mutual insurance company is very large, its members will not face any risk. Each member's contribution will almost always be very close to πL. The risk of a loss of L is eliminated through risk pooling. At this point, the captains agree to form the mutual insurance company, and they select Isaac Mutant as President and CEO.

The ability of the risk-pooling mechanism to eliminate risk has been discussed within the context of a mutual insurance company, but the same mechanism can eliminate the risk that the shareholders of a stock insurance company face from very large losses, thereby reducing the R component of cost to zero if the number of policy holders is sufficiently large.

The ability of the risk-pooling mechanism to reduce risk hinges on the assumption that the losses are independent events. If the losses are positively correlated, then the risk-pooling mechanism's ability to reduce risk is impaired, but not entirely eliminated. In the extreme case, where losses are perfectly correlated—if one individual has a loss, then they all suffer losses—the risk-pooling mechanism is completely ineffective in reducing risk.

The risk-pooling mechanism operates when the potential loss from a large number of different risks can be combined. Another mechanism is also available to ameliorate the risk for a unique event.

Risk Spreading

The costs and benefits of a given risky project can be shared or *spread* over a number of individuals. If the net return on the project is uncorrelated with individuals' wealth from other sources, then the total cost of risk bearing goes to zero as the number of individuals who share in the net return on the project becomes very large. This is known as the **Arrow–Lind Theorem.**

Suppose that Connie could invest in a research project that may lead to a desk-top nuclear fusion reactor. The cost of the research project is C. If the project is successful, desk-top fusion will yield a return of S and Connie's wealth will be $W + S - C$. If the project fails to produce a viable desk-top fusion reactor, the project will not generate any return and Connie's wealth will be $W - C$. The probability of success is π, and therefore Connie's expected wealth, if she invests in the project, is $EW = W + \pi S - C$. To determine whether she should invest in the project, Connie compares her expected utility with the project to her expected utility without the project. If she does not invest, her expected utility is $U(W)$. It is assumed that the project would raise her expected wealth, but that it is so risky that her expected utility with the project is less than $U(W)$. This situation is shown in Figure 9.4. In this context the horizontal distance, k_1, between EW and Connie's CEW with the project can be considered the cost of bearing the risk for this project when she is the only investor.

Suppose Connie were to share the costs and the benefits from the desk-top fusion project with another investor, Bjorn. It will be assumed for convenience that Connie and Bjorn exhibit the same degree of risk aversion and have the same wealth, W, if they do not invest in the project. Both individuals will contribute half of the cost and receive half of the gross return if it is successful. Therefore, each individual's wealth would be $W + (S - C)/2$ if the project is a success and $W - C/2$ if it is a failure. Figure 9.5 shows each individual's expected utility. Note that in this case, EU exceeds $U(W)$ and therefore Connie and Bjorn would be willing to invest in the desk-top fusion research project. The key point is that by sharing in the gains and the losses from the project, the investors have reduced the cost of risk bearing. In Figure 9.5, the cost of risk bearing is the distance k_2. Not only is $k_2 < k_1$ and therefore the cost of risk bearing per investor reduced, but careful inspection reveals that $2k_2 < k_1$. That is, the total cost of risk bearing has been reduced. If the project were shared by n investors, the total cost of risk bearing would be nk_n where k_n is the cost of risk bearing to any one of the individuals. Arrow and Lind (1970) showed that nk_n approaches zero as n becomes very large.

Figure 9.4

Connie's Evaluation of Desk-Top Fusion

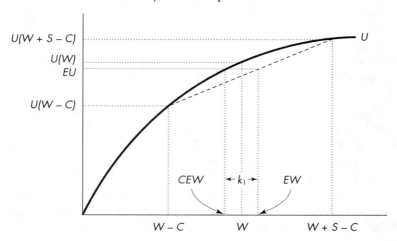

Figure 9.5

Connie's Evaluation of Desk-Top Fusion When She Shares the Project with Bjorn

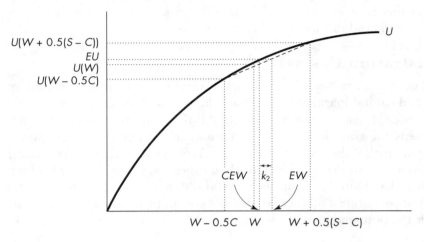

The Arrow–Lind Theorem implies that a project whose net return is uncorrelated with the return on other assets should be undertaken if the expected net return is positive. No risk premium is required by investors in such projects because the total cost of risk bearing can be completely eliminated through the risk-spreading mechanism. This mechanism allows firms with many shareholders to undertake projects that would be too risky for an individual or a small group of investors to undertake. Lloyd's of London provides insurance coverage for a wide variety of special risks by spreading the risk among a syndicate of "names," wealthy individuals who agree to cover losses in exchange for a share of the premiums. Governments can also use the risk-spreading mechanism to eliminate risk if the costs and benefits of a project are spread over the population through the government's tax and expenditure system. For example, governments can sponsor basic scientific research into finding a cure for cancer without worrying that such research activity is highly risky in the sense that it may fail to produce significant results. As long as the expected benefit from the research exceeds its expected cost, then the research should be undertaken. The riskiness of the research can be ignored because the benefits will be shared by all citizens (if they face a reduced risk of cancer) and the costs are spread over all taxpayers.

As with the risk-pooling mechanism, risk spreading cannot be used to eliminate the risk from projects where their returns are positively correlated with labour income or the returns on other assets. In this case, the project would tend to be a success when the returns on other assets are high, and therefore the marginal utility of wealth is relatively low, and it would tend to be a failure when the returns on other assets are low and the marginal utility of wealth is relatively high. Spreading the net returns from the project across many investors in this case would not eliminate the risk premium that investors would require to hold this asset in their portfolios.

Administration Costs

Of course, even if the risk-pooling and risk-spreading mechanisms are used by insurance and capital markets to eliminate the need for the risk premium, R, the insurance contract will not be purchased if the administration cost of the policy exceeds the consumer surplus from actuarially fair insurance. Recall that G will be small if the probability of a loss is either very high or very small, or if the magnitude of the loss is small. Under these circumstances, it is likely that G will be less than A, and insurance will not be provided for these risks. This does not constitute a market failure. The cost of providing the policy simply exceeds the potential gain.

For some risks, the magnitude of a loss may be a random variable—a collision with another vehicle can result in damages that range from a minor scrape to a total write-off. The gain from being insured against a small loss may be less than the cost of administering a small claim, and therefore the insured will want a **deductible** in the insurance policy so that small losses are not insured, and these administration costs are avoided. With a deductible of D, only losses in excess of D are insured. The use of a deductible in an insurance contract helps to economize on administration costs, but the policy still provides protection against large losses. The individual only has partial coverage, but this should not be construed as a market failure.

SOURCES OF MARKET FAILURE

Under what conditions do private markets fail to provide appropriate insurance coverage? When is the provision of social insurance by government warranted?

Inability to Pool Risks

As we have seen, the risk-pooling mechanism is impaired when losses are positively correlated. Should governments provide social insurance when risks are positively correlated? It is useful to consider this issue within the context of unemployment insurance because unemployment is a cyclical phenomenon. When the unemployment rate is high in one industry or region, it is usually high in other industries or regions.[4] Suppose private firms provided unemployment insurance. An insurance company would run a surplus in the years in which claims were low, and this surplus would be held as a reserve to pay for claims when the unemployment rate was high. In a major recession, claims might exceed premiums and reserves, and the insurance company would have to borrow to meet its obligations. Even a very large and well-run insurance company would be unable to borrow enough to pay all the private UI claims during a major recession, and therefore would be forced to default on its claims and declare bankruptcy.[5] One of the advantages that most governments have in the provision of UI is that they have a greater capacity to borrow than even the largest private corporations. Unlike the shareholder in a private insurance company, the taxpayers' liability is not limited. Therefore, governments can provide social insurance for losses that the private sector would not cover because of the inability to pool risks.

Increasing Returns to Scale in the Provision of Insurance

We have seen that the ability to reduce risk through risk pooling increases with the number of individuals who are insured. Therefore, at least one component of an insurance company's average cost declines as the number of policies increases, making insurance a potential natural monopoly. However, studies of returns to scale in the insurance industry suggest that for most forms of property and casualty insurance the economies of scale from risk pooling are exhausted at relatively low volumes of insurance. The property and casualty insurance industry generally has relatively low barriers to entry and relatively low concentration ratios. For example, there were more than one hundred firms in the automobile insurance industry in Alberta in 1982, and the four largest firms had 31 percent of the market (see Dahlby, 1992). On the other hand, it is often claimed that provincial health insurance has lower average costs than comparable private insurance companies operating in the United States. These cost differences may be due to economies of scale in administration, different administration procedures (U.S. hospitals have to keep detailed records of the costs incurred in treating patients in order to bill the private insurers), or the exercise of monopsony power in the purchase of inputs in providing health care.

---

[4] For example, over the period 1975 to 1990, correlation coefficients between provincial unemployment rates were 0.49 for Ontario and Newfoundland, 0.86 for British Columbia and Ontario, and 0.90 for British Columbia and Newfoundland.

[5] In the early 1980s, a private company began offering "executive" unemployment insurance. Unfortunately, the company entered the market just before the 1982 recession. Within six months it was unable to pay the claims on its policies and was forced into bankruptcy.

Asymmetric Information

To this point, we have considered insurance markets where the buyer and the seller of the insurance policy have the same information concerning the probability and the magnitude of the loss. In many situations the purchaser of the insurance policy has more information about π and L than the insurance company, and this gives rise to a situation of asymmetric information—the buyer and the seller of a product do not possess the same information about the quality of the product. Asymmetric information can occur in a wide variety of markets, but it seems to be particularly important in insurance markets. Two basic types of asymmetric information problems can be distinguished. Adverse selection occurs when the insured has more accurate information concerning his or her loss probability than the insurance company. Moral hazard occurs when the insured can influence the magnitude or the probability of a loss. The implications of these phenomena for the operation of private insurance markets are considered below.

Adverse Selection

Suppose there is a large group of risk-averse individuals. Each has wealth equal to W and faces a possible loss of L. There are two types of individuals—high risks and low risks. The loss probability is π_h for a high-risk individual and π_l for a low-risk individual. Let h represent the fraction of the population that is in the high-risk group. The average probability of a loss is $\bar{\pi} = h\pi_h + (1 - h)\pi_l$, and therefore $0 < \pi_l < \bar{\pi} < \pi_h < 1$. In the absence of insurance, the expected utility of a low-risk individual is EU_l and the expected utility of a high-risk individual is EU_h shown in Figure 9.6.

Would a private insurance industry be able to provide full insurance coverage in this market? To simplify the analysis, it is assumed that the individuals' losses are independent events and that there are no administration costs in running an insurance company. Hence A and R are zero, and competition in the insurance market will ensure that premiums are equal to the expected claims. If an insurance company can distinguish high-risk individuals from low-risk individuals, it would offer two full coverage policies. Members of the high-risk group would be charged a premium equal to $\pi_h L$, and members of the low-risk group would be charged a lower premium, equal to $\pi_l L$.

Now suppose each individual knows his risk group, but the insurance company cannot distinguish a high-risk individual from a low-risk individual. Clearly, the insurance company cannot continue to offer two full coverage insurance policies with different premiums because everyone would claim to be a member of the low-risk group and pay $\pi_l L$. The average claim per policy

Figure 9.6

Adverse Selection

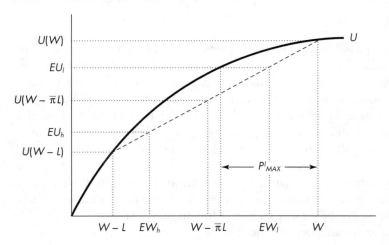

would be $\bar{\pi}L$, and the insurance company would lose money on each policy. Eventually, it would have to raise its premium or go out of business. Suppose the insurance company raised its premium to $\bar{\pi}L$, which would cover the expected claims if the policy were purchased by both risk groups. Would the insurance company be able to sell this policy to both risk groups? Not necessarily. Figure 9.6 shows a situation in which the maximum premium that the low-risk individuals would pay for a full coverage insurance policy, P^l_{MAX}, is less than $\bar{\pi}L$. Thus, only the high-risk individuals would purchase the full coverage policy, and the insurance company would have to raise the premium to $\pi_h L$ in order for the premiums to cover the expected losses. High-risk individuals would be willing to pay this premium for full coverage, but the low-risk individuals would not because $\pi_h L > \bar{\pi}L > P^l_{MAX}$.[6]

Does this mean that the low risks would not receive any insurance coverage? Again, not necessarily. Insurance companies would recognize that there are low-risk individuals who would be willing to buy some insurance coverage as long as the premium is not driven up because high-risk individuals purchase it. Therefore, insurance companies may offer a partial coverage policy with a deductible D that is large enough so that the high-risk individuals prefer the full coverage policy at $\pi_h L$ (see Rothschild and Stiglitz, 1976). However, it is

---

[6] If $P^l_{MAX} > \bar{\pi}L$, the low risks would still prefer a partial coverage policy.

possible that when the administration costs of providing insurance are taken into account, the premium for the partial coverage policy may be so high, relative to the protection that it provides, that the low risks would rather remain uninsured.

To summarize, one possible outcome of adverse selection in an insurance market is a situation where full coverage policies are offered, but the premiums are very high because they reflect the loss experience of high-risk individuals. Partial coverage policies, which expose the individual to some risk, may be offered at much lower premiums, and these will be purchased by low-risk individuals. When administration costs are relatively high, the low-risk individuals may be better off with no insurance coverage.

Before considering whether government intervention is warranted when there is adverse selection in an insurance market, we will consider some other private market responses to adverse selection. One market response is to provide insurance coverage to all the members of a particular group such as the employees of a firm. Group coverage circumvents the adverse selection problem because all of the members of the group are covered, and not just those who think that they have a high probability of a loss. Thus, group health insurance or group life insurance can be provided to all of the employees of a firm at premiums that are lower than in the open market, which is subject to an adverse selection process. The problem with group coverage is that it is only available to individuals who are members of large groups that qualify for such coverage. The employees of small firms or the self-employed cannot obtain group coverage, and this may distort individuals' decisions concerning whether to work for a large or a small firm. It also means that individuals risk losing their insurance coverage if they are laid off by their employer.

Another response to the adverse selection problem is that insurance companies may categorize individuals according to some observable characteristic—such as age, sex, or marital status—which is an *imperfect* indicator of an individual's risk type. For example, private automobile insurers charge a 20-year-old male a higher premium than a 20-year-old female because on average young males have a higher claim frequency than young females. This does not mean that all 20-year-old males are high-risk drivers or that all 20-year-old females are low-risk drivers. Each group contains high and low risks, but there is a higher proportion of high-risk drivers among the 20-year-old male population than among the 20-year-old female population. While an insurance company may not be able to distinguish who is a high or low risk, it can tell males from females, and it may decide to use these imperfect indicators of loss probability to charge different premiums to males and females. The use of these imperfect indicators helps to create more homogeneous risk groups, but it raises ethical issues regarding discrimination. The Supreme Court has ruled that sex-based automobile insurance premiums do not contravene the Canadian Charter of Rights and Freedoms because the insurance industry has demonstrated that its use of these categories is based on statistical evidence that young males have higher loss probabilities than young females. However, many people feel uncomfortable with such rationalizations and wonder whether discrimination on the basis of race or religion would also be accepted if it were supported by statistical evidence. It is well known that the elderly, on average, incur higher health care expenditures than the rest of the population. Private health insurers would charge higher premiums to the elderly and, indeed, to anyone with a history of illness. The insurance industry's use of information obtained from genetic testing to predict individuals' likelihood of contracting hereditary diseases raises many important ethical and economic issues. In summary, categorizing risks and charging them different premiums would reduce the scope for insurance coverage for many groups. Individuals may prefer a social insurance scheme that does not discriminate among individuals according to some observable characteristics that are correlated with expected losses.

One of the primary characteristics of social insurance programs is that they are compulsory. This means that they are not subject to the adverse selection process that arises when individuals can use their private information regarding their loss probability to choose their insurance coverage. The welfare implications of adopting compulsory social insurance in order to overcome an adverse selection problem are examined below. Suppose that the private market provides full coverage to high-risk individuals at a premium equal to $\pi_h L + A$, which covers their expected losses and administration costs, and that low-risk individuals do not purchase any insurance coverage. When the social insurance program is introduced, it provides full coverage for the entire population. All individuals will have to contribute, either in premiums or in taxes, an amount equal to $\bar{\pi} L + A$ to cover the expected cost of the claims and the administration costs of the program. (It is assumed that the administration cost per policy, A, is independent of the amount of coverage and the same for private and public insurance.) High-risk individuals, who previously purchased full coverage from the private sector, will be better off with the social insurance scheme because their premium or contribution will decline from $\pi_h L + A$ to $\bar{\pi} L + A$. Low-risk individuals will be made worse off because they prefer zero coverage to full coverage at a premium of $\bar{\pi} L + A$. Therefore, a compulsory full coverage insurance program will not be a Pareto improvement over the private market outcome. It will make the high-risk individuals better off, but it will make the low-risk individuals worse off. It can be shown, however, that a compulsory partial coverage policy may be able to achieve a Pareto improvement over the private market equilibrium.[7]

If a compulsory full coverage social insurance scheme does not represent a Pareto improvement over the private market outcome, can it be justified on other grounds? First, consider the distributional effects of a compulsory social insurance program. Even though the high risks receive full coverage with private insurance, they are less well off than the low risks who are not insured because $U(W - (\pi_h L + A)) < EU_l$. Otherwise the low risks would purchase the full coverage policy that is offered in the market. Thus, it can be argued that compulsory full coverage insurance improves distributional equity. Furthermore, it can be shown that with the compulsory full coverage policy the high-risk individuals gain more than the low-risk individuals lose. The per capita net gain is $h(\pi_h - \bar{\pi})L + (1 - h)(P^l_{MAX} - \bar{\pi}L - A)$ where the first term is positive and represents the per capita gain to the high-risk individuals from the reduction in their premiums. The second term is negative and represents the per capita loss to the low risks from being forced to contribute to a full coverage insurance policy. Their loss is the difference between the value that they place on full coverage insurance, P^l_{MAX}, and the amount that they have to contribute, $\bar{\pi}L + A$. By adding and subtracting $(1 - h)\pi_l L$ to the above expression, it can be shown that the net gain from compulsory full coverage insurance is $(1 - h)(P^l_{MAX} - \pi_l L - A)$. Thus, as long as the maximum premium that a low-risk individual would pay for full insurance exceeds his or her actuarially fair premium and administration cost, there is an net social gain from compulsory insurance. Therefore, as Akerlof (1970) speculated in his seminal article on adverse selection, compulsory insurance can be justified on a cost–benefit basis when the private market is afflicted with an adverse selection problem.

Moral Hazard

A moral hazard problem arises in an insurance market when an individual can influence the probability or the magnitude of a loss by undertaking some action, and that action is not observable by the insurance company.[8] Actions that affect the magnitude of an individual's loss are called *self-insurance* activities. Actions that affect the probability of an individual's loss are called *self-protection* activities. Examples of self-insurance and self-protection activities are given in Table 9.1. In some cases, the actions affect both the magnitude and probability of a loss.

---

[7] See Dahlby (1981).
[8] We will treat adverse selection and moral hazard as separate phenomena, but in many situations both moral hazard and adverse selection will be present in the market.

Table 9.1

Examples of Self-Insurance and Self-Protection Activities

TYPE OF INSURANCE	ACTION
Fire	Installation of a sprinkler system
Unemployment	Intensity of job search by an unemployed worker
Health and Pensions	Amount of physical exercise taken
Automobile	Driving speed
Automobile and Health	Consumption of alcohol
Health and Pensions	Number of cigarettes consumed

In analyzing the effect of moral hazard on insurance markets, we will focus on self-protection activities. We begin by examining the choice of self-protection activity in the absence of insurance.

Self-Protection Activity in the Absence of Insurance

Suppose that an individual can reduce the probability of a loss by undertaking an activity x that costs ρ dollars per unit. The effect of the activity on the individual's loss probability is shown in Figure 9.7. If x is zero the loss probability, $\pi(0)$, is less than one. More x always reduces the loss probability, but at a decreasing rate. The expenditure on self-protection, ρx, is made before the

Figure 9.7

Loss-Prevention Activity

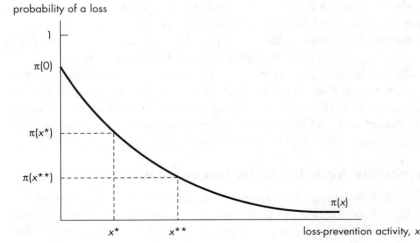

individual knows whether a loss will occur. The individual chooses x in order to maximize expected utility:

$$EU = \pi(x)U(W - L - \rho x) + (1 - \pi(x))U(W - \rho x) \qquad (9.13)$$

The level of self-protection activity that maximizes the individual's expected utility occurs where the marginal benefit from additional x, MB_x, equals ρ. The MB_x is equal to the marginal reduction in the probability of a loss, MRP, which is the absolute value of the slope of the tangent to the $\pi(x)$ curve, multiplied by a dollar measure of the gain from avoiding the loss, GU. The condition for the optimal amount of self-protection activity and the components of the MB_x are expressed below:

$$MB_x = MRP \cdot GU = \rho \qquad (9.14)$$

where

$$MRP = \frac{\Delta \pi}{\Delta x} \qquad (9.15)$$

$$GU = \frac{U(W - \rho x) - U(W - L - \rho x)}{EU'} \qquad (9.16)$$

The utility gain from avoiding a loss, $U(W - \rho x) - U(W - L - \rho x)$, is converted into a dollar figure by dividing it by the expected marginal utility of wealth, EU'. For a risk-neutral individual, EU' is a constant and GU is the magnitude of the loss, L. Therefore, MB_x^N is $MRP \cdot L$. In Figure 9.8, a risk-neutral individual would choose x^*. This level of loss-prevention activity would minimize $\pi(x)L + \rho x$, the sum of the expected loss and the cost of the loss-prevention activity. In general, it will not be optimal for a risk-neutral individual to reduce π to zero by increasing x even if this were possible. The amount of loss-prevention activity that a risk-averse individual will undertake is more difficult to determine because GU may be greater or smaller than L. In the situation portrayed in Figure 9.8, a risk-averse individual would choose loss-prevention activity equal to x^{**}, which would exceed the amount chosen by a risk-neutral individual. However, at a higher price for loss-prevention activity, a risk-averse individual may choose a level of loss-prevention activity that is less than x^*.

Self-Protection Activity with Insurance

If an individual is risk averse, there are potential gains from purchasing insurance. We begin by considering the case where an insurance company can observe the insured's level of loss-prevention activity. It will be assumed for

Figure 9.8

Choice of the Level of Loss-Prevention Activity

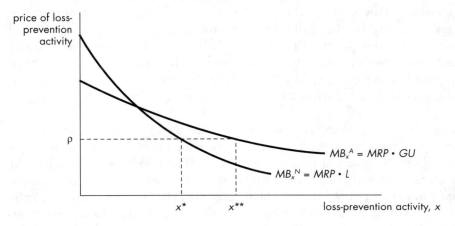

simplicity that there are no administration costs and that losses are uncorrelated. Since x is observable, the insurance contract will specify the level of x, along with the deductible, D, and the premium, P. In this context, the optimal insurance contract will have the following specification: $D = 0$, $x = x^*$, and $P = \pi(x^*)L$. In other words, the insurance industry would offer a full coverage contract and specify that the insured has to undertake the level of loss-prevention activity that minimizes the sum of the expected loss and the cost of the loss-prevention activity. The premium would be the expected loss, given the level of loss-prevention activity x^*. This implies that the optimal insurance contract when x is observable may specify either more or less loss-prevention activity than a risk-averse individual would undertake in the absence of insurance. If, in the absence of insurance, a risk-averse individual would choose $x^{**} > x^*$, then the loss probability would increase under the full coverage policy because prevention activity would decline. The increased frequency of losses would represent an improvement in the allocation of resources in the economy because we would be using the risk-pooling mechanism, instead of loss-prevention activity, to reduce risks. For example, in the absence of insurance coverage against theft, individuals might invest in very expensive security devices to protect their property. If the expenditure on security devices exceeded the amount that would minimize the expected loss plus the cost of the devices, then society would be better off with a somewhat higher loss probability, risk reduction provided by the risk-pooling mechanism, and more resources available for other productive purposes. Although it may seem paradoxical, insurance may serve a useful role in reducing loss-prevention activity and, as a consequence, increasing the frequency of losses.

The preceding analysis was based on the assumption that the insurance company could observe the insured's level of self-protection activity. If x is not observable by the insurance company, its value cannot be specified in the insurance contract. This leads to the problem of moral hazard. If the insurance industry continued to offer full insurance contracts, the optimal level of x for the insured individual would be 0, not x^*. If all of the insured individuals reduced their provision of x to 0, the premium for full coverage insurance would have to increase to $\pi(0)L$. With this higher premium, the full insurance contract may be less attractive than no insurance.

However, the insurance industry is not restricted to full coverage contracts. It can offer partial coverage insurance contracts, which give the insured an incentive to engage in some self-protection activity. When there is a moral hazard problem, the optimal insurance contract will be a partial coverage contract that specifies D and P, but not x. The insured will choose x to satisfy the condition $MB_x = \rho$. A larger deductible will induce the insured to choose more loss-prevention activity (thereby reducing expected losses and allowing the insurance company to offer the policy at a lower premium), but a higher deductible will also impose a larger financial penalty on the insured if a loss occurs. *With the optimal deductible, the additional gain from providing the insured with a greater incentive to engage in self-protection activity equals the additional loss in expected utility from reducing insurance coverage by increasing the deductible by one dollar.*

Does moral hazard cause market failure? Is social insurance warranted when an insurance market is affected by a moral hazard problem? These issues are complex and have not been fully resolved by economists. First consider the question of whether moral hazard provides a justification for social insurance. It should be emphasized that, if a moral hazard problem exits, it will affect the public sector as much as the private sector. In general, the public sector does not have any advantage over the private sector in monitoring the loss-prevention activity of the insured. If the public sector provides social insurance, it should be a partial coverage, so that individuals have some incentive to reduce expected losses.[9] The optimal deductible under social insurance would be determined according to the same criteria as under private insurance. Therefore, moral hazard does not provide a strong rationale for the provision of social insurance.

---

[9] For example, if an unemployed worker can increase his or her probability of finding a new job by devoting more effort to searching for a job, then the optimal unemployment insurance system should not replace all of the unemployed worker's lost earnings.

There are, however, other forms of government intervention that may improve the private sector's allocation of resources when there is a moral hazard problem. Arnott and Stiglitz (1986) showed that a Pareto improvement in the allocation of a resource is possible if the government can subsidize the price of loss-prevention activity. The insured will engage in more loss-prevention activity, thereby permitting the insurance industry to increase its insurance coverage and moving the allocation of resources closer to the full insurance contracts that would be provided in the absence of the moral hazard problem. Similar arguments can be used to justify other forms of government intervention that affect individuals' loss-prevention or self-protection activity. In terms of the examples presented in Table 9.1, the allocation of resources in the economy may be improved by enforcing regulations that sprinkler systems be installed in some types of buildings, by subsidizing the cost of providing unemployed workers with information on job vacancies at government employment centres, by subsidizing the provision of recreation facilities, by enforcing speed limits and the wearing of seat-belts, and by taxing alcohol and cigarettes. A more complete discussion of the welfare implications of moral hazard is contained in Arnott and Stiglitz (1990).

CONCLUSIONS

We began this chapter by noting that many important government programs—unemployment insurance, health insurance, and public pensions—provide insurance coverage. Social insurance programs have four primary characteristics: they are compulsory, financed by contributions, triggered by undesirable events, and not means-tested.

To understand the rationale for social insurance and the context in which social insurance programs operate, we have reviewed an economic model of the demand for insurance. We have seen that if individuals are risk averse they are willing to pay more than their expected loss for a full coverage insurance policy. The private insurance industry can provide insurance coverage for some losses, especially if the collective risk can be reduced or eliminated through risk pooling or risk spreading. However, it may not be worthwhile to insure some risks if their administration cost is high, the loss is relatively small, or the probability of a loss is either very high or very low.

The private sector may not be able to provide insurance coverage when risks are highly correlated. In cases such as unemployment insurance, the public sector may be able to provide a form of insurance because of its superior ability to borrow in the event that there are very high losses.

Asymmetric information may also provide a rationale for social insurance. Adverse selection occurs when individuals differ in their loss probabilities, but insurance companies cannot distinguish high-risk individuals from low-risk individuals. As a consequence, many low-risk individuals may purchase little or no insurance coverage because the presence of the high risks drives up the insurance premiums. Adverse selection also gives rise to segmented insurance markets where some individuals can obtain group coverage, usually through their employer. Other individuals are assessed premiums based on observable characteristics, such as age, sex, or claims history, which are imperfect indicators of an individual's risk group. Compulsory social insurance programs solve the adverse selection problem, but full coverage policies will generally make the low-risk individuals worse off and benefit high-risk individuals. However, this may be viewed as acceptable on equity grounds.

Moral hazard occurs when the insured can affect the magnitude or the probability of a loss, but the insurance company cannot directly monitor the individual's actions. The optimal insurance contract will be a partial coverage contract, which provides the insured with some incentive to reduce expected losses, but that does not expose the insured to large financial penalty if a loss occurs. Moral hazard does not provide a strong rationale for compulsory social insurance, but it may influence the design of social insurance programs, and it justifies the use of regulation, taxes, and subsidies to influence the behaviour of individuals who are covered by public or private insurance.

It is possible that some social insurance programs are motivated by the perception of market failure. However, social insurance programs may also be desired as an instrument for achieving certain distributional goals. In the next chapter, we examine some of the conceptual issues concerning the design of income redistribution programs, and then consider the use of other instruments, such as in-kind transfers and social insurance, to supplement the more traditional transfer mechanisms.

SUMMARY

- The actuarially fair premium for an insurance policy is equal to the insured's expected loss. The maximum premium that an insured will pay for an insurance policy is the premium that makes the individual indifferent between having the policy and being uninsured.

- Individuals are considered to be risk averse if they are willing to pay more than the actuarially fair premium for an insurance policy. The maximum premium that a risk-averse individual will pay approaches the actuarially fair premium when the probability of a loss is very high or very low.

- The private insurance industry is able to offer insurance policies at relatively attractive premiums if the administration costs of the policies are relatively low and if the risk borne by the insurance company can be reduced to an acceptable level through the risk-pooling and the risk-spreading mechanisms.

- To economize on administration costs, insurance policies may contain deductibles so that small losses are not covered.

- The ability of the risk-pooling mechanism to eliminate risk is impaired if the losses are positively correlated.

- Social insurance may be a response to market failure. The main reasons why the private sector may fail to provide an appropriate level of insurance are:

  - an inability to pool risks;
  - increasing returns to scale in the provision of insurance; and
  - adverse selection.

- Adverse selection is the problem of hidden information. It occurs in an insurance market when:

  - the population is not homogeneous with respect to the probability of a loss;
  - each individual knows his or her own loss probability; and
  - an insurance company does not know an individual's loss probability.

- With adverse selection, the bad risks drive up insurance premiums. The good risks respond by purchasing insurance policies with low coverage, i.e., high deductibles. The policies with high deductibles are less attractive to high-risk individuals, and therefore low-risk individuals can purchase them at relatively low premiums, which reflect their low-loss probability. Some low risks may choose to go without insurance coverage.

- The adverse selection problem may also cause private insurance companies to categorize individuals according to some observable characteristic, such as age, sex, or marital status, which is an *imperfect* indicator of an individual's risk type.

- The adverse selection problem may justify compulsory social insurance, but it is likely that compulsory full coverage insurance would make the low-risk individuals worse off.

- Moral hazard is the problem of hidden action. A moral hazard problem arises in an insurance market when:

  - the individual can influence the probability and/or the magnitude of a loss by undertaking some action; and
  - an insurance company cannot observe the individual's action.

- If the loss-prevention activity could be monitored by an insurance company, the optimal full coverage insurance contract would specify that the insured undertake the level of activity that would minimize the expected loss and the cost of the loss-prevention activity. In the absence of insurance, a risk-averse individual may engage in more or less loss-prevention activity than the level that minimizes the expected loss and the cost of the loss-prevention activity.

- If the insurance company cannot monitor the individual's loss-prevention activity, the insurance company will offer a partial coverage insurance policy that provides the insured with some incentive to engage in loss-prevention activity. The level of insurance coverage will be determined by the trade-off between providing the insured with greater security from losses and with an incentive to engage in some self-protection activity that will reduce expected losses.

- Moral hazard does not in itself justify social insurance programs, but it may provide a rationale for regulations, taxes, or subsidies that may modify the insured's behaviour and affect the probability or the magnitude of losses.

DISCUSSION QUESTIONS

1. Suppose that an individual, with wealth equal to W, is offered a lottery ticket where the prize is $1,000,000 (tax free). Suppose that the probability of winning the prize is 1/100,000 if one purchases one ticket.

   a. Calculate the actuarially fair price for this lottery ticket.
   b. Show that a risk-averse individual would never be willing to purchase a lottery ticket if its price is equal to or greater than its actuarially fair price.

2. Suppose that two individuals have the same W in the absence of an accident, have the same degree of risk aversion, and face the same expected loss if an accident occurs. Individual 1 faces a larger loss than individual 2, $L_1 > L_2$, but with a lower probability such that $\pi_1 L_1 = \pi_2 L_2$. Using a diagram, show that with an actuarially fair insurance policy individual 1 obtains a larger consumer surplus than individual 2.

3. Three individuals each face a one-third probability of suffering a loss of L. Suppose they form a mutual insurance company and agree to share their losses. Calculate their expected contribution to total loss and plot a histogram of the probability distribution of each individual's contribution if the losses are independent events.

4. Suppose that individuals use the following utility function to evaluate their expected utility in the absence of insurance:

$$EU = \pi ln(W - L) + (1 - \pi)ln(W)$$

Each individual's wealth, W, is 100, and the magnitude of a loss, L, is 30.

a. Calculate the actuarially fair insurance premium for a full coverage policy if the loss probability, π, is 0.10.

b. Calculate the maximum premium that this individual would pay for a full coverage policy.

5. Explain why the private sector may not provide full coverage insurance at an actuarially fair premium for the following types of insurance coverage:

a. Automobile collisions.

b. Medical malpractice.

c. Home (including fire and theft).

6. The federal and provincial governments provide farmers with crop insurance. What problems or issues may explain why governments, rather than the private sector, provide crop insurance?

REFERENCES

Akerlof, G. "The Market for Lemons: Qualitative Uncertainty and the Market Mechanism." *Quarterly Journal of Economics* 84 (1970): 488–500.

Arnott, R., and J. Stiglitz. "The Welfare Economics of Moral Hazard," in *Risk, Information, and Insurance*, ed. H. Louberge. Boston: Kluwer Academic Publishers, 1990, pp. 91–121.

Arnott, R., and J. Stiglitz. "Moral Hazard and Optimal Commodity Taxation." *Journal of Public Economics* 29 (1986): 1–24.

Arrow, Kenneth J. "Uncertainty and the Welfare Economics of Medical Care." *American Economic Review* 53 (December 1963): 941–73.

Arrow, K.J., and R. Lind. "Uncertainty and the Evaluation of Public Investments." *American Economic Review* 60 (1970): 364–78.

Dahlby, B. "Price Adjustment in an Automobile Insurance Market: A Test of the Sheshinski-Weiss Model." *Canadian Journal of Economics* 25 (August 1992): 564–83.

Dahlby, B. "Adverse Selection and Pareto Improvement through Compulsory Insurance." *Public Choice* 37 (1981): 547–58.

Pindyck, Robert S., and Daniel L. Rubinfeld. *Microeconomics*, 4th ed. Upper Saddle River, NJ: Prentice-Hall, 1998.

Rothschild, M., and J. Stiglitz. "Equilibrium in Competitive Insurance Markets: An Essay on the Economics of Imperfect Information." *Quarterly Journal of Economics* 90 (1976): 629–50.

Varian, Hal R. *Intermediate Microeconomics: A Modern Approach*. New York: W.W. Norton, 1987.

APPENDIX

Derivation of Equation (9.12)

If X and Y are random variables and a and b are constants, then:

$$Var(aX + bY) = a^2Var(X) + b^2Var(Y) + 2abCov(X,Y)$$

where:

$$Cov(X,Y) = E((X - EX)(Y - EY)) = \rho_{xy}(var(X)var(Y))^{1/2}$$

and ρ_{xy} is the correlation coefficient between X and Y. For the mutual insurance company, $Cov(L_i, L_j) = \rho_{ij}\pi(1 - \pi)L^2$. Suppose that the individuals' losses are statistically independent, i.e., $\rho_{ij} = 0$. Consequently,

$$Var(S/n) = \sum_{i=1}^{n}(1/n)^2Var(L_i) = (1/n)^2nVar(L_i) = \frac{\pi(1 - \pi)L^2}{n}$$

Note that if n is large, $Var(S/n)$ becomes small. Thus, if the mutual insurance company is large, its members will not face any risk. Uncertainty is eliminated through risk pooling.

Chapter 10

Income Redistribution

A decent provision for the poor is the true test of civilization.

–Samuel Johnson

"*I*n general, the art of government consists in taking as much money as possible from one class of citizens to give to the other." While Voltaire's assertion is an overstatement, it is true that virtually every important political issue has implications for the distribution of income. Even when they are not explicit, questions of who will gain and who will lose lurk in the background of public policy debates. This chapter presents a framework for thinking about the normative and positive aspects of government income redistribution policy. This framework is used in Chapter 12 to analyze major government programs for maintaining the incomes of the poor.

Before proceeding, we should discuss whether economists ought to consider distributional issues at all. Not everyone thinks they should. Notions concerning the "right" income distribution are value judgments, and there is no "scientific" way to resolve differences in matters of ethics. Therefore, some argue that discussion of distributional issues is detrimental to objectivity in economics and that economists should restrict themselves to analyzing only the efficiency aspects of social issues (see Kristal, 1980).

This view has two problems. First, as emphasized in Chapter 4, the theory of welfare economics indicates that efficiency by itself cannot be used to evaluate a given situation. Criteria other than efficiency must be brought to bear when comparing alternative allocations of resources. Of course, one can assert that only efficiency matters, but this in itself is a value judgment.

In addition, decision makers care about the distributional implications of policy. If economists ignore distribution, then policy makers will ignore economists. Policy makers may thus end up focusing only on distributional issues and pay no attention at all to efficiency. The economist who systematically takes distribution into account can keep policy makers aware of both efficiency and distributional issues. Although training in economics certainly does not confer a superior ability to make ethical judgments, economists are skilled at drawing out the implications of alternative sets of values and measuring the costs of achieving various ethical goals.

A related question is whether government ought to be involved in changing the income distribution. As noted in Chapter 1, some important traditions of political philosophy suggest that government should play no redistributive role. However, even the most minimal government action conceivably influences income distribution. For example, when the government purchases materials for public goods, some firms receive contracts and others do not; presumably the owners of the firms receiving the contracts enjoy increases in their relative incomes. More generally, the government's taxing and spending activities are both bound to change the distribution of real income. Distributional issues are part and parcel of the government's functioning.

DISTRIBUTION OF INCOME

We begin by examining recent trends in average family income. Figure 10.1 shows the average family income, measured in 1995 dollars, over the 1980 to 1995 period. Average family income was $55,247 in 1995. This represented a 4.8 percent decline from the peak of $58,024 recorded in 1989, and it was only slightly higher than average family income in 1980. Thus, the recessions of the early 1980s and 1990s have produced prolonged declines in Canadians' average incomes and little or no improvement in the average standard of living over the last fifteen years. The distribution of family income in 1995 is shown in Figure 10.2. Just under 2 percent of families had incomes of less than $10,000, and 9.7 percent had incomes between $10,000 and $20,000. The median family income was $48,079. (Fifty percent of families had more than the median and 50 percent received less.) Just under 9 percent of families received more than $100,000. These figures give some impression of the extent of income inequality in Canada. Before examining the trends in income inequality, we will discuss the data that are used to measure income, the definitions of households, and the time frame that is used to measure income.

Figure 10.1

Average Family Income in Constant 1995 Dollars

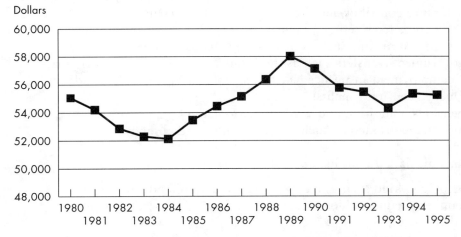

SOURCE: Statistics Canada, *Income Distributions by Size in Canada, 1995*, Table I, p. 23.

Figure 10.2

Percentage Distribution of Families by Income Groups in 1995

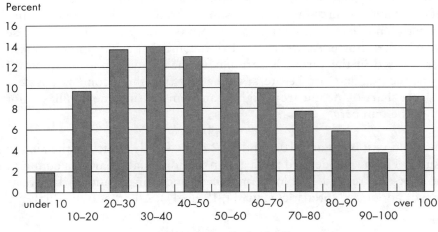

SOURCE: Statistics Canada, *Income Distributions by Size in Canada, 1995*, Table 1, pp. 60–61.

The income data are based on Statistics Canada's annual Survey of Consumer Finances. Total income includes:

- wages and salaries before the deduction of income taxes, unemployment insurance contributions, etc.;
- net income from self-employment;
- investment income such as interest, dividends, and net rent;
- government transfers such as the Child Tax Benefit, Old Age Security, Unemployment Insurance benefits, social assistance, and Canada and Quebec Pension benefits;
- pensions, annuities, and superannuation; and
- miscellaneous income such as scholarships and alimony.

The income data do not include:

- income in kind such as meals, accommodation, and fringe benefits;
- gambling gains and losses;
- inheritances;
- capital gains and losses; and
- the implicit rental income from owner-occupied housing.[1]

The exclusion of these forms of income may understate the incomes received by some groups. For example, capital gains are disproportionately received by high-income earners, and the implicit rental income from owner-occupied housing may be relatively large for seniors who have paid off their mortgages. Another important source of in-kind income is the value of the time that adults devote to their households. The official data miss important differences in the levels of economic resources available to single-parent versus two-parent families and between two-parent families with both parents working versus those with one parent at home. Another source of income that is likely not reported or underreported in the survey is earnings in the "underground economy." Finally, the income data are before-tax. The fact that the income tax system takes a larger share of income from high- than from low-income families is not reflected in the numbers.

The household unit in Figures 10.1 and 10.2 is the family, which in the Survey of Consumer Finances is defined as "a group of individuals sharing a common dwelling unit and related by blood, marriage (including common law relationships) or adoption" (Statistics Canada, 1996: 41). All other individuals are

---

[1] A house provides its owner with a flow of housing services. The value of these services is the cost to the home-owner of renting a comparable dwelling.

referred to as unattached individuals, who are either living alone or living in a household with other unrelated individuals. In 1995, average income for unattached individuals was $24,166 compared to average family income of $55,247. Comparing the standard of living of families and unattached individuals is difficult because families have to spread their income among several individuals. The average family in 1995 had 3.07 members. Since there are economies for individuals living together as a family, especially in the consumption of housing, equivalence scales are sometimes used to compare the standard of living of households of different sizes. For example, in constructing its low-income measures Statistics Canada assumes that a second adult adds 40 percent to the needs of a household and each child adds 30 percent to the household expenditure needs. Thus, a two-parent family with one child would have the equivalent needs of 1.7 unattached individuals, and if they received the average family income of $55,247 they would have the equivalent standard of living of an unattached individual receiving $32,498. Obviously, adjusting family income for size is highly judgmental, but some adjustments should be made when we compare households of different sizes.

The data in the figures refer to annual income, but it is not obvious what time frame should be used. A daily or weekly measure of income would be absurd, because even rich individuals could have zero incomes during some short time periods. It makes much more sense to measure the flow of income over a year, as is customarily done. However, even annual measures may not reflect an individual's true economic position. After all, there can be unexpected fluctuations in income from year to year. From a theoretical point of view, lifetime income would have advantages, but the practical problems in estimating it are enormous.

Although distinguishing between different time periods may seem a mere academic quibble, it is really quite important. People tend to have low incomes when they are young, more when they are middle-aged, and less again when they are old and in retirement. Therefore, people who have identical lifetime incomes but are in different stages of the life cycle can show up in the annual data as having unequal incomes. Measures of inequality based on annual income will indicate much more inequality than those constructed on the more appropriate lifetime basis.

Bearing in mind the problems that arise from the actual measures of income, the size and composition of the household unit, and the time frame used to measure income, we will proceed with our examination of the trends in the distribution of income in Canada. Table 10.1 shows the distribution of total income among families and unattached individuals since 1951. The bottom quintile represents the 20 percent of households with the lowest incomes. In 1995, they received 4.7 percent of total income, up from 4.4 percent in 1951 and 3.6 percent in 1971. On the other hand, the richest fifth of the population received 44.1 percent of total income in 1995, up from 41.1 percent in 1961. At first glance, the data seem to indicate that the distribution of income is very stable. The largest change is the 3.0 percentage point increase in the top quintile's share between 1961 and 1995. The quintile income shares have remained relatively constant in spite of the major changes in employment patterns across regions and industries, levels of education and training, labour force participation rates by females, and the introduction and enhancement of social assistance and social insurance programs. It might be thought that an expansion of government transfer programs since World War II would have reduced income inequality, assuming of course that low-income households receive most of the benefits from these programs. However, it could be the case that the expansion of the transfers has been caused by the need to offset the changes in the distribution of factor market income, which would have increased income inequality. On the other hand, more generous transfer programs may have produced greater inequality in earnings, by creating disincentives to work and earn income, leading to little overall change in the distribution of income.

Some small shifts in the income distribution can be discerned. Since 1951, the top 40 percent of households have increased their income shares by 2.5 percentage points at the expense of the lower- and middle-income groups, and since 1981 the income share of the fourth quintile has declined, suggesting an increasing polarization in the income distribution. However, the income share of the bottom quintile has increased, by a relatively modest 0.3 percentage

Table 10.1

Distribution of Income among Families and Unattached Individuals

YEAR	BOTTOM QUINTILE	SECOND QUINTILE	THIRD QUINTILE	FOURTH QUINTILE	TOP QUINTILE
1951	4.4	11.2	18.3	23.3	42.8
1961	4.2	11.9	18.3	24.5	41.1
1971	3.6	10.6	17.6	24.9	43.3
1981	4.6	10.9	17.6	25.2	41.8
1991	4.7	10.3	16.6	24.7	43.8
1995	4.7	10.2	16.4	24.5	44.1

SOURCE: David Ross, *The Canadian Fact Book on Income Distribution* (Toronto: Canadian Council on Social Development, 1980), Table 1, p. 12, and Statistics Canada, *Income Distributions by Size in Canada, 1995* (December 1996), Table 55, p. 159. Reprinted with permission.

points since 1951 and 0.1 percentage points since 1981, and therefore the gains by the richest 20 percent have *not* been at the expense of the bottom 20 percent, as has been the case in the United States.[2]

As the quotation by Samuel Johnson at the beginning of this chapter indicated, most people focus on the economic position of the poor in assessing whether income inequality is high or low, increasing or decreasing. In Canada and other countries, it has become a common practice to compute the number of people below the **poverty line,** a fixed level of real income considered enough to provide a minimally adequate standard of living. The most widely used poverty lines are Statistics Canada's Low Income Cut-Off lines.[3] (Statistics Canada does not refer to them as poverty lines, and they have no official status.) The 1995 low-income cut-off lines are based on an analysis of the 1992 expenditure pattern of households, and define the income level at which families usually spent 54.7 percent or more on food, shelter, and clothing. The low-income cut-off lines are adjusted using an equivalence scale for the size of the household and the size of the community in which the household lives. The 1995 low-income cut-off line was $16,874 for an unattached individual living in an urban area exceeding 500,000, and $11,661 in a rural area. For a family of three, it was $26,232 in the large urban area, and $18,129 in a rural area. While there is clearly some arbitrariness in determining what is an adequate standard of living, the notion of a poverty line still provides a useful benchmark.

Figure 10.3 shows the percentage of the total population that was below Statistics Canada's Low Income Cut-Off lines (LICO) from 1980 to 1995. The trend in the incidence of low income over this period is the mirror image of the trend in average family income. It increased from 15.6 percent in 1980 as average real family income declined in the early 1980s, and then decreased after 1984 as the economy recovered. Since 1989 when the economy went into a recession, the percentage of the population below the LICO has increased from 14.1 percent to 17.8 percent by 1995. The incidence of poverty among two groups—the young and the old—is a special concern for most people. Figure 10.3 shows the incidence of low incomes among children was slightly higher than for the population as a whole up until 1989. Since then it has rapidly increased and reached 21.3 percent in 1993. Among the elderly there

---

[2] See Beach and Slotsve (1996) on trends in the income distributions in Canada and the United States.

[3] Other poverty lines have been devised by other groups. The Fraser Institute publishes poverty lines based on the cost of acquiring a basic level of subsistence. The Canadian Council on Social Development publishes poverty lines based on one-half the average income of a family of three, with other adjustments for the size of the family. See Ross, Shillington, and Lochhead (1994: ch. 2) for a comparison of the various poverty lines.

Figure 10.3

The Incidence of Low Incomes

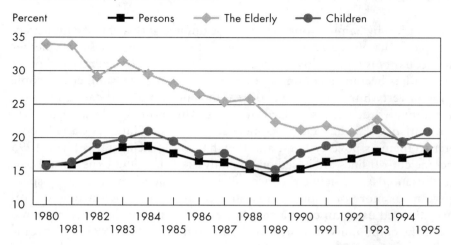

SOURCE: Statistics Canada, *Income Distributions by Size in Canada, 1995*, Table III, pp. 26–27.

has been a long-term decline in the proportion who are poor, from 28 percent in 1980 to 18.7 percent in 1995. This decline in the incidence of low incomes among the elderly is the result of the improvement in public and private pension benefits. The decline in the poverty rate among the elderly obscures the fact that the poverty rate among elderly individuals who live alone was 45.1 percent in 1995. Finally, the incidence of poverty is higher among women than it is among men. In summary, while progress has been made in reducing the poverty rate among the elderly, there is still a high poverty rate among some groups, and the rising incidence of poverty among children is an increasingly important issue.

Measuring the proportion of the population that is poor may obscure the severity of the poverty problem because a household is classified as poor if it is $1 or $10,000 below the poverty line. The income deficiency concept measures how much income would have to be transferred to low-income households to lift their incomes to the poverty line (assuming the transfers had no effects on the recipients' work effort). The average income deficiency in 1995 was $6,659, down from $6,990 in 1980, but the aggregate income deficiency was $17.9 billion in 1995, up from $14.1 billion in 1980.[4]

---

[4] All of the income deficiency figures are measured in constant (1993) dollars. See Statistics Canada (1996: Tables V and VI, pp. 34–37).

Table 10.2 shows the incidence of low incomes by province, the number of earners in the household, and education level in 1991. The poverty rate among families was lowest in Prince Edward Island, 9.9 percent, and highest in Manitoba, at 17.0 percent, followed closely by Newfoundland and Quebec. Not surprisingly, households where no one earned income had very high poverty rates. For families, adding a second paycheque reduced the incidence of poverty from 21.7 to 5.9 percent. These figures reflect a basic reality for many Canadian families—both parents have to work in order for the family to have a "reasonable" standard of living. It also means that some households are choosing to be poor when they decide that one parent, usually the mother,

Table 10.2

Percentage of Families or Individuals below Low-Income Cut-offs in 1991

CHARACTERISTICS	FAMILIES	UNATTACHED INDIVIDUALS
Canada	**13.0%**	**36.6%**
Newfoundland	16.4	41.3
Prince Edward Island	9.9	40.5
Nova Scotia	12.7	35.5
New Brunswick	12.2	35.8
Quebec	15.9	44.0
Ontario	11.3	31.8
Manitoba	17.0	38.2
Saskatchewan	13.4	34.5
Alberta	13.1	33.4
British Columbia	11.1	35.9
Number of Earners		
0	34.8	56.5
1	21.7	23.2
2	5.9	n.a.
3 or more	2.5	n.a.
Education		
0–8 years	20.1	54.8
9–10 years	22.3	48.0
11–13 years	15.6	34.8
some postsecondary	16.7	39.5
postsecondary cert./diploma	8.7	25.8
university degree	6.1	22.1

SOURCE: D. Ross, E.R. Shillington, and C. Lochhead, *The Canadian Fact Book on Poverty* (Toronto: Canadian Council on Social Development, 1994), Table 5.3, p. 59. Reprinted with permission.

will stay home to devote full time to raising young children. The figures on the incidence of poverty by education level are consistent with the widely held perception that those with little education have a greater likelihood of being poor.

The question of why there are large disparities in income has long occupied a central place in economics and is far from definitively settled.[5] The most important reason for inequality in family incomes appears to be differences in the wages and salaries of the family heads. Differences in property income (interest, dividends, etc.) account for only a relatively small proportion of overall income inequality. While very important, this observation does not explain income inequality—one must still account for the large differences in earnings. Earned income depends on items as diverse as physical strength, intelligence, effort, health, education, marriage decisions, the existence of race and sex discrimination, the presence of public welfare programs, and luck. Many economists believe that a key factor driving the increase in inequality in recent years is an increase in the financial returns to education—because of changes in technology such as the widespread introduction of computers into the workplace, workers with college educations are now earning relatively more than their low-education counterparts. But no single item can account for every case of poverty. As we see later, this fact has bedevilled attempts to formulate sensible policies for redistributing income.

RATIONALES FOR INCOME REDISTRIBUTION

While there is no doubt that income is distributed unequally, there is a lot of controversy concerning whether, and to what extent, the government should undertake policies to change that distribution. This section discusses several different views on this matter.

Utilitarianism

Conventional welfare economics posits that the welfare of society is defined by the well-being of its members. Algebraically, if there are n individuals in society and the ith individual's utility is U_i, then social welfare, W, is some function $F(\cdot)$ of individuals' utilities[6]:

$$W = F(U_1, U_2, \ldots, U_n) \qquad (10.1)$$

---

[5] For an excellent survey of alternative theories, see Atkinson (1983).
[6] This discussion ignores the problems that arise if the members of a society cannot agree on a social welfare function. See Chapter 11 under "Direct Democracy."

It is assumed that an increase in any of the U_is, other things being the same, increases W. A change that makes someone better off without making anyone worse off increases social welfare.

The nineteenth-century utilitarian philosophers, such as Jeremy Bentham and John Stuart Mill, argued that public policies should be guided by the principle of the greatest good for the greatest number. This utilitarian maxim is usually interpreted by economists as implying a social welfare function that is simply the sum of individuals' utilities. It is referred to as an additive social welfare function:

$$W = U_1 + U_2 + \ldots + U_n. \tag{10.2}$$

What does utilitarianism say about whether the government should redistribute income? The answer is straightforward—redistribute income as long as it increases W. Alone, this social welfare function tells us little about the appropriate redistribution policy. However, if a few assumptions are made, strong results can be obtained. Assume:

1. Individuals have identical utility functions that depend only on their incomes.
2. These utility functions exhibit diminishing marginal utility of income—as individuals' incomes increase, they become better off, but at a decreasing rate.
3. The total amount of income available is fixed.

Under these assumptions and the additive social welfare function of Equation (10.2), the government should redistribute income so that *complete equality* is obtained. To prove this, assume that the society consists of only two people, Peter and Paul. (It is easy to generalize the argument to cases where there are any number of people.)

In Figure 10.4, the horizontal distance OO' measures the total amount of income available in society. Paul's income is measured by the distance to the right of point O; Peter's income is measured by the distance to the left of point O'. Thus, any point along OO' represents some distribution of income between Paul and Peter. The problem is to find the "best" point.

Paul's marginal utility of income is measured vertically, beginning at point O. Following assumption 2, the schedule relating Paul's marginal utility of income to his level of income is downward sloping. It is labelled MU_{Paul} in Figure 10.4.

Figure 10.4

Model of the Optimal Distribution of Income

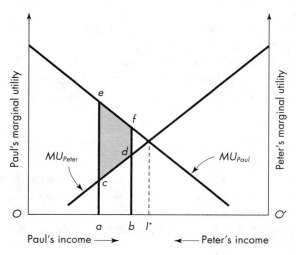

Peter's marginal utility of income is measured vertically, beginning at point O'. His marginal utility of income schedule is denoted MU_{Peter}. (Remember that movements to the left on the horizontal axis represent *increases* in Peter's income.) Because Peter and Paul have identical utility functions, MU_{Peter} is a mirror image of MU_{Paul}.

Assume that initially Paul's income is Oa and Peter's is $O'a$. Is social welfare as high as possible, or could the sum of utilities be increased if income were somehow redistributed between Paul and Peter? Suppose that ab dollars are taken from Peter and given to Paul. Obviously, this makes Peter worse off and Paul better off. However, the crucial question is what happens to the *sum* of their utilities. Because Peter is richer than Paul, Peter's loss in utility is smaller than Paul's gain, so the sum of their utilities goes up. Geometrically, the area under each person's marginal utility of income schedule measures the change in his utility induced by the income change. Distributing ab dollars to Paul increases his utility by area *abfe*. Taking the ab dollars from Peter decreases his utility by area *abdc*. The sum of their utility therefore increases by shaded area *cefd*.

Similar reasoning suggests that as long as incomes are unequal, marginal utilities will be unequal, and the *sum* of utilities can be increased by distributing income to the poorer individual. Only at point I^*, where incomes and marginal utilities are equal, is social welfare maximized. Full income equality should be pursued.

The policy implications of this result are breathtaking, so the assumptions behind it require scrutiny.

Assumption 1. The validity of the notion that individuals have identical utility functions is fundamentally impossible to determine. It simply cannot be known whether individuals derive the same amount of satisfaction from the consumption of goods, because satisfaction cannot be objectively measured. There are, however, two possible defences for the assumption. First, although it cannot be *proved* that people derive the same utility from equal amounts of income, it is a reasonable guess. After all, if people generally do not vary wildly in their observable characteristics—weight, height, and so on—why should their utility functions differ? Second, one can interpret the assumption not as a psychological statement, but as an *ethical* one. Specifically, in designing a redistributional policy, government ought to act *as if* all people have the same utility functions, whether they do or not.

Clearly, neither of these defences would convince a skeptic, and the assumption remains troublesome.

Assumption 2. A more technical, but equally important objection concerns the assumption of decreasing marginal utility of income. While it may be that the marginal utility of any given *good* decreases with its consumption, it is not clear that this is true for *income* as a whole. In Figure 10.4, the results change drastically if the marginal utility of income schedules fail to slope down. Suppose the marginal utility of income is instead constant at all levels of income. Then MU_{Peter} and MU_{Paul} are represented by an identical horizontal line. Whenever a dollar is taken from Peter, the loss in his utility is exactly equal to Paul's gain. Thus, the value of the sum of their utilities is independent of the income distribution. Government redistributive policy cannot change social welfare.

Assumption 3. By this assumption, the total amount of income in the society, distance OO', is fixed. The size of the pie does not change as the government redistributes its pieces. Suppose, however, that individuals' utilities depend not only on income, but also on leisure. Each individual chooses how much leisure to surrender (how much to work) to maximize his or her utility. The taxes and subsidies enacted to redistribute income generally change people's work decisions and diminish total real income. Thus, a society whose goal is to maximize the sum of utilities faces an inescapable dilemma. On one hand, it prefers to equalize the distribution of income. However, in doing so, it reduces the total amount of income available. The optimal income distribution must take into account the costs (in lost real income) of achieving more equality.[7]

To consider how distortionary taxation affects the optimal income distribution, suppose that all income is earned by Peter and that a transfer to Paul is financed by a proportional income tax on Peter's income. In order to transfer more income to Paul, a higher tax rate has to be imposed on Peter, and it is assumed that the disincentive effects of the higher tax rate cause him to generate less income. As defined in Chapter 5, the marginal cost of public funds, MCF, measures the cost to a society in raising an additional dollar of tax revenue. With a distortionary tax system, the MCF will be greater than one. The optimal income distribution from a utilitarian perspective occurs where the gain to Paul from an additional dollar of transfers, MU_{Paul}, equals the cost imposed on Peter in raising that additional dollar, $MCF \cdot MU_{Peter}$, or in other words where[8]:

$$\frac{MU_{Paul}}{MU_{Peter}} = MCF \qquad (10.3)$$

Since the MCF is greater than one, MU_{Paul} is greater than MU_{Peter}, and this means that Paul's income is less than Peter's income. The more the tax distorts Peter's decision to earn income, the greater the MCF, and the more inequality there will be with the optimal income distribution. Thus, even if we are willing to accept the assumption of identical utility functions and a utilitarian social welfare function, we cannot conclude that the goal of government distributional policy should be to obtain complete equality. The answer depends on the methods used to redistribute income and their effects on people's behaviour.

The Maximin Criterion

The form of the social welfare function plays a crucial role in determining the appropriate governmental redistribution policy. So far, we have examined the utilitarian social welfare function according to which society is indifferent to the distribution of utilities.[9] If a unit of utility (or "util") is taken away from

---

[7] Some studies suggest these costs may be substantial. See Browning (1993) for a study of the marginal cost of redistribution using Canadian data. Research on this topic is still in the formative stage, and there are some unresolved methodological issues. See Dahlby and Ruggeri (1996).

[8] For a formal derivation of this condition, see Sandmo (1991).

[9] Equation (10.2) does not imply that society is indifferent to the distribution of incomes, as was proved in the preceding section.

one individual and given to another, the sum of utilities is unchanged, and by definition, so is social welfare.

Other kinds of social welfare functions do not carry this implication, and hence yield different policy prescriptions. Consider the following social welfare function:

$$W = Minimum(U_1, U_2, \ldots, U_n) \tag{10.4}$$

According to Equation (10.4), social welfare depends only on the utility of the person who has the lowest utility. This social objective is often called the **maximin criterion** because the objective is to maximize the utility of the person with the minimum utility. The maximin criterion implies that the income distribution should be perfectly equal, *except* to the extent that departures from equality increase the welfare of the worst-off person. Consider a society with a rich person, Peter, who employs a poor person, Paul. The government levies a tax on Peter, and distributes the proceeds to Paul. However, when Peter is taxed, he cuts production and fires Paul. Moreover, the income that Paul receives from the government is less than his job-related income loss. In this hypothetical economy, satisfaction of the maximin criterion would still allow for income disparities.

The maximin criterion has received considerable attention, principally because of philosopher John Rawls's (1971) assertion that it has a special claim to ethical validity. Rawls's argument relies on his notion of the **original position,** an imaginary situation in which people have no knowledge of what their place in society is to be. Because of this ignorance as to whether ultimately they will be rich or poor, Rawls believes that in the original position, people's opinions concerning distributional goals are impartial and fair. Rawls then argues that in the original position, people adopt the maximin social welfare function because of the insurance it provides against disastrous outcomes. People are frightened that they may end up at the bottom of the income distribution, and therefore want the level at the bottom as high as possible.

Rawls's analysis is controversial. One important issue is whether decisions that people would make in the hypothetical original position have any superior claim to ethical validity. Why should the amoral and selfish views that individuals have in the original position be given special moral significance? Further, granted Rawls's view on the ethical validity of the original position, it is not obvious that rational self-interest would lead to the maximin criterion. Rawls's decision makers are so averse to risk that they are unwilling to take any chances. However, people might be willing to accept a small probability of being very poor in return for a good chance of receiving a high income.

Finally, critics have noted that the maximin criterion has some peculiar implications. Feldstein (1976: 84) considers the following scenario: "A new opportunity arises to raise the welfare of the least advantaged by a slight amount, but almost everyone else must be made substantially worse off, except for a few individuals who would become extremely wealthy." Because *all* that is relevant is the welfare of the worst-off person, the maximin criterion indicates that society should pursue this opportunity. Intuitively, however, such a course seems unappealing.

Pareto Efficient Income Redistribution

In our discussion of both utilitarian and maximin social welfare functions, we assumed that redistribution makes some people better off and others worse off. Redistribution was never a Pareto improvement—a change that allowed all individuals to be at least as well off as under the status quo. This is a consequence of the assumption that each individual's utility depends on his or her income only. In contrast, imagine that high-income individuals are **altruistic**, so their utilities depend not only on their own incomes, but those of the poor as well. Under such circumstances, redistribution can actually be a Pareto improvement.

Assume that if (rich) Peter were to give a dollar of income to (poor) Paul, then Peter's increase in satisfaction from doing a good deed would outweigh the loss of his own consumption. At the same time, assume that Paul's utility would increase if he received the dollar. Both individuals would be made better off by the transfer. Indeed, efficiency requires that income be redistributed until Peter's gain in utility from giving a dollar to Paul just equals the loss in Peter's utility caused by lower consumption.[10] Suppose that it is difficult for Peter to bring about the income transfer on his own, perhaps because he lacks enough information to know just who is really poor. Then if the government costlessly does the transfer for Peter, efficiency is enhanced. In a formal sense, this is just an externality problem. Paul's behaviour (his consumption) affects Peter's welfare in a way that is external to the market. As usual in such cases, government may be able to increase efficiency.

Pushing this line of reasoning to its logical extreme, the income distribution can be regarded as a public good, because everyone's utility is affected by the degree of inequality.[11] Suppose that each person would feel better off if the income distribution were more equal. No individual acting alone, however, is willing to transfer income to the poor because of the free-rider problem. If the

---

[10] See Hochman and Rodgers (1969).
[11] See Thurow (1971).

government uses its coercive power to force *everyone* who is wealthy to redistribute income to the poor, economic efficiency increases.

Although altruism doubtless plays an important part in human behaviour, it does not follow that altruistic motives explain the majority of government income redistribution programs. This argument *assumes* that in the absence of coercion, people will contribute less than an efficient amount to the poor. Some argue, however, that if people really want to give to the poor, they do so—witness the millions of dollars in charitable contributions made each year.

There are other reasons self-interest might favour income redistribution. For one, there is always some chance that through circumstances beyond your control, you will become poor. An income distribution policy is a bit like insurance. When you are well off, you pay "premiums" in the form of tax payments to those who are currently poor. If bad times hit, the "policy" pays off, and you receive relief. The idea that government should provide a safety net is an old one. The seventeenth-century political philosopher Thomas Hobbes (1963/1651: 303–4) noted, "And whereas many men, by *accident* become unable to maintain themselves by their labour; they ought not to be left to the charity of private persons; but to be provided for, as far forth as the necessities of nature require, by the laws of the Commonwealth" (emphasis added).

In addition, some believe that income distribution programs help purchase social stability. If poor people become *too* poor, they may engage in antisocial activities such as crime and rioting. The link between social stability and changes in income distribution is not totally clear, however. Improvement in the well-being of the poor may increase their aspirations and lead to demands for more radical change.

Nonindividualistic Views

The views of income distribution discussed so far have quite different implications, but they share a common characteristic. In each, social welfare is some function of individuals' utilities, and the properties of the optimal redistribution policy are *derived* from the social welfare function. Some thinkers have approached the problem by specifying what the income distribution should look like independent of individuals' tastes. As Fair (1971: 552) notes, Plato argued that in a good society the ratio of the richest to the poorest person's income should be at the most four to one. Others have suggested that as a first principle, incomes should be distributed equally.[12]

---

[12] This view is considerably stronger than that of Rawls, who allows inequality as long as it raises the welfare of the worst-off individual.

Fairness as a Process

The positions discussed earlier take for granted that individuals' incomes are common property that can be redistributed as "society" sees fit. No attention is given to the fairness of either the processes by which the initial income distribution is determined or of the procedures used to redistribute it. In contrast, some argue that a just distribution of income is defined by the *process* that generated it. For example, many believe that if "equal opportunity" (somehow defined) were available to all, then the ensuing outcome would be fair, *regardless* of the particular income distribution it happened to entail. Hence, if the process generating income is fair, there is no scope for government-sponsored income redistribution.

Arguing along these lines, the philosopher Robert Nozick (1974) has attacked the use of social welfare functions to justify changes in the distribution of income. He argues that how "society" should redistribute its income is a meaningless question because "society" per se has no income to distribute. Only *people* receive income, and the sole possible justification for government redistributive activity is when the pattern of property holdings is somehow improper. Nozick's approach shifts emphasis from the search for a "good" social welfare function to a "good" set of rules to govern society's operation. The problem is how to evaluate social processes. It is hard to judge a process independent of the results generated. If a "good" set of rules consistently generates outcomes that are undesirable, how can the rules be considered good?

An alternative argument against the government undertaking redistribution policies is that, with sufficient social mobility, the distribution of income is of no particular ethical interest. Suppose that those at the bottom of the income distribution (or their children) will occupy higher rungs on the economic ladder in future years. At the same time, some other people will move down, at least in relative terms. Then, even distributional statistics that remain relatively constant over time will conceal quite a bit of churning within the income distribution. Even if people at the bottom are quite poor, it may not be a major social problem if the people who are there change over time. In a study of income mobility in Canada, the Economic Council of Canada (1992) tracked the incomes of a sample of families between 1982 and 1986. They found that "39 percent of those who were in the lowest quintile in 1982 had climbed to a higher quintile by 1986. Conversely, 40 percent of those who were in the lowest quintile in 1986 had dropped down from the higher quintile they occupied in 1982" (p. 13). There was also evidence of mobility among high-income groups. Over 30 percent of those who were in the top quintile of the income distribution in 1982 had moved into a lower quintile by 1986 (Economic Council of Canada, 1992: Figure 7, p. 14). However, while there is evidently considerable income mobility in Canada, it is probably not enough to convince most observers that income inequality is unimportant.

CASH VERSUS IN-KIND TRANSFERS

To this point, it has been assumed that cash transfers are made to the poor. However, many transfer programs, such as public housing, involve either the provision or the subsidization of a specific commodity. In addition, many people support public education and health care programs because they think that these programs result in a more equitable distribution of well-being in our society. We will begin by considering the relative merits of cash and in-kind transfers when a society respects the preferences of the poor and there is no uncertainty about who deserves a transfer.

Suppose Jones has income equal to Y. Let H be the quantity of housing consumed, measured in square metres, and p_H be the rental price for housing in dollars per square metre. The maximum amount of housing that Jones can consume is Y/p_H. Let C denote Jones's expenditure on the consumption of all other goods. In Figure 10.5, her budget line is AB, and she obtains the maximum utility by consuming H_1 units of housing and spending C_1 on all other goods. Jones is considered to be poor and deserving of a transfer. Suppose the government subsidizes Jones's consumption of housing by paying a fraction, s, of her total rent. This program would reduce the effective price of housing for Jones to $(1 - s)p_H$, and she would now maximize her utility by choosing the H and C combination at point E_2 on her new budget line AB'. As a result of the housing subsidy, her consumption of housing would increase from H_1 to H_2 and her expenditure on all other goods would increase from C_1 to C_2. (These changes mean that her demand curve for housing has a negative slope and that the price elasticity of her housing demand is less than one. Our results do not depend on these assumptions.) In the absence of the subsidy, if Jones had consumed H_2, she would only have been able to spend C'_2 on other goods. The fact that she can purchase C_2 instead of C'_2 means that the government is providing her with the additional purchasing power $C_2 - C'_2$. Therefore, the total cost of the housing subsidy to the government is equal to $C_2 - C'_2$ or equivalently the vertical distance X.

Now suppose that instead of the housing subsidy, the government gave her the equivalent lump-sum cash subsidy X. This would increase her total income to $Y + X$, and her new budget line would be ZZ'. Note that this budget line will also go through the point E_2, but it is steeper than AB' because it reflects the full price of housing rather than the subsidized price. As a consequence, the budget line ZZ' intersects the indifference curve I_2 at E_2. It is not tangent to I_2.

Figure 10.5

Cash versus In-kind Transfers

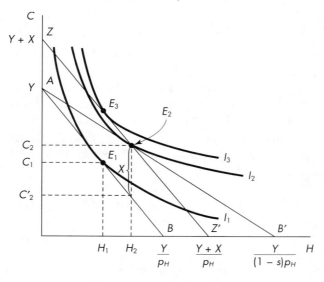

Jones's preferred combination on ZZ' will be at a point such as E_3 where the budget line is tangent to the indifference curve I_3. Note that E_3 will always be to the left of E_2, and I_3 will always lie above I_2. Therefore, Jones is *better off* with the lump-sum subsidy of X dollar than she would be with a housing subsidy that also costs X dollars. This suggests that, for a given total expenditure, the poor should be given a cash transfer rather than an in-kind transfer if society wants to improve the well-being of the poor by the maximum amount. Another problem with in-kind transfer programs is that they may involve higher administrative costs than an equivalent cash transfer. Blanchard et al. (1982: ii) estimated that administrative costs of the U.S. food stamp program could be reduced by about 36 percent if beneficiaries simply received cheques instead of coupons redeemable for food.

If cash transfers are superior to in-kind transfers, why are in-kind transfers widely used? Why are medicare and public education frequently viewed as appropriate tools for redistributing income?

Asymmetric Information

We will begin by considering the effect of imperfect information on the instruments that governments' use to improve the well-being of the poor. A government may have difficulty in distinguishing the "truly needy" who deserve a cash transfer from others who might try to take advantage of a cash transfer program by pretending to be needy. In these cases, an in-kind transfer may help to screen the truly needy from the pretenders. The following model, which is based on Blackorby and Donaldson (1988), illustrates how in-kind transfers can serve this purpose.

Suppose that a society consists of two individuals—Able who is physically fit and Bacchus who has a back problem. For simplicity, it is assumed that the marginal utility of consumption is constant and equal to one for both individuals. If both individuals have the same income, Able has a higher level of utility than Bacchus because Able can enjoy more physical activities than Bacchus. If Bacchus receives physiotherapy treatments, he can enjoy a wider range of physical activities and attain a higher level of utility. The individuals' utility functions are given below:

$$U_A = C_A + H \qquad\qquad (10.5)$$

$$U_B = C_B + h \cdot T \qquad\qquad (10.6)$$

where C_A is Able's consumption of goods. H is the dollar value that Able attaches to being healthy, and it is the amount of money that Able would be prepared to spend to stay physically active. C_B is Bacchus's consumption of goods. T is the expenditure on Bacchus's therapy, and h is the marginal utility of a dollar spent on therapy. It is assumed that h is constant, but less than one. In other words, therapy improves Bacchus's well-being, but he would rather spend an additional dollar on consumption because the marginal utility of consumption is one. Let the total value of resources available to this society be R. It is assumed that R is fixed and that transferring income between the two individuals does not affect the amount of resources that are available, i.e., there are no disincentive effects from taxes and transfers. The available resources can either be used to provide consumption for Able, consumption for Bacchus, or therapy for Bacchus. (Since Able does not have a bad back, he would never want to have therapy.) Therefore $R = C_A + C_B + T$.

If society can identify those who have a bad back, it can give different lump-sum transfers to Able and Bacchus. The society's utility possibilities curve is the line $\alpha\delta$ shown in Figure 10.6. (Recall from Chapter 4 that the utility possibilities curve shows the maximum utility that one individual can obtain for any given utility level obtained by the other individual.) Along the utility possibilities curve $\alpha\delta$, no resources are devoted to therapy because, given our assumption that h is less than one, providing Bacchus with a dollar of therapy is an inefficient way of raising Bacchus's utility. He would be better off with another

Figure 10.6

Cash and In-kind Transfers under Asymmetric Information

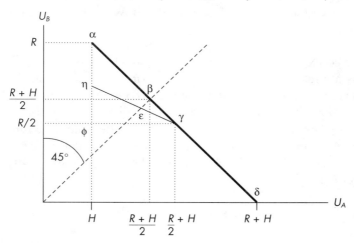

dollar of income, which he would spend on the consumption of goods. Some particular points on the utility possibilities curve can be discerned. At α, all of the society's resources are used for Bacchus's consumption, and therefore $U_B = R$ and $U_A = H$. At β, where the two individuals have the same utility level, Bacchus's income, $(R + H)/2$, exceeds Able's income, $(R - H)/2$, by the amount H. In other words, we equalize their utility levels by giving them unequal incomes. At γ, both individuals receive the same income, $R/2$, but Able has a higher level of utility than Bacchus because he has good health. At δ, all of the society's resources are devoted to Able's consumption. The preferred distribution of income will depend on the ethical preferences that are used to evaluate distributional issues. For example, given that there are no disincentive effects from income transfers and that the marginal utility of consumption is constant and the same for both individuals, a Rawlsian would choose the equal utility level at β, whereas a utilitarian would be indifferent as to how income was distributed. For a utilitarian, all points on $\alpha\delta$ are equally desirable because it has been assumed that the marginal utility of consumption is a constant and the same for both individuals. The key point, however, is that regardless of the ethical preferences, cash transfers would be used for redistribution and an in-kind transfer—therapy—would not be used.

Now suppose that we cannot distinguish between someone who has a bad back and someone who pretends to have a bad back. If income transfers were based on whether an individual had a bad back, Able would pretend to have a bad back if it meant that he would receive a higher income. Consequently, the maximum income that Bacchus can receive is $R/2$, the equal income point. We can't raise Bacchus's cash income above $R/2$ because then Able would pretend to have back pain so that he would qualify for a higher income, and this society does not have enough resources to provide both individuals with incomes in excess of $R/2$. On the other hand, Bacchus cannot pretend to be Able, and therefore society could provide Able with more income than Bacchus. This means that, given the asymmetric information problem, the society's utility possibilities curve is $\phi\gamma\delta$ if only lump-sum income transfers are used for redistribution.

Is it possible to raise Bacchus's utility level above $R/2$ by providing him with an in-kind transfer, in this case therapy? The answer is yes as long as a dollar spent on therapy raises Bacchus's utility by more than 0.5. To see this, suppose that, starting at the point γ, we reduce each individual's income by \$0.50 and use the dollar to provide Bacchus with therapy free of charge. While Bacchus's consumption is reduced by 0.5, which reduces his utility by 0.5, he will be better off as long as the marginal utility from therapy, h, exceeds 0.5.[13] In Figure 10.6, it is assumed that $0.5 < h < 1$, and the line $\eta\gamma$, which has a slope of $1 - 2h$, shows the utility combinations that can be achieved by providing an in-kind transfer, therapy, to anyone with back pain. The utility combinations along $\eta\gamma$ cannot be achieved without the in-kind transfer, and the points along $\eta\gamma$ are Pareto optimal. The preferred point on the utilities possibilities curve $\eta\gamma\delta$ will depend on one's ethical preferences. A utilitarian would continue to prefer any allocation along $\gamma\delta$, whereas a Rawlsian would prefer the equal utility combination at ε where H/h is spent on therapy.[14] The key point is that, with asymmetric information, in-kind transfers may be an efficient policy tool.

Commodity Egalitarianism

Tobin (1970) has suggested that only certain commodities should be distributed equally, a position sometimes called **commodity egalitarianism**. In some cases, this view has considerable appeal. Most people believe that the right to vote should be distributed equally to all, as should the consumption of certain essential foodstuffs during times of war. Other types of commodity egalitarianism are more controversial. Should all Canadian children consume the same quality of primary school education? Should everyone receive the same type of

---

[13] More generally, the expenditure on therapy will raise the utility of individuals with back pain as long as h is greater than the fraction of the population with back pain.
[14] If utility is equalized, $C_A + H = C_B + hT$. Along $\eta\gamma$, the individuals have equal incomes so that $C_A = C_B$. Therefore, hT will equal H at ε. In other words, at ε the individuals will have the same consumption of goods and the same health status.

health care, or should the rich be able to purchase better quality care? Clearly, limiting the range of the "special" commodities is a difficult problem.

Paternalism

A paternalistic attitude toward the poor, a position that in some cases resembles commodity egalitarianism, can provide a rationale for in-kind transfers within the framework of conventional welfare economics. Assume that Henry cares about Catherine's welfare. Specifically, Henry's utility depends on his own income as well as Catherine's level of *food consumption*, as opposed to her *income*. (This might be due to the fact that Henry does not approve of the other commodities Catherine might consume.) In effect, then, Catherine's food consumption generates a positive externality. Following the logic developed in Chapter 8 on externalities, efficiency may be enhanced if Catherine's food consumption is subsidized, or perhaps if food is provided to her directly. In short, when donors care about recipients' consumption of certain commodities, a policy of redistributing income via these commodities can be viewed as an attempt to correct an externality.

In-kind transfers may also be attractive politically because they help not only the beneficiary, but also the producers of the favoured commodity. A transfer program that increases the demand for housing benefits the building industry, which therefore becomes willing to lend its support to a political coalition in favour of the program. In the same way, the public employees who administer the various in-kind transfer programs can be expected to put their political support behind them. These explanations for in-kind transfers are not mutually exclusive, and they probably have all influenced policy design.

OVERVIEW

We began by surveying a wide range of opinions concerning whether the government should adopt explicit policies to redistribute income. The views run the gamut from engineering complete equality to doing nothing. The scope of disagreement is not surprising. Setting a distributional objective is no less than formalizing one's views of what a good society should look like, and this is bound to be controversial. Theories on optimal income distribution are normative rather than positive. Actual government redistributive policies may be guided by a number of these considerations, but it is not obvious that this is the case. As we see, finding a coherent explanation of Canadian income distribution practices is not easy.

We also stressed the difficulties involved in measuring income accurately and in defining the appropriate time period over which it should be measured.

Many important types of income are ignored because of measurement difficulties. Transfers often take the form of in-kind payments on which it is difficult to put a dollar value. There is a widely held view among economists that in-kind transfers are less efficient than cash transfers, but in-kind transfers may be efficient policy instruments if it is difficult to identify the needy or if one does not accept the individuals' preferences as the basis for making transfers.

SUMMARY

- Economists analyze distributional issues to determine the consequences of alternative distributional policies and to draw out the implications of various ethical goals.

- If (1) social welfare is the sum of identical utility functions that depend only on income; (2) there is decreasing marginal utility of income; and (3) the total amount of income is fixed; then income should be equally distributed. These are quite strong assumptions, and weakening them gives radically different results.

- The maximin criterion states that the best income distribution maximizes the utility of the person who has the lowest utility. The ethical validity of this proposition is controversial.

- The income distribution may be like a public good—everyone derives utility from the fact that income is equitably distributed, but government coercion is needed to accomplish redistribution. Pareto efficient redistribution occurs when no one is made worse off as a result of a transfer.

- Other views of income distribution do not follow the utilitarian framework. Some believe it is a first principle that income, or at least certain goods, be distributed equally. Others argue that the distribution of income is irrelevant as long as the distribution arises from a "fair" process.

- Income is hard to measure correctly. Some forms of income, such as capital gains and the implicit rental income from owner-occupied housing, are not included in the official statistics. Moreover, it is not clear what time period—month, year, lifetime—or what unit of observation—individual, household, family—is appropriate.

- Many government programs provide goods and services (in-kind transfers) instead of cash. The value of the in-kind transfer to the recipient will often be less than the market price.

- The prevalence of in-kind transfer programs may be due to asymmetric information, paternalism, commodity egalitarianism, administrative feasibility, or political attractiveness.

DISCUSSION QUESTIONS

1. Are the concepts of fairness and equality in the distribution of income synonymous? To what extent is income inequality consistent with fairness? What are the implications of your answer for government expenditure policy?

2. Suppose there are only two people, Simon and Charity, who must split a fixed income of $100. For Simon, the marginal utility of income is:

$$MUs = 400 - 2Is$$

while for Charity, marginal utility is:

$$MUc = 400 - 6Ic$$

where Ic, Is are the amounts of income to Charity and Simon, respectively.

   a. What is the optimal distribution of income if the social welfare function is additive?
   b. What is the optimal distribution if society values only the utility of Charity? What if the reverse is true? Comment on your answers.
   c. Finally, comment on how your answers change if the marginal utility of income for both Simon and Charity is constant:

$$MUc = 400$$

$$MUs = 400$$

3. "Mobility should play a bigger role in our thinking about poverty. The current standard, preoccupied with income snapshots, only echoes the current welfare formula, with its emphasis on supporting people in poverty rather than helping them to get out" (Jenkins, 1992: A10). Do you agree with this statement? In your answer, discuss how the quote relates to utilitarian criteria for evaluating government distributional problems and to the difficulties present in official statistics on the poverty rate.

4. Suppose that the government requires employers to provide day care centres for their workers. Suppose further that the market value of the day care centre provided by a particular employer is $5,000 per year. Can we conclude that an employee who takes advantage of the day care centre is better off by $5,000 per year? (Hint: Analyze a model in which the individual chooses between two commodities, "hours of day care" and "all other goods.")

5. Consider the following government programs. How might each program affect the distribution of income?

   a. Subsidies to biotechnology firms.
   b. Purchase of helicopters for the Air Force.

6. Philip's demand curve for housing is shown in the figure below. (Assume that quantity of housing is measured simply by the number of square metres. Other aspects of quality are ignored.) The market price of housing is P_1; Philip can purchase as much housing as he desires at that price. Alternatively, Philip can live in public housing for a price of P_2 per square metre, but the only apartment available to him has H_2 square metres. Will Philip choose public housing or rent on the private market? Explain carefully. (Hint: Compare consumer surplus—see the appendix to Chapter 4—under both possibilities.)

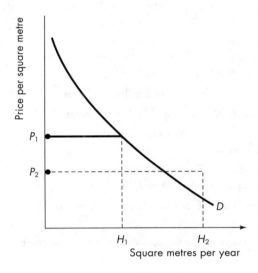

REFERENCES

Atkinson, A.B. *The Economics of Inequality.* Oxford: Oxford University Press, 1983.

Beach, Charles M., and George A. Slotsve. *Are We Becoming Two Societies?: Income Polarization and the Middle Class in Canada.* Toronto: C.D. Howe Institute, 1996.

Blackorby, C., and D. Donaldson. "Cash Versus Kind, Self-Selection, and Efficient Transfers." *American Economic Review* 78 (1988): 691–700.

Blanchard, Lois, J.S. Butler, T. Doyle, R. Jackson, J. Ohls, and Barbara Posner. *Final Report, Food Stamp SSI/Elderly Cash-out Demonstration Evaluation.* Princeton, NJ: Mathematica Policy Research, 1982.

Browning, Edgar K. "The Marginal Cost of Redistribution." *Public Finance Quarterly* 21 (1993): 3–32.

Dahlby, Bev G., and Guiseppe C. Ruggeri. "The Marginal Cost of Redistribution: Comment." *Public Finance Quarterly* 24 (1996): 44–62.

Economic Council of Canada. *The New Face of Poverty: Income Security Needs of Canadian Families.* Ottawa: Ministry of Supply and Services Canada, 1992.

Fair, Ray C. "The Optimal Distribution of Income." *Quarterly Journal of Economics* 85 (1971): 551–79.

Feldstein, Martin S. "On the Theory of Tax Reform." *Journal of Public Economics* 6 (1976): 77–104.

Hobbes, Thomas. *Leviathan.* New York: Meridian Books, 1963 (1651).

Hochman, H.M., and J.D. Rodgers. "Pareto Optimal Redistribution." *American Economic Review* 59 (1969): 542–57.

Jenkins, Holman, Jr. "The 'Poverty' Lobby's Inflated Numbers." *The Wall Street Journal,* December 14, 1992, p. A10.

Kristal, Irving. "Some Personal Reflections on Economic Well-Being and Income Distribution," in *The American Economy in Transition,* ed. Martin Feldstein. Chicago: University of Chicago Press, 1980, pp. 479–86.

Nozick, Robert. *Anarchy, State, and Utopia.* Oxford: Basil Blackwell, 1974.

Rawls, John. *A Theory of Justice.* Cambridge, MA: Harvard University Press, 1971.

Ross, David. *The Canadian Fact Book on Income Distribution.* Toronto: Canadian Council on Social Development, 1980.

Ross, D., E.R. Shillington, and C. Lochhead. *The Canadian Fact Book on Poverty.* Toronto: Canadian Council on Social Development, 1994.

Sandmo, A. "Economists and the Welfare State." *European Economic Review* 35 (1991): 213–39.

Statistics Canada. *Income Distributions by Size in Canada, 1995.* Ottawa, December 1996.

Thurow, Lester C. "The Income Distribution as a Pure Public Good." *Quarterly Journal of Economics* (May 1971): 327–36.

Tobin, James. "On Limiting the Domain of Inequality." *Journal of Law and Economics* 13 (1970): 263–77.

Chapter 11

Public Choice

Monarchy is like a sleek craft, it sails along well until some bumbling captain runs it into the rocks: democracy, on the other hand, is like a raft. It never goes down but, dammit, your feet are always wet.

—Fisher Ames

*T*extbook discussions of market failures and their remedies tend to convey a rather rosy view of government. With a tax here, an expenditure there, the state readily corrects all market imperfections, meanwhile seeing to it that incomes are distributed in an ethically desirable way. Such a view is at variance with apparent widespread public dissatisfaction with government performance. In a 1990 opinion poll, 70 percent of Canadians agreed with the statement "I don't think that the government cares much what people like me think," and 82 percent agreed with the statement that "most candidates in federal elections make campaign promises they have no intention of fulfilling."[1] Humorist P.J. O'Rourke probably summarized the sentiments of many when he quipped, "Giving money and power to government is like giving whiskey and car keys to teenage boys."

Perhaps this is merely gratuitous whining. As a matter of definition, in a democracy we get the government we want. Another possibility, however, is that it is inherently difficult for even democratically elected governments to respond to the public interest. This chapter discusses and evaluates various mechanisms for making public choices. At the outset, we examine direct democracies and how well they translate the preferences of their members into

---

[1] Blais and Gidengil (1991: 35).

collective action. We then turn to the complications that arise when decisions are made not by individuals themselves, but by their elected representatives.

DIRECT DEMOCRACY

In democratic societies, various voting procedures are used to decide what quantities of public goods to provide. This section looks at some of these procedures.

Unanimity Rules

The irony of the free-rider problem is that everyone could be better off if the public good were provided efficiently, but because people act in their narrow self-interest, not enough is provided. This suggests that in principle, if a vote were taken on whether to provide the good in an efficient quantity, consent would be unanimous as long as there was a suitable tax system to finance it. A procedure designed to elicit such unanimous agreement was proposed in the early twentieth century by Lindahl (1919/1958).

To understand Lindahl's procedure, assume again there are two individuals, Adam and Eve, and one public good, rockets for fireworks (r). Suppose Adam is told that his share of the cost of rocket provision will be 30 percent. Then if the market price per rocket is P_r, Adam's price per rocket is $.30 \times P_r$. Given this price, the prices of other goods, his tastes, and his income, there is some quantity of rockets that Adam will want to consume. More generally, let S^A denote Adam's share of the cost of rocket provision. For any particular value of S^A, Adam demands some quantity of rockets. As his tax share increases and rockets become more expensive for him, he demands a smaller quantity.

In Figure 11.1, the horizontal axis measures the quantity of rockets. Adam's tax share is measured by the vertical distance from point O. The curve D_r^A shows how the quantity of rockets demanded by Adam decreases as his tax share increases.

In the same way, define S^E as Eve's share of the cost of rockets. (By definition, $S^A + S^E = 1$.) When S^E goes up, the quantity demanded by Eve decreases. In Figure 11.1, Eve's tax share increases as we move down along the vertical axis from O'. (Thus, the distance OO' is 1.) Her demand schedule is denoted D_r^E. It slopes upward because upward movements along the vertical axis represent a lower price to her.

An obvious similarity exists between the role of tax shares in the Lindahl model and market prices in the usual theory of demand. But there is an important difference. Instead of each individual facing the same price, each faces a

Figure 11.1

Lindahl's Model

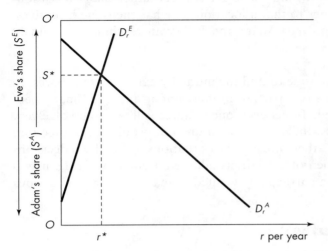

personalized price per unit of public good, which depends on his or her tax share. The tax shares are referred to as **Lindahl prices.**

An equilibrium is a set of Lindahl prices such that at those prices each person votes for the same quantity of the public good. In Figure 11.1, this occurs when Adam's tax share is $OS*$ and Eve's tax share is $O'S*$. At these Lindahl prices, both parties agree that $r*$ rockets should be provided.

Feasibility of unanimity rules. The Lindahl model shows the tax shares and level of public good provision that are agreeable to all members of society. The big question is how the economy reaches the equilibrium. Imagine that an auctioneer announces some initial set of tax shares. On the basis of their respective demand schedules, Adam and Eve vote for the number of rockets they want. If agreement is not unanimous, the auctioneer announces another set of tax shares. The process continues until Adam and Eve unanimously agree on the quantity of rockets ($r*$, in Figure 11.1). The determination of the quantity of public goods, then, is quite similar to the market process. Like the market outcome, it can be shown that the allocation is Pareto efficient.[2]

---

[2] Intuitively, assume $P_r = 1$. Then Eve sets $S^E P_r = MRS_{ra}^{Eve}$, and Adam sets $S^A P_r = MRS_{ra}^{Adam}$. Therefore, $MRS_{ra}^{Eve} + MRS_{ra}^{Adam} = S^E P_r + S^A P_r = P_r(S^E + S^A) = P_r$. But P_r represents MRT_{ra}, so $MRS_{ra}^{Eve} + MRS_{ra}^{Adam} = MRT_{ra}$, which is the necessary condition for Pareto efficiency of Equation (7.2). For further details, see Mueller (1989).

As a practical method for providing public goods, Lindahl's procedure has two main problems. First, it assumes people vote sincerely. If Adam can guess the maximum amount that Eve would spend for rockets rather than do without them, he can try to force her to that allocation. Eve has the same incentives. Strategic behaviour may prevent Adam and Eve from reaching the Lindahl equilibrium.

Second, it may take a lot of time to find the mutually agreeable tax shares. In this example, there are only two parties. In most important cases, many people are likely to be involved. To get everyone to agree is likely to involve very high decision-making costs. Indeed, although unanimity rules guarantee that no one will be "exploited," they often lead to situations in which *no* decisions are made. Historically, when organizations adopted a unanimity rule, it was often expressly because the participants wanted to make sure that no actions were taken![3]

Majority Voting Rules

Unanimity is clearly difficult to attain. As a result, voting systems not requiring unanimity may be desirable. With a **majority voting rule**, one more than half of the voters must favour a measure for it to be approved.

Although the mechanics of majority voting are familiar, it is useful to review them carefully. Consider a community with three voters, Denise, Rudy, and Theo, who have to choose among three levels of missile provision, A, B, and C. Level A is small, level B is moderate, and level C is large. The voters' preferences are depicted in Table 11.1. Each column shows how the voter ranks the choices. For example, Rudy most prefers level C, but given a choice between B and A, would prefer B.

Suppose an election were held on whether to adopt A or B. Denise would vote for A, while Rudy and Theo would vote for B. Hence, B would win by a vote of 2 to 1. Similarly, if an election were held between B and C, B would win by a vote of 2 to 1. Level B wins any election against its opposition, and thus is the option selected by majority rule. Note that the selection of B is independent of the order in which the votes are taken.

[3] In seventeenth-century Poland, the structure of government was essentially feudal. None of the nobles wanted to lose any power to the monarch. Hence, the monarch had to promise to take no action unless he received the unanimous consent of the Polish parliament (see Massie, 1980: 228).

Table 11.1

Voter Preferences that Lead to an Equilibrium

	VOTER		
CHOICE	DENISE	RUDY	THEO
First	A	C	B
Second	B	B	C
Third	C	A	A

Majority decision rules do not always yield such clear-cut results. Suppose the preferences for various levels of missile provision are as depicted in Table 11.2. Again, imagine a series of paired elections to determine the most preferred level. In an election between A and B, A would win by a vote of 2 to 1. If an election were held between B and C, B would win by a vote of 2 to 1. Finally, in an election between A and C, C would win by the same margin. This is a disconcerting result. The first election suggests that A is preferred to B; the second that B is preferred to C. Conventional notions of consistency suggest that A should therefore be preferred to C. But in the third election, just the opposite occurs. Although each individual voter's preferences are consistent, the community's are not. This phenomenon is referred to as the **voting paradox**.

Moreover, with the preferences in Table 11.2, the ultimate outcome depends crucially on the order in which the votes are taken. If the first election is between propositions A and B and the winner (A) runs against C, then C is the ultimate choice. On the other hand, if the first election is B versus C, and the winner (B) runs against A, then A is chosen. Under such circumstances, the ability to control the order of voting—the agenda—confers great power. **Agenda manipulation** is the process of organizing the order of votes to assure a favourable outcome.

Table 11.2

Voter Preferences that Lead to Cycling

	VOTER		
CHOICE	DENISE	RUDY	THEO
First	A	C	B
Second	B	A	C
Third	C	B	A

A related problem is that paired voting can go on forever without reaching a decision. After the election between *A* and *B*, *A* wins. If *C* challenges *A*, then *C* wins. If *B* then challenges *C*, *B* wins. The process can continue indefinitely, a phenomenon called **cycling**. Many important historical cases of cycling have been identified. A good example concerns the seventeenth amendment to the U.S. Constitution, which provides for direct election of U.S. senators. Adoption "was delayed for 10 years by parliamentary maneuvers that depended on voting cycles involving the status quo (the appointment of senators by the state legislature) and two versions of the amendment" (Blair and Pollak, 1983: 88).

Clearly, the majority rule does not have to suffer from these problems. After all, the elections associated with Table 11.1 went smoothly. Why the difference? It turns on the structure of individual preferences for various levels of missile procurement. Consider again the people in Table 11.2. Because Denise prefers *A* to *B* to *C*, it follows that *A* gives Denise more utility than *B*, and *B* more than *C*. The schedule denoted Denise in Figure 11.2 depicts this relationship. The schedules labelled Rudy and Theo do the same for the other voters.

We define a **peak** in an individual's preferences as a point at which all the neighbouring points are lower.[4] A voter has **single-peaked preferences** if, as she

Figure 11.2

Graphing the Preferences from Table 11.2

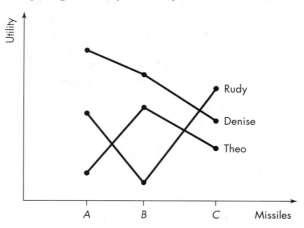

---

[4] For this analysis, the absolute amount of utility associated with each alternative is irrelevant. The vertical distances could change, but as long as the pattern of peaks stays unchanged, so does the outcome of the election.

moves away from her most preferred outcome in any and all directions, her utility consistently falls. She has **double-peaked preferences** if, as she moves away from the most preferred outcome, utility goes down, but then goes up again. Thus, Denise has a single peak at point *A*; Theo has a single peak at point *B*; and Rudy has two peaks, one at *A* and one at *C*. It turns out that Rudy's preferences are the ones that lead to the voting paradox. If Rudy had *any* set of single-peaked preferences, majority voting would lead to a consistent decision. This is why no voting paradox emerges from Table 11.1. There, each voter has single-peaked preferences. More generally, if all voters' preferences are single peaked, no voting paradox occurs.

Because multipeaked preferences can throw a wrench into majority voting, it is important to know whether they are likely to be important as a practical matter. Consider again Rudy in Table 11.2, whose preferences have two peaks. She prefers either very large or very small missile expenditures to a quantity in the middle. Although such preferences are not necessarily irrational, they do seem a bit peculiar.[5]

Suppose, however, that instead of missiles, voters are choosing among expenditure levels for a public park—a good for which there are private substitutes. Assume that in the presence of small or medium public park expenditures, voter Smith will join a private country club, but given large expenditures, he will use the public park. Provided that Smith's tax burden increases with park expenditure, he prefers a small to a medium park—since neither of these options benefits Smith, he prefers the one with the smaller tax burden. But his most preferred outcome might be the large-expenditure public park. (This depends in part on the associated tax burden compared to the country club membership fee.) In short, Smith may prefer either the small or large public park to the medium-sized one. Thus, when there are private substitutes for a publicly provided good, a multipeaked pattern like Rudy's in Figure 11.2 can easily emerge.

Moreover, when issues are not based on a single dimension, multipeaked preferences are also a serious possibility.[6] Suppose that a community is trying to decide how to use a vacant building. Choice *A* is an abortion clinic, choice *B* is an adult book store, and choice *C* is an armed forces recruitment office. Unlike the choice between different levels of missile expenditure, here the alter-

---

[5] Perhaps Rudy believes that moderate numbers of missiles will provide little if any real protection, so that unless expenditures are large, they might as well be close to nothing.
[6] Atkinson and Stiglitz (1980: 306) explain how the notion of a "peak" is generalized to a multidimensional setting.

natives do not represent more or less of a single characteristic. It is easy to imagine multipeaked preferences emerging.

The median voter theorem. Let us now return to the simple case in which all alternatives being considered represent smaller or greater amounts of a single characteristic. People rank each alternative on the basis of this single characteristic. An example is how much of some public good to acquire. Define the **median voter** as the voter whose preferences lie in the middle of the set of all voters' preferences; half the voters want more of the good than the median voter, and half want less. The **median voter theorem** states that as long as all preferences are single peaked, the outcome of majority voting reflects the preferences of the median voter.[7]

To demonstrate the median voter theorem, assume there are five voters: Donald, Daisy, Huey, Dewey, and Louie. They are deciding how large a party to give together, and each of them has single-peaked preferences for party sizes. The most preferred level for each voter is noted in Table 11.3. *Because preferences are single peaked,* the closer an expenditure level is to a given voter's peak, the more he or she prefers it. A movement from zero party expenditure to $5 would be preferred to no money for parties by all voters. A movement from $5 to $100 would be approved by Daisy, Huey, Dewey, and Louie, and from $100 to $150 by Huey, Dewey, and Louie. Any increase beyond $150, however, would be blocked by at least three voters: Donald, Daisy, and Huey. Hence, the majority votes for $150. But this is just the amount preferred by Huey, the median voter. The election results mirror the median voter's preferences.

To summarize: When all preferences are single peaked, majority voting yields a stable result, and the choice selected reflects the preferences of the median

Table 11.3

Preferred Level of Party Expenditure

VOTER	EXPENDITURE
Donald	$ 5
Daisy	100
Huey	150
Dewey	160
Louie	700

[7] See Mueller (1989). With an even number of voters, there may be a tie between two median voters, which must be broken arbitrarily.

voter. However, when all voters' preferences are not single peaked, a voting paradox may emerge.[8] Because multipeaked preferences may be important in many realistic situations, majority voting cannot be depended on to yield consistent public choices. Moreover, as we shall see below, even when majority voting leads to consistent decisions, it may not be efficient in the sense that overall benefits exceed costs.

Econometric application of the median voter theorem. Despite its imperfections, the median voter theorem provides a useful framework for empirical investigation of the demand for public goods. Assume each community's preferences for public goods coincide with the preferences of its median voter. Suppose that for a sample of communities we have data on the quantity of public goods (G), the relative price per unit of public good (P), and the median voter's income (I). Then by examining how G depends on P and I, we can compute the demand curve for public goods. Specifically, we can estimate a regression equation in which the quantity of some public good, G, is the dependent variable, and P and I appear as explanatory variables. The responsiveness of public goods demand to changes in price and income can then be inferred from the coefficients on P and I, respectively.[9]

Several problems arise in implementing this procedure. First, standard data sources do not reveal the identity of the voter with median preferences for the public good; hence, we do not know his or her income. The typical procedure is to assume that the median income in the community is also the income of the median voter. While in many cases this is probably a good assumption, it need not always be correct. To see why, suppose that poor people have a relatively low demand for *public* education, and that as income increases, the demand goes up. However, suppose further that as people's incomes become very high, they choose to send their children to private schools, so the demand for public education falls with income. Thus, both high- and low-income people have relatively low demands for education, and the demand for public education by the person with median income might exceed the demand of the person with median preferences for education.

A second problem is measuring the price of the public good. Think of P as the median voter's cost of purchasing an additional unit of G. This depends on the

---

[8] The presence of one or more voters with multipeaked preferences does not *necessarily* lead to a voting paradox. It depends on the number of voters and the structure of their preferences. See Discussion Question 1 at the end of this chapter.

[9] It is necessary to include on the right-hand side variables that might affect the community's tastes for public goods. For example, the size of the school-aged population influences preferences for education.

resource cost of purchasing an additional unit of G, and the share of the cost that must be paid by the median voter. The share, in turn, depends on how taxes are raised in the community. For example, assume that all community revenues are raised by proportional taxes on housing. Thus, if the median voter's house is worth V and the tax rate is t, then the tax liability is tV. The median voter's share of total community taxes is $tV/t\Sigma V$ where ΣV is the total value of all houses in the community. Because the t's divide out, the median voter's share of the resource cost is simply the value of his or her house relative to the value of all houses in the community. Thus, information on the tax system together with data on the community's resource cost for public goods can be used to construct P.

Many econometric studies have used this framework. The demands for education, hospitals, parks, police protection, and public works have been analyzed. Naturally, the results differ depending on the particular item being studied. In general, however, both the implied income and price elasticities tend to be small. For example, in his survey of results on the demand for education, Rubinfeld (1987) reports that most studies find income elasticities that are less than one, and price elasticities in the range of -0.2 to -0.4. Thus, demands for education (as well as most other public goods) are relatively unresponsive to changes in their prices. Such results are helpful in answering a number of policy questions, such as how the provision of local public goods might change if their prices were subsidized by the federal government.

Logrolling

A possible problem with simple majority voting is that it does not allow people to register how strongly they feel about the issues. Whether a particular voter just barely prefers A to B or has an enormous preference for A has no influence on the outcome. **Logrolling** systems allow people to trade votes and hence register how strongly they feel about various issues. Suppose that voters Smith and Jones prefer not to have more missiles, but this preference is not strongly felt. Brown, on the other hand, definitely wants more missiles. With a logrolling system, Brown may be able to convince Jones to vote for more missiles if Brown promises to vote for a new road to go by Jones's factory.

Vote trading is controversial. Its proponents argue that trading votes leads to efficient provision of public goods, just as trading commodities leads to efficient provision of private goods. Proponents also emphasize its potential for revealing the intensity of preferences and establishing a stable equilibrium. Moreover, the compromises implicit in vote trading are necessary for a democratic system to function. As the English statesman Edmund Burke noted, "All government—indeed, every human benefit and enjoyment, every virtue and every prudent act—is founded on compromise and barter." (Married readers will believe this!)

A numerical example helps illustrate these advantages of logrolling. Suppose a community is considering three projects, a hospital, a library, and a swimming pool. The community has three voters, Melanie, Rhett, and Scarlet. Table 11.4 shows their benefits for each project. (A minus sign indicates a net loss; that is, the costs exceed the benefits.)

The first thing to notice about the table is that the total net benefit for each project is positive. Thus, by definition, the community as a whole would be better off if each project were adopted.[10] But what would happen if the projects were voted on *one at a time?* Melanie would vote for the hospital because her net benefit is positive, but Rhett and Scarlet would vote against it because their benefits are negative. The hospital would therefore lose. Similarly, the library and the swimming pool would go down in defeat.

Vote trading can remedy this situation. Suppose Melanie agrees to vote for the library if Rhett consents to vote for the hospital. Melanie comes out ahead by 160 (= 200 – 40) with such a trade; Rhett comes out ahead by 100 (= 150 – 50). They therefore strike the deal, and the hospital and library pass. In the same way, Melanie and Scarlet can make a deal in which Melanie's support for the pool is given in return for Scarlet's vote for the hospital. Thus, logrolling allows all three measures to pass, a desirable outcome.

On the other hand, opponents of logrolling stress it is likely to result in special-interest gains not sufficient to outweigh general losses. Large amounts of waste can be incurred. For example, Allan MacEachen was able to get an oil

Table 11.4

Logrolling Can Improve Welfare

PROJECT	VOTER			TOTAL NET BENEFITS
	MELANIE	RHETT	SCARLET	
Hospital	200	–50	–55	95
Library	–40	150	–30	80
Pool	–120	–60	400	220

[10] We assume the absence of externalities or any other considerations that would make private costs and benefits unequal to their social counterparts.

refinery and a heavy water plant located in his home province of Nova Scotia through collecting political IOUs during his time as House Leader for the Trudeau government.[11]

A numerical example can illustrate situations in which logrolling leads to such undesirable outcomes.[12] Assume we have the same three voters and three projects under consideration as in Table 11.4, but now the various net benefits are as depicted in Table 11.5. Every project has a negative net benefit. Each should therefore be rejected, as would be the case if the projects were voted on one at a time.

However, with logrolling, some or all of these inefficient projects could pass. Suppose Melanie offers to support the library in return for Rhett's vote for the hospital. The deal is consummated because both of them come out ahead— Melanie by 160 (= 200 – 40) and Rhett by 40 (= 150 – 110). With the support of Melanie and Rhett together, both projects pass. In the same way, Rhett and Scarlet can trade votes for the pool and the library, so both of those projects are adopted.

To understand the source of this outcome, consider again Melanie and Rhett's vote trading over the hospital and the library. Note that Scarlet comes out behind on both projects. This demonstrates how with logrolling, a majority of voters can form a coalition to vote for projects that serve their interests, but whose costs are borne mainly by the minority. Hence, despite the fact that the benefits of the projects to the majority exceed the costs, this is not true for society as a whole. We conclude that although logrolling can sometimes improve on the results from simple majority voting, this is not necessarily the case.

Table 11.5

Logrolling Can Also Lower Welfare

PROJECT	VOTER			TOTAL NET BENEFITS
	MELANIE	RHETT	SCARLET	
Hospital	200	–110	–105	–15
Library	–40	150	–120	–10
Pool	–270	–140	400	–10

---

[11] Savoie (1990: 200).
[12] For further details, see Buchanan and Tullock (1962).

Arrow's Impossibility Theorem

We have shown that neither simple majority voting nor logrolling has entirely desirable properties. Many other voting schemes have also been considered, and they, too, are flawed.[13] An important question is whether *any* ethically acceptable method for translating individual preferences into collective preferences escapes these problems. It depends on what is meant by "ethically acceptable." Nobel laureate Kenneth Arrow (1951) proposed that in a democratic society, a collective decision-making rule should satisfy the following criteria[14]:

1. It can produce a decision whatever the configuration of voters' preferences. Thus, for example, the procedure must not fall apart if some people have multipeaked preferences.

2. It must be able to rank all possible outcomes.

3. It must be responsive to individuals' preferences. Specifically, if every individual prefers A to B, then society's ranking must prefer A to B.

4. It must be consistent in the sense that if A is preferred to B and B is preferred to C, then A is preferred to C.[15]

5. Society's ranking of A and B depends only on individuals' rankings of A and B. Thus, the collective ranking of defence expenditures and foreign aid does not depend on how individuals rank either of them relative to research on a cure for AIDS. This assumption is sometimes called the **independence of irrelevant alternatives.**

6. Dictatorship is ruled out. Social preferences must not reflect the preferences of only a single individual.

Taken together, these criteria seem quite reasonable. Basically, they say that society's choice mechanism should be logical and respect individuals' preferences. Unfortunately, the stunning conclusion of Arrow's analysis is that in general it is *impossible* to find a rule that satisfies all these criteria.[16] A democratic society cannot be expected to be able to make consistent decisions.

---

[13] These include point voting (each person is given a fixed number of points that are cast for the different alternatives), plurality voting (the alternative with the most votes wins), Borda counts (each alternative is ranked by each voter, and the ranks are totalled to choose), Condorcet elections (the alternative that defeats the rest in paired elections wins), and exhaustive voting (the proposal favoured least by the largest number of voters is repeatedly removed until only one remains). See Mueller (1989) for further details.

[14] Arrow's requirements have been stated in a number of different ways. This treatment follows Blair and Pollak (1983).

[15] More precisely, in this context *preferred to* means *better than or just as good as*.

[16] The proof involves fairly sophisticated mathematics. The procedure of proof is to show that if all six conditions are imposed, phenomena like the voting paradox can arise.

This result, sometimes called Arrow's Impossibility Theorem, thus casts doubt on the very ability of democracies to function. Naturally, the theorem has generated debate, much of which has focused on whether other sets of criteria might allow formation of a social decision-making rule. It turns out that if any of the six criteria is dropped, a decision-making rule that satisfies the other five *can* be constructed. But whether or not it is permissible to drop any of the criteria depends on one's views of their ethical validity.

Arrow's theorem does not state that it is *necessarily* impossible to find a consistent decision-making rule. Rather, the theorem only says it cannot be guaranteed that society will be able to do so. For certain patterns of individual preferences, no problems arise. An obvious example is when members of society have identical preferences. Some radical theorists have suggested that the real significance of Arrow's theorem is that it shows the need for a virtual uniformity of tastes if a democracy is to function. They then argue that many capitalist institutions have the express purpose of moulding people's tastes to make sure that uniformity emerges. An example is mandatory public education.

Others have argued that Arrow's theorem does not really have much to say about the viability of democratic processes. Another Nobel prize winner, James Buchanan (1960: 83), views the inconsistencies of majority voting as having beneficial aspects:

> Majority rule is acceptable in a free society precisely because it allows a sort of jockeying back and forth among alternatives, upon none of which relative unanimity can be obtained.... It serves to insure that competing alternatives may be experimentally and provisionally adopted, tested, and replaced by new compromise alternatives approved by a majority group of ever-changing composition. This is [the] democratic choice process.

Another important question raised by Arrow's theorem concerns use of a social welfare function in economic analysis. Recall from Chapter 4 that a social welfare function is a rule that evaluates the desirability of any given set of individuals' utilities. In a democratic society, the social welfare function must be chosen collectively. But Arrow's theorem says that it may be impossible to make such decisions, and hence we cannot assume that a social welfare function really exists. However, if it does not exist, how can economists use the social welfare function to rank alternative states? Some economists have therefore rejected the function's use. They argue that it is merely a way of introducing value judgments and not a representation of "society's" preferences. As such, a social welfare function does not isolate the correct allocation of resources. However, most economists believe that the function is an important tool. It may not provide "the" answer, but it can be used to draw out the implications of alternative sets of value judgments. With this interpretation, the social welfare function provides valuable insights.

REPRESENTATIVE DEMOCRACY

Although the discussion of public decision making thus far sheds light on some important questions, it is based on a very unrealistic view of government. Government is essentially a big computer that elicits from citizens their preferences and uses this information to produce social decisions. The state has no interests of its own; it is neutral and benign.

In fact, of course, government is done by people—politicians, judges, bureaucrats, and others. To understand the realities of public choice, one must study the goals and behaviour of the people who govern. This section discusses some models of government action based on these individuals' motivations and behaviour. These models assume that people in government attempt to maximize their self-interest. Two points are important regarding this assumption:

- Selfishness does not necessarily lead to inefficient outcomes. As we saw in Chapter 4, under certain conditions the marketplace harnesses self-interest to serve a social end. The question is what, if anything, performs that role in the "political market."
- While the maximization assumption may not be totally accurate, just as in more conventional settings, it provides a good starting point for analysis.

Elected Politicians

Our earlier discussion of direct democracy led to the median voter theorem: If individual preferences are single peaked and can be represented along a single dimension, the outcome of majority voting reflects the preferences of the median voter. In reality, direct referendums on fiscal matters are most unusual. More commonly, citizens elect representatives who make decisions on their behalf. Nevertheless, under certain assumptions, the median voter theory can help explain how these representatives set their positions.

Consider an election between two candidates, Smith and Jones. Assume voters have single-peaked preferences along the spectrum of political views. Voters cast ballots to maximize their own utility, and candidates seek to maximize the number of votes received. What happens? Downs (1957) argues that under these conditions, a vote-maximizing politician adopts the preferred program of the median voter—the voter whose preferences are exactly in the middle of the distribution of preferences. To see this, assume voters rank all positions on the basis of whether they are "conservative" or "liberal." Figure 11.3 shows a hypothetical distribution of voters who most prefer each point in the political spectrum. Suppose that Candidate Jones adopts position M, at the median, and Candidate Smith chooses position S to the right of centre. Because all voters have single-peaked preferences and want to maximize utility, each supports the candidate whose views lie closest to his or her own. Smith will win all the votes to the right of S, as well as some of the votes between S and M. Because M is the median, one-half of the voters lie to the left of M. Jones will receive all of these votes and some of those to the right of M, guaranteeing him a majority. The only way for Smith to prevent himself from being "outflanked" is to move to position M himself. Therefore, it pays both candidates to place themselves as close as possible to the position of the median voter.

This model has two striking implications. First, successful political parties offer policies that are in the "centre" of the political spectrum. The wisdom of this strategy was reflected in the words of retiring B.C. premier Bill Bennett to his successor, Bill Vander Zalm: "Bill, I got a piece of advice for you. Please. Stay in the middle! Don't go too far to the right. Stay in the middle."[17] Or in the words of Pierre Elliott Trudeau, one of Canada's longest-serving prime

Figure 11.3

Median Voter Theorem for Elections

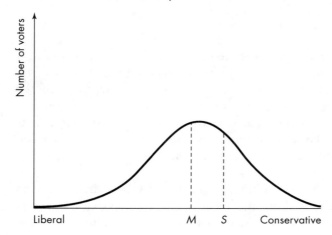

---

[17] Quoted in Olive (1993: 100).

Chapter II: Public Choice

ministers and, in that sense, one of our most successful politicians—"We are in the extreme centre, the radical middle. That is our position."[18]

Second, the replacement of direct referendums by a representative system will have *no* effect on the outcome. Both simply mirror the preferences of the median voter. Thus, government spending cannot be "excessive" because political competition for votes leads to an expenditure level that is exactly in accord with the median voter's wishes.

Before taking these rather optimistic results too much to heart, however, several aspects of the analysis require careful examination.

Single-dimensional rankings. If all political beliefs cannot be ranked along a single spectrum, the median voter theorem falls apart because the identity of the median voter depends on the issue being considered. The median voter with respect to feminist questions may not be the same person as the median voter on atomic energy issues. Similarly, just as in the case of direct referendums, if preferences are not single peaked, there may not be a stable voting equilibrium at all.

Ideology. While it is assumed that politicians are simple vote maximizers, they may care about more than just winning elections. The tension between maintaining ideological purity and winning power by adopting a less doctrinaire platform with a broad electoral appeal was a constant source of conflict in the Co-operative Commonwealth Federation (CCF), the forerunner of the New Democratic Party. One proponent of ideological purity was Carlyle King, a professor of English and president of the CCF in Saskatchewan, who argued:

> The trouble is that socialist parties have gone a-whoring after the Bitch Goddess. They have wanted Success, Victory, Power; forgetting that the main business of socialist parties is not to form governments but to change minds. When people begin to concentrate on success at the polls, they become careful and cautious; and when they become careful and cautious, the virtue goes out of them.[19]

Personality. The assumption that voters' decisions depend only on issues may be unrealistic. Personalities may sometimes be more important. Prime

---

[18] Quoted in Olive (1993: 115).
[19] Quoted in Walter Young (1969: 127).

Minister Brian Mulroney's low popularity at the end of his time in office was due largely to perceived arrogance.

Leadership. In the model, politicians passively respond to voters' preferences. But these preferences may be influenced by the politicians themselves. This is just another way of saying that politicians provide leadership. Indeed, at times in history, rational calculations of voter self-interest have apparently given way altogether to the appeals of charismatic politicians. "Politics is magic. He who knows how to summon forces from the deep, him they will follow."[20]

Decision to vote. The analysis assumes every eligible citizen chooses to exercise his or her franchise. If the candidates' positions are too close, however, some people may become too apathetic to vote. Individuals with extreme views may fail to vote out of alienation. The model also ignores the costs of acquiring information and voting. A rational voter makes a determination on the suitability of a candidate's platform, the probability that the candidate will be able and willing to keep his or her promises, and so forth. The fact that these costs may be high, together with the perception that a single vote will not influence the outcome anyway, may induce a self-interested citizen to abstain from voting. A free-rider problem emerges—each individual has an incentive not to vote, but unless a sizable number of people do so, a democracy cannot function (see Downs, 1957). Part of the answer may be the success with which the educational system instils the idea that the citizen's obligation to vote transcends narrow self-interest.

Public Employees

The next group we consider is public employees, also referred to as bureaucrats. Donald Savoie (1990: 207) gives the following example of the federal bureaucracy's influence on public policies:

> When the Mulroney government came to office, it quickly indicated its desire to transfer a number of industrial incentive programs to provincial governments. The intent was to transfer not just the programs but also a set spending level. The proposed transfer, however, meant that a number of officials would either have to transfer with the programs or be declared redundant. Two things happened. First federal officials slowed the process down—deliberately, some insist. After several months, key ministers (status participants) began to lose their desire to transfer the programs and began to express deep concern over the likely loss of public visibility for spending. Secondly, while discussions were taking place about the pro-

---

[20] Hugo von Hofmannsthal, quoted in Schorske (1981: 172).

posed transfer, policy papers were being prepared outlining the "new role" for officials previously delivering the programs. In future, the policy papers argued, they would be freed from the time-consuming task of processing applications so that they could do what they ought to have been doing all along. That is, to assist business people to identify new business opportunities, to guide them towards new technologies, and to identify new markets abroad. In the end, however, the programs were never transferred.

Bureaucrats have been the target of much bitter criticism. They are blamed for being unresponsive, creating excessive red tape, and intruding too much into the private affairs of citizens. Remember, however, that a modern government simply cannot function without bureaucracy. Bureaucrats provide valuable technical expertise in the design and execution of programs. Moreover, the fact that their tenures in office often exceed those of elected officials provides a continuity in government that would otherwise be lacking.

On the other hand, it would be naive to assume a bureaucrat's only aim is to interpret and passively fulfil the wishes of the electorate and its representatives. Having said this, we are still left with the problem of specifying the bureaucrat's goals. Niskanen (1971) argued that in the market-oriented private sector, an individual who wants to "get ahead" does so by making his or her company as profitable as possible. The individual's salary rises with the firm's profits. In contrast, bureaucrats tend to focus on such items as perquisites of office, public reputation, power, and patronage because opportunities for monetary gains are minimal.[21] In the words of a student who was attempting to enter the civil service in India, becoming a bureaucrat "means a lot of power ... power in the sense of whatever you feel like doing.... They have a lot of hold over what the government does" (Gargan, 1993: A4). Niskanen suggested that power, status, and so on are positively correlated with the size of the bureaucrat's budget and concluded that the bureaucrat's objective is to maximize his or her budget.

To assess the implications of this hypothesis, consider Figure 11.4. The output of a bureaucracy, Q, is measured on the horizontal axis. Q might represent the number of units of housing subsidized by Canada Mortgage and Housing Corporation or the number of tanks stockpiled by the Department of National Defence. Dollars are measured on the vertical axis. The curve VV represents the total value placed on each level of Q by the legislative sponsor who controls the budget. The slope of VV is the marginal social benefit of the output;

---

[21] Obviously, this distinction is blurred in the real world. Firm executives care about power and job perks as well as money. Nevertheless, the distinction is useful for analytical purposes.

Figure 11.4

Niskanen's Model of Bureaucracy

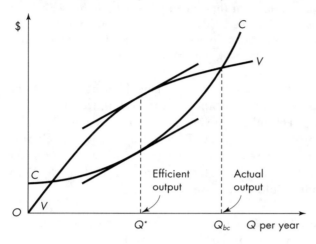

it is drawn on the reasonable assumption of diminishing marginal benefit. The total cost of providing each output level is *CC*. Its slope measures the marginal cost of each unit of output. *CC* is drawn on the assumption of increasing marginal cost.

Suppose the bureaucrat knows that the sponsor will accept any project whose total benefits exceed total costs. Then the bureaucrat (*bc*) proposes Q_{bc}, the output level that maximizes the size of the bureau subject to the constraint that *CC* not be above *VV*. Q_{bc}, however, is an inefficient level of output. Efficiency requires that a unit of output be produced only as long as the additional benefit from that output exceeds the additional cost. Hence, the efficient output is where marginal cost equals marginal benefit, *not* total cost equals total benefit. In Figure 11.4, the efficient level is Q^*, where the *slopes* of *VV* and *CC* are equal. Thus, the bureaucrat's desire to build as large an "empire" as possible leads to an inefficiently large bureaucracy.

An important implication of Niskanen's model is that bureaucrats have incentives to expend effort on promotional activities to increase the sponsor's perceptions of the bureau's benefits—to shift up the *VV* curve. This is analogous to the use of advertising in the private sector. If such efforts succeed, the equilibrium value of Q_{bc} moves to the right. Hence, officials in the Department of National Defence are expected to emphasize security threats and their counterparts in the Department of Human Resources Development to promote awareness of the poverty problem. Note also that an unscrupulous bureaucrat may ask for more funds than needed to achieve a given output level and/or to overstate the benefits of the program. However, the tendency of bureaucracies to exceed their efficient size does not depend on such outright trickery.

An obvious question is why the sponsor allows the bureaucrat to operate at Q_{bc} rather than Q^*. In essence, Niskanen assumes that the bureaucrat can present his or her output to the sponsor as an all-or-nothing proposition: take Q_{bc} or none at all. But, if the sponsor is well informed and cares about efficiency, he or she should require output Q^* and insist that it be produced at minimum cost. One impediment is that it may be difficult for the sponsor to know just what is going on. The process of producing the bureaucratic output is likely to be complicated and to require specialized information that is not easily obtainable by the sponsor. Just consider the technical expertise required to monitor production of electronic guidance systems for missiles.

Are government bureaucracies more likely to operate at points Q_{bc} or Q^*? One way to find out would be to compare the costs and outputs of a government bureau to a private firm producing the same product. Unfortunately, in many important cases, such as defence, there is no private sector counterpart. Moreover, as noted in Chapter 7, government bureaucracies tend to produce outputs that are very hard to measure. Thus, the widespread suspicion that bureaucrats' main concern is empire building is hard to confirm or deny. After surveying studies of the determinants of bureaucrats' salaries in Canada, the United States, and the United Kingdom, Robert Young (1991: 52) concluded that "there exists little relationship between the growth of bureaus and the career prospects of bureaucrats. There is no strong empirical support for the view that civil servants obtain higher salary increases and faster promotions when they are in bureaucracies that are growing faster than normal."

Special Interests

We have been assuming so far that citizens who seek to influence government policy can act only as individual voters.[22] In fact, people with common interests can exercise disproportionate power by acting together. The source of the group's power might be that its members tend to have higher voter participation rates than the population as a whole. Alternatively, members might be willing to use their incomes to make campaign contributions and/or pay bribes. For example, in 1993 registered political parties received $53.8 million in campaign contributions (Chief Electoral Officer of Canada, 1993: Table 1).

---

[22] Much of this section is based on the excellent treatment by Musgrave (1980).

On what bases are these interest groups established? There are many possibilities.

Source of income: capital or labour. According to orthodox Marxism, people's political interests are determined by whether they are capitalists or labourers. This view is too simple to explain interest-group formation in contemporary Canadian society. Even though there is a tendency for those with high incomes to receive a disproportionate share of their income from capital, much of the income of the rich is also derived from labour. Thus, it is difficult even to identify who are the capitalists and the labourers.

Size of income. On many economic policy issues, the rich and the poor have different views, independent of the sources of their incomes. The poor favour redistributive spending programs and the rich oppose them. Similarly, each group supports implicit or explicit subsidies for goods they tend to consume intensively. Hence, the rich support tax deductible retirement savings while the poor favour noncontributory public pensions.

Source of income: industry of employment. Both workers and owners have a common interest in government support for their industry. A good example is the automobile industry where both the Canadian auto workers union and the Big Three auto producers lobby for limits on the importation of automobiles from Japan.

Region. Residents of geographical regions often share common interests. Albertans want favourable tax treatment for the oil and gas industry; Quebeckers want protection for the dairy industry; and the residents of Atlantic Canada want enhanced unemployment insurance benefits. "Given Canada's vast geography, its uneven economic development, and the lack of strong ideologies or even policy preferences in our political parties, the regional factor is perhaps more important in Canadian politics than in any other country" (Savoie, 1990: 195).

Demographic and personal characteristics. The elderly favour public health care and generous public pensions; young married couples are interested in good schools and low payroll taxes. Religious beliefs play a major role in debates over the funding of abortion and provincial funding of private schools. Ethnic groups differ on the propriety of government expenditure for bilingual education programs. Gender is becoming an important basis for interest-group formation.

The list could go on indefinitely. Given the numerous bases on which interest groups can be established, it is no surprise that people who are in opposition on one issue may be in agreement on another; "politics makes strange bedfellows" is more or less the order of the day.

This discussion has ignored the question of how individuals with common interests actually manage to organize themselves. Belonging to a group may require membership fees, donation of time, and so forth. Each individual has an incentive to let others do the work while he or she reaps the benefits, becoming a free rider. Stigler (1974) suggests that the probability that a group will actually form increases when the number of individuals is small, and it is possible to levy sanctions against nonjoiners. But perhaps the role of rational financial self-interest should not be relied on too heavily as an explanation in this context. It is only necessary to observe the debate over abortion to realize the influence of ideology and emotion on the decision to join a group.

Another obvious question is why bills that only benefit the members of a special interest group receive majority support in the House of Commons. One reason is that interest groups and bureaucrats may be well organized and armed with information, while those who will bear the costs are not organized and may not even be aware of what is going on. Even if those citizens who will bear the costs are well informed, it may not be worth their while to fight back. Because the costs of the program are spread over the population as a whole, any given citizen's share is low, and even if total costs exceed total benefits, it would not be worth the time and effort to organize opposition. In contrast, the benefits are relatively concentrated, making political organization worthwhile for potential beneficiaries (see Olson, 1982). Another reason is that a successful political party, such as the federal Liberal Party, may be a coalition of interest groups. In return for having its pet project included in the party platform, an interest group agrees to support other interest groups' pet projects. "The making of governmental decisions is not a majestic march of great majorities united upon certain matters of basic policy. It is the steady appeasement of relatively small groups. Even when these groups add up to a numerical majority at election time it is usually not useful to construe that majority as more than an arithmetic expression" (Dahl, 1956: 146).

The iron law of Canadian politics. "For every government action there is an interest-group reaction."[23] Over the last thirty years there has been a remarkable increase in the number of interest groups holding press conferences, testifying before parliamentary committees, issuing policy papers, and engaged in other related activities. Many of these advocacy groups are funded by the fed-

---

[23] Susan Delacourt, *The Globe and Mail*, Saturday, April 1, 1995.

eral government. John Bryden (MP for Hamilton–Wentworth) investigated fourteen of the publicly funded special interest groups, such as the Canadian Council of Multicultural Health, the Canadian Council on Smoking and Health, the Canadian Ethnocultural Council, the Canadian Labour Council, the National Anti-Poverty Organization, and Pollution Probe. Bryden concluded that "the practice of using general tax revenues to finance groups with particular axes to grind has created a multimillion-dollar system of bureaucratic patronage that operates with little accountability to ministers, members of Parliament, the media or to taxpayers."[24] Parliament exercises little control over the grants received by advocacy groups, and the system allows the bureaucracy to "pump up" the demand for particular programs or policies by funding advocacy groups. The government can then appear to respond to public pressures by adopting those policies. The defenders of advocacy group funding argue that public funding allows disadvantaged groups, such as the poor who lack the power and money of the large corporations, to have their interests and concerns articulated in the public policy processes. Whether interest groups should be publicly funded depends on whether the groups represent the truly disadvantaged, whether the interests represented by the groups are "narrow" or "broad," and whether "levelling the playing field" is worth the potential for abuse.

Other Actors

Without attempting to be exhaustive, we list a few other parties who affect government fiscal decisions.

The judiciary. Court decisions on the legality of various taxes have major effects on government finance. For example, in Canada the judiciary has interpreted provincial retail sales taxes as "direct taxes" and therefore the provincial governments have been allowed to levy them. In contrast, in Australia retail sales taxes were ruled to be indirect taxes and therefore the state governments were prohibited from levying them. The judiciary also affects the expenditure side of the budget. For example, the courts have ruled that governments must provide the same benefits to same-sex couples that they provide to heterosexual couples.

Journalists. The ability to bring certain issues to public attention gives the press considerable influence. For example, the widespread publicity given to crumbling bridges and roads has induced a number of jurisdictions to increase spending on infrastructure. Politicians, bureaucrats, and special interest groups often try to use the media to influence the outcome of debates on fiscal issues.

---

[24] Quoted in Susan Delacourt, *The Globe and Mail*, Saturday, April 1, 1995.

For example, in recent years advocacy for those with AIDS or HIV has brought this issue to public attention by numerous media events. This attention contributed to increased federal subsidies for research on AIDS.

Experts. Information is potentially an important source of power. Legislative aides who gain expertise on certain programs often play important roles in drafting statutes. They can also affect outcomes by virtue of their ability to influence which items are put on the legislative agenda. Of course, there are also experts outside the government. Many academic social scientists have sought to use their expertise to influence economic policy. Economists love to quote John Maynard Keynes's (1965/1936: 383) famous dictum that "the ideas of economists and political philosophers, both when they are right and when they are wrong, are more powerful than is commonly understood. Indeed, the world is ruled by little else." However, it is extremely difficult to determine whether social science research influences policy, and if so, through what channels this influence operates.

EXPLAINING GOVERNMENT GROWTH

Much of the concern about whether government operates efficiently has been stimulated by the rate of growth in government. As documented in Chapter 2, over the long run government expenditures in Canada have grown enormously, both in absolute terms and proportionately. A growing public sector is not a uniquely Canadian experience, as the figures for a few other Western countries in Table 11.6 indicate. Thus, as we search for explanations for the growth in government, care must be taken not to rely too heavily on events and institutions that are peculiar to Canada. Also, the various explanations are not necessarily mutually exclusive. No single theory accounts for the whole phenomenon. Indeed, even taken together, they still leave much unexplained. Some of the most prominent theories follow.

Citizen preferences. Growth in government expenditure is an expression of the preferences of the citizenry. Suppose the median voter's demand for public sector goods and services (G) is some function (f) of the relative price of public sector goods and services (P) and income (I):

$$G = f(P,I). \tag{11.1}$$

There are many different ways such a demand function can lead to an increasing proportion of income spent on public sector goods and services. Suppose that when income increases by a given percentage, the quantity demanded of public goods and services increases by a greater percentage—the income elas-

Table 11.6

Government Expenditure as a Percentage of GDP
in Selected Countries

	POST–WORLD WAR I (ABOUT 1920)	PRE–WORLD WAR II (ABOUT 1937)	POST–WORLD WAR II (ABOUT 1960)	(1980)	(1990)	(1994)
Canada	13.3	18.6	28.6	38.8	46.0	47.4
France	27.6	29.0	34.6	46.1	49.8	54.9
Germany	25.0	42.4	32.4	47.9	45.1	49.0
Italy	22.5	24.5	30.1	41.9	53.2	53.9
Japan	14.8	25.4	17.5	32.0	31.7	35.8
Netherlands	13.5	19.0	33.7	55.2	54.0	55.4
Spain	9.3	18.4	18.8	32.2	42.0	45.6
Sweden	8.1	10.4	31.0	60.1	59.1	68.8
United Kingdom	26.2	30.0	32.2	43.0	39.9	42.9
United States	7.0	8.6	27.0	31.8	33.3	33.5

SOURCE: Table 1, in Vito Tanzi and Ludger Schuknecht, "The Growth of Government and the Reform of the State in Industrial Countries," in *Social Inequality*, edited by Andres Solimano (Ann Arbor: University of Michigan, forthcoming).

ticity of demand is greater than one. If so, the process of income growth by itself leads to an ever-increasing share of income going to the public sector, other things being the same.[25] Similarly, if the price elasticity of demand for G is less than one and P increases over time, an increase in government's share of income may also occur.

The important point is that the relative increase in the size of the public sector does not necessarily imply something is "wrong" with the political process. Government growth could well be a consequence of the wishes of voters, who rationally take into account its opportunity cost in forgone consumption in the private sector. The question then becomes whether the actual changes in P and I over time can account for the actual historical changes in G. Paul Boothe (1995: 83) analyzed the determinants of the growth of eleven categories of provincial government spending in Alberta between 1968 and 1991 and found that they were "reasonably well explained by economic variables such as real

---

[25] The hypothesis that government services rise at a faster rate than income is often called **Wagner's Law**, after Adolph Wagner, the nineteenth-century economist who formulated it.

per capita income, the tax price of government services, and the unemployment rate."[26] He also found that political variables such as the government's share of the popular vote and the size of its legislative majority seemed to affect the level of some kinds of government spending. This suggests that more is going on than a simple median voter story can explain.

Political-economic interaction. Some Marxist theories view the rise of state expenditure as inherent to the political-economic system.[27] In the Marxist model, the private sector tends to overproduce, so the capitalist-controlled government must expand expenditures to absorb this production. Typically, this is accomplished by augmenting military spending. At the same time, the state attempts to decrease worker discontent by increasing spending for social services. Eventually, rising expenditures outpace tax revenue capacity, and the government collapses.

Musgrave (1980: 388) argues that the historical facts are inconsistent with this analysis: "There is little evidence ... [that] expenses directed at appeasing social unrest [have] continuously increased." It is also noteworthy that in Western Europe the enormous increase in the size and scope of government in the post–World War II era has been accompanied by anything but a resurgence in militarism. The main contribution of this Marxist analysis is its explicit recognition of the links between the economic and political systems as sources of government growth.

Chance events. In contrast to the theories that view government growth as inevitable are those that consider it as the consequence of chance events. In "normal" periods there is only moderate growth in public expenditure. Occasionally, however, external shocks to the economic and social system "require" higher levels of government expenditure and novel methods of financing. Even after the shock disappears, higher levels continue to prevail because of inertia. Peacock and Wiseman (1967) call this the *displacement effect*. Examples of shocks are the Great Depression and World War II.

Societal attitudes. In popular discussions, it is sometimes suggested that specific changes in societal attitudes have encouraged government growth. Lubar (1980) argued that social trends encouraging personal self-assertiveness lead people to make extravagant demands on the political system. At the same

---

[26] The tax price of government spending was defined as the proportion of spending that Albertans would finance through taxes. Interest income from the Alberta Heritage Saving Trust Fund and natural resource revenue were assumed to reduce the price of government spending for Albertans.

[27] These theories are surveyed by Musgrave (1980), on which this discussion is based.

time, widespread television advertising has created unrealistically high expectations, leading to a "Santa Claus mentality" that causes people to lose track of the fact that government programs do have an opportunity cost.

However, one could just as well argue that people undervalue the benefits of government projects instead of their costs. In this case, the public sector is too small, not too big. More generally, although recent social phenomena might account for some movement in the growth of government expenditure, it has been going on for too many years and in too many places for this explanation to have much credibility.

Income redistribution. As George Bernard Shaw observed, "A Government which robs Peter to pay Paul can always depend on the support of Paul."[28] It has been hypothesized that government grows because low-income individuals use the political system to redistribute income toward themselves (see Meltzer and Richard, 1981). The idea is that politicians can attract voters whose incomes are at or below the median by offering benefits that impose a net cost on those whose incomes are above the median. As long as average income exceeds the median, and the mechanisms used to bring about redistribution are not too detrimental to incentives, politicians have an incentive to increase the scope of government-sponsored income distribution. Suppose, for example, that there are five voters whose incomes are $5,000, $10,000, $15,000, $25,000, and $40,000. The median income is $15,000 and the average income is $19,000. A politician who supports government programs that transfer income to those with less than $25,000 will win in majority voting.

If this is the case, it must still be explained why the share of public expenditures increases *gradually* (as in Table 2.2). Why not a huge once-and-for-all transfer as the poor confiscate the incomes of the rich? One reason is because, in Western countries, property and/or status requirements for voting have *gradually* been abolished during the last century. Extension of the right to vote to those at the bottom of the income scale increases the proportion of voters likely to support politicians promising redistribution. Hence, the gradual extension of the franchise leads to continuous growth in government, rather than a once-and-for-all increase.

One problem with this theory is that it fails to explain the methods used by government to redistribute income. If it is correct, most income transfers should go to the poor and should take the form that would maximize their welfare, that is, direct cash transfers. Instead, many transfers in Canada are in-

---

[28] Quoted in Smith (1993: 14).

kind transfers, such as subsidized tuition at universities, which mainly benefit the middle- and upper-income classes.

Government programs that benefit different income classes can exist simultaneously, so various views of government redistribution are not necessarily mutually exclusive. The important point here is their common theme. Government growth occurs when individuals use the political system to redistribute income toward themselves. Generically, these activities are called **rent seeking**—using the government to obtain higher than normal returns ("rents"). Via the iron law of Canadian politics discussed previously, coalitions of politicians, rent-seeking special interest groups, and bureaucrats vote themselves programs of ever-increasing size.

We have examined several different hypotheses for explaining the growth of the state's economic role. Unfortunately, the chances for testing them econometrically seem remote. To begin with, it is very difficult to measure the size of government (see Chapter 2). In addition, it is hard to quantify many of the variables that are important in the politically oriented theories—how, for example, can "bureaucratic power" be measured? Thus, the relative importance of each theory is likely to remain open to question.

Bringing Government under Control

Substantial growth in the public sector need not imply that anything is wrong with the political budgetary process. For those who believe that public sector fiscal behaviour is more or less at the size desired by the median voter, bringing government under control is a non-issue.[29] On the other hand, for those who perceive growth in government as a symptom of flaws in the political process, bringing government under control is very much a problem.

Two types of argument are made in the controllability debate. One view is that the basic problem results from commitments made by government in the past, so there is very little current politicians can do to change the rate of growth or composition of government expenditures. Federal transfers to persons, businesses, crown corporations, and other levels of government were estimated to be $78.4 billion in 1996–97 out of a total of program spending of $107.9 billion.[30] When interest payments on the public debt are included, about 80 percent of federal expenditure is uncontrollable.

---

[29] Of course, the composition of government expenditure is at issue, not just its total size. Some believe defence expenditures are too high and social welfare expenditures are too small. Others argue to the contrary.
[30] Treff and Cook (1995: Table 2.4).

Are these expenditures really uncontrollable? If legislation created entitlement programs, it can take them away. In theory, then, many of the programs can be reduced or even removed. In reality, both moral and political considerations work against reneging on past promises to various groups in the population. Any serious reductions are likely to be scheduled sufficiently far into the future so that people who have made commitments based on current programs will not be affected.

According to the second argument, our political institutions are fundamentally flawed, and bringing things under control is more than just a matter of changing the entitlement programs. One remedy that has been proposed is to change bureaucratic incentives. Niskanen, who views bureaucracy as a cause of unwarranted government growth, suggests that financial incentives be created to mitigate bureaucrats' empire-building tendencies. For example, the salary of a government manager could be made to depend negatively on changes in the size of his or her agency. A bureaucrat who cut the agency's budget would get a raise. (Similar rewards could be offered to budget-cutting legislators.) However, such a system could lead to undesirable results. To increase his or her salary, the bureaucrat might reduce the budget beyond the point at which marginal benefits equal marginal costs.

Niskanen also suggests expanding the use of private firms to produce public goods and services, although the public sector would continue to finance them. The question of whether privatization is likely to reduce the costs of services that are currently produced by the government was already discussed in Chapter 6.

CONCLUSIONS

Public decision making is complicated and not well understood. Contrary to simple models of democracy, there appear to be forces pulling government expenditures away from levels that would be preferred by the median voter. However, critics of the current budgetary process have not come up with a satisfactory alternative. The formulation of meaningful rules and constraints for the budgetary process, either at the constitutional or statutory level, is an important item on both the academic and political agendas for the years ahead. In this context it should be stressed that the judgment that government currently may be inequitable or inefficient does not necessarily imply that government as an institution is "bad." People who like market-oriented approaches to resource allocation can nevertheless seek to improve markets. The same goes for government.

SUMMARY

This chapter examines the problems of public choice in both direct and representative democracy.

Direct Democracy

- Economists have studied several methods for choosing levels of public goods:

  - Lindahl pricing results in a unanimous decision to provide an efficient quantity of public goods, but relies on honest revelation of preferences.
  - Majority voting may lead to inconsistent decisions regarding public goods if some people's preferences are not single peaked.
  - Logrolling allows voters to express the intensity of their preferences by trading votes. However, minority gains may come at the expense of greater general losses.

- Arrow's Impossibility Theorem states that, in general, it is impossible to find a decision-making rule that simultaneously satisfies a number of apparently reasonable criteria. The implication is that democracies are inherently prone to inconsistency regarding public goods and other decisions.

Representative Democracy

- Explanations of government behaviour require studying the interaction of elected officials, public employees, and special interest groups.

- Under restrictive assumptions, the actions of elected officials mimic the wishes of the median voter.

- Public employees have an important impact on the development and implementation of economic policy. One theory predicts that bureaucrats attempt to maximize the size of their agencies' budgets, resulting in oversupply of the service.

- Rent-seeking private citizens form groups to influence government activity. Special interests can form on the basis of income source, income size, industry, region, or personal characteristics.

- The growth of government has been rapid by any measure. Explanations of this phenomenon include:

  - Citizens simply want a larger government.
  - The public sector must expand to absorb private excess production.
  - Random events (such as wars) increase the growth of government, while inertia prevents a return to previous levels.
  - Unrealistic expectations have resulted in increasing demands that ignore the opportunity costs of public programs.

- Certain groups in the population use the government to redistribute income to themselves.

- Proposals to control the growth in government include decentralization to reduce bureaucratic power and encouraging private sector competition.

DISCUSSION QUESTIONS

1. Suppose there are five people—1, 2, 3, 4, and 5—who rank projects A, B, C, and D as follows:

1	2	3	4	5
A	A	D	C	B
D	C	B	B	C
C	B	C	D	D
B	D	A	A	A

    a. Sketch the preferences, as in Figure 11.2.
    b. Will any project be chosen by a majority vote rule? If so, which one? If not, explain why.

2. Suppose that in a given referendum, the conditions required for the median voter rule are satisfied. Construct an example to demonstrate that the outcome can be inefficient, that is, that Equation (7.2) is violated. (Hint: Write down marginal benefits and marginal costs for each voter, and remember that the marginal costs [tax burdens] can differ across voters.)

3. Industries in the country of Technologia invest in new equipment that annually increases productivity of private workers by 3 percent. Government employees do not benefit from similar technical advances.

    a. If wages in the private sector are set equal to the value of the marginal product, how much will they rise yearly?
    b. Government workers annually receive increases so that wages remain comparable to those in the private sector. What happens to the price of public services relative to privately produced goods?
    c. If the same quantity of public services is produced each year, what happens to the size of the government (measured by spending)?

4. Voting directly on laws in a referendum enables citizens to circumvent the normal legislative process. If the assumptions of the median voter model hold, how would the introduction of direct referendums affect provincial government expenditures in Canada? If the iron law model holds, how would expenditures be affected?

5. Governments can either provide subsidies to private day care operations, fund public day care facilities, or require employers to provide day care

services for their employees. Discuss how these alternatives affect measured size of government and attempts to limit the size of the government.

6. In 1993, the people of Puerto Rico held a referendum in which there were three choices—retain commonwealth status, become a U.S. state, or become independent. Discuss the problems that can arise when people vote over three options.

7. Develop a special interest group theory to explain the existence of laws that require motorcycle riders to wear helmets. Who would favour such laws, and who would oppose them? How might you test your theory?

REFERENCES

Arrow, Kenneth J. *Social Choice and Individual Values*. New York: John Wiley and Sons, 1951.

Atkinson, Anthony B., and Joseph E. Stiglitz. *Lectures on Public Economics*. New York: McGraw-Hill, 1980.

Blair, Douglas H., and Robert A. Pollak. "Rational Collective Choice." *Scientific American* 249, no. 2 (August 1983): 88–95.

Blais, André, and Elisabeth Gidengil. *Making Representative Democracy Work: The Views of Canadians*. Volume 17 of the research studies of the Royal Commission on Electoral Reform and Party Financing. Ottawa: Ministry of Supply and Services Canada, 1991.

Boothe, Paul. *The Growth of Government Spending in Alberta*. Canadian Tax Paper No. 100. Toronto: Canadian Tax Foundation, 1995.

Buchanan, James M. "Social Choice, Democracy, and Free Markets," in *Fiscal Theory and Political Economy—Selected Essays,* ed. James M. Buchanan. Chapel Hill: University of North Carolina Press, 1960, pp. 75–89.

Buchanan, James M., and Gordon Tullock. *The Calculus of Consent*. Ann Arbor: University of Michigan Press, 1962.

Chief Electoral Officer of Canada. *Contributions and Expenses of Registered Political Parties and Candidates*. Thirty-fifth General Election. Ottawa: Elections Canada, 1993.

Dahl, Robert Alan. *A Preface to Democratic Theory*. Chicago: University of Chicago Press, 1956.

Delacourt, Susan. "Losing Interest." *The Globe and Mail,* Saturday, April 1, 1995, p. D1.

Downs, Anthony. *An Economic Theory of Democracy*. New York: Harper and Row, 1957.

Gargan, Edward A. "A Student's Prayer: Let Me Join the Ruling Class." *The New York Times*, December 6, 1993, p. A4.

Keynes, John Maynard. *The General Theory of Employment, Interest, and Money*. New York: Harcourt Brace and World, 1965 (1936).

Lindahl, E. "Just Taxation—A Positive Solution," in *Classics in the Theory of Public Finance,* ed. R.A. Musgrave and A.T. Peacock. New York: St. Martin's Press, 1958.

Lubar, Robert. "Making Democracy Less Inflation-Prone." *Fortune,* September 22, 1980, pp. 78–86.

Massie, Robert K. *Peter the Great—His Life and World.* New York: Random House, 1980.

Meltzer, Allan H., and Scott F. Richard. "A Rational Theory of the Size of Government." *Journal of Political Economy* 89, no. 5 (October 1981): 914–27.

Mueller, Dennis C. *Public Choice II.* Cambridge: Cambridge University Press, 1989.

Musgrave, Richard A. "Theories of Fiscal Crises: An Essay in Fiscal Sociology," in *The Economics of Taxation,* ed. Henry J. Aaron and Michael J. Boskin. Washington, DC: Brookings Institution, 1980.

Niskanen, William A., Jr. *Bureaucracy and Representative Government.* Chicago: Aldine, 1971.

Olive, David. *Canadian Political Babble.* Toronto: John Wiley and Sons, 1993.

Olson, Mancur. *The Rise and Decline of Nations: Economic Growth, Stagflation, and Social Rigidities.* New Haven, CT: Yale University Press, 1982.

Peacock, A.T., and J. Wiseman. *The Growth of Public Expenditure in the United Kingdom,* 2nd ed. London: Allen and Unwin, 1967.

Rubinfeld, Daniel. "The Economics of the Local Public Sector," in *Handbook of Public Economics,* vol. II, ed. Alan J. Auerbach and Martin Feldstein. Amsterdam: North-Holland, 1987, ch. 11.

Savoie, Donald J. *The Politics of Public Spending in Canada.* Toronto: University of Toronto Press, 1990.

Schorske, Carl E. *Fin-de-Siècle Vienna—Politics and Culture.* New York: Vintage Books, 1981.

Smith, Julie P. *Taxing Popularity: The Story of Taxation in Australia.* Canberra: Federalism Research Centre, Australian National University, 1993.

Stigler, George J. "Free-Riders and Collective Action." *Bell Journal of Economics* 5 (1974): 359–65.

Tanzi, Vito, and Ludger Schuknecht. "The Growth of Government and the Reform of the State in Industrial Countries," in *Social Inequality,* ed. Andres Solimano. Ann Arbor: University of Michigan, (forthcoming).

Treff, Karin, and Ted Cook. *Finances of the Nation, 1995.* Toronto: Canadian Tax Foundation, 1995.

Young, Robert A. "Budget Size and Bureaucratic Careers," in *The Budget-Maximizing Bureaucrat: Appraisals and Evidence,* ed. André Blais and Stéphane Dion. Pittsburgh: University of Pittsburgh Press, 1991, pp. 33–58.

Young, Walter D. *The Anatomy of a Party: The National CCF, 1932–61.* Toronto: University of Toronto Press, 1969.

Part 4

Public Expenditures in Canada

*H*aving analyzed the circumstances in which market outcomes are either inefficient or unfair, we now examine some of the major expenditure programs of Canadian governments. The specific areas that we examine are income security, health care, and education. These programs are the core activities of government and collectively represent 55 percent of total public expenditures. We use the framework provided by welfare economics to analyze the reasons for government intervention in these programs and to evaluate the strengths and weaknesses of the various programs.

In 1994–95, Canadian governments spent about $200 billion on income security, health, and education. Figure 1 shows that $96.2 billion was spent on income security programs in 1994–95, and they have increased from 6.2 percent of GDP in 1970–71 to 12.65 percent in 1994–95. The federal government is responsible for about two-thirds of the total spending on income security programs, with the remaining one-third funded either fully or partially by provincial governments. The main federal income security programs are Old Age Security, Employment Insurance, the Child Tax Benefit, and social assistance programs for veterans and registered Indians. The Canada Pension Plan (CPP) is administered by the federal government, but the provincial governments also have significant involvement in policy development and financing. Social assistance programs are administered by

Figure 1

Health, Education, and Income Security Programs in Canada

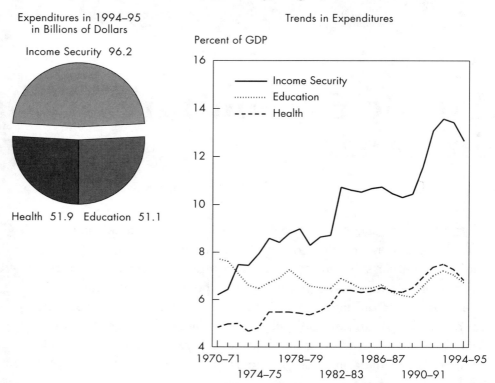

Expenditures in 1994–95
in Billions of Dollars

Income Security 96.2

Health 51.9   Education 51.1

Trends in Expenditures

Percent of GDP

——— Income Security
············ Education
----- Health

SOURCE: Human Resources Development Canada, Social Security Expenditures and Welfare Expenditures, Canada, 1994–95. Reproduced with permission of the Minister of Public Works and Government Services, Canada.

the provincial governments, but the federal government provides transfers to the provinces to help finance these programs. The provincial governments provide other income security programs, such as the Ontario GAINS-A program, to those with low incomes, and are also responsible for worker's compensation programs. The government of Quebec controls the Quebec Pension Plan, which is the counterpart of the Canada Pension Plan. Unemployment insurance, worker's compensation, the Canada Pension Plan, and the Quebec Pension Plan are financed by earmarked payroll taxes. The other income security programs are financed out of general revenues.

Income security in Canada is provided by a range of programs, which are aimed at different age groups or provide income security for individuals who have different needs or face different risks. Analysis of income security programs in Canada is complicated because:

- Many of the programs are motivated by the desire to redistribute income and by the need to provide insurance coverage for income losses that may not be provided by the private insurance market.
- There are important interactions between the programs. For example, the duration of unemployment insurance benefits affects the number of individuals who have to apply for welfare programs if they are unemployed for a long period of time and exhaust their unemployment insurance benefits.
- There are overlapping federal and provincial responsibilities in the provision of income security programs, which has resulted in the need for federal–provincial coordination and intergovernmental grants.

In Chapter 12 we describe the provision of welfare programs, which anchor Canada's social safety net. Then in Chapter 13 we examine the unemployment insurance program, which provides income security for workers due to layoffs. In Chapter 14 we review the main public pension programs in Canada, the Canada and Quebec Pension Plans and the Old Age Security program.

Health care and education are the other major spending areas for government. While both of these areas fall under provincial responsibility, federal transfers to the provinces and provincial transfers to local school boards and hospital districts have played a significant role in financing these programs. Figure 1 shows that relative to GDP there has been a marked upward trend in health care spending and a slight downward trend in education spending over the past twenty-five years. Chapter 15 deals with health care, and Chapter 16 deals with education.

Chapter 12

Social Welfare Programs

As for me, welfare has been a beautiful gift from my county. It permitted me to escape from a nightmarish situation and to survive even when in poor health. Perhaps even more important, it gave my children a full-time parent when they needed one most. While I expect that many people will always be rigid and judgmental about welfare, I hope that at least some facts can be made clear. Welfare recipients do not have great bundles of money to live on each month. A welfare cheque is, believe me, barely adequate for survival and is well below the poverty lines. Furthermore, it is a system which seems to be designed to keep you down once you are down. It would help if people could remember that most welfare recipients do not want to be in that position and would gladly change places with anyone who is not.

—Anonymous welfare recipient, quoted in National Council of Welfare, *Welfare in Canada* (1987)

There is a consensus in our society that no Canadian should live in abject poverty. While there may be disagreements as to what constitutes a basic standard of living or how income support for the poor should be provided, most Canadians agree that the provision of a social safety net is an essential activity of government.[1] Our welfare programs express in a concrete way the fundamental values of Canadian society. The strengths and weaknesses of the welfare system are eloquently expressed by an anonymous welfare recipient in the above quotation.

---

[1] In a 1989 Gallop poll, 84 percent of the respondents agreed with the statement: "The government has a responsibility to insure that all citizens have the basic necessities of life, regardless of circumstances." See Peters (1995: Table 16, p. 105).

This chapter examines the social welfare programs that are a basic component of our social safety net. These programs have been under pressure in recent years because of the rapid expansion in the number of welfare recipients in Canada. An increasing number of welfare recipients are classified as unemployed employable persons, causing some to question whether the receipt of welfare should be conditional on participation in job training and/or community employment programs. Some think that welfare rates are "too high," making welfare more attractive than work. These concerns may have motivated the highly controversial 20 percent reductions in welfare rates in Alberta in 1993 and in Ontario in 1995, and the implementation of a three-month residency requirement for eligibility for welfare in British Columbia at the end of 1995. Others have blamed tight monetary policy, public expenditure cuts, and free trade for the decline in the real earnings of low-skilled workers, resulting in the increased reliance on social assistance programs.

In this chapter, we provide the background to welfare reform in Canada. We describe how the social welfare programs operate, the characteristics of welfare recipients, and the factors that may have contributed to the growth in the number of people on welfare. We also discuss the effects that welfare programs have on work incentives by reviewing the theory of labour–leisure choice, and the empirical evidence on the disincentive effects of social welfare programs. Finally, we examine two widely discussed alternatives to welfare—a negative income tax and workfare.

WELFARE PROGRAMS: DESCRIPTIONS AND TRENDS

Under the Canadian Constitution, the provincial governments are responsible for the provision of social welfare programs. However, the federal government has played a significant role in the financing and the design of social welfare programs through the Canada Assistance Plan (CAP). This program began in 1966 and provided grants to the provinces equal to 50 percent of their expenditures on social welfare that satisfied certain federal guidelines. The most important of these guidelines was that the provinces could not impose residency requirements and that provincial welfare benefits were to be provided on the basis of need. The latter requirement has been interpreted as ruling out workfare because workfare makes receipt of benefits conditional on performance of certain activities and not on the basis of need. The federal government's 50 percent matching grant for all eligible welfare expenditures to all provinces ended in fiscal year 1990–91 when the federal government imposed a 5.0 percent ceiling on the growth of CAP payments to the "have" provinces—Alberta, British Columbia, and Ontario.[2] It is estimated that the federal government's total payments under CAP to the provinces and territories in 1995–96 was $7.275 billion. In 1996–97, the Canada Health and Social Transfer (CHST) replaced the Canada Assistance Plan and the Established Program Financing (EPF) grants that were made to the provinces to help support their expenditures on health care and postsecondary education. A more extensive discussion of CAP and other federal–provincial grants is contained in Chapter 6.[3]

Subject to the general guidelines established by the federal government under CAP or CHST, the provincial governments have complete control over the design and delivery of social welfare programs. As a result, there are significant differences in the benefit levels and the administration of welfare across provinces. For example, municipalities in Ontario, Manitoba, and Nova Scotia play a significant role in the financing and administration of social assistance. One common characteristic of the welfare programs supported under CAP is that social assistance payments are made to individuals or families on the basis of their needs. This means that their basic needs for food, shelter, clothing, household supplies, and personal care, as well as any special needs such as medications or dental care, have to be assessed. Then the financial resources of the family—income from employment or other sources, such as unemployment insurance or worker's compensation—are calculated. The assets of potential recipients are also taken into account, with exemptions for household furniture, automobiles, homes, and tools of employment, and exemptions for liquid financial assets, such as funds in savings accounts, below certain limits (up to $2,500 for a single employable individual). Social assistance payments are then calculated as the difference between assessed needs and available resources.

The Level of Social Assistance Benefits

Figure 12.1 shows the annual welfare incomes of four types of households in 1995 as estimated by the National Council of Welfare (1997: Table 2). These welfare incomes are based on the maximum regular social assistance benefits available in each province, the Child Tax Benefit of $1,233 for one child or $2,040 for two children, the GST tax credit, which ranges from $199 for a single individual to $608 for a couple with two children, and other provincial

---

[2] In 1992–93 the federal government's CAP payments represented only 28 percent of Ontario's social assistance expenditures. Grady (1995: 65).

[3] See Courchene (1995: 69–76) for a discussion of some of the potential effects on provincial welfare programs of replacing CAP by CHST.

Figure 12.1

Welfare Incomes in 1995

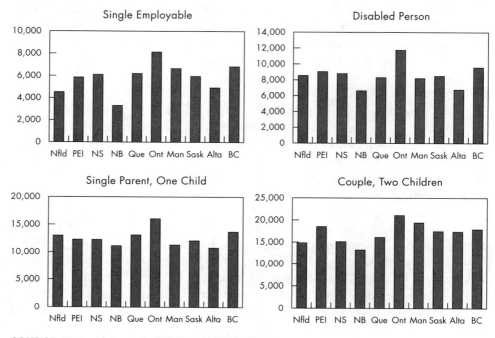

SOURCE: National Council of Welfare (1997: Table 2).

benefits and tax credits. The calculations do not include any payments for special needs, such as dental care, and are based on the assumption the individual or family has no other financial resources. The figure indicates that there is considerable variation in the social assistance benefits that are paid to a given type of household in different provinces. For example, the welfare income of a single employable person in 1995 ranged from $3,295 in New Brunswick to $8,126 in Ontario. For a single parent with one child, the welfare income ranged from $10,800 in Alberta to $16,042 in Ontario. Some of the variation in social assistance rates may be due to variations in the cost of living or the fiscal capacities of provinces such as New Brunswick and Ontario. However, there are variations in welfare rates between provinces, such as between Prince Edward Island and New Brunswick or between Saskatchewan and Alberta, which cannot be explained in terms of the cost of living or fiscal capacity, and therefore some of the variation in welfare rates is due to different preferences, as expressed through the political process, for welfare programs. Ontario had the highest welfare rates in 1995. It should be noted that these data are based on the assumption that the welfare recipient received assistance from January 1 to December 31, 1995. Therefore, the welfare incomes for Ontario only partially reflect the 21.6 percent reduction in social assistance levels that occurred in October 1995.

Are the welfare incomes adequate? Do they prevent welfare recipients from being impoverished? The answer to these questions depends, of course, on where we draw the poverty line.[4] If we use Statistics Canada's Low Income Cut-Off lines (LICO), then the 1995 welfare incomes in all of the provinces were below the poverty line. For example, in Ontario, which provided the highest welfare income, the welfare income of a single employable person was only 51 percent, and the welfare income of a single parent with one child was only 75 percent, of the LICO line.[5] However, if one uses the concept of poverty developed by Sarlo (1992), which is based on the notion of absolute deprivation, then the welfare income for a single parent with one child in New Brunswick was above the poverty line (see Courchene, 1994: Table 23, p. 153). Consequently, the adequacy of social welfare benefits in Canada depends on whether one thinks that welfare income should only protect against extreme deprivation, or whether it should provide a reasonable standard of living in line with prevailing norms in Canadian society.

Who Are the Welfare Recipients?

Figure 12.2 describes some of the characteristics of social assistance recipients in March 1993. Note that the elderly represent only about 1 percent of the heads of welfare families. The OAS/GIS/SPA, CPP, QPP, and other provincial programs that provide income support for the elderly have eliminated the need for social assistance for the vast majority of seniors. By contrast, over one-third of the heads of welfare families were less than 30 years of age in 1993. In fact, children (37.3 percent) and single parents (14.8 percent) represented more than half of the total number of welfare recipients. Single persons represented 31.1 percent of the total. Lone parents with small children represented 28 percent of the heads of welfare families, and the disabled represented 20 percent.

Trends in Welfare Case Loads

One of the most striking trends in the composition of the welfare case load is the increasing proportion of the heads of welfare families who are classified as unemployed employable persons. In the early 1970s, unemployed employable persons represented 10 to 20 percent of the case load.[6] They now constitute

---

[4] See Chapter 10 for a discussion of the measurement of poverty lines.
[5] National Council of Welfare (1997: Table 3, p. 26).
[6] Hobson and St-Hilaire (1993: 131).

Figure 12.2

Characteristics of Social Assistance Recipients, March 1993

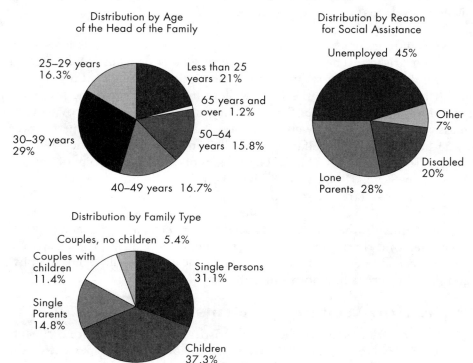

Distribution by Age
of the Head of the Family

Distribution by Reason
for Social Assistance

25–29 years
16.3%

Less than 25
years 21%

65 years and
over 1.2%

50–64
years 15.8%

30–39 years
29%

40–49 years 16.7%

Unemployed 45%

Other
7%

Disabled
20%

Lone
Parents 28%

Distribution by Family Type

Couples, no children 5.4%

Couples with
children
11.4%

Single
Parents
14.8%

Single Persons
31.1%

Children
37.3%

SOURCE: Human Resources Development Canada (1994a: 12–13) and (1994b: 12). Reproduced with permission of the Minister of Public Works and Government Services, Canada.

almost 50 percent of the total. The other striking trend is that the percentage of the population receiving social assistance has increased from 6.6 percent in 1971 to 10.6 percent in 1994. Because of the increase in the proportion of heads of welfare families who are classified as unemployed employable persons, it is interesting to compare the trend in the percentage of the population receiving social assistance with the trend in the unemployment rate. As Figure 12.3 indicates, the percentage of the population receiving social assistance declined from 6.6 percent in 1971 to 5.4 percent in 1980 in spite of the increase in the unemployment rate that occurred over this period. During the recession of the early 1980s, the percentage on welfare increased from 5.4 percent in 1980 to 7.4 percent in 1985. Between 1985 and 1990, the unemployment rate fell by 2.4 percentage points, but the percentage of the population receiving welfare benefits declined only by half of a percentage point. The

Figure 12.3

Trends in the Percentage of the Population Receiving Social Assistance and the Unemployment Rate

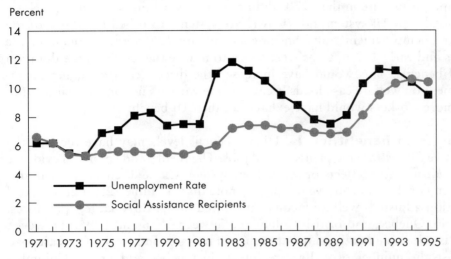

SOURCE: Human Resources Development Canada, Social Security Statistics, Table 361, and Statistics Canada, *The Labour Force*, November 1995.

sharp increase in the unemployment rate in the 1991–93 recession resulted in a dramatic increase in the percentage of the population receiving social assistance benefits.

While the linkage between higher unemployment rates and rising welfare case loads is evident in the early 1980s and 1990s, the experience of the 1970s indicates that rising unemployment rates do not necessarily imply increasing welfare case loads, and the experience of the latter half of the 1980s indicates that falling unemployment rates do not necessarily lead to declines in the welfare case load. Obviously, other factors besides the unemployment rate have had an important influence on the number of social assistance recipients.[7] We will consider three factors—changes in the UI program, in welfare benefits, and in real wages—in more detail.

Changes to the unemployment insurance program. As discussed in more detail in the next chapter, there have been significant changes in the cov-

---

[7] See Brown (1995) for an analysis of the trend in welfare case loads.

erage, benefit levels, duration of benefits, and qualifying periods for unemployment insurance during the last twenty-five years. In 1971 the coverage and the generosity of the UI program were greatly enhanced. The increase in the level and duration of UI benefits may explain in part why the increase in the unemployment rate in the 1970s did not put upward pressure on the welfare case load. The UI system, not the welfare system, absorbed the shock of the higher unemployment rate.[8] Starting in the late 1970s and throughout the 1980s and early 1990s, steps were taken to reduce the level and the duration of UI benefits. This would have increased the direct effect of higher unemployment on welfare case loads because some workers no longer qualified for, and more workers would have exhausted, their UI benefits.

Changes in benefit levels. Higher benefit levels may have reduced the incentive for welfare recipients to find jobs. The theory and empirical evidence on the disincentive effects of the welfare system will be discussed later in this chapter. For the moment, we will simply note that, as Table 12.1 indicates, real (inflation adjusted) welfare incomes increased in the three largest provinces, Ontario, Quebec, and British Columbia, between 1986 and 1995.[9] However, there is no simple relationship between welfare rates and the welfare case load because the number of welfare recipients in Quebec and British Columbia declined by 19.9 percent and 15.5 percent respectively, while the number of welfare recipients in Ontario increased by 39 percent, between 1986 and 1990.

The effects of reductions in welfare benefits on social assistance case loads in Alberta in 1993 and in Ontario in 1995 have generated a lot of public attention. In Alberta, the social assistance case load dropped from 95,000 in 1993 to under 50,000 in 1996. Boessenkool (1997) has analyzed the decline in the social assistance case load in Alberta and concluded that, while the reduction in benefit levels helped to reduce the case load, a major factor was the change in the administration of the welfare program. New applicants were directed to training and work projects. Between 1993 and 1996, "more than 35,000 former and potential welfare clients went through various work, training and education programs" (Boessenkool, 1997: 16). Most of the reduction in the case load was achieved by reducing the inflow of new cases (especially by young single employable individuals) and not by increasing the rate at which existing recipients left the welfare rolls. Welfare became a program of last

---

[8] Some have argued that it contributed to the increase in the unemployment rate. See Chapter 13.

[9] These data are based on the assumption that the welfare recipient received assistance for the entire year. Therefore, the calculations for Ontario do not fully reflect the 21.6 percent reduction in social assistance levels that occurred in October 1995.

Table 12.1

Percentage Change in Real Welfare Incomes, 1986–1995

PROVINCE	A SINGLE EMPLOYABLE PERSON (% CHANGE)	A SINGLE PARENT WITH ONE CHILD (% CHANGE)
Newfoundland	–4.4	–0.7
Prince Edward Island	–32.9	–8.8
Nova Scotia	–4.4	–1.3
New Brunswick	1.7	3.7
Quebec	87.3[a]	6.9
Ontario	15.3	16.7
Manitoba	–4.9	–8.2
Saskatchewan	1.3	–11.0
Alberta	–41.6	–22.4
British Columbia	14.8	14.9

[a] The large increase in welfare rates for single employables in Quebec was due to reforms that "raised welfare rates for single employable people under 30 to the same level as rates for people 30 and over." National Council of Welfare (1997: 31).

SOURCE: National Council of Welfare (1997: Table 5).

resort, and applicants had to demonstrate that they had exhausted all other avenues of income support before they were provided with assistance.

Changes in real wage rates for low-income workers. Even if real social assistance benefit levels had not increased in the three largest provinces, many low-income workers in those provinces would have found that work was becoming less attractive than welfare because of the decline in their real wage incomes. Data in Brown (1995: Table 1, p. 45) indicate that the average real earnings of a male, in the first decile of the income distribution and working full-time for a full year in 1990–92, were only 72.2 percent of the average real income of a comparable male in 1975. The decline in real average earnings of low-income males was even greater than this in Ontario and British Columbia, but somewhat lesser in Quebec. Combined with the increase in benefit levels, data in Brown (1995: Table 4, p. 49) indicate the ratio of social assistance benefits to earnings by low-income males almost doubled between 1975 and 1990–92.

In summary, rising unemployment rates, amendments to the unemployment insurance program, increases in real welfare rates, and declines in the real wage rates of low-income workers may all have contributed to the upward trend in social assistance rates. To gain a better appreciation of the role that these factors may have played in the growth of welfare dependency in Canada, we will review economic theory and empirical evidence concerning disincentive effects of welfare programs.

WELFARE PROGRAMS AND WORK INCENTIVES

The Theory

Consider Jane Doe, who is deciding how much of her time to devote each month to work and how much to nonmarket activity, which we call leisure. In Figure 12.4, the horizontal axis measures the number of hours of leisure.[10] Even if Doe does not work, there is an upper limit to the amount of leisure she can consume, because there are just so many hours in a month. This number of hours, referred to as the time endowment, is distance *TO* in Figure 12.4. We assume all time not spent on leisure is devoted to work in the market. Any point on the horizontal axis, therefore, simultaneously indicates hours of leisure and hours of work. For example, at point *a*, *Oa* hours are devoted to leisure, and the difference between that and the time endowment, *TO*, represents time spent at work, *aT*.

Figure 12.4

Budget Constraint for the Leisure/Income Choice

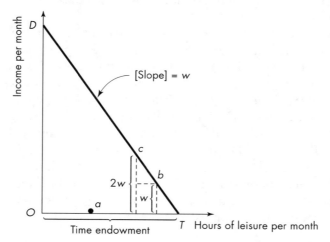

Our first problem is to illustrate how Doe's income, which is measured on the vertical axis, varies with her hours of work. Assume that she can earn a wage of $w per hour. Also, for the moment, assume that no welfare is available. Then her income for any number of hours worked is just the product of $w and the number of hours. Suppose, for example, Doe does not work at all. If labour is her only source of income, her income is simply zero. This option of zero work and zero income is represented by point T.

If Doe works one hour each week, her consumption of leisure equals her time endowment minus one hour. This point is one hour to the left of T on the horizontal axis. Working one hour gives her a total of $w. The combination of one hour of work with a total income of $w is labelled point b. If Doe works two hours—moves two hours to the left of T—her total income is 2 × $w, which is labelled point c. Continuing to compute the income associated with each number of hours of work, we trace out all the leisure/income combinations available to Doe—straight line TD, whose slope, in absolute value, is the wage rate. TD is the analog of the budget constraint in the usual analysis of the choice between two goods. Here, however, the goods are income and leisure. The price of an hour of leisure is its opportunity cost (the income forgone by not working that hour), which is just the wage.

To know which point on TD Doe chooses, we need information on her tastes. In Figure 12.5 we reproduce the budget constraint TD. Assume that prefer-

Figure 12.5

Utility-Maximizing Choice of Leisure and Income

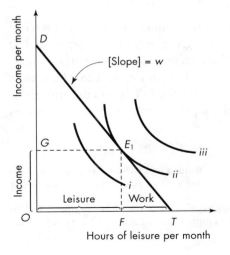

ences for leisure and income can be represented by normal, convex-to-the-origin indifference curves. Three such curves are labelled *i*, *ii*, and *iii* in Figure 12.5. Utility is maximized at point E_1, where Doe devotes OF hours to leisure, works FT hours, and earns income OG.

Suppose now that Doe becomes eligible to receive a social assistance benefit of $500 per month. However, suppose that her benefits are reduced by $1 for each dollar she earns. How does the social assistance program modify her budget constraint? In Figure 12.6, clearly one option that social assistance makes available to Doe is point P, which is associated with zero hours of work and an income of $500 from welfare. Now suppose that Doe works one hour. Graphically, she moves one hour to the left from P. When Doe works one hour, she receives a wage of w from her employer, but simultaneously her welfare is reduced by the same amount. The hour of work has netted her nothing—her total income is $500. This is shown by point P_1, where there is one hour of work and total income is $500. In effect, Doe's earnings are being taxed at a rate of 100 percent. Additional hours of work continue to produce no net gain in income, so the budget constraint is flat. This continues until point R, at which point Doe's earnings exceed $500, so that she is out of the welfare system altogether. Beyond that point, each hour of work raises her income by $w.[11] Thus, the budget constraint is the kinked line PRD, whose segment PR has zero slope, and whose segment RD has a slope whose absolute value is w.

How will Doe respond to such incentives? Figure 12.7 shows one distinct possibility: she maximizes utility at point P, at which no labour is supplied. In no case will a rational person work between zero and PR hours. This should come as no surprise. Why should someone work if she can receive the same income by not working?[12]

Of course, the welfare system does not necessarily induce an individual to stop working. If the indifference curves are flat enough, a point along segment RD may be chosen. Figure 12.8 depicts the leisure/income choice of Esther Jones, who faces exactly the same budget constraint as Doe in Figure 12.7. However, Jones maximizes utility at point E_2, where she works MT hours per month. If her income falls below the poverty line, then a person such as Jones is a member of the working poor.

---

[11] If Doe becomes subject to the income tax, her take-home wage will be less than $w. This consideration is unimportant in the current context and is discussed in Chapter 21 under "Labour Supply."

[12] In a more complicated model, an individual might select a point along segment RD to develop her skills or to signal her quality to future employers by maintaining a continuous work history.

Figure 12.6

Budget Constraint under a Welfare System with a 100 Percent Tax Rate on Additional Earnings

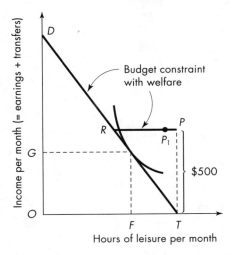

Figure 12.7

Work Decision under a Welfare System with a 100 Percent Tax Rate on Additional Earnings

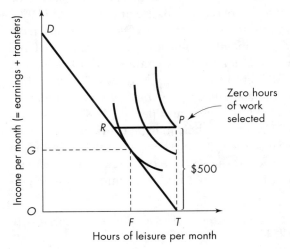

Figure 12.8

An Individual Chooses to Work in the Presence of a Welfare System

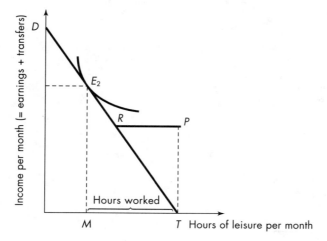

Empirical Evidence on Disincentive Effects

Figures 12.7 and 12.8 depict a classical welfare system in which the implicit tax rate on additional earnings is 100 percent. The provincial governments have recognized that a 100 percent marginal tax rate on earnings creates an extreme disincentive to work. Therefore, they generally allow welfare recipients to keep all of their earnings below some exemption level, and then welfare benefits are reduced by less than a dollar for each additional dollar earned. For example, in British Columbia in 1992 the exempt earnings level was $100 per month for singles and $200 for families, and the benefit reduction rate on earnings above these thresholds was 75 percent.[13] Battle and Torjman (1993) analyzed the marginal tax rate on low-income earners in Ontario arising from the interaction of the federal and provincial income and payroll taxes (UI and CPP) and the benefit reduction rates under social assistance and other income transfer programs, such as the GST credit and the Child Tax Benefit. Their results are shown in Figure 12.9. For a single employable individual, the marginal tax rate was 75 percent at $1,000 per year and peaked at 87 percent on earnings of $9,000. Above $13,000, the implicit marginal tax rate dropped from 83 percent to 33 percent because the individual was no longer eligible for welfare and therefore was not subject to the welfare tax back rate. For a single parent with a 2-year-old child, the marginal tax rate jumped from 2 per-

---

[13] See Grady (1995: Table 9, pp. 67–68) for the treatment of earnings under the social assistance programs of each province in 1992.

cent on annual earnings of $1,000 to 68 percent on $1,500, and then gradually increased to 95 percent on earnings of $19,000 to $21,000. The marginal tax rate dropped to 46 percent when the single parent earned $27,000 and was no longer eligible for welfare. Thus, Battle and Torjman's analysis indicates that while welfare recipients are not subject to the 100 percent marginal tax rate indicated in Figures 12.7 and 12.8, the marginal tax rates are nonetheless very high and could significantly reduce work incentives.[14]

The disincentives to work are also affected by the level of welfare payments compared to the potential earnings of low-income workers. Figure 12.10 shows the difference in annual net incomes for individuals or families working full-time at the minimum wage rate in each province in 1992 and the welfare income that they could receive. For a single employable individual and a two-earner couple with two children, full-time full-year earnings at the mini-

Figure 12.9

Effective Marginal Tax Rates on Low-Income Earners in Ontario, 1992

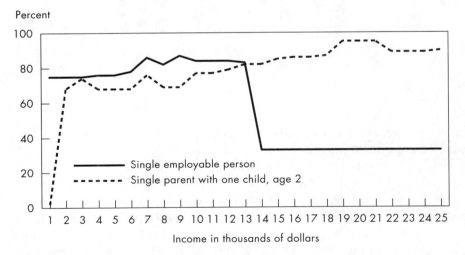

SOURCE: Ken Battle and Sherri Torjman, "The Welfare Wall: The Interactions of the Welfare and Tax Systems" (Ottawa: Caledon Institute of Social Policy, Summer 1993).

---

[14] Marginal tax rates can exceed 100 percent if individuals no longer qualify for in-kind benefits, such as rent subsidies, dental care, or drug plans, when their earnings increase. If the loss of welfare payments and in-kind benefits exceeds the increase in earnings, then the marginal tax rate exceeds 100 percent and individuals are worse off if they earn an extra dollar. The Ontario government has avoided this problem by allowing low-income workers to retain their in-kind benefits. See Brown (1995).

Figure 12.10

Net Income Differentials Working at the Minimum Wage versus Welfare in 1992

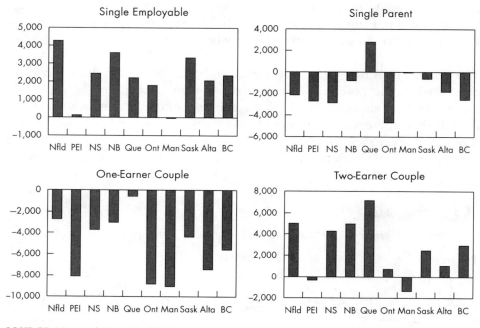

SOURCE: National Council of Welfare (1993).

mum wage rate exceeded welfare incomes in all provinces, except Prince Edward Island and Manitoba where the income differentials were negligible for a single employable person. For a single parent with one child, a welfare income was higher than a minimum wage income in all provinces except for Quebec. For a one-earner couple with two children, welfare incomes were higher in all provinces, and the income differential was over $8,000 in Ontario and Manitoba. Clearly, in one-earner families with children, welfare provides a higher income than working at the minimum wage. The parents in these families, motivated by the desire to provide a higher standard of living for their children, would choose to go on welfare. Even for a single employable individual, welfare may be more attractive than work at the minimum wage because, even though working provides a higher income, the net return from working is relatively low. For example, in Alberta, working at the minimum wage made a single employable person better off by about $2,000 compared to welfare, but this was a net return of about $1.00 per hour worked. When the costs associated with working, such as transportation and clothing, are taken into account, the net return per hour could be considerably lower, and we should not be surprised if some individuals find that welfare is more attractive than work.

While the relatively high marginal tax rates on earnings and relatively high benefit levels compared to earnings at the minimum wage rate suggest that the social welfare system may have created significant disincentives to work, the extent of the problem can only be assessed through statistical studies of the determinants of welfare participation. Allen (1993) and Charette and Meng (1994), using cross-section data from 1986 and 1989, analyzed the effect of higher welfare rates on welfare participation by women. Both studies found that higher welfare rates increased the probability of welfare participation. Allen's study indicated that a $1,000 per year increase in welfare benefits would increase the number of women on welfare by about 100,000. Brown (1995) analyzed the effects of welfare benefit rates and unemployment rates on the percentage of the population receiving welfare in British Columbia, Alberta, and Ontario over the period 1989 to 1993. He found that benefit rates and unemployment had positive, but relatively small, effects on the number of single employable individuals on welfare, but that the effects were generally not statistically significant for single parents and families. Fortin, Lacroix, and Roberge (1995) examined the lengths of the welfare spells of single individuals aged 18 to 30 in Quebec between 1979 and 1993. They found that higher social assistance benefits and unemployment rates reduced the rate at which individuals leave welfare. Thus, a number of recent Canadian studies have found that higher welfare benefits are associated with higher welfare participation rates or longer welfare spells.

Putting work incentives in perspective. Public concern over how much welfare recipients work may be somewhat misplaced. True, an important aspect of any welfare system is the incentive structure it creates. But if the goal of welfare policy were only to maximize work effort, the government could simply force the poor into workhouses, as was done under the English Poor Law of 1834. Using the tax-transfer system to provide a social safety net inevitably means that individuals' economic decisions are distorted. Designing a good transfer system means that there should be a careful balancing of incentive and equity considerations.

Welfare Dependence

The public concern over the welfare system has encompassed broader issues than just hours of work per month. One such issue is whether receipt of social assistance reduces the chances that a recipient will ever become self-supporting. In terms of the economist's standard framework for analyzing work deci-

sions, the question is whether the receipt of welfare changes the slopes of an individual's leisure/income indifference curves—people become "lazier" if they are on welfare for an extended period of time—or whether their labour market skills atrophy when they are not employed. Barrett and Cragg (1995) examined the length of time that individuals were on welfare in British Columbia over the period 1980 to 1992. They found that 75 percent of spells on welfare were for less than six months and less than 10 percent of the welfare spells lasted more than a year, indicating that only a small proportion of welfare recipients were continuously dependent on welfare. Barrett and Cragg (1995: 16) also found that "a quarter of welfare recipients are back on the welfare rolls within three months of leaving, while a full 50 percent return within a year." Fortin, Lacroix, and Roberge (1995) found that the rate at which 25- to 30-year-old individuals leave the welfare system declined after the individual had been on welfare for four months, but the exit rate for younger individuals (18–24 years) was not affected by the length of time on welfare. They also found that individuals who had previously been on welfare had higher exit rates from welfare. Thus, the evidence from the Fortin, Lacroix, and Roberge study indicated that, at least for young people, contact with the welfare system does not generate increasing welfare dependency.

Another way that social assistance might create long-term welfare dependence is through its effects on family structure. The impact of welfare on family structure has been fiercely debated in the United States because the most important welfare program, Aid to Families with Dependent Children (AFDC), is generally only available for one-parent families. It is argued that this induces fathers to leave their families. Mothers left to fend for themselves can neither earn enough money to bring the family out of poverty nor provide a proper environment for raising children. In Canada, the impact of welfare on family structure is perceived to be less of a problem because a two-parent family is eligible for welfare if it satisfies the needs test. Still, there are concerns that the Canadian welfare system affects the incentives for a single parent to marry and also the divorce rate among low-income families. This subject has not been extensively studied in Canada. The study by Allen (1993) indicated single-parenthood and divorce are positively associated with higher welfare benefits, and a study by Dooley (1995: Table 45) indicated that the proportion of lone mothers under age 35 who have never married has increased from less than one-quarter in the 1970s to almost one-half in the 1990s. However, the welfare system's effect on family structure does not seem to have played a major role in the increase in the welfare case load because most of the growth has been in unattached individuals and married couples. More studies are required to understand the complex forces that are changing the nature of the family in Canada before we can assess the impact of the welfare system on family structure.

ALTERNATIVES TO WELFARE

Concerns about the current welfare system are sufficiently serious that a number of alternative approaches have been considered. We discuss two of these: the negative income tax and workfare.

Negative Income Tax

A negative income tax (NIT) is an income support program in which all individuals or families are guaranteed a basic annual income, even if they have zero earnings. If they have positive earnings their grants are reduced only by some fraction of their earnings. A NIT scheme differs from a classical welfare scheme in that the implicit marginal tax rate on earnings is less than 100 percent, and benefits are determined on the basis of income deficiency rather than on the assessment of need. Because NIT schemes contain an implicit guarantee that an individual's or a family's income will not fall below a certain level, such schemes are also known as Guaranteed Annual Income (GAI) schemes.

A NIT scheme would operate as follows. Suppose that the basic monthly grant is $400, and the system has a tax rate on additional earnings of 50 percent. If Doe earns $180, her grant is reduced by $90 (= .50 × $180) to $310. Doe's total monthly income is then the sum of $310 (from grant) plus $180 (from earnings) or $490. Figure 12.11 shows how this NIT scheme would affect Doe's budget constraint. As before, in the absence of an income support program, Doe works FT hours and earns OG. In the presence of the negative income tax, one option is point Q, where no labour is supplied and Doe receives $400 per month. If Doe works one hour, she receives w from her employer. Simultaneously, her grant is reduced by $1/2w$, still leaving her ahead by $1/2w$. Thus, another point on the budget constraint is U, which is one hour to the left of Q, and $1/2w$ above it. Similarly, Doe continues to receive an effective hourly wage of $1/2w$ until she works VT hours, at which point her earnings are high enough that her net grant is zero. At point S, Doe is earning $800 monthly. She receives no benefits at this, or any higher, level of earnings because the amount taxed away exhausts the basic grant of $400. Thus, the budget constraint is the kinked line QSD. Segment QS has a slope in absolute value of $1/2w$; segment SD has a slope of w.

Algebraically, the benefit received (B) is related to the basic grant (G), tax rate (t), and level of earnings (E) by $B = G - tE$. It follows that the benefit is zero $(B = 0)$ when $E = G/t$ or at any higher level of E. The earnings level, G/t, is referred to as the break-even earnings under a NIT scheme.

Figure 12.11

Budget Constraint under a Negative Income Tax

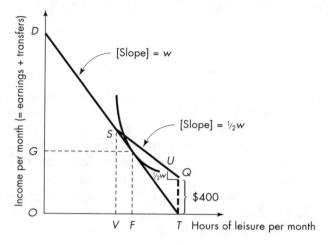

As usual, the ultimate work decision depends on the shapes of the individual's indifference curves. As drawn in Figure 12.12, Doe works fewer hours under the NIT scheme than she would in the absence of an income support program, that is, *KT* hours as opposed to *FT* hours. However, a more relevant comparison of work incentives is with the classical welfare system depicted in Figure 12.7, where she opts out of the labour force altogether. To be sure, we could also draw Doe's indifference curves in Figure 12.12 such that the maximum utility under the NIT is reached at zero hours of work. But because the implicit tax rate is less than 100 percent, this outcome is less likely under the negative income tax than it is under a classical welfare system.

The Canadian income security system has some components that operate like a NIT scheme. The Guaranteed Income Supplement (GIS) program, which is described in Chapter 14, is a NIT scheme for those over 65 years of age, and the Child Tax Benefit and GST tax credit have the characteristics of a NIT.

A universal NIT was proposed for Canada in the 1971 Senate "Report on Poverty" and by the 1985 Macdonald Royal Commission. The proponents of a universal NIT stress the following benefits:

- Welfare recipients would have more incentive to work because the marginal tax rate on their earnings would be lower.
- The working poor would receive some income support if they earn less than the break-even earnings.

Figure 12.12

Labour Supply Decision under a Negative Income Tax

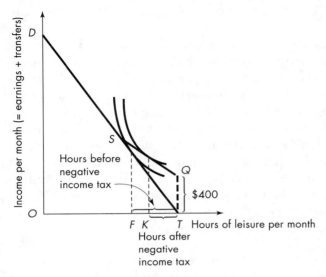

- The administration of the welfare system could be simplified by eliminating the assessment of needs under the current social assistance programs and by eliminating the duplication and overlap with other income security programs such as the GST credit, the GIS, the Child Tax Benefit, housing subsidies, and possibly unemployment insurance.

There are, however, a number of perceived problems with a universal NIT scheme. The first problem is that a universal NIT would be very costly if it were to provide both incentives to work through low tax rates and a reasonably high guaranteed annual income to support those who cannot work.[15] The calculation of the break-even earnings level indicates the fundamental dilemma in designing a negative income tax—there is a trade-off between the size of the basic grant and the tax rate on additional earnings. For a given program cost, a lower tax rate means that the basic grant must also be lower. A system with good work incentives might provide little money for those who are unable to work,

---

[15] Grady (1995) has calculated that 1.6 million households would have been eligible for benefits under a NIT scheme in 1993 if its tax rate was 50 percent and if it provided a guaranteed income of $5,000 to a single individual, $8,000 to a family of two, $10,000 to a family of three, and $12,000 to a family of four or more. The total gross cost of the scheme would have been $6.2 billion, but the net cost would have been reduced to $3.2 billion if social assistance payments were reduced.

such as the severely disabled. A system that has low tax rates and high guaranteed incomes will have a high break-even earnings level, which means that a substantial portion of the population will qualify for benefits, and this means that the rest of the population will have to pay high taxes in order to finance it.

A second problem with a NIT scheme is that, while it could increase the work incentive for current welfare recipients, it would likely reduce the work incentive for the working poor who would become eligible for benefits. The working poor would face higher marginal tax rates on their earnings than under the current system, generating a substitution effect in favour of leisure, and the guaranteed income would generate an income effect that would also favour increased consumption of leisure. The effects of NIT schemes on labour supply have been extensively studied in a series of major social experiment schemes in Canada and the United States.[16] The Manitoba Basic Annual Income Experiment (known as Mincome) was conducted between 1975 and 1979 and studied the labour supply behaviour of over one thousand families in Winnipeg, Dauphin, and rural areas of Manitoba. The study compared the labour supplies of a control group of households with individuals and families who were enrolled in NIT schemes with marginal tax rates of 35, 50, and 75 percent. Hum and Simpson (1991 and 1993) found reductions in the hours of work (1 percent for men, 3 percent for married women, and 4 percent for single women) in households enrolled in the Mincome experiment. However, it is difficult to know whether the labour supply responses to any particular NIT scheme introduced in the latter half of the 1990s would have comparable labour supply responses.

A third problem with a universal NIT scheme is that it would not be as simple as its proponents describe. Special provisions would have to be made for individuals with special needs, such as those with disabilities, and this would increase the complexity and the administration cost. Furthermore, the implementation of a universal NIT in Canada would require a high degree of federal and provincial cooperation—something that has not been exhibited in recent years.

A fourth problem with a NIT scheme is that, like a conventional welfare scheme, it is a passive income support scheme. Financial support is provided

---

[16] Aaron's (1984: 13) analysis of the U.S. NIT experiments suggests that "few men who were offered cash assistance actually quit their jobs and that the reduction in the number of hours they worked was under 10 percent. But the tests also suggested that for every $100 provided to male-headed families, earnings would fall $25 to $50." In short, while the labour supply responses are not huge, neither are they small enough to ignore.

so that basic material needs are met, but recipients are not provided with the opportunities to improve their skills, through formal training or on-the-job work experience, which would allow them to become self-sufficient. Furthermore, there is no reciprocal responsibility for the welfare/NIT recipient to try to become a more productive member of society. Dissatisfaction with passive income support programs has led to increased interest in workfare programs.

Workfare

Conventional welfare and negative income tax programs allow welfare recipients to choose their hours of work. If the receipt of the benefit lowers hours of work, so be it. An alternative scheme is workfare. Able-bodied individuals receive transfer payments only if they agree to participate in a work-related activity and accept employment, if offered. Proponents of workfare argue that it has a number of advantages: (1) Requiring welfare recipients to work may make the program more popular politically and hence lead to more generous benefits; (2) by making it harder to collect welfare, it will reduce the number of welfare recipients and lower the costs of welfare; and (3) it gives people the opportunity to gain work experience and skills, allowing them ultimately to escape from poverty. A study by Fortin, Truchon, and Beausejour (1993), which simulated labour supply responses to changes in Quebec's tax-transfer system, indicated that there are workfare programs that are potentially superior to the existing welfare system.

A number of skeptical questions have been raised about workfare: Is such a system an affront to the dignity of the poor? Can useful jobs be found for recipients? In light of the huge case loads that welfare administrators have to handle, can they differentiate between people who are able-bodied and those who are not? Are the costs of administering workfare prohibitive? Obviously there is great deal of controversy about the effectiveness and the morality of workfare programs. Recent essays on the pros and cons of workfare are contained in Krashinsky (1995) and Lightman (1995).

Because work-for-welfare programs were not eligible for funding under the Canada Assistance Plan, Canadian commentators on workfare have had to rely on the U.S. experience, where a number of states have introduced programs that are variants on the workfare theme. A review of the U.S. experience by Gueron (1993: 171) concludes that: "(1) implementing participation mandates is feasible but difficult; and (2) such programs result in positive and cost-effective—although modest—gains but do not lift large numbers of people out of poverty."

In 1996, the government of Ontario introduced the Ontario Works program, which requires social assistance recipients (excluding seniors, persons with disabilities, and single parents with young children) to participate in community projects or job training. The program started in September 1996 in twenty municipalities, and it is to be extended to the entire province in 1998. The impact of this program on social assistance case loads and the employability of social assistance recipients will be closely monitored by other provinces that are contemplating similar reforms to their welfare systems.

HAVE WELFARE PROGRAMS HELPED?

A reasonable way to begin an evaluation of the welfare system is to examine its impact on poverty. A study by Hanratty and Blank (1992) has shown that the Canadian social security system prevented the rapid deterioration in the standard of living of the bottom quintile of the income distribution that occurred in the 1980s and early 1990s. In the face of deteriorating labour market conditions for low-skilled workers, our social safety net worked. That success has come at a high financial cost, which taxpayers in the higher income brackets may not be willing to continue to support. While reforms may be necessary to lower expenditures and improve incentives, Canadian society will remain committed to preserving a social safety net for the disadvantaged.

SUMMARY

- Welfare programs are the responsibility of the provincial governments, but the federal government has played a significant role in the financing and design of the programs through the Canada Assistance Plan (CAP) and the Canada Health and Social Transfer (CHST).

- Eligibility for social assistance has been based on need. The level of social assistance benefits varies widely from province to province.

- Children and single parents represent more than half the total number on welfare, but single employable persons are the most rapidly growing component of the welfare system.

- The percentage of the population on welfare increased from 5.4 percent in 1980 to 10.4 percent in 1995. Changes in the unemployment insurance program, the level of welfare benefits, and the real wages and unemployment rates of low-income workers contributed to this trend.

- Welfare programs impose high marginal tax rates on earnings by welfare recipients. Economic theory suggests that this may discourage work, and this hypothesis is confirmed by empirical research.

- A negative income tax is an income support program in which individuals or families are guaranteed a basic annual income. Benefits are reduced as earnings increase. The main problem in designing a negative income tax is to choose the trade-off between adequate support and good work incentives.

- Under workfare, able-bodied individuals only receive benefits if they work or enrol in a training program. Preliminary evidence on these programs is mixed.

DISCUSSION QUESTIONS

1. Elizabeth's wage rate is $5 per hour. She faces a welfare system that pays a monthly benefit of $150. The benefit is reduced by 25 cents for each dollar of earnings.

    a. Sketch the budget constraint in a leisure/income diagram. How many hours does she have to work before her benefit is reduced to zero?
    b. Sketch a set of indifference curves consistent with Elizabeth's participating in the labour market and working 60 hours. What is her monthly welfare benefit?
    c. Draw your diagram for part (a) again, and now sketch a set of indifference curves consistent with Elizabeth's not participating in the market.
    d. Suppose the government introduces a workfare program that requires welfare recipients to work 100 hours per month. If welfare recipients work 100 hours they keep their earnings and receive $100 in benefits. The welfare benefits are reduced by 25 cents for each dollar of earnings after the recipient works 100 hours. Draw Elizabeth's budget constraint with the workfare program.
    e. Is Elizabeth better off under the workfare program than she was under the welfare program?

2. Suppose you wanted to conduct an econometric study of the impact of job-training programs on future earnings. What data would you need? Suggest a specific estimating equation.

3. Discuss: "Workfare is an efficient way to transfer income if the quantity of leisure consumed by the recipient appears in the utility function of the donor."

REFERENCES

Aaron, Henry J. "Six Welfare Questions Still Searching for Answers." *Brookings Review* 3, no. 1 (Fall 1984): 12–17.

Allen, Douglas. "Welfare and the Family: The Canadian Experience." *Journal of Labour Economics* 11, no. 1 (1993): S201–23.

Barrett, Gary F., and Michael I. Cragg. "Dynamics of Canadian Welfare Participation." Discussion Paper No. 95-08. Department of Economics, University of British Columbia, 1995.

Battle, Ken, and Sherri Torjman. "The Welfare Wall: The Interactions of the Welfare and Tax Systems." Ottawa: Caledon Institute of Social Policy, 1993.

Boessenkool, Kenneth J. *Back to Work: Learning from the Alberta Welfare Experiment.* C.D. Howe Institute Commentary 90. Toronto: C.D. Howe Institute, 1997.

Brown, D.M. "Welfare Case Load Trends in Canada," in *Helping the Poor: A Qualified Case for "Workfare,"* ed. J. Richards and W.G. Watson. Toronto: C.D. Howe Institute, 1995, pp. 37–90.

Charette, M., and R. Meng. "The Determinants of Welfare Participation of Female Heads of Households in Canada." *Canadian Journal of Economics* 27, no. 2 (1994): 290–306.

Courchene, Thomas J. *Redistributing Money and Power: A Guide to the Canada Health and Social Transfer.* Observation 39. Toronto: C.D. Howe Institute, 1995.

Courchene, Thomas J. *Social Canada in the Millennium.* Toronto: C.D. Howe Institute, 1994.

Dooley, Martin. "Lone-Mother Families and Social Assistance Policy in Canada," in *Family Matters: New Policies for Divorce, Lone Mothers, and Child Poverty,* ed. J. Richards and W.G. Watson. Toronto: C.D. Howe Institute, 1995, pp. 35–104.

Fortin, B., G. Lacroix, and H. Roberge. "The Dynamics of Welfare Spells in Quebec." Department of Economics, Laval University, 1995.

Fortin, Bernard, Michel Truchon, and Louis Beausejour. "On Reforming the Welfare System: Workfare Meets the Negative Income Tax." *Journal of Public Economics* 51, no. 2 (June 1993): 119–51.

Grady, Patrick. "Income Security Reform and the Concept of a Guaranteed Annual Income," in *Redefining Social Security.* Government and Competitiveness Project, School of Policy Studies, Queen's University, 1995.

Gueron, Judith M. "Welfare Reform in the United States: Strategies to Increase Work and Reduce Poverty," in *Income Security in Canada: Changing Needs, Changing Means,* ed. Elisabeth B. Reynolds. Montreal: Institute for Research on Public Policy, 1993, pp. 171–87.

Hanratty, Maria J., and Rebecca M. Blank. "Down and Out in North America: Recent Trends in Poverty Rates in the United States and Canada." *Quarterly Journal of Economics* 107, no. 1 (February 1992): 233–54.

Hobson, Paul A., and France St-Hilaire. "The Financing and Delivery of Social Policy: Fiscal Transfers for Social Assistance and Social Services," in *Income Security in Canada: Changing Needs, Changing Means,* ed. Elisabeth B. Reynolds. Montreal: Institute for Research on Public Policy, 1993, pp. 117–47.

Hum, Derek, and W. Simpson. "Economic Response to a Guaranteed Annual Income: Experience from Canada and the United States." *Journal of Labour Economics* 11, no. 1 (1993): S263–96.

Hum, Derek, and Wayne Simpson. *Income Maintenance, Work Effort, and the Canadian Mincome Experiment.* Ottawa: Economic Council of Canada, 1991.

Human Resources Development Canada. *Basic Facts on Social Security Programs.* Ottawa: Ministry of Supply and Services Canada, November 1994a.

Human Resources Development Canada. *Reforming the Canada Assistance Plan: A Supplementary Paper.* Ottawa: Ministry of Supply and Services Canada, November 1994b.

Krashinsky, Michael. "Putting the Poor to Work: Why 'Workfare' Is an Idea Whose Time Has Come," in *Helping the Poor: A Qualified Case for "Workfare,"* ed. J. Richards and W.G. Watson. Toronto: C.D. Howe Institute, 1995, pp. 91–120.

Lightman, Ernie S. "You Can Lead a Horse to Water; but ...: The Case against Workfare in Canada," in *Helping the Poor: A Qualified Case for "Workfare,"* ed. J. Richards and W.G. Watson. Toronto: C.D. Howe Institute, 1995, pp. 151–83.

National Council of Welfare. *Welfare Incomes 1995.* Ottawa: Ministry of Supply and Services Canada, 1997.

National Council of Welfare. *Incentives and Disincentives to Work.* Ottawa: Ministry of Supply and Services Canada, 1993.

Peters, Suzanne. *Exploring Canadian Values: Foundations for Well-Being.* CPRN Study No. F01, rev. ed. Ottawa: Canadian Policy Research Network, 1995.

Sarlo, C.A. *Poverty in Canada.* Vancouver: Fraser Institute, 1992.

Chapter 13

Unemployment Insurance

The UI program is designed to provide workers with earnings-related benefits in the event of unemployment: it is not designed to provide all Canadians with a minimum level of income: nor is UI designed to redistribute incomes on a vertical basis.

—Canadian Labour Congress

For us. Unemployment Insurance is a federal social assistance program. whose purpose is to protect against temporary interruption of earnings.

—Fédération des femmes du Québec

I don't see UI as a problem. I see that $1 million a week coming into the Miramichi economy as a God-send. as a matter of fact. UI is not the problem. It is one of the strengths of the economy.

—Miramichi Regional Development Corporation

The unemployment insurance system plays a central role in Canada's income security system. It provided income protection for 13.1 million Canadians, and over 913,000 people received benefits in 1996. It is the largest single expenditure program of the federal government. In 1994, $12.002 billion was spent on regular benefits, $1.703 billion was spent on sickness, maternity, adoption, and parental benefits, $0.249 billion was spent on fishing benefits, and $1.837 billion was spent on training, work sharing, job creation, and self-employment assistance.

Unemployment insurance is also one of the most controversial programs. Every decade there has been a major review of the program. The most recent review resulted in some significant changes in 1996, including a name change —Employment Insurance. Part of the reason for the controversy, and the continual search for reforms, is that there are very different views about the role of unemployment insurance in the Canadian income security program. The lead quotes for this chapter were drawn from submissions to the Forget Commission of Inquiry on Unemployment Insurance in the mid-1980s, and they express different views about the role of unemployment insurance. The Canadian Labour Congress emphasized the insurance role of the UI program, the Fédération des femmes du Québec emphasized the fact that it was a *federal* (as opposed to a provincial) social assistance program, albeit for temporary income losses, and the Miramichi Regional Development Corporation emphasized the importance of UI as a support for the Miramichi region. Given these diverse views, it is little wonder that there has been an ongoing debate about the purpose of the unemployment insurance program. In this chapter, we review the history of the program and reasons why unemployment insurance is provided by the public sector. We examine the effects of the UI system on unemployment rates and the redistributional effects among industries, regions, and income groups. Finally, we describe the 1996 reforms, which set the stage for the current Employment Insurance system. We begin by examining the nature and trends of unemployment in Canada.

UNEMPLOYMENT IN CANADA

Unemployment is measured by Statistics Canada's Labour Force Survey. Around 50,000 households are contacted by the survey each month, and individuals over 15 years of age are asked a variety of questions about their labour market behaviour.[1] Individuals are considered to be **unemployed** if they did not have a job at the time of the survey, but were available for work and made an effort to find a job during the previous four weeks. They are also counted as unemployed if they were available for work and were waiting to be recalled to a job from which they had been laid off within the last twenty-six weeks or were waiting to report to a new job within four weeks. Individuals who had a job—regardless of the number of hours worked—or who were off work because of illness, vacation time, or an industrial dispute are considered to be employed. The **labour force** is defined as the total number of individuals who are employed and unemployed. The **unemployment rate** is the percentage of the labour force that is unemployed. Those who did not have a job and did not actively search for employment, such as full-time students, are classified as **not in the labour force**.

---

[1] The labour force survey also excludes persons living on Indian reserves, members of the military, and people living in institutions such as prisons.

Figure 13.1

Average Monthly Labour Force Flows, 1976–1991 (in thousands)

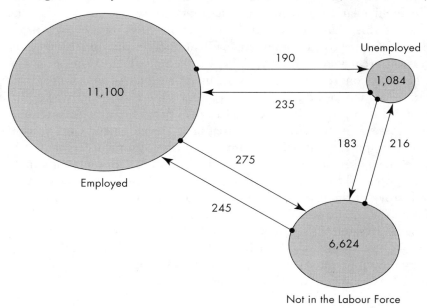

SOURCE: Jones (1993: Table 1, p. 3). Reprinted with permission of *Canadian Public Policy/Analyse de Politiques.*

Figure 13.1 shows the average number of individuals in the three categories of labour market activity over the period 1976 to 1991. The average number of employed persons was 11.1 million, and the average number of unemployed was 1.08 million. The labour force averaged 12.2 million, and the average unemployment rate was (1.08/12.2) × 100 or 8.9 percent. The **labour force participation rate**, which measures the labour force as a percentage of the working-age population, averaged 64.8 percent over this period. The **employment rate**, which measures total employment as a percentage of the working-age population, averaged 59 percent.

Figure 13.1 also shows the average monthly flows among the categories of employed, unemployed, and those not in the labour force. On average, 190,000 individuals (1.7 percent of the employed) quit their jobs or were laid off and became unemployed each month. On the other hand, 235,000 unemployed individuals (22.2 percent of the total unemployed) found jobs each month. At the same time, 183,000 unemployed individuals stopped looking for work and dropped out of the labour market. Some of these may have been

discouraged workers who stopped looking for work, not because they were no longer interested in gaining employment, but because they thought that their chances of getting employment were so low that it was not worthwhile searching for a job. On the other hand, some of those who dropped out of the labour force may have decided that another activity, such as going back to school or raising children full-time, was more important than looking for employment. On average 275,000 individuals left employment each month and dropped out of the labour force. At the same time, 245,000 individuals, who in the previous month had not been looking for employment, found a job. It is interesting to note that the average monthly flows between the employed and the not in the labour force categories are even larger than the flows between the employed and the unemployed categories.

In summary, Figure 13.1 indicates that the level of unemployment depends on:

- the rate at which individuals are laid off or quit their jobs, but continue to search for new jobs;
- the rate at which unemployed individuals find acceptable job offers and become employed;
- the rate at which unemployed individuals drop out of the labour force;
- the rate at which individuals enter or re-enter the labour force and look for employment.

The data in the figure also indicate that while month-to-month changes in total unemployment may be small, the turnover rate among the unemployed may be relatively high, and that movements in and out of the labour force can have a significant effect on the measured level of unemployment.

Defining and measuring the "true" unemployment rate is very difficult. As we have seen, discouraged workers are not counted as unemployed. On the other hand, there may be other "unemployed" individuals who, in practice, make very little effort to find a job and yet report that they are looking for employment. There is no definition or standard concerning the amount of effort or the actions that an individual must take in order to qualify as unemployed. Individuals differ in how they describe their effort or their aspirations to find a job, and this means that the measured unemployment rate may understate or overstate the "actual" level of unemployment. Because of the individual differences in self-reporting, some economists feel that the employment rate is a better measure of the state of the labour market. One difficulty with both the employment rate and the unemployment rate is that individuals with a job are considered to be employed even if they would like to work more hours. Part-time employment is becoming increasingly common, and many individuals with part-time jobs report that they would like to work more hours, but are

Figure 13.2

Labour Market Trends

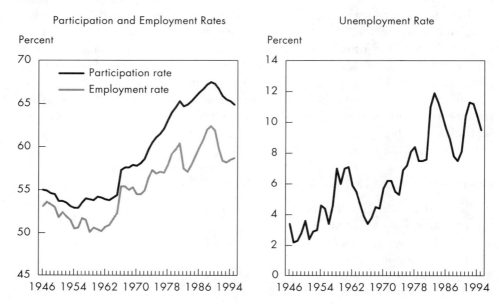

SOURCE: Statistics Canada, *The Labour Force* (Ottawa: November 1995).

not able to do so. Such individuals can be viewed as partially unemployed, but this aspect of unemployment is not reflected in the official unemployment rate.[2] Unemployment is a complex social and economic phenomenon. There are significant conceptual problems in defining it and practical difficulties in measuring it. A good deal of caution has to exercised in interpreting these labour market statistics.

Figure 13.2 shows trends in the participation rate, the employment rate, and the unemployment rate since 1946. There has been a upward trend in the labour force participation rate from 54.1 percent in 1965 to a peak of 67.5 percent in 1989. The increase in labour force participation over this period has been due to the dramatic increase in the participation rate of married females. The figure also shows that there have been fluctuations in the employment rate, as a result of expansions and contractions in the Canadian economy, and these are mir-

---

[2] The analysis in Gower (1990: Table 1, p. 76) indicated that an "hours-based" unemployment rate exceeded the official unemployment rate by 15 percent for men and 40 percent for women in 1988.

rored by fluctuations in the unemployment rate. While there has been a secular increase in the employment rate from 53.1 percent in 1946 to 64.2 percent in 1989, there has also been a significant upward trend in the unemployment rate. During the 1950s, the average unemployment rate was 4.2 percent, in the 1960s it was 5.0 percent, in the 1970s it was 6.7 percent, in the 1980s it was 9.4 percent, and over the period 1990 to 1995 it averaged 10.2 percent. The upward trend in the unemployment rate has been a major concern for Canadians.

While a number of Western countries have experienced rising unemployment rates, the Canadian experience has been quite different from that of the United States, our largest trading partner and a country with similar labour market institutions. Average unemployment rates in Canada and the United States were similar in the 1950s and 1960s. However, since the 1980s the average unemployment rate in Canada has been about two percentage points higher than in the United States, and in 1995 it was four points higher. Card and Riddell (1993) found that the unemployment rates diverged in the 1980s because individuals who are not working are more likely to be classified as unemployed in Canada than in the United States.

Regional variations in the unemployment rate are very important in Canada. As Table 13.1 indicates, the Atlantic provinces and Quebec have experienced above-average unemployment rates, while Ontario and the Prairie provinces have generally experienced below-average unemployment rates. Variations in the unemployment rate can be due to variations in the incidence of unemployment—the percentage of individuals who become unemployed during a year—and the duration of a spell of unemployment. Table 13.1 shows that, in 1985, 25.4 percent of the labour force experienced unemployment at some point during the year and that the average duration of an unemployment spell was 17.7 weeks. These data indicate that the incidence of unemployment in Atlantic Canada was much higher than in the rest of Canada, and that the average duration of unemployment was also somewhat higher. Average unemployment rates are generally higher in rural areas than in urban areas.

In evaluating the severity of a country's unemployment, economists often focus on the duration of unemployment because long periods of unemployment may be particularly damaging to the skills and self-esteem of a worker. While in recent years Canada's unemployment rate has been comparable to a number of Western European countries, long-term unemployment has been less of a problem. For example, in Canada in 1995, 13.8 percent of the unemployed were without a job for more than a year, while in France and Germany the percentages were 45.6 and 48.3 percent respectively. In the United States, only 9.7 percent of the unemployed were without a job for more than one year (OECD, 1997).

Table 13.1

Unemployment Rates, Incidence, and Duration by Province

	AVERAGE UNEMPLOYMENT RATE, 1976–1996	INCIDENCE OF UNEMPLOYMENT IN 1985 (PERCENT)	AVERAGE NUMBER OF WEEKS UNEMPLOYED IN 1985
Newfoundland	17.4	39.9	20.8
Prince Edward Island	13.5	31.8	19.8
Nova Scotia	11.8	28.9	20.2
New Brunswick	12.8	34.7	20.2
Quebec	11.2	28.3	20.1
Ontario	7.9	21.3	14.5
Manitoba	7.6	21.5	15.3
Saskatchewan	6.6	20.1	15.9
Alberta	7.5	25.2	15.9
British Columbia	10.1	29.7	20.3
Canada	9.3	25.4	17.7

SOURCE: Statistics Canada and Forget Report (1986: Figure 2.16, p. 54).

Unemployment rates also vary according to individuals' demographic characteristics. Table 13.2 indicates that in 1995, males had a higher average unemployment rate than females, and their average duration of unemployment was also higher. Young people, on average, have higher unemployment rates than older workers, but the average duration of unemployment is higher for older workers. In general, unemployment rates are lower for workers with more education and training (Forget, 1986: Figure 2.17, p. 55).

THE RATIONALE FOR PUBLIC UNEMPLOYMENT INSURANCE

Why should the public sector provide unemployment insurance? First, we examine the possibility of market failure, and then we consider the role of unemployment insurance as an income redistribution program.

Market Failure in the Provision of Unemployment Insurance

Recall from Chapters 5 and 9 that private markets may fail to provide adequate amounts of insurance in situations where **adverse selection** and **moral hazard** are important. First consider adverse selection. As the tables in the pre-

Table 13.2

Demographic Characteristics and Unemployment

DEMOGRAPHIC CHARACTERISTIC	UNEMPLOYMENT RATE IN 1995	AVERAGE DURATION OF UNEMPLOYMENT IN NOVEMBER 1995 (IN WEEKS)
Sex:		
Male	9.8	25.8
Female	9.2	22.3
Age:		
15–24 years	15.6	15.5
25–44 years	8.9	24.8
45 years and older	7.3	33.2

SOURCE: Statistics Canada, *The Labour Force* (Ottawa: November 1995) and CANSIM Matrix 2064.

ceding section indicate, individual workers face different probabilities of being unemployed for different lengths of time. Those workers who have the highest probability of becoming unemployed for long periods of time will have the highest demand for unemployment insurance. Therefore, private insurance firms would have to charge relatively high premiums to make a profit, which would make private unemployment insurance unattractive for many low-risk individuals. At the same time, unemployment insurance is subject to a moral hazard problem because workers and their employers can influence, to some extent, the probability and the magnitude of a loss. For example, a firm can affect the probability that its workers will be unemployed by deciding whether to lay off workers during a recession. Workers can affect the duration of a spell of unemployment (the magnitude of the loss) by deciding how much effort to put into searching for a new job or deciding whether to accept a new job at a lower rate of pay or in a new region. Because it is difficult for the insurer to determine whether, or to what extent, a layoff or a spell of unemployment is the fault of a firm or a worker, a private unemployment insurance company would have to pay out large amounts of money for a "full coverage" policy. To reduce the incentive to collect unemployment insurance, a private firm would offer "partial coverage" policies where only part of the lost wages of an unemployed worker would be covered. It might also charge higher premiums to those workers who made more frequent claims.

As noted in the earlier chapters, a compulsory government insurance program avoids the adverse selection problem. Premiums can be based on the average expected loss for the entire labour force, and this is especially beneficial for those who face an above-average risk of unemployment. (See Chapter 9 on the welfare effects of compulsory insurance.) However, government provision does not eliminate the moral hazard problem, and the unemployment insurance system should be designed to reduce the incentives for layoffs and lengthy spells of unemployment. For example, unemployment insurance systems often do not cover the first few weeks of unemployment, and the benefit rate is usually only a fraction of the worker's employment earnings. These features are equivalent to deductibles and coinsurance clauses in more conventional insurance policies.

Another reason why the private sector may not be able to provide unemployment insurance is that the unemployment insurance claims increase dramatically during recessions and decline during economic expansions. As discussed in Chapter 9, the cyclical nature of unemployment means that the risk-pooling mechanism cannot eliminate the risk from the cost of providing unemployment insurance. A national government has a greater capacity to borrow than a private corporation to finance unemployment insurance claims during a recession, and therefore it has an important advantage in the provision of unemployment insurance.

Unemployment Insurance as an Income Redistribution Program

Alternatively, many think that unemployment insurance is primarily an income redistribution program and not an insurance program that happens to be provided by the public sector because of market failure. Conflicting views over the purpose of social insurance programs have been a recurring element in the debate over the design of social insurance programs in Canada, as the following quote from the 1943 *Report on Social Security for Canada* (the Marsh Report) indicates:

> The understanding of social insurance ... is still confused because too much emphasis is placed on the second word and too little on the first word of the phrase. Social insurance brings in the resources of the state, i.e., the resources of the community as a whole, or in a particular case that part of the resources which may be garnered together through taxes or contributions. It does not mean ... that there must be a precise actuarial adjustment of premiums to risk in each individual case.[3]

In discussing the issue of whether unemployment insurance should be treated as an insurance or an income redistribution program, it is important to dis-

---

[3] Marsh (1975: 10–11).

tinguish between **ex ante redistribution** and **ex post redistribution**. All insurance programs, including privately provided insurance, redistribute wealth from those that did not suffer a loss to those that did. Therefore, insurance always changes the distribution of wealth compared to what it would have been in the absence of insurance. This type of redistribution is called ex post redistribution because we only know who are the winners and losers after the insured event has occurred. An alternative type of redistribution occurs when an individual's contribution or premium differs from his or her expected payout from the insurance coverage. Recall from Chapter 9 that an actuarially fair premium is the expected payout from an insurance policy. For example, if Sam faces a 20 percent probability of being unemployed for ten weeks each year, during which time he would collect $4,000 in unemployment insurance benefits, then the actuarially fair premium for this unemployment insurance coverage is $800. If Sam's actual contribution or premium is less than $800, then Sam receives an ex ante subsidy. If his actual premium is more than $800, then he makes an ex ante net contribution to the unemployment insurance system. Competition among private insurance companies means that there is no ex ante redistribution among their policy holders. If an identifiable group were charged more than the expected cost of their insurance coverage, another company could offer them a lower premium. In contrast, a social insurance program, such as unemployment insurance, can involve ex ante redistribution because such programs are usually compulsory, and there is no competitive pressure from alternative suppliers to force premiums in line with expected benefits. Thus, unemployment insurance can be considered an income redistribution program if it leads to ex ante redistribution. Ex ante redistribution can occur either within the unemployment insurance system if, for example, all of the insured make the same contributions, but some of the insured have higher claim frequencies or draw larger benefits, or if the total contributions from the insured do not cover the benefits that are paid out, and the deficiency is financed from other government revenues. Consequently, both the way that unemployment insurance benefits are structured and the way that they are financed will determine whether the unemployment insurance system involves ex ante redistribution.

In a later section, we will consider whether the Canadian unemployment insurance system has resulted in ex ante redistribution. For the present, we will consider whether it is desirable to have ex ante redistribution through unemployment insurance. Those who think that unemployment insurance should function as an income redistribution program argue that social insurance programs help to supplement social assistance programs. Henry Richardson (1960: 63) argued that since:

the community as a whole gains substantial advantages from social insurance, it is reasonable that it should make a contribution towards the cost. Provision of social insurance benefits would reduce the number of people who would otherwise have to ask for public assistance, and any resultant savings could be used as a social insurance contribution.

In other words, all taxpayers should subsidize unemployment insurance because unemployment insurance benefits reduce the amount that governments would otherwise have to spend on social assistance. Unemployment insurance also allows governments to provide income support, which is linked to labour market activity, and therefore the disincentives to return to work are not as great as they are under welfare programs where the implicit tax rate on earnings is often very high. As Lars Osberg (1995: 224) has noted:

> UI is much closer to "workfare" than to traditional social assistance. In requiring that individuals, even in very depressed local labour markets, somehow repeatedly come up with 12 weeks of paid employment, the UI system now forces individuals into repeated job search and repeated contact with employment (usually in the private sector). A purely passive income transfer system [such as a negative income tax scheme] does not require any job search or work effort.

Having an income support system with two different programs—unemployment insurance for those who normally have full-time employment and social assistance for those with only limited ability to be self-supporting—means that each program can be geared to a different segment of the population, and this allows the social assistance system to be more generous than it otherwise would be if it were the only income support program.[4]

Critics of the notion that the unemployment insurance system is primarily an income redistribution program argue that in practice the unemployment insurance program does a poor job of redistributing income to the poor, it violates the goals of horizontal and vertical equity, and it has caused major distortions in labour market decisions of firms and workers because it lacks an insurance orientation. Before considering these criticisms further, we will review the main features of the unemployment insurance system in Canada.

---

[4] Recall from the previous chapter that for a given level of expenditure, there is a trade-off between the level of benefits and the marginal tax rate under a negative income tax.

THE HISTORY OF THE CANADIAN UNEMPLOYMENT INSURANCE SYSTEM

The Creation of the UI Program

The unprecedented increase in unemployment during the 1930s inflicted enormous suffering on Canadian workers and their families. In 1933, approximately 25 percent of the labour force was unemployed, and 15 percent of the population was "on relief," which was largely funded by the provincial and municipal governments. These tragic events convinced many Canadians that the federal government should be involved in the provision of social insurance programs. However, the social insurance program enacted by Prime Minister R.B. Bennett's Conservative government in 1935 was ruled *ultra vires*, that is, outside the jurisdiction of the federal government. With the agreement of the provinces, the BNA Act (now the Constitution Act, 1867) was amended to give the federal government exclusive jurisdiction over the provision of unemployment insurance, and Prime Minister William Lyon Mackenzie King's Liberal government passed the 1940 Unemployment Insurance Act, which established a program of unemployment benefits based on insurance principles. Coverage was limited to those in jobs for which there was a moderate risk of unemployment. "Jobs with high rates of turnover or seasonality were excluded, and those from which people were not likely to be laid off were also out" (HRDC, 1996). Specifically excluded were "high risk" jobs in agriculture, forestry, and fishing and "low risk" jobs in the police, the armed forces, and government employment. Persons who earned more than $2,000 per year were also excluded. As a result of these limitations, only 42 percent of the labour force was covered by the unemployment insurance system. Nonetheless, the program was the largest social insurance program enacted by a Canadian government up to that time. It was financed mainly by contributions from employers and employees, with the federal government paying 20 percent of the total contributions plus the administration costs out of general revenue. The unemployment insurance benefits were "approximately one-half of the wage-rate with a 15 per cent supplement for a married claimant" (Guest, 1980: 108). The maximum duration of benefits was "one day of benefit for each five daily contributions made in the previous five years, less one day for each three days of benefits received in the previous three years" (HRDC, 1996). The reduction in the benefit period if benefits were received in the previous three years was intended to curtail the use of the program by the seasonally unemployed.

Table 13.3 shows how some of the important characteristics of the unemployment insurance system have evolved over the last fifty years. In the 1950s, coverage was expanded to provide some seasonal unemployment benefits, and

Table 13.3

Characteristics of Unemployment Insurance in Canada, 1946–1991

YEAR	PERCENTAGE OF LABOUR FORCE COVERED	AVERAGE EARNINGS REPLACEMENT RATE (PERCENT)	MINIMUM NUMBER OF WEEKS TO QUALIFY	MAXIMUM NUMBER OF WEEKS FOR MINIMALLY QUALIFIED CLAIMANT
1946	44	47	30	6
1951	58	38	30	6
1961	62	38	30	15
1966	61	31	30	15
1971	63	35	8	28–44
1976	91	41	8	28–44
1981	89	37	10–14	10–42
1986	91	42	10–14	10–42
1991	92	46	10–20	10–42

SOURCE: Lazar (1994: Table 3, p. 52).

in 1956 unemployment insurance benefits were extended to "self-employed" fishermen. These amendments to the program represented important departures from the "insurance principles" upon which the original program had been based. In 1962, the Gill Committee, which had been established by Prime Minister John Diefenbaker's government to study the unemployment insurance system, acknowledged that the program had moved away from its insurance principles and become part of Canada's income security system, and it recommended the establishment of a coordinated income security system.

The 1971 Reforms

No major changes were made to the unemployment insurance system until 1971 when the Unemployment Insurance Act (Bill C-229) was passed. This bill expanded UI coverage to 93 percent of the labour force, excluding the self-employed, and increased the generosity of the unemployment insurance system. The minimum requirements for eligibility were reduced to eight weeks of employment, and the benefit rate was increased to two-thirds of previous insurable earnings (75 percent for those with dependents) up to the maximum insurable earnings level, which was initially set at $150 per week. Sickness and maternity benefits were enhanced. The duration of benefits was linked to the number of weeks worked in the qualifying period, and it also increased when the national unemployment rate exceeded 4 percent and when the unemployment rate in the worker's region exceeded the national average by one to three percentage points. This feature of the unemployment insurance system is known as **regional extended benefits**. For example, if the national unemployment rate was 5.5 percent, then a worker who lived in a region with an unemployment rate of 9 percent was eligible for forty-four weeks of benefits if he or she worked eight weeks. The regular benefits, maternity, sickness, and retirement benefits, and the administration costs of the system were financed by contributions collected from employers and employees. In 1972, employees paid $0.90 for each $100 of insurable earnings, and employers paid 1.4 times this amount. The federal government paid for the unemployment insurance benefits that were attributable to a national unemployment rate in excess of 4 percent, the regional extended benefits, the training benefits, and the benefits for self-employed fishermen out of general revenues.

Between 1971 and 1972, with the introduction of the new unemployment insurance program, the number of persons covered by unemployment insurance increased from 5.439 million to 7.845 million; the number of weeks of paid benefits increased from 22.6 million to 30.5 million; and the average weekly payment increased from $40.28 to $61.79.[5] The total expenditure on unemployment insurance benefits more than tripled, from $0.590 billion to $1.868 billion, even though the average rate of unemployment, 6.2 percent, was the same in both years. As a result of the enhanced benefits and increased coverage, expenditure on unemployment insurance benefits soared from 0.8 percent of GNP in 1971 to 2.1 percent of GNP in 1975. This prompted a number of reforms that were aimed at reducing the generosity of the system and curtailing abuse. In 1975, the disqualification period for those who had quit their job without just cause or were fired for misconduct was increased from three to six weeks. The age limit for unemployment insurance coverage was reduced from 70 to 65. The 75 percent benefit rate for those with dependents was eliminated. The financing of unemployment insurance was also changed. The national unemployment rate at which the federal government funded benefits out of general revenue was changed to an eight-year moving average, instead of 4 percent. Further amendments in 1977 increased the number of weeks of insurable employment that new entrants and re-entrants to the labour force and people with repeat claims needed in order to establish a claim, but there was an exemption for repeat claimants in high-unemployment regions. The benefit rate was also reduced from two-thirds of insurable earnings to 60 percent. High-income earners were subject to a claw-back of 30 percent of their UI benefits if their net income exceeded 1.5 times the maximum insurable earnings.

---

[5] See Statistics Canada (1995: Table 10, p. 37).

UI in the 1980s

During the recession of the early 1980s, the unemployment rate increased from 7.6 percent in 1981 to 11.9 percent in 1983, and unemployment insurance benefits jumped from $4.757 billion to $10.063 billion. The reform of unemployment insurance was a major concern of the Macdonald Royal Commission on the Economic Union and Development Prospects for Canada, which released its report in 1985. The commission argued that the unemployment insurance system was in part responsible for the increase in unemployment rates in Canada since 1971 and that the UI system should be re-established on insurance principles. It was argued that the income redistribution component of the UI system should instead be met through a negative income tax (NIT) system, which would provide all Canadians with a guaranteed annual income. The Forget Commission of Inquiry on Unemployment Insurance, which issued its report in 1986, also recommended that regional extended benefits be abolished and that they be replaced with an earnings supplementation program similar to a NIT. Both of these reports met with considerable opposition, especially from Atlantic Canada and from representatives of the labour movement who issued their own minority report as an addendum to the Forget Report. As a result, the recommendations of the Macdonald Royal Commission and the Forget Report were largely ignored. During the latter half of the 1980s, the unemployment rate slowly declined, but unemployment insurance benefits remained in the $9 to $11 billion range.

The next major change to the UI program occurred in 1989 with Bill C-21, which expanded the use of unemployment insurance funds for training, relocation assistance, and other employment measures. The impetus for these changes was the view that the long-term unemployed or repeat users had to be provided with additional training or assistance in relocation if they were to become less dependent on the UI system for income support. "Active" labour market intervention, and not just "passive" income support measures, was necessary to break the dependence on the unemployment insurance system. Expenditures on training programs expanded from around 3 percent of total UI expenditure to over 8 percent by 1992.[6] Other significant changes in 1989 were the repeal of the qualification provisions for repeat users of the UI system and the cessation of the federal government's contributions toward the financing of unemployment insurance. Starting in fiscal year 1991–92, the unemployment insurance system was entirely financed by employer and employee contributions.

---

[6] See Lazar (1994: Table 5, p. 55).

UI in the 1990s

During the 1990–92 recession, the unemployment rate increased to 11.3 percent. The sharp increase in unemployment insurance claims meant that the UI account had a large deficit, and the government increased the employee contribution rate from $2.25 to $2.80 effective July 1, 1991. In 1992, the contribution rates were further increased to $3.00 for employees and $4.20 for employers. The 33 percent increase in the employer contribution rate during the recession may have increased the number of layoffs and exacerbated the unemployment problem.

In 1993, the federal government also reduced the benefit rate from 60 percent to 57 percent, and those who voluntarily quit their jobs without just cause became ineligible for UI benefits. In 1994, further measures were taken to reduce the generosity of the UI system. The minimum entrance requirement for UI eligibility in high-unemployment regions (more than 13 percent) was increased from ten weeks to twelve weeks. (The minimum entrance requirement in a region with an unemployment rate of 6.0 percent or less was twenty weeks.) Claimants could receive benefits for seventeen to fifty weeks depending on the number of weeks worked and the regional unemployment rate. The benefit rate was reduced to 55 percent, but a higher benefit rate of 60 percent for low-income recipients with dependents was reintroduced. The employee contribution rate was increased to $3.00 per $100 of insurable earnings up to the maximum insurable earnings of $780.00 per week.

A major review of Canadian social security programs was launched by Prime Minister Jean Chrétien's government in 1994. The review culminated in the 1996 Employment Insurance Act. The provisions of the new Employment Insurance (EI) system will be described after we have discussed the efficiency and distributional effects of the UI system that it replaced.

THE LABOUR MARKET EFFECTS OF UI

As we have seen, there has been an ongoing debate in Canada about whether the unemployment insurance system should be structured as an insurance program or as an income redistribution program. Whichever concept is used to justify a system of unemployment insurance, the effects of the unemployment insurance system on the labour market behaviour of firms and workers and its redistributional impact are important characteristics of the system. These characteristics of the UI system will be evaluated in this section.

Moral Hazard

The concept of moral hazard provides a useful framework for thinking about the labour market impacts of the UI system, even if the primary purpose of unemployment insurance is to "redistribute" income rather than to "insure" income. A moral hazard problem exists if the insured individual can alter his or her behaviour in unobservable ways that affect the probability, or the magnitude, of a loss. The provision of insurance will in general cause individuals to change their behaviour so that the expected loss increases. The features of the insurance program can be altered so that a balance is struck between the change in behaviour of the insured and the provision of benefits when earnings are reduced due to unemployment. As was indicated in Chapter 9, it is very difficult to design a system of incentives that balances these competing objectives. Economists have been primarily concerned with trying to understand how the unemployment insurance system affects labour market behaviour, and in particular with its effect on the unemployment rate, but they have not made much headway on the question of the optimal design of the unemployment insurance system. This, of course, has not prevented them from making recommendations regarding the reform of the system.

A couple of aspects of the moral hazard problem, as it applies to unemployment insurance, should be borne in mind. First, moral hazard refers to the changes in the behaviour of individuals and firms, operating within the rules and guidelines of the system, that increase the expected payouts from the UI system. Moral hazard is not primarily concerned with the abuse of the system by individuals or firms who break the rules for personal gain. Cheating the UI system is undoubtedly a problem, just as tax evasion is a problem. (See Chapter 19 for an analysis of tax evasion.) Investigation and enforcement measures can help to reduce the amount of cheating that takes place. Second, even though the unemployment insurance system only insures workers, an employer's behaviour may be affected by the unemployment insurance system and therefore subject to a moral hazard problem. Employers and employees may agree, explicitly or implicitly, to alter the nature of their employment arrangements to take advantage of the provisions of the UI system.

Canadian economists first became concerned with the effect of the unemployment insurance system on the level of unemployment in the mid-1970s in the wake of the 1971 reforms, which dramatically increased the UI system's generosity and coverage, and in view of the steady rise in the unemployment rate. Studies by Grubel, Maki, and Sax (1975) and Green and Cousineau (1976) examined the effect of the 1971 changes on the unemployment rate in Canada using aggregate time series data. They concluded that the 1971 reforms increased the aggregate unemployment rate by between 0.4 and 0.8 of a percentage point. A number of other studies have investigated this issue, and as is often the case in economics, some of the subsequent studies yielded similar results while others found that the 1971 reforms had no effect on the unemployment rate.

There are a number of reasons why it is has been difficult to reach a consensus on the effects of the 1971 reforms. First, unemployment insurance is an extremely complicated program with many different provisions that affect the "generosity" of the system. For example, generosity is affected not only by the benefit replacement rate, but also by the maximum and minimum insurable earnings, the number of weeks of work that are required to become eligible for benefits, the number of weeks of benefits that are paid, and the penalties, if any, that are imposed on those who quit their jobs without cause or repeatedly apply for benefits. It is extremely difficult to measure the generosity of the UI system using a single variable such as the benefit replacement rate. Furthermore, some provisions of the UI system only affect certain regions with high unemployment or certain workers (such as self-employed fishermen), and therefore the system may have important impacts on particular labour markets, but relatively small effects on the aggregate unemployment rate. A second problem is that other factors, such as the oil price increases in the 1970s and the high real interest rates since the early 1980s, may have contributed to the rise in the unemployment rate. It is difficult to disentangle the effects of the changes in the unemployment insurance system on the unemployment rate from the effects of these shocks to the economy and the other, more subtle, long-term trends, such as changes in labour force participation behaviour, technological change, and international competitiveness.

Miles Corak (1994: 146–47) has prepared an extensive review of the recent Canadian studies of the effects of unemployment insurance on the unemployment rate, and he has concluded that "macro-level research conducted since the mid-1980s does not appear to offer conclusive evidence that changes in the UI program since 1970 have increased the aggregate unemployment rate or altered its dynamics." He went on to note that "the finding that UI has no effect in the aggregate should not be taken to imply that it is not in fact having an effect on behavior. The efficiency and distributional consequences of the program could very well be quite great without there being any aggregate effect at all."

To help organize the discussion of the effects of the UI system on the unemployment rate, we will use the schema shown in Table 13.4. The effects can be divided into direct effects, systemic effects, and macroeconomic effects. The direct effects of the UI system are the effects on the flows between the unemployed, the employed, and the not in the labour force categories that were identified in Figure 13.1. The systemic effects refer to changes in the economic environment that determine employment patterns in the economy. The macroeconomic effects refer to the way that the UI system affects the transmission of economic shocks to the economy and their impact on the unemployment rate.

Table 13.4

The Labour Market Effects of the Canadian UI System

DIRECT EFFECTS

- Layoffs
- Quits
- Duration of unemployment
- Labour force participation

SYSTEMIC EFFECTS

- Industrial mix
- Labour mobility
- Education, training, and occupational choices

MACROECONOMIC EFFECTS

- Automatic stabilizing effects

Direct Effects

The flows between employment and unemployment are affected by the rate at which firms lay off workers and employees voluntarily quit their jobs and the rate at which unemployed workers are hired by firms. Layoffs and hiring occur because of (a) seasonal variations in the demand for labour, (b) fluctuations in aggregate demand over the business cycle, and (c) long-term secular changes in the economy as some industries expand and others contract due to changes in technology, international competitiveness, and consumer spending patterns. Even under "normal" economic conditions, some firms will be "downsizing" and laying off workers while other firms will be expanding and hiring more labour. The reallocation of labour among firms, perhaps in different industries and in different regions, is neither instantaneous nor costless, and unemployment will occur in even a well-functioning labour market.

Of the three sources of labour demand fluctuations, an insurance-based UI system is primarily intended to deal with unemployment caused by the business cycle. Seasonal layoffs, insofar as they are highly predictable, do not represent an insurable risk. On the other hand, the long-term secular changes in the economy often mean that workers have to acquire new skills or move to a new region, and these adjustments are not adequately addressed by a temporary income replacement. Older workers, and those who are unable to acquire new skills or move to new places of employment, may suffer permanent reductions in their real incomes and require either long-term financial assistance or subsidies to acquire new skills or to relocate. Other income transfer programs or education and training programs are better suited to deal with the unemployment problems caused by secular changes in the economy.

Layoffs. Over the period 1980 to 1988, about 58 percent of job separations were classified as permanent layoffs, 21 percent were temporary layoffs, and 21 percent resulted from workers voluntarily quitting their jobs (Baker, Corak, and Heisz, 1996: Table 3). First consider the effect of the UI system on the number of temporary layoffs in the economy. When it faces a downturn in the demand for its products, a firm will generally cut back production and reduce its use of inputs, including labour. A reduction in the demand for labour can be achieved through a reduction in the number of hours worked by each worker or by reducing the number of workers. UI, which provides workers with replacement income in the event of a layoff but not when hours of work are reduced, makes laying off workers more attractive than cutting hours of work, thus increasing the measured unemployment rate.

It has also been alleged that some workers and firms find it in their interest to create jobs that last just long enough to qualify the workers for UI benefits. In regions of high unemployment, only twelve weeks of employment were required in 1996 to qualify a worker for thirty-two weeks of benefits. The effect of the variable entrance requirement on length of jobs has been studied by Christofides and McKenna (1995) and Green and Riddell (1995). The former study found that 5 to 6 percent of all jobs ended when the entrance requirement was satisfied, and that the reduced entrance requirements in the high-unemployment regions reduced the length of these jobs by about 20 percent. Most of these job separations were due to layoffs and not to quits. Green and Riddell (1995) found that the increase in the entrance requirement from ten weeks to fourteen, which occurred in the high-unemployment areas of Canada in 1990, was responsible for "a 0.4 percent drop in the unemployment rate and for a 1.5 week increase in the average length of employment" (Corak, 1994: 122). Thus, the entrance requirements of the UI system seem to affect the length of employment spells. This behaviour is not restricted to the private sector. Some provincial governments have created jobs in order to qualify workers for UI, thereby transferring them from provincially funded social assistance programs to the nationally financed unemployment insurance program.

Quits. The effect of the UI system on the behaviour of job quitters can be discerned to some extent by comparing the duration of unemployment in Canada with that of the United States. Prior to 1993, Canadians who quit their jobs were eligible for UI, whereas Americans who quit their jobs were not eligible for UI. Over the period 1980 to 1988, Baker, Corak, and Heisz (1996: Table

3) found that, while job quits represent about the same proportion of total job separations in Canada as in the United States, the average duration of unemployment for a quitter was 20.6 weeks in Canada, whereas it was 11.2 weeks in the United States. Thus, extending UI coverage to job quitters tends to increase the unemployment rate through its effect on the job search behaviour of those who quit rather than increasing the number of quits.

Duration of unemployment. The effect of UI benefits on the length of time that unemployed individuals search for a new job has been extensively studied by economists. The higher the UI benefit replacement rate, the lower the opportunity cost of turning down a low-paying job in the hope of eventually finding a better-paying job. Thus, labour market search models predict that a higher UI replacement rate will increase the expected duration of a worker's unemployment spell. Empirical studies of the duration of unemployment in Canada by Ham and Rea (1987) and Corak (1992) have concluded that the UI replacement rate has "no effect on the duration of insured unemployment for males, but [seems] to have a strong effect for females" and that "while there is some tendency for UI recipients to search more intensively as exhaustion [of UI benefits] is impending, this tendency affects only a minority of claimants and is not strong" (Corak, 1994: 119). It can also be argued that UI-induced increases in the length of time that workers spend searching for a job can improve labour market performance and help to reduce the overall unemployment rate if a longer period of search generates a better "match" or "fit" between the worker and the firm. If workers are under pressure to accept the first available job, many workers will accept jobs that do not fully utilize their skills, and they will quit these jobs as soon as they can find a position that better matches their skills. This would result in more job turnover and higher recruitment costs for firms.

Labour force participation. The UI system can affect the number of individuals who decide to join the labour force and seek employment. Since all workers pay the same UI premium, the decision to work is effectively subsidized if the marginal entrant has an above-average probability of becoming unemployed and collecting UI benefits. Holding the number of jobs constant, an increase in the labour force participation rate means that the unemployment rate will increase. Studies by Rea (1977) and Sharir and Kuch (1978) have indicated that the UI system increases the labour force participation rate, especially for married females. Green and Riddell (1993) found that the 1975 amendments to the UI program, which reduced the eligibility age for UI from 75 to 65, significantly reduced the labour force participation rate of workers over the age of 65.

Systemic Effects

The UI system can also increase the unemployment rate by altering the mix of industries in the economy, by affecting workers' incentives to move from high-unemployment regions or industries to regions or industries with low-unemployment rates, and by changing the training, education, and occupational choices that workers make.

Industrial mix. The premium rate structure that is used to finance the UI system is the same for all workers and all firms in Canada. Premiums vary with the wage rate that the worker earns up to the maximum insurable earnings. Premiums are not based on the expected UI benefits for individual workers or the likelihood that a firm will lay off its workers. Figure 13.3 shows the ratios of the UI benefits received to UI premiums paid by industry in Canada over the period 1986 to 1990. The industries with a high benefit to tax ratio, such as agriculture, forestry, fishing, and construction, tend to be seasonal industries or industries that are subject to volatile swings in market demand. In general, small firms have higher benefit–tax ratios than large firms. In 1988, workers in firms with fewer than five employees had a benefit–tax ratio of 2.59,

Figure 13.3

Relative Benefit–Tax Ratios by Industry and Province, 1986–1990

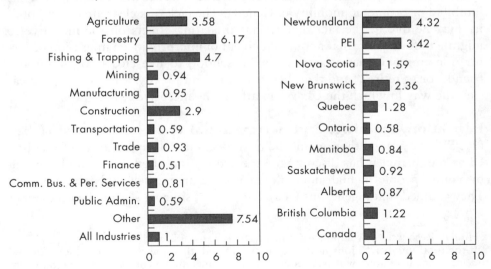

Industry	Ratio
Agriculture	3.58
Forestry	6.17
Fishing & Trapping	4.7
Mining	0.94
Manufacturing	0.95
Construction	2.9
Transportation	0.59
Trade	0.93
Finance	0.51
Comm. Bus. & Per. Services	0.81
Public Admin.	0.59
Other	7.54
All Industries	1

Province	Ratio
Newfoundland	4.32
PEI	3.42
Nova Scotia	1.59
New Brunswick	2.36
Quebec	1.28
Ontario	0.58
Manitoba	0.84
Saskatchewan	0.92
Alberta	0.87
British Columbia	1.22
Canada	1

SOURCE: Corak and Pyper (1995: Table 3, p. 14).

whereas it was only 0.44 for firms with more than 5,000 employees.[7] The UI system can be viewed as subsidizing employment in the seasonal and more volatile sectors of the economy and taxing employment in sectors that provide more stable employment. This pattern of implicit taxes and subsidies increases the overall unemployment rate in the economy.

Labour mobility. The unemployment rate in a country may be reduced if individuals migrate from high- to low-unemployment regions.[8] Therefore, the UI system can affect the unemployment rate if it has an effect on labour mobility. In theory, the UI system can either encourage or discourage labour mobility. On the one hand, UI benefits can help unemployed workers to finance a move to another region where the prospects of obtaining a job are better. Furthermore, the UI system may encourage migration when employment opportunities in other regions are uncertain because it provides income support in the event that the migrant does not get a job when he or she moves. On the other hand, UI benefits reduce the income gain from migration, and this reduces the incentive to move from high-unemployment regions. This disincentive is reinforced when unemployment benefits are more generous (lower entrance requirements and longer benefit periods) in high-unemployment regions. There have been a number of empirical studies of the effect of UI on interprovincial migration in Canada. An early study by Winer and Gauthier (1982) found that the UI system reduced mobility, but recent studies by Osberg, Gordon, and Lin (1994) and Lin (1995) did not find any evidence that the UI system affected mobility. Thus, there is no clear evidence that the UI system has inhibited or promoted mobility in Canada. The lack of a clear effect on mobility may be due to the fact that UI has offsetting effects on the incentive to migrate to find work, that about 70 percent of interprovincial migration occurs for non-employment reasons (to go to school, to live closer to family and friends, or to retire),[9] and that, because of its complexity, it is difficult to measure the way in which the UI system affects the incentives to migrate.

Education, training, and occupational choices. May and Hollett (1995) have argued that one of the most detrimental aspects of the Canadian UI system is that it has discouraged the acquisition of education and training by young people in high-unemployment-rate areas such as Newfoundland. They claimed that a generous UI system, by subsidizing seasonal employment

---

[7] Human Resources Development Canada (1994: Table 6.2, p. 87).
[8] If the total number of jobs in the economy is fixed, then migration from high- to low-unemployment regions will not reduce the total unemployment rate. For migration to reduce the national unemployment rate, at least some of the migrants to a low-unemployment region must be employed.
[9] See Lin (1995: Table 7, p. 17).

and "make-work" projects, increases the opportunity cost of acquiring education or training and makes the "pogey" lifestyle more attractive. "Far too often, young people view this lifestyle as an occupational choice: that is, they see that they can quit school, get a job on a local makework project, and then qualify for UI" (May and Hollett, 1995: 45). Osberg (1995: 226) has acknowledged that "May and Hollett may be right in arguing that, in the 1970s, unemployment insurance was partly responsible for maintaining the overpopulation of rural Atlantic Canada and that we are now facing, in the 1990s, the social costs of the educational and occupation decisions of 20 years ago," but he pointed out that the current generation of young people in Atlantic Canada are staying in school and acquiring education. The high school drop-out rate in Atlantic Canada has dramatically declined over the last twenty years. In 1991, "in the 20–24 age cohort, a *higher* percentage of Atlantic Canadians had attended university than the national average" (Osberg, 1995: 217; emphasis in original).

Macroeconomic Effects

Automatic stabilizing effects. The UI system can act as an automatic stabilizer, if total benefit payments increase and total UI premiums decrease during a recession, thereby helping the unemployed to maintain their expenditures on goods and services. During a boom, total UI benefits decline and total premiums collected increase as employment expands, and this helps to reduce inflationary pressures. The stabilizing effect of the UI system occurs without any deliberate policy decisions by governments and therefore has many advantages over discretionary fiscal policies aimed at stabilizing the economy.

The UI system will act as an automatic stabilizer if the UI fund records a deficit during a recession and a surplus during a boom. Figure 13.4 shows that the UI program incurred a deficit during the recession of the early 1980s, a surplus during the expansion that occurred in the latter half of the 1980s, and then another deficit during the recession of the early 1990s. A study by Dungan and Murphy (1995: 7) indicated that the UI system reduced the contraction in output during the 1981–82 recession by about 13 percent. However, the effectiveness of the UI system as an automatic stabilizer has been reduced because the federal government increased the UI premium rates during the 1981–83 and the 1990–92 recessions. Dungan and Murphy (1995: 30) estimated that if the "1989 premium rate had been held through 1990–1992, GDP would have been over 2 percent higher in 1992 and there would have been over 180,000 more jobs." Consequently, legislation that requires the UI fund not to run a deficit for an extended period has resulted in tax increases during recessions, which have increased the cost of hiring labour when the demand for labour was declining and reduced the net incomes of those who continued to have

Figure 13.4

Revenue Minus Expenditure on Unemployment Insurance

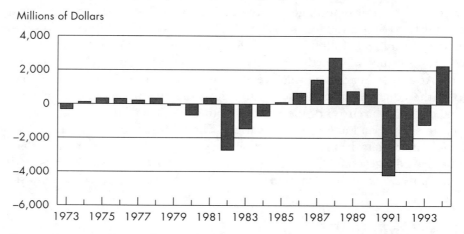

Millions of Dollars

Revenue is net contributions from employers and plus the federal contribution to UI.

SOURCE: Statistics Canada UI Statistics, 1995, Table 21.

employment. Allowing the UI fund to run larger deficits during recessions would help to improve its performance as an automatic stabilizer.

THE DISTRIBUTIONAL EFFECTS OF UI

The extent to which UI alleviates poverty and redistributes income from the affluent to the less well-off depends on how the benefits are distributed and how the program is financed. We will begin by considering the distribution of UI benefits and then examine UI financing.

The Distribution of UI Benefits

Table 13.5 shows the percentage of UI claimants at various income levels in 1992. If all individuals were equally likely to collect UI, then the percent of UI claimants in any income bracket would equal their proportion of the labour force. The table shows that slightly over 50 percent of UI claimants had individual incomes of $10,000 to $25,000, whereas this income group represented only 31.6 percent of the labour force. Individuals earning more than $25,000 were a lower percentage of UI claimants than their share of the labour force. While these statistics indicate that a relatively high percentage of UI claimants have relatively low incomes, the distribution of benefits is not as pro-poor as

Table 13.5

Distribution of UI Claimants Compared to Labour Force, 1992

INDIVIDUAL TOTAL INCOME (INCLUDING UI BENEFITS)	PERCENT OF LABOUR FORCE	PERCENT OF UI CLAIMANTS
less than $10,000	20.9	19.8
$10,000 to $25,000	31.6	50.5
$25,000 to $50,000	35.7	27.0
$50,000 to $75,000	9.2	2.4
$75,000 to $100,000	1.7	0.2
over $100,000	0.9	0.1

SOURCE: Human Resources Development Canada (1994: Table A.3, p. 99). Reproduced with the permission of the Minister of Public Works and Government Services Canada, 1997.

the distribution of claimants, because higher-income workers are generally entitled to receive higher benefits.

While low-income workers are, on average, more likely to receive UI benefits than high-income workers, there are problems with the distribution of UI benefits if it is viewed as an income redistribution program. First, the UI program provides relatively few benefits to the lowest-income households because the lowest-income households often have relatively little attachment to the labour market due to disability, age, or other responsibilities (single mothers with small children), and because those working less than fifteen hours per week were not eligible for UI benefits. Second, UI benefits go to members of families who are not poor. For example, May and Hollett (1995: Table 2, p. 34) examined the distribution of UI benefits in Atlantic Canada in 1992 among households where at least one of the family received UI. They found that in "UI households" with disposable incomes between $70,000 and $80,000 the average after-tax UI benefit was $8,131, whereas it was only $6,246 in UI households with disposable incomes of $20,000 to $30,000. Thus, in spite of the claw-back of UI benefits for high-income individuals, substantial benefits go to households that are not poor, and the UI program is a relatively inefficient way of redistributing income.[10] Third, there are significant horizontal inequities—unequal treatment of equals—in the distribution of UI benefits. For example, two individuals who earn the same wage rate and make the same

---

[10] If an individual's income exceeds 1.5 times the maximum insurable earnings, the UI benefits are subject to a 30 percent claw-back.

contributions to the UI fund, but live in regions with different unemployment rates, receive different expected benefits because the qualifying and benefit periods are based on the regional unemployment rate. Another example of inequitable treatment is the fact that self-employed fishermen in Newfoundland are entitled to receive UI while self-employed farmers in Saskatchewan are not. In short, viewed as an income redistribution program, UI does not provide support for the poor who are unable to work or for the working poor who are employed but earn low wages. UI benefits are received by high-income households, and benefit entitlement is subject to complex rules that do not provide the same treatment to individuals with the same needs. Because of these shortcomings, many feel that the UI program should be replaced, or at least supplemented, by a negative income tax, which they argue would be more effective in distributing benefits to those low-income households (see May and Hollett, 1995: ch. 5).

Financing UI

UI benefits are financed by premiums that are collected from employees and employers. In 1996, the employee contribution rate was $2.95 for every $100 of insurable earnings, and the employer contribution rate was 1.4 times the employee rate or $4.13 per $100 of insurable earnings. The maximum annual contribution was $1,150.76 for an employee and $1,610.96 for an employer. The UI premiums are not related to the employee's history of claims or the past layoffs of the firm. The uniformity, and compulsory nature, of the UI premiums means that they are essentially payroll taxes that are "earmarked" to finance a particular program. The degree to which the UI system redistributes income depends, in part, on who bears the burden of these payroll taxes.

The incidence of taxes is discussed in detail in Chapter 17, and therefore the discussion of the incidence of payroll taxes in this section will be very brief. An employee payroll tax will be borne by workers unless there is an increase in their wage rates. Most workers do not have the power to increase their own wage rates to offset the effect of a tax increase. In addition, a payroll tax does not create labour shortages, which would lead to higher wage rates, because the supply of labour is usually considered to be quite inelastic—an individual's desired hours of work are relatively unresponsive to changes in the after-tax wage rate. Therefore, economists have generally concluded that employees will bear the burden of an employee payroll tax.

The burden of the employer payroll tax can be analyzed in the same framework. An increase in an employer payroll tax will push up the cost of hiring workers and reduce the number of workers employed by firms. In a competitive labour market, the reduced demand for labour will put downward pressure on wage rates. If the supply of labour is completely inelastic, the wage rate will decline by the full amount of the employer payroll tax, and the entire burden of the employer payroll tax will be shifted to workers. However, the burden of an employer payroll tax may not be shifted to *all* workers. Low-income workers who earn the minimum wage rate may not bear the burden of the employer payroll tax because employers are unable to reduce wage rates. These low-wage workers may bear part of the burden through reduced employment opportunities. At the other extreme, high-income workers who are represented by strong unions may be able to prevent employers from shifting the burden of the employer payroll tax to them. Overall, the theoretical and empirical studies tend to support the notion that most of the burden of the employer payroll tax is shifted to workers.[11]

Figure 13.5 shows the payroll tax burden as a percentage of household income at various income levels in 1986 under the assumption that employer and employee contributions to UI (and the Canada and Quebec Pension Plans) are ultimately borne by workers. The relationship between payroll tax burden

Figure 13.5

Payroll Taxes as a Percentage of Income, 1986

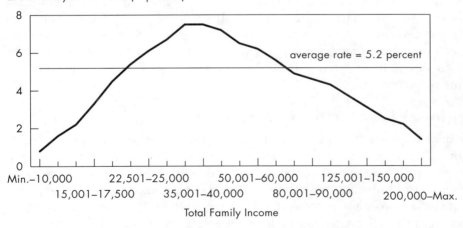

SOURCE: Ruggeri et al. (1994: Figure 5c, p. 440). Reproduced with permission from the Canadian Tax Foundation.

---

[11] See Dahlby (1993) for a review of the evidence regarding the shifting of payroll taxes.

and income is an inverted *U* shape. At low-income levels, most households obtain a high proportion of their income from government transfers (such as social assistance and Old Age Security), and therefore payroll taxes are a relatively small proportion of total income. The payroll tax burden increases as a percentage of income until workers earned $30,000 to $35,000 in 1986, at which point they paid the maximum premium. Workers who earn more than the maximum insurable earnings pay the same amount, and the payroll tax burden as a percentage of income declines above this level of income.

Recall from Chapter 5 that a tax is classified as **regressive** or **progressive** if the tax burden as a percentage of income decreases or increases as income increases. Figure 13.5 indicates that UI premiums can be viewed as a progressive tax over the lower-income range and as a regressive tax over the upper-income range. This has important implications for the amount of redistribution that can occur through the UI program. Since the benefits are financed by a tax that is regressive over the upper-income range, the redistribution that occurs through the UI program is mainly from middle-income families to lower-middle-income families. The program does not redistribute income to the lowest income groups in Canadian society because the lowest income households often have relatively little attachment to the labour market because of disability, age, or other factors. The UI program does not lead to much redistribution from the highest income groups because of the upper limit on UI contributions and because the richest households receive a substantial proportion of their income from self-employment and investment income that is not taxed to finance UI. If one views the UI program as an income redistribution program, then the current method of financing, with an upper bound on contribution by insured workers and no contributions by high-income self-employed workers or the recipients of capital income, is a major shortcoming.

Regional Redistribution through UI

The distributional effects of UI by region and industry are also significant. As Figure 13.3 indicated, the UI system redistributes income from west to east. Except for British Columbia, workers in provinces west of the Ottawa Valley are net contributors, and workers in Quebec and the Atlantic provinces are net beneficiaries. Workers in Newfoundland received $4.32 in benefits for every dollar that they contributed, while in Quebec they received $1.28. In 1993, Newfoundland received a net transfer (benefits minus contributions) of $691 million or $1,335 per capita through the UI system. Quebec received a net transfer of $1.231 billion or $775 per capita. These regional net transfers are almost as large as the intergovernmental transfers that occur through the federal equalization program.[12] Attempts to reform the UI program have frequently been opposed by the provincial governments of eastern Canada because, in spite of UI's potentially harmful effects on resource allocation and its inequitable treatment of individuals, it has become an important source of income for the residents of Quebec and the Atlantic provinces.

The UI program can also be viewed as transferring income to workers in the primary industries (agriculture, forestry, fishing, and trapping) and construction from workers in other sectors of the economy. While average earnings in the primary industries are relatively low, construction workers earn relatively high incomes. The UI system means that a low-wage clerk in the finance sector subsidizes a high-wage carpenter in the construction sector.

Experience Rated Premiums

Some of these inequitable cross-subsidies would be eliminated if UI were financed through a system of experience rated premiums. Under this system, which is used to finance UI in the United States, employers pay higher premiums the more frequently they lay off workers. This premium structure is similar to private automobile insurance where those who make more frequent claims have to pay higher premiums. Adopting experience rated premiums in Canada would mean that premiums would go up in industries, such as construction, where layoffs are common, and workers' wage rates in these industries would probably decline at least to some degree. In other industries where layoffs are less common, premiums would decline, and workers' wage rates would tend to increase. To the extent that high-wage industries, such as construction, have high-layoff rates and are subsidized by low-wage and low-layoff industries, the switch to experience rated UI premiums would increase the fairness of the UI system. However, many of the sectors with high-layoff rates are also low-wage industries, and a switch to experience rated premiums would impose significant burdens on many low-wage workers in these industries.

Experience rated premiums might also help to reduce the overall unemployment rate through changes in firms' incentives to lay off workers and through changes in the distribution of the cost of UI across industries. Experience rated premiums would provide firms with an incentive to reduce layoffs during a recession or off-season. Industries where firms continued to have high layoff

---

[12] Franke and Hermanutz (1996: Table 2, p. 11) calculated that the equalization program in 1993 resulted in a net transfer of $794 million to Newfoundland and $2.121 billion to Quebec. The net UI transfer to Prince Edward Island exceeded its net transfer under equalization.

rates would face higher costs than those with low layoff rates, and over time the high-layoff industries would contract and the low-layoff industries would expand. More employment would occur in the stable, nonseasonal sectors of the economy, and the overall unemployment rate would be expected to decline. It has been argued that incomplete experience rating has contributed to higher unemployment rates in the United States,[13] and therefore the absence of any experience rating in Canada has presumably had a large effect on unemployment rates in Canada. However, a study by Betcherman and Leckie (1995) that compared the layoff behaviour of Canadian and U.S. firms in 1993 found that the degree of experience rating did not seem to affect firms' layoff behaviour. Even if experience rating does not have a significant effect on firms' layoff behaviour, the change in the distribution of the costs of the UI program under experience rating would improve the allocation of labour in the long run, but this policy option would increase the unemployment rate in the short term because it would take time for workers displaced from the current high benefit–tax ratio industries to be absorbed by the current low benefit–tax ratio industries. Experience rating would have a detrimental effect in Quebec and the Atlantic provinces because the high benefit–tax ratio industries are concentrated in these provinces, and therefore there would be considerable opposition to any UI reforms that would increase premiums and reduce job opportunities in these regions.

FROM UI TO EI: THE 1996 REFORMS

In 1996, the federal government introduced a series of reforms and changed the name of the program from Unemployment Insurance to Employment Insurance. The major changes included[14]:

Hours-based eligibility. Under the new Employment Insurance (EI) system, eligibility is based on the number of hours worked during the last fifty-two weeks. The minimum required number of hours for eligibility ranges from 700 hours, if the regional unemployment rate is 6.0 percent or less, to 420 hours if the regional unemployment rate exceeds 13.1 percent. For new entrants to the work force and for those who are re-entering the labour market after an absence of two years, the minimum eligibility requirement is 910 hours. To qualify for sickness, maternity, or parental benefits, workers will require 700 hours. Those who earn less than $2,000 per year and do not work enough hours to be eligible for EI will receive a premium refund. The maximum number of weeks of benefits was reduced to forty-five from fifty.

---

[13] See Feldstein (1976) and Topel (1990).
[14] See Nakamura (1996) for further discussion of the EI reform.

The shift to the hours-based eligibility requirement from the previous weeks-based eligibility requirement is based on the recognition that fewer workers have the "standard" thirty-five to forty hour work week. Part-time employment has become increasingly important, but the percentage of people working more than fifty hours per week has also been increasing. Under the old UI system, workers had to work at least fifteen hours per week to be eligible. It is estimated that 90,000 individuals who were not eligible for UI will be eligible for EI. The reform also means that people who work long hours over a short period of time, a situation that is common in some seasonal industries, will be eligible for additional weeks of benefits.

Maximum insurable earnings. The annual maximum insurable earnings (MIE) was reduced from $42,380 in 1995 to $39,000 in 1996, and it will remain at that level until the year 2000. Previously, the MIE was increased each year on the basis of the annual rate of increase in earnings over the previous eight years (with a two-year lag because of data availability). Up until the early 1980s, the MIE was very close to average earnings, but since then the MIE has grown faster than current annual earnings, and by 1994 the MIE exceeded average industrial earnings by 36 percent. The relative increase in the MIE was one of the reasons for the growth in UI spending. The reduction in the MIE will lower and stabilize total EI expenditures until the year 2000. It will also reduce contributions for employees who earn more than the new MIE. The employee contribution rates for 1997 and 1998 were reduced to $2.90 and $2.80 respectively per $100 of insurable earnings, with employers continuing to pay 1.4 times the employee rate.

The benefit rate and family income supplement. The EI benefit rate, for most claimants, will continue to be 55 percent of insurable earnings. Low-income claimants with children will receive more generous benefits. If they earn less than $25,921 per year, they can receive up to 65 percent of insurable earnings as Family Income Supplement in 1997, and this maximum rate will increase by five percentage points a year until it reaches 80 percent in the year 2000. Approximately 15 percent of all EI claimants will be eligible for the Family Income Supplement. High-income claimants will have their benefits clawed back. For every dollar of annual income in excess of $48,750, EI benefits will be reduced by 30 cents.

The intensity rule. The benefit rate was also reduced for frequent EI claimants. Those who have collected more than twenty weeks of benefits over the previous five years will have their benefit rate reduced by one percentage point for every twenty weeks of benefits, with a maximum reduction of five percentage points. Only claims incurred since July 1996 will be used in computing the reduction in the benefit rate, and therefore the intensity rule will not take effect until 2001. Those who receive the Family Income Supplement will not be subject to the intensity rule. The claw-back of benefits for claimants who are subject to the intensity rule will be even more severe. The income threshold at which their claw-back starts will be $39,000, and the claw-back rate will increase with the number of weeks of benefits received in the previous five years, until it reaches 100 percent for 120 weeks of benefits in the previous five years.

The intensity rule and the claw-back will introduce an element of experience rating into the EI system, especially for claimants with above-average incomes. However, unlike the system in the United States where employers' premiums are based on previous layoffs, EI will adjust employees' benefits based on their history of claims. Since individuals may be able to control, at least to some degree, the length of their employment spells, experience rating benefits may reduce the duration of some unemployment spells. Furthermore, it will reduce the attractiveness of employment in seasonal industries and with firms that engage in frequent layoffs. Over time, the intensity rule may shift employment patterns in favour of the more stable industries and employers.

Employment and training subsidies. In conjunction with the provinces, the EI program will fund a variety of wage subsidy, self-employment assistance, job creation, earning supplementation, and job training programs. More than $2 billion will be spent on these programs by the fiscal year 2000–01. Overall, the federal government has projected that the EI reforms will result in savings of $1.2 billion by the fiscal year 2000–01.

CONCLUSION

The Employment Insurance program, like its predecessor, is a compromise between an insurance program and an income redistribution program. As an insurance program, only contributors are covered, and the benefits are larger for those who have higher earnings because they suffer larger losses when they are unemployed. As an income redistribution program, the benefits for low-income households are enhanced through the Family Income Supplement, and the payouts to high-income claimants are reduced through the claw-back. Consequently, EI benefits are based on both the insured's loss and the household's need. EI financing also contains elements of the insurance and income redistribution concepts. Premiums are collected from the insured, but they do not vary with the size of the insured's risk or history of claims. This results in some pro-poor redistribution, but the amount of vertical redistribution is limited because there is an upper bound on the contributions by high-income earners, and there are many situations where some low-income workers end up subsidizing higher-income workers. Financing EI, at least in part, with personal income tax revenues would be more consistent with its redistributive role.

The dual nature of the EI program—part insurance, part income support—means that it may not perform either of these functions very well. It has often been suggested that the insurance and redistribution functions should be performed by two separate programs, with EI run on strict insurance principles to provide all workers with coverage against income losses due to unemployment, and with the income redistribution function performed by a negative income tax program. While the separation of functions would have many advantages from the perspective of equity and efficiency, there are serious obstacles to this type of reform. First, there would always be interactions between the insurance program and the redistribution program—people who received more insurance benefits would receive less from the redistribution program—and the terms and conditions of one program would likely influence the design of the other program. Thus, it is unlikely that EI could ever be a "pure" insurance program. The second problem is that any negative income tax program would have to be coordinated with provincial welfare programs. The provinces might object to the federal government establishing a negative income tax program and prefer federal grants to enhance their own welfare programs. Consequently, it is very difficult for the federal government to divide the EI program into separate insurance and income support programs. While many of the EI reforms, such as the move to hours-based eligibility and the intensity rule, are significant improvements in the design of the program, the major issues and tensions that have been present in the UI program for more than twenty-five years will remain.

SUMMARY

- Since the 1950s, there has been a steady upward trend in the rate of unemployment, with year-to-year fluctuations caused by the business cycle.

- The rise in the unemployment rate has meant that the UI program plays a central role in the provision of income security in Canada, but it has also raised questions: Has the UI program contributed to the high unemployment rates? Does the UI program provide income security in an effective and equitable manner?

- Public provision of unemployment insurance can be justified on the basis of market failure due to adverse selection. The public sector can also provide UI more effectively than the private sector because of its greater ability to borrow to finance benefits in the event of a major recession. Moral hazard issues mean that UI programs should be designed so that firms and workers have some incentive to reduce the number of layoffs and the duration of unemployment spells.

- UI may affect the unemployment rate through its effects on layoffs, quits, the duration of unemployment spells, the labour force participation rate, the industrial mix, labour mobility, education and training choices, and its automatic stabilizing effects.

- Unemployment insurance redistributes income to the extent that a worker's expected UI benefits exceed the UI premium. In Canada, UI premiums are not experience rated, and there are significant net UI transfers to the primary industries—agriculture, forestry, and fishing—and to the construction industry and the small business sector. There are substantial net transfers to workers in Quebec and the Atlantic region. In 1992, about 40 percent of UI claimants were members of families with incomes in excess of $50,000.

- The Employment Insurance program, which was introduced in 1996, bases eligibility on the number of hours that individuals work, and it has introduced some experience rating in benefits through the intensity rule and the claw-back of benefits.

DISCUSSION QUESTIONS

1. a. Show that the unemployment rate, *ur*, is related to the employment rate, *er*, and labour force participation rate, *pr*, as follows:

$$ur = \left(1 - \frac{er}{pr}\right)$$

   b. Suppose the labour market is in equilibrium when the labour force participation rate is 0.60 and the employment rate is 0.55. What is the unemployment rate in this economy?
   c. Suppose that an increase in unemployment insurance benefits causes the participation rate to increase to 0.61. What would be the effect on the unemployment rate? Use a diagram to illustrate your answer and explain your assumptions.

2. a. Show that the unemployment rate, *ur*, is related to the layoff rate (the proportion of employees who are laid off each month), *lr*, and average duration of an unemployment spell, *du*, as follows:

$$ur = \frac{lr \cdot du}{1 + lr \cdot du}$$

b. Suppose the layoff rate is 0.02 and the average duration of a spell of unemployment is four and a half months. What is the unemployment rate in this economy?

c. Suppose that an increase in unemployment insurance benefits causes the layoff rate to increase to 0.021. What would be the effect on the unemployment rate and why would it change?

d. Suppose that an increase in unemployment insurance benefits causes the average duration of a spell of unemployment to increase by one week. What would be the effect on the unemployment rate and why would it change?

3. What problems would arise in setting experience rated unemployment insurance premiums with regard to the following?

a. Distinguishing between quits and layoffs.
b. Setting rates for new businesses.
c. Setting rates for small businesses with only a couple of employees.
d. Firms declaring bankruptcy.

4. Consider an individual whose earnings are taxed at a rate of 25 percent under the personal income tax and at a combined rate of 10 percent under the Canada Pension Plan and Employment Insurance payroll taxes. Suppose that if the individual becomes unemployed, EI replaces 50 percent of his or her before-tax earnings. (Note that EI benefits are subject to income tax, but not payroll taxes.) What percentage of the individual's *after*-tax income is replaced by EI? What are the implications for the effects of EI on unemployment?

REFERENCES

Baker, Michael, Miles Corak, and Andrew Heisz. "Unemployment in the Stock and Flow." Discussion Paper No. 97, Business and Labour Market Analysis. Ottawa: Statistics Canada, 1996.

Betcherman, Gordon, and Norm Leckie. *Employer Responses to UI Experience Rating: Evidence from Canadian and American Establishments.* Unemployment Insurance Evaluation Series, Human Resources Development Canada. Ottawa: Ministry of Supply and Services, 1995.

Card, David, and Craig Riddell. "A Comparative Analysis of Unemployment in Canada and the United States," in *Small Differences that Matter: Labor Markets and Income Maintenance in Canada and the United States,* ed. David Card and Richard Freeman. Chicago: University of Chicago Press and National Bureau of Economic Research, 1993.

Christofidies, L.N., and C.J. McKenna. *Employment Patterns and Unemployment Insurance.* Unemployment Insurance Evaluation Series, Human Resources Development Canada. Ottawa: Ministry of Supply and Services, 1995.

Corak, Miles. "Unemployment Insurance, Work Disincentives, and the Canadian Labor Market: An Overview," in *Unemployment Insurance: How to Make It Work*, ed. John Richards and William G. Watson. Toronto: C.D. Howe Research Institute, 1994, pp. 86–159.

Corak, Miles. "The Duration of Unemployment Insurance Payments." Economic Council of Canada Working Paper 42. Ottawa: Economic Council of Canada, 1992.

Corak, Miles, and Wendy Pyper. *Firms, Industries and Cross-subsidies: Patterns in the Distribution of UI Benefits and Taxes.* Unemployment Insurance Evaluation Series, Human Resources Development Canada. Ottawa: Ministry of Supply and Services, 1995.

Dahlby, Bev. "Payroll Taxes," in *Business Taxation in Ontario*, ed. Allan Maslove. Published for the Ontario Fair Tax Commission by the University of Toronto Press, Toronto, 1993, pp. 80–170.

Dungan, Peter, and Steve Murphy. *The UI System as an Automatic Stabilizer in Canada.* Unemployment Insurance Evaluation Series, Human Resources Development Canada. Ottawa: Ministry of Supply and Services, 1995.

Feldstein, Martin. "Temporary Layoffs in the Theory of Unemployment." *Journal of Political Economy* 84 (October 1976).

Forget, Claude. *Report of the Commission of Inquiry on Unemployment Insurance.* Ottawa: Supply and Services Canada, 1986.

Franke, Oliver, and Derek Hermanutz. "Unemployment Insurance Reform: A Focused Approach to Social Policy." Mimeo. Edmonton: Alberta Treasury, 1996.

Gower, David. "Time Lost: An Alternative View of Unemployment." *Perspectives* (Spring 1990): 73–77.

Green, Christopher, and Jean-Michel Cousineau. *Unemployment in Canada: The Impact of Unemployment Insurance.* Ottawa: Economic Council of Canada, 1976.

Green, David, and Craig Riddell. "Qualifying for Unemployment Insurance: An Empirical Analysis for Canada." Unemployment Insurance Evaluation Series, Human Resources Development Canada. Ottawa: Ministry of Supply and Services, 1995.

Green, David, and Craig Riddell. "The Economic Effects of Unemployment Insurance in Canada: An Empirical Analysis of UI Disentitlement." *Journal of Labor Economics* 11 (January 1993).

Grubel, Herbert, Dennis Maki, and Shelley Sax. "Real and Insurance Induced Unemployment in Canada." *Canadian Journal of Economics* 8 (May 1975).

Guest, Dennis. *The Emergence of Social Security in Canada.* Vancouver: University of British Columbia Press, 1980.

Ham, John, and Samuel A. Rea, Jr. "Unemployment Insurance and Male Unemployment Duration in Canada." *Journal of Labor Economics* 5 (July 1987).

Human Resources Development Canada. "History of Unemployment Insurance." http://www.hrdc-drhc.gc.ca/hrdc/ei/insuran/histui/hrdc.html, 1996.

Human Resources Development Canada. *From Unemployment Insurance to Employment Insurance: A Supplementary Paper.* Ottawa: Ministry of Supply and Services, 1994.

Jones, Stephen. "Cyclical and Seasonal Properties of Canadian Gross Flows of Labour." *Canadian Public Policy* 19, no. 1 (March 1993): 1–17.

Lazar, Fred. "UI as a Redistributive Scheme and Automatic Fiscal Stabilizer," in *Unemployment Insurance: How to Make It Work,* ed. John Richards and William G. Watson. Toronto: C.D. Howe Research Institute, 1994, pp. 36–85.

Lin, Zhengxi. *Interprovincial Labour Mobility in Canada: The Role of Unemployment Insurance and Social Assistance.* Unemployment Insurance Evaluation Series, Human Resources Development Canada. Ottawa: Ministry of Supply and Services, 1995.

Marsh, Leonard Charles. *Report on Social Security for Canada.* Toronto: University of Toronto Press, 1975. This report was originally published in 1943 by the government of Canada.

May, Doug, and Alton Hollett. *The Rock in a Hard Place.* The Social Policy Challenge 9. Toronto: C.D. Howe Institute, 1995.

Nakamura, Alice. *Employment Insurance: A Framework for Real Reform.* Commentary 85. Toronto: C.D. Howe Institute, 1996.

OECD. *Labour Force Statistics: 1975–1995.* Paris: OECD, 1997.

Osberg, Lars. "Is Unemployment or Unemployment Insurance the Problem in Atlantic Canada?" in *The Rock in a Hard Place,* ed. Doug May and Alton Hollett. The Social Policy Challenge 9. Toronto: C.D. Howe Institute, 1995, pp. 213–28.

Osberg, Lars, Daniel Gordon, and Zhengxi Lin. "Interregional Migration and Interindustry Labour Mobility in Canada: A Simultaneous Approach." *Canadian Journal of Economics* 27, no. 1 (February 1994): 58–80.

Rea, S. "Unemployment Insurance and Labour Supply: A Simulation of the 1971 Unemployment Insurance Act." *Canadian Journal of Economics* 10 (May 1977): 263–78.

Richardson, J. Henry. *Economic and Financial Aspects of Social Security: An International Survey.* Toronto: University of Toronto Press, 1960.

Ruggeri, G.C., D. Van Wart, and R. Howard. "The Redistributional Impact of Taxation in Canada." *Canadian Tax Journal* 42, no. 2 (1994): 417–51.

Sharir, S., and P. Kuch. "Contributions to Unemployment of Insurance-Induced Labour Force Participation." *Economic Letters* 1 (1978): 271–74.

Statistics Canada. *Canadian Economic Observer.* Historical Statistical Supplement 1994/95. Ottawa, 1995.

Topel, Robert. "Financing Unemployment Insurance: History, Incentives, and Reform," in *Unemployment Insurance: The Second Half-Century,* ed. W. Lee Hansen and J.F. Byers. Madison: University of Wisconsin Press, 1990.

Winer, Stanley, and Denis Gauthier. *Internal Migration Data: An Econometric Study of the Determinants of Interprovincial Migration in Canada.* Ottawa: Economic Council of Canada, 1982.

Chapter 14

Public Pensions

You lied to us. You made us vote for you and then good–bye Charlie Brown.

–Solange Denis, "the erstwhile Joan of Ark of the fight against the partial indexation of the Old Age Security in 1985" (Battle, 1996: 188)

A ll societies have to provide for the elderly who can no longer earn income. In traditional societies, a few individuals could accumulate enough assets during their working lives to finance their consumption in their declining years. For most individuals who managed to survive to old age, the family provided the income support and other services such as nursing care. In the twentieth century, with the decline in the extended family and the increase in life expectancy, the public sector has emerged as the most important source for retirement income for most Canadians.

The Canadian retirement income system consists of three "pillars": the Old Age Security Program, the Canada and Quebec Pension Plans, and tax-assisted private savings and pensions. The Old Age Security Program, which consists of the Old Age Security Pension (OAS), Guaranteed Income Supplement (GIS), and Spouse's Allowance (SA) programs, provided $22 billion in benefits in 1996. These federal programs are financed out of general revenues and provide basic income support for the elderly. In 2001, these programs will be amalgamated in the new Seniors Benefit (SB) program. The second pillar consists of the Canada Pension Plan (CPP) and Quebec Pension Plan (QPP), which are compulsory, earnings-related pension schemes that also provide other benefits such as payments for disability. They are financed by earmarked payroll taxes that are levied on employers and employees. These programs provided approximately $22 billion in benefits in 1996. The third pillar consists of the Registered Pension Plan (RPP) and the Registered Retirement Savings Plan (RRSP), which receive special tax treatment under the Canadian income tax system. These programs generated about $32 billion in private pension and retirement income in 1996.

This chapter focuses on the first two pillars of the retirement income system. (The third pillar—RPPs and RRSPs—is discussed in Chapter 21.) Canadians are very concerned about the long-term viability of these components of the retirement income system because of the projected rapid increase in pension expenditures when the baby-boom generation retires. A Gallup poll conducted in October 1994 indicated that less than 30 percent of respondents who were under 49 years of age were confident that they would receive OAS and CPP/QPP benefits in the future. Will future generations be able to afford the projected increases in public pensions and health care costs caused by an aging population? Even if future generations can afford them, will they be willing to bear the high tax rates and make the large intergenerational transfer that will be required? These concerns have led to changes in the Old Age Security Program, which will be replaced by the Seniors Benefit program in 2001, and to proposals by the federal and provincial governments in 1997 that will increase the CPP contribution rates and reduce some benefits.

This chapter examines the issues surrounding the reform of the public pension system in Canada. We begin by considering the following questions: Why should the public sector intervene in the provision of retirement income? If there are legitimate reasons for intervening, what type of intervention is warranted? We then consider in more detail the history and structure of the OAS and CPP, the reasons why reforms are required, and the implications of some of these proposals.

PUBLIC INTERVENTION IN THE PROVISION OF RETIREMENT INCOMES

Among the "usual suspects" for market failure, paternalism, redistribution, and adverse selection in the market for annuities are the most prominent issues as far as the provision of retirement income is concerned. There are also other features of the pension market—the absence of inflation indexation in private pensions and annuities, the Samaritan's dilemma, and the possibility that the public sector can provide a higher rate of return than the private sector—that have to be considered.

Paternalism. Some individuals are myopic and will not save enough for their retirement. They will live to regret the excessive consumption spending of their youth. This argument raises two issues. First, is it true that people

would fail to provide adequately for their retirement years? To find out requires estimating how people would behave in the absence of the public pension programs. This is very difficult to do. Second, even if it is true, it does not necessarily follow that the government should step in. Those with a highly individualistic philosophical framework believe that people should be left to make their own decisions, even if this occasionally results in mistakes.

Miscalculation and decision-making costs. Even if individuals are not myopic, they may underestimate how much they must save in order to have a reasonable level of consumption in their retirement years. For example, if an individual's earnings increase at 2 percent a year and if she wants her consumption level in retirement to be two-thirds of her pre-retirement consumption level, then over a thirty-year period she will have to save 17 percent of her annual disposable income if the real rate of return on her savings is 3 percent and she lives for fifteen years after retirement.[1] If the individual underestimates the required savings rate, she may not be aware of her mistake until it is too late to correct it. Hiring a professional adviser may be costly. If public decision makers select an appropriate retirement program for everyone, individuals do not have to waste resources on making their own decisions. A clear criticism here is that there is no reason to believe the government would necessarily choose the right kind of policy. After all, different people have different needs, so it might be better to promote public education and retirement counselling and to let people choose their own retirement scheme.

Redistribution. The preceding discussion assumed that individuals can earn enough during their working lives to be able to save for an adequate level of consumption during their retirement. However, some individuals' incomes are so low during their working lives that they are unable to save for their retirement. These individuals will be destitute when they retire, and society has an obligation to prevent them from falling into abject poverty. A noncontributory pension scheme, such as Old Age Security, ensures that all seniors have a basic level of income. One might question whether the elderly need a special income redistribution program, aside from the fact that Old Age Security is a federal program and therefore the cost of providing income support for the elderly is borne by all Canadians, whereas welfare programs are funded by the provinces.

A separate income redistribution program for the elderly may be desirable for three reasons. First, the elderly have characteristics, such as their ability to work, that set them apart from younger welfare recipients. Therefore, an

---

[1] See Diamond (1977: 288).

income redistribution program for the elderly can be designed with their special needs and characteristics in mind. Second, providing income support in the form of a "pension" may reduce the stigma that is often associated with welfare. Third, a society may want to engage in intergenerational redistribution if, for example, an entire generation was unable to save for their retirement because economic depression or a war wiped out their savings or reduced their potential earnings. Thus, the income redistribution motive can justify a public "pension" scheme that is financed out of current tax revenues.

The Samaritan's dilemma. Given that a society has income redistribution programs for the poor and the elderly, some young people may decide not to save for their old age, gambling that they will be supported by the public sector when they retire. Society may frown on such behaviour, but be unwilling to withhold benefits from those who have taken advantage of the system if it would mean that they would fall into abject poverty. To prevent individuals from planning to take advantage of the retirement income support system, society may force individuals to save for their retirement by introducing a compulsory contributory pension scheme. Individuals' contributions during their working lives could either be included in a common pension fund, which would be invested by the public sector's fund managers, or they could be segregated in a private fund, similar to an RRSP. The individual, when he reaches the age of retirement, would then use the accumulated fund to purchase an annuity, which is a contract in which an insurance company agrees to pay the individual a given sum each month as long as the individual lives.

Adverse selection in the market for annuities. An individual who saves for her retirement runs the risk of outliving her savings. By purchasing an annuity, she can ensure that she will always receive some income as long as she lives. The market for annuities is, however, subject to an adverse selection process. Individuals probably know more about their health status than an insurance company. Those individuals who expect to live for a long period of time are willing to pay a higher price for an annuity than are individuals who expect to live only a short length of time. Thus, those who have the longest life expectancy are the ones who are most likely to demand annuities. Because the price of an annuity must reflect the life expectancy of the average annuity purchaser, the adverse selection process drives up the price that must be charged, and as a result individuals will reduce the amount of their retirement fund that they convert to annuities, exposing themselves to a greater risk of outliving their savings. A compulsory contributory public pension scheme overcomes the adverse selection problem if everyone is forced to participate, and the pension payouts can be based on the life expectancy of the entire population and not just those who anticipate living a long life. Therefore, a compulsory contributory pension scheme has the potential of offering individuals a higher rate of return on their contributions than they could get in the private market when the purchase of annuities is voluntary.

Private annuity markets will try to use observable information on individuals' life expectancies in setting annuity prices. Women are charged higher prices for an annuity than men because the life expectancy of a woman at age 65 is nineteen years, whereas it is fourteen years for a 65-year-old man.[2] Many view this form of statistical discrimination as offensive, especially because women generally have lower retirement incomes and are more likely to be impoverished in their old age. A public sector pension plan in which contributions and benefits are the same for both sexes can overcome this problem.

Inflation indexation. Another problem with annuity contracts and private employer-sponsored pension plans is that they do not provide benefits that are indexed to the cost of living. Even a relatively modest annual inflation rate of 3.0 percent will reduce the purchasing power of a fixed annual income by one-third in 13.5 years. Thus, the elderly face the risk that the purchasing power of their pensions and annuities will be eroded through inflation. The public sector has less difficulty than the private sector in providing inflation-indexed pensions because tax revenues normally increase as rapidly as the inflation rate, and perhaps even more rapidly if the income tax system is not indexed. It is often argued that the public sector can help the private sector in providing inflation-indexed pensions if the public sector issues inflation-indexed bonds. The private pension funds can purchase these bonds and use the income from them to provide inflation-indexed pensions. The government of Canada issues inflation-indexed bonds, but the demand for these bonds has been rather modest, perhaps because the rate of inflation has declined in recent years and other investments have offered very attractive real rates of return.

Pay-as-you-go financing versus fully funded pensions. Public sector pensions can be funded on a pay-as-you-go basis, which means that the benefits paid to current retirees come from payments made by those who are currently working. There is no need to accumulate a fund in order to pay the pension benefits. With private sector pension schemes, workers' contributions are accumulated in a fund, and a worker's expected benefits when he retires are equal to his accumulated contributions and investment income on the fund. The private sector can only offer funded pensions because it cannot force the current generation of workers to pay for the pensions of those who are cur-

---

[2] Statistics Canada (1993: Figure 7, p. 28).

rently retired. The public sector can utilize pay-as-you-go financing because the state can make contributions to its pension scheme compulsory.

Pay-as-you-go financing can be an attractive method of financing pensions if the economy's total wages and salaries (the contribution base) is growing faster than the rate of return on investments that are held by pension funds. Under these conditions, if the contribution rate is the same for each generation, then the ratio of a generation's pension benefit to its contributions will be higher under the pay-as-you-go financing scheme than it would be with the same contribution rate under a fully funded pension scheme. The superiority of the pay-as-you-go financed pension was proclaimed by Nobel laureate Paul Samuelson:

> The beauty of social insurance is that it is actuarially unsound. Everyone who reaches retirement age is given benefit privileges that far exceed anything he has paid in…. How is this possible? It stems from the fact that the national product is growing at compound interest and can be expected to do so for as far ahead as the eye can see. Always there are more youths than old folks in a growing population. More important, with real incomes growing at some three percent a year, the taxable base upon which benefits rest in any period are much greater than the taxes paid historically by the generation now retired…. A growing nation is the greatest Ponzi game ever contrived.[3]

In the 1960s, when Samuelson wrote these words and when the CPP and QPP were established, the real growth rate of wages and salaries exceeded the real interest rate, and pay-as-you-go seemed to be the best way to finance these programs (see Figure 14.1). In the 1970s, the gap between the growth rate of wages and salaries and real interest rates declined, and since the 1980s the real interest rate has exceeded the growth rate of wages and salaries, mainly because of much lower rates of productivity growth and slower growth in employment. With hindsight, the choice of pay-as-you-go financing for the CPP and QPP was not wise, and the decline in productivity growth and employment growth will force major changes in these programs. These changes will be discussed later in this chapter.

Most countries with public pension schemes use pay-as-you-go financing because it is politically attractive, when the pension scheme is initiated, to be able to offer the first generation of pensioners benefits that are far in excess of

---

[3] Quoted in Oreopoulos (1996: 6); reprinted by permission of the publisher. A Ponzi game is an illegal pyramid investment scheme where the returns to the initial investors are financed by the capital contributed by later investors. Such schemes may produce high rates of return for early investors, but they inevitably collapse because there is nothing to guarantee that later investors will get their investment back, let alone receive a return.

Figure 14.1

Growth of Total Wages and Salaries and Real Interest Rates

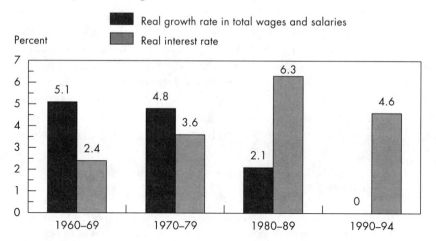

■ Real growth rate in total wages and salaries

■ Real interest rate

SOURCE: Federal, Provincial, and Territorial Governments of Canada, *An Information Paper for Consultations on the Canada Pension Plan*, February 1996, p. 23. Reproduced with the permission of the Minister of Public Works and Government Services Canada, 1997.

their contributions. In some cases, this intergenerational transfer may be justified if that generation had low retirement income prospects because of a war or an economic depression. In other cases, it may not be justified on equity grounds, but giving a large net benefit to one group of voters, while imposing potential burdens on future generations who are not yet born, let alone voters, has been irresistible to politicians in all countries. The potential effects of pay-as-you-go public pensions on individuals' economic decisions are assessed in the next section.

EFFECTS OF PUBLIC PENSIONS ON ECONOMIC BEHAVIOUR

Some economists have argued that a public pension influences people's behaviour in a way that is detrimental to the economy's efficient operation. Most of the discussion has focused on the impact of public pensions on saving behaviour and labour supply decisions. As we shall see, all the difficulties in doing empirical work that were explained in Chapter 3 arise here with a vengeance. The impact of public pensions on behaviour remains a controversial subject, so this section is best regarded as a report on research in progress, rather than a compendium of definitive conclusions.

Saving Behaviour

The starting point for most work on public pensions and saving is the life-cycle theory of savings, which suggests that individuals' consumption and saving decisions are based on lifetime considerations. During their working lives, individuals save some portion of their incomes to accumulate wealth from which they can finance consumption during retirement.[4] Such funds can be invested until they are needed, thus increasing the economy's capital stock or its net holding of foreign assets.

The introduction of a public pension system can substantially alter the amount of lifetime saving. Such changes are the consequences of three effects. First, workers realize that in exchange for their public pension contributions, they will receive a guaranteed retirement income. The value of future public pension benefits is an important part of a family's assets and is often referred to as public pension wealth. If workers view the taxes levied to finance the public pension as a means of "saving" for these future benefits, they will tend to save less on their own. This phenomenon is referred to as the wealth substitution effect. As emphasized earlier, with pay-as-you-go financing, the contributions are not all saved—almost all is paid out immediately to the current beneficiaries. Thus, there is no public saving to correspond to some of the loss of private saving, which means a reduction in total savings.

Second, a public pension may induce people to retire earlier than they would have, if to receive benefits they have to reduce their participation in the labour force. However, if the length of retirement increases, the individual has more nonworking years during which consumption must be financed, but fewer working years to accumulate funds. This retirement effect tends to increase saving.

Finally, suppose an important reason for saving is the bequest motive—people want to leave inheritances for their children. Suppose, in addition, people realize that a public pension system tends to shift income from children (worker/taxpayers) to parents (retiree/benefit recipients). Then parents may save more to increase bequests to their children and hence offset the distributional effect of social security. In essence, people increase their saving to undo the impact of social security on their children's incomes. This is referred to as the bequest effect.

---

[4] Of course, savings are also accumulated for other reasons as well: to finance the purchase of durables, to use in case of a rainy day, and so forth. For a more complete discussion of the life-cycle theory, see Modigliani (1986).

Given that the three effects work in different directions, theory alone cannot tell us how public pensions affect saving. Econometric analysis is necessary. The first step is to specify a mathematical relationship that shows how the amount of saving depends on public pension wealth and other variables that might have an effect. Alternatively, an investigator can just as well posit a relation that explains the amount of consumption as a function of the same variables, because by definition, saving and consumption are opposite sides of the same coin—anything that raises consumption by a dollar must lower saving by the same amount.

In a controversial study, Feldstein (1974) assumed that consumption during a given year is a function of private wealth at the beginning of the year, disposable income during the year, and public pension wealth (also referred to as social security wealth), among other variables. Income and private wealth are included because they are measures of the individual's capacity to consume.

Feldstein estimated the regression equation with annual U.S. data from 1929 to 1976, using statistical methods similar to those described in Chapter 3. For our purposes, the key question is the sign and magnitude of the parameter multiplying the social security wealth variable. Feldstein found a positive and statistically significant value of 0.018.[5] This positive sign suggests that increases in social security wealth increase consumption and, hence, decrease saving. Thus, the wealth substitution effect dominates the retirement and bequest effects. If Feldstein's results are correct, the pay-as-you-go nature of the U.S. social security system has reduced personal saving by 40 percent.[6]

Feldstein's study spawned a considerable amount of controversy, much of which centred on whether his equation contains all the explanatory variables that it should. In particular, Feldstein's regression did not include the rate of unemployment, but Munnell (1977) has suggested that it is an important determinant of the aggregate amount of saving, because during years of high unemployment, people are likely to draw on their savings to maintain their standard of living. She argued further that Feldstein's failure to include the unemployment rate in the equation tends to make his coefficient on the social security wealth variable appear higher than it actually is. This is because through time, social security wealth and unemployment have tended to move

---

[5] This estimate is from a revision and update of the 1974 paper. See Feldstein (1982).
[6] Interestingly, when social security was introduced in the United States during the 1930s, the perception that it decreased saving was regarded as a virtue. This was because of the belief that a major cause of the Great Depression was the failure of people to consume enough.

in opposite directions. (During the 1930s, social security wealth in the United States was zero for most of the years, and the unemployment rate was very high. Later on, social security wealth increased while the unemployment rate came down.) Thus, part of the variation in saving that might be caused by fluctuations in unemployment is reflected in the coefficient of the social security wealth variable. When Munnell estimated an equation similar to Feldstein's, but included the rate of unemployment, she found that social security wealth still reduces personal saving, but the magnitude is only about 10 percent of that found by Feldstein. Obviously, the implications for saving are much less portentous. Other studies have used different data sets and methods of estimation. Leimer and Lesnoy (1982) found evidence that social security in the United States might even have increased saving.

In view of recent evidence that Canadians' saving rates do not vary with age, Burbidge (1996: 116) has concluded that "a revenue-neutral expansion of public pensions probably does not reduce aggregate saving much, because those paying the taxes and those receiving the transfers probably do not have dramatically different savings rates out of disposable income." He notes, however, that an increase in public pensions, financed by increased borrowing from foreigners, will reduce the well-being of future generations.

Retirement Decisions

A public pension plan can create an incentive for early retirement if it increases a worker's public pension wealth and if his or her earnings are subject to a claw-back of benefits. The public pension wealth effect enhances a worker's ability to retire at an early age, and the claw-back of benefits reduces his or her incentives to work. The public wealth created by the pay-as-you-go financing of the CPP and QPP and the claw-back of benefits under the Guaranteed Income Supplement program may have induced some workers to take early retirement.[7] In 1961, 50.4 percent of men over the 65 to 69 age cohort participated in the labour force. By 1981, the participation rate for this group was 21.9 percent, and by 1993 it was 16.6 percent.[8] Many investigators believe that changes to the Canadian public pension system have played an important role in the dramatic change in retirement patterns, but other factors such as rising incomes, changing life expectancies, changes in the demand for different occupations, inflation, and the amount of wealth accumulated in private pensions have been at least as important.

---

[7] Up until the mid-1980s, the CPP may have induced workers to delay retirement because the phasing-in of benefits meant that postponing retirement led to significantly higher pensions.

[8] Burbidge (1996: 111).

Implications

Some economists believe that the public pension system depresses both work effort and saving. However, the evidence is murky, and many others are unconvinced. Even if the system does distort economic decisions, this is not necessarily a bad thing. If society wants to achieve some level of income security for its members, then presumably it should be willing to pay for that security in terms of some loss of efficiency. On the other hand, efforts should be made to structure the system so that work and saving incentives are adversely affected as little as possible.

THE OLD AGE SECURITY PROGRAM

The federal government's involvement in the provision of public pensions began with the Old Age Pension Act of 1927 in which the federal government agreed to pay half (and in 1931 three-quarters) of the cost of means-tested pensions administered by the provinces. In 1952, the federal government introduced a universal pension of $40 per month to all Canadians over the age of 70 under the Old Age Security Act. Figure 14.2 shows the OAS benefit (in 1995 dollars) from 1952 to 1995. Benefits increased sharply from 1957 to 1967. The decline in real benefits after 1967 was due to the fact that benefits were only partially indexed to inflation. The age of eligibility was gradually reduced to 65 in 1970. Full indexation to the consumer price index (CPI) was introduced in 1973, and benefit levels have been relatively constant in real terms since that time. In 1985, the Mulroney government attempted to reintroduce partial indexation by limiting indexation to CPI increases in excess of 3 percent. The resulting political uproar, which pushed the diminutive Solange Denis into the national spotlight, resulted in the withdrawal of this proposal. OAS pensions are taxed under the personal income tax, and for an individual with annual income in excess of $53,215 there is an additional $15 claw-back of benefits for each additional $100 earned above this threshold. The full pension, which is provided to those who have lived in Canada for at least forty years after age 18, was $400.71 per month in January 1997.

Guaranteed Income Supplement, which was introduced in 1967, operates like a negative income tax program. Single individuals with no income other than the OAS pension received $476.20 per month, and a married couple each received $310.18 a month in January 1997. Benefits are reduced by 50 cents for each dollar of income (other than OAS pension) that the individual or couple receives. Thus, the combination of OAS and GIS ensured that a single senior had a minimum monthly income of $876.91 in January 1997, and the GIS benefit was reduced to zero when the individual had other non-OAS income equal to $952.40. GIS benefits are nontaxable and indexed to the CPI.

Figure 14.2

Old Age Security Benefits per Pensioner in 1995 Dollars

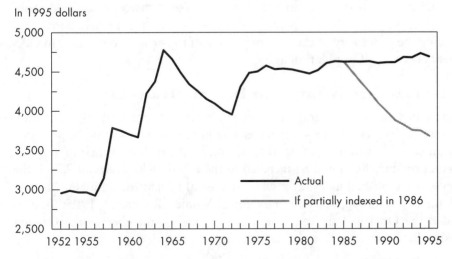

In 1995 dollars

SOURCE: Battle (1996: Figure 3, p. 143). "A New Old Age Pension," in *Reform of Retirement Income Policy: International and Canadian Perspectives*, edited by Keith G. Banting and Robin Boadway, School of Policy Studies, Queen's University, Kingston, Ontario.

Spouse's Allowance, which was introduced in 1975, is an income-tested benefit that is paid to the spouse of an OAS pensioner, or to a widow or widower. The recipient must be 60 to 64 years of age and have lived in Canada for at least ten years after the age of 18. The maximum SA was $710.89 in January 1997, and the benefit is reduced by 75 cents for each dollar of non-OAS income received by the recipient or the couple. Benefits are not taxable and are indexed to the CPI. In 1996, 3.5 million individuals received OAS, 1.4 million received GIS, and 105,000 received SA. Of the approximately $22 billion in payments, OAS pensions accounted for just over 75 percent of the total, GIS was about 22 percent, and SA was about 2 percent.

The Old Age Security Program, in conjunction with the CPP and QPP and the provincial income support programs for seniors, has helped to lower the incidence of poverty among those over age 65. The poverty rate among families headed by someone over age 65 has fallen from 41.1 percent in 1969 to 7.1 percent in 1994. For single seniors, the poverty rate has declined from 69.1 percent in 1969 to 47.6 percent in 1994.[9] The dramatic decline in the incidence

---

[9] Battle (1996: 152).

of poverty among the elderly must be counted as one of the most remarkable successes of the Canadian public pension system.

The Old Age Security Program has also been beset by two interrelated problems—targeting the OAS pension to those who need income assistance and reducing the generosity of the system in view of the projected increase in OAS benefits because of population aging.

Universal versus Targeted Income Transfers

If one views the OAS program as primarily an income redistribution program for the elderly, then the question arises whether the benefit should be provided as a universal flat-rate payment to all recipients regardless of their income, or whether the benefit should be targeted to the elderly who are poor. When the OAS was established in 1952, it was a universal benefit for seniors. This type of transfer has its supporters. For example, Monica Townsend (1995: 3), who headed the Ontario Fair Tax Commission and is a member of the Canada Pension Plan Advisory Board, has argued:

> The rationale for Old Age Security as a universal, flat-rate benefit paid to all seniors, was that seniors had made a contribution to society and that society as a whole would acknowledge that by paying them benefits in their older years. It is widely recognized that such programs promote social solidarity and are far less vulnerable to cutbacks than social assistance type benefits which are income- or means tested. Because everyone benefits from them, they usually have wide public support.

Critics of universal transfer programs point to the inequity of providing transfers to everyone, including middle- and upper-income groups, that have to be financed by general taxes, some of which are borne by those with low incomes. The critics argue that a negative income tax scheme, such as GIS, is a fairer and more efficient transfer mechanism than a lump-sum transfer, such as OAS, when it has to be financed by distortionary taxation. They note that if universal transfers are to achieve widespread support they must be financed by highly progressive taxes that fall mainly on the rich so that the median voter, who is probably in the middle-income range, is a net beneficiary. The problem is that highly progressive taxes are also very distortionary and may not raise enough revenue to finance a large transfer program. If a society decides that it is not willing or able to impose highly progressive taxes, then the median voter will be a net contributor, and the alternative of providing a targeted transfer to those with low incomes will be more attractive. (This assumes that the transfer program is motivated by altruism toward the elderly poor as well as self-interest.) A claw-back of OAS benefits and Family Allowance was introduced in 1989, and Ken Battle (1996: 147) views this as "a milestone in the history of Canadian social policy. It spelled the end of the universal foundation of the child and elderly benefit systems, one of the sacred principles of the universalist welfare state."[10]

The introduction of the OAS claw-back in 1989 was more symbolic than real. The OAS pension was reduced by 15 cents for each dollar that an individual's income exceeded $53,215. Thus, a single senior with $60,000 of income would have his or her OAS pension reduced by $1,018, but would still receive a net pension of over $3,700 per year. A couple where each received $50,000 of income would still be entitled to the full OAS pension. In the view of many, the 1989 claw-back of OAS pensions did not go far enough in targeting the pension to low-income seniors.

Population Aging

The second problem confronting the OAS program is the projected increase in expenditures as the baby-boom generation reaches age 65 in the year 2010. Figure 14.3 shows the percentage of the population over age 65 from 1951 to 2031. From 1951 to 1971, the percentage of the population over age 65 increased only modestly because the increase in the life expectancy of the elderly was offset by the very high birth rate that occurred in Canada between 1945 and 1965. The "baby bust," which followed the baby boom, will have a major repercussion on the age composition of the population in the twenty-first century—the percentage of the population over age 65 is projected to almost double between 1991 and 2031 when the last of the baby boomers turns 65. The ratio of the economically active population, aged 20 to 64, to the 65-plus age group will decrease from 5.26 in 1991 to 2.44 in 2031.[11] The increase in the number of seniors, from 3.7 million in the mid-1990s to 8.8 million in 2030, implies that OAS/GIS/SA expenditures, net of federal income tax and the claw-back, will increase from $21 billion to $77 billion.[12]

Not everyone is convinced that the OAS/GIS/SA expenditures will impose a heavy burden on taxpayers in the twenty-first century. Wolfson and Murphy (1996: Table 2, p. 84) project that OAS/GIS/SA expenditures will increase from 5.5 percent of aggregate wages in 1994 to 9.5 percent in 2036 in absence of real economic growth, but will *decline* to 3.7 percent of aggregate wages in

---

[10] In 1993, the Mulroney government replaced the Family Allowance and child tax credit with the income-tested Child Tax Benefit.

[11] Statistics Canada (1993: Table A3).

[12] Government of Canada (1996: 34).

Figure 14.3

Percentage of the Population Aged 65 and Over

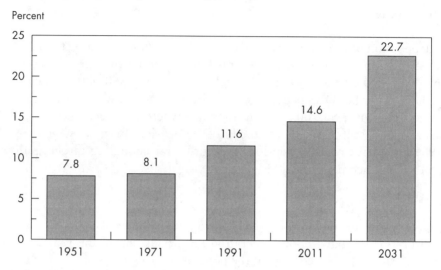

SOURCE: Statistics Canada (1993: Table A33).

2036 if the economy achieves a 2.0 percent annual average growth rate over the next forty years. When coupled with the fact that the baby-boom genera-tion will be paying income taxes on its RRSP withdrawals and RPP income and sales taxes on its consumption expenditures, the authors conclude that "there is no particular affordability problem with current programs" (1996: 95).

The affordability of OAS/GIS/SA depends on the future rates of economic growth, but also upon the expenditure burdens that will be imposed by CPP and QPP and health care costs for the elderly. In any event, the federal gov-ernment announced in the 1996 federal budget that the OAS and GIS pro-grams will be replaced by the new Seniors Benefit program starting in 2001.[13]

The Seniors Benefit

Under the new program, a single senior will receive $11,420 per year and a cou-ple will receive $18,440 if in either case they have no other source of income. The benefit will be tax free, but will be subject to a claw-back based on the single indi-vidual's income or the combined family income in the case of a couple. The ben-

---

[13] In 2001, the age and pension income tax credits will also be eliminated. The Spouse's Allowance program will be retained.

efit will be reduced by 50 cents for each dollar of income received until the benefit is $5,160 for a single senior or $10,320 for a couple. The benefits will remain at these levels until the annual income of the single senior or couple reaches $25,921. Then the benefits will be reduced by an additional 20 cents for each additional dollar of income. A single senior will not receive any Seniors Benefit if his or her income exceeds $52,000, and senior couples will not receive any benefit if their combined income exceeds $78,000. The benefits and the income thresholds that trigger benefit reductions will be fully indexed to inflation.

Figure 14.4 shows the projected Seniors Benefit levels and the OAS/GIS at various income levels for a single individual and a couple. The figure indicates that seniors with incomes of less than $38,000 and couples with less than $42,000 will generally be better off with the Seniors Benefit than they would have been with the OAS/GIS. Anyone who was 60 or older on December 31, 1995, will be able to choose whether they want to switch to the new Seniors Benefit or retain the OAS/GIS benefits. The federal government estimates that "75 per cent of single seniors and couples will receive the same or higher benefits. Nine out of 10 single senior women will be better off under the new system."[14]

Figure 14.4

Comparison of the OAS/GIS and the Seniors Benefit in 2001

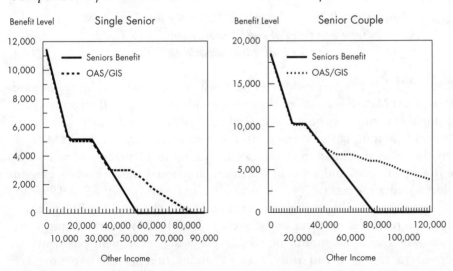

SOURCE: Government of Canada, *The Seniors Benefit* (1996: Tables 1 and 2).

---

[14] Government of Canada (1996: 7).

Overall, the reforms will continue the process of increased targeting of bene-fits on the basis of income. The other major innovations include the use of fam-ily income, instead of individual income, in determining the benefits for couples and the indexation of the income thresholds, which means that infla-tion will not start to push increasing numbers of seniors into the claw-back income range. It is projected that the new Seniors Benefit will cost $69.1 bil-lion in 2030, a saving of $8.2 billion or 10.7 percent over the expenditure under the OAS/GIS system.

THE CANADA PENSION PLAN

The Canada Pension Plan, established in 1966, is a compulsory earnings-related public pension scheme financed on a pay-as-you-go basis. Ten million Canadians contribute toward, and 3.5 million Canadians receive benefits from, the CPP. About three million Quebeckers contribute to the QPP, which provides similar benefits for about one million people. Changes to the CPP require the approval of the federal government and two-thirds of the provinces containing two-thirds of the population. CPP benefits consist of retirement benefits, disability benefits, and survivor benefits.

Retirement benefits. A contributor is entitled at age 65 to a pension, which is based on the following formula:

$$CPP \ pension = 0.25 \times (average \ YMPE \ for \ the \ previous \ three \ years)$$
$$\times \ (average \ ratio \ of \ pensionable \ earnings \ to \ YMPE$$
$$for \ the \ individual's \ working \ life) \qquad (14.1)$$

where YMPE is the Yearly Maximum Pensionable Earnings. Since the mid-1980s, the YMPE has equalled the average industrial wage. If a contributor's pensionable earnings in any year exceed the YMPE, then the ratio is set equal to one. In computing the average ratio of pensionable earnings to YMPE, an individual may eliminate from the calculation up to 15 percent of years with the lowest earnings and years in which the individual was providing care for children under the age of 7 years. An individual who turned 65 in 1996 and who earned the YMPE or higher over his or her entire working life would be entitled to receive 25 percent of the average YMPE in 1994, 1995, and 1996, which was $727.08 a month or $8,725 per year. Subsequent payments are indexed to the CPI and fully taxable under the personal income tax. Individuals may elect to receive their pension as early as age 60 or as late as age 70. The annual pension is permanently reduced by 6 percent for each year that it is received before age 65, and it is increased by 6 percent a year for each year that it is postponed after age 65. The average age at which CPP pension

benefits begin is 62.5 years. In 1996, CPP retirement benefits amounted to $10.9 billion and represented over two-thirds of total CPP expenditures.

Disability benefits. Individuals who are unable to work because of physical or mental disability are entitled to disability benefits until age 65, at which point they receive their retirement benefits. The disability benefit is a flat rate plus 75 percent of the CPP retirement pension that the individual would have been entitled to at age 65. Additional benefits are also paid if the disabled individual has children under the age of 18 or who are 18 to 25 and attending an educational establishment. In 1996, disability benefits were $3.3 billion or 17 percent of total CPP expenditures.

Survivor benefits. At the death of the CPP contributor, there is a one-time payment of a death benefit to the estate of the deceased. In 1996, the maximum death benefit was $3,540. The surviving spouse of a deceased contributor who is between the ages of 45 and 65, or less than 45 with dependent children, is entitled to a pension, which is a fixed rate plus 37.5 percent of the CPP retirement pension that the deceased would have received. The maximum benefit in 1996 was $399.70 At age 65, the surviving spouse is entitled to a pension equal to 60 percent of the pension entitlement of the deceased. An orphan's benefit is also paid to the children of a deceased CPP contributor if the child is less than 18 years old or between 18 and 25 years and attending an educational institution full-time. In 1996, total survivor benefits represented $2.8 billion or 16 percent of total CPP expenditures.

Contributions. A self-employed individual whose pensionable earnings are less than YMPE makes contributions to the CPP according to the following formula:

$$CPP\ contribution =$$
$$contribution\ rate \times (pensionable\ earnings - YBE) \qquad (14.2)$$

where YBE is the Year's Basic Exemption, which is equal to 10 percent of the YMPE (rounded to the nearest $100). In 1996, the YMPE was $35,400, the YBE was $3,500, and the contribution rate was 5.6 percent. An individual whose pensionable earnings exceeded the YMPE in 1996 paid the maximum contribution of 0.056 ($35,400 – $3,500) or $1,786. An employed individual pays half this amount, and his or her employer pays the other half.

When the CPP was established in 1966, the contribution rate was set at 3.6 percent, and it remained at that level until 1986. From 1987 to 1996 the contribution rate was increased by 0.2 percentage points per year. Figure 14.5 shows

Figure 14.5

CPP Contribution Rates

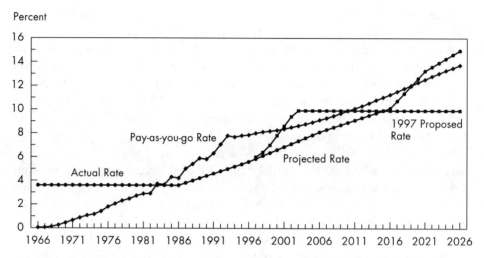

SOURCE: Office of the Superintendent of Financial Institutions (1995: Table 1A and p. 19).

the actual contribution rates over the period 1966 to 1996, and the contribution rates that are projected into the twenty-first century by the chief actuary of the Canada Pension Plan. The figure also shows past and projected pay-as-you-go contribution rates where the pay-as-you-go contribution rates are the rates that would be required to finance the CPP expenditures in a given year. These contribution rates are projected to increase to 14.2 percent in 2030. Finally, the figure shows the contribution rates proposed by the federal government and eight of the ten provinces in 1997 as part of the reform of the CPP.

From 1966 to 1982, the actual contribution rate exceeded the pay-as-you-go contribution rate, and the surplus of revenue over expenditure was used to establish the Canada Pension Plan reserve fund, which was invested in provincial government bonds. The CPP reserve fund is now equal to about $40 billion, or about two years' worth of benefits. The primary function of the reserve fund is to provide a cushion so that the contribution rate does not have to fluctuate wildly from year to year in the event of economic fluctuations. The CPP is not a funded pension plan. If the CPP had been designed as a funded pension plan at its inception, it would have required $600 billion in assets in 1995 to finance the projected expenditure. The difference between $600 billion and the $40 billion that the fund actually has is referred to as the unfunded liability of the Canada Pension Plan.

Since 1983, the contribution rate has been below the pay-as-you-go contribution rate. The difference was financed by the investment earnings from the reserve fund. Since 1993, CPP expenditures have exceeded contributions plus the fund's investment income, and therefore the fund has begun to decline. Even with the projected increase in the contribution rate, it is anticipated that the reserve fund will continue to decline and be exhausted by the year 2015.

Analysis of CPP Contribution Increases

The anticipated increases in the CPP contribution rates, from 5.60 percent in 1996 to around 14.2 percent in the year 2030, has led to major concerns about the affordability and the political viability of the CPP in the twenty-first century. We will begin by examining the factors that have led to the rapid increase in the projected CPP contribution rates, and then we will examine some of the proposed reforms.

When the CPP was established in 1966, it was anticipated that the pay-as-you-go contribution rate would increase to 5.5 percent in 2030. Table 14.1 shows the four main factors that are responsible for the increase in the pay-as-you-go rate from 5.5 percent to the 14.2 percent that is anticipated in 2030 by the chief actuary of the CPP in his *Fifteenth Actuarial Report*.[15] The first is the change in demographics. When the CPP was established in 1966, the birth rate had just started to decline, and the implication of this for the age composition of the population in the twenty-first century was not foreseen. CPP pensions are financed by the contributions of the current working population. The decline in the average number of workers per pensioner from 6.7 in the 1960s to 2.4 in 2030 means that the contribution rate that has to be levied on the earnings of the working generation will be higher than anticipated. In addition, the elderly are living longer. When the CPP was established, life expectancy at age 65 was 15.3 years. It is now anticipated that the life expectancy at age 65 will increase to 19.4 years in 2015. Therefore, pensions will have to be paid for 4.1 years longer than anticipated. These demographic changes will increase the pay-as-you-go rate by 2.6 percentage points in 2030 and account for about 30 percent of the total increase in the pay-as-you-go rate.

The second factor is the change in economics. As we have seen, pay-as-you-go financing is attractive when the total wages and salaries (the contribution base of the working generation) is growing faster than the rate of return on assets that are normally held by pension plans. As Figure 14.1 indicated, total wages and salaries were increasing rapidly in the 1960s, and these trends were

---

[15] See Office of the Superintendent of Financial Institutions (1995).

Table 14.1

Decomposition of the Pay-as-you-go Rate Increase for the Canada Pension Plan

	PAY-AS-YOU-GO CONTRIBUTION RATE
Rate in 2030 as projected when the CPP started	5.5
Change in Demographics	2.6
Change in Economics	2.2
Enrichment of Benefits	2.4
Increase in Disability Claims	1.5
Rate in 2030 as projected by the Chief Actuary in 1995	14.2

SOURCE: Federal, Provincial, and Territorial Governments of Canada, *An Information Paper for Consultations on the Canada Pension Plan*, February 1996, p. 20. Reproduced with the permission of the Minister of Public Works and Government Services Canada, 1997.

extrapolated into the future, implying that future contribution rates would be relatively modest. Since the mid-1970s, productivity growth rates have plunged, and the chief actuary, in forecasting the pay-as-you-go rate for 2030, has assumed that productivity will grow by 1 percent per year. The slower than anticipated productivity growth rate means that the pay-as-you-go rate in 2030 will be 2.2 percentage points higher than anticipated, accounting for about 25 percent of the total increase in the pay-as-you-go rate.

The third factor is the enhancement of CPP benefits since its inception. These enhancements include[16]:

- full indexation of benefits in 1975;
- provision of survivor benefits to widowers in 1975;
- dropping retirement and earnings tests in 1975[17];
- allowing the child-rearing drop-out provision in calculating contributions in 1978;
- enhanced benefits and reduced contribution requirements for disability claims;
- allowing recipients of survivor benefits to retain benefits upon remarriage.

---

[16] See Federal, Provincial, and Territorial Governments of Canada, *An Information Paper for Consultations on the Canada Pension Plan*, February 1996, pp. 23–24.

[17] "Originally, contributors aged 65 to 69 could only receive their retirement benefits if they passed a retirement test, and their subsequent benefit up to age 70 was reduced if they earned more than a set amount." Ibid., p. 23.

All of these changes have increased the generosity of the CPP system. They will add 2.4 percentage points to the pay-as-you-go rate in 2030 and account for 28 percent of the total increase in the pay-as-you-go rate.

The fourth factor is the unanticipated increase in disability claims. The surge in disability claims, especially by women, is a relatively recent phenomenon.[18] Between 1989 and 1994 the incidence of new disability cases increased from 4.28 to 6.34 per thousand for males and from 2.99 to 5.79 per thousand for females. Part of the reason for the increase in the number of claims is the administrative guidelines that were issued in 1989, which allowed adjudicators to take into account the unemployment rate in the applicant's region, the availability of jobs, and the person's skills in determining eligibility for disability benefits. The recession of the early 1990s increased the number of applicants who could qualify on the basis of labour market conditions. In addition, the Canada Pension Plan Advisory Board has noted that private insurers and the provincial governments increased their efforts to get individuals to apply for CPP disability benefits. For a provincial government, shifting the disabled from provincial social welfare and worker's compensation to the CPP is attractive because it means that the cost of supporting the disabled is borne by all Canadian workers (outside Quebec) and not just the province's own taxpayers.

Intergenerational Redistribution through the CPP

The relatively low contribution rates in the early years of the CPP have resulted in a substantial intergenerational income transfer. Figure 14.6 shows calculations by Oreopoulos (1996) of the ratio of the present value of the CPP benefits to contributions that various generations will receive with current benefit rates and contribution rates similar to those projected by the chief actuary in the *Fifteenth Actuarial Report*. The generation that was born in 1915 and turned 65 in 1980 is expected to receive about $5.50 in benefits for every dollar that it contributed to the CPP. Individuals born between 1950 and 1955 are expected to break even. The present value of their benefits will be approximately equal to the present value of their contributions. Those who are born after 1975 will receive less than 50 cents for every dollar contributed to the CPP.

These benefit–contribution ratios are based on the assumption that there will be no major changes to the CPP benefits, but CPP benefits could be arbitrarily reduced by some future governments. This may be a politically attractive option for governments after the year 2020 because, even with the increase in the percentage of the population over age 65, a majority of the voters will be

---

[18] See Office of the Superintendent of Financial Institutions (1995: 56).

Figure 14.6

CPP Lifetime Benefit–Contribution Ratios by Age Cohort

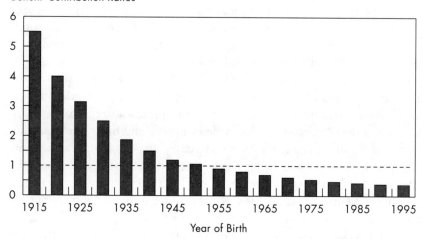

SOURCE: Oreopoulos (1996).

contributors and would be better off with a cut in CPP benefits.[19] To avoid an abrupt loss of benefits in the future, many argue that the CPP should be reformed now.

Options for Reforming the Canada Pension Plan

A number of reforms have been suggested that will reduce the contribution rates required to finance the CPP after 2010. Some of these reforms are discussed below.

"Ramp up" the contribution rate. A more rapid increase in the contribution rate over the period to 2010 would allow the CPP to build up a larger reserve fund and to lower the "steady state" contribution.[20] For example, a steady state contribution rate of 10.9 percent could be achieved if the contribution rate were progressively increased to this level by 2002. A higher steady state contribution rate of 11.1 percent would be achieved if the contribution

---

[19] See Robson (1996) for an analysis of the incentives to vote for the winding up of the CPP by different age groups.
[20] The steady state contribution rate is defined as "the constant contribution rate which would maintain an approximately constant proportion of funding over the next century." Federal, Provincial, and Territorial Governments, *An Information Paper* (1996: 55).

rate were progressively increased to this level by 2005. Thus, a more rapid increase in the contribution rate leads to a lower steady state contribution rate. Policy makers have to trade off the potentially harmful effects of the rapid payroll tax increase on the economy's output and employment with the potential longer-term gain of having a lower steady state contribution rate.

Investment policy of the CPP reserve fund. The more rapid the increase in the contribution rate, the more the CPP reserve fund will grow, and the more important the rate of return on the reserve fund becomes for bringing down the steady state contribution rate. The reserve fund has been invested in the debt issued by the provincial governments, and the interest rate on these bonds has been set at the federal government's borrowing rate. This policy has been criticized because the rate of return on the fund has been relatively low, 8.0 percent over the period 1967 to 1989 compared to the 10.3 percent rate of return earned by private investment funds over the same period,[21] and it may have encouraged the provincial governments to borrow more than they otherwise would have because they had a captive source of funds at a relatively low rate of interest. Increasing the range of assets that the reserve fund could hold to include domestic and foreign equities would increase the rate of return that the reserve fund could generate, without unduly increasing the risk, but many feel that a publicly managed fund might make politically motivated investment decisions, such as investing in a company because it is located in a particular area of the country.

Reducing CPP retirement benefits. One way of bringing down the contribution rate is to reduce retirement benefits. It has been estimated that reducing the pension benefit rate from 25 percent of earnings to 22.5 percent of earnings would reduce the pay-as-you-go contribution rate in 2030 from 14.2 percent to 12.95 percent. Any pension reduction would almost certainly not apply to current CPP pension recipients, and it would have to be phased in over a number of years so that workers will have a chance to adjust their savings and retirement decisions to the new lower pension benefits. One criticism of reducing CPP retirement benefits is that the public pensions are the major source of income for low- and middle-income workers, and therefore reducing the CPP retirement pension is inequitable.

To assess the distribution effect of a cut in CPP retirement benefits, it is important to take into account how a CPP pension reduction would affect payments under the Seniors Benefit and personal income tax payments. Table 14.2 shows

---

[21] Lam, Cutt, and Prince (1996: 115).

how a hypothetical $1,000 reduction in the maximum CPP retirement benefit in the year 2001 would affect Tom, Dick, and Harry, three single Albertans who retire at age 65 in 2001. It is assumed that the 1996 federal and Alberta income tax rates continue to apply and that the maximum CPP pension benefit is reduced from $10,000 to $9,000 in 2001. Tom's only sources of income are the Seniors Benefit and his CPP pension. The $1,000 reduction in the CPP retirement pension is offset by a $500 increase in Tom's nontaxable Seniors Benefit and a reduction in personal income tax paid on the CPP pension. As a result, Tom's after-tax income declines by only $268. Dick has $10,000 of income in addition to his CPP pension and Seniors Benefit. In Dick's case, the $1,000 reduction in CPP benefits is not offset by an increase in the Seniors Benefit because he is in the income range where income changes have no effect on the Seniors Benefit (see Figure 14.4). As a result, Dick's after-tax income would decline by $743. Harry has $30,000 of private pension income. His after-tax income is reduced by only $409 dollars because he is in the income range where a $1,000 reduction in income increases the Seniors Benefit by $200. These examples show that a reduction in CPP retirement benefits will have its greatest impact on individuals with relatively modest private pension or RRSP income. The impact of a CPP reduction on those with little or no private income will be largely offset by changes in the Seniors Benefit. It also means that "fixing" the CPP by reducing retirement benefits will increase the expenditures under the Seniors Benefit program, and any reduction in the CPP contribution rate may be at least partially offset by increases in other tax rates

Table 14.2

Effect of a Hypothetical Reduction in the CPP Retirement Pension in 2001

	OTHER INCOME	CPP PENSION	SENIORS BENEFIT	PERSONAL INCOME TAX	AFTER-TAX INCOME	REDUCTION IN AFTER-TAX INCOME
Tom	0	10,000	6,240	677	15,563	
	0	9,000	6,740	445	15,295	268
Dick	10,000	10,000	5,160	3,519	21,641	
	10,000	9,000	5,160	3,262	20,898	743
Harry	30,000	10,000	2,350	10,059	32,291	
	30,000	9,000	2,550	9,668	31,882	409

Note: The personal income tax is calculated for a single individual with no dependents or other deductions using the 1996 Alberta income tax rates.

SOURCE: Calculation by the authors.

that are required to finance the increase in the Seniors Benefit and the reduction in personal income tax on CPP pensions.

Reducing or eliminating the year's basic exemption. The deduction of the YBE from pensionable earnings in computing CPP contributions reduces the effective tax contribution rate below the statutory contribution rate. As pensionable earnings increase, the effective contribution rate increases—making the CPP contribution a progressive tax—up to the point where income equals YMPE. Then, the effective contribution rate declines as pensionable earnings increase above YMPE. If one views the CPP contribution as a benefit tax, then contributions should be proportional to earnings up to YMPE because retirement benefits are proportional to earnings up to YMPE. From the benefit perspective, the YBE should be eliminated because it lowers the effective contribution rate for those with low earnings. However, if one views CPP contributions as an earmarked tax that is used to finance an intergenerational income redistribution program, then one would want to finance it with a progressive tax, and the YBE introduces some progressivity into the financing of the CPP.

Removing the "drop-out" provision in calculating the retirement pension. In calculating the CPP pension benefit, a contributor can drop out of the calculation any years in which the contributor was caring for children under 7 years of age and up to 15 percent of the remaining years (to a maximum of seven years) in which his or her earnings were relatively low. This provision gives a larger pension to individuals (mainly women) who have had their lifetime earnings reduced because of child care responsibilities and to those who have had periods of low earnings because of unemployment or education and training. These provisions introduce some "progressivity" into the provision of CPP benefits. This is appropriate if one views the CPP as an income redistribution program, but it is more appropriate to provide income support for the elderly, with reduced lifetime earnings, through the OAS/GIS/SA or the Seniors Benefit programs.

Raising the age of entitlement. When the CPP was established in 1966, the average life expectancy at age 65 was 15.3 years. It is currently 19.4 years, and by 2030 it is expected to increase to 19.8 years. Individuals are living longer and are choosing to retire at a younger age. As we have seen, the provision of a public pension system may have contributed to the trend in early retirement. The longer life expectancy and presumably improved health of today's 65 year olds suggests that they should be able to work for a longer period and enjoy the same length of retirement as previous generations. Gradually increasing the retirement age to 67, as the United States has done, would reduce pension expenditures and the steady state contribution rate by just over half a percentage point. It is sometimes argued that delaying the age of entitlement would increase unemployment because older workers would postpone retirement and retain the jobs that would otherwise be filled by younger workers. However, after 2010 the Canadian economy may have less difficulty in providing jobs for workers of all ages as the ratio of workers to the retired population sharply declines.

Reducing or removing disability benefits from the CPP. The rapid increase in disability benefits is one of the main factors contributing to the expansion in CPP expenditures. Changes in the guidelines for the administration of the program have ruled out "socioeconomic" factors in adjudicating claims, but it is likely that a further tightening of the system could be justified. It can also be argued that the provision of disability benefits to the working-age population should not be part of the CPP. The provision of income protection for the disabled should be the responsibility of the provincial governments through their social assistance and worker's compensation programs. Making the provinces solely responsible for income redistribution because of disability would reduce federal–provincial overlap and duplication, which may have contributed to the expansion of the disability case load. More federal grants to the provinces may be necessary if the provincial governments acquire the additional responsibilities for disability from the Canada Pension Plan.

Partial indexation for inflation. The CPP could return to the pre-1975 policy of only indexing CPP benefits to some maximum value, say 2 percent. This would reduce the real value of retirement pensions and the contribution rates required to finance them to the extent that the inflation rate exceeds the threshold rate. This policy could impose severe hardship on some seniors if we again experience the high rates of inflation that were observed in the 1970s and early 1980s. Partial indexation would impose a heavier burden on women than on men because women tend to live longer than men. If the intention is to reduce CPP expenditures, a reduction in the benefit rate from 25 percent of previous earnings would be fairer and create less uncertainty than partial indexation.

Reforms Proposed in *Securing the Canada Pension Plan*

In February 1997, the federal government and eight of the ten provinces proposed a series of amendments to the CPP.[22] The governments proposed that the contribution rate be increased to a steady state rate of 9.9 percent in 2003 (see Figure 14.5). They also proposed freezing the YBE at $3,500. Over time, this

---

[22] See HRDC (1997). British Columbia and Saskatchewan did not agree to the proposals.

will increase the effective contribution rate as pensionable earnings increase. As a result of these measures, the CPP reserve fund will grow from around two years of CPP expenditures to five years of expenditures by 2017. This larger fund will be invested in a diversified portfolio of securities by an independent CPP Investment Board.

Benefit reductions were also proposed. New retirement pensions will be based on the average YMPE over the previous five years instead of over the previous three years. Averaging the YMPE over five years instead of three years will reduce pension benefits if, as seems likely, the YMPE increases over time due to inflation and productivity growth. If the YMPE increases at 4.5 percent per year (the rate of growth of earnings assumed by the chief actuary), then the shift from three-year averaging to five-year averaging is equivalent to cutting the benefit rate from 25 percent to 24 percent of the average YMPE over the previous three years. The magnitude of the effective reduction in the CPP benefit will be larger the higher the rate of inflation. The administration of the disability benefit is to be tightened, the retirement pension for disability beneficiaries will be reduced because it will be based on the YMPE at the time of disability, instead of when the individual turns 65, and more stringent eligibility requirements will be imposed. Finally, the maximum death benefit will be reduced from $3,580 to $2,500 and frozen at this level. In summary, the proposed reforms rely on a rapid increase in the contribution rate over a seven-year period, combined with some benefit reductions, to keep the contribution rate below 10 percent after the year 2015.

CONCLUSION

In this chapter, we have considered two of the pillars of Canada's retirement income system. The OAS–Seniors Benefit program is primarily an income redistribution program for the elderly. The CPP is primarily an earnings-related public pension scheme. Its existence (but not its pay-as-you-go financing) can be justified on the basis of market failure—paternalism, the Samaritan's dilemma, adverse selection in the market for annuities, and inflation indexation. The introduction of these programs in the 1950s and 1960s resulted in a significant decline in poverty among the elderly, but it may have had adverse effects on savings rates and retirement decisions. The massive intergenerational wealth transfers that are inherent in these programs have called into question their long-term viability, and major changes to both programs have been announced in recent years.

The new Seniors Benefit will be more focused on its redistributive role, continuing the trend away from a universal benefit. Canada is not the only country that has moved from universal to targeted transfers. Australia, Denmark, Finland, Holland, Iceland, Sweden, and New Zealand have also introduced claw-backs of pension benefits for middle- and upper-income pensioners. As Myles and Quadango (1996: 248) have noted, "'Need' is replacing 'citizenship' as the criterion for eligibility" in many countries.

Demographic and economic changes are responsible for just over half of the increase in the projected costs of CPP. These factors were beyond the control of the designers of the CPP, but the implications of these changes for the financing of the CPP have been clear for some time, and governments have been very slow in initiating reform. Indeed, the actions taken in the 1970s and 1980s— enhancing benefits and making it easier to collect disability benefits—were made at a time when the worsening financial position of the CPP should have been recognized and have contributed to the problem.

Our political system has difficulty in reforming public sector pensions. Governments often have a very short time horizon. A week is a long time in politics, but the decisions made in that week may have profound effects on public sector pensions, and the contributions required to finance them, in seventy years' time. The temptation to put off unpopular decisions, or to consider only those reforms that make a majority of the current voting population better off, pushes the problems and the costs onto future generations. Pensioners are a potent interest group. They have high voter turnout rates, and they are often portrayed in the media as a particularly deserving group. In some respects, however, the political economy of pension reform is unique. Paul Pierson (1966: 280) argues that "in comparison with say, welfare benefits, where an 'us' versus 'them' mentality is easy to construct, pension recipients are rarely seen as 'them.' Those paying for pensions are both the children of pensioners and future pension recipients. The political outcry against even quite substantial intergenerational redistribution is likely to remain relatively muted." The first decades of the twenty-first century will tell whether Pierson's prediction is correct.

SUMMARY

- Canada's retirement income system consists of three pillars: Old Age Security, the Canada and Quebec Pension Plans, and tax-assisted private savings and pensions.

- Public provision of pensions can be justified on the basis of market failure. The causes of market failure include paternalism, redistribution, adverse selection in the market for annuities, the absence of inflation indexation with private pensions and annuities, and the Samaritan's dilemma.

- With pay-as-you-go financing, the current working generation pays the pension of the retired generation. There is no need for a pension fund. Pay-as-you-go financing is superior to a funded pension scheme when the growth rate of total real wages and salaries exceeds the real interest rate on assets held in pension funds.

- Pay-as-you-go pensions may reduce private saving—the wealth substitution effect—or increase saving—the retirement and bequest effects. A reasonable conclusion on the basis of the econometric results is that saving has been reduced, but by how much is not clear.

- The percentage of retired older workers has increased dramatically since the 1950s, and the introduction of the public pension programs may have contributed to this trend.

- The Seniors Benefit, which will replace the OAS/GIS program in 2001, will continue the trend from universal to targeted income transfers. Family income will be used to establish eligibility.

- CPP contribution rates are projected to increase because of population aging, the slow-down in the growth rate of real wages, the enhancement of benefits that occurred in the 1970s and 1980s, and the increase in disability claims.

- The CPP has resulted in a large intergenerational transfer of income, because the age cohorts that were born before 1950 will receive benefits that are far in excess of their contributions.

- A number of reforms to the CPP are under consideration, including more rapid contribution rate increases, benefit reductions, reducing disability benefits and eligibility, and raising the age of eligibility for pension benefits.

DISCUSSION QUESTIONS

1. "Public pensions improve economic welfare. Because the system distributes current earnings of the young (which they would save anyway) to the old, the old are better off and the young are unaffected." Discuss carefully.

2. Will an increase in the Canada Pension Plan contribution rate increase the national savings rate?

3. Why do we have two public pension systems, OAS/GIS/SA and CPP/QPP? Discuss the rationale for having two pension systems and the relationship between them.

4. Calculate the total marginal tax rates on income received by Tom, Dick, and Harry in the example shown in Table 14.2. Which individual faced the largest disincentive to save for retirement and to work beyond age 65?

REFERENCES

Battle, Ken. "A New Old Age Pension," in *Reform of Retirement Income Policy: International and Canadian Perspectives*, ed. Keith G. Banting and Robin Boadway. School of Policy Studies, Queen's University, Kingston, Ontario, 1996, pp. 135–90.

Burbidge, John B. "Public Pensions in Canada," in *When We're 65: Reforming Canada's Retirement Income System*, ed. John Richards and William G. Watson. Toronto: C.D. Howe Institute, 1996, pp. 93–128.

Diamond, Peter A. "A Framework for Social Security Analysis." *Journal of Public Economics* 8, no. 3 (December 1977): 275–98.

Federal, Provincial, and Territorial Governments of Canada. *An Information Paper for Consultations on the Canada Pension Plan.* Ottawa: February 1996.

Feldstein, Martin S. "Social Security and Private Saving: Reply." *Journal of Political Economy* 90, no. 3 (June 1982): 630–42.

Feldstein, Martin S. "Social Security, Induced Retirement, and Aggregate Capital Accumulation." *Journal of Political Economy* 82, no. 5 (September–October 1974): 905–26.

Government of Canada. *The Seniors Benefit: Securing the Future.* Ottawa: 1996.

Human Resources Development Canada. *Securing the Canada Pension Plan: Agreement on Proposed Changes to the CPP.* Ottawa: 1997.

Lam, Newman, James Cutt, and Michael Prince. "The Canada Pension Plan: Retrospect and Prospect," in *Reform of Retirement Income Policy: International and Canadian Perspectives*, ed. Keith G. Banting and Robin Boadway. School of Policy Studies, Queen's University, Kingston, Ontario, 1996, pp. 105–34.

Leimer, Dean R., and Selig D. Lesnoy. "Social Security and Private Saving, New Time-Series Evidence." *Journal of Political Economy* 90, no. 3 (June 1982): 606–29.

Modigliani, Franco. "Life Cycle, Individual Thrift, and The Wealth of Nations." *American Economic Review* 76, no. 3 (June 1986): 297–313.

Munnell, Alicia H. *The Future of Social Security.* Washington, DC: Brookings Institution, 1977.

Myles, John, and Jill Quadango. "Recent Trends in Public Pension Reform: A Comparative View," in *Reform of Retirement Income Policy: International and Canadian Perspectives*, ed. Keith G. Banting and Robin Boadway. School of Policy Studies, Queen's University, Kingston, Ontario, 1996, pp. 247–72.

Office of the Superintendent of Financial Institutions. *Canada Pension Plan: Fifteenth Actuarial Report as at 31 December 1993.* Ottawa: 1995.

Oreopoulos, Philip. "Bad Tasting Medicine: Removing Intergenerational Inequity from the CPP." *Choices* 2, no. 7 (November 1996). Institute for Research on Public Policy, Montreal, Quebec.

Pierson, Paul. "The Politics of Pension Reform," in *Reform of Retirement Income Policy: International and Canadian Perspectives*, ed. Keith G. Banting and Robin Boadway. School of Policy Studies, Queen's University, Kingston, Ontario, 1996, pp. 273–94.

Robson, William B.P. "Ponzi's Pawns: Young Canadians and the Canada Pension Plan," in *When We're 65: Reforming Canada's Retirement Income System*, ed. John Richards and William G. Watson. Toronto: C.D. Howe Institute, 1996, pp. 27–56.

Statistics Canada. *Population Ageing and the Elderly: Current Demographic Analysis.* Catalogue 91-533E. Ottawa: Ministry of Industry, Science and Technology, 1993.

Townsend, Monica. *Our Aging Society: Preserving Retirement Incomes into the 21st Century.* Ottawa: Canadian Centre for Policy Alternatives, 1995.

Wolfson, Michael, and Brian Murphy. "Aging and Canada's Public Sector: Retrospect and Prospect," in *Reform of Retirement Income Policy: International and Canadian Perspectives*, ed. Keith G. Banting and Robin Boadway. School of Policy Studies, Queen's University, Kingston, Ontario, 1996, pp. 69–98.

Chapter 15

Health Care

Newspaper headlines regularly suggest that the health care system is in crisis. Conflicts are escalating between health care providers and governments. People see hospitals closing, and they are told that waiting lists for surgery are getting longer and that physicians are leaving the country.... Can medicare survive? Will it be there for our children?

–National Forum on Health

Many Canadians believe that the Canadian health system is one of the best in the world, but they are concerned that it may not be one of the best for much longer. As one of the major public services provided by government, it faces the same pressures faced by all government programs in the 1990s as governments seek to restore fiscal balance. In this chapter we begin by asking what makes health care different from other government services. We then compare the Canadian health system to health systems in other parts of the world. Next we examine the role played by the Canada Health Act. Finally, we focus on some key challenges and future directions for the Canadian health system.

WHAT'S SPECIAL ABOUT HEALTH CARE?

To some people, it seems obvious that health care is a unique commodity. After all, receiving health care can be a matter of life and death. But food and shelter are also crucial for survival, and the country is not debating whether private markets are a good way to provide these commodities. Another possible reason one might think of the health care sector as being unique is the way it has been expanding in recent years. Health expenditures were less than 6 percent of gross domestic product in 1960, and they are now almost 10 percent. But in itself, the fact that people are spending proportionately more on a commodity is neither unique nor alarming. Expenditures on personal computers and compact disk players have also been going up dramatically in recent years, but no one seems terribly upset about it.

When economists consider what is special about the health care market, they ask why that market is unlikely to provide health care in socially optimal amounts. The reasons include those outlined below.

Poor information. We normally assume that consumers are fairly well informed about the commodities they purchase—when you buy an apple, you have a pretty good idea of how it will taste and how much satisfaction it will give you. In contrast, when you are ill, you may not have a very good sense of what medical procedures are appropriate. To make things more complicated, the person on whom you are likely to rely for advice in such a situation, your physician, is also the person who is selling you the commodity.

Adverse selection and moral hazard. Health care costs can be unpredictable and very large. In such a situation, people will want insurance. Most of the general arguments in Chapter 9 for why problems are likely in private insurance markets would apply if health insurance were privately provided.

When an insurance company sets a price for a policy for individuals in a given class (for example, middle-aged urban females), the policy tends to be purchased by those individuals within the class who have the highest risk. For example, if Thelma believes that she is at high risk in terms of her health and Louise does not, then if they are offered insurance at the same price, Thelma is more likely to purchase it. This adverse selection problem causes the average buyer of insurance to have a higher risk than the average person in his or her class. But with a lot of its policy holders becoming ill, the insurance company finds itself losing money. To break even, the company must therefore raise premiums. With higher premiums, individuals with a relatively low risk of becoming ill leave the market. (Facing the higher premium, Thelma purchases the insurance only if she really believes that she is at high risk.) The spiral continues, with more and more people deciding to opt out of purchasing insurance. A private market is likely to underprovide health insurance, other things being the same.

Even in the absence of adverse selection, public or private health insurance may distort people's incentives. First, if people know that they have insurance, they may take less care to avoid risks. Thus, people with insurance may adopt more unhealthy lifestyles (eating a lot of junk food and not exercising much) because the negative consequences of doing so are reduced by insurance.

Second, people have incentives to overconsume health care, because the insurance pays for some or all of the cost. These incentive problems are referred to as moral hazard.

Moral hazard can be analyzed using a conventional supply-and-demand diagram. In Figure 15.1, the market demand curve for medical services in the absence of insurance is labelled D_m. For simplicity, assume that the marginal cost of producing medical services is a constant, P_0. Hence, the supply curve, S_m, is a horizontal line at P_0. As usual, equilibrium is at the intersection of supply and demand; the equilibrium price and quantity are P_0 and M_0, respectively. Total expenditure in the market is the product of the price per unit times number of units, that is, OP_0 times OM_0, or rectangle P_0OM_0a (the darker-shaded area in the diagram).

Before proceeding, we should note one possible objection to Figure 15.1—the downward-sloping demand curve. When people are sick, don't they just follow the doctor's orders, regardless of price? Would you haggle with your surgeon in the midst of an appendicitis attack? The implication of this view is that the demand curve for medical services is perfectly vertical, not downward sloping. Such reasoning ignores the fact that many medical procedures are discretionary. Patients make the initial decision whether to seek health care. And despite the conflict-of-interest issue referred to above, patients do not always comply with their doctor's advice. Pauly (1986) surveyed a number of empir-

Figure 15.1

Market for Medical Services

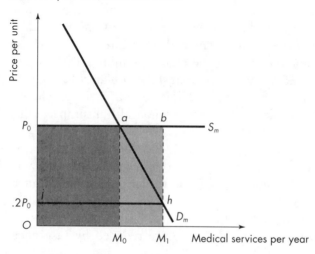

ical studies suggesting that when the price of medical services goes down, the quantity demanded does increase.

How does the introduction of insurance affect the market? To keep things simple, assume that the policy pays for 80 percent of the health costs, leaving the patient to pay for 20 percent.[1] The key to analyzing the impact of insurance is to realize that a 20 percent coinsurance rate is equivalent to an 80 percent reduction in the price facing the patient—if the incremental cost to the hospital for a day's stay is \$800, the patient pays only \$160. In Figure 15.1, the price confronted by the patient is no longer P_0, but only .2 times P_0. Given this lower price, the quantity demanded increases to M_1, and the patient spends area $OjhM_1$ on medical services.

Note that at the new equilibrium, although the patient is paying $.2P_0$ per unit, the marginal cost of providing health services is still P_0; the difference $(.8P_0)$ is paid by the insurance. Hence, total expenditures are OP_0 times OM_1, or the rectangle P_0OM_1b, with the insurance company paying P_0bhj. Thus, as a consequence of the insurance, health care expenditures increase from P_0OM_0a to P_0OM_1b, or the grey area aM_0M_1b.

Of course, the actual amount by which expenditures increase depends on the shape of the demand curve, the precise provisions of the insurance policy, and so on. But the general point is clear—with insurance, consumers do not confront the full marginal costs of their health care, which leads to an increase in both the quantity demanded and total expenditure.

Paternalism. People may not understand how insurance works, or they may lack the foresight to purchase it. Paternalistic arguments suggest that people should be forced into a medical insurance system for their own good.

Income redistribution. There does indeed appear to be a strong societal consensus that everyone should have equal access to necessary medical services, regardless of their ability to pay. In Canada, the health system is an important vehicle for redistributing income from higher- to lower-income groups.

Externalities. Health services received by an individual may also improve the health of others by reducing the spread of infectious diseases. Not properly accounting for these externalities may cause individuals to underconsume health services if they are privately provided.

---

[1] Even with medicare, some health services, such as drugs, are not fully insured. The proportion not covered is called the coinsurance rate.

COMPARING HEALTH SYSTEMS AROUND THE WORLD

How does the Canadian health system look in comparison with other countries? A good place to start is to examine the data provided in Table 15.1. In this table we present selected health statistics from seven OECD countries. In the first column we look at an important characteristic of each country—the proportion of seniors in the population (defined as persons 65 years of age and over). Since seniors are the biggest consumers of health care services, this statistic gives us an indication of the demand for health services in each country. We see that of the seven countries considered, Canada has one of the youngest populations. Only New Zealand has a smaller proportion of seniors in its population.

The second column reports the number of practising doctors per 1,000 residents. This statistic gives us an indication of the supply of health services[2] by country. Canada is in the middle of the range with 2.2 doctors per 1,000 residents. Germany, Sweden, and the United States have substantially more, while Japan and the United Kingdom have fewer.

The next two columns provide some information on the output of the health care system—measures of the health of the population. The first statistic is average life expectancy. For the seven countries considered, Canada is near the

Table 15.1

Selected Health Statistics in 1994

COUNTRY	POP. >64	DOCTORS PER 1,000	LIFE EXPECTANCY	INFANT MORTALITY	COST
Canada	11.9	2.2	78.1	0.68	2,010
Germany	15.2	3.3	76.6	0.56	1,869
Japan	14.0	1.8	79.8	0.42	1,473
New Zealand	11.5	2.1	76.0	0.73	1,226
Sweden	17.4	3.0	78.8	0.44	1,348
U.K.	15.7	1.5	76.8	0.62	1,211
U.S.	12.4	2.5	75.7	0.79	3,516

Note: Some data taken from 1993.

SOURCE: "Striking a Balance Working Group Synthesis Report," NFOH, vol. II (1997: 8).

---

[2] Clearly there are other indicators one would include in a more in-depth treatment of this issue. Physicians are only one of many different health care providers, and different countries could well have the same services delivered by different providers.

top with Japan and Sweden, while the United States, the United Kingdom, and New Zealand are at the bottom. The second statistic is infant mortality. Here Canada ranks in the middle, with Japan and Sweden substantially better than the other five countries and the United States at the bottom.

The fifth column compares the expenditures on health services across countries. Of the seven countries considered, Canada's per capita expenditures are second highest.[3] On average, Americans spend about 75 percent more per capita than Canadians, while Swedes spend 33 percent less. Interestingly, American health outcomes are substantially worse than Canadian outcomes in both life expectancy and infant mortality, while Swedish health outcomes are substantially better, despite the greater proportion of seniors in the Swedish population. Consistent with this finding, research has shown that many factors unrelated to the health care system are important determinants of health outcomes. One factor that seems especially important is income disparities.

THE HISTORY OF CANADIAN HEALTH CARE FINANCING

Until the 1940s, hospital and medical care in Canada was largely privately funded. Individual patients paid doctors for their services, and many hospitals were run by religious or voluntary organizations, where ability to pay was taken into account. Constitutionally, the public provision of health care is the responsibility of the provinces. In 1947, the government of Saskatchewan became the first province to introduce a program of provincial hospital insurance. The federal government offered health grants to the provinces in 1948 to help pay for hospital services. This was followed by the Hospital Insurance and Diagnostic Services Act in 1957, through which the federal government offered to share the cost of hospital services. By 1961, all provinces had hospital insurance plans, with the federal government contributing about 50 percent of the cost on average.

While provinces were developing insurance schemes to cover the cost of hospital services, payments to physicians were still largely private. However, under Premier Tommy Douglas, Saskatchewan once again took the lead by introducing a provincial medicare scheme that included payments to doctors. Opposition by doctors led to a bitter strike in 1962 (and the subsequent defeat of the CCF government of Premier Lloyd in the next provincial election), but the Saskatchewan approach was soon adopted by other provinces, in part

---

[3] Among OECD countries, Canada's per capita expenditures are actually third highest, behind the United States and Switzerland.

because the federal government once again offered to share the cost through the Medical Care Act of 1966. By 1971 all provinces had programs, with the federal government contributing about one-half of the cost. Provincial shares were paid from general tax revenues and, in some cases, health care premium charges.

In 1977, the federal government combined its support for medicare and post-secondary education into a single grant, which was converted from a shared-cost to a "block" grant. The new grant, known as Established Program Financing (EPF),[4] was no longer designed to pay one-half of the cost of provincial health programs, but rather were to be equal per capita grants to provinces scheduled to grow at the same rate as Canadian GDP. Only five years after EPF was introduced, the federal government began to change it unilaterally. Over the period 1982 to 1995, changes were made to limit its growth, and to change the distribution of grants to favour provinces eligible for equalization payments.

On the legislative side, the federal government passed the Canada Health Act in 1984. The act laid out five general conditions that provincial health plans were required to meet to qualify for federal support. EPF transfers would be withheld from provinces not complying (as determined by the federal government) with the conditions of the act. Later, in an attempt to maintain some measure of control over health care as EPF transfers were being reduced for budgetary reasons, the federal government announced that penalties for noncompliance could be applied to other federal transfers as well.

In 1996, the federal government announced the termination of EPF grants and the creation of a new block grant to support health, education, and postsecondary education—the Canadian Health and Social Transfer (CHST) (see Chapter 6). This block grant, which retained the conditions of the Canada Health Act, was scheduled to decline from more than $18 billion in 1995 to $12.5 billion in 1998.

CHANGES IN THE PATTERN OF HEALTH SPENDING

One of the ways to see how the Canadian health system is changing is to look at changes in the pattern of health spending. Table 15.2 compares the pattern of spending in 1994 with spending in 1975. Over time there has been a sub-

---

[4] Thus, the federal government used a shared-cost grant to encourage provinces to adopt programs, and then moved to a block grant once the programs were "established." See Chapter 6 for a discussion of these grants.

Table 15.2

How Canadians Spend Their Health Dollars (percent)

	1975	1994	CHANGE
Hospitals	44.9	37.2	−7.7
Other institutions	9.2	9.8	0.6
Physicians	15.0	14.2	−0.8
Other providers	7.3	8.5	1.2
Drugs	8.8	12.7	3.9
Other	14.8	17.6	2.8

SOURCE: "Striking a Balance Working Group Synthesis Report," NFOH, vol. II (1997: 13).

stantial drop in the share spent on the largest expenditure item—hospitals—reflecting the trend to deliver more services in the community and the home. The other notable change is the increased share of spending on drugs. In addition to the increasing cost of drugs, this trend probably reflects scientific advances in the development of drugs to treat more illnesses more effectively, and also the aging population, since seniors are relatively large consumers of pharmaceuticals. The share of spending on physician services has remained relatively stable at 14 to 15 percent.

Another way to look at the health system is to divide spending into its public and private components. Table 15.3 shows the share of public spending in each of the six health expenditure categories. As we see, spending on physicians' services is almost exclusively public. Spending on hospital services remains largely public, although it has declined by about 4 percentage points over the past twenty years to its current value of 90 percent. The most noteworthy is

Table 15.3

Public Share of Health Spending in Canada (percent)

	1975	1994	CHANGE
Hospitals	94	90	−4
Other institutions	71	70	−1
Physicians	99	99	—
Other providers	15	14	−1
Drugs	15	32	17
Other	70	70	—
Total	76	72	−4

SOURCE: "Striking a Balance Working Group Synthesis Report," NFOH, vol. II (1997: 15).

the tremendous increase in the public share of spending on drugs. This reflects the trend toward publicly funded drug plans, especially for seniors. Overall, the public share of total health spending has declined somewhat from 76 to 72 percent over the past twenty years.

THE CANADA HEALTH ACT

The Canada Health Act was passed by the federal Parliament in 1984. The act lays out five conditions or principles that provincial health plans must follow to be eligible for federal grants. The five conditions are:

1. *Universality*. All residents are entitled to health insurance coverage.
2. *Accessibility*. There can be no financial or other barriers to receiving medically necessary hospital and physician services (defined by provinces). Reasonable compensation for physicians and hospitals must be paid, and extra billing (beyond payments made by the provincial plans) is prohibited.
3. *Comprehensiveness*. All medically necessary services must be insured. However, the definition of medically necessary services is left to the provinces.
4. *Portability*. Coverage must be maintained when a resident moves within Canada or travels outside the country. Out-of-country coverage is limited to payment at existing provincial rates.
5. *Public administration*. The administration of the health insurance plan must be on a nonprofit basis by a public authority.

All provinces have affirmed their support of the conditions of the Canada Health Act on numerous occasions, and public support for the act is very strong. Despite the act, however, per capita health spending and the range of services insured varies greatly by province.[5] Figure 15.2 illustrates the wide variation in per capita health spending across provinces.

Some advocates for a strong federal role in health care have argued that maintaining the federal government's ability to levy financial penalties on provinces is critical to enforcing adherence to the five principles of the Canada Health Act. However, when they have been invoked by the federal government, financial penalties have been small relative to the size of provincial health spending. Boothe and Johnston (1993) have argued that the Canada Health Act is not

---

[5] See Boothe and Johnston (1993).

Figure 15.2

*Health Care Spending by Province, Fiscal Year 1991/92
(percent deviation from national average)*

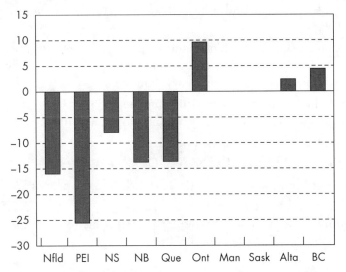

SOURCE: Calculations based on Statistics Canada, *Public Finance Historical Data*, cat. no. 68-512
(Ottawa, 1992); and data supplied by Canada, Department of Finance.

really much of a financial constraint to provinces—rather it is the broad public support for the five principles that maintains adherence to the act.

CHALLENGES AND FUTURE DIRECTIONS

As we noted at the beginning of the chapter, Canadians value their health system highly, but they are concerned about whether it will survive in the future
because of rapidly rising costs and the need for fiscal balance. In this section
we look at the current state of the health system and consider some likely
directions for the health system in the future.

Over the past decade the number of acute-care hospital beds in Canada has
declined by 27 percent. The number of chronic-care and rehabilitation facility
beds has declined by 35 percent. The average length of stay in an acute-care
hospital has dropped from nine to seven days over the same period.[6] Does this
suggest that the Canadian health system is in decline?

[6] Mitchell (1997: A8).

If one focuses on the ultimate goal of any health system—to maintain and enhance the health of the population—the answer seems to be no. Consider the following facts published by the federal Department of Health and Welfare[7]:

1. Canadians' rating of their own health has remained virtually unchanged over the past ten years.

2. Life expectancy is increasing for both men and women, and men are gradually catching up to women in this measure. Canadian women currently live, on average, 1.5 more disability-free years than men.

3. The proportion of the population reporting that health problems limit their daily activities is declining, especially among older Canadians.

4. There is a declining trend in work-related injuries.

5. The rate of low-birthweight babies has been stable since the 1980s.

6. There has been a significant increase since the mid-1980s in the proportion of overweight adults, particularly women.

7. Death rates from most major causes, particularly deaths due to heart disease and injuries, have declined since the 1970s.

Thus, considering the impact of the health care system on health outcomes (and recognizing that many other factors are important determinants of health), there seems to be little evidence to support the view that the Canadian health system is in decline.

In addition, seven of ten provinces have conducted health system reviews in the past five years. After examining the findings of these reviews, the National Forum on Health (1997: 5) concluded: "... without exception, all reviews have concluded that the health care system needs better management, not more money." Indeed, some of the key features and trends in the current system were singled out for particular praise. For example, the research reviewed by the National Forum indicated that at the macro level, the size of the public share of total health spending in a jurisdiction was positively correlated with effective cost control in the health system. At the micro level, movement toward shorter hospital stays in a jurisdiction was correlated with effective cost control in the health system.

Despite these promising signs, the Canadian health system is facing important cost pressures. The aging population is expected to increase the demand

---

[7] Health and Welfare Canada (1996: ch. 2).

for health care services substantially over the next three decades. Improving technology has acted to reduce the cost of some health services (allowing, for example, shorter hospital stays), but also to increase the range of available services (some of which are costly). Finally, technological innovation has been especially apparent in the area of drugs. While new drugs can contribute greatly to treatment, many of them are also very costly. Coupled with the trend toward publicly funded drug plans, especially for seniors, we can understand both the growth in drugs as a share of total health spending and the increasing role played by the public sector in those expenditures.

What will the Canadian health system look like in the future? A number of important debates are currently in progress:

Changing incentives. The question here is: Does the current fee-for-service method of paying physicians (especially for primary care) provide the best incentive to deliver the right amount of health care at the lowest cost? Currently, some provinces are experimenting with alternative remuneration schemes for physicians to compare both the health and cost outcomes.

Defining medically necessary services. The Canada Health Act leaves the definition of medically necessary services to the individual provincial health insurance schemes. We currently observe wide variations in per capita spending on health and the range of insured services across provinces. Some provinces are currently examining the idea of developing an explicit list of medically necessary services (and thus a corresponding list of services that could be provided privately outside of the Canada Health Act). Currently, only non-insured services are explicitly defined. The National Forum on Health has recommended that pressure to develop such lists be resisted, arguing that medical necessity of a given service will vary across individual patients.

A national pharmacare program. As we saw earlier, the trend in Canada has been to spend more on drugs overall, and to increase the public share of that spending. The National Forum on Health recommended that drugs be included as part of the publicly funded health system. The federal government responded by indicating some interest in a national pharmacare program, which would be a partnership between federal and provincial governments and the private sector. Currently about half of the $6.5 billion spent annually on prescription drugs comes from employee benefit plans.[8] A detailed federal proposal has yet to be developed.

---

[8] Coutts (1997: A10).

SUMMARY

- Health care services may be different from other commodities and services for a number of reasons, including adverse selection, moral hazard, and society's desire to act paternalistically, to redistribute income, or to internalize externalities.

- Compared with health systems in selected OECD countries, Canada's health system produces average or above-average outcomes at above-average cost.

- Health care insurance is a provincial government responsibility. The federal government contributes transfers to support health care services, but these transfers are declining.

- The Canada Health Act lays out five conditions that must be met for provincial health insurance schemes to qualify for federal transfers. The federal government may unilaterally reduce transfers if it decides that a provincial scheme is not meeting the conditions of the Canada Health Act.

- As we look at the future of the Canadian health care system, we note that the health of Canadians is generally improving over time.

- Health experts agree that better management rather than more funding is needed to adapt the Canadian health system to future needs.

- Significant future public cost pressures will come as a result of the aging population, technical advances in health sciences, which will expand the range of health problems that can be treated, and the increasing reliance on public funding for drugs.

- Current debates about future directions for the Canadian health care system centre around changing incentives faced by physicians and other health care providers, defining a list of medically necessary services, and the value of a national pharmacare program.

DISCUSSION QUESTIONS

1. Spending on health care services in Canada has been rising as a share of GDP. Is this a cause for concern? Why is the demand for health care services different from the demand for other kinds of services?

2. Judging from media reports, the Canadian health system is operating under tremendous financial pressure, and is in danger of collapse. As an economist advising the federal Minister of Health, what evidence would you collect to determine if the concerns reported in the media were justified?

3. What role has the Canada Health Act played in shaping the evolution of the Canadian health system?

REFERENCES

Boothe, Paul, and Barbara Johnston. *Stealing the Emperor's Clothes: Deficit Offloading and National Standards in Health Care.* Toronto: C.D. Howe Institute, 1993.

Coutts, Jane. "Business Key to Grits' Pharmacare Plan." *The Globe and Mail*, May 7, 1997, p. A10.

Health and Welfare Canada. *Report on Health of Canadians.* Ottawa: Minister of Public Works and Government Services, 1996.

Mitchell, Alanna. "Cutbacks Not the Only Cause of Vanishing Hospital Beds." *The Globe and Mail*, April 22, 1997, p. A8.

National Forum on Health. "Striking a Balance Working Group Synthesis Report," in *Canadian Health Action: Building on the Legacy, Volume II of the Report of the National Forum on Health.* Ottawa: Minister of Public Works and Government Services, 1997.

Pauly, Mark. "Taxation, Health Insurance and Market Failure in the Medical Economy." *Journal of Economic Literature* 24, no. 2 (June 1986): 629–75.

Chapter 16

Education

*The enormous investment in education over the years has paid dividends....
But our past commitment to education cannot guarantee our nation's continuing economic success.*

–Government of Canada (1994: 57–58)

*There are few areas of public finance—and certainly few within the sphere
of "social expenditures"—which seem more ripe for application of the benefit principle than postsecondary education.*

–Richard M. Bird (1976: 225)

INTRODUCTION

Education is one of the most important public sector expenditure items.
In Canada, the combined spending of local, provincial, and federal
governments was $44 billion ($30 billion for elementary and secondary and
$11 billion for postsecondary) in 1994. This was 12.3 percent of all government spending, and 5.9 per cent of GDP (see Table 16.1). About nineteen out of every twenty Canadian children are educated in *public* elementary
and secondary schools.[1]

Canada is unique among industrialized countries in that it does not have a
central agency with oversight responsibilities in the area of education.

---

[1] Total spending on education in Canada in 1996 was $58.2 billion. This includes fees
paid to private schools for education and training, tuition in the postsecondary sector,
expenditures on education provided directly by private institutions, and expenditures
financed by gifts and endowment income.

Table 16.1

Public Expenditures on Education as a Share of Total Public
Expenditure and of GDP, 1933 to 1994

| | EDUCATION | AS A PERCENTAGE OF | |
| | EXPENDITURES | GOVERNMENT | |
YEAR	(IN MILLIONS)	EXPENDITURES	GDP
1933	$ 107	11.3	2.9
1945	186	3.3	1.5
1950	442	10.7	2.3
1955	746	10.6	2.6
1960	1,579	14.6	4.0
1965	2,982	17.3	5.2
1970	6,089	19.0	6.8
1975	10,654	14.8	6.2
1980	18,096	13.7	5.8
1985	28,502	12.7	6.0
1990	38,911	12.3	5.8
1994	43,920	12.3	5.9

SOURCE: Calculated from data in Statistics Canada, *Public Sector Finance, 1995–1996* (Ottawa:
March 1996); *Public Finance Historical Data, 1965/66–1991/92* (Ottawa: March 1992); *Canadian
Economic Observer, Historical Statistical Supplement 1995/96* (Ottawa: July 1996); and M.C.
Urquhart and K.A.H. Buckley, *Historical Statistics of Canada*, 2nd ed. (Ottawa: Minister of Supply
and Services, 1983), p. H148-160.

Responsibility for education is assigned to the provinces by the Constitution
Act of 1867, and the federal government plays a minor role in primary and secondary education.[2] Each province has chosen to meet its responsibility in a different manner, with substantial variation among provinces in methods of
financing and managing public education. Since the end of World War II, the
federal government has provided significant funding for postsecondary education—over $8 billion in fiscal 1994. The federal government also plays a sig-
nificant role in vocational training; federal spending for vocational training in
fiscal 1990 was more than twice that of the provinces.[3]

---

[2] The federal government has responsibility for elementary and secondary education of
children of armed forces personnel, for inmates of federal institutions, and for Indians and
Inuit.
[3] In fiscal 1990 the federal government accounted for 60 percent of the $3.5 billion in pub-
lic spending on vocational education. Private spending on in-house training by business is
not well documented. See Kitchen and Auld (1995: ch. 9).

Elementary and Secondary Education

In New Brunswick and Prince Edward Island, public education is paid for by the provincial governments. Local taxes are not used. Revenues from provincial property taxes are not earmarked for education, and funding is from general revenues. Provincial governments in Quebec and Newfoundland also account for nearly all school funding, but local school boards retain some responsibility and flexibility to supplement provincial funds. The situation is different in Ontario, where local governments use property taxes to fund the majority of spending on public schools. In the western provinces, local governments also share responsibility for funding education, and local property taxes are used to meet this responsibility. Table 16.2 shows the breakdown in funding sources for public elementary and secondary education in Canada in 1973 and 1992. Although the figures reflect relative overall stability, a substantial shift to greater provincial responsibility for funding education occurred in Nova Scotia and Quebec during this period. The opposite occurred in Ontario and three western provinces. Table 16.3 shows per student expenditures by province in 1993/94.

Table 16.2

Composition of School Board Revenues by Province, 1973 and 1992

	1973			1992		
PROVINCE	LOCAL TAXES	PROVINCIAL FUNDING	OTHER	LOCAL TAXES	PROVINCIAL FUNDING	OTHER
Newfoundland	1.9	92.3	5.8	3.3	94.9	1.9
PEI	–	98.8	1.2	–	99.5	0.5
Nova Scotia	41.7	56.4	1.9	17.0	79.9	3.1
New Brunswick	–	100.0	–	–	98.2	1.8
Quebec	31.3	66.5	2.2	10.4	85.1	4.4
Ontario	38.0	59.6	2.4	57.1	40.0	2.9
Manitoba	40.5	58.2	1.3	43.4	51.9	4.7
Saskatchewan	44.6	51.7	3.7	49.5	46.3	4.1
Alberta	40.1	56.2	3.7	44.6	50.7	4.7
British Columbia	35.2	59.3	5.5	31.0	64.8	4.1
Yukon	–	99.3	0.7	–	98.1	1.9
NWT	2.9	96.7	0.4	6.1	90.0	3.9
Weighted Average for Canada	34.7	62.6	2.7	38.4	58.0	3.6

SOURCE: Data for 1973 from Harry Kitchen and Douglas Auld, *Financing Education and Training in Canada*, Canadian Tax Paper No. 99 (Toronto: Canadian Tax Foundation, 1995), p. 10. 1992 data are for the 1992/93 fiscal year and are calculated from data in Statistics Canada, *Education in Canada, 1995*, Cat. no. 81-229-XPB (February 1996), pp. 184–85.

Table 16.3

Expenditures on Education per Student, by Province and Level of Schooling, 1993/94

| | ELEMENTARY AND SECONDARY | | POSTSECONDARY* | |
PROVINCE	PER STUDENT EXPENDITURE	PERCENT OF NATIONAL AVERAGE	PER STUDENT EXPENDITURE	PERCENT OF NATIONAL AVERAGE
Newfoundland	$5,480	83.1	$13,676	98.5
PEI	5,448	82.6	14,581	105.1
Nova Scotia	5,680	86.1	13,195	95.1
New Brunswick	5,855	88.8	14,966	107.8
Quebec	6,735	102.1	13,571	97.8
Ontario	6,716	101.8	11,673	84.1
Manitoba	6,465	98.0	16,299	117.4
Saskatchewan	5,292	80.2	16,003	115.3
Alberta	5,979	90.7	15,409	111.0
British Columbia	6,303	95.6	18,590	133.9
Canada	6,595	100.0	13,880	100.0

*Expenditures on postsecondary education are divided by the number of full-time students plus 0.3 times the number of part-time students.

SOURCE: Calculated from data in Statistics Canada, *Education in Canada, 1995*, Cat. no. 81-229-XPB (February 1996), pp. 18–19.

There are other differences among the provinces. In some provinces—Quebec, Ontario, Saskatchewan, and Alberta—local and provincial taxes support public *and* separate (religiously affiliated) school systems, while in others, such as Nova Scotia, public funds are used *only* for public schools. Although school boards are elected in most provinces, in Nova Scotia a third of each school board is appointed by the provincial government and a third by the municipal council.

Another difference among provinces is the use of public funds to support private schools. No provincial support is provided to private elementary and secondary schools in Newfoundland, the Maritime provinces, or Ontario, while Manitoba provides some support for private secondary but not private elementary schools. In contrast, Quebec, Saskatchewan, Alberta, and British Columbia partially fund private schools that meet government standards.

Postsecondary Education

Although postsecondary education is also a provincial responsibility, federal government involvement occurred as early as 1885 with the land grant for the establishment of the University of Manitoba. Activities of the National Research Council, created in 1916, included funding of university research. With the return of armed forces personnel after World War II, the federal government made per student grants based on the number of enrolled veterans, and when these grants ceased in 1951 the federal government made grants to universities based on the population of the provinces. From 1967 to 1976, federal grants to provinces covered 50 percent of the operating expenses of postsecondary institutions. These open-ended grants ceased in 1977 when the federal government reduced the grant and provided more tax room for the provinces by freeing up tax points for provincial use. This cut the link between the amount of grant and the amount spent by a province. Although the federal government continued to provide substantial funding, purportedly for postsecondary education, from 1977 onward there has been no requirement that the funds be spent on higher education. This has led to a federal concern that in some provinces the funds have been otherwise employed, with the federal government receiving inadequate recognition for its contribution to higher education.

Employee Training

Canadian companies spent $1.4 billion on training according to a 1987 Statistics Canada survey covering 750,000 companies, and federal and provincial government expenditures on vocational training exceeded $3.5 billion in 1991–92. Nonetheless, comparative data for industrialized countries indicates that the percentage of Canadian workers who benefit from on-the-job training and the share of the wage bill spent on such training is much below that of other countries (Gunderson and Thirsk, 1994). This evidence, combined with slow productivity growth and competition from abroad, has caused policy makers to suggest that more government action may be needed to stimulate expenditures on training in Canada. Yet, in truth, we have no hard evidence on whether Canada is currently under- or overinvesting in training. In the "market failure" section below, we further discuss on-the-job training.[4]

MARKET FAILURE AND THE PUBLIC PROVISION OF EDUCATION

The framework of welfare economics suggests we begin with a fundamental question: Why is the government so extensively involved in education, rather than leaving its provision to the market? As we saw in Chapter 5, markets do

---

[4] Gunderson and Thirsk (1994: 84) conclude that "relatively low investment in worker training (in Canada) appears to be rooted in such non-tax factors as rigid minimum wage laws and generous unemployment insurance." This may contribute to firms' inability to internalize all benefits from training expenditures.

not provide goods efficiently when those goods are public goods, when they give rise to externalities, when they are provided by a monopoly, or when there is asymmetric information concerning the quality of the good. At first glance, education seems to be primarily a *private* good, improving students' welfare by enhancing their ability and contributing to higher incomes. We will now examine this more closely.

Let's use the theory of public goods to analyze government spending on education. Which of the three reasons discussed in Chapter 5—market power, asymmetric information, externalities—provides the basis for government involvement? Externalities are a frequently mentioned reason for public sector involvement in education. Market power and asymmetric information may also be important reasons in certain circumstances.

Monopoly Power

Where transportation costs are high, local schools have an element of monopoly power, but this argument is not very persuasive, except perhaps in rural areas. In small communities or rural settings, economies of scale may create a natural monopoly, and public control may be required to obtain schooling of an acceptable quality at a reasonable price. In a highly urbanized country such as Canada, most schooling is provided in settings where the potential for competition exists. Fear of monopoly power does not provide a strong argument for public provision of education in many Canadian settings.

Asymmetric Information

Insufficient information for informed decisions. Education, if entirely based on decisions by parents, will depend on information available to parents and on parental values. Parents who are unaware of high private returns to education may choose to spend little on education, limiting future opportunities available to their children. Decisions become more complex when there is a diversity of schooling opportunities. Only parents who possess the interest, ability, and capacity to assimilate the required information will benefit from increased choice. Government involvement, greater uniformity in schools, and compulsory schooling to a certain age protect students (to some extent) against uninformed, short-sighted, or self-serving decisions by parents.

Imperfect capital markets. If education is not adequately subsidized or provided by governments, students from poorer families may bear the brunt of the burden. Poor families, and students without family support, may find it especially difficult to obtain loans from the private sector. Without slavery, it may be difficult for poor families to provide adequate collateral for loans for investments in "human capital," and markets for these loans may not materialize. Imperfect capital markets, as an argument for public involvement, has some merit. One possible remedy for this market failure is for government loan programs to ensure that loans are available to students, or to their parents, at the going rate of interest. But even here, in the case of elementary and secondary students, parents would have to assume substantial debt with no assurance the children—those who realize the higher income resulting from education—will assist in the repayment. In other words, those who would benefit most may not have the legal authority to take out the loan, and underspending may still occur. In the case of postsecondary students it is likely that the benefiting student has the authority to assume the obligation of repayment.

Education as a signal. The acquisition of detailed information about a potential employee's abilities is often costly, and educational qualifications may provide a useful signal to potential employers. Innate ability is required to move through the educational system, with the result that the correlation between the level of formal education and innate ability is likely to be relatively strong. Consequently, some companies only consider applicants who possess certain academic qualifications for a job because those who have the qualifications have a higher innate ability than those who do not.

This relation of innate ability to the level of education attained has two interesting effects. First, estimates of social rates of return to education investments that are based on higher salaries may be overstated. Part of the higher income associated with more education may be due to enhanced productivity and part may be due to the fact that education is a screening device that identifies for prospective employers those individuals with high innate ability. (We return to this problem of estimating the rate of return to education later in the chapter.) Second, students may pursue further education not because it will enhance their performance in a certain job, but because it gives them access to the job. The higher salary in this case is also due to innate ability. If those with high innate ability would be highly productive, whether or not they received an education, then there is a tendency to overinvest in education. In other words, too many resources are devoted to education if education only determines how the "economic pie" is distributed and not how much is produced. On the other hand, signals may have social value if they enhance society's productivity by, for example, preventing "round pegs from being put in square holes."

To summarize, "education as a signal" suggests that the market may devote too many resources to education when signalling does not enhance productivity. Government intervention could be required to reduce expenditure on education in such circumstances.

Externalities

One rationalization for subsidizing all levels of education is the existence of externalities. Primary, secondary, and postsecondary education each increase earning capacity, but also contribute to the literate and well-informed populace that supports a smoothly functioning modern democracy. That education increases productivity may be true, but *as long as the earnings reflect their higher productivity, there is no externality*. The magnitude of the externalities accompanying education are not well documented. Yet the existence of externalities appears to be the main argument for extensive public involvement in education. What are these externalities?

One argument is that public schools are a powerful socialization force in a society with large numbers of recent immigrants and a diverse ethnic mix. Another is that education is vital to a successful democratic process—a literate and educated electorate contributes to political stability. As the Greek historian Plutarch wrote in his *Morals*, "The very spring and root of honesty and virtue lie in good education." Further, education may facilitate the adoption of new technologies and contribute to lower crime rates through higher levels of employment and income. Each of these arguments points to externalities associated with education, and an argument that if left to private decisions alone, too little education will be produced and consumed.[5]

Figure 16.1

Externalities and the Demand for Education

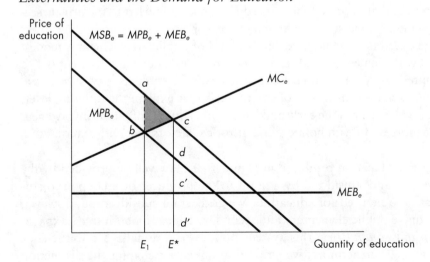

---

[5] For a brief review of these arguments, see Poterba (1994).

Although the individual, as with other private goods, realizes most of the benefits from education in the form of higher wages or a richer life, public good characteristics, along with redistribution objectives and capital market imperfections, have led to government activity in Canada as well as elsewhere. Figure 16.1 demonstrates that if education generates positive externalities it will be underprovided if left to the private sector. MPB_e is the marginal private benefit from education, and MC_e is the marginal cost of education. The amount of education provided in a year will be E_1 without government involvement. MEB_e is the marginal external benefit from education that is due to externalities associated with education. MSB_e reflects the marginal social benefit from education—the sum of the private benefit (MPB_e) and the marginal externality (MEB_e). MEB_e may either increase or decrease as education expenditures increase. It is assumed to remain constant in Figure 16.1. Since efficiency is achieved when $MC_e = MSB_e$, the amount of education that should be provided equals E^*, rather than E_1. In order to achieve this result it is necessary for government to provide a subsidy equal to the marginal social benefit, in this case cd (or $c'd'$) in Figure 16.1. The added cost of moving from E_1 to E^* is equal to the area E_1E^*cb, while the added benefit equals E_1E^*ca, with a net gain in welfare of abc.

In Figure 16.1 the externalities as measured by marginal social benefit, cd, are greater than zero. Little work has been done to measure the size of this benefit, and only if it outweighs the cost of government involvement, including excess burdens associated with taxes required for financing, should the public sector become involved.

It is interesting that in preschool years education is largely left to the private sector, to families. Public subsidies to education for those age 5 and under occur through tax credits for child care, but the level of public involvement is modest compared with elementary and secondary education. Public involvement is also more limited for postsecondary education, where students pay substantial tuition. We lack clear measures of externalities that explain the differing levels of public involvement in the early and later years. Patterns of public involvement may have more to do with political and historical factors that with externalities.

Note that the education produced in Figure 16.1 may well be provided by the private sector, and subsidized by a grant to the producer or a coupon to students that is to be used for education. We go beyond subsidization, however, when we make public elementary and secondary education both *free* (taxpayer financed) and *compulsory*; this system cannot be rationalized on efficiency grounds alone. Furthermore, we stressed in an earlier chapter the distinction between government provision (i.e., financing) of a good and government production of that good. What is so special about education that leads the government not only to fund it, but to produce it as well? One theory is that public education produces human capital while simultaneously inculcating belief in the existing political system. Because individuals care about their human capital but receive no private gains from belief in the political system, private schools in competition for students would devote all their resources to producing human capital. According to this view, the development of a common commitment to established democratic processes is more easily carried out in a system of public schools protected from competition. Indoctrination that has occurred through public schools in totalitarian states must not be lost sight of in considering whether this is a positive reason for government involvement.

On-the-job training is also an area where externalities are often cited as reason for public sector involvement. Here it is a case of "third-party effects"—a private company financing the training realizes only part of the benefits. Where portable skills are provided, employees may either "walk" or "be poached" by competitors. Employers, unable to "internalize" all of the benefit, will underinvest in training.

Inability to "internalize" benefits from on-the-job training has led to the suggestion that public policies should encourage private companies to spend more on training. Figure 16.1 represents this situation, and $c'd'$ is the subsidy required to get the right amount of private spending. Such a subsidy can be delivered through the tax system or through direct expenditures. Tax credits may be allowed for expenditures on training, as in Quebec. This permits larger credits for small firms that are less likely to provide training, in part because small companies may find retention more difficult given more limited opportunities within the firm. Other possible programs include direct payments to companies with trainees, as in Sweden, or direct payments to trainees to reduce company wage costs, as in Germany (Gunderson and Thirsk, 1994).

There is little solid evidence in Canada on the increased productivity that is likely to result from greater private or public expenditure on training. Nor is there much good evidence on the rate of return to government programs that encourage increased training, or on subsidy programs designed to have an impact at the margin without subsidizing expenditures already being made. Much work remains to be done in this area (Betcherman, 1993).

INCOME REDISTRIBUTION AND EDUCATION
Elementary and Secondary Education

Welfare economics suggests that equity must also be considered, and here, too, arguments can be made for public education. Because access to education is an important source of social mobility, it is an important good to be made available to all citizens. Differences in parental resources would lead to differences in education if education were left to the private sector. This would lead to unequal job and income opportunities over a lifetime. Provision of public education for all is a step toward *equality of opportunity*.

In countries such as Canada, Australia, and the United States, public education systems have enabled immigrants and their children to move upward within the economic and social structure. This contributes to movement from lower incomes to higher incomes and greater equality in lifetime incomes. Recall from an earlier chapter the notion of **commodity egalitarianism**. Because of the value placed on equal opportunity, and society's view of the role of education, citizens value education beyond any monetary return it yields to them as individuals, and required levels of education are mandated.

The government could support education in a number of ways. It could transfer funds directly to parents with children, allowing them to choose how much to spend on education. It could provide vouchers or funds to be used for no other purpose than to pay for a child's education; and parents may be allowed to choose a public or private school. Or the government could fund only public schools and require students to attend up to a certain age. Mandating public education or providing vouchers reflects a wish to guarantee that public funds are used to the benefit of children—that redistribution occurs from the old to the young, and that a particular target population benefits. They ensure that all students have reasonably uniform opportunities that are not dependent on family resources. The choice between vouchers and publicly provided education will be discussed at the end of this chapter.

Local governments have long had major responsibility for education. This conflicts with the "redistribution" motive for government intervention because redistribution is normally the responsibility of higher levels of government. There is, however, evidence that greater local responsibility may enable educational objectives to be achieved more efficiently (see Hoxby, 1995). Nonetheless, provincial responsibilities over student participation, curriculum content, and growing involvement with funding (see Table 16.2) reflect concern over equality of opportunity.

None of the above arguments precludes the use of vouchers to increase school choice. Nor do these arguments counter the concern that strong interest groups that benefit from in-kind transfers, such as teachers' unions, may cause excessive reliance on publicly provided education services.

Postsecondary Education

Public support for postsecondary education in Canada takes the form of subsidized tuition fees. Setting tuition at the same level for all programs subsidizes some students to a much greater extent than others, depending upon the actual costs of the programs. Public subsidies for some university programs, such as medicine, dentistry, and engineering, far exceed the subsidies for the arts, commerce, law, and the basic sciences. Private rates of return on university education in the former areas may be double or more those in the latter areas (Kitchen and Auld, 1995: 89; Vaillancourt, 1995: 549). Higher subsidies may be justified if externalities are much greater in the high-cost disciplines. But with little evidence in support of such differential subsidies, there is a strong argument for varying tuition fees so as to equalize private rates of return across areas of study.

It is observed that if the subsidies were cut, and tuition is raised, fewer people would attend university. This is probably true, but alone does not justify the subsidies.[6] If there were subsidies for young people who wanted to open auto repair shops and these were cut, then the number of auto repair shops would also decline. Why should a potential car mechanic be treated differently from a potential classicist or physician?

The theory of welfare economics recognizes that an inefficient program can be justified if it produces "desirable" effects on income distribution. Subsidies for university students represent a transfer from taxpayers as a whole to university students. Views on the appropriateness of such a transfer are likely to be affected by whether one looks at *lifetime* income or *annual* income. Students, to the extent that they have withdrawn from the labour force, are likely to have temporarily low incomes. On this basis the transfer may seem appropriate. However, university students in Canada continue to be disproportionately from families with above-average incomes, and university graduates have higher lifetime incomes. Thus, when one looks at the family incomes of students, or expected lifetime incomes, the argument for transfers through heavily subsidized tuition fees or subsidized loans is much weakened. Transfer policies that subsidize individuals with university educations could lead to greater inequality in the income distribution.[7] In the absence of persuasive evidence on externalities, the benefit to society as a whole is not clear.

---

[6] See Levin (1990) for a discussion of the limited effect that higher tuition fees are likely to have on university enrolments.

[7] However, to the extent that the loans go to people who would not otherwise have gone to college, the program may increase income equality.

Imperfections in capital markets, especially as confronted by families with low incomes and little wealth, may justify government-established student loan programs. The government may run its own loan program or work through private lending institutions. Unless the existence of a positive externality can be established, there is no efficiency basis for subsidizing the interest rate. The extent of the subsidy should depend on the size of the externality. What about the problem of paying back the debt after graduation? As Passell (1985) notes, "The prospect of heavy debt after graduation would no doubt discourage some students from borrowing. But that may be the wisest form of restraint. Someone finally has to pay the bill, and it is hard to see why that should be the taxpayers rather than the direct beneficiary of the schooling."

The federal government, in its 1994 discussion paper, suggested that consideration be given to programs that make the rate of repayment of student loans contingent on income after graduation.[8] The rationale for this appears to be related to equity considerations. Briefly consider a program that ties the rate of repayment to income levels after graduation. So long as market rates of interest continue to accumulate on the unpaid debt, this is a way to permit individuals to smooth their consumption pattern over a lifetime. However, if repayment schedules and interest rates are structured to increase government subsidies to those earning low incomes after graduation, this may encourage students and society to invest unwisely in some forms of education. In the absence of externalities associated with the subsidies, or income distribution objectives that cannot be better achieved by other means, such subsidies would be inefficient.

Government grants continue to account for around 70 percent of operating income of Canadian colleges and universities, with tuition accounting for around 20 percent.[9] This reflects a sizable government subsidy for those in many college and university programs. Further subsidization occurs through student loan programs financed by public funds. Faced with scarce resources, these subsidies are appropriate only where positive externalities or distributional effects are sufficiently large to justify them. Without evidence to these effects, the argument for higher college and university tuition, covering a larger share of the full cost of these programs, appears strong. This said, such tuition increases will only make sense if government loan programs overcome imperfections in capital markets caused by asymmetric information.

---

[8] See Government of Canada (1994: 63–64).
[9] As late as the 1950s, tuition was accounting for 40 to 50 percent of university revenues.

THE CONTROL AND FUNDING OF EDUCATION
Why Local Control?

One argument for the decentralized provision of a good is that it can be tailored to local tastes. Because many parents hold strong views about the education of their children and these views differ across communities, this is an important argument for the leading role played by local governments in providing education. One could, of course, allow local discretion over school policy while having funding come from provincial governments. This is, to a degree, the route taken in New Brunswick, for example, where locally elected school boards have little or no ability to add to what is spent on education, but retain power to make expenditure decisions. However, it may be difficult to maintain meaningful control of the schools if the financing comes from a higher level of government—he who pays the piper, calls the tune.

Local governments raise money for education primarily through property taxation; there are wide variations in the amount of property wealth available to school districts. Variations in the property tax base, if not equalized through provincial taxes and funding, can be associated with huge differences in funding for school districts. An egalitarian view of education calls for funding by provinces that redistributes resources across local boundaries, regardless of the possible effects on local autonomy. As Table 16.2 clearly reflects, provincial funding plays an important role in school finance in *all* provinces, with local school boards making decisions even in New Brunswick where no funding comes from local taxes.

Individuals living within a school district are the ones who benefit most from spending on local schools. To the extent that the benefits are localized, as with other goods and services, it is reasonable to levy taxes and fees on those who benefit. Efficient allocation of resources occurs where the marginal benefit equals the marginal cost. Some of those benefiting from the education system may not have children—local citizens benefit from well-educated neighbours, and a home-owner without children may see an increase in house value as the quality of nearby schools improves.

Consider, for example, the decision of a local jurisdiction on whether or not to spend more on schooling. Higher taxes, when capitalized (see Chapter 17), decrease the value of a property. But it is possible that an improved education system (or other service) increases the demand for housing in an area and contributes more to property values than the taxes detract from the values. Indeed, this is the basis for many public services, as locally elected public officials attempt to maximize property values for local stakeholders—those citizens who will vote in the next election. Hence, local citizens may want more spent on education even when it means higher taxes. Provincial systems that dictate school board spending deprive citizens of local autonomy, and limit possible gains from local choice and diversity.

There is also the question of whether there has been adequate accountability with respect to spending on education. Easton (1988: 32) concluded with regard to elementary and secondary education that "it seems to be a major omission for governments that pour billions into this kind of education not to be willing to systematically examine the results both over time and across provincial education systems." Accountability is likely to be enhanced when there exists a strong link between those who pay and those who benefit, in other words, when decisions regarding tax-financed education are made by those expected to benefit. This link is strongest for the consumption of private goods, but local taxes paid for local benefits can be a close approximation. A link between local property taxes and education costs may lead to greater scrutiny of increasing costs, and increased accountability, than will such spending from the province's general revenues.

There is, in addition, some evidence that suggests when provincial standardization occurs across local jurisdictions, higher levels of spending and higher costs may result.[10] Rather than moving high spending areas down to the average, the tendency is to move the average up. Likewise, standardization of cost factors such as teacher salaries may also raise averages. Competitiveness among local jurisdictions in the provision of local services, which may include public schooling, may help to control costs. However, there is the possibility that tax competition between local jurisdictions may lead to underspending on education and other services. Lower taxes, which are needed to attract new businesses and jobs, bring immediate political payoffs, but result in lower spending on education, which does not reflect returns to individuals and society over the longer run.

Why Provincial Funding?[11]

Disparities in income and property wealth across school districts would likely lead to disparate school quality if local taxes on property or other local tax

---

[10] Easton (1988: 55–56). A recent U.S. study adds support to this argument. Hoxby (1995, no page numbers) found that "increases in states' shares of school funding have been associated with significant increases in per-pupil schooling costs," and that "a higher state share of school funding not only does not appear to improve educational attainment, but worsens it by a small but statistically significant amount."

[11] This discussion draws on the much more detailed discussion found in Kitchen and Auld (1995: 26–41).

bases were heavily relied on for school finance. To overcome this problem, provinces have assumed a large role in financing elementary and secondary education. The benefits of public education extend well beyond local boundaries. Employers in Hamilton have a strong interest in education systems in Toronto or Kingston, which affect the supply of available skilled workers. Strong local education systems contribute to the economic and social development of the province as a whole.

But to what extent, and how, should provincial governments be involved in the funding and delivery of primary and secondary education? The answer has differed from province to province. All provinces make grants to local public school boards. This is consistent with commodity egalitarianism and with externalities associated with education. Not all provinces make grants to private schools, although these schools are likely to have some of the same positive externalities that exist for public schools. Although school boards with locally elected members make education expenditure decisions in all provinces, in Newfoundland, the Maritimes, and Quebec, 80 to 100 percent of funding for elementary and secondary education comes from provincial general revenues—not from local taxes controlled by school boards. Other provincial governments provided from 40 to 65 percent of total funding in 1992. Some economists (e.g., Bird and Slack, 1983) see complete provincial takeover as "an eminently logical extension of the apparent trend of educational policy in Canada since the Second World War" (p. 95). This view is supported by those who believe that public education of a well-defined quality should be available to all, that **wealth neutrality** should exist in the provision of education, and that benefits from local control and variation are likely to be modest. Wealth neutrality is a situation where ability to pay, defined by factors such as the property tax base or income levels, has no effect on the quality of education in local jurisdictions. So long as local governments are free to raise local taxes to enhance their public education system, wealth neutrality cannot exist. All provinces have adopted policies that contribute to wealth neutrality (within the province) and have a major impact on local school expenditures.

Provinces providing less than full funding may encourage a specific level of per student spending on education through **foundation grant** programs. Foundation grants seek to assure a minimum level of expenditure per student, regardless of local property wealth. This form of grant is similar to those used in Alberta, Saskatchewan, and Prince Edward Island. Foundation grants are basically conditional (that is, they must be spent on education) nonmatching grants. The amount of grant per student depends on local property wealth. The wealthier a district, the smaller the grant received from the province. Neither the district's own spending on education nor its property-tax rate affects the

Figure 16.2

Education Expenditures with Foundation Grant

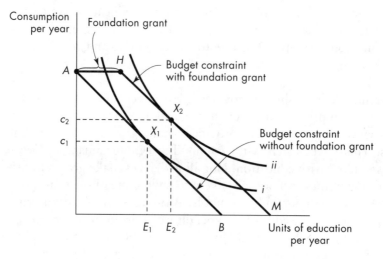

amount of the transfer received from the province. Such grants are expected to have an *income effect* but no *substitution effect* on local spending. This is depicted in Figure 16.2, where the amount of the grant is AH. The budget constraint line is shifted from AB to AHM by the foundation grant, and the amount spent on education increases from E_1 to E_2 because of the grant. The income effect results in an increase in other consumption as well, from c_1 to c_2.

Under a foundation grant program, the amount of the grant per student may be specified as

$$G_i = (E_p - t_p B_i),$$

where G_i is the per student grant in the ith jurisdiction, E_p is the provincially set per student expenditure level, t_p is a provincially determined tax rate, and B_i is the per student tax base in the ith jurisdiction. If P_i represents the number of students in the ith jurisdiction, the amount of the grant to the ith jurisdiction is $P_i \times G_i$. Although the formula specifies the grant, it does not determine total funds available to a school board. The province has several options, moving from more to less local autonomy: (1) it may leave the local jurisdiction free to set the local tax rate to be applied to B_i, (2) it may allow the local jurisdiction to set a local tax rate equal to or higher than t_p, or (3) it may specify that the local tax rate must be set at t_p, neither higher nor lower, ensuring that funds available for each student are equal in all jurisdictions.

The foundation grant is independent of the level of local spending. There is no recognition of externalities that may accompany an additional dollar of local spending on education. Alternatively, where additional spending by a local jurisdiction is accompanied by benefits that extend beyond local borders, a province may wish to provide per student grants that increase as local spending increases. Ontario has used this form of grant. Such grants may be referred to as **percentage equalization grants**. The grant, as a share of per student spending on education, increases as the per student tax base decreases. These grants, too, are conditional and must be spent on education. Whether in a rich or a poor jurisdiction, local decisions to spend more will increase the size of the grant as well as require more locally raised revenues.

The percentage equalization grant as a share of a local jurisdiction's total spending on education can be specified as $\%_I = 1 - [L \times (B_i/V)]$. $\%_I$ is the share of spending to be provided by the province to the ith jurisdiction. L represents the share of funding to be provided by the local school board with an average per student tax base. Say this is 60 percent, so $L = 0.6$. B_i is the per student tax base in the ith jurisdiction, and V is the per student tax base for a jurisdiction with an average per student tax base. Thus, B_i/V equals 1 for a jurisdiction with an average per student tax base, and the share of spending funded by the province is $1 - 0.6$, or 40 percent. Where a jurisdiction has 1.5 times the average tax base per student, perhaps because a petrochemical complex is located there, the share funded by the province decreases to $1 - (0.6 \times 1.5)$, or 10 percent. In a poor jurisdiction, with half the average tax base per student, the province's share would be $1 - (0.6 \times 0.5)$, or 70 percent.

In the case of these equalization grants, both an income effect and a substitution effect lead to increased spending on education by local jurisdictions. This is seen in Figures 16.3A and 16.3B, as the equalization grant shifts the budget constraint from GA to GB in a poor jurisdiction, and from $G'A'$ to $G'B'$ in a rich jurisdiction, altering the price of education services to the local jurisdiction as well as increasing available revenues. Due to the substitution effect caused by the "percentage equalization," the price of education falls relative to consumption goods with the result that less may be spent on consumption, c'_2 rather than c'_1 in Figure 16.3B, as local funds are diverted to education. More is spent on both education *and* consumption in Figure 16.3A, where the income effect outweighs the substitution effect.

In the foregoing discussion the size of the grant is linked only to the revenue raising capacity and/or spending level of local jurisdictions, and does not recognize that substantial cost differences may exist among local jurisdictions. Grants can also be linked, as in British Columbia, to cost factors such as teachers' salaries.

Figure 16.3

Education Expenditures with Percentage Equalization Grants

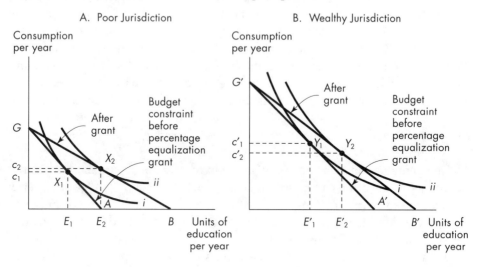

A. Poor Jurisdiction

B. Wealthy Jurisdiction

We have not addressed the question of how a province might finance a program of grants to local school boards; so far the grants to local school boards appear to be a free lunch. This is not the case. The higher provincial taxes required to finance a grant program will have a negative income effect on spending on private and public goods and services, including education. Budget constraint lines in Figures 16.2 and 16.3 shift down and to the left due to the higher taxes. The net effect on education spending in any jurisdiction depends on the size of this negative income effect relative to the positive income and substitution effects of grant programs. Rich jurisdictions may experience an overall fall in spending on education given the combined effect of the higher taxes and grants. In other words, *HM* in Figure 16.2 (after the grant and after taxes used to finance the grant) is to the *left* of *AB* (the budget constraint line before the grant program). The net effect in poorer jurisdictions is more likely to result in increased spending on education, but even here the effect of the higher taxes must be considered.

What do grants for education accomplish? Provincial grants to local school districts transfer resources into poorer districts. But do they affect educational outcomes? There are two questions here. The first is: Do grants lead to higher expenditures on education? As the above analysis indicates, this is likely in many jurisdictions, but may not occur in some. Figures 16.1, 16.2, and 16.3 indicate that spending may increase; but spending on education may fall in wealthier jurisdictions as provinces attempt to redistribute.[12]

Where grants increase school expenditures, we must confront the second question: Do higher expenditures lead to better education? After all, we are ultimately concerned with educational outcomes for students, not educational expenditures per se. According to the econometric evidence, discussed later in this chapter, it is not at all clear that more spending, particularly if due to increased provincial funding, leads to better outcomes.

Why Federal Funding?

The federal government's involvement in education has been primarily at the postsecondary level, although, as noted earlier, it has responsibility for public schooling for the families of armed forces personnel, those in federal penitentiaries, and for Indians and Inuit. Table 16.4 provides detail on federal support for postsecondary education in 1993/94.

Strong postsecondary systems in the Atlantic provinces and in Saskatchewan have for years exported their graduates to rapidly growing parts of the country such as Toronto, Vancouver, and Calgary. During industrial booms, edu-

Table 16.4
Federal Support for Postsecondary Education, 1993/94

	($ MILLIONS)
Contributions to provinces and territories	
Established Programs Financing (EPF)	$6,108
Direct federal support for research	
NSERC, MRC, and SSHRC	828
National Research Council	45
Canada student loans	293
All other programs	786
TOTAL	8,060

SOURCE: Canada, Department of the Secretary of State, *Federal and Provincial Support to Post-Secondary Education in Canada: A Report to Parliament, 1993–94* (Ottawa: 1995), p. 21, table 3.

---

[12] See Bird and Slack (1978: Appendix E). A recent U.S. econometric study indicates that for each $1 of grants received, spending on education increased by 32 cents (Case, Hines, and Rosen, 1993).

cation has facilitated successful moves to Ontario; and with the resource boom of the 1970s, talented professionals and tradespeople moved to Alberta. Provinces do not capture part of the return to higher education—future income streams and taxes that flow from the education—and underspending on post-secondary education may occur if left to the provinces alone.[13] Ease of trans-ferability among postsecondary institutions also contributes to labour force flexibility. This is important when part-time studies are common, extend over a lengthy period, and may be interrupted by job changes. Thus, high levels of education and national standards facilitate mobility and contribute to social and economic development, and to a sense of nationhood. Since benefits of higher education extend beyond provincial borders, important externalities accompany provincial spending.

That a strong postsecondary system is a national priority is reflected in the $6.1 billion transferred to provinces in tax points and cash in 1994/95.[14] This was about 29 percent of the $21 billion spent by provinces on postsecondary and vocational education. Note, however, that $6.1 billion is not conditional upon provincial standards or spending. It becomes part of provincial general revenues, with a possible income effect on postsecondary spending, but no substitution effect.

Federal funding for research, about $900 million, is much more direct. These funds flow directly to institutions and are conditional in that the research must be carried out. The information forthcoming from research is a public good, and we have seen that centralized provision or subsidization of public goods can avoid the free-rider problem that might arise at the local level. One concern is that federal research grants rarely cover the full costs of institutional infrastructure that the research requires. Institutional resources may, therefore, be diverted from other uses, such as undergraduate teaching, because of the substitution effects created by research grants.

---

[13] Dickson, Milne, and Murrell (1996: 322) estimate the internal rate of return to the New Brunswick government for its 1990 expenditures on universities at 2.6 percent for males and 1.4 percent for females. This reflects that 36 percent of alumni no longer reside in the province. The province's return is in the form of higher income tax and sales tax revenues due to the higher incomes of graduates. However, the complete picture of the return on public spending must include the higher income taxes and sales taxes that flow to the federal government; the combined return to the provincial and federal governments is estimated at about 7 percent for both men and women. What are the implications of these estimates? If funding were left to the province alone, the low returns would encourage reduced provincial spending on universities. The significant returns beyond provincial borders provide reason for federal support for higher education.

[14] $6.1 billion is the cash transfer plus tax points related to postsecondary education. This is part of the total EPF transfer for 1993 of about $22.5 billion.

ARE WE SPENDING WISELY ON EDUCATION?

One of the dominant issues in debates over public education is whether spending on it is high enough. Such debates force us to confront two crucial questions: (1) Do higher expenditures lead to better education?, and (2) Are we receiving an adequate rate of return on existing education expenditures?

More Spending, Better Performance?

We are ultimately concerned with educational outcomes for students, not educational expenditures per se. If we knew the production function for education, we would know the relationship between inputs purchased and the amount of education produced. Attempts to measure the relationship between various inputs to education, such as teachers' years of experience and the number of teachers available per student, have faced major difficulties. Part of the difficulty comes in defining, let alone measuring, the output "education."

Some measures that have been used to capture the increased human capital imparted through education are test scores, attendance records, drop-out rates or continuation rates to higher levels of schooling, and labour market outcomes such as unemployment rates and earnings. Hanushek (1986: 1150–52) surveys 147 statistical estimates of the relationship between input usage and various measures of educational attainment. The inputs considered are the teacher/pupil ratio, teacher education, teacher experience, teacher salary, and expenditures per pupil. He reaches the startling conclusion that the data support virtually no correspondence between input usage per student and the quality of the educational experience.[15]

What are we to make of these results? We do not conclude schooling is unimportant; there are clearly effective and ineffective schools. However, the research indicates that we cannot predict which schools will be effective simply by looking at data on their purchased inputs. The same is true of teachers; data on degrees held or years of teaching experience do not usefully discriminate between effective and ineffective teachers.

One particularly notable result emerges from the research on class size. It appears that, over a wide range, class size does not matter. Given the conventional methods of measuring education, teaching to a class of twenty appears no more effective than teaching to a class of thirty (Hanushek, 1986: 1161). This research has tremendous policy implications for public expenditures, particularly in light of the declining pupil/teacher ratios, and salary scales that

---

[15] A few studies have reached different conclusions. See, for example, Sander (1993).

have been tied to longevity and additional course credits. Table 16.5 illustrates the sharp fall in the pupil/teacher ratio since 1960 in all provinces, with close to a 40 percent decrease for the country as a whole. Teachers' salaries, which equalled manufacturing wages in 1960, had risen to 155 percent of manufacturing wages by 1983 (Easton, 1988: 49). With teachers' salaries accounting for about 60 percent of the $31 billion spent by public school boards in 1994, the reader is left to consider what would have been required had class size remained unchanged from 1960 to 1994 and teacher salaries equal to wage levels in the manufacturing sector. Increasing teacher salaries and decreasing class sizes resulted in a more than fourfold increase in *real* per student expenditures from 1960 to 1992 (see Table 16.6). Real per capita GDP little more than doubled during this same period. Rising costs and limited evidence of improved student performance have contributed to pressures to more effectively control public spending on education.

In cost–benefit terms, one cannot support the position that class sizes should be reduced. This does not mean all expenditures are futile. For example, there is evidence that, while classes of twenty are not measurably better than classes of thirty, classes of three or fewer students are better, especially if the students are in the early grades and are performing at below-average levels.

Table 16.5

Student/Teacher Ratios by Province for Public Elementary and Secondary Schools, 1960 to 1993

PROVINCE	1960	1980	1993	PERCENTAGE CHANGE 1960 TO 1993
Newfoundland	29.9	19.2	14.6	−51.2
PEI	25.2	19.6	17.2	−31.7
Nova Scotia	26.9	17.5	16.6	−38.3
New Brunswick	26.0	19.6	16.6	−36.2
Quebec	24.0	16.1	15.1	−37.1
Ontario	28.2	20.0	15.1	−46.5
Manitoba	25.4	18.3	15.2	−40.2
Saskatchewan	24.2	18.9	17.7	−26.9
Alberta	25.0	19.4	17.5	−30.0
British Columbia	27.1	19.4	17.0	−37.3
Yukon	25.3	18.2	12.6	−50.2
NWT	27.1	18.2	12.3	−54.6
Canada	26.1	18.6	15.7	−39.2

SOURCE: Stephen T. Easton, *Education in Canada* (Vancouver: The Fraser Institute, 1988), p. 47, and Statistics Canada, *Education in Canada, 1995*, Cat. no. 81-229-XPB (February 1996), p. 171.

Table 16.6

Average Cost per Elementary and Secondary Student in Public Schools (in 1981 dollars), 1960/61 to 1992/93

YEAR	1960	1970	1980	1992
Average cost	$900	$1,760	$2,865	$3,701

SOURCE: Stephen T. Easton, *Education in Canada* (Vancouver: The Fraser Institute, 1988), p. 41, and Statistics Canada, *Education in Canada, 1995*, Cat. no. 81-229-XPB (February 1996), pp. 34 and 180.

Well-targeted class size reductions below the levels considered in the studies reviewed by Hanushek (1986), such as tutoring sessions, might have significant payoffs.

The Rate of Return on Education Expenditures

Society has alternative uses for its resources. If public sector investment in education does not yield a reasonable return, say 7 to 10 percent, spending should be reallocated to other public services or taxes should be cut in order to increase resources available for private use. Estimating returns to education expenditures is understandably complex. It requires the researcher to distinguish between returns to innate abilities and those to formal education, and (usually arbitrary) values must be assigned to externalities.

The discussion of the marginal cost of funds in Chapter 5 indicates that it may cost more than $1, perhaps $1.50 or more, to raise an additional dollar of tax revenues because of the **excess burden** of a tax. Even if there are externalities, the cost of raising public funds may outweigh any benefits.

Table 16.7 shows social rates of return on education expenditures as estimated by Constantatos and West (1991). This table recognizes that part of the higher incomes that accompany more education may be due to innate ability—in other words higher income (compared to others) would have been achieved without the additional formal education. Moving from left to right in Table 16.7, the share of the increased income that is due to "ability" rather than to "education" increases from 0 to 0.35. The table also recognizes that the rate of return to public spending depends on the cost of raising an additional tax dollar. If this cost is $1.50 rather than $1, the returns on investments in public education are lower. The first two rows show that the rate of return to spending on elementary education falls from 18.4 percent to 12.2 percent when the share of the income differential due to "ability" rises from 0 to 0.35 percent and the cost of raising a tax dollar is $1.50 instead of $1.

Table 16.7

Social Rate of Return to Canadian Education Expenditures, 1980

MARGINAL COST OF PUBLIC FUNDS	PROPORTION OF DIFFERENTIAL INCOME DUE TO ABILITY			
	0	0.15	0.25	0.35
Elementary Education				
1.0	18.4	17.1	16.6	15.0
1.5	15.3	14.1	13.2	12.2
High School (4 years)*				
1.0	13.1	11.8	10.8	9.7
1.5	11.2	10.0	9.1	8.2
University Degree*				
1.0	9.9	8.9	8.3	7.6
1.5	8.8	7.9	7.3	6.6

*This assumes that forgone earnings are 66 percent of the earnings of workers with the immediately lower level of education.

SOURCE: Taken from Table 4 of Constantatos and West (1991: 132).

In sum, if part of the higher income is due to factors other than the additional education, such as innate ability, the return on the investment in education is lower. Similarly, if the cost of the public investment in education is higher (due to a high marginal cost of funds), a given income flow from the investment reflects a lower rate of return.

The estimated rates of return in Table 16.7 are similar to results from other recent studies; see, for example, Vaillancourt and Henriques (1986), Easton (1988), and Vaillancourt (1995). Based on their results and returns to alternative investments, Constantatos and West conclude that while returns to elementary and secondary education may justify current and higher spending levels, it is difficult to argue for more tax-financed spending on public universities.

New Directions for Public Education

Economic growth in some countries, particularly in the Far East, has been much more rapid than in Canada in recent decades. Canada's unemployment rate has been around 10 percent and persistently higher than in more rapidly growing countries. Students in other countries have outperformed Canadian students in a variety of subject areas. This has occurred at a time when large increases in real per student expenditure in Canada have not been accompanied by any perception of improved educational quality. In such an environment, school reform is a widely debated issue.

If simply spending more on education won't improve the situation, what will? Economists are often quick to consider whether any market in trouble might not benefit from an infusion of competition. This is true in the debate over what to do about Canada's elementary and secondary schools, as well as its colleges and universities. Some economists are convinced schools would improve if forced to compete with one another to attract students. The essence of competition is that consumers can choose among suppliers. In contrast, the elementary and secondary public school system has often operated on a take-it-or-leave-it basis: the only public school available to a student is the one assigned to the student's neighbourhood. Important exceptions are school systems where there is open enrolment, which permits (usually to a limited degree) students to choose the school they wish to attend. In these cases, schools may develop and market strengths that appeal to particular students.

Recently, much attention has been paid to ways to improve public school quality by increasing dramatically the scope of choice. The basic approach is to provide financial support to students rather than directly to schools. Each student could be given a tuition voucher, for example, that could be redeemed at whatever qualified school the student's family liked best. The theory is that the effects of competition would be as salutary in the education market as they are in other markets. Terrible schools would have few enrollees and would be forced to reform or to close.

If a government provides vouchers to students, the government must decide if the vouchers can be used for both public and private schooling. Where use is limited to public schools, this is similar to existing situations where students choose their school and funding is based on the number of students enrolling. However, where public authorities are reluctant to close existing physical facilities and have limited ability to hire and fire, efficiency will not be achieved. The willingness of some provinces (but not others) to partially fund private schools, with funding based on student enrolment, is a move to increase the choice of parents and to increase competition. But so long as funding for private schools is substantially below that for public schools, competitive forces will be limited. Funding differentials that favour public schools reduce the ability of private entrepreneurs to establish new schools in areas where existing schools are of poor quality.

Many issues are involved in designing a voucher system. How much latitude can schools have in designing their curricula? Can schools hire teachers who lack professional credentials? Who establishes the appropriate credentials for teachers? What criteria can oversubscribed schools use to choose which students will be enrolled? Can parents donate extra resources to the schools of their choice, or would this violate standards of equal education? How will students' families be informed about the different schooling choices available to them? Who has responsibility for accepting and integrating disruptive children into the classroom?

Critics of market-oriented schemes offer a number of objections. Principal among them is that consumers in the education market are not well informed so the competitive outcome would be far from satisfactory. Supporters of this view point to the proliferation of vocational schools of dubious value that prey on students eligible for student loans and grants. Further, they argue that if weaker public schools were replaced by what turned out to be even worse private schools, it may further delay the steps needed to establish a reasonably strong system of public schools in the area.

In response, supporters of choice note that the quality of public schools appears to be static or declining despite massive increases in spending. They argue that just because people are poor doesn't mean they are unwilling or unable to seek out the best opportunities available for their children.[16] Provincial support for the establishment of private or charter schools (perhaps initially limited in number) that compete directly with public schools should help inform future, and much needed, debates over competition in the market for education. They also note that strong interest groups that benefit from in-kind transfers, such as teachers' unions, may cause excessive reliance on publicly provided education services.

SUMMARY

- Education is a provincial responsibility. Provincial governments in Prince Edward Island and New Brunswick have assumed full responsibility for financing public education, and in Quebec, Newfoundland, and Alberta most of the financing responsibility rests at the provincial level. In the other provinces, local revenues (primarily from property taxes) are an important source for financing education.

- All provinces provide grants to ensure a minimum level of per pupil expenditure by public school boards. This contributes to greater **wealth neutrality** in the provision of education.

- Although generally publicly provided, much of the return to education is in the form of privately realized higher incomes.

---

[16] See Chubb and Moe (1990) for further arguments along these lines.

- To the extent that externalities accompany education expenditures, education has public good qualities. Education's role in providing equal opportunity is one reason for government involvement. Other reasons include public education's role in the socialization of a culturally diverse population, its contribution to labour mobility and technological progress, and to stable democratic processes. We have little empirical data on the size of the subsidies that are justified by the importance of these externalities.

- Estimates of social returns to education in Canada may justify current levels of spending on elementary and secondary education. Evidence is less clear for postsecondary education where the social rates of return are marginal.

- Much of the benefit from postsecondary education is in the form of higher incomes for individuals. These private returns, coupled with questionable distributional effects of existing public subsidies, are arguments for higher tuition, more effective loan programs, and possibly lower public funding.

- Real per pupil spending on elementary and secondary education increased fourfold from 1960 to 1992. Statistical research suggests that the link between spending and educational outcomes is, at best, very weak.

- Demands for new ways to deliver education and enhance student performance have increased public interest in vouchers, private schools, and charter schools.

- Local responsibility for education can be justified on the basis of different tastes across communities, and because externalities from education primarily affect the local community. However, equity considerations and inefficiencies that may result from tax competition justify provincial involvement in the distribution of resources available for elementary and secondary education. Externalities associated with university research and a highly skilled and mobile work force justify federal involvement in postsecondary education. However, evidence that links the size of federal transfers for postsecondary education with the size of externalities is scarce.

DISCUSSION QUESTIONS

1. Suppose you are asked to determine whether public or private schools produce at lower cost. What kind of data would you need? Suggest an econometric strategy.

2. Higher property taxes may, in some circumstances, be accompanied by a rise in local property values. Discuss the circumstances that may lead to such an outcome.

3. Universities argue that federal research grants should cover the full cost of the research, including research infrastructure. Using a diagram such as that

in Figure 16.2 and the concept of conditional matching grants, explain how research grants that cover only a portion of the full cost may divert university resources away from undergraduate teaching.

4. The federal government's 1994 discussion paper suggests that the rate of repayment of loans to university students should be based on income after graduation. Explain on what basis you would, or would not, support such a program.

5. There is evidence that the private rate of return to university education differs substantially depending on the area of study. Tuition fees that differ substantially from program to program would result in more equal private rates of return from area to area. Explain why you would, or would not, support a move that set higher tuition for some areas than for others.

REFERENCES

Betcherman, Gordon. "Research Gaps Facing Training Policy-Makers." *Canadian Public Policy* 19, no. 1 (March 1993).

Bird, Richard M. *Charging for Public Services*. Toronto: Canadian Tax Foundation, 1976. See Chapter 19 on postsecondary education.

Bird, Richard M., and Enid Slack. *Urban Public Finance in Canada*. Toronto: Butterworths, 1983.

Bird, R.M., and N.E. Slack. *Residential Property Tax Relief in Ontario*. Toronto: University of Toronto Press, 1978.

Case, Anne C., James R. Hines, and Harvey S. Rosen. "Budget Spillovers and Fiscal Policy Interdependence: Evidence from the States." *Journal of Public Economics* 52 (October 1993): 285–305.

Chubb, John E., and Terry M. Moe. *Politics, Markets, and America's Schools*. Washington, DC: Brookings Institution, 1990.

Constantatos, C., and E.G. West. "Measuring Returns from Education: Some Neglected Factors." *Canadian Public Policy* 17, no. 2 (June 1991).

Dickson, Vaughan, William J. Milne, and David Murrell. "Who Should Pay for University Education? Some Net Benefit Results by Funding Source for New Brunswick." *Canadian Public Policy* 22, no. 4 (December 1996).

Easton, Stephen T. *Education in Canada: An Analysis of Elementary, Secondary and Vocational Schooling*. Vancouver: The Fraser Institute, 1988.

Government of Canada. *Improving Social Security in Canada*. Ottawa: October 1994.

Gunderson, Morley, and Wayne R. Thirsk. "Tax Treatment of Human Capital," in *Taxes as Instruments of Public Policy*, ed. Allan M. Maslove. Toronto: University of Toronto Press, 1994.

Hanushek, Eric A. "The Economics of Schooling: Production and Efficiency in Public Schools." *Journal of Economic Literature* 24, no. 3 (September 1986): 1141–77.

Hoxby, Caroline M. "Is There an Equity-Efficiency Trade-off in School Finance? Tiebout and a Theory of the Local Public Goods Producer." Working Paper No. 5265. Cambridge, MA: National Bureau of Economic Research, September 1995.

Kitchen, Harry, and Douglas Auld. *Financing Education and Training in Canada.* Toronto: Canadian Tax Foundation, 1995.

Levin, Benjamin. "Tuition Fees and University Accessibility." *Canadian Public Policy* 16, no. 1 (March 1990).

Passell, Peter. "Lend to Any Student." *The New York Times*, April 1, 1985, p. A20.

Poterba, James M. "Government Intervention in the Markets for Education and Health Care: How and Why." Working Paper No. 4916. Cambridge, MA: National Bureau of Economic Research, November 1994.

Sander, William. "Expenditures and Student Achievement in Illinois: New Evidence." *Journal of Public Economics* 52 (October 1993): 403–16.

Vaillancourt, Francois. "The Private and Total Returns to Education in Canada, 1985." *Canadian Journal of Economics* 28, no. 3 (August 1995).

Vaillancourt, Francois, and Irene Henriques. "The Returns to University Schooling in Canada." *Canadian Public Policy* 12, no. 3 (September 1986).

Part 5

A Framework for
Tax Analysis

*B*oth politicians and economists have long searched for a set of principles to guide tax policy. Several centuries ago, the French statesman Jean-Baptiste Colbert suggested, "The art of taxation is the art of plucking the goose so as to get the largest possible amount of feathers with the least possible squealing."[1] Modern economics takes a somewhat less cynical approach, emphasizing how taxes should be levied to enhance economic efficiency and to promote a "fair" distribution of income. These are the topics of the next three chapters. Our goal is to construct a theoretical framework for thinking about tax policy. A thorough discussion of actual Canadian tax institutions is deferred to Part 6.

---

[1] George Armitage-Smith, *Principles and Methods of Taxation* (London: John Murray, 1907), p. 36.

Chapter 17

Taxation and Income Distribution

Struggle and contrive as you will, lay your taxes as you please, the traders will shift it off from their own gain.

–John Locke

*I*n recent years, Canadian policy debates about the tax system have been dominated by the question of whether its burden is distributed fairly. A sensible discussion of this normative issue requires some understanding of the positive question of how taxes affect the distribution of income. A simple way to determine how taxes change the income distribution would be to conduct a survey in which each person is asked how many dollars he or she pays to the tax collector each year. Simple—but usually wrong. An example demonstrates that assessing correctly the burden of taxation is a complicated problem.

Suppose the price of a bottle of wine is $10. The government imposes a tax of $1 per bottle, to be collected in the following way: Every time a bottle is purchased, the tax collector (who is lurking about the store) takes a dollar out of the wine seller's hand before the money is put into the cash register. A casual observer might conclude that the wine seller is paying the tax.

However, suppose that a few weeks after its imposition, the tax induces a price rise to $11 per bottle. Clearly, the proprietor receives the same amount per bottle as he did before the tax. The tax has apparently made him no worse off. The entire amount of the tax is being paid by consumers in the form of higher prices. On the other hand, suppose that after the tax the price increases to only $10.30. In this case, the proprietor keeps only $9.30 for each bottle sold; he is worse off by 70 cents per bottle. Consumers are also worse off, however, because they have to pay 30 cents more per bottle.[1] In this case, producers and consumers share the burden of the tax. Yet another possibility is that after the tax is imposed, the price stays at $10. If this happens, the consumer is no worse off, while the seller bears the full burden of the tax.

The **statutory incidence** of a tax indicates who is legally responsible for the tax. All three cases in the preceding paragraph are identical in the sense that the statutory incidence is on the seller. But the situations differ drastically with respect to who really bears the burden. Because prices may change in response to the tax, knowledge of statutory incidence tells us *essentially nothing* about who is really paying the tax. In contrast, the **economic incidence** of a tax is the change in the distribution of private real income brought about by a tax.[2] Our focus in this chapter is on the forces that determine the extent to which statutory and economic incidence differ—the amount of **tax shifting**.

TAX INCIDENCE: GENERAL REMARKS

Several observations should be kept in mind in any discussion of how taxes affect the distribution of income.

Only People Can Bear Taxes

The Canadian legal system treats certain institutions as if they were people. The most prominent example is the corporation. Although for many purposes this is a convenient fiction, it sometimes creates confusion. From an economist's point of view, people—stockholders, workers, landlords, consumers—bear taxes. A corporation cannot. Thus, when some politicians declare "business must pay its fair share of taxes," it is not clear what, if anything, this means.

Given that only people can bear taxes, how should they be classified for purposes of incidence analysis? Often their role in production—what inputs they supply to the production process—is used. (Inputs are often referred to as *factors of production*.) The focus is on how the tax system changes the distribution of income among capitalists, labourers, and landlords. This is referred to as the **functional distribution of income**.

---

[1] Actually, the change in the prices faced by consumers and producers is only part of the story. There is also a burden due to the tax-induced distortion of choice. See Chapter 18.
[2] Note the similarity to the problem of *expenditure incidence* introduced in Chapter 10.

Framing the analysis this way may seem a bit old-fashioned. In eighteenth-century England, it may have been the case that property owners never worked and workers owned no property. But in contemporary Canada, many people who derive most of their income from labour also have savings accounts and/or common stocks. (Often, these assets are held for individuals in pensions.) Similarly, some people own huge amounts of capital and also work full-time. Thus, it seems more relevant to study how taxes affect the way in which total income is distributed among people: the **size distribution of income**. Given information on what proportion of people's income is from capital, land, and labour, changes in the factor distribution can be translated into changes in the size distribution. For example, a tax that lowers the relative return on capital tends to hurt those at the top of the income distribution because a relatively high proportion of the incomes of the rich is from capital.[3]

Other classification schemes might be interesting for particular problems. When the Trudeau government enacted the National Energy Program in October 1980, the incidence by region received a great deal of attention. (The shift in income from Alberta to Central Canada involved tens of billions of dollars.) Alternatively, when proposals are made to change the taxation of income from pensions, analysts often look at incidence by age. It is easy to think of further examples based on sex, ethnicity, and so forth.

Both Sources and Uses of Income Should Be Considered

In the previous wine tax example, it is natural to assume that the distributional effects of the tax depend crucially on people's spending patterns. To the extent that the price of wine increases, the people who tend to consume a lot of wine are made worse off. Further thought suggests, however, that if the tax reduces the demand for wine, the factors employed in wine production may suffer income losses. Thus, the tax may also change the income distribution by affecting the *sources* of income. Suppose that poor people spend a relatively large proportion of their incomes on wine, but that vineyards tend to be owned by the rich. Then on the *uses* of income side, the tax redistributes income away from the poor, but on the sources side, it redistributes income away from the rich. The overall incidence depends on how both the sources and uses of income are affected. This distinction plays an important role in the debate over hotel room taxes and other taxes on "tourism." Proponents focus on the uses side arguing that relatively well-to-do "tourists" bear the tax, while opponents

---

[3] However, some low-income retirees also derive the bulk of their income from capital.

may point to the lower-income wage earners and small business people adversely affected on the sources side.

In practice, economists commonly ignore effects on the sources side when considering a tax on a commodity and ignore the uses side when analyzing a tax on an input. This procedure is appropriate if the most *systematic* effects of a commodity tax are on the uses of income and those of a factor tax on the sources of income. The assumption simplifies analyses, but its correctness must be considered for each case.

Incidence Depends on How Prices Are Determined

We have emphasized that the incidence problem is fundamentally one of determining how taxes change prices. Clearly, different models of price determination may give quite different answers to the question of who really bears a tax. This chapter considers several different models and compares the results.

A closely related issue is the time dimension of the analysis. Incidence depends on changes in prices, but change takes time. In most cases, one expects responses to be larger in the long run than the short run. Thus, the short- and long-run incidence of a tax may differ, and the time frame that is relevant for a given policy question must be specified.

Incidence Depends on the Disposition of Tax Revenues

Balanced-budget incidence computes the combined effects of levying taxes and government spending financed by those taxes. In general, the distributional effect of a tax depends on how the government spends the money. Expenditures on AIDS research have a very different distributional impact than spending on hot lunches for school children. Some studies assume the government spends the tax revenue exactly as the consumers would if they had received the money. This is equivalent to returning the revenue as a lump sum and letting consumers spend it.

In most cases, tax revenues are not earmarked for particular expenditures. It is then desirable to be able to abstract from the question of how the government spends the money. The idea is to examine how incidence differs when one tax is replaced with another, holding the government budget constant. This is called **differential tax incidence**. Because differential incidence looks at changes in taxes, it is useful to have a reference point. The hypothetical "other tax" used as the basis of comparison is often assumed to be a **lump-sum tax**—a tax for which the individual's liability does not depend upon behaviour. (For example, a 10 percent income tax is *not* a lump-sum tax because it depends on how much the individual earns. But a head tax of $500 independent of earnings is a lump-sum tax.)

Finally, **absolute tax incidence** examines the effects of a tax when there is no change in either other taxes or government expenditure. Absolute incidence is of most interest for macroeconomic models in which tax levels are changed to achieve some stabilization goal.

Tax Progressiveness Can Be Measured in Several Ways

Suppose that an investigator has managed to calculate every person's real share of a particular tax—the economic incidence as defined above. The bottom line of such an exercise is often a characterization of the tax as proportional, progressive, or regressive. The definition of **proportional** is straightforward; it describes a situation in which the ratio of taxes paid to income is constant regardless of income level.[4]

Defining progressive and regressive is not easy, and unfortunately, ambiguities in definition sometimes confuse public debate. A natural way to define these words is in terms of the **average tax rate**, the ratio of taxes paid to income. If the average tax rate increases with income, the system is **progressive**; if it falls, the tax is **regressive**.[5]

Confusion arises because some people think of progressiveness in terms of the **marginal tax rate**—the *change* in taxes paid with respect to a change in income. To illustrate the distinction, consider the following very simple income tax structure. Each individual computes his or her tax bill by subtracting $3,000 from income and paying an amount equal to 20 percent of the remainder. (If the difference is negative, the individual gets a subsidy equal to 20 percent of the figure.) Table 17.1 shows the amount of tax paid, the average tax rate, and the marginal tax rate for each of several income levels. The average rates increase with income. However, the marginal tax rate is constant at 0.2 because for each additional dollar earned, the individual pays an additional 20 cents, regardless of income level. People could disagree about the progressiveness of this tax system and each be right according to their own definitions. It is therefore very important to make the definition clear when using the terms *regressive* and *progressive*. In the remainder of this book, we assume they are

---

[4] However, the definition of income is not straightforward; see Chapter 20.
[5] As a matter of convention, taxes are generally referred to as progressive, regressive, or proportional in relation to income. Alternatively, they might be viewed in relation to consumption or wealth.

Table 17.1

Tax Liabilities under a Hypothetical Tax System

INCOME	TAX LIABILITY	AVERAGE TAX RATE	MARGINAL TAX RATE
$ 2,000	$ –200	–0.10	0.2
3,000	0	0	0.2
5,000	400	0.08	0.2
10,000	1,400	0.14	0.2
30,000	5,400	0.18	0.2

defined in terms of average tax rates. Measuring the *degree* of progressivity of a tax system is more difficult and controversial than defining progressivity.

PARTIAL EQUILIBRIUM MODELS

With preliminaries out of the way, we turn now to the fundamental issue of this chapter: how taxes affect the income distribution. We have argued that the essence of the problem is that taxes induce changes in relative prices. Knowing how prices are determined is therefore a key ingredient in the analysis. In this section we analyze **partial equilibrium models** of price determination—models that look only at the market in which the tax is imposed and ignore the ramifications in other markets. This kind of analysis is most appropriate when the market for the taxed commodity is relatively small compared to the economy as a whole. The vehicle for our analysis is the supply and demand model of perfect competition.

Unit Taxes on Commodities

We study first the incidence of a **unit tax**, so named because it is levied as a fixed amount per unit of a commodity sold. For example, the federal government imposes a tax on wine of $0.51 per litre and a tax on cigarettes of $1.36 per pack.[6] Suppose that the price and quantity of wine are determined competitively by supply (S_c) and demand (D_c) as in Figure 17.1. Before imposition of the tax, the quantity demanded and price are Q_0 and P_0, respectively.

---

[6] The federal cigarette tax in 1996 was $10.86 per carton of 200, or $1.36 per pack for a pack of 25 short cigarettes. This tax rate was applied in Newfoundland, Manitoba, Saskatchewan, Alberta, British Columbia, and the territories in 1996. To deal with a serious smuggling problem across the U.S. border, federal unit taxes on cigarettes were lower in some provinces—$0.81 per pack in Quebec and $0.86 in Ontario. The federal tax for Nova Scotia, New Brunswick, and Prince Edward Island was $1.11 per pack.

Figure 17.1

Price and Quantity before Taxation

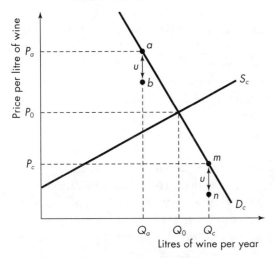

Now suppose that a unit tax of $\$u$ per litre is imposed on each purchase, and the statutory incidence is on buyers. A key step in incidence analysis is to recognize that in the presence of a tax, the price paid by consumers and the price received by suppliers differ. Previously, we could use a supply–demand analysis to determine the *single* market price. Now, this analysis must be modified to accommodate two different prices, one for buyers and one for sellers.

We begin by determining how the tax affects the demand schedule. Consider an arbitrary point a on the demand curve. Recall that this point indicates that the *maximum* price per litre that people would be willing to pay for Q_a litres is P_a. After the unit tax of u is imposed, the most that people would be willing to spend for Q_a is *still* P_a. There is no reason to believe the tax affects the underlying valuation people place on wine. However, when people pay P_a per litre, producers no longer receive the whole amount. Instead, they receive only $(P_a - u)$, an amount that is indicated as point b in Figure 17.1. In other words, after the unit tax is imposed, a is no longer a point on the demand curve *as perceived by suppliers*. Point b is on the demand curve as perceived by suppliers, because they realize that if Q_a is supplied, they receive only $(P_a - u)$ per litre. It is irrelevant to the suppliers how much consumers pay per litre; all that matters to suppliers is the amount they receive per litre.

Of course, point a was chosen arbitrarily. At any other point on the demand curve, the story is just the same. Thus, for example, after the tax is imposed, the price received by suppliers for output Q_c is at point n, which is found by subtracting the distance u from point m. Repeating this process at every point along the demand curve, we generate a new demand curve located exactly u dollars below the old one. In Figure 17.2, the demand curve so constructed is labelled D'_c. Schedule D'_c is relevant to suppliers because it shows how much they receive for each unit sold.

We are now in a position to find the equilibrium quantity of wine after the unit tax is imposed. The equilibrium is where the supply equals demand as perceived by suppliers. In Figure 17.2, this occurs at output Q_1. Thus, the tax lowers the quantity sold from Q_0 to Q_1.

The next step is to find the new equilibrium price. As noted earlier, there are really two prices at the new equilibrium: the price received by producers, and the price paid by consumers. The price received by producers is at the intersection of their effective demand and supply curves, which occurs at P_n. The price paid by consumers is P_n plus u, the unit tax. To find this price geometrically, we must go up from P_n a vertical distance exactly equal to u. But by construction, the distance between schedules D_c and D'_c is equal to u. Hence, to find the price paid by consumers, we simply go up from the intersection of D'_c and S_c to the original demand curve D_c. The price so determined is P_g. Because P_g includes the tax, it is often referred to as the price gross of tax. On the other hand, P_n is the price net of tax.

Figure 17.2

Incidence of a Unit Tax Imposed on the Demand Side

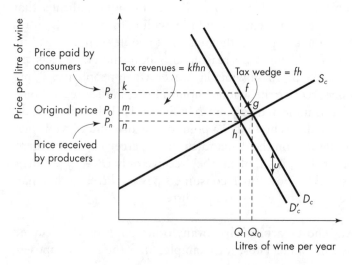

Consumers are made worse off by the tax because P_g, the new price they face, is higher than the original price P_0. But the consumers' price does not increase by the full amount of the tax—$(P_g - P_0)$ is less than u. Producers also pay part of the tax in the form of a lower price received per litre. Producers now receive only P_n, while before the tax they received P_0. Thus, both producers and consumers are made worse off by the tax.[7] Notice that consumers and producers "split" the tax in the sense that the increase in the consumer price $(P_g - P_0)$ and the decrease in the producer price $(P_0 - P_n)$ just add up to \$$u$.

By definition, revenues collected are the product of the number of units purchased, Q_1, and the tax per unit, u. Geometrically, Q_1 is the width of rectangle *kfhn* and u is its height, so tax revenues are the area of this rectangle.

This analysis has two important implications:

1. *The incidence of a unit tax is independent of whether it is levied on consumers or producers.* Suppose the same tax u had been levied on the suppliers of wine instead of the consumers. Consider an arbitrary price P_i on the original supply curve in Figure 17.3. The supply curve indicates that for suppliers to produce Q_i units, they must receive at least P_i per unit. After the unit tax, suppliers still must receive P_i per unit. For them to do so, however, consumers must pay price $P_i + u$ per unit, which is shown geometrically as point *j*. It should now be clear where the argument is heading. To find the supply curve as it is perceived by consumers, S_c must be shifted up by the amount of the unit tax. This new supply curve is labelled S'_c. The post-tax equilibrium is at Q'_1, where the schedules S'_c and D_c intersect. The price at the intersection, P'_g, is the price paid by consumers. To find the price received by producers, we must subtract u from P'_g, giving us P'_n. A glance at Figure 17.2 indicates that $Q'_1 = Q_1$, $P'_g = P_g$, and $P'_n = P_n$. Thus, the incidence of the unit tax is independent of the side of the market on which it is levied.

   This is the same as our statement that the statutory incidence of a tax tells us nothing of the economic incidence of the tax. It is irrelevant whether the

---

[7] In terms of surplus measures, consumers are worse off by area *mkfg* and producers are worse off by *mghn*. The loss of total surplus exceeds the tax revenues by triangle *fhg*; this is the excess burden of the tax, as explained in Chapter 18. Area *mghn* is the loss in producer surplus. Just as consumer surplus is the area between the demand curve and a horizontal line at the going price, producer surplus is the area between the supply curve and a horizontal line at the going price. For a review of consumer surplus, see the Appendix to Chapter 4.

Figure 17.3

Incidence of a Unit Tax Imposed on the Supply Side

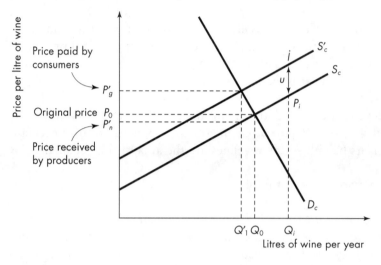

tax collector (figuratively) stands next to consumers and takes u dollars every time they pay for a litre of wine or stands next to sellers and collects u dollars from them whenever they sell a litre. Figures 17.2 and 17.3 prove that what matters is the size of the disparity the tax introduces between the price paid by consumers and the price received by producers, and not on which side of the market the disparity is introduced. The tax-induced difference between the price paid by consumers and the price received by producers is referred to as the **tax wedge** (the distance between P'_n and P'_g in Figure 17.3).

2. *The incidence of a unit tax depends on the elasticities of supply and demand.* In Figure 17.2, consumers bear the brunt of the tax—the amount they pay goes up much more than the amount received by producers goes down. This result is strictly determined by the shapes of the demand and supply curves. In general, the more elastic the demand curve, the less the tax borne by consumers, *ceteris paribus*. Similarly, the more elastic the supply curve, the less the tax borne by producers, *ceteris paribus*. Intuitively, elasticity provides a rough measure of an economic agent's ability to escape the tax. The more elastic the demand, the easier it is for consumers to turn to other products when the price goes up, and therefore more of the tax must be borne by suppliers. Conversely, if consumers purchase the same amount regardless of price, the whole burden can be shifted to them. Similar considerations apply to the supply side.

Illustrations of extreme cases are provided in Figures 17.4 and 17.5. In Figure 17.4, commodity X is supplied perfectly inelastically. When a unit tax is imposed, the effective demand curve becomes D'_X. As before, the price received by producers (P_n) is at the intersection of S_X and D'_X. Note that P_n is exactly u less than P_0. Thus, the price received by producers falls by exactly the amount of the tax. At the same time, the price paid by consumers, P_g ($= P_n + u$), remains at P_0. When supply is perfectly inelastic, producers bear the entire burden. Figure 17.5 represents an opposite extreme. The supply of commodity Z is perfectly elastic. Imposition of a unit tax leads to demand curve D'_Z. At the new equilibrium, quantity demanded is Z_1 and the price received by producers, P_n,

Figure 17.4

Tax Incidence When Supply is Perfectly Inelastic

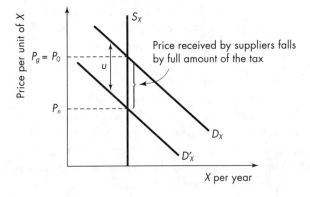

Figure 17.5

Tax Incidence When Supply is Perfectly Elastic

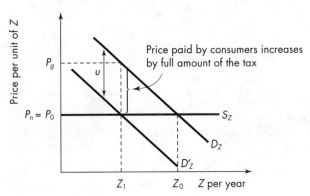

is still P_0. The price paid by consumers, P_g, is therefore $P_0 + u$. In this case, consumers bear the entire burden of the tax.[8]

Ad Valorem Taxes

We now turn to the incidence of an **ad valorem** tax, a tax with a rate given as a *proportion* of the price. For example, clothing in Toronto is taxed at 15 percent of its price—a combination of a 7 percent federal Goods and Services Tax (GST) and an 8 percent provincial retail sales tax. The provincial retail sales taxes are all ad valorem taxes.

Luckily, the analysis of ad valorem taxes is very similar to that of unit taxes. The basic strategy is still to find out how the tax changes the effective demand curve and compute the new equilibrium. However, instead of moving the curve down by the same absolute amount for each quantity, the ad valorem tax lowers it in the same *proportion*. To show this, consider the demand (D_f) and supply (S_f) curves for clothing in Figure 17.6. In the absence of taxation, the equilibrium price and quantity are P_0 and Q_0, respectively. Now suppose that a tax of 25 percent of the gross price is levied on the consumption of clothing.[9] Consider point m on D_f. After the tax is imposed, P_m is still the most that consumers will pay for Q_m of clothing; the amount producers will receive is 75 percent of the vertical distance between point m and the horizontal axis, which is labelled point n. Hence, point n is one point on the demand curve perceived by producers. Similarly, the price at point r migrates down one-quarter of the way between it and the horizontal axis to point s. When this exercise is repeated for every point on D_f, the effective demand curve facing suppliers is determined as D'_f in Figure 17.7. From here, the analysis proceeds exactly as for a unit tax: The equilibrium is at the intersection of S_f and D'_f, with the quantity exchanged Q_1, the price received by clothing producers P_n, and the price paid by consumers P_g. As before, the incidence of the tax is determined by the elasticities of supply and demand. (An ad valorem tax can also be analyzed with a shift in the supply curve, as from S_f to S'_f.)

---

[8] Note that as long as input costs are constant, the *long-run* supply curve for a competitive market is horizontal as in Figure 17.5. Hence, under these conditions, in the long run consumers bear the entire burden of the tax.

[9] A fundamental ambiguity is involved in measuring ad valorem tax rates. Is the tax measured as a percentage of the net or gross price? In this example, the tax is 25 percent of the gross price, which is equivalent to a rate of 33 percent of net price. To see this, note that if the price paid by the consumer were $1, the tax paid would be 25 cents, and the price received by producers would be 75 cents. Expressing the 25 cent tax bill as a fraction of 75 cents gives us a 33 percent rate as a proportion of the net price.

Figure 17.6

Introducing an Ad Valorem Tax

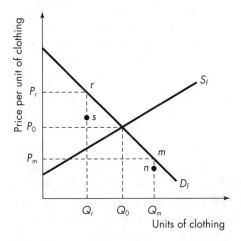

Figure 17.7

Incidence of an Ad Valorem Tax

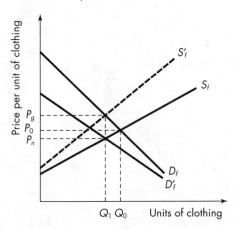

Taxes on Factors

So far we have discussed taxes on goods, but the analysis can also be applied to factors of production.

The payroll tax. Consider the payroll tax used to finance the Canada Pension Plan (CPP). As noted in Chapter 14, in 1996 a tax equal to 2.6 percent of workers' pensionable earnings was paid by their employers and a tax at the same rate paid by the workers themselves—a total of 5.2 percent.[10] This division has a long history and is a consequence of our lawmakers' feeling that the payroll tax should be shared by employers and employees. It is important to realize that the *statutory distinction between workers and bosses is irrelevant.* As suggested earlier, the incidence of this labour tax is determined only by the wedge the tax puts between what employees receive and employers pay.

This point is illustrated in Figure 17.8, where D_L is the demand for labour and S_L is the supply of labour. For purposes of illustration, assume S_L to be perfectly inelastic. Before taxation, the wage is w_0. The ad valorem tax on labour moves the effective demand curve to D'_L. As usual, the distance between D'_L and D_L is the wedge between what is paid for an item and what is received by those who supply it. After the tax is imposed, the wage received by workers falls to w_n. On the other hand, w_g, the price paid by employers, stays at w_0. In this example, despite the statutory division of the tax, the wage rate received by workers falls by exactly the amount of the tax—they bear the entire burden.

Of course, we could have gotten just the opposite result by drawing the supply curve as perfectly elastic. The key point to remember is that nothing about

Figure 17.8

Incidence of a Payroll Tax with an Inelastic Supply of Labour

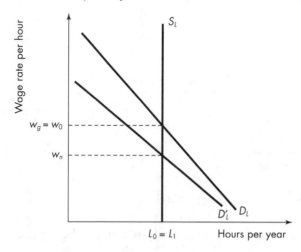

the incidence of a tax can be known without information on the relevant behavioural elasticities. In fact, there is some evidence that the elasticity of the total supply of hours of work is about zero.[11] At least in the short run, labour probably bears most of the payroll tax, despite the continuing debates on the "fair" distribution of the burden.

Capital taxation in an open economy. The strategy for analyzing a tax on capital is essentially the same as that for analyzing a tax on labour—draw the supply and demand curves, shift or pivot the relevant curve by an amount depending on the size of the tax, and see how the after-tax equilibrium compares with the original one. In an economy that is closed to trade, it is reasonable to assume that the demand curve will slope downward (firms demand less capital when its price goes up), and that the supply of capital will slope upward (people supply more capital [i.e., save more] when the return to saving increases).[12] In this case, the owners of capital will bear some of the burden of the tax, the precise amount depending on the supply and demand elasticities.

Suppose now that the economy is open and capital is perfectly mobile across countries. In effect, there is a single world market for capital, and if suppliers of capital cannot earn the going world rate of return in a particular country, they will take it out of that country and put it in another. In terms of a supply and demand diagram, the supply of capital to a particular country is perfectly elastic—its citizens can purchase all the capital they want at the going rate of return, but none whatsoever at a lower rate. The implications for the incidence of a tax on capital are striking. As in Figure 17.5, the before-tax price paid by the users of capital rises by exactly the amount of the tax, and the suppliers of capital bear no burden whatsoever. Intuitively, capital will simply move abroad if it has to bear any of the tax; hence, the rate of return has to rise.

Now, even in today's highly integrated world economy, capital is not perfectly mobile across countries. However, for a country like Canada whose capital market is small relative to the world market, the supply curve is much more horizontal than for the United States. Policy makers who ignore world trade and capital flows will tend to overestimate their ability to place the burden of taxation on owners of capital. To the extent that capital is internationally mobile, taxes on capitalists are shifted to others, and the apparent progressivity of taxes on capital proves to be illusory. Capital escapes the tax by migrating to other

---

[11] According to Phipps (1993: 40): "Modern empirical labour economics concludes that the labour-supply behaviour of men *and* women is inelastic—highly inelastic if we focus on the most recent estimates using the best available data."

[12] However, saving need not increase with the rate of return. See Chapter 21.

jurisdictions, and less mobile factors such as labour, having less capital with which to work, are less productive and bear the burden of the tax on capital.

Commodity Taxation without Competition

The assumption of competitive markets has played a major role in our analysis. We now discuss how the results might change under alternative market structures.

Monopoly. The polar opposite of competition is monopoly—one seller.[13] Figure 17.9 depicts a monopolist that produces commodity X. Before any taxation, the demand curve facing the monopolist is D_X, and the associated marginal revenue curve is MR_X. The marginal cost curve for the production of X is MC_X, and the average total cost curve, ATC_X. As usual, the condition for profit maximization is that production be carried to the point where marginal revenue equals marginal cost, at output X_0 where the price charged is P_0. Economic profit per unit is the difference between average revenue and average total cost, distance ab. The number of units sold is db. Hence, total profit is ab times db, which is the area of rectangle $abdc$.

Now suppose that a unit tax of u is levied on X. For exactly the same reasons as before, the effective demand curve facing the producer shifts down by a ver-

Figure 17.9

Equilibrium of a Monopolist

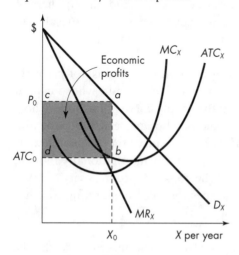

---

[13] See Baumol and Blinder (1982: ch. 25) for a review of price and output determination under monopoly.

tical distance equal to u.[14] In Figure 17.10, this demand curve is labelled D'_x. At the same time, the marginal revenue curve facing the firm also shifts down by distance u because the firm's incremental revenue for each unit sold is reduced by the amount of the tax. The new effective marginal revenue curve is labelled MR'_x.

The profit-maximizing output, X_1, is found at the intersection of MR'_x and MC_x. Using output X_1, we find the price received by the monopolist by going up to D'_x, the facing demand curve, and locate price P_n. The price paid by consumers is determined by adding u to P_n, which is shown as price P_g on the diagram. After-tax profit per unit is the difference between the price *received by the monopolist* and average total cost, distance fg. Number of units sold is if. Therefore, monopoly economic profits after tax are measured by area $fghi$.

What are the effects of the tax? Quantity demanded goes down ($X_1 < X_0$); the price paid by consumers goes up ($P_g > P_0$); and the price received by the monopolist may go either up or down, depending on the shapes of the marginal revenue and marginal cost curves. In Figure 17.10, the price received by the monopolist goes down ($P_n < P_0$). Note that monopoly profits are lower under the tax—area $fghi$ in Figure 17.10 is smaller than area $abdc$ in Figure 17.9. Despite its market power, a monopolist is in general made worse off by

Figure 17.10

Imposition of a Unit Tax on a Monopolist

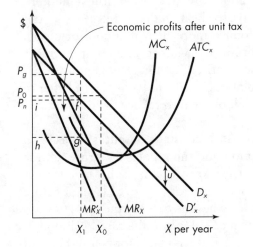

a unit tax on the product it sells. In public debate it is often assumed that a firm with market power can simply pass on all taxes to consumers. This analysis shows that even a completely greedy and grasping monopolist must bear some of the burden. As before, the precise share of the burden borne by consumers depends on the elasticity of the demand schedule.

It is straightforward to repeat the exercise for an ad valorem tax on the monopolist (D_x and MR_X pivot instead of moving down in a parallel fashion); this is left as an exercise for the reader.

Oligopoly. Between the polar extremes of perfect competition and monopoly is the oligopoly market structure in which there are a "few" sellers. Unfortunately, there is no well-developed theory of tax incidence in oligopoly. The reason for this embarrassing fact is simple: Incidence depends primarily on how relative prices change when taxes are imposed, but there is no generally accepted theory of how oligopolistic prices are determined.

Still, we can get a sense of the issues involved by imagining the problem faced by the firms in an oligopolistic market. From the firms' point of view, the ideal situation would be for them to collude and jointly produce the output that maximizes the profits of the entire industry. This output level is referred to as the *cartel solution*. (A cartel is just a group of producers who act together to maximize profits. The international oil cartel OPEC is the most famous example.) The cartel solution requires each firm to cut its output to force up the market price. The problem for the firms is that the cartel solution is very difficult to obtain. Why? Once an agreement about how much each firm should produce is reached, each firm has an incentive to cheat on that agreement—to take advantage of the higher price and produce more than its quota of output. (Again, think about OPEC, and the problems it has in keeping its members from producing "too much" oil.) Consequently, output in an oligopolistic market is typically higher than the cartel solution. The firms would all be better off if there were some mechanism to force all of them to reduce their output.

Now let us consider what happens when this industry's output is subjected to a tax. As is the case both for competition and monopoly, the firms contract their output. However, unlike the other market structures, this is not necessarily bad for the oligopolistic firms. To be sure, for any given level of before-tax profits, the firms are worse off, because they have to pay the tax. However, as the firms contract their outputs, they move closer to the cartel solution, so their before-tax profits increase. It is theoretically possible for before-tax profits to increase by so much that even after paying the tax the firms are better off (see Besley, 1989). Of course, it is also possible for the firms to be worse off.

One needs more information on just how much the firms cut back their output to obtain a definitive answer.

The U.S. cigarette industry provided a case study of an excise tax increase in an oligopolistic situation in the 1980s (Harris, 1987). Taxes on cigarettes rose by 8 cents per package in 1983. The 8 cents increase was known in advance, and was accompanied by an increase of 16 cents in the wholesale price of cigarettes, inclusive of tax. In other words, prices rose by roughly double the amount of the tax increase, contrary to what would be expected in a competitive situation; operating profits of cigarette companies also rose sharply. According to Harris (p. 88), the "tax increase appears to have served as a focal point for coordinating oligopoly price increases by sellers."[15] This example is illustrative of the difficulties, in Canada or elsewhere, in predicting the incidence of commodity taxes in an oligopolistic situation.[16]

As economic behaviour under oligopoly becomes better understood, improved models of incidence will be developed. In the meantime, most economists feel fairly comfortable in relying on the predictions produced by competitive models, although they realize these are only approximations.

Profits Taxes

So far we have been discussing taxes based on sales. Firms can also be taxed on their **economic profits**, defined as the return to owners of the firm in excess of the opportunity costs of the factors used in production. (Economic profits are also referred to as *supranormal* or *excess* profits.) We now show that as long as firms are profit maximizing, a tax on economic profits cannot be shifted—it is borne only by the owners of the firm.

Consider first a perfectly competitive firm in short-run equilibrium. The firm's output is determined by the intersection of its marginal cost and marginal revenue schedules. A tax of a given rate on economic profits changes neither marginal cost nor marginal revenue. Therefore, no firm has the incentive to change its output decision. Because output does not change, neither does the price paid by consumers, so they are no worse off. The tax is completely absorbed

---

[15] The effect of the $360 billion (over twenty-five years) in penalties imposed on the U.S. cigarette companies in 1997 may have a similar effect. This may account for the small impact the imposition of these large penalties appears to have had on the price of tobacco stocks.
[16] Although the overall demand for cigarettes and alcohol is relatively inelastic, young smokers and young drinkers appear to be quite price sensitive—price elasticities for this group may be well in excess of unity. Thus, higher taxes may significantly reduce smoking and drinking by youth. See Grossman et al. (1993).

by the firms. Another way to get to the same result is this: If the tax rate on economic profits is t_p, the firm's objective is to maximize after-tax profits, $(1 - t_p)\pi$, where π is the pretax level of economic profits. But it is just a matter of arithmetic that whatever strategy maximizes π is identical to the one that maximizes $(1 - t_p)\pi$. Hence, output and price faced by consumers stay the same, and the firm bears the whole tax.

In long-run competitive equilibrium, a tax on economic profits has no yield, because economic profits are zero—they are all competed away. For a monopolist, there may be economic profits even in the long run. But for the same reasons given in the preceding paragraph, the tax is borne by the owners of the monopoly. If a firm is maximizing profits before the profits tax is imposed, the tax cannot be shifted.[17]

Because they distort no economic decisions, taxes on economic profits might appear to be very attractive policy alternatives. However, profits taxes have received very little support from public finance specialists. The main reason is the tremendous problems in making the theoretical notion of economic profits operational. For example, excess profits are often computed by examining the rate of return that a firm makes on its capital stock and comparing it to some "basic" rate of return set by the government. Clearly, how the capital stock is measured is important. Should the original cost be used, or the cost of replacing it? And what if the rate of return is high not because of excess profits, but because the enterprise is very risky and investors have to be compensated for this risk? Considerations such as these lead to major difficulties in administration and compliance.[18]

Tax Incidence and Capitalization

"An old tax is a good tax" is a familiar adage to economists. The reason is that the burden of the tax will have been borne by a previous owner or generation. For example, if a tax was imposed on land or buildings before purchase by the existing owner, he or she would have paid less because of the tax's effect on the after-tax income from the property. To eliminate or lower the tax unexpectedly now would lead to a "windfall gain," and an unexpected increase in the tax would cause a "windfall loss."[19] Let's now look more closely at a tax on land.

---

[17] On the other hand, if the firm is following some other goal, it may raise the price in response to a profits tax. One alternative to profit maximization is revenue maximization; firms try to make their sales as large as possible, subject to the constraint that they earn a "reasonable" rate of return.

[18] See Gillis and McLure (1979) for further details.

[19] This concept is developed further in the discussion of horizontal equity in Chapter 19.

Early in the twentieth century several western Canadian provinces taxed only land, and not the buildings and other improvements on the land. Since then there has been continuing discussion of whether tax rates on the value of land should be higher than those on the value of improvements. In other words, should taxes on land be raised and those on improvements lowered?

This question leads us to consider the special issues that arise when land is taxed. For these purposes, the distinctive characteristics of land are that it is fixed in supply and it is durable.[20] Suppose the annual rental rate on land is $\$R_0$ this year. It is known that the rental will be $\$R_1$ next year, $\$R_2$ two years from now, and so on. How much should someone be willing to pay for the land? If the market for land is competitive, the price of land is just equal to the present discounted value of the stream of the rents. Thus, if the interest rate is r, the price of land (P_R) is

$$P_R = \$R_0 + \$R_1/(1 + r) + \$R_2/(1 + r)^2 + \dots + \$R_T/(1 + r)^T \qquad (17.1)$$

where T is the last year the land yields its services (possibly infinity).

Assume it is announced that a tax of $\$u_0$ will be imposed on land now, $\$u_1$ next year, $\$u_2$ two years from now, and so forth. From Figure 17.4 we know that because land is fixed in supply, the annual rental received by the owner falls by the full amount of the tax. That means that the landlord's return initially falls to $\$(R_0 - u_0)$, in year 1 to $\$(R_1 - u_1)$, and in year 2 to $\$(R_2 - u_2)$. Prospective purchasers of the land take into account the fact that if they purchase the land, they buy a future stream of tax liabilities as well as a future stream of returns. Therefore, the most a purchaser is willing to pay for the land after the tax is announced (P'_R) is

$$P'_R = \$(R_0 - u_0) + \$(R_1 - u_1)/(1 + r) + \$(R_2 - u_2)/(1 + r)^2$$
$$+ \dots + \$(R_T - u_T)/(1 + r)^T. \qquad (17.2)$$

Comparing Equations (17.2) and (17.1), we see that as a consequence of the tax, the price of land falls by

$$u_0 + u_1/(1 + r) + u_2/(1 + r)^2 + \dots + u_T/(1 + r)^T.$$

Thus, at the time the tax is imposed, the price of the land falls by the present value of *all future tax payments*. This process by which a stream of taxes becomes incorporated into the price of an asset is referred to as **capitalization**.

---

[20] Hence, the analysis of this section applies to any commodity or input with these characteristics.

Because of capitalization, the person who bears the full burden of the tax forever is the landlord at the time the tax is levied. To be sure, future landlords
make payments to the tax authorities, but such payments are not really a "burden" because they just balance the lower price paid at purchase. Capitalization
complicates attempts to assess the incidence of a tax on a durable item that is
fixed in supply. Knowing the identities of current owners is not sufficient—one
must know who the landlords were at the time the tax was imposed. In light
of this analysis, it's no wonder that significant changes in taxes on real property, and land in particular, lead to strong taxpayer resistance.[21]

GENERAL EQUILIBRIUM MODELS

A great attraction of partial equilibrium models is their simplicity—examining
only one market at a time is a relatively uncomplicated affair. In some cases,
however, ignoring feedback into other markets leads to an incomplete picture
of a tax's incidence. Suppose, for example, that a tax is levied on all capital
used in the construction of housing. Partial equilibrium analysis of this tax
would involve analyzing only the supply and demand curves for housing capital. But suppose that the tax induces some people who formerly invested in
housing to invest their capital in factories instead. As new capital flows into
the manufacturing sector, the rate of return to capital employed there falls.
Thus, capitalists in the manufacturing sector may end up bearing part of the
burden of a tax imposed on the housing sector.

More generally, when a tax is imposed on a sector that is "large" relative to
the economy, looking only at that particular market may not be enough.
General equilibrium analysis takes into account the ways in which various
markets are interrelated.

Another problem with partial equilibrium analysis is that it gives insufficient
attention to the question of just who the "producers" of a taxed commodity
are. The "producer" is a composite of entrepreneurs, capitalists, and workers.
In many cases, the division of the tax burden among these groups is important.
General equilibrium analysis provides a framework for investigating it.

Before turning to the specifics of general equilibrium analysis, note that the
fundamental lesson from partial equilibrium models still holds: Because of rel-

---

[21] If a land tax is anticipated before it is levied, then presumably it is borne at least in part
by the owner at the time the anticipation becomes widespread. In theory, then, even finding out the identity of the landowner at the time the tax was imposed may not be enough.
Further, at the fringes of urban areas that are adjacent to farmland, the supply of urban
land can be extended, so the incidence is not entirely on landlords.

ative price adjustments, the statutory incidence of a tax generally tells *nothing* about who really bears its burden.

Tax Equivalence Relations

The idea of dealing with tax incidence in a general equilibrium framework at first appears daunting. After all, thousands of different commodities and inputs are traded in the economy. How can we keep track of all their complicated interrelations? Luckily, for many purposes, useful general equilibrium results can be obtained from models in which there are only two commodities, two factors of production, and no savings. For illustration, call the two commodities food (F) and manufactures (M), and the two factors capital (K) and labour (L). There are nine possible ad valorem taxes in such a model:

t_{KF} = *a tax on capital used in the production of food.*

t_{KM} = *a tax on capital used in the production of manufactures.*

t_{LF} = *a tax on labour used in the production of food.*

t_{LM} = *a tax on labour used in the production of manufactures.*

t_F = *a tax on the consumption of food.*

t_M = *a tax on consumption of manufactures.*

t_K = *a tax on capital in both sectors.*

t_L = *a tax on labour in both sectors.*

t = *a general income tax.*

The first four taxes, which are levied on a factor in only some of its uses, are referred to as **partial factor taxes**.

Certain combinations of these taxes are equivalent to others. One of these equivalences is already familiar from the theory of the consumer. Taxes on food (t_F) and manufactures (t_M) at the same rate are equivalent to an income tax (t).[22] To see this, just note that equiproportional taxes on all commodities have the same effect on the consumer's budget constraint as a proportional income tax. Both create a parallel shift inward.

Now consider a proportional tax on both capital (t_K) and labour (t_L). Because in this model all income is derived from either capital or labour, it is a simple

---

[22] Note that given the assumption that all income is consumed, an income tax is also equivalent to a tax on consumption expenditure.

matter of arithmetic that taxing both factors at the same rate is also equivalent to an income tax (t).

Perhaps not so obvious is the fact that partial taxes on both capital and labour in the food sector at a given rate ($t_{KF} = t_{LF}$) are equivalent to a tax on food (t_F) at the same rate. Because capital and labour are the only inputs to the production of food, making each of them more expensive by a certain proportion is equivalent to making the food itself more expensive in the same proportion.

More generally, any two sets of taxes that generate the same changes in relative prices have equivalent incidence effects. All the equivalence relations that can be derived using similar logic are summarized in Table 17.2. For a given ad valorem tax rate, the equivalences are shown by reading across the rows or down the columns. To determine the incidence of all three taxes in any row or column, only two have to be analyzed in detail. The third can be determined by addition or subtraction. For example, from the third row, if we know the incidence of taxes on capital and labour, then we also know the incidence of a tax on income.

In the next section, we discuss the incidence of four taxes: a food tax (t_F), an income tax (t), a general tax on labour (t_L), and a partial tax on capital in manufacturing (t_{KM}). With results on these four taxes in hand, the incidence of the other five can be determined by using Table 17.2.

The Harberger Model

The pioneering work in applying general equilibrium models to tax incidence is that by Harberger (1974). The principal assumptions of his model are as follows:

1. *Technology.* Firms in each sector use capital and labour to produce their outputs. The technologies in each sector are such that a simultaneous dou-

Table 17.2

Tax Equivalence Relations

t_{KF}	and	t_{LF}	are equivalent to	t_F
and		and		and
t_{KM}	and	t_{LM}	are equivalent to	t_M
are		are		are
equivalent		equivalent		equivalent
to		to		to
t_K	and	t_L	are equivalent to	t

SOURCE: Charles E. McLure, Jr., "The Theory of Tax Incidence with Imperfect Factor Mobility," *Finanzarchiv* 30 (1971): 29.

bling of both inputs leads to a doubling of output, constant returns to scale.[23] However, the production technologies may differ across sectors. In general, the production technologies differ with respect to the ease with which capital can be substituted for labour (the **elasticity of substitution**) and the ratios in which capital and labour are employed. For example, it has been calculated that the capital–labour ratio in the production of food is about 1.3 times that used in the production of appliances.[24] The industry in which the capital–labour ratio is relatively high is characterized as **capital intensive**; the other is **labour intensive**.

2. *Behaviour of factor suppliers*. Suppliers of both capital and labour maximize total returns. Moreover, capital and labour are perfectly mobile—they can freely move across sectors according to the wishes of their owners. Consequently, the net marginal return to capital must be the same in each sector, and so must the net marginal return to labour. Otherwise, it would be possible to reallocate capital and labour in such a way that total net returns could be increased.

3. *Market structure*. Firms are competitive and maximize profits, and all prices (including the wage rate) are perfectly flexible. Therefore, factors are fully employed, and the return paid to each factor of production is the value of its marginal product—the value to the firm of the output produced by the last unit of the input.

4. *Total factor supplies*. The total amounts of capital and labour available to the economy are fixed. But, as already suggested, both factors are perfectly free to move between sectors.

5. *Consumer preferences*. All consumers have identical preferences. A tax therefore cannot generate any distributional effects by affecting people's uses of income. This assumption allows us to concentrate on the effect of taxes on the sources of income.

6. *Tax incidence framework*. The framework for the analysis is differential tax incidence: We consider the substitution of one tax for another. Therefore, approximately the same amount of income is available before and after the tax, so it is unnecessary to consider how changes in aggregate income may change demand and factor prices.

Clearly, these assumptions are somewhat restrictive, but they serve to simplify the analysis considerably. Later in this chapter, we consider the consequences

---

[23] It is also assumed the production function is homogeneous, a technical condition that means each ratio of factor prices is uniquely associated with a given ratio of capital to labour.

[24] See Devarajan, Fullerton, and Musgrave (1980: 167).

of dropping some of them. We now employ Harberger's model to analyze several different taxes.

Analysis of Various Taxes

A commodity tax (t_F). When a tax on food is imposed, its relative price increases (although not necessarily by the amount of the tax). Consumers are thereby induced to substitute manufactures for food. Consequently, less food and more manufactures are produced. As food production falls, some of the capital and labour formerly used in food production are forced to find employment in manufacturing. Because the capital–labour ratios differ between the two sectors, the relative prices of capital and labour have to change for manufacturing to be willing to absorb the unemployed factors from food production. For example, assume that food is the capital-intensive sector. (Canadian agriculture does, in fact, use relatively more capital equipment—tractors, combines, and so forth—than many types of manufacturing.) Therefore, relatively large amounts of capital must be absorbed in manufacturing. The only way for all this capital to find employment in the manufacturing sector is for the relative price of capital to fall—including capital already in use in the manufacturing sector. In the new equilibrium, then, *all* capital is relatively worse off, not just capital in the food sector. More generally, a tax on the *output* of a particular sector induces a decline in the relative price of the *input* used intensively in that sector.

To go beyond such qualitative statements, additional information is needed. The greater the elasticity of demand for food, the more dramatic will be the change in consumption from food to manufactures, which ultimately induces a greater decline in the return to capital. The greater the difference in factor proportions between food and manufactures, the greater must be the decrease in capital's price for it to be absorbed into the manufacturing sector. (If the capital–labour ratios for food and manufactured goods were identical, neither factor would suffer relative to the other.) Finally, the harder it is to substitute capital for labour in the production of manufactures, the greater the decline in the rate of return to capital needed to absorb the additional capital.

Thus, on the sources side of the budget, the food tax tends to hurt people who receive a proportionately large share of their incomes from capital. Given that all individuals are identical (assumption 5), there are no interesting effects on the uses side. However, were we to drop this assumption, then clearly those people who consumed proportionately large amounts of food would tend to bear relatively larger burdens. The total incidence of the food tax then depends on both the sources and uses sides. For example, a capitalist who eats a lot of food is worse off on both counts. On the other hand, a labourer who eats a lot

of food is better off from the point of view of the sources of income, but worse off on the uses side.

An income tax (*t*). As already noted, an income tax is equivalent to a set of taxes on capital and labour at the same rate. Since factor supplies are completely fixed (assumption 4), this tax cannot be shifted. It is borne in proportion to people's initial incomes. The intuition behind this result is similar to the analogous case in the partial equilibrium model; since the factors cannot "escape" the tax (by opting out of production), they bear the full burden.

A general tax on labour (*t_L*). A general tax on labour is a tax on labour in all its uses, in the production of both food and manufactures. As a result, there are no incentives to switch labour use between sectors. Further, the assumption of fixed factor supplies implies labour must bear the entire burden.

A partial factor tax (*t_{KM}*). When capital used in the manufacturing sector only is taxed, there are two initial effects:

1. *Output effect.* The price of manufactures tends to rise, which decreases the quantity demanded by consumers.
2. *Factor substitution effect.* As capital becomes more expensive in the manufacturing sector, producers there use less capital and more labour.

A flowchart for tracing the implications of these two effects is presented in Figure 17.11.

The output effect is described on the left side. As its name suggests, the output effect is a consequence of reductions in the production of manufactures. When the price of manufactures increases and less is demanded, capital and labour are released from manufacturing and must find employment in the production of food. If the manufacturing sector is labour intensive, then (relatively) large amounts of labour have to be absorbed in the food sector, and the relative price of capital increases. If, on the other hand, the manufacturing sector is capital intensive, the relative price of capital falls. Thus, the output effect is ambiguous with respect to the final effect on the relative prices of capital and labour.

This ambiguity is not present with the factor substitution effect, as depicted in the right-hand side of Figure 17.11. As long as substitution between capital and labour is possible, an increase in the price of capital induces manufacturers to use less capital and more labour, tending to decrease the demand for capital and its relative price.

Figure 17.11

Incidence of a Partial Factor Tax (t_{KM}) in a General Equilibrium Model

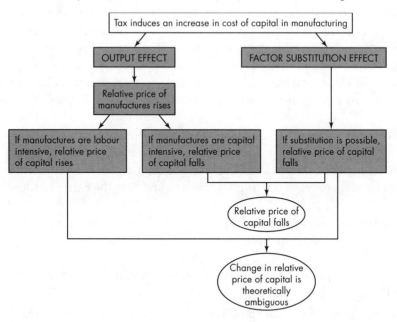

Putting the two effects together, we see that if manufacturing is capital intensive, both effects work in the same direction, and the relative price of capital must fall. But if the manufacturing sector is labour intensive, the final outcome is theoretically ambiguous. Even though the tax is levied on capital, it can make labour worse off! More generally, as long as factors are mobile between uses, a tax on a given factor in one sector ultimately affects the return to *both* factors in *both* sectors. Such insights cannot be obtained with the partial equilibrium models discussed earlier in this chapter.

Much of the applied research on incidence in general equilibrium models has focused on the corporation income tax. Such work assumes that the two sectors are "corporate" and "noncorporate," and that the corporation income tax is an ad valorem tax on capital only on its use in the corporate sector.[25] Given the theoretical ambiguity of the effect of a partial factor tax on the demand for capital, empirical work is required to find its incidence. Although

---

[25] Specifically, it is assumed the capital is financed by selling shares of stock as opposed to borrowing. As we see in Chapter 24, this is a somewhat controversial view.

different studies have reached different conclusions, in an open economy such as Canada's it is unlikely that the corporate income tax results in a fall in the after-tax return to capital owners. Capital can easily be moved to other locations, and the tax is likely to fall on workers who will have less capital to work with, or on consumers where producers are able to raise prices on goods not subject to international competition.[26]

Some Qualifications

Changes in the assumptions underlying the general equilibrium model can modify its implications for tax incidence in the following ways.

Differences in individuals' tastes. By assumption 5, all consumers have the same preferences for the two goods. When they do not, tax-induced changes in the distribution of income change aggregate spending decisions and hence relative prices and incomes. Consider a general tax on labour. As noted, in the model with fixed factor supplies, this is borne entirely by labourers. However, if labourers consume different commodities from capitalists, those commodities favoured by labourers face a decrease in demand. Resources are then allocated away from these commodities, and the factor used intensively in their production receives a lower return. If labourers tend to consume capital-intensive goods disproportionately, capital can end up bearing part of the burden of a general tax on labour.

Immobile factors. By assumption 2, resources are free to flow between sectors, seeking the highest rate of return possible. However, for institutional or technological reasons, some factors may be immobile. For example, if certain land is zoned for residential use, it cannot be used in manufacturing, no matter what the rate of return. Abandoning perfect mobility can dramatically affect the incidence implications of a tax. For example, earlier we showed that if factors are mobile, the incidence of a partial factor tax is ambiguous, depending on the outcome of several conflicting effects. If the factor is immobile, however, the incidence result is clear-cut: The taxed factor bears the whole burden. Intuitively, this is because the factor cannot "escape" taxation by migrating to the other sector. Note also that because the return to the taxed

---

[26] The most typical finding for a large economy such as the United States is that much of the tax is shifted to the owners of all capital, not just owners of capital in the corporate sector (U.S. Department of the Treasury, 1992: 147; Gravelle, 1995). The effect of the tax may be quite different in Canada where higher taxes may cause capital to relocate to the large U.S. market, causing less mobile factors to bear a significant part of the burden (McKenzie and Mintz, 1992).

immobile factor falls by just the amount of the tax, the prices of capital and labour in the untaxed sectors are unchanged, as is the price of the good in the taxed sector.

Variable factor supplies. By assumption 4, the total supplies of both factors are fixed. In the long run, however, the supplies of both capital and labour to the economy are variable. Allowing for growth can turn conclusions from the static model completely on their heads. Consider a general factor tax on capital. When the capital stock is fixed, this tax is borne entirely by the capital's owners. In the long run, however, less capital may be supplied due to the tax.[27] To the extent this occurs, the economy's capital–labour ratio decreases, and the return to labour falls. (The wage falls because labour has less capital with which to work, and hence is less productive, *ceteris paribus*.) Thus, labour can be made worse off as a result of a general tax on capital.

Because the amount of calendar time that must elapse before the long run is reached may be substantial, short-run effects should not be regarded as inconsequential. On the other hand, intelligent policy also requires consideration of the long-run consequences of taxation.

Applied Incidence Studies

In a recent study, Vermaeten et al. (1994) used the theory of tax incidence as a framework to estimate how the Canadian system of federal, provincial, and local taxation affected the distribution of income in 1988. It should by now be clear that all incidence results depend crucially on the underlying models. The income definition, the period considered (annual or lifetime), and shifting assumptions all affect the outcome. Vermaeten et al. examined tax burdens using several alternative models and compared the results. Using a "broad income" concept that included transfer payments and imputed income, and measuring incidence based on annual income, they employed the following set of shifting assumptions for their standard case:

- personal income taxes borne by the taxpayer with no shifting,
- corporate income taxes borne totally by owners of corporations,
- sales and excise taxes borne by consumers in proportion to consumption expenditures,
- payroll taxes borne by labour, whether paid by employer or employee, and in proportion to wages and salaries that are subject to tax,

---

[27] However, the supply of capital does not necessarily decrease. See Chapter 21.

- property taxes on land borne by landowners, and taxes on structures borne by consumers of services from structures (e.g., a retailer is assumed to pass any property tax on the structure on to consumers of goods or services).

Table 17.3 and Figure 17.12 show the results for the tax system as a whole, based on these assumptions. Figure 17.13 provides a view of the incidence of various taxes—personal income tax, corporate income tax, sales and excise taxes, payroll taxes, property taxes, and other taxes. Figure 17.14 gives the overall results for federal, provincial, and local taxes. Vermaeten et al. summarize their findings for 1988 as follows:

> The total Canadian tax system is slightly progressive up to the median broad income level, beyond which it is more or less proportional with a hint of progressivity for the richest one percent of families. This overall tax incidence pattern is composed of a federal tax system that is clearly progressive (especially up to the median income), a provincial tax system that is more or less proportional, and a local tax system that is regressive throughout the income scale.[28]

The incidence of the different types of taxes is illustrated in Figure 17.13. The personal income tax is progressive over all but the highest income levels, while commodity taxes, property taxes, and other taxes are regressive across the income spectrum. Payroll taxes, initially progressive, turn regressive around $50,000 in 1988. The corporate income tax adds a progressive element at the highest income levels. Again, we refer the reader to the "standard case" assumptions on which these results are based. Although there is considerable variation among taxes, Vermaeten et al. found the 1988 Canadian tax system to be roughly proportional over much of the income range. Hence, the tax system does not have much effect on the distribution of income.[29]

---

[28] In another paper, Vermaeten et al. (1995) examine changes in Canadian tax incidence for the period 1951 to 1988, comparing tax incidence for the years 1951, 1961, 1969, and 1988.

[29] Using a different income base and shifting assumptions, Ruggeri et al. (1994) find that the Canadian tax system provides significant redistribution of income and is more progressive than Vermaeten et al. conclude. For example, Ruggeri et al. do not include gifts and inheritances in income, and they adjust taxes shifted to consumption for indexing of government transfers to persons for inflation. Both of these procedures increase the progressivity of the tax system. Whalley (1984) reached the same conclusion in his detailed examination of Canadian tax incidence for 1972. Whalley also found that alternative assumptions lead to substantially different results in the distribution of the tax burden. For an interesting and careful analysis based on (and justifying) assumptions leading to progressive results for the U.S. system, see Browning and Johnson (1979).

Table 17.3

Effective Tax Rate by Broad Income Class—by Type of Tax, Government Level, and Type of Assumptions, 1988

INCOME LEVEL (IN 000'S)	1–10	10–20	20–30	30–40	40–50	50–60	60–70	70–80	80–90	90–100	100–150	150–300	300+	ALL
Type of Tax (standard assumptions used)														
Personal income tax	0.7	4.4	7.6	9.9	11.5	12.9	13.7	14.0	14.2	14.7	15.5	16.2	14.5	13.1
Corporate income tax	0.3	0.5	0.6	0.6	0.7	0.8	0.8	0.9	1.0	1.1	1.3	3.8	12.3	2.2
Commodity taxes	14.6	11.9	11.1	10.7	10.0	9.5	8.9	8.3	7.8	7.7	7.0	6.1	4.2	8.2
Payroll taxes	2.2	3.6	5.1	6.1	6.3	6.5	6.3	6.0	5.8	5.5	4.8	3.0	0.8	4.9
Property tax	7.0	5.6	4.6	4.2	3.8	3.5	3.3	3.2	3.1	2.9	2.8	2.5	2.4	3.3
Other taxes	5.3	3.2	2.4	2.0	1.8	1.7	1.5	1.4	1.4	1.3	1.2	1.1	1.2	1.6
Total taxes	30.1	29.2	31.4	33.5	34.2	34.9	34.5	33.8	33.2	33.3	32.6	32.7	35.3	33.4
Level of Government (standard assumptions used)														
Federal	8.7	10.9	13.8	15.8	16.6	17.4	17.5	17.3	17.2	17.3	17.2	17.8	19.0	16.8
Provincial	13.9	12.3	12.7	13.3	13.5	13.8	13.5	13.2	12.7	12.9	12.4	12.2	13.8	13.0
Local	7.5	5.9	4.9	4.4	4.1	3.7	3.5	3.3	3.3	3.1	3.0	2.6	2.5	3.5
Total taxes	30.1	29.2	31.4	33.5	34.2	34.9	34.5	33.8	33.2	33.3	32.6	32.7	35.3	33.4
Assumptions														
Standard	30.1	29.2	31.4	33.5	34.2	34.9	34.5	33.8	33.2	33.3	32.6	32.7	35.3	33.4
Progressive	19.6	22.1	25.3	27.4	28.6	29.3	29.5	29.1	28.6	29.2	29.4	32.7	42.3	30.2
Regressive	42.2	37.4	36.9	37.7	37.4	37.0	36.3	35.2	35.0	33.9	33.8	33.4	33.0	35.5

SOURCE: Reproduced with the permission of the Canadian Tax Foundation from Frank Vermaeten, W. Irwin Gillespie, and Arndt Vermaeten, "Tax Incidence in Canada," *Canadian Tax Journal* 42, no. 2 (1994): 414–15.

Figure 17.12

Effective Tax Rate, Total Taxes, by Broad Income, Canada, 1988

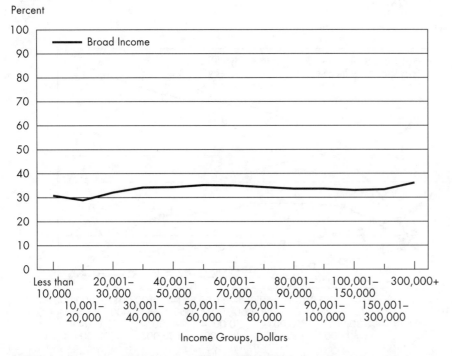

Income Groups, Dollars

SOURCE: Reproduced with the permission of the Canadian Tax Foundation from Frank Vermaeten, W. Irwin Gillespie, and Arndt Vermaeten, "Tax Incidence in Canada," *Canadian Tax Journal* 42, no. 2 (1994) at 372, figure 2.

Note that in *all* of their analyses, Vermaeten et al. assume there is no shifting of the personal income tax. This assumption is a common one and helps to simplify the problem considerably. But the theory of tax incidence suggests that it is questionable, especially in the long run.[30]

Vermaeten et al. demonstrate the extent to which a change in assumptions alters the outcome. For example, if capital flows freely between sectors, corporate capital will not bear the entire burden of the corporation income tax; where imperfect competition exists, corporations may pass on corporate income taxes to consumers through higher prices; union power may prevent employers from

[30] See, for example, Schaafsma (1992) for a discussion of the extent to which Canadian dentists shift personal income taxes onto dental patients in the form of higher dental fees.

Figure 17.13

Effective Tax Rate, by Revenue Source, Broad Income, Standard Case, Canada, 1988

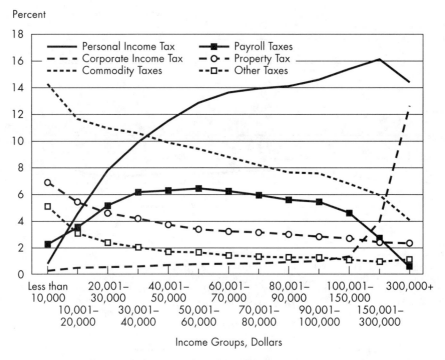

SOURCE: Reproduced with the permission of the Canadian Tax Foundation from Frank Vermaeten, W. Irwin Gillespie, and Arndt Vermaeten, "Tax Incidence in Canada," *Canadian Tax Journal* 42, no. 2 (1994) at 374, figure 4.

fully shifting payroll taxes onto employees; and where capital is less than perfectly mobile, capital owners may bear part of the tax on structures. Changing assumptions may lead to sharply different outcomes, and Figure 17.15 shows the results of "progressive" and "regressive" assumptions made by Vermaeten et al.

Another problem with placing too much reliance on an analysis such as the above is the use of "annual" incomes of families. Using some measure of lifetime income would be more appropriate and could change the results importantly. To see why, we begin by noting that a substantial amount of empirical research suggests people's consumption decisions are more closely related to some lifetime income measure than the value of income in any particular year. Just because a family's income is *temporarily* high or low in a year does not have that great an impact on consumption decisions (see Friedman, 1957).

Figure 17.14

Effective Tax Rate, by Level of Government, Broad Income, Canada, 1988

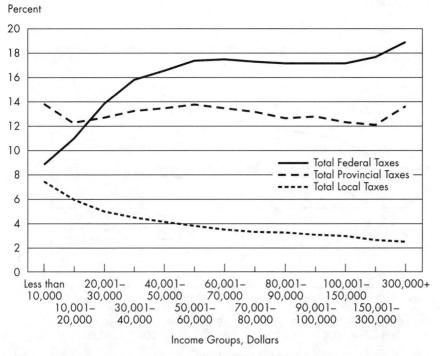

SOURCE: Reproduced with the permission of the Canadian Tax Foundation from Frank Vermaeten, W. Irwin Gillespie, and Arndt Vermaeten, "Tax Incidence in Canada," *Canadian Tax Journal* 42, no. 2 (1994) at 374, figure 3.

Assume that the consumption of commodity X is proportional to lifetime income. Assume further that the supply curve for X is horizontal, so that consumers bear the entire burden of any tax on X. Then a tax on X would be proportional with respect to lifetime income. However, in any particular year, some people have incomes that are temporarily higher than their permanent values and some lower. A person with a temporarily high income spends a relatively small proportion of his annual income on X because he does not increase his consumption of X due to the temporary increase in income. Similarly, a person with a temporarily low income devotes a relatively high proportion of her income to good X. In short, based on annual income, good X's budget share appears to fall with income, and a tax on X looks regressive. Consistent with this theory, several investigators have found that incidence results are sensitive to whether *lifetime* or *annual* measures are employed. For example, in their analysis of Canadian tax incidence, Davies, St-Hilaire, and

Figure 17.15

Effective Tax Rate, by Shifting Assumption Model, Broad Income, Canada, 1988

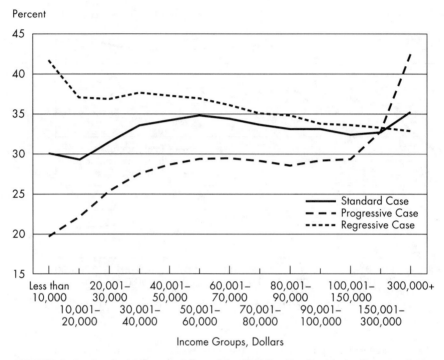

SOURCE: Reproduced with the permission of the Canadian Tax Foundation from Frank Vermaeten, W. Irwin Gillespie, and Arndt Vermaeten, "Tax Incidence in Canada," *Canadian Tax Journal* 42, no. 2 (1994) at 377, figure 6.

Whalley (1984: 643) found that sales and excise taxes were 27.2 percent of the annual incomes in the lowest income decile, and 8.5 percent in the highest decile—a decidedly regressive pattern. Using lifetime income, however, the regressivity is substantially reduced, with sales and excise taxes taking 15.0 percent of lifetime income in the lowest decile, and 12.4 percent in the highest decile. Table 17.4 illustrates the difference in results for all taxes, as well as the more striking results for sales and excise taxes.[31] We conclude that even though

---

[31] Recent evidence from the United States reinforces this conclusion. In his analysis of U.S. state and local sales taxes, Metcalf (1993) finds that sales taxes are 1.90 percent of the *annual* incomes of the lowest income decile, and 1.07 percent in the highest decile—a very regressive pattern. Using lifetime income, the pattern is reversed, with sales taxes equal to 1.03 percent of lifetime income in the lowest decile, and 1.74 percent in the highest decile.

Table 17.4

"Lifetime" Incidence versus "Annual" Incidence

	TAXES AS A PERCENT OF LIFETIME INCOME		TAXES AS A PERCENT OF ANNUAL INCOME	
INCOME DECILE	SALES & EXCISE TAXES	ALL TAXES	SALES & EXCISE TAXES	ALL TAXES
1	15.0	30.9	27.2	35.4
2	14.3	35.5	20.3	28.4
3	14.1	35.9	15.8	30.1
4	13.9	37.7	14.6	31.9
5	13.8	38.1	14.0	32.6
6	13.5	39.3	13.4	33.6
7	13.6	39.8	13.5	33.7
8	13.3	42.2	13.2	35.0
9	13.2	41.3	12.8	36.8
10	12.4	46.5	8.5	46.0

SOURCE: J. Davies, F. St-Hilaire, and J. Whalley, "Some Calculations of Lifetime Tax Incidence," *American Economic Review* 74, no. 4 (September 1984): 643. Reproduced by permission.

empirical work of the sort done by Vermaeten et al. is suggestive, the results must be viewed with caution (see Davies, 1992).

The foregoing discussion has focused entirely on the incidence of taxes. It has ignored the incidence of government expenditures. The negative effect of taxes on those with low incomes may be much more than offset by the positive effect of government transfer payments and benefits from other government programs. The reverse may be true for those with high incomes.[32]

CONCLUSIONS

We began this chapter with an innocent question: Who bears the burden of a tax? It led us to an analysis of the sometimes complicated relationships among various markets. We have seen that price changes are the key to finding the burden of a tax, but that price changes depend on a lot of things: market structure, elasticities of supply and demand, movements of factors of production, and so on. At this stage, an obvious question is: What do we really know?

---

[32] Studies of the overall incidence of tax and expenditure systems are complex and quite rare. One Canadian study found the combined incidence of government taxes and expenditures to be progressive (see Gillespie, 1976).

For taxes that may reasonably be analyzed in isolation, the answer is, "Quite a bit." To do a partial equilibrium incidence analysis, one needs only to know the market structure and the shapes of the supply and demand curves. In cases other than a clear-cut monopoly, the competitive market paradigm has proved to be a sensible choice of market structure. Estimates of supply and demand curves can be obtained using the empirical methods discussed in Chapter 3. Incidence analysis is on firm ground.

Even in general equilibrium models, incidence analysis is straightforward for a tax on an immobile factor—the incidence is entirely on the taxed factor. More generally, though, if a tax affects many markets, incidence depends on the reactions of numerous supply and demand curves for goods and inputs. The answers are correspondingly less clear.

Unfortunately, it seems that many important taxes such as the corporate tax fall into the last category. Why is this? It may be for the very reason that the incidence is hard to find. (What are the political chances of a tax that clearly hurts some important group in the population?) Complicated taxes may actually be simpler for a politician because no one is sure who actually ends up paying them.

In any case, the models in this chapter tell us exactly what information is needed to understand the incidence even of very complex taxes. To the extent that this information is currently unavailable, the models serve as a measure of our ignorance. This is not altogether undesirable. As St. Jerome noted, "It is worse still to be ignorant of your ignorance."

SUMMARY

- Statutory incidence refers to the legal liability for a tax, while economic incidence shows the actual sacrifice of income due to the tax. Knowledge of the legal incidence usually tells us little about economic incidence.

- Economic incidence is determined by the way price changes when a tax is imposed. The incidence of a tax ultimately falls on individuals via both their sources and uses of income.

- Depending on the policy being considered, it may be appropriate to examine balanced budget, differential, or absolute incidence.

- In partial equilibrium competitive models, tax incidence depends on the elasticities of supply and demand. The same general approach can be used to study incidence in a monopolized market. For oligopoly, however, there is no single accepted framework for tax analysis.

- Due to capitalization, the burden of future taxes may be borne by current owners of an inelastically supplied durable commodity such as land.

- General equilibrium incidence analysis is often conducted using a two-sector, two-factor model. This framework allows for nine possible taxes. Certain combinations of these taxes are equivalent to others.

- Taxing a single factor in its use only in a particular sector changes relative factor prices and, hence, the distribution of income. The particular outcome depends on factor intensities, ease of substitution in production, mobility of factors, and elasticities of demand for outputs.

- Finally, a cautionary note: It is essential to keep in mind that income distribution is affected more by government expenditures and regulations than by taxation. The incidence of these activities, as well as taxation, must be examined to gain a fuller understanding of the government's impact on income distribution.

DISCUSSION QUESTIONS

1. In the province of Alberta, the tax on hotel rooms is 5 percent. Supporters of this tax argue that the tax benefits the province because its victims are largely out-of-province tourists. Use the theory of tax incidence to analyze this claim.

2. Higher payroll taxes may be required to finance the Canada Pension Plan as the population ages. If employers are asked to pay all of any such increase, rather than sharing the increase equally between employers and employees, how would this affect wages and employment? Would businesses likely end up paying for the increase in CPP premiums?

3. For commodity X, average cost is equal to marginal cost at every level of output. Assuming that the market for X is competitive, analyze the effects when a unit tax of u dollars is imposed. Now analyze the effects of the same tax assuming that the market for X is a monopoly. Discuss the income differences.

4. Assume that the capital–labour ratios are identical in all sectors of the economy. What determines the incidence of a tax on the output of any single sector?

5. Suppose that the demand for cigarettes in a hypothetical country is given by $Q_c^D = 2,000 - 200\, P_c$, where Q_c^D is the number of packs demanded and P_c is the price per pack. The supply of cigarettes is $Q_c^S = P_c \times 200$.

   a. Find the price and quantity of cigarettes, assuming the market is competitive.
   b. In an effort to reduce smoking, the government levies a tax of $2 per pack. Compute the quantity of cigarettes after the tax, the price paid by

consumers, and the price received by producers. How much revenue does the tax raise for the government?

REFERENCES

Baumol, William J., and Alan S. Blinder. *Economic Principles and Policy*, 2nd ed. New York: Harcourt Brace Jovanovich, 1982.

Besley, Timothy. "Commodity Taxation and Imperfect Competition: A Note on the Effects of Entry." *Journal of Public Economics* 40, no. 3 (December 1989): 359–68.

Browning, E.K., and W.R. Johnson. *The Distribution of the Tax Burden*. Washington, DC: American Enterprise Institute for Public Policy Research, 1979.

Davies, James B. "Tax Incidence: Annual and Lifetime Perspectives in the United States and Canada," in *Canada–U.S. Tax Comparisons*, ed. John B. Shoven and John Whalley. Chicago: University of Chicago Press, 1992, pp. 151–88.

Davies, J., F. St-Hilaire, and J. Whalley. "Some Calculations of Lifetime Tax Incidence." *American Economic Review* 74, no. 4 (September 1984).

Devarajan, S., D. Fullerton, and R. Musgrave. "Estimating the Distribution of Tax Burdens: A Comparison of Alternative Approaches." *Journal of Public Economics* 13 (1980): 155–82.

Friedman, Milton. *A Theory of the Consumption Function*. Princeton, NJ: Princeton University Press, 1957.

Gillespie, W. Irwin. "On the Redistribution of Income in Canada." *Canadian Tax Journal* 24, no. 4 (July–August 1976): 419–50.

Gillis, Malcolm, and Charles E. McLure. "Excess Profits Taxation: Post-Mortem on the Mexican Experience." *National Tax Journal* 32, no. 4 (December 1979): 501–11.

Gravelle, Jane G. "The Corporate Income Tax: Economic Issues and Policy Options." *National Tax Journal* 48, no. 2 (1995): 267–77.

Grossman, Michael, J.L. Sindelar, J. Mullahy, and R. Anderson. "Policy Watch: Alcohol and Cigarette Taxes." *Journal of Economic Perspectives* 7, no. 4 (Fall 1993): 211–22.

Harberger, Arnold C. "The Incidence of the Corporation Income Tax," in *Taxation and Welfare*, ed. Arnold C. Harberger. Boston: Little, Brown, 1974, pp. 135–62.

Harris, Jeffrey E. "The 1983 Increase in the Federal Cigarette Excise Tax," in *Tax Policy and the Economy, Volume 1*, ed. Lawrence H. Summers. Cambridge, MA: MIT Press, 1987, pp. 87–111.

McKenzie, Kenneth, and Jack Mintz. "Tax Effects on the Cost of Capital," in *Canada–U.S. Tax Comparisons*, ed. John B. Shoven and John Whalley. Chicago: University of Chicago Press, 1992.

Metcalf, Gilbert E. "The Life-time Incidence of State and Local Taxes: Measuring Changes during the 1980s." Working Paper No. 4252. Cambridge, MA: National Bureau of Economic Research, January 1993.

Phipps, Shelley A. "Does Unemployment Insurance Increase Unemployment?" *Canadian Business Economics* 1, no. 3 (Spring 1993): 37–50.

Ruggeri, G.C., D. Van Wart, and R. Howard. "The Redistributional Impact of Taxation in Canada." *Canadian Tax Journal* 42, no. 2 (1994): 417–51.

Schaafsma, Joseph. "Forward Shifting of the Personal Income Tax by Self-Employed Canadian Dentists." *Canadian Journal of Economics* 25, no. 3 (August 1992): 636–51.

U.S. Department of the Treasury. *Integration of the Individual and Corporate Tax Systems.* Washington, DC: U.S. Government Printing Office, 1992.

Vermaeten, Arndt, W. Irwin Gillespie, and Frank Vermaeten. "Who Paid the Taxes in Canada, 1951–1988?" *Canadian Public Policy* 21, no. 3 (September 1995): 317–43.

Vermaeten, Frank, W. Irwin Gillespie, and Arndt Vermaeten. "Tax Incidence in Canada." *Canadian Tax Journal* 42, no. 2 (1994): 348–416.

Whalley, John. "Regression or Progression: The Taxing Question of Incidence Analysis." *Canadian Journal of Economics* 17, no. 4 (November 1984): 654–82.

Chapter 18

Taxation and Efficiency

Waste always makes me angry.

–Rhett Butler in *Gone With the Wind*

*T*axes impose a cost on the taxpayer. It is tempting to view the cost as simply the amount of money that he or she hands over to the tax collector. However, an example indicates that this is just part of the story.

Consider Richard Dove, a citizen who typically consumes ten ice cream cones each week, at a price of 80 cents per cone. The government levies a 25 percent tax on his consumption of ice cream cones, so now Dove faces a price of $1.[1] In response to the price hike, Dove reduces his ice cream cone consumption to zero, and he spends the $8 per week on other goods and services. Obviously, because Dove consumes no ice cream cones, the ice cream tax yields zero revenue. Do we want to say that Dove is unaffected by the tax? The answer is no. Dove is worse off because the tax has induced him to consume a less desirable bundle of goods than previously. We know that the after-tax bundle is less desirable because, before tax, Dove had the option of consuming no ice cream cones. Since he chose to buy ten cones weekly, this must have been preferred to spending the money on other items. Thus, despite the fact that the tax raised zero revenue, it made Dove worse off.

---

[1] As emphasized in Chapter 17, the price paid by the consumer generally does not rise by the full amount of the tax. This assumption, which is correct if the supply curve is horizontal, is made here only for convenience.

This example is a bit extreme. Normally, we expect that an increase in price diminishes the quantity demanded but does not drive it all the way to zero. Nevertheless, the basic result holds: Because a tax distorts economic decisions, it brings about an **excess burden**—a loss of welfare above and beyond the tax revenues collected. Excess burden is sometimes referred to as *welfare cost* or *deadweight loss*. In this chapter we discuss the theory and measurement of excess burden, and explain why it is an important concept for evaluating actual tax systems.

EXCESS BURDEN

Ruth has a fixed income of I dollars, which she spends on only two commodities: barley and corn. The price per pound of barley is P_b and the price per pound of corn is P_c. There are no taxes or "distortions" such as externalities or monopoly in the economy, so the prices of the goods reflect their social marginal costs. For convenience, these social marginal costs are assumed to be constant with respect to output. In Figure 18.1, Ruth's consumption of barley is measured on the horizontal axis and her consumption of corn on the vertical. Her budget constraint is the line AD, which has slope $-P_b/P_c$ and horizontal intercept I/P_b. Assuming Ruth wants to maximize her utility, she chooses a point like E_1 on indifference curve i, where she consumes B_1 kilograms of barley and C_1 kilograms of corn.

Figure 18.1

Effect of a Tax on the Budget Constraint

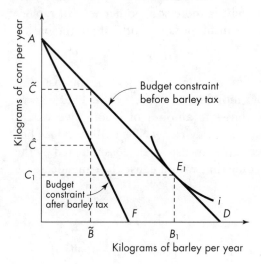

Now suppose the government levies a tax at a percentage rate of *tb* on barley so the price Ruth faces becomes $(1 + t_b)P_b$. (The before-tax price is unchanged because of our assumption of constant marginal social costs.) Imposition of the tax changes Ruth's budget constraint. It now has a slope of $-[(1 + t_b)P_b/P_c]$ and horizontal intercept $I/[(1 + t_b)P_b]$. This is represented in Figure 18.1 as line *AF*. (Because the price of corn is still P_c, lines *AF* and *AD* have the same vertical intercept.)

Note that for any given consumption level of barley, the vertical distance between *AD* and *AF* shows Ruth's tax payments measured in corn. To see this, consider an arbitrary quantity of barley *B* on the horizontal axis. Before the tax was imposed, Ruth could have both $\tilde{B}$ kilograms of barley and $\tilde{C}$ kilograms of corn. After the tax, however, if she consumed $\tilde{B}$ kilograms of barley, the most corn she could afford would be $\hat{C}$ kilograms. The difference (distance) between $\tilde{C}$ and $\hat{C}$ must therefore represent the amount of tax collected by the government measured in kilograms of corn. If we choose, we can convert tax receipts to dollars by multiplying the distance $\tilde{C}\hat{C}$ by the price per kilogram of corn, P_c. For convenience, we can choose to measure corn in units such that $P_c = 1$. In this case, the distance $\tilde{C}\hat{C}$ measures tax receipts in corn *or* dollars.

So far, we have not indicated which point Ruth chooses on her new budget constraint, *AF*. Figure 18.2 shows that her most preferred bundle is at E_2 on indifference curve *ii*, where her consumption of barley is B_2, her consumption of corn is C_2, and her tax bill is the associated vertical distance between *AD* and *AF*, GE_2. Clearly, Ruth is worse off at E_2 than she was at E_1. However, *any* tax would have put her on a lower indifference curve.[2] The important question is whether the barley tax inflicts on Ruth a greater utility loss than is necessary to raise revenue GE_2. Alternatively, is there some other way of raising revenue GE_2 that would cause a smaller utility loss to Ruth? If so, the barley tax has an excess burden.

To investigate this issue, we need to find a dollar equivalent of the loss that Ruth suffers by having to move from indifference curve *i* to *ii*. One way to measure this is the **equivalent variation**—the amount of income we would have to take away from Ruth (before the barley tax was levied) to induce her to move from *i* to *ii*. The equivalent variation measures the loss inflicted by the tax as the size of the reduction in income that would cause the same decrease in utility as the tax.

---

[2] This ignores benefits that might be obtained from the expenditures financed by the tax.

Figure 18.2

Effect of a Tax on the Consumption Bundle

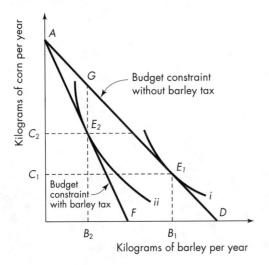

To depict the equivalent variation graphically, recall that taking away income from an individual is represented by a parallel movement inward of her budget line. Hence, to find the equivalent variation, all we have to do is shift *AD* inward, until it is tangent to indifference curve *ii*. The amount by which we have to shift *AD* is the equivalent variation. In Figure 18.3, budget line *HI* is parallel to *AD* and tangent to indifference curve *ii*. Hence, the vertical distance between *AD* and *HI*, ME_3, is the equivalent variation. Ruth is indifferent between losing ME_3 dollars and facing the barley tax.

Note that the equivalent variation ME_3 exceeds the barley tax revenues of GE_2. To see why, just observe that ME_3 equals *GN*, because both measure the distance between the parallel lines *AD* and *HI*. Hence, ME_3 exceeds GE_2 by distance E_2N. This is really quite a remarkable result. It means that the barley tax makes Ruth worse off by an amount that actually exceeds the revenues it generates. In Figure 18.3, the amount by which the loss in welfare (measured by the equivalent variation) exceeds the taxes collected—the excess burden—is distance E_2N.

Does *every* tax entail an excess burden? Define a **lump-sum tax** as a certain amount that must be paid regardless of the taxpayer's behaviour. If the government levies a $100 lump-sum tax on Ruth, there is nothing she can do to avoid paying the $100, other than to leave the country or die. In contrast, the

Figure 18.3

Excess Burden of the Barley Tax

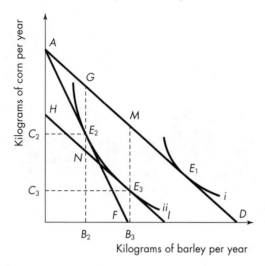

barley tax is not a lump-sum tax, because the revenue yield depends on Ruth's barley consumption.

Let us analyze a lump-sum tax that leaves Ruth as well off as the barley tax. To begin, we must sketch the associated budget line. It must have two characteristics. First, it must be parallel to AD. (Because a lump-sum tax simply takes away money from Ruth, it does not change the relative prices of barley and corn; two budget lines embodying the same price ratio must be parallel.) Second, because of the stipulation that Ruth attain the same utility level as under the barley tax, the budget line must be tangent to indifference curve ii.

Budget line HI in Figure 18.3, which is tangent to indifference curve ii at point E_3, satisfies both these criteria. If confronted with this budget line, Ruth would consume B_3 kilograms of barley and C_3 kilograms of corn. The revenue yield of the lump-sum tax is the vertical distance between E_3 and the before-tax budget constraint, or distance ME_3. But we showed earlier that ME_3 is also the equivalent variation of the move from indifference curve i to ii. This comes as no surprise, since a lump-sum tax is just a parallel shift of the budget line. Because the revenue yield of a lump-sum tax equals its equivalent variation, *a lump-sum tax has no excess burden.*

In short, a lump-sum tax that leaves Ruth on the *same indifference curve* as the barley tax generates more revenue for the government. Alternatively, if we

compared a lump-sum tax and a barley tax that raised the *same revenue*, the lump-sum tax would leave Ruth on a higher indifference curve.

The skeptical reader may suspect that this result is merely an artifact of the particular way the indifference curves are drawn in Figure 18.3. This is not the case. It can be shown that as long as the indifference curves have the usual shape, a tax that changes relative prices generates an excess burden.[3] Alternatively, a tax that changes relative prices is inefficient in the sense that it lowers individual utility more than is necessary to raise a given amount of revenue.

EXCESS BURDEN: QUESTIONS AND ANSWERS

The previous section's discussion of excess burden raises some important questions.

If lump-sum taxes are so efficient, why aren't they widely used? Lump-sum taxation is an unattractive policy tool for several reasons. Suppose the government announced that every person's tax liability was $2,000 per year. This is a lump-sum tax, but most people would consider it unfair for everyone to pay the same tax regardless of their economic circumstances. In 1990, the government of British Prime Minister Margaret Thatcher implemented a tax that in some ways resembled a lump-sum tax. The property tax that had financed local government was replaced by a head tax; in each local jurisdiction the amount depended on that jurisdiction's per capita revenue needs. The tax was lump sum in the sense that a person's tax liability did not vary with the amount of income earned or property owned; it did vary, however, with a person's choice of where to live. The perceived unfairness of that tax was one of the factors that led to Mrs. Thatcher's downfall in 1990, and it was repealed in 1991 by her successor, John Major.

As a way of producing more equitable results, one might consider making people pay different lump-sum taxes based on their incomes. A rich person might be required to pay $20,000 annually, independent of his or her economic decisions, while a poor person would pay only $500. The problem with this proposal is that people entering the work force would soon realize that their eventual tax burden depended on their incomes. They would then adjust their work and savings decisions accordingly. In short, because the amount of income individuals earn is at least in part under their control, the income-based tax is not a lump-sum tax.

---

[3] For a proof see Diamond and McFadden (1974).

Ultimately, to achieve an equitable system of lump-sum taxes, it would be necessary to base the tax on some underlying "ability" characteristic that measured individuals' *potential* to earn income. In this way, high- and low-potential people could be taxed differently. Because the base is potential, an individual's tax burden would not depend on behaviour. Even if such an ability measure existed, however, it could not possibly be observed by the taxing authority. Thus, individual lump-sum taxes are best viewed as standards of efficiency, but not as major policy options in a modern economy.

Are there any results from welfare economics that would help us understand why excess burdens arise? Recall from Chapter 4 that a necessary condition for a Pareto efficient allocation of resources is that the marginal rate of substitution of barley for corn in consumption (MRS_{bc}) equals the marginal rate of transformation of barley for corn in production (MRT_{bc}). Under the barley tax, consumers face a price of barley of $(1 + t_b)P_b$. Therefore, they set

$$MRS_{bc} = [(1 + t_b)P_b]/P_c. \qquad (18.1)$$

Equation (18.1) is the algebraic representation of the equilibrium point E_2 in Figure 18.3.

Producers make their decisions by setting the marginal rate of transformation equal to the ratio of the prices *they receive*. Even though Ruth pays $(1 + t_b)P_b$ per kilogram of barley, the barley producers receive only P_b—the difference goes to the tax collector. Hence, profit-maximizing producers set

$$MRT_{bc} = P_b/P_c. \qquad (18.2)$$

Clearly, as long as t_b is not zero, MRS_{bc} exceeds MRT_{bc}, and the necessary condition for an efficient allocation of resources is violated.

Intuitively, when MRS_{bc} is greater than MRT_{bc}, the marginal utility of substituting barley consumption for corn consumption exceeds the change in production costs necessary to do so. Thus, utility would be raised if such an adjustment were made. However, in the presence of the barley tax there is no *financial* incentive to do so. The excess burden is just a measure of the utility loss. The loss arises because the barley tax creates a wedge between what the consumer pays and what the producer receives. In contrast, under a lump-sum tax, the price ratios faced by consumers and producers are equal. There is no wedge, so the necessary conditions for Pareto efficiency are satisfied.

Does an income tax entail an excess burden? Figure 18.3 showed the imposition of a lump-sum tax as a downward parallel movement from *AD* to *HI*. This movement could just as well have arisen via a tax that took some proportion of Ruth's income. Like the lump-sum tax, an income reduction moves the intercepts of the budget constraint closer to the origin but leaves its slope unchanged. Perhaps, then, lump-sum taxation and income taxation are equivalent. In fact, if income were fixed, an income tax *would* be a lump-sum tax. However, when people's choices affect their incomes, an income tax is *not* generally equivalent to a lump-sum tax.

Think of Ruth as consuming *three* commodities, barley, corn, and leisure time, *l*. Ruth gives up leisure (supplies labour) to earn income that she spends on barley and corn. In the production sector, Ruth's leisure is an input to the production of the two goods. The rate at which her leisure time can be transformed into barley is MRT_{lb} and into corn MRT_{lc}. Just as a utility-maximizing individual sets the marginal rate of substitution between two commodities equal to their price ratio, the *MRS* between leisure and a given commodity is set equal to the ratio of the wage (the price of leisure) and the price of that commodity.

Again appealing to the theory of welfare economics, the necessary conditions for a Pareto efficient allocation of resources in this three-commodity case are

$$MRS_{lb} = MRT_{lb}$$

$$MRS_{lc} = MRT_{lc}$$

$$MRS_{bc} = MRT_{bc}$$

A proportional income tax, which is equivalent to a tax at the same rate on barley and corn, leaves the third equality unchanged, because producers and consumers still face the same *relative* prices for barley and corn. However, it introduces a tax wedge in the first two conditions. To see why, suppose that Ruth's employer pays her a before-tax wage of w, and the income tax rate is t. Ruth's decisions depend on her after-tax wage, $(1 - t)w$. Hence, she sets $MRS_{lb} = (1 - t)w/P_b$. On the other hand, the producer's decisions are based on the wage rate he or she pays, the before-tax wage, w. Hence, the producer sets $MRT_{lb} = w/P_b$. Consequently, $MRS_{lb} \neq MRT_{lb}$. Similarly, $MRS_{lc} \neq MRT_{lc}$. In contrast, a lump-sum tax leaves all three equalities intact. Thus, income and lump-sum taxation are generally not equivalent.

The fact that the income tax breaks up two equalities while taxes on barley and corn at different rates break up all three is in itself irrelevant for determining which system is more efficient. Once *any* of the equalities fails to hold, a loss of efficiency results, and the sizes of the welfare losses cannot be compared merely by counting wedges. Rather, the excess burdens associated with each tax regime must be computed and then compared. There is no presumption that income taxation is more efficient than a system of commodity taxes at different rates—differential commodity taxation. It *may* be true, but this is an empirical question that cannot be answered on the basis of theory alone.[4]

If the demand for a commodity does not change when it is taxed, does this mean that there is no excess burden? The intuition behind excess burden is that it results from distorted decisions. If there is no change in the demand for the good being taxed, one might conclude there is no excess burden. This conjecture is examined in Figure 18.4. Naomi, the individual under consideration, begins with the same income as Ruth and faces the same prices and taxes. Hence, her initial budget constraint is *AD*, and after the barley tax it is *AF*. However, unlike Ruth, Naomi does not change her barley consumption after the barley tax; that is, $B_1 = B_2$. The barley tax revenues are E_1E_2. Is there an excess burden? The equivalent variation of the barley tax is RE_3. This exceeds

Figure 18.4

Excess Burden of a Tax on a Commodity Whose Ordinary Demand Curve is Perfectly Inelastic

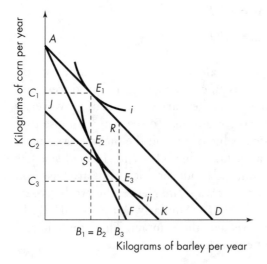

[4] Income taxation is necessarily more efficient than differential commodity taxation only when the underlying structure of consumer preferences has a very particular property. See Sandmo (1976).

the barley tax revenues of E_1E_2 by E_2S. Hence, even though Naomi's barley consumption is unchanged by the barley tax, it still creates an excess burden of E_2S.

The explanation of this paradox begins with the observation that even though Naomi's barley consumption doesn't change, her corn consumption does (from C_1 to C_2). When the barley tax changes barley's relative price, the marginal rate of substitution is affected, and the composition of the commodity *bundle* is distorted.

A more rigorous explanation requires that we distinguish between two types of responses to the barley tax. The movement from E_1 to E_2 is the **uncompensated response**. It shows how consumption changes because of the tax and incorporates effects due to both losing income and the tax-induced change in relative prices. Now, we can imagine decomposing the move from E_1 to E_2 into a move from E_1 to E_3, and then from E_3 to E_2. The movement from E_1 to E_3 shows the effect on consumption of a lump-sum tax. This change, called the **income effect**, is due solely to the loss of income because relative prices are unaffected. In effect, then, the movement from E_3 to E_2 is strictly due to the change in relative prices. It is generated by giving Naomi enough income to remain on indifference curve *ii* even as barley's price rises due to the tax. Because Naomi is being compensated for the rising price of barley with additional income, the movement from E_3 to E_2 is called the **compensated response**, also sometimes referred to as the **substitution effect**.

The compensated response is the important one for calculating excess burden. Why? By construction, the computation of excess burden involves comparison of tax collections at points E_2 and E_3 on indifference curve *ii*. But the movement from E_3 to E_2 along indifference curve *ii* is precisely the compensated response. Note also that it is only in moving from E_3 to E_2 that the marginal rate of substitution is affected. As shown earlier, this change violates the necessary conditions for a Pareto efficient allocation of commodities.

An ordinary demand curve depicts the uncompensated change in the quantity of a commodity demanded when price changes. A **compensated demand curve** shows how the quantity demanded changes when price changes *and* simultaneously income is compensated so that the individual's commodity bundle stays on the same indifference curve. A way of summarizing this discussion is to say that excess burden depends on movements along the compensated rather than the ordinary demand curve.

Although these observations may seem like theoretical nit-picking, they are actually quite important. In many policy discussions, attention is focused on whether or not a given tax influences observed behaviour, with the assumption that if it does not, no serious efficiency problem is present. For example, some would argue that if hours of work do not change when an income tax is imposed, then the tax has no adverse efficiency consequences. We have shown that such a notion is fallacious. A substantial excess burden may be incurred even if the uncompensated response of the taxed commodity is zero.

EXCESS BURDEN MEASUREMENT WITH DEMAND CURVES

The concept of excess burden can be reinterpreted using (compensated) demand curves. This interpretation relies heavily on the notion of consumer surplus—the difference between what people would be *willing* to pay for a commodity and the amount they actually have to pay. As shown in the appendix to Chapter 4, consumer surplus is measured by the area between the demand curve and the horizontal line at the market price. Assume that the compensated demand curve for barley can be represented by the straight line D_b in Figure 18.5. For convenience, we continue to assume that the social marginal cost of barley is constant at P_b, so that the supply curve is the horizontal line marked S_b.[5] In equilibrium, q_1 kilograms of barley are consumed. Consumer surplus, the area between the price and the demand curve, is *aih*.

Figure 18.5

Excess Burden of a Commodity Tax

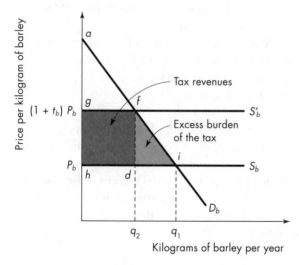

---

[5] The analysis is easily generalized to the case when the supply curve slopes upward. See footnote 6.

Again suppose that a tax at percentage rate t_b is levied on barley, so the new price, $(1 + t_b)P_b$, is associated with supply curve S'_b. Supply and demand now intersect at output q_2. Observe the following characteristics of the new equilibrium:

1. Consumer surplus falls to the area between the demand curve and S'_b, *agf*.

2. The revenue yield of the barley tax is rectangle *gfdh*. This is because tax revenues are equal to the product of the number of units purchased (*hd*) and the tax paid on each unit: $(1 + t_b)P_b - P_b = gh$. But *hd* and *gh* are just the base and height, respectively, of rectangle *gfdh*, and hence their product is its area.

3. The sum of post-tax consumer surplus and tax revenues collected (area *hafd*) is less than the original consumer surplus (*ahi*) by area *fid*. In effect, even if we returned the tax revenues to barley consumers as a lump sum, they would still be worse off by triangle *fid*. The triangle, then, is the excess burden of the tax.

This analysis provides a convenient framework for computing an actual dollar measure of excess burden. The area of triangle *fid* is one-half the product of its base (the tax-induced change in the quantity of barley) and height (the tax per kilogram). Some simple algebra leads to the conclusion that this product, which estimates the excess burden (*EB*), can be written

$$EB = 1/2\,\eta^c P_b q_1 t_b^2 \qquad (18.3)$$

where η^c is the absolute value of the compensated price elasticity of demand for barley.[6] (A proof is provided in Appendix A at the end of this chapter.)

A high (absolute) value of η^c indicates that the compensated quantity demanded is quite sensitive to changes in price. Thus, the presence of η^c in Equation (18.3) makes intuitive sense—the more the tax distorts the (compensated) consump-

---

[6] The formula is an approximation that holds strictly only for an infinitesimally small tax levied in the absence of any other distortions. When the supply curve is upward sloping rather than horizontal, the excess-burden triangle contains some producer surplus as well as consumer surplus. The formula for excess burden then depends on the elasticity of supply as well as the elasticity of demand. Bishop (1968) shows that in this case, the excess burden is

$$EB = [1/2\ P_b q t_b^2]/[(1/\eta^c)+(1/\varepsilon^c)]$$

where ε^c is the compensated elasticity of supply. Note that as ε^c approaches infinity, this expression collapses to Equation (18.3). This is because an ε^c of infinity corresponds to a horizontal supply curve as in Figure 18.5.

tion decision, the higher the excess burden. $P_b \times q_1$ is the total revenue expended on barley initially. Its inclusion in the formula shows that the greater the initial expenditure on the taxed commodity, the greater the excess burden.

Finally, the presence of $t_b{}^2$ suggests that as the tax rate increases, excess burden goes up with its square. Doubling a tax quadruples its excess burden, other things being the same. Because excess burden increases with the square of the tax rate, the *marginal* excess burden from raising one more dollar of revenue exceeds the *average* excess burden. That is, the incremental excess burden of raising one *more* dollar of revenue exceeds the ratio of total excess burden to total revenues. This fact has important implications for cost–benefit analysis. Suppose, for example, that the average excess burden per dollar of tax revenue is 20 cents, but the marginal excess burden (MEB) per additional dollar of tax revenue is 40 cents. (These may be plausible figures for Canada. For personal income taxes, Dahlby (1994) found the marginal excess burden per additional dollar to range from 40 cents in Alberta to 99 cents in Quebec, and Fortin and Lacroix (1994) estimated the marginal excess burden for Quebec to be between 39 and 53 cents.)[7] The social cost of each dollar raised for a given public project is the dollar *plus* the incremental excess burden of 40 cents. Thus, a public project must produce marginal benefits of more than $1.40 per dollar of explicit cost if it is to improve welfare.

Concern over excess burden was one major reason that the federal government replaced the manufacturers' sales tax (MST) with the GST in 1991. Many goods and services were excluded from the MST tax base, resulting in a narrow base and high tax rates. Whalley and Fretz (1990) estimated the MEB to be 35 cents for the MST, while that for a more broadly based sales tax such as the GST was 7.3 cents.[8]

Pre-existing Distortions

This analysis has assumed no distortions in the economy other than the tax under consideration. In reality, when a new tax is introduced, there are already other distortions: monopolies, externalities, and pre-existing taxes. This complicates the analysis of excess burden.

Suppose that consumers regard gin and rum as substitutes. Suppose further that rum is currently being taxed, creating an excess burden "triangle" like

---

[7] Calculations by Jorgenson and Yun (1991) for the U.S. tax system supported average and marginal excess burdens of 18 cents and 39 cents.

[8] Whalley and Fretz (1990: 49) estimated that an efficiency gain of $849 million (1980 dollar), or $30 per capita, would accompany the replacement of the MST by a broadly based sales tax.

that in Figure 18.5. Now the government decides to impose a tax on gin. What is the excess burden of the gin tax? In the gin market, the gin tax creates a wedge between what gin consumers pay and gin producers receive. As usual, this creates an excess burden. But the story is not over. If gin and rum are substitutes, the rise in the consumers' price of gin induced by the gin tax increases the demand for rum. Consequently, the quantity of rum demanded increases. Now, because rum was taxed under the status quo, "too little" of it was being consumed. The increase in rum consumption induced by the gin tax helps move rum consumption back toward its efficient level. There is thus an efficiency gain in the rum market that helps offset the excess burden imposed in the gin market. In theory, the gin tax could actually lower the overall excess burden. (A graphical demonstration of this phenomenon is contained in Appendix B at the end of this chapter.)

We have shown, then, that the efficiency impact of a given tax or subsidy cannot be considered in isolation. To the extent that there are other markets with distortions, and the goods in these markets are related (either substitutes or complements), then the overall efficiency impact depends on what is going on in all the markets. To compute the overall efficiency impact of a set of taxes and subsidies, it is generally incorrect to calculate separately the excess burdens in each market and then add them up. The aggregate efficiency loss is not equal to the "sum of its parts."

This result can be quite discomfiting because, strictly speaking, it means that *every* market in the economy must be studied to assess the efficiency implications of *any* tax or subsidy. In most cases, practitioners simply assume that the amount of interrelatedness between the market of their concern and other markets is sufficiently small that cross-effects can safely be ignored.[9] Although this is clearly a convenient assumption, its reasonableness must be evaluated in each particular case.

The Excess Burden of a Subsidy

Commodity subsidies are important components of the fiscal systems of many countries. In effect, a subsidy is just a negative tax, and like a tax, it is associated with an excess burden. To illustrate the calculation of the excess burden of a subsidy, we consider the subsidy for owner-occupied housing provided by the federal government via certain provisions of the personal income tax. (See Chapter 21 for details of the law.)

[9] For an exception, see Fullerton and Rogers (1993).

Assume that the demand for owner-occupied housing services is the straight line D_h in Figure 18.6. Supply is horizontal at price P_h, which measures the marginal social cost of producing housing services. Initially, the equilibrium quantity is h_1. Now suppose that the government provides a subsidy of s percent to housing producers. The new price for housing services is then $(1 - s)P_h$ and the associated supply curve is S'_h. The subsidy increases the quantity of housing services consumed to h_2. If the purpose of the subsidy was to increase housing consumption, then it has succeeded. But if its goal was to maximize social welfare, is it an appropriate policy?

Before the subsidy, consumer surplus was area *mno*. After the subsidy, consumer surplus is *mqu*. The benefit to housing consumers is the increase in their surplus, area *nouq*. But at what cost is this benefit obtained? The cost of the subsidy program is the quantity of housing services consumed, *qu*, times the subsidy per unit, *nq*, or rectangle *nvuq*. Thus, the cost of the subsidy actually exceeds the benefit—there is an excess burden equal to the difference between areas *nvuq* and *nouq*, which is the shaded area *ovu*.

How can subsidizing a good thing like housing be inefficient? Recall that any point on the demand curve for housing services measures how much people value that particular level of consumption. To the right of h_1, although individuals do derive utility from consuming more housing, its value is less than P_h, the marginal cost to society of providing it. In other words, the subsidy

Figure 18.6

Excess Burden of a Housing Subsidy

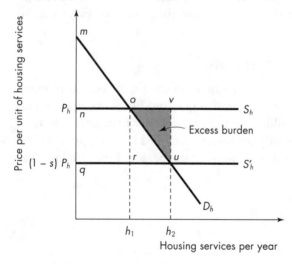

induces people to consume housing services that are valued at less than their cost—hence, the inefficiency.[10]

A very important policy implication follows from this analysis. One often hears proposals to help some group of people by subsidizing a commodity that they consume heavily. We have shown that this is an inefficient way to aid people. Less money could make them as well off if it were given to them as a direct grant. In Figure 18.6, people would be indifferent between a housing subsidy program costing *nvuq* and a direct grant of *nouq*, even though the subsidy program costs the government more money.[11] This is one of the reasons many economists prefer direct income transfers to commodity subsidies.

The Excess Burden of Income Taxation

The theory of excess burden that we have developed for taxing commodities applies just as well to factors of production. In Figure 18.7, Jacob's hours of work are plotted on the horizontal axis and his hourly wage on the vertical.

Figure 18.7

Excess Burden of a Tax on Labour

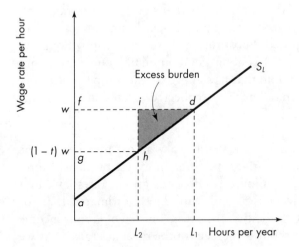

---

[10] Alternatively, after the subsidy the marginal rate of substitution in consumption depends on $(1 - s)P_h$, while the marginal rate of transformation in production depends on P_h. Hence, the marginal rate of transformation is not equal to the marginal rate of substitution, and the allocation of resources cannot be efficient.

[11] This result is very similar to that obtained when we examined in-kind subsidy programs in Chapter 10. That chapter also discusses why commodity subsidies nevertheless remain politically popular.

Jacob's compensated labour supply curve, which shows the smallest wage that would be required to induce him to work each additional hour, is labelled S_L. Initially, Jacob's wage is w and the associated hours of work L_1. In the same way that consumer surplus is the area between the demand curve and the market price, worker surplus is the area between the supply curve and the market wage rate. When the wage is w, Jacob's surplus is therefore area *adf*.

Now assume that an income tax at a rate t is imposed. The after-tax wage is then $(1 - t)w$, and given supply curve S_L, the quantity of labour supplied falls to L_2 hours. Jacob's surplus after the tax is *agh*, and the government collects revenues equal to *fihg*. The excess burden due to the tax-induced distortion of the work choice is the amount by which Jacob's loss of welfare (*fdhg*) exceeds the tax collected: area *hid* (= *fdhg* – *fihg*). In analogy to Equation (18.3), area *hid* is approximately

$$1/2\varepsilon^c wL_1 t^2 \qquad\qquad (18.4)$$

where ε^c is the compensated elasticity of hours of work with respect to the wage.

Recent calculations suggest that for an adult married male, a reasonable value for ε^c is about 0.2.[12] For illustrative purposes, suppose that before taxation, Jacob works 2,000 hours per year at a wage of $20 per hour. A tax on earnings of 40 percent is then imposed. Substituting these figures into Equation (18.4), the excess burden of the tax is about $640 annually. One way to put this figure into perspective is to note that it is approximately 4 percent of tax revenues. Thus, on average, each dollar of tax collected creates an excess burden of 4 cents.

Of course, wage rates, tax rates, and elasticities vary across members of the population, so different people are subject to different excess burdens. Moreover, the excess burden of taxing labour also depends on tax rates levied on other factors of production. Jorgenson and Yun (1991) estimated that for plausible values of the relevant elasticities, the excess burden of labour income taxation in the United States is about 30 percent of the revenues raised. As we show in Chapter 21, however, there is considerable uncertainty about the values of some of the key elasticities. Hence, this particular estimate must be

---

[12] See Phipps (1993: 38), who, upon reviewing the literature, finds that for Canadian men the gross own-wage elasticity of labour supply ranged from a low of –0.05 to +0.46. Also see Browning (1985), who provides an edifying discussion of the pitfalls involved in calculating excess burdens.

regarded cautiously. Still, evidence indicates that the excess burden of labour income taxation, relative to revenues raised, may be higher in Canada than in the United States. Dahlby (1994) reported that the excess burden of one more dollar from the personal income tax averaged 66 percent in 1993.[13]

DIFFERENTIAL TAXATION OF INPUTS[14]

In the income tax example just discussed, we assumed that labour income was taxed at the same rate regardless of where the labour was supplied. But sometimes the tax levied on a factor of production depends on where it is employed. For instance, because of the corporate income tax, some argue that capital employed in the corporate sector faces a higher rate than capital in the non-corporate sector. Another example is the differential taxation of labour in the household and market sectors. If an individual does housework, valuable services are produced but not taxed.[15] On the other hand, if the same individual works in the market, the services are subject to the income and payroll taxes. The fact that labour is taxed in one sector and untaxed in another distorts people's decisions on how much time to spend on each. The efficiency cost can be measured using a model developed by Harberger (1974). In Figure 18.8A, hours of work in the household sector are measured on the horizontal axis, and dollars are measured on the vertical. Now define the **value of the marginal product** (VMP) of hours worked in the household sector as the dollar value of the *additional* output produced for each hour worked. The schedule VMP_x in Figure 18.8A represents the value of the marginal product of household work. It is drawn sloping downward, reflecting the reasonable assumption that as more hours are spent in the home, the incremental value of those hours decreases. This is just an example of the law of diminishing marginal returns.

Similarly, schedule VMP_z in Figure 18.8B shows the value of the marginal product of hours worked in the market sector. Although we also expect VMP_z to slope downward, there is no reason to expect that its shape should be identical to that of VMP_x.

---

[13] Fortin and Lacroix (1994) estimated the cost of raising an additional dollar in Quebec through the personal income tax to be from $1.39 to $1.53, indicating an excess burden of 39 to 53 percent for the marginal dollar.

[14] This section can be skipped without loss of continuity.

[15] The value of housework was expressed nicely by a biblical author who wrote during an era in which it was assumed homes were managed only by females. In Proverbs, he discusses in detail the many tasks performed by the woman who "looketh well to the ways of her household" (Prov. 31:27). His general conclusion is that "her price is far above rubies" (Prov. 31:10). Unfortunately, price data on rubies during the biblical era are unavailable. Chandler (1994) estimates the value of household work in Canada, using opportunity cost and replacement cost methods, at between 31 and 46 percent of GDP in 1992.

Figure 18.8

The Allocation of Time between Housework and Market Work

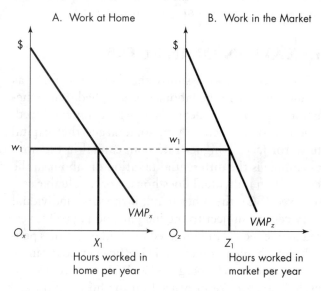

For simplicity, assume that the total number of hours of work available is fixed, so that the only question is how to divide the work between the market and household sectors. Assume further that individuals allocate their time between housework and market work to maximize their total incomes. As a result of this allocation process, the value of the marginal product of labour is the same in both sectors. If it were not, it would be possible for people to reallocate labour between the sectors to increase their incomes. In Figure 18.8, the initial equilibrium occurs where X_1 hours are devoted to housework and Z_1 hours to market work. The value of the marginal product of labour in both sectors is w_1 dollars. Competitive pricing ensures that the wage in the market sector is equal to the value of the marginal product.

Now assume that a tax of t is levied on income from market work, but the return to housework is untaxed. Immediately after the tax is levied, the net return to market work declines to $(1 - t)w_1$. The original allocation is no longer desirable to individuals because the return to the last hour of work in the household (w_1) exceeds the comparable rate in the market, $(1 - t)w_1$. As a result, people begin working less in the market and more at home. As individuals devote less time to the market sector, VMP_z begins to rise; as they enter the household sector, VMP_x falls. Equilibrium is reached when the *after-tax* value of marginal product in the market sector equals the value of marginal product in the household sector. In Figure 18.9, this occurs when people work X_2 hours in the home and Z_2 hours in the market. Because the total hours of work are fixed, the increase in hours in the household sector exactly equals the decrease in the market sector—distance X_1X_2 equals distance Z_2Z_1.

At the new equilibrium, the after-tax *VMP*s in the two sectors are both equal to $(1 - t)w_2$. However, the *before-tax VMP* in the market sector, w_2, is greater than the *VMP* in the household sector $(1 - t)w_2$. This means that if more labour were supplied to the market sector, the increase in income there (w_2) would exceed the loss of income in the household sector, $(1 - t)w_2$. But there is no incentive for this reallocation to occur, because individuals are sensitive to the returns they receive *after tax*, and these are already equal. The tax thus creates a situation in which there is "too much" housework being done and "not enough" work in the market. In short, the tax leads to an inefficient allocation of resources in the sense that it distorts incentives to employ inputs in their most productive uses. The resulting decrease in real income is the excess burden of the tax.

To measure the excess burden, we must analyze Figure 18.9 closely. Begin by observing that as a result of the exodus of labour from the market, the value

Figure 18.9

Differential Factor Taxation

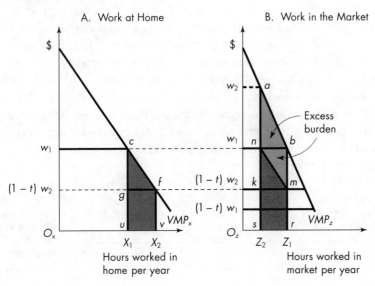

A. Work at Home   B. Work in the Market

of output there goes down by *abrs*, the area under VMP_z between Z_1 and Z_2.[16] On the other hand, as labour enters the household sector, the value of output increases by *cfvu*, the area under the VMP_x curve between X_1 and X_2. Therefore, the excess burden is area *abrs* minus area *cfvu*. Because $X_1X_2 = Z_2Z_1$ (remember, the total supply of hours is fixed), it follows that area *cfvu* equals area *nmrs*. Hence, the difference between *abrs* and *cfvu* is simply *abmn*. This area, which is the excess burden of the tax, has a convenient algebraic representation:

$$1/2(\Delta Z)tw_2,$$

where ΔZ is the change in hours worked in the market sector.[17] The greater the change in the allocation of labour (ΔZ) and the greater the tax wedge (tw_2), the greater the excess burden.

In general, whenever a factor is fixed in total supply and is taxed differently in different uses, a misallocation of factors between sectors and hence an efficiency loss is generated. In the case of housework versus market work just discussed, Boskin (1975) estimated the cost of the distortion as between 6 and 13 percent of tax revenues in the United States. Somewhat higher personal income tax rates in Canada may mean that the cost of the distortion in Canada would be toward the higher end of this estimate.

DOES EFFICIENT TAXATION MATTER?

Every year dozens of documents relating to the details of government spending and taxation are published. You would look in vain, however, for an "excess burden budget" documenting the distortionary impact of government fiscal policies. The reason for this is not hard to understand. Excess burden does not appear in anyone's bookkeeping system. It is conceptually a rather subtle notion and is not easy to make operational. Nevertheless, although the losses in real income associated with tax-induced changes in behaviour are hidden, they are real, and according to some estimates, they are very large. We have emphasized repeatedly that efficiency considerations alone are never enough to determine policy. Still, it is unfortunate that policy makers often seem to ignore efficiency altogether.

---

[16] The vertical distance between *VMP* and the horizontal axis at any level of input gives the value of marginal product for that level of input. Adding up all these distances gives the value of the total product. Thus, the area under *VMP* gives the value of the total product.

[17] Proof: Area *abmn* is the sum of two triangles *abn* and *nbm*. Triangle *abn* = $1/2(nb)(an)$ = $1/2\Delta Z(an)$. Triangle *nbm* = $1/2(nb)(bm)$ = $1/2(\Delta Z)(bm)$. Their sum is $1/2(\Delta Z)(an + bm)$ = $1/2(\Delta Z)tw_2$.

The fact that a tax generates an excess burden does not mean that the tax is bad. One hopes, after all, that it will be used to obtain something beneficial for society either in terms of public goods or income redistribution. But to determine whether or not the supposed benefits are large enough to justify the costs, intelligent policy requires that excess burden be included in the calculation as a social cost.[18] Moreover, as we see in the next chapter, excess burden is extremely useful in comparing alternative tax systems. Providing estimates of excess burden is an important role for the economist.

SUMMARY

- Taxes generally impose an excess burden—a cost beyond the tax revenue collected.

- Excess burden is caused by tax-induced distortions in behaviour. It may be examined using either indifference curves or compensated demand curves.

- Lump-sum taxes do not cause distortions, but are unattractive as policy tools. Nevertheless, they are an important standard against which the excess burdens of other taxes can be compared.

- Excess burden may result even if observed behaviour is unaffected, because it is the compensated response to a tax that determines its excess burden.

- When a single tax is imposed, the excess burden is proportional to the compensated elasticity of demand, and to the square of the tax rate.

- In cost–benefit analysis, the marginal excess burden of raising funds by taxation should be included as a cost.

- Excess-burden calculations typically assume no other distortions. If other distortions exist, the incremental excess burden of a new tax depends on its effects in other markets.

- Subsidies also create excess burdens because they encourage people to consume goods valued less than the marginal social cost of production.

- The differential taxation of inputs creates an excess burden. Such inputs are used "too little" in taxed activities and "too much" in untaxed activities.

---

[18] The excess burden may be quite high depending on the elasticity of labour supply and the level of existing tax rates upon which the change is being imposed. Assuming an uncompensated elasticity of 0.2, Browning and Johnson (1984: 175) found that "the disposable money income of the upper income quintiles of households is depressed by $9.51 for each dollar increase in the disposable money income of lower-income quintiles." Thus, even with low labour supply elasticities, excess burden accompanying greater equality may be large if tax rates are already quite high.

DISCUSSION QUESTIONS

1. Which of the following is likely to impose a large excess burden?

   a. A tax on land.
   b. A subsidy for personal computers.
   c. An annual tax of $125 on each television you own. (They actually do this in the United Kingdom.)
   d. A subsidy for investment in "high-tech" companies.
   e. A tax on economic profits.

2. The combined federal and provincial taxes on a carton of 200 cigarettes were reduced from $24 to $10 in Ontario in February 1994. Describe how you would compute the reduction in excess burden that results from this lowering of the tax.

3. "In the formula for excess burden given in Equation (18.3), the tax is less than one. When it is squared, the result is smaller, not bigger. Thus, having t^2 instead of t in the formula makes the tax less important." Comment.

4. Since the tax system is only partially indexed for inflation, Canadian taxpayers (in Ontario) with unchanged *real* incomes may experience an increase in their marginal tax rate from about 26 percent to 40 percent as their *nominal* income exceeds $29,590 in 1995. By what factor would this change in tax rates increase their excess burdens?

5. Recall Harberger's general equilibrium model presented in Chapter 17 under "General Equilibrium Models." In that model, there are two commodities and two factors of production, and the total supply of each factor of production is fixed. What is the excess burden of a proportional income tax? What is the excess burden of a proportional tax on one of the two factors?

REFERENCES

Bishop, Robert L. "The Effects of Specific and Ad Valorem Taxes." *Quarterly Journal of Economics* (May 1968): 198–218.

Boskin, Michael J. "Efficiency Aspects of the Differential Tax Treatment of Market and Household Economic Activities." *Journal of Public Economics* 4 (1975): 1–25.

Browning, Edgar K. "A Critical Appraisal of Hausman's Welfare Cost Estimates." *Journal of Political Economy* 93, no. 5 (October 1985): 1025–34.

Browning, Edgar K., and William R. Johnson. "The Trade-Off between Equality and Efficiency." *Journal of Political Economy* 92, no. 2 (April 1984): 175–203.

Chandler, William. "The Value of Household Work in Canada, 1992." *Canadian Economic Observer* (April 1994).

Dahlby, Bev. "The Distortionary Effect of Rising Taxes," in *Deficit Reduction: What Pain, What Gain?* ed. W. Robson and W. Scarth. Toronto: C.D. Howe Institute, 1994, pp. 43–72.

Diamond, Peter A., and Daniel L. McFadden. "Some Uses of the Expenditure Function in Public Finance." *Journal of Public Economics* 3 (1974): 3–21.

Fortin, B., and G. Lacroix. "Labour Supply, Tax Evasion, and the Marginal Cost of Public Funds: An Empirical Investigation." *Journal of Public Economics* 55 (November 1994): 407–31.

Fullerton, Don, and Diane Lim Rogers. *Who Bears the Lifetime Tax Burden?* Washington, DC: Brookings Institution, 1993.

Harberger, Arnold C. "Efficiency Effects of Taxes on Income from Capital," in *Taxation and Welfare*, ed. Arnold C. Harberger. Boston: Little, Brown, 1974, pp. 163–70.

Jorgenson, Dale W., and Kun-Young Yun. "The Excess Burden of Taxation in the United States." *Journal of Accounting, Auditing and Finance* 6, no. 4 (Fall 1991): 487–508.

Phipps, Shelley A. "Does Unemployment Insurance Increase Unemployment?" *Canadian Business Economics* (Spring 1993): 37–50.

Sandmo, Agnar. "Optimal Taxation—An Introduction to the Literature." *Journal of Public Economics* 6 (1976): 37–54.

Tresch, Richard W. *Public Finance: A Normative Theory.* Plano, Texas: Business Publications, 1981.

Whalley, John, and Deborah Fretz. *The Economics of the Goods and Services Tax.* Toronto: Canadian Tax Foundation, 1990.

APPENDIX A

Formula for Excess Burden

This appendix shows how the excess burden triangle *fdi* of Figure 18.5 may be written in terms of the compensated demand elasticity. The triangle's area, A, is given by the formula

$$A = 1/2 \times base \times height \qquad (18A.1)$$
$$= 1/2 \times (di) \times (fd).$$

fd is just the difference between the gross and net prices (ΔP_b):

$$fd = \Delta P_b = (1 + t_b) \times P_b - P_b = t_b \times P_b. \qquad (18A.2)$$

di is the change in the quantity (Δq) as a result of the price rise:

$$di = \Delta q \qquad (18A.3)$$

Now, note that the definition of the compensated price elasticity, η^c, is

$$\eta^c \equiv [\Delta q/\Delta P_b] \times [P_b/q]$$

so that

$$\Delta q = \eta^c[q/P_b]\Delta P_b. \tag{18A.4}$$

We saw in (18A.2) that $\Delta P_b = t_b \times P_b$, so that (18A.4) yields

$$\Delta q = \eta^c \times q/P_b \times (t_bP_b) = \eta^c \times q \times t_b. \tag{18A.5}$$

Finally, recall that $di = \Delta q$ and substitute both (18A.5) and (18A.2) into (18A.1) to obtain

$$
\begin{aligned}
A &= 1/2(di)(fd) \\
&= 1/2(\eta^cqt_b) \times (t_bP_b) \\
&= 1/2 \times \eta^c \times P_b \times q \times (t_b)^2,
\end{aligned}
$$

as in the text.

APPENDIX B

Multiple Taxes and the Theory of the Second Best

This appendix discusses the measurement of excess burden when a tax is imposed in the presence of a pre-existing distortion.

In Figure 18.10, we consider two goods, gin and rum, whose demand schedules are D_g and D_r, and whose before-tax prices are P_g and P_r, respectively. (The prices represent marginal social costs and are assumed to be constant.) Rum is currently being taxed at a percentage rate t_r so its price is $(1 + t_r)P_r$. This creates an excess burden in the rum market, triangle *abc*. Now suppose that a tax on gin at rate t_g is introduced, creating a wedge between what gin consumers pay and gin producers receive. This creates an excess burden in the gin market of *efd*. But this is not the end of the story. If gin and rum are substitutes, the increase in the consumers' price of gin induced by the gin tax shifts the demand curve for rum to the right, say to D'_r. As a consequence, the quantity of rum demanded increases from r_2 to r_3, distance *cg*. For each bottle of rum purchased between r_2 and r_3, the amount that people pay $[(1 + t_r)P_r]$ exceeds the social cost (P_r) by distance *cb*. Hence, there is a social gain of *cb* per bottle of rum times *cg* bottles, or area *cbhg*.

Figure 18.10

Excess Burden of a Tax in the Presence of an Existing Tax

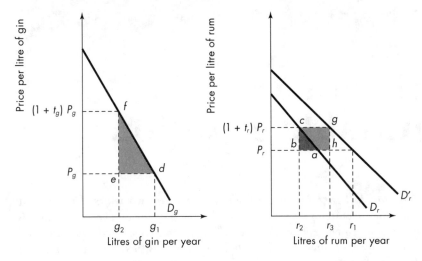

To summarize: Given that the tax on rum was already in place, the tax on gin creates an excess burden of *efd* in the gin market *and* simultaneously decreases excess burden by *cbhg* in the rum market. If *cbhg* is sufficiently large, the tax can actually reduce overall excess burden. This is an example of the **theory of the second best**: In the presence of existing distortions, policies that in isolation would increase efficiency can decrease it and vice versa.

This discussion is a special case of the result that the excess burden of a *set* of taxes generally depends on the whole set of tax rates, as well as on the degree of substitutability and complementarity among the various commodities. Specifically, suppose that *n* commodities are subject to taxation. Let P_i be the before-tax price of the *i*th commodity; t_i the ad valorem tax on the *i*th commodity; and S_{ij}, the compensated response in the demand of the *i*th good with respect to a change in the price of the *j*th good. Then it can be shown (see Tresch, 1981: ch. 15) that the overall excess burden is

$$-1/2 \sum_{i=1}^{n} \sum_{j=1}^{n} t_i P_i t_j P_j S_{ij}$$

For example, in the two-good case just discussed, where the goods are *g* and *r*, the overall excess burden is

$$-1/2(t_r^2 P_r^2 S_{rr} + 2t_r P_r t_g P_g S_{rg} + t_g^2 P_g^2 S_{gg}).$$

Chapter 19

Efficient and Equitable Taxation

A nation may fall into decay through taxation in two ways. In the first case, when the amount of the taxes exceeds the powers of the nation and is not proportioned to the general wealth. In the second case, when an amount of taxation, proportioned on the whole to the powers of the nation, is viciously distributed.

—Pietro Verri

The last two chapters focused on the positive question: How do taxes affect the distribution of income and economic efficiency? We turn now to the normative question: How should a tax system be designed if it is to yield efficient and fair outcomes? Our goal is to establish a set of criteria that can be used to evaluate real-world tax systems.

OPTIMAL COMMODITY TAXATION

The premier of your province has asked you for advice on how to design a tax system. At what rates should various goods be taxed? The purpose of the theory of optimal commodity taxation is to provide a framework for answering this question. Of course, before going to work, it would be fair for you to ask the premier a question in return: What goal do you seek? At the outset, we assume that the premier's only goal is to finance the province's given expenditure level with a minimum of excess burden and without using any lump-sum taxes. We return later to issues that arise when there are concerns about distribution as well as efficiency.

To begin, consider the situation of Stella, a representative citizen who consumes only two commodities, X and Y, as well as leisure, l. The price of X is P_x, the price of Y is P_y, and the wage rate (which is the price of leisure) is w. The maximum number of hours per year that Stella can work—her **time endowment**—is fixed at T. (Think of T as the amount of time left over after sleep.) It follows that hours of work are $(T - l)$—all time not spent on leisure is devoted to work. Income is the product of the wage rate and hours of work—$w(T - l)$. Assuming that Stella spends her entire income on commodities X and Y (there is no saving), her budget constraint is

$$w(T - l) = P_x X + P_y Y. \qquad (19.1)$$

The left-hand side gives total earnings, and the right-hand side shows how the earnings are spent. Equation (19.1) can be rewritten as

$$wT = P_x X + P_y Y + wl \qquad (19.2)$$

The left-hand side of (19.2) is the value of the time endowment. It shows the income that Stella could earn if she worked every waking hour.

Now, suppose that it is possible to tax X, Y, and l at the same ad valorem rate, t. The tax raises the effective price of X to $(1 + t)P_x$, of Y to $(1 + t)P_y$, and of l to $(1 + t)w$. Thus, Stella's after-tax budget constraint is

$$wT = (1 + t)P_x X + (1 + t)P_y Y + (1 + t)wl. \qquad (19.3)$$

Dividing through Equation (19.3) by $(1 + t)$, we have

$$[1/(1 + t)] \times wT = P_x X + P_y Y + wl \qquad (19.4)$$

Comparison of (19.3) and (19.4) points out the following fact: a tax on all commodities including leisure, at the same percentage rate, t, is equivalent to reducing the value of the time endowment from wT to $[1/(1 + t)] \times wT$. For example, a 25 percent tax on X, Y, and l is equivalent to a reduction of the value of the time endowment by 20 percent. However, because w and T are fixed, their product, wT, is also fixed; for any value of the wage rate, an individual cannot change the value of his or her time endowment. Therefore, a tax that reduces the value of the time endowment is in effect a lump-sum tax. From Chapter 18 we know that lump-sum taxes have no excess burden. We conclude that a tax at the same rate on all commodities, *including leisure*, is equivalent to a lump-sum tax and has no excess burden.

In practice, putting a tax on leisure time is impossible. The only available tax instruments are taxes on commodities X and Y. Therefore, some excess burden generally is inevitable. The goal of optimal commodity taxation is to select tax rates on X and Y in such a way that the excess burden of raising the required tax revenue is as low as possible. It is popular to suggest that the solution to this problem is to tax X and Y at the same rate—so-called **neutral taxation**.[1] We will see that, in general, neutral taxation is *not* efficient.

The Ramsey Rule

To raise the revenue with the least excess burden possible, how should the tax rates on X and Y be set? To minimize overall excess burden, the marginal excess burden of the last dollar of revenue raised from each commodity must be the same. Otherwise, it would be possible to lower overall excess burden by raising the rate on the commodity with the smaller marginal excess burden, and vice versa.

To explore the consequences of this typical example of marginal analysis in economics, suppose for simplicity that for our representative consumer, X and Y are unrelated commodities—they are neither substitutes nor complements for each other. Hence, a change in the price of either commodity affects its own demand and not the demand for the other. Figure 19.1 shows Stella's compensated demand for X, D_x. Assume that she can buy all the X she wants at the price P_0, so the supply curve of X is horizontal.

Suppose that a small unit tax of u_x is levied on X. As proven in the last chapter, the excess burden of the tax is the area of triangle *abc*. The height of the triangle is the change in the price induced by the tax, u_x, and the base is the change in the (compensated) demand for X, which we denote ΔX. Hence, the excess burden is

$$1/2 u_x \Delta X \tag{19.5}$$

The revenues raised by the tax are found by multiplying the tax per unit (u_x) by the number of units sold (X_1), *or*

$$u_x X_1 \tag{19.6}$$

Recall that excess burden minimization requires information on the *marginal* excess burden on the last dollar of revenue collected. To derive an explicit

---

[1] In light of the tax equivalence relations in Table 17.2, in this model a tax on X and Y at the same rate is equivalent to an income tax.

Figure 19.1

Marginal Excess Burden

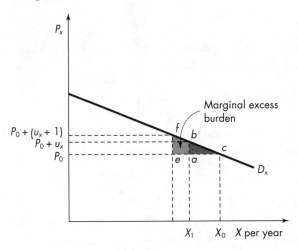

expression for this, our strategy is to imagine increasing the unit tax rate by a dollar. Step 1 is to find the marginal excess burden induced by the tax increase. Step 2 is to compute the associated increase in revenues. Step 3 is simply to divide the step 1 result by that from step 2. By definition, this gives us the marginal excess burden per incremental dollar of revenue collected.

Step 1. If the unit tax increases from u_x to $(u_x + 1)$, then according to Equation (19.5) excess burden increases to approximately $1/2(u_x + 1)\,\Delta X$. The marginal excess burden is just the difference between the excess burdens before and after the tax increase. Thus, we subtract $1/2\,u_x\Delta X$ from $1/2(u_x + 1)\,\Delta X$, which gives us

$$1/2\Delta X = \textit{marginal excess burden.} \qquad (19.7)$$

Graphically, this is approximately the difference between the excess burden associated with the tax rate $(u_x + 1)$ (triangle *fec* in Figure 19.1), and the original excess burden (*abc*), or trapezoid *feab*.

Step 2. Note from Equation (19.6) that when the unit tax increases from u_x to $(u_x + 1)$, revenues increase approximately from u_xX_1 to $(u_x + 1)\,X_1$. Therefore, marginal tax revenues are just $(u_x + 1)\,X_1$ minus u_xX_1, or

$$X_1 = \textit{marginal tax revenue.} \qquad (19.8)$$

Step 3. Marginal excess burden per additional dollar of tax revenue is Equation (19.7) divided by (19.8) or

$$[1/2\Delta X]/X_1.$$

Exactly the same reasoning indicates that if a unit tax of u_y is levied on Y, the marginal excess burden per last dollar of revenue is

$$[1/2\Delta Y]/Y_1$$

Because the condition for minimizing overall excess burden is that the marginal excess burden per last dollar of revenue be the same for each commodity, we must set

$$[1/2\Delta X]/X_1 = [1/2\Delta Y]/Y_1$$

Multiplying both sides of the equation by two yields

$$\Delta X/X_1 = \Delta Y/Y_1. \qquad (19.9)$$

To interpret Equation (19.9), note that the change in a variable divided by its total value is just the percentage change in the variable. Hence, Equation (19.9) says that to minimize total excess burden, tax rates should be set so that the percentage reduction in the quantity demanded of each commodity is the same.[2] This result, called the **Ramsey rule**, after its discoverer Frank Ramsey (1927), also holds even for cases when X, Y, and l are related goods—substitutes or complements.

But why should efficient taxation induce equiproportional changes in quantities demanded rather than equiproportional changes in prices? Because excess burden is a consequence of distortions in quantities. To minimize total excess burden requires that all these changes be in the same proportion.

A reinterpretation of the Ramsey rule. It is useful to explore the relationship between the Ramsey rule and demand elasticities. Let η_x be the compensated elasticity of demand for X. Let t_x be the tax rate on X, this time expressed as an ad valorem rate rather than a unit tax.[3] Now, by definition of

---

[2] The result holds strictly only for infinitesimal taxes.

[3] In a competitive market, any unit tax can be represented by a suitably chosen ad valorem tax, and vice versa. For example, suppose a commodity is subject to a unit tax of 5 cents, and the price paid by consumers is 50 cents. Then the resulting excess burden is the same as that which would be induced by an ad valorem tax at a rate of 10 percent of the after-tax price.

an ad valorem tax, t_x is the percentage increase in the price induced by the tax. Hence, $t_x\eta_x$ is the percentage change in the price times the percentage change in quantity demanded when the price increases by 1 percent. This is just the percentage reduction in the demand for X induced by the tax. Similarly, defining t_y and η_y analogously to t_x and η_x, then $t_y\eta_y$ is the proportional reduction in Y induced by the tax. The Ramsey rule says that to minimize excess burden, these percentage reductions in quantity demanded must be equal:

$$t_x\eta_x = t_y\eta_y. \qquad (19.10)$$

Now divide both sides of the equation by $t_y\eta_x$ to obtain

$$t_x/t_y = \eta_y/\eta_x \qquad (19.11)$$

Equation (19.11) is the **inverse elasticity rule**: As long as goods are unrelated in consumption, tax rates should be inversely proportional to elasticities. That is, the higher is η_y relative to η_x, the lower should be t_y relative to t_x.[4] Efficiency does not require that all rates be set uniformly.

The intuition behind the inverse elasticity rule is straightforward. An efficient set of taxes should distort decisions as little as possible. The potential for distortion is greater the more elastic the demand for a commodity. Therefore, efficient taxation requires that relatively high rates of taxation be levied on relatively inelastic goods.

The Corlett–Hague rule. Corlett and Hague (1953) proved an interesting implication of the Ramsey rule: When there are two commodities, efficient taxation requires taxing the commodity that is complementary to leisure at a relatively high rate. To understand this result intuitively, recall that *if* it were possible to tax leisure, a "first-best" result would be obtainable—revenues could be raised with no excess burden. Although the tax authorities cannot tax leisure, they *can* tax goods that tend to be consumed jointly *with* leisure, indirectly lowering the demand for leisure. If yachts are taxed at a very high rate,

---

[4] A more careful demonstration requires a little calculus. Recall from Equation (18.3) that the excess burden on commodity X is $1/2\eta_x P_x X t^2_x$. Similarly, the excess burden on Y is $1/2\eta_y P_y Y t^2_y$. Then the total excess burden is $1/2\eta_x P_x X t^2_x + 1/2\eta_y P_y Y t^2_y$. (We can just add up the two expressions because, by assumption, X and Y are unrelated.) Now, suppose the required tax revenue is R. Then t_x and t_y must satisfy the relation $P_x X t_x + P_y Y t_y = R$. Our problem is to choose t_x and t_y to minimize $1/2\eta_x P_x X t^2_x + 1/2\eta_y P_y Y t^2_y$ subject to $R - P_x X t_x - P_y Y t_y = 0$. Set up the Lagrangian expression $\mathcal{L} = 1/2\eta_x P_x X t^2_x + 1/2\eta_y P_y Y t^2_y + \lambda[R - P_x X t_x - P_y Y t_y]$ where λ is the Lagrange multiplier. (The method of Lagrangian multipliers is reviewed in Henderson and Quandt, 1980: 381–83.) Taking $\partial\mathcal{L}/\partial t_x$ yields $\eta_x t_x = \lambda$ and $\partial\mathcal{L}/\partial t_y$ yields $\eta_y t_y = \lambda$. Hence, $\eta_x t_x = \eta_y t_y$, and Equation (19.11) follows immediately.

people consume fewer yachts and spend less time at leisure. In effect, then, taxing complements to leisure at high rates provides an indirect way to "get at" leisure and, hence, move closer to the perfectly efficient outcome that would be possible if leisure were taxable.[5]

Equity Considerations

At this point the reader may suspect that efficient tax theory has unpleasant policy implications. For example, the inverse elasticity rule says inelastically demanded goods should be taxed at relatively high rates. Is this fair? Do we really want a tax system that collects the bulk of its revenue from taxes on insulin?

Of course not. Efficiency is only one criterion for evaluating a tax system; fairness is just as important. In particular, it is widely agreed that a tax system should have **vertical equity**: It should distribute burdens fairly across people with different abilities to pay. The Ramsey rule has been modified to consider the distributional consequences of taxation. Suppose, for example, that the poor spend a greater proportion of their income on commodity X than do the rich, and vice versa for commodity Y. X might be bread, and Y caviar. Suppose further that the social welfare function puts a higher weight on the utilities of the poor than on those of the rich. Then even if X is more inelastically demanded than Y, optimal taxation may require a higher rate of tax on Y than X (Diamond, 1975). True, a high tax rate on Y creates a relatively large excess burden, but it also tends to redistribute income toward the poor. Society may be willing to pay the price of a higher excess burden in return for a more equal distribution of income. In general, the extent to which it makes sense to depart from the Ramsey rule depends on:

1. The strength of society's egalitarian preferences. If society cares only about efficiency—a dollar to one person is the same as a dollar to another, rich or poor—then it may as well strictly follow the Ramsey rule.

2. The extent to which the consumption patterns of the rich and poor differ. If the rich and the poor consume both goods in the same proportion, taxing the goods at different rates cannot affect the distribution of income. Even if society has a distributional goal, it cannot be achieved by differential taxation of X and Y.

---

[5] As Auerbach (1985) notes, what is "special" about leisure in this model is that it is the only good with an endowment (T) that cannot be taxed independently of its consumption.

Overview

If lump-sum taxation were available, taxes could be raised without any excess burden at all. Optimal taxation would need to focus only on distributional issues. Lump-sum taxes are not available, however, so the problem becomes how to collect a given amount of tax revenue with as small an excess burden as possible. In general, minimizing excess burden requires that taxes be set so that the (compensated) demands for all commodities are reduced in the same proportion. For unrelated goods, this implies that tax rates should be set in inverse proportion to the demand elasticities. This has provided a good argument for maintaining the *individual* as the unit for income taxation in Canada.

Application to Taxation of the Family

Consider the case where the *family* is the unit for income taxation, as was recommended by the Royal Commission on Taxation in 1966.[6] In this case, a husband and wife would be taxed on the sum of their incomes. Regardless of whether the wife or the husband earns an extra dollar, it would be taxed at the same rate. Would this be efficient? In other words, would the family's excess burden be minimized by taxing each spouse's income at the same rate?

Imagine the family as a unit whose utility depends on the quantities of three "commodities": total family consumption, husband's hours of work, and wife's hours of work. Family utility increases with family consumption, but decreases with each spouse's hours of work. Each spouse's hours of work depend on his or her wage rate, among other variables. A tax on earnings distorts the work decision, creating an excess burden. (See Chapter 18, Figure 18.7.) How should tax rates be set so the family's excess burden is as small as possible?

Assume for simplicity that the husband's and wife's hours of work are approximately "unrelated goods"—an increase in the husband's wage rate has very little impact on the wife's work decision and vice versa. This assumption is consistent with much empirical research. Then application of the inverse elasticity rule suggests that a higher tax should be levied on the commodity that is relatively inelastically supplied. To enhance efficiency, whoever's labour supply is relatively inelastic should bear a relatively high tax rate. Numerous econometric studies suggest that the *primary earner's* supply of labour is considerably less elastic than that of the *secondary earner*. Efficiency would therefore be gained if higher marginal tax rates were applied to primary earners than to sec-

---

[6] This recommendation of the royal commission was not accepted. Discussion in this section is based on Boskin and Sheshinski (1979).

ondary earners.[7] This is possible, and occurs to some degree, under the existing Canadian system where the *individual* is the unit for income taxation.

Again, we emphasize that efficiency is only one consideration in tax design. However, if society's distributional goals are related to the family, departures from efficient taxation rules may be appropriate in this case as well.

OPTIMAL USER FEES

So far we have assumed that all production occurs in the private sector. The government's only problem is to set the tax rates that determine consumer prices. Sometimes, the government itself is the producer of a good or service. In such cases, the government must directly choose a **user fee**—a price paid by users of a good or service provided by the government. As usual, we would like to determine the "best" possible user fee. Analytically, the optimal tax and user fee problems are closely related. In both cases, the government sets the final price paid by consumers. In the optimal tax problem, this is done indirectly by choice of the tax rate, while in the optimal user fee problem, it is done directly.

When does the government choose to produce a good instead of purchasing it from the private sector? Government production is likely when the production of some good or service is subject to continually decreasing average costs—the greater the level of output, the lower the cost per unit. Under such circumstances, it is unlikely that the market for the service is competitive. A single firm can take advantage of economies of scale and supply the entire industry output, at least for a sizable region. This phenomenon is often called **natural monopoly**.[8] Examples are highways, bridges, electricity, and television. In some cases, these commodities are produced by the private sector and regulated by the government (electricity); and in others they are produced by the public sector (highways). Although we study public production here, many of the important insights apply to regulation of private monopolies.

Figure 19.2 measures the output of the natural monopoly, Z, on the horizontal axis, and dollars on the vertical. The average cost schedule is denoted AC_Z. By assumption, it decreases continuously over all relevant ranges of output. Because average cost is decreasing, marginal cost must be less than average.

---

[7] See Ballard, Shoven, and Whalley (1985) for a review of several econometric studies on labour supply. Note that the important distinction here is not between *husband* and *wife*, but between *primary earner* and *secondary earner*. In families where the wife has the lower supply elasticity, efficiency requires that she have the higher tax rate.

[8] It is also possible that the industry can end up as an oligopoly (few sellers). We focus on the analytically simpler case of monopoly.

Figure 19.2

A Natural Monopoly

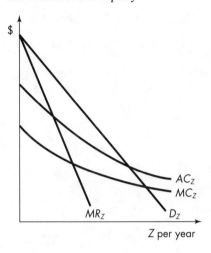

Therefore, the marginal cost (MC_Z) curve, which shows the incremental cost of providing each unit of Z, lies below AC_Z. The demand curve for Z is represented by D_Z. The associated marginal revenue curve is MR_Z. It shows the incremental revenue associated with each level of output of Z.

To illustrate why decreasing average costs often lead to public sector production or regulated private sector production, consider what would happen if Z were produced by an unregulated monopolist. The monopolist seeking to maximize profits produces up to the point that marginal revenue equals marginal cost, output level Z_m in Figure 19.3. The associated price, P_m, is found by going up to the demand curve, D_Z. Monopoly profits are equal to the product of number of units sold times the profit per unit and are represented geometrically by the light-shaded rectangle.

Is output Z_m efficient? According to the theory of welfare economics, efficiency requires that price equal marginal cost—the value that people place on the good must equal the incremental cost to society of producing it. At Z_m, price is *greater* than marginal cost. Hence, Z_m is inefficient. This inefficiency plus the fact that society may not approve of the existence of the monopoly profits provides a possible justification for government taking over the production of Z.[9]

---

[9] The usual caveat applies: just because government intervention can improve the status quo does not mean it will.

Figure 19.3

Alternative Pricing Schemes for a Natural Monopoly

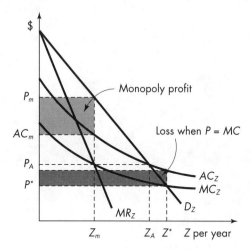

The obvious policy prescription seems to be for the government to produce up to the point where price equals marginal cost. In Figure 19.3, the output at which $P = MC$ is denoted Z^*, and the associated price is P^*. There is a problem, however: at output Z^*, the price is less than the average cost. Price P^* is so low that the operation cannot cover its costs, and it continually suffers losses. The total loss is equal to the product of the number of units sold, Z^*, times the loss per unit, measured as the vertical distance between the demand curve and AC_Z at Z^*. Geometrically, the loss is the darker-shaded rectangle in Figure 19.3.

How should the government confront this dilemma? Several solutions have been proposed.

Average cost pricing. By definition, when price equals average cost, there are neither profits nor losses—the enterprise just breaks even. The operation no longer has to worry about a deficit. Geometrically, this corresponds to the intersection of the demand and average cost schedules in Figure 19.3, where output is Z_A and price is P_A. However, note that Z_A is less than Z^*. Although average cost pricing leads to more output than at the profit-maximizing level, it still falls short of the efficient amount.

Marginal cost pricing with lump-sum taxes. Charge $P = MC$, and make up the deficit by levying lump-sum taxes. Charging $P = MC$ ensures efficiency in the market for Z; financing the deficit with lump-sum taxes on the rest of society guarantees that no new inefficiencies are generated by meeting the deficit. However, there are two problems with this solution.

First, as previously noted, lump-sum taxes are generally unavailable. It is more likely that the deficit will have to be financed by distorting taxes, such as income or commodity taxes. If so, the distortion in the market where the tax is levied may more than outweigh the efficiency gain in the market for Z.

Second, there is also a widespread belief that fairness requires consumers of a publicly provided service to pay for it—the so-called **benefits-received principle**. If this principle is taken seriously, it is unfair to make up the deficit by general taxation. If the Canadian Coast Guard rescues me from a stormy sea, why should you pay for it?

Two-part tariff. A **two-part tariff** involves a lump-sum charge to gain permission to use the service, plus a price equal to marginal cost for each unit of the service consumed. To see how this works, suppose there are 1,000 users of service Z. Under the simplest version of the scheme, each user would be charged one one-thousandth of the deficit just for the privilege of having the option to purchase Z. Once this lump-sum entrance fee was paid, Z could be freely purchased at a price equal to its marginal cost. Hence, the deficit is made up by a nondistorting tax on the users of the service, who are then given incentives to consume it in efficient quantities. Two-part tariffs may seem like a peculiar idea, but they are fairly common. Just think of a telephone or electric company, which charges each user a monthly sum plus an additional fee for each minute of calling time or each unit of power used.[10]

A problem with the two-part tariff is that the entrance fee may deter some users so that consumption falls below the efficient level. Whether this is an important problem depends on the commodity in question. In a country such as Canada, it may not be a major problem for natural monopolies such as water and electricity. In the case of telephones, two sources of inefficiency can be identified—a person may be willing to pay the marginal cost of the extra phone call, but unwilling to pay for the "entrance fee," and the costs to those unable to connect to the phoneless person.

Another problem is that the entrance fee is essentially an equal lump-sum tax on all users, rich and poor alike. If society cares about income distribution, this

---

[10] This is not to imply that the structure of telephone or other companies' two-part tariffs are necessarily optimal.

will be undesirable. Feldstein (1972) shows how the two-part tariff can be modified when society has distributional objectives. Suppose that Z is consumed in disproportionately high amounts by the rich and that society places a relatively high weight on the welfare of the poor. Then it is optimal to set the price per each unit of Z above marginal cost. When the price is greater than marginal cost, the deficit is less than the darker-shaded area in Figure 19.3. Because the rich consume Z in proportionately large amounts, they account for the bulk of the reduction of the deficit. Thus, by charging a price above marginal cost, some efficiency is lost, but some equity is gained. There is an obvious similarity to the optimal tax problem discussed earlier. In both cases, departures from full efficiency may be appropriate in the presence of distributional objectives.

Overview

Of the various possibilities for dealing with decreasing costs, which has Canada chosen? In many cases, average cost pricing has been selected both for publicly owned and regulated private enterprises. Tresch (1981: 203–6) argues that although average cost pricing is inefficient, it is probably a reasonable compromise. It has the virtue of being fairly simple and adheres to the popular benefits-received principle.[11] There are, however, a good many cases where two-part tariffs are used.

OPTIMAL INCOME TAXATION

Thus far, we have assumed that a government can levy taxes on all commodities and factors of production. We now turn to the question of how to design systems in which tax liabilities are based on people's incomes. Income taxation is an obvious candidate for special attention because of its importance in the revenue structures of most developed countries. In addition, some argue that income is an especially appropriate tax base because it is the best measure of an individual's ability to pay. For the moment, we merely assume that society has somehow decided that an income tax is desirable, and ask how to structure it. In subsequent chapters, we discuss whether income really is a particularly desirable tax base.

Edgeworth's Model

At the end of the nineteenth century, Edgeworth (1959/1897) examined the question of optimal income taxation using a simple model based on the following assumptions.

---

[11] There are problems in administering average cost pricing in regulated industries. See Tresch (1981: ch. 10).

1. Subject to the revenues required, the goal is to make the sum of individuals' utilities as high as possible. Algebraically, if U_i is the utility of the ith individual and W is social welfare, the tax system should maximize

$$W = U_1 + U_2 + \ldots + U_n, \qquad (19.12)$$

   where n is the number of people in the society.

2. Individuals have identical utility functions that depend only on their levels of income. These utility functions exhibit diminishing marginal utility of income; as income increases, an individual becomes better off, but at a decreasing rate.

3. The total amount of income available is fixed.

Edgeworth's assumptions are virtually identical to the assumptions behind the optimal income distribution model presented in Chapter 10 under "Rationales for Income Redistribution." There we showed that with these assumptions, maximization of social welfare requires that each person's marginal utility of income be the same. When utility functions are identical, equal marginal utilities of income occur only at equal levels of income. The implications for tax policy are clear: Taxes should be set in such a way that the after-tax distribution of income is as equal as possible. In particular, income should be taken first from the rich because the marginal utility lost is smaller than that of the poor. If the government requires more revenue even after complete equality has been reached, the additional tax burden should be evenly distributed.

Edgeworth's model, then, implies a radically progressive tax structure—incomes are levelled off from the top until complete equality is reached. In effect, marginal tax rates on high-income individuals are 100 percent. However, as stressed in Chapter 10, each of the assumptions underlying this analysis is subject to question. Beginning in the 1970s, economists began investigating how Edgeworth's results change when certain of the assumptions are relaxed.

Modern Studies

One of the most vexing problems with Edgeworth's analysis is the assumption that the total amount of income available to society is fixed. Confiscatory tax rates are assumed to have no effect on the amount of output produced. More realistically, suppose that individuals' utilities depend not only on income, but on leisure as well. Then income taxes distort work decisions and create excess burdens (Chapter 18). A society with a utilitarian social welfare function thus faces an inescapable dilemma. On the one hand, it desires to allocate the tax burden to equalize the after-tax distribution of income. However, in the process of doing so, it reduces the total amount of real income available. Design of an optimal income tax system must consider the costs (in excess burden) of achieving more equality. In Edgeworth's model, the cost of obtaining more equality is zero, which explains the prescription for a perfectly egalitarian outcome.

How does Edgeworth's result change when work incentives are taken into account? Stern (1976) studied a model similar to Edgeworth's, except that individuals choose between income and leisure. To simplify the analysis, Stern assumed that the amount of tax revenues collected from a person is given by

$$Revenues = -\alpha + t \times Income, \tag{19.13}$$

where α and t are positive numbers. For example, suppose that $\alpha = \$3,000$ and $t = .25$. Then a person with income of $20,000 would have a tax liability of $2,000 (= −$3,000 + .25 × $20,000). A person with an income of $6,000 would have a tax liability of *minus* $1,500 (= −$3,000 + .25 × $6,000). Such a person would receive a $1,500 grant from the government.

In Figure 19.4, we graph Equation (19.13) in a diagram with income measured on the horizontal axis and tax revenues on the vertical. When income is zero, the tax burden is negative—the individual receives a lump-sum grant from the government of α dollars. Then, for each dollar of income, the individual must pay t dollars to the government. Thus, t is the marginal tax rate, the proportion of an additional dollar that must be paid in tax. Because the geometric

Figure 19.4

A Linear Income Tax

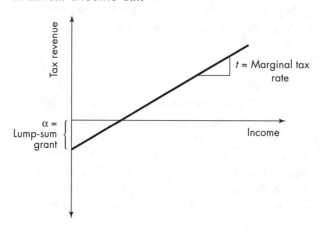

interpretation of Equation (19.13) is a straight line, it is referred to as a **linear income tax schedule**. In popular discussions, a linear income tax schedule is often referred to as a **flat tax**. Note that even though the marginal tax rate for a linear tax schedule is constant, the schedule is progressive in the sense that the higher an individual's income, the higher the proportion of income paid in taxes.[12] Just how progressive depends on the precise values of α and t. Greater values of t are associated with more progressive tax systems. However, at the same time that high values of t lead to more progressiveness, they create larger excess burdens. The optimal income tax problem is to find the "best" combination of α and t—the values that maximize social welfare [Equation (19.12)] subject to the constraint that a given amount of revenue (above the required transfers) be collected.

Stern (1976) finds that allowing for a modest amount of substitution between leisure and income, and with required government revenues equal to about 20 percent of income, a value of t of about 19 percent maximizes social welfare.[13] This is considerably less than the value of 100 percent implied by Edgeworth's analysis. Even quite modest incentive effects appear to have important implications for optimal marginal tax rates. Incidentally, Stern's calculated rate is also much smaller than the actual marginal tax rates found in many Western countries. For example, under the Canadian personal income tax system, the highest statutory (federal plus provincial) marginal income tax rate is 54.2 percent in British Columbia in 1996; at times it has been 84 percent.

More generally, Stern showed that the more elastic the supply of labour, the lower the optimal value of t, other things being the same. Intuitively, the cost of redistribution is the excess burden it creates. The more elastic the supply of labour, the greater the excess burden from taxing it; see Equation (18.4). More elastic labour supply therefore means a higher cost to redistribution, so that less should be done.

Stern also investigated how alternative social welfare functions affect the results, focusing on the impact of giving different social weights to the utilities of the rich and the poor. In Equation (19.12), more egalitarian preferences are represented by assigning the utilities of poor people higher weights than utilities of the rich. An interesting extreme case is the maximin criterion, according to which the only individual who receives any weight in the social welfare

---

[12] See the discussion of the definition of progressive in Chapter 17.
[13] Specifically, the result reported here assumes the elasticity of substitution between leisure and income is 0.6. In Stern's model, this corresponds to a small positive elasticity of labour supply with respect to the net wage, about 0.1.

function is the person with the minimum utility (see Chapter 10). Stern found that the maximin criterion calls for a marginal tax rate of about 80 percent. Not surprisingly, if society has extremely egalitarian objectives, high tax rates are called for. Even here, though, the rates fall short of 100 percent.

One limitation of Stern's analysis is that it constrains the income tax system to have only a single marginal tax rate. Slemrod, Yitzhaki, Mayshar, and Lundholm (1994) investigated a generalization of Stern's model that allowed for two marginal tax rates. The most interesting finding to emerge from their analysis is that if a second bracket is used, people in the higher-income bracket should face a *lower* marginal tax rate than people in the lower bracket. In contrast, in most real-world income tax systems, marginal tax rates increase with income. For example, in Canada, the marginal tax rate on the lowest income bracket is zero, and on the highest it is 54.2 percent (in British Columbia).[14] The intuition behind the result is that, by lowering the marginal tax rate on high-income people, they are induced to supply more labour, and the increased tax revenue can be used to lower the tax burdens on low-income individuals. Importantly, although marginal tax rates fall with income, average tax rates rise with income, so the optimal tax system is still progressive.

This cataloguing of results may convey a somewhat false sense of precision as to what economists really know about the optimal tax system. After all, there are many controversial value judgments behind the utilitarian social welfare that the optimal tax system seeks to maximize. Moreover, as explained in Chapter 21, there is substantial uncertainty about the behavioural elasticities that are crucial to analyzing the trade-off between efficiency and equity. Nevertheless, it is extremely informative to have explicit calculations of what the optimal tax rates would be under alternative sets of assumptions.

The theory and computation of optimal tax rates continues to be of great interest to economists. The basic models have been expanded to see how optimal tax rates are affected by new complications. This literature cannot be expected to produce a blueprint of the optimal tax system. As has been stressed, the answer depends to a large extent on value judgments, and economics does not provide definitive answers to ethical questions. The contribution of the literature on optimal taxation is systematically to draw out the implications of alternative ethical and behavioural assumptions, thus allowing coherent discussions of tax policy.

---

[14] Top marginal tax rates in other provinces in 1996 range from 46.1 percent in Alberta to 52.9 percent in Ontario and 53.3 percent in Newfoundland.

POLITICS AND THE TIME INCONSISTENCY PROBLEM

Optimal taxation is a purely normative theory. It does not purport to predict what real-world tax systems look like, or to explain how these tax systems emerge. The theory pays little attention to the institutional and political setting in which tax policy is made. Brennan and Buchanan (1977) argue that actual tax systems may look more reasonable when political realities are considered than they do from an optimal tax perspective.

Assume that in a certain society, there are three commodities, X, Y, and leisure. Labour is totally fixed in supply, and therefore, income is fixed. Currently, this society levies a tax on X, but its constitution forbids taxing Y. Viewing this situation, a student of optimal tax theory might say something like this: "You are running an inefficient tax system. Because labour is totally fixed in supply, you could have no excess burden if you taxed X and Y at equal rates—an income tax. I recommend that you lower the tax on X and impose a tax at the same rate on Y. Set the rates so that the same amount of revenue is collected as before."

Suppose, however, that the citizens suspect that if they allow Y to be taxed, their politicians and bureaucrats will *not* lower the tax rate on X. Rather, they will simply take advantage of the opportunity to tax something new to make tax revenues as large as possible. As we saw in Chapter 11 under "Explaining Government Growth," certain theories of the public sector suggest that those who run the government can and will maximize tax revenues despite the wishes of the citizenry. Therefore, by constitutionally precluding the taxation of Y, the citizens may be rationally protecting themselves against an inefficiently large public sector. In other words, if citizens do not trust the government, what looks inefficient from the point of view of optimal commodity taxation may be efficient in a larger setting.[15]

This situation is related to a more general phenomenon called the **time inconsistency of optimal policy**. Suppose the government announces that it will place a 10 percent tax on the value of capital in place today, but promises that no tax on capital will be levied at any time in the future. While capitalists presumably would not be pleased to pay the tax, it would appear to have no impact on their current incentives to save for the future. Such a tax is in effect a lump-sum levy and therefore fully efficient.

---

[15] Hettich and Winer (1985) provide further comparisons between optimal tax theory and the Buchanan–Brennan approach.

There is a problem, however. The government has an incentive to renege on its promise and pull exactly the same trick next year. That way the government can again attempt to raise revenue without an excess burden. Thus, the stated tax policy will be inconsistent with the government's incentives over time. Even worse, the capitalists realize the government has an incentive to renege. They will change their saving behaviour to reflect the expectation that the more they save now, the more they will be taxed next year. Because the expected tax changes behaviour, it introduces an inefficiency.

In short, unless the government can *credibly* promise not to renege, it cannot conduct the fully efficient tax policy. To avoid this time-inconsistency problem, the government must be able to commit itself to behave in certain ways in the future. How can this be done? One possible approach is to enact constitutional provisions that would forbid the government to go back on its promises. However, as long as the government has an underlying incentive to renege, suspicions will remain, frustrating attempts to run an efficient policy. These considerations suggest that the credibility of the political system must be considered before making recommendations based on optimal tax theory.

OTHER CRITERIA FOR TAX DESIGN

As we have seen, optimal taxation depends on the trade-off between "efficiency" and "fairness." However, the use of these concepts in optimal tax theory does not always correspond closely to lay usage. In the context of optimal tax theory, a fair tax is one that guarantees a socially desirable distribution of the tax burden; an efficient tax is one with a small excess burden. In public discussion, on the other hand, a fair tax is often one that imposes equal liabilities on people who have the same ability to pay, and an efficient tax system is one that keeps down administrative and compliance expenses. These alternative notions of fairness and efficiency in taxation are the subject of this section.

Horizontal Equity

A traditional criterion for good tax design is **horizontal equity**: "People in equal positions should be treated equally" (Musgrave, 1959: 160). Horizontal equity appeals to a fundamental sense of justice. However, to use this notion, *equal position* must be defined. Customarily, some observable index of ability to pay, such as income, expenditure, or wealth, defines equal position.

Unfortunately, these measures represent the *outcomes* of people's decisions and are not really suitable measures of equal position. Consider two individuals, both of whom can earn $10 per hour. Mr. *A* chooses to work 1,500 hours each year, while Ms. *B* works 2,200 hours each year. *A*'s income is $15,000 and *B*'s is $22,000, so that in terms of income, *A* and *B* are not in "equal positions." In an important sense, however, *A* and *B* *are* the same, because their earning capacities are identical—*B* just happens to work harder. Thus, because work effort is at least to some extent under people's control, two individuals with different incomes may actually be in equal positions. Similar criticism would apply to expenditure or wealth as a criterion for measuring equal positions.

These arguments suggest that the individual's wage *rate* rather than income be considered as a candidate for measuring equal positions, but this idea has problems too. First, investments in human capital—education, on-the-job training, and health care—can influence the wage rate. If Mr. *A* had to go to university to earn the same wage that Ms. *B* is able to earn with only a high school diploma, is it fair to treat them the same? Second, computation of the wage rate requires division of total earnings by hours of work, but the latter is not easy to measure. (How should time spent on coffee breaks be counted?) Indeed, for a given income, it would be worthwhile for a worker to exaggerate hours of work to be able to report a lower wage rate and pay fewer taxes. Presumably, bosses could be induced to collaborate with their employees in return for a share of the tax savings.

As an alternative to measuring equal position either in incomes or wage rates, Feldstein (1976) suggests it be defined in utilities. Hence, the **utility definition of horizontal equity:** (a) if two individuals would be equally well off (have the same utility level) in the absence of taxation, they should also be equally well off if there is taxation; and (b) taxes should not alter the utility ordering—if *A* is better off than *B* before taxation, he should be better off after.

To assess the implications of Feldstein's definition, first assume all individuals have the same preferences, that is, identical utility functions. In this case, individuals who consume the same commodities (including leisure) should pay the same tax, or, equivalently, all individuals should face the same tax schedule. Otherwise, individuals with equal before-tax utility levels would have different after-tax utilities.

Now assume that people have diverse tastes. For example, let there be two types of individuals, Gourmets and Sunbathers. Both groups consume food (which is purchased using income) and leisure, but Gourmets put a relatively high value on food, as do Sunbathers on leisure time. Assume further that before any taxation, Gourmets and Sunbathers have identical utility levels. If the same proportional income tax is imposed on everybody, Gourmets are necessarily made worse off than Sunbathers, because the former need relatively large amounts of income to support their food habits. Thus, even though this income tax is perfectly fair judged by the traditional definition of horizontal equity, it is not fair according to the utility definition. Indeed, as long as tastes for leisure differ, *any* income tax violates the utility definition of horizontal equity.

Of course, the practical difficulties involved in measuring individuals' utilities preclude the possibility of having a utility tax. Nevertheless, the utility definition of horizontal equity has some provocative policy implications. Assume again that all individuals have the same preferences. Then it can be shown that *any* existing tax structure does not violate the utility definition of horizontal equity *if* individuals are free to choose their activities and expenditures.

To see why, suppose that in one type of job a large part of compensation is in the form of amenities that are not taxable. These might include pleasant offices, access to a swimming pool, and so forth. In another occupation, compensation is exclusively monetary, all of which is subject to income tax. According to the traditional definition, this situation is a violation of horizontal equity, because a person in the job with a lot of amenities has too small a tax burden. But, if both arrangements coexist and individuals are free to choose, then the net after-tax rewards (including amenities) must be the same in both jobs. Why? Suppose that the net after-tax reward is greater in the jobs with amenities. Then individuals migrate to these jobs to take advantage of them. But the increased supply of workers in these jobs depresses their wages. The process continues until the *net* returns are equal. In short, although people in the different occupations pay unequal taxes, there is no horizontal inequity because of adjustments in the *before-tax* wage.

Some suggest that certain tax advantages available only to the rich are sources of horizontal inequity. According to the utility definition, this notion is wrong. If these advantages are open to everyone with high income, and all high-income people have identical tastes, then the advantages may indeed reduce tax progressiveness, but they have no effect whatsoever on horizontal equity.

We are led to a striking conclusion: Given common tastes, a pre-existing tax structure cannot involve horizontal inequity. Rather, all horizontal inequities arise from changes in tax laws. This is because individuals make commitments based on the existing tax laws that are difficult or impossible to reverse. For example, people may buy larger houses because of the preferred tax treatment for owner-occupied housing.[16] When the tax laws are changed, their welfare goes down, and horizontal equity is violated. Many of the initiatives to

---

[16] See Chapter 21.

broaden the tax base in Finance Minister MacEachen's 1981 tax reform were attacked on the basis that "desirable incentives" had suddenly become "unattractive loopholes." These observations give new meaning to the dictum, "The only good tax is an old tax."[17]

The fact that tax changes may generate horizontal inequities does not necessarily imply that they should not be undertaken. After all, tax changes may lead to improvements from the points of view of efficiency and/or vertical equity. However, the arguments suggest that it might be appropriate somehow to ease the transition to the new tax system. For example, if it is announced that a given tax reform is not to go into effect until a few years subsequent to its passage, people who have based their behaviour on the old tax structure will be able to make at least some adjustments to the new regime. The problem of finding fair processes for changing tax regimes (transitional equity) is very difficult, and not many results are available on the subject.

The very conservative implications of the utility definition of horizontal equity should come as no great surprise, because implicit in the definition is the notion that the pretax status quo has special ethical validity. (Otherwise, why be concerned about changes in the ordering of utilities?) However, it is not at all obvious why the status quo deserves to be defended. A more general feature of the utility definition is its focus on the *outcomes* of taxation. In contrast, some have suggested that the essence of horizontal equity is to put constraints on the *rules* that govern the selection of taxes, rather than to provide criteria for judging their effects. Thus, horizontal equity excludes capricious taxes, or taxes based on irrelevant characteristics. For example, we can imagine the government levying special lump-sum taxes on people with red hair, or putting very different taxes on angel food and chocolate cakes. The rule definition of horizontal equity would presumably exclude such taxes from consideration, even if they somehow had desirable efficiency or distributional effects.

However, identifying the permissible set of characteristics on which to base taxation is a problem. Most people would agree that religion and race should be irrelevant for purposes of determining tax liability. On the other hand, there is continuing disagreement as to whether or not marital status should influence tax burdens (see Chapter 20 under "Choice of Tax Unit"). And even once there is agreement that certain characteristics are legitimate bases for discrimination, the problem of how much discrimination is appropriate still remains. Everyone agrees that serious physical impairment should be taken into account in determining personal tax liability. But how much must your

---

[17] See the discussion of tax capitalization in Chapter 17.

vision be impaired before you are eligible for special tax treatment as blind? And by what amount should your tax bill be reduced?

We are forced to conclude that horizontal equity, however defined, is a rather amorphous concept. Yet it continues to have enormous appeal as a principle of tax design. Notions of fairness among equals, regardless of their vagueness, will continue to play an important role in the implementation of tax policy.

Costs of Running the Tax System

An implicit assumption in the models we have been studying is that collecting taxes involves no costs. However, contrary to this assumption, tax administration is not a costless activity. Rather, gathering taxes requires the consumption of resources by the taxing authorities. At the same time, taxpayers incur costs in complying with the tax system. These include outlays for accountants and tax lawyers, as well as the value of taxpayers' time spent filling out tax returns and keeping records. The controversy surrounding the introduction of the GST in 1991 highlighted this reality.

The costs of administering the personal income and payroll taxes in Canada are fairly low. For example, Vaillancourt (1989) found that the government spends only about $1 to raise each $100 in tax revenues.[18] However, the compliance costs of personal income taxes and payroll taxes are quite substantial. Vaillancourt estimated that in 1986 the average Canadian taxpayer devoted about 5.5 hours in order to prepare his or her own return. Those paying to have their tax returns prepared spent an average of $69 for professional assistance. The average cost per taxpayer was estimated by Vaillancourt (1989: 83) to be $122.50 in 1986. Multiplying this by 15.9 million taxpaying units in 1986 gives a total cost of $1.95 billion, or 2.5 percent of the personal income and payroll taxes collected. To this we must add the compliance costs of employers, estimated at $2.75 billion or 3.5 percent of revenues. Total administrative and compliance costs—government, individuals, employers—equalled about 7 percent of revenues, or $5.5 billion, in 1986.

Clearly, the choice of tax and subsidy systems should take account of administrative and compliance costs. Even systems that appear fair and efficient (in the excess burden sense) might be undesirable because they are excessively complicated and expensive to administer. Consider the possibility of taxing output produced in the home—housecleaning, child care, and so on. As sug-

---

[18] These cost estimates are for the personal income tax, and for unemployment insurance and Canada Pension Plan premiums collected from employees and employers.

gested in Chapter 18, the fact that market work is taxed but housework is not creates a sizable distortion in the allocation of labour. Moreover, an argument could be made that taxing differentially on the basis of choice of workplace violates some notions of horizontal equity. Nevertheless, the difficulties involved in valuing household production would create such huge administrative costs that the idea is infeasible.

Unfortunately, in many cases, administrative problems receive insufficient attention. A classic case is that of the combined federal and provincial excise taxes on tobacco products at the end of 1993 and into 1994.[19] Early in 1994 taxes on cigarettes had reached a level (between $2.75 and $3 per pack of twenty-five) at which smuggling across the Canada–U.S. border was rampant. Perhaps two-thirds of all cigarettes in Quebec were purchased illegally. The smuggling problem was also serious in Ontario and other eastern provinces. Cigarette taxes were subsequently cut by as much as 60 percent in Quebec and Ontario, with lesser reductions in other provinces, to reduce the incentive to evade the taxes. An additional 350 customs inspectors were hired, and the number of RCMP antismuggling agents was doubled.[20]

The Goods and Services Tax (GST) has also proved to have higher than anticipated compliance and administrative costs. One study found GST *compliance* costs to be 17 percent of tax collected for businesses with annual sales of $100,000 or less and 2.65 percent for those with yearly sales over $1 million. Revenue Canada estimated *administrative* costs at 3 percent of the revenues, much higher than for similar taxes in other countries (House of Commons, 1994).

Obviously, no tax system is costless to administer; the trick is to think carefully about whether or not the administrative costs are worth the benefits. In some cases, it may be necessary to trade off excess burden against administrative costs. For example, it might be very cumbersome to administer a sales tax system in which each commodity has its own rate, despite the fact that this is the general tack prescribed by the Ramsey rule. Any reductions in excess burden that arise from differentiating the tax rates must be compared to the incremental administrative costs.

---

[19] This discussion is based on information found on pages 8:5 to 8:7 in *The National Finances, 1994*.

[20] This addressed the problem of smuggling in Central Canada, but with big differences in cigarette taxes between provinces in the East and West ($4.11 per pack in British Columbia versus $1.21 in Ontario) that have resulted, there is an increased incentive for illegal cigarette traffic among provinces.

Tax Evasion

We now turn to one of the most important problems facing any tax administration—cheating. First, it is important to distinguish between tax avoidance and tax evasion. **Tax avoidance** is changing your behaviour so as to reduce your legal tax liability. There is nothing illegal about tax avoidance:

> Over and over again courts have said that there is nothing sinister in so arranging one's affairs so as to keep taxes as low as possible. Everybody does so, rich or poor; and all do right, for nobody owes any public duty to pay more than the law demands.... To demand more in the name of morals is mere cant. (Judge Learned Hand, *Commissioner v. Newman*, 1947)

In contrast, **tax evasion** is failing to pay legally due taxes. If a tax on mushrooms is levied and you sell fewer mushrooms, it is tax avoidance. If you fail to report your sales of mushrooms to the government, it is tax evasion. Tax evasion is not a new problem. Centuries ago Plato observed, "When there is an income tax, the just man will pay more and the unjust less on the same amount of income." In recent years, however, the phenomenon of tax evasion has received a large amount of public attention.

Tax cheating is extremely difficult to measure. Although Revenue Canada has not published estimates on tax cheating, the Minister of National Revenue has publicly acknowledged it as an important issue.

There are several common ways to commit tax fraud:

1. *Keep two sets of books to record business transactions.* One records the actual business and the other is shown to the tax authorities. Some evaders use two cash registers.
2. *Moonlight for cash.* Of course, there is nothing illegal in working an extra job. In many cases, however, the income received on such jobs is paid in cash rather than by cheque. Hence, there is no legal record, and the income is not reported to the tax authorities.
3. *Barter.* "I'll fix your car if you bake me five loaves of bread." When you receive payment in kind instead of money, it is legally a taxable transaction. However, such income is seldom reported.
4. *Deal in cash.* Paying for goods and services with cash and cheques made out to "cash" makes it very difficult for Revenue Canada to trace transactions.

At one time, tax evasion was associated with millionaires who hid their capital in Swiss bank accounts. Now the current image of a tax evader may well be a repairer whose income comes from "unofficial" work not reported for tax purposes, or a small business where cash transactions are common.

We first discuss the positive theory of tax evasion, and then turn to the normative question of how public policy should deal with it.

Positive analysis of tax evasion. Assume Al cares only about maximizing his expected income.[21] He has a given amount of earnings and is trying to choose R, the amount that he hides from the tax authorities. Suppose Al's marginal income tax rate is 0.3; for each dollar shielded from taxable income, his tax bill falls by 30 cents. This is the marginal benefit to him of hiding a dollar of income from the tax authorities. More generally, when Al faces a marginal income tax rate t, the marginal benefit of each dollar shielded from taxation is t.

The tax authority does not know Al's true income, but it randomly audits all taxpayers' returns. As a result, there is some probability, ρ, that Al will be audited. If he is caught cheating, Al pays a penalty that increases with R at an increasing rate. Note that if it were costless to monitor Al every second of every day, there would be no opportunities for evasion. The fact that such monitoring is infeasible is the fundamental source of the problem.

Assuming that Al knows the value of ρ and the penalty schedule, he makes his decision by comparing the marginal costs and benefits of cheating. In Figure 19.5, the amount of income not reported is measured on the horizontal axis, and dollars on the vertical. The marginal benefit (MB) for each dollar not reported is t, the amount of tax saved. The expected marginal cost (MC) is the amount by which the penalty goes up for each dollar of cheating (the marginal penalty) times the probability of detection. For example, if the additional penalty for hiding the thousandth dollar is $1.50 and the probability of detection is 1 in 3, then the *expected* marginal penalty is 50 cents. The "optimal" amount of cheating is where the two schedules cross, at R^*. R^* is optimal in the sense that *on average* it is the policy that maximizes Al's income. In a world of uncertainty, finding the best policy in this "expected value" sense is a reasonable way to proceed. It is possible, of course, that it will be optimal not to cheat at all. For the individual in Figure 19.6, the marginal cost of cheating exceeds the marginal benefit for all positive values of R, so the optimum is equal to zero.

---

[21] This model is similar in structure to those that have been used to describe criminal behaviour in general. See Becker (1968) and Cowell (1990).

Figure 19.5

Optimal Tax Evasion is Positive

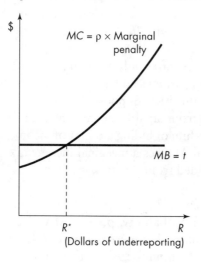

The model implies that cheating increases when marginal tax rates go up. This is because a higher value of t increases the marginal benefit of evasion, shifting up the marginal benefit schedule so the intersection with marginal cost occurs at a higher value of R.[22] On the basis of such reasoning, many people thought the increase in marginal tax rates on average Canadians that occurred from 1950 through the early 1980s contributed to an increase in tax cheating, and that the reductions in marginal rates in the tax reforms of 1981 and 1987 would help address the problem. A further implication of the model is that cheating decreases when the probability of detection goes up and when the marginal penalty rate increases. Both of these steps raise the expected marginal cost of cheating.

Although this model yields useful insights, it ignores some potentially important considerations.

Psychic costs of cheating. Simply put, tax evasion may make people feel guilty. One way to model this phenomenon is by adding psychic costs to the marginal

---

[22] This prediction is borne out by the econometric work of Clotfelter (1983), who estimated for the United States that the elasticity of underreported income with respect to the marginal tax rate is about 0.84. This means that for a 10 percent increase in the marginal tax rate, say from 30 to 33 percent, unreported income increases by 8.4 percent.

Figure 19.6

Optimal Tax Evasion is Zero

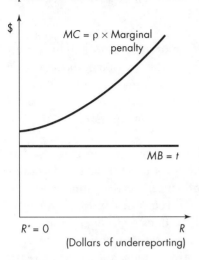

cost schedule. For some very honest people, the psychic costs are so high they would not cheat even if the expected marginal penalty were zero.

Risk aversion. Figures 19.5 and 19.6 assume people care only about expected income, and that risk per se does not bother them. To the extent that individuals are risk averse, their decisions to engage in what is essentially a gamble may be modified.

Work choices. The model assumes the only decision is how much income to report. The type of job and the amount of before-tax income are taken as given. In reality, the tax system may affect hours of work and job choices. For example, high marginal tax rates might induce people to choose occupations that provide substantial opportunities for evading taxation, the so-called **underground economy**.[23] This includes economic activities that are legal but easy to hide from the tax authorities (home repairs) as well as work that is criminal per se (prostitution, selling drugs). Based on a random survey carried out in the region of Quebec City, Lemieux, Fortin, and Frechette (1994) found that when marginal tax rates increase, so does the probability of participating in the underground sector.

---

[23] However, this is not necessarily the case; see Sandmo (1981).

The range of estimates on the size of the underground economy is quite wide. Statistics Canada estimates that the underground economy is, at most, 5.2 percent of GDP, or $40 billion in 1994 (Smith, 1994). Other estimates are in the range of 10 to 12 percent of GDP, or $75 to $90 billion.[24]

Changing probabilities of audit. In our simple analysis, the probability of an audit is independent of both the amount evaded and the size of income reported. However, in Canada audit probabilities depend on occupation and the size of reported income. Tax returns received by e-mail are also more likely to be audited. This complicates the model, but does not change its essential aspects.

It is clear that cheating is a more complicated phenomenon than Figures 19.5 and 19.6 suggest. Nevertheless, the model provides us with a useful framework for thinking about the factors that influence the decision to evade. Unfortunately, by its very nature, it is difficult to do empirical work on tax evasion. Consequently, it is not known whether high fines or frequent audits are more effective ways of deterring cheating. One tentative result that emerges from several econometric studies is that, for most groups, audits do increase the probability of subsequent compliance, but the magnitude of the effect is small (Beron, Tauchen, and Witte, 1990).

Normative analysis of tax evasion. Most public discussions of the underground economy assume that it is a bad thing and that policy should be designed to reduce its size. Although possibly correct, this proposition is worth scrutiny.

An important question in this context is whether or not we care about the welfare of tax evaders. In the jargon of welfare economics, do the utilities of participants in the underground economy belong in the social welfare function? Assume for the moment that they do. Then under certain conditions, the existence of an underground economy raises social welfare. For example, if the supply of labour is more elastic to the underground economy than to the regular economy, optimal tax theory suggests that the former be taxed at a relatively low rate. This is simply an application of the inverse elasticity rule, Equation (19.11). Alternatively, suppose that participants in the underground economy tend to be poorer than those in the regular economy, and that the underground economy permits employment of individuals who would be unemployed if normal taxes and other regulations (e.g., minimum wages)

---

[24] A wide variety of methods have been used to estimate the underground economy. See Mirus et al. (1994) and Spiro (1994) for a literature review and recent estimates.

applied. Then to the extent society has egalitarian income redistribution objectives, leaving the underground economy intact might be desirable.

Of course, there is no proof that either of these assertions is correct. The important point is that the usual utilitarian welfare analysis leads to ambiguous results about the desirability of an underground economy.[25]

Consider now the policy implications when evaders are not given any weight in the social welfare function, and the goal is simply to eliminate cheating at the lowest administrative cost possible. Figure 19.5 suggests a fairly straightforward way to accomplish this objective. The expected marginal cost of cheating is the product of the penalty rate and the probability of detection. The probability of detection depends on the amount of resources devoted to tax administration; if Revenue Canada has a big budget, it can catch a lot of cheaters. However, even if the tax authorities have a small budget so that the probability of detection is low, the marginal cost of cheating can still be made arbitrarily high if the penalty is large enough. If only one tax evader were caught each year, but he or she were publicly hanged for the crime, the *expected* cost of tax evasion would deter many people. The fact that such a draconian policy has never been seriously proposed in Canada is indicative of the fact that existing penalty systems try to incorporate *just retribution*.[26] Contrary to the assumptions of the utilitarian framework, society cares not only about the end result (getting rid of cheaters), but also the processes by which the result is achieved.

In their search for a socially acceptable way to deal with tax evaders, state governments in the United States have declared periods of **tax amnesty**. During a tax amnesty, people can pay delinquent taxes without facing criminal charges for their previous tax evasion. It is difficult to assess the likely impact on tax collections of a tax amnesty. Tax amnesties in the United States have often been accompanied by an announced intention to increase enforcement efforts, and the success of many "tax amnesty programs" may be due partly to increased enforcement. A further problem in assessing the success of tax amnesty programs lies in the long-term effects of tax amnesties on tax compliance. When tax amnesties are declared repeatedly, the knowledge that an amnesty is forthcoming can lower taxpayers' perceived chances of being prosecuted for future tax evasion. By lowering the expected costs of future tax evasion, an amnesty

---

[25] For further discussion along these lines, see Sandmo (1981).
[26] Other nations have not been so constrained in enforcing economic honesty. In China, for example, embezzlement can be a capital offence.

program that brings with it an expectation of future amnesties may actually *increase* tax evasion.

OVERVIEW

Traditional analysis of tax systems elucidated several "principles" of tax design: taxes should have horizontal and vertical equity, be "neutral" with respect to economic incentives, be administratively easy, and so on. In recent years, public finance economists have integrated these somewhat ad hoc guidelines with the principles of welfare economics. The optimal tax literature *derives* the criteria for a good tax using an underlying social welfare function.

On some occasions, optimal tax analysis has corrected previous errors. For example, it may *not* be efficient for all tax rates to be the same (neutral)—taxing additive tobacco products more heavily than other goods may be efficient. Furthermore, optimal tax theory has clarified the trade-offs between efficiency and equity in tax design. As a by-product, the various definitions of "equity" have been scrutinized.

The result of this work is not a blueprint for building a tax system, if for no other reason than the economic theory forming the basis for optimal tax theory has its own problems (see Chapter 4). In this context two comments are cogent. First, optimal tax theory generally ignores political and social institutions. An "optimal" tax may easily be ruined by politicians or be overly costly to administer. Second, while the optimal tax approach points out that the concept of horizontal equity is difficult to make operational, the fact remains that *equal treatment of equals* is an appealing ethical concept. Horizontal equity is difficult to integrate with optimal tax theory because of the latter's focus on outcomes rather than processes.

Thus, optimal tax theory has used the tools of welfare economics to add analytical strength to the traditional discussion of the goals of tax design. Nevertheless, it is wedded to the utilitarian welfare approach in economics. As such, it is open to criticisms concerning the adequacy of this ethical system.

SUMMARY

- Efficient commodity tax theory studies how to raise a given amount of revenue with a minimum of excess burden.

- The Ramsey rule stipulates that to minimize excess burden, tax rates should be set so that the proportional reduction in the quantity demanded of each good is the same.

- When goods are unrelated in consumption, the Ramsey rule implies that relative tax rates should be inversely related to compensated demand elasticities.

- Choosing optimal user fees for government-produced services is quite similar to choosing optimal taxes. In particular, there are efficiency and distributional considerations in choosing an optimal two-part tariff.

- Income taxation is a major source of revenue in developed countries. Edgeworth's early study of optimal income taxes stipulated that after-tax incomes be equal. However, when the excess burden of distorting the leisure–income trade-off is included, marginal tax rates of far less than 100 percent are optimal. A surprising result of optimal income tax theory is that if marginal tax rates are allowed to vary, in general, the marginal tax rate on the highest income should be zero.

- Tax systems may be evaluated by standards other than those of optimal tax theory. Horizontal equity, the costs of administration, incentives for tax evasion, and political constraints all affect the design of tax systems.

- Traditional definitions of horizontal equity rely on income as a measure of "equal position" in society. However, it is not clear that income as conventionally measured does an adequate job. The utility definition is more precise, but leads to radically different policy provisions and contains an inherent bias toward the pretax status quo. Other definitions of horizontal equity focus on the rules by which taxes are chosen.

- The costs of running a tax system are ignored in most theoretical analyses. However, administrative and compliance costs affect the choice of tax base, tax rates, and the amount of tax evasion.

DISCUSSION QUESTIONS

1. "If the compensated demand for a single commodity is completely inelastic, the most socially desirable ad valorem tax rate on this commodity will be higher than the tax rates on other commodities." Comment.

2. Early in 1994 the combined federal and provincial excise taxes on cigarettes in Canada were about $3 per pack of twenty-five. Discuss the efficiency, equity, and administrability of cigarette taxes at this level.

3. Prior to 1988, Revenue Canada permitted business meals and entertainment expenses to be fully deducted in calculating taxable income. Since then, the allowed deduction has been reduced to 50 percent of the expense. This affects those who incur such expenses as part of normal business activity. Evaluate this change in tax policy using the alternative criteria for horizontal equity.

4. "If tips must be reported as taxable income, restaurants will go out of business, costing jobs. In addition, it's too hard to find out how much in tips waiters and waitresses actually receive. Besides, most of the people who earn tips have low incomes and shouldn't be taxed anyway." Discuss the equity and efficiency aspects of the problem of taxing tips.

REFERENCES

Auerbach, Alan J. "The Theory of Excess Burden and Optimal Taxation," in *Handbook of Public Economics*, vol. 1, ed. Alan J. Auerbach and Martin S. Feldstein. Amsterdam: North-Holland, 1985, pp. 61–128.

Ballard, Charles L., John B. Shoven, and John Whalley. "General Equilibrium Computations of the Marginal Welfare Costs of Taxes in the United States." *American Economic Review 75*, no. 1 (March 1985): 128–38.

Becker, Gary S. "Crime and Punishment: An Economic Approach." *Journal of Political Economy 76* (March–April 1968): 169–217.

Beron, K.J., H.V. Tauchen, and A.D. Witte. "The Effect of Audits and Socioeconomic Variables on Compliance." Mimeograph. Wellesley, MA: Wellesley College, 1990.

Boskin, Michael J., and Eytan Sheshinski. "Optimal Tax Treatment of the Family: Married Couples." Working Paper 368. Cambridge, MA: National Bureau of Economic Research, 1979.

Brennan, Geoffrey, and James M. Buchanan. "Toward a Tax Constitution for Leviathan." *Journal of Public Economics 8*, no. 3 (December 1977): 255–74.

Canadian Tax Foundation. *The National Finances, 1994.* Toronto: Canadian Tax Foundation, 1994.

Clotfelter, Charles T. "Tax Evasion and Tax Rates: An Analysis of Individual Returns." *Review of Economics and Statistics 65*, no. 3 (August 1983): 363–73.

Corlett, W.J., and D.C. Hague. "Complementarity and the Excess Burden of Taxation." *Review of Economic Studies 21* (1953): 21–30.

Cowell, Frank A. *Cheating the Government.* Cambridge, MA: MIT Press, 1990.

Diamond, Peter A. "A Many-Person Ramsay Tax Rule." *Journal of Public Economics 4* (1975): 335–42.

Edgeworth, F.Y. "The Pure Theory of Taxation," reprinted in *Readings in the Economics of Taxation*, ed. Richard A. Musgrave and Carl S. Shoup. Homewood, IL: Richard D. Irwin, 1959, pp. 258–96.

Feldstein, Martin S. "On the Theory of Tax Reform." *Journal of Public Economics 6* (1976): 77–104.

Feldstein, Martin S. "Equity and Efficiency in Public Sector Pricing: The Optimal Two-Part Tariff." *Quarterly Journal of Economics 86* (1972): 175–87.

Henderson, James M., and Richard E. Quandt. *Microeconomic Theory: A Mathematical Approach*, 3rd ed. New York: McGraw-Hill, 1980.

Hettich, Walter, and Stanley Winer. "Blueprints and Pathways: The Shifting Foundations of Tax Reform." *National Tax Journal* 38, no. 4 (December 1985): 423–46.

House of Commons, Standing Committee on Finance. *Replacing the GST: Options for Canada.* June 1994.

Lemieux, Thomas, Bernard Fortin, and Pierre Frechette. "The Effect of Taxes on Labor Supply in the Underground Economy." *American Economic Review* 84, no. 1 (March 1994): 231–54.

Mirus, Rolf, Roger S. Smith, and Vladimir Karoleff. "Canada's Underground Economy Revisited: Update and Critique." *Canadian Public Policy* 20, no. 3 (1994): 235–52.

Musgrave, Richard A. *The Theory of Public Finance.* New York: McGraw-Hill, 1959.

Ramsay, Frank P. "A Contribution to the Theory of Taxation." *Economic Journal* 37 (1927): 47–61.

Sandmo, Agnar. "Income Tax Evasion, Labour Supply, and the Equity-Efficiency Trade-off." *Journal of Public Economics* 16, no. 3 (December 1981): 265–88.

Slemrod, Joel, Shlomo Yitzhaki, Joram Mayshar, and Michael Lundholm. "The Optimal Two-Bracket Linear Income Tax." *Journal of Public Economics* 53 (February 1994): 269–90.

Smith, Philip. "Assessing the Size of the Underground Economy: The Statistics Canada Perspective." *Canadian Economic Observer* (May 1994): 3.16–33.

Spiro, Peter S. "Estimating the Underground Economy: A Critical Evaluation of the Monetary Approach." *Canadian Tax Journal* 42, no. 4 (1994): 1059–81.

Stern, Nicholas H. "On the Specification of Models of Optimal Income Taxation." *Journal of Public Economics* 6, nos. 1 and 2 (July–August 1976): 123–62.

Tresch, Richard W. *Public Finance: A Normative Theory.* Plano, TX: Business Publications, 1981.

Vaillancourt, Francois. *The Administrative and Compliance Costs of the Personal Income Tax and Payroll Tax System in Canada, 1986.* Toronto: Canadian Tax Foundation, 1989.

Part 6

The Canadian Revenue System

The next five chapters describe and analyze the major sources of revenue in the Canadian fiscal system. This involves some bad news and some good news. The bad news is that it is hard to know just how long the descriptive material will be correct. The 1987 tax reform, which included the introduction of the Goods and Services Tax in January 1991, was the most recent major revision of Canada's taxes. Significant changes to our tax system are continually under consideration, and adjustments will continue to be made even if major change does not occur in the new few years. The good news is that after seeing the tools of public finance applied to the existing tax institutions, the reader will be in a position to analyze any new taxes that may arise. Moreover, we discuss some major proposed modifications for each of the existing taxes.

Describing each tax individually seems to be the only feasible expositional technique. Nevertheless, keep in mind that the various taxes do interact. For example, audits for federal Goods and Services Tax may improve income tax compliance while simultaneously increasing, at least in some cases, the incentive to evade federal taxes. More generally, failure to consider more than one tax at a time gives a misleading picture of the overall magnitude of the tax burden.

Chapter 20

The Personal Income Tax

It was true as taxes is. And nothing's truer than them.

–Charles Dickens, *David Copperfield*

The personal income tax is the workhorse of the Canadian tax system. In 1994, over 20.1 million tax returns were filed by a Canadian population of 29.3 million. Personal income taxes generated $62.0 billion in revenue for the federal government and $40.5 billion for provincial governments in fiscal 1994/95. The personal income tax accounted for 45 percent of federal revenues, 31 percent of provincial own-source revenues, and 34 percent of consolidated (including local government) revenues.[1]

Personal income tax revenues grew rapidly in the postwar period, as shown in Table 20.1. The number of returns rose from about 3.2 million, 16 percent of Canada's population in 1946, to about 20.2 million, 69 percent of the population, in 1994. Federal plus provincial revenues increased from $671 million in 1946 to about $102.5 billion in 1994. This was a per capita increase from $356 to $2,733 in constant 1986 dollars, an eightfold increase. The personal income tax grew rapidly as a share of GDP, from 5.5 percent to 13.7 percent, and as a share of total government revenues, from 17.2 percent in 1946 to 33.8 percent by 1994. Relative to other countries, Table 20.2 shows that Canada's reliance on the personal income tax grew rapidly.

---

[1] Computed from Statistics Canada, *Public Sector Finance, 1995–1996*, Cat. no. 68-212-XPB (Ottawa: March 1996).

Table 20.1

Personal Income Tax Revenues in Canada, 1933 to 1994

| | | | | PIT AS % OF | |
YEAR	NUMBER OF RETURNS (THOUSANDS)	PIT REVENUES (MILLIONS)	PER CAPITA 1986 $*	TOTAL REVENUES (PERCENT)	GDP (PERCENT)
1933		$ 38	32	5.1	1.0
1946	3,162	671	356	17.2	5.5
1955	4,923	1,318	247	19.2	4.5
1965	7,163	3,477	642	22.6	6.0
1975	12,002	19,023	1,774	30.3	11.1
1985	15,864	56,594	2,265	31.5	11.8
1994	20,154	102,488	2,733	33.8	13.7

* The deflator used was the GDP price index for personal expenditure for consumer goods and services.

SOURCE: M.C. Urquhart and K.A.H. Buckley, *Historical Statistics of Canada*, 2nd ed. (Ottawa: Minister of Supply and Services, 1983), pp. H52–74; Statistics Canada, *Public Finance Historical Data 1965/66–1991/92*, Cat. no. 68-512 occasional (Ottawa: March 1992), pp. 162–63; Statistics Canada, *Public Sector Finance 1995–1996*, Cat. no. 68-212 annual (Ottawa: March 1996), p. 167; Statistics Canada, *Canadian Economic Observer, Historical Statistical Supplement 1995/96*, Cat. no. 11-210-XPB, vol. 10 (July 1996), pp. 3, 25, 41; Revenue Canada, *Tax Statistics on Individuals, 1996 Edition* (Ottawa: Revenue Canada, 1996), p. 241.

Provincial revenues from the individual income tax have increased particularly rapidly in the past thirty years.[2] Personal income taxes rose from 11 percent of provincially raised revenues in 1965/66 to 31 percent by 1994/95, and the provinces' share of personal income tax revenues increased from 24 percent to 40 percent.

This chapter discusses problems associated with designing a personal income tax system, how Canada has dealt with them, and the efficiency and equity of the results. Since its inception in 1917, the income tax law has been revised many times. We devote some attention to explaining and evaluating the changes that have been made in recent years.

BASIC STRUCTURE

The federal Income Tax Act requires Canadians to file an annual tax return that computes their previous year's tax liability. The individual is the taxable unit.

[2] Income taxes are not used by local governments in Canada. Income taxes are, however, a major source of revenues for local governments in countries such as Sweden and Japan. They are also an important revenue source for several major U.S. cities, including New York City and Philadelphia. Both large and small local jurisdictions in Ohio and Pennsylvania derive revenues from local income taxes.

Table 20.2

Personal Income Taxes as a Percentage of GDP, OECD Countries, 1965 to 1994

YEAR	CANADA	U.S.	OECD EUROPE
1965	5.9	7.9	7.2
1975	10.6	9.5	10.4
1985	11.6	10.2	11.1
1994	13.4	9.8	10.5

SOURCE: Organization for Economic Cooperation and Development, *Revenue Statistics of OECD Member Countries, 1965–1995* (Paris: OECD, 1996), p. 79.

Individuals who are resident in Canada for at least 183 days during the year are taxable on their worldwide income. The tax return is due every April 30.

All Canadian provinces, with the exception of Quebec, levy their income tax as a percentage of the federal tax and have signed a collection agreement with the federal government. This permits individuals to complete one tax form and submit payment of both the federal and provincial tax to Revenue Canada. This has simplified administration and compliance and enhances public understanding of a complex form of taxation. One of the strengths of the Canadian income tax system has been integration and harmonization of the federal and provincial income taxes.[3]

The calculation of tax liability requires a series of steps summarized in Figure 20.1. The first step is to compute "total income." Total income is defined as income from all taxable sources. Taxable sources include (but are not limited to) wages, dividends, interest, realized capital gains, alimony, rents, royalties, income from pensions (including QPP and CPP), Unemployment Insurance (UI) and Old Age Security (OAS) benefits, and business profits including those from farming and fishing. In the calculation of business profits, the taxpayer may deduct expenses incurred in earning income such that total income includes only net business income.

---

[3] This harmonization comes at a cost, a cost that Quebec has been unwilling to pay. Therefore, Quebec (like many states in the United States) uses separate forms to collect its income taxes, permitting greater deviation from the federal tax, both its base and its rate structure. Provincial reliance on the federal tax base limits the use that provinces can make of the personal income tax for policy purposes. This has led provinces, Ontario and Alberta in particular, to consider following Quebec's example and collecting their own tax. With the provincial role growing relative to the federal role, and the cutback in federal transfers to provinces, provinces continue to press for greater freedom within the Tax Collection Agreement. The greater policy flexibility such freedom provides to provinces is likely to come at a cost of increased complexity, which raises administrative and compliance costs.

Other benefits also add to taxable income. These include gratuities, the value of room and board, the value of personal use of an employer's car, allowances for personal living expenses, the value of below-market interest rates on loans provided by employers, benefits from share purchases at below-market rates, benefits under deferred benefit plans, and allowances for personal living expenses.

Income in a number of forms is not taxed. This includes employers' contributions to employee pension plans in the year the contribution is made; nor is the income on these plans taxed in the year earned. Employer payments to group dental and medical plans, to group life insurance plans (up to $25,000 per employee), and to supplemental unemployment benefit plans are not taxed to the employee. Nor is the value of counselling services for mental and physical health, or the winnings from lotteries or other gambling, taxed. Finally, several forms of income from government are excluded from taxable income: disability payments and payments from provincial Worker's Compensation Boards, and "income-tested" payments from governments, such as federal Guaranteed Income Supplements (GIS) and provincial social assistance. Several major sources of untaxed income are discussed in the following sections.

Not all of "total income" is subject to tax. The second step is to convert total income to taxable income—the amount of income subject to tax. This is done by subtracting various amounts called deductions from total income. Some deductions recognize additional expenses of earning income, and others are used by the government to encourage private savings. The former include union dues, child care expenses, moving expenses, and some other employment expenses. The latter include contributions to retirement savings plans such as RRSPs and RPPs. Since alimony payments are included in the income of the recipient, a deduction is permitted to a taxpayer required to make such payments. Deductions are discussed more fully later.

The third step is to calculate the amount of tax due before tax credits. Federal tax rates are applied to taxable income. The fourth and final step is to calculate and subtract "nonrefundable"[4] tax credits and other tax credits. These credits reduce taxes that would otherwise be due, and recognize factors that affect the taxpayer's ability to pay. However, as with deductions, credits are also used to encourage certain taxpayer behaviour. The credits recognize:

- the number of individuals supported by the taxpayer, including the taxpayer,

---

[4] The credits are nonrefundable in that if the credits exceed taxes payable, the government does not pay the difference to the taxpayer.

Figure 20.1

Computation of Personal Income Tax Liability

STEP 1:
ADD: Income from taxable sources:
- wages and other employment income
- interest
- dividends
- rent
- taxable capital gains
- alimony received
- royalties
- pension and unemployment insurance benefits
- net business income
- ...
  = Total Income

STEP 2:
SUBTRACT: Deductions:
- union dues and certain employment expenses
- child care expenses
- moving expenses
- interest expenses
- eligible RRSP and RPP contributions
- alimony payments
  = Taxable Income

STEP 3:
APPLY: Tax rate schedule to Taxable Income
    = Income tax **before** tax credits

STEP 4:
SUBTRACT: Nonrefundable tax credits for:
- taxpayer and dependents
- medical expenses and disabilities
- age and pension income
- contributions to QPP and CPP
- premiums paid for UI
- eligible tuition and education expenses
- gifts to charities and to the Crown
- and any other tax credits
  = **Federal tax payable**

STEP 5:
CALCULATE: Provincial tax payable based on federal tax payable

- age of the taxpayer, and the existence of medical expenses or disabilities,
- required contributions by the taxpayer to the Canada or Quebec Pension Plans and to Unemployment Insurance,
- voluntary expenditures for education or contributions for charitable purposes.

The tax credits are subtracted to obtain the taxpayer's "federal tax." The provincial tax is a percentage of the federal tax.[5]

For most taxpayers, some tax is withheld out of each paycheque during the year. The amount that actually has to be paid on April 30 is the difference between the tax liability and the accumulated withholding payments. If more has been withheld than is owed, the taxpayer is entitled to a refund.

It sounds fairly straightforward, but in reality complications arise in every step of the process. We now discuss some of the major problems.

DEFINING INCOME

Clearly, the ability to identify "income" is necessary to operate an income tax. A natural way to begin this section would be to discuss and evaluate the definition of income in the Income Tax Act. However, the law provides no definition. It does indicate that income subject to tax includes that from employment in the form of wages and salaries, income from a business, income from investments, including capital gains, and income from sources such as alimony, pensions, unemployment benefits, and royalties.[6]

---

[5] With a federal surtax, provincial surtaxes, and flat-rate taxes, as well as credits for political contributions and for foreign taxes paid, even for the simplest cases the situation is more complex than described here.

[6] The definition in the Income War Tax Act (1917) is as follows: " 'Income' means the annual net profit or gain or gratuity, whether ascertained and capable of computation as wages, salary, or other fixed amount, or unascertained as being fees or emoluments, or as being profits from a trade or commercial or financial or other business or calling, directly or indirectly received by a person from any office or employment, or from any profession or calling, or from any trade, manufacture or business, as the case may be; and shall include interest, dividends or profits directly or indirectly received from money at interest upon any security or without security, or from stocks, or from any other investment and, whether such gains or profits are divided or distributed or not, and also the annual profit or gain from any other source; including the income from but not the value of property acquired by gift, bequest, or devise or descent; and including the income from but not the proceeds of life insurance policies paid upon the death of the person insured, or payments made or credits to the insured on life insurance endowment or annuity contracts upon the maturity of the term mentioned in the contract or upon the surrender of the contract." Statutes of Canada, 12 Parliament, 7 Session, ch. 28, p. 171.

Public finance economists have traditionally used their own standard, the so-called Haig–Simons (H-S) definition: Income is the money value of the net increase to an individual's power to consume during a period.[7] This is equal to the amount actually consumed during the period plus net additions to wealth. Net additions to wealth—saving—must be included in income because they represent an increase in potential consumption. This comprehensive definition of income was behind recommendations in the 1966 *Report* of the Royal Commission on Taxation (Carter Commission).

Importantly, the H-S criterion requires the inclusion of all sources of potential increases in consumption, regardless of whether the actual consumption takes place, and regardless of the form in which the consumption occurs. At the same time, the H-S criterion implies that any decreases in an individual's potential to consume should be subtracted in determining income. An example is expenses that have to be incurred to earn income. If the gross revenues from an individual's business are $100,000, but business expenses are $95,000, the individual's potential consumption has only increased by $5,000.

Items Included in H-S Income

The H-S definition encompasses those items ordinarily thought of as income: wages and salaries, business profits, rents, royalties, dividends,[8] and interest. However, the criterion also includes certain unconventional items:

Employer contributions to pensions and other retirement plans. Such payments, even though not made directly to the recipient, represent an increase in the long-run potential to consume.

Employer contributions for employees' insurance. Even if compensation is paid to an employee in the form of a certain commodity (in this case, an insurance policy) instead of cash, it is still income.

Transfer payments, including CPP/QPP retirement benefits, UI benefits, and worker's compensation payments. Any receipt, be it from the government or an employer, is income.

---

[7] Named after Robert M. Haig and Henry C. Simons, economists who wrote in the first half of the twentieth century. See Simons (1938).

[8] While dividends are included in taxable income, Canada's "dividend tax credit" makes some provision for the fact that income from which the dividends are paid may have been subject to the corporate income tax. Detailed discussion of the dividend tax credit is deferred to Chapter 24.

Capital gains. Increases in the value of an asset are referred to as capital gains, decreases as capital losses. Suppose Brutus owns some shares of Imperial Oil stock that increase in value from $10,000 to $12,500 over the course of a year. Then he has enjoyed a capital gain of $2,500. This $2,500 represents an increase in potential consumption and, hence, belongs in income.[9] If Brutus sells the Imperial Oil stock at the end of the year, the capital gain is said to be realized; otherwise it is unrealized. From the H-S point of view, it is absolutely irrelevant whether a capital gain is realized or unrealized. It represents potential to consume and, hence, is income. If Brutus does not sell his Imperial Oil stock, in effect he chooses to save by reinvesting the capital gain in Imperial Oil. Because the H-S criterion does not distinguish between different uses of income, the fact that Brutus happens to reinvest is irrelevant. All the arguments for adding in capital gains apply to subtracting capital losses. If Casca's Northern Telecom stock decreases in value by $4,200 during a given year, this $4,200 should be subtracted from other sources of income.

Income in kind. Some people receive part or all of their incomes in kind— in the form of goods and services rather than cash. Farmers provide field hands with food; corporations give employees subsidized lunches or access to company fitness centres. One important form of income in kind is the annual rental value of owner-occupied homes. A home-owner receives a stream of services from a dwelling. The net monetary value of these services—imputed rent— is equal to the rental payments that would have been received had the owner chosen to rent the house out, after subtracting maintenance expenses, taxes, and so on.

Gifts and inheritances. Receipt of a gift or inheritance increases a taxpayer's potential to consume, and based on the H-S criterion should be included in taxable income. That the donor, deceased or not, may have previously paid tax on these funds is no more relevant than the fact that purchases of goods that contribute to the income of a shopkeeper have been made from post-tax income. Admittedly, this is not the way much of the public perceives this matter.

In all these cases, from the H-S point of view, it makes no difference whether benefits are received in monetary form, or in the form of goods and services. They are all income.

---

[9] Only the real value of capital gains constitutes income, not gains due merely to inflation. This issue is discussed later.

Some Practical and Conceptual Problems

A number of difficulties arise in attempts to use the Haig–Simons criterion as a basis for constructing a tax system.

- The criterion makes it clear that only income net of business expenses increases potential consumption power. But it is often hard to distinguish between consumption expenditures and costs of obtaining income. If Calpurnia buys a desk to use while working at home, but the desk is also a beautiful piece of furniture, to what extent is the desk a business expense? What portion of a "three-martini lunch" designed to woo a client is consumption, and what portion is business? (According to current law, the answer to the latter question is 50 percent is consumption. Fifty percent of business-meal expenses are deductible.)
- Capital gains and losses may be very difficult to measure, particularly when they are unrealized. For assets that are traded in active markets, the problem is fairly manageable. Even if Brutus does not sell his shares of Imperial Oil common stock, it is easy to determine their value at any time by consulting the financial section of the newspaper. It is not nearly as easy to measure the capital gain on a piece of art that has appreciated in value. One possibility would be to find a comparable piece that had recently been sold, a task that would be difficult if only a few sales were being made. Alternatively, art owners could be required to hire professional appraisers to value their collections each year, but this would be expensive, and different appraisers might produce widely different estimates.
- Inflation contributes to measurement problems. For example, changes in the general price level alter the real value of assets and liabilities, such as loans, specified in nominal dollars. It is difficult to include such changes in net worth in the annual income of individuals.
- Imputed income from durables also presents measurement difficulties. For example, it may be hard to estimate the market rent of a particular owner-occupied dwelling. Each, in some way, is unique. Similarly, measuring the imputed rental streams generated by other durables such as cars, compact disk players, and motor boats is not feasible.
- In-kind services are hard to value. One important example is the income produced by people who do housework rather than participate in the market. These services—housecleaning, cooking, child care—are clearly valuable.[10] However, even though markets exist for purchasing these

---

[10] Recall that the most recent estimates by Statistics Canada value housework at between 31 and 46 percent of GDP in 1992, between $200 billion and $300 billion (Chandler, 1994).

services, it would be difficult to estimate whether a given homemaker's services were equal to the market value.

- Gifts take different forms, many of which it would be difficult or inappropriate to tax. Few would argue for inclusion of the value of food, clothing, and education opportunities in the taxable income of the recipient when the donee is a minor child and the donor the parent. Yet if the parent chooses to spend less on a young child, then gives the child $10,000 when she has left home and established her own household, many more will agree that this should be taxable. Provision of postsecondary and professional education, gifts of valuable household furnishings that have been in the family, and access to valuable vacation property owned by the parent are some of the areas in which arbitrary lines would have to be drawn.

Evaluation of H-S Criterion

Numerous additional difficulties involved in implementing the H-S criterion can be listed, but the main point is clear. No definition of income can make the administration of an income tax simple and straightforward. Arbitrary decisions about what should be included in income are inevitable. Nevertheless, the Haig–Simons criterion has often been regarded as an ideal toward which policy makers should strive: Income should be defined as broadly as is feasible, and all sources of income received by a particular person should be taxed at the same rate. The Carter Commission recommendations, based on these principles, were viewed very favourably by many academics and commentators. And the tax reforms of 1971, 1981, and 1987, at least in part, drew upon these principles.[11]

Why is the H-S criterion so attractive? There are two reasons. First, the criterion appeals to a sense of justice. Recall the traditional definition of horizontal equity from Chapter 19—people with equal incomes should pay equal taxes. For this dictum to make any sense, all sources of income must be included in the tax base. Otherwise, two people with identical abilities to pay could end up with different tax liabilities.

On the other hand, Feldstein (1976) has argued that as long as people's abilities to earn income differ, the H-S criterion cannot produce fair outcomes. Suppose that Popeye is endowed with a lot of brains, and Bluto with a lot of brawn. Suppose further that the work done by brawny people is less pleasant, and in far less pleasant surroundings, than that available to brainy individu-

---

[11] See Bird (1970: 444–78), and Royal Commission on Taxation (1966).

als. In that case, if Bluto and Popeye have the same income, then Popeye has more utility. Is it fair to tax them as equals?

The second reason for the appeal of the Haig–Simons criterion is efficiency. Defenders of the criterion argue that it has the virtue of neutrality—it treats all forms of income the same and, hence, does not distort the pattern of economic activity. Following this reasoning, it is argued that the failure to tax imputed rent from owner-occupied housing leads to excessive investment in housing, other things being the same.

It is doubtless true that many departures from the Haig–Simons criterion create inefficiencies. But it does not follow that equal tax rates on all income, regardless of source, would be most efficient. Consider income from rent on unimproved land. The supply of such land is perfectly inelastic, and hence no excess burden would be created by taxing it at a very high rate.[12] An efficient tax system would tax the returns to such land at higher rates than other sources of income, and not tax all sources at the same rate, as dictated by the Haig–Simons criterion. More generally, the optimal tax literature discussed in Chapter 19 suggests that as long as lump-sum taxes are ruled out, efficiency is enhanced when relatively high tax rates are imposed on those activities with relatively inelastic supply. "Neutrality," in the sense of equal tax rates on all types of income, generally does not minimize excess burden.

Where does this leave us? Sunley (1977: 272) points out that we cannot be sanguine about the possibilities for using optimal tax theory as a framework for designing the tax base: "If one follows this efficiency logic, … one would end up with a highly differentiated tax system that would strike most people as unjust, unworkable, and having no obvious appeal." It would be unwise, therefore, to abandon the Haig–Simons criterion altogether. On the other hand, there is no reason to regard the criterion as sacred. Departures from it should be considered on their merits and should not be viewed prima facie as unfair and inefficient.

EXCLUDABLE FORMS OF MONEY INCOME

We have seen that some income sources that would be taxable according to the Haig–Simons criterion are omitted from the tax base for practical reasons. In addition, several forms of income that would be administratively relatively easy to tax are partially or altogether excluded from adjusted gross income.

---

[12] This fact has long been recognized. See George (1914).

Capital Gains

Currently, for most taxpayers, three-quarters of realized capital gains are taxed as normal income. There is a trail of many changes over the past twenty-five years as we have come to this point, and further change may occur.[13]

Prior to 1971, capital gains were exempt and not included in taxable income. The Carter Commission recommended that realized capital gains be fully taxable, and the 1971 tax reform included half of capital gains in taxable income. The 1985 budget provided for a lifetime exemption of $500,000 in capital gains for each taxpayer (in addition to the exemption provided for principal residences). This exemption was reduced to $100,000 in the 1987 tax reform and subsequently was eliminated for real estate in 1992 and for all other assets in the 1994 budget.[14]

The 1987 reforms also changed the share of capital gains to be included in taxable income. The share of realized gains to be included in taxable income rose from one-half to two-thirds in 1988. This was further increased to three-quarters in 1990 and thereafter. Realized capital losses—decreases in the value of an asset—can be offset only against a realized gain. Thus, if a $10,000 gain is realized on the sale of Imperial Oil common stock, and a $5,000 loss on the sale of Northern Telecom, the taxable gain for the year is $5,000. Moreover, capital losses in excess of capital gains in any year cannot be subtracted from ordinary income. Such losses can be carried back three years and carried forward indefinitely, but can only be used to offset capital gains.

With the taxation of three-quarters of capital gains, and the elimination of the lifetime exemptions, substantial movement toward the Haig–Simons criterion for capital gains has occurred. However, other aspects of the tax treatment of capital gains depart from the H-S criterion in important ways.

Only realizations taxed. Unless a capital gain is actually realized—the asset is sold—no tax is levied. In effect, the tax on a capital gain is deferred until the gain is realized. The mere ability to postpone taxes may not seem all that important, but its consequences are enormous. Consider Cassius, who purchases an asset for $100,000 that increases in value by 12 percent each year. After the first year, it is worth $100,000 × (1 + .12) = $112,000. After the

---

[13] Tax competition with the United States is among the factors that may contribute to further change in Canada. Changes to capital gains taxation in the United States, where realized gains are now fully taxed, continue under active discussion in 1997.

[14] The $500,000 capital gain exemption for farms and small business remains, but is under review.

second year, it is worth $112,000 \times (1 + .12) = \$100,000 \times (1 + .12)^2 = \$125,440$. Similarly, by the end of twenty years, it is worth $\$100,000 \times (1 + .12)^{20} = \$964,629$. If the asset is sold at the end of twenty years, Cassius realizes a capital gain of $\$864,629$ (= $\$964,629 - \$100,000$). Three-quarters of this, or $\$648,472$, is taxable. Assume that the tax rate applied to the taxable gain is 50 percent. Then Cassius's tax liability is $\$324,236$ (= $\$648,472 \times 0.5$), and his net gain (measured in dollars twenty years from now) is $\$540,393$ (= $\$864,629 - \$324,236$).

Now assume that the 50 percent rate on the taxable share of the capital gains is levied as the capital gains accrue, regardless of whether they are realized. This means that $\$9,000$ of the $\$12,000$ gain in the first year is subject to the 50 percent tax rate. At the end of the first year, Cassius has $\$107,500$ [= $\$100,000 \times (1 + .075)$]. (Remember, $\$4,500$ of the $\$12,000$ gain goes to the tax collector.) Assuming that the $\$7,500$ after-tax gain is reinvested in the asset, at the end of two years, Cassius has $\$107,500 \times (1 + .075) = \$100,000 \times (1.075)^2 = \$115,563$. Similarly, by the end of twenty years, he has $\$100,000 \times (1.075)^{20} = \$424,785$. Cassius's after-tax capital gain is $\$324,785$ (= $\$424,785 - \$100,000$). Comparing this to the previous amount of $\$540,393$ makes clear that the seemingly innocent device of letting the gains accrue without tax makes a big difference. This is because the deferral allows the investment to grow geometrically at the before-tax rather than the after-tax rate of interest. In effect, the government gives the investor an interest-free loan on taxes due.[15]

It should now be clear why a favourite slogan among tax accountants is "taxes deferred are taxes saved." Many very complicated tax-shelter plans are nothing more than devices for deferring payment of taxes.

Because only realized capital gains are subject to tax, taxpayers who are considering switching or selling capital assets must take into account that doing so will create a tax liability. As a consequence, they may be less likely to change their portfolios. This phenomenon is referred to as the **lock-in effect**, because the tax system tends to lock investors into their current portfolios.[16] This leads to a misallocation of capital, because it no longer flows to where its return is highest. There have been several econometric studies of the tax treatment of capital gains realizations in the United States. A number of them have found

---

[15] A method proposed by Auerbach (1991), while taxing only realized gains, would levy an interest charge on past gains when realization occurs, and thereby reduce or eliminate the incentive to defer realization.

[16] Note that while the deferral of taxes lowers the effective tax rate on capital gains, this is somewhat offset by the fact that the lock-in effect prevents investors from reallocating their portfolio optimally when economic conditions change.

that cuts in capital gains tax rates would significantly increase the realization of long-term capital gains, although the magnitude of the response is controversial (see Auten and Cordes, 1991).

Gains realized at death. Canadian law provides for the realization of gains at time of death. At death, the capital assets of an individual are deemed to be disposed of at their current market value, and three-quarters of the capital gains are taken into income in the year of death. This is particularly important in Canada since there are no death taxes.[17]

Evaluation of capital gains rules. We conclude that in terms of the Haig–Simons criterion, the tax treatment of capital gains is mixed. The criterion requires that all capital gains be taxed, whether realized or unrealized. Whereas substantial movement has occurred toward the H-S criterion since 1971, the tax system still taxes only three-quarters of realized gains as ordinary income. Further, unrealized capital gains can accrue without taxation, and significant exemptions exist for gains on principal residences, on farms, and on small businesses.

The optimal tax literature does not provide any more justification for preferential treatment of capital gains than the Haig–Simons criterion.[18] However, several rationalizations have been proposed for preferential treatment of this form of capital income. Some argue that capital gains are not regular income, but rather windfalls that occur unexpectedly. Fairness requires that such unexpected gains not create a tax liability. Moreover, because investing requires the sacrifice of abstaining from consumption, it is only fair to reward this sacrifice. However, it could just as well be asserted that labour income should be treated preferentially, because it involves the unpleasantness of work, while those who receive capital gains need only relax and wait for their money to flow in. Ultimately, it is impossible to argue convincingly that production of one source of income or another requires more sacrifice and should therefore be treated preferentially.

---

[17] In contrast, U.S. law permits for the transfer of assets to heirs without the capital gain being realized and taxed at death. Moreover, the cost basis for any capital gain realized by the heir is on a "stepped-up basis," equal to the market price of the asset at the time the heir receives it. In this way capital gains on assets held to the death of the owner are never taxed. However, there are estate taxes in the United States, and assets in excess of $600,000 in an estate are subjected to rates ranging from 37 to 55 percent. State death duties may be on top of this.

[18] However, under certain conditions, optimal tax theory suggests that no forms of capital income should be taxed. See Chapter 22 under "Personal Consumption Tax."

Another justification for preferential taxation of capital gains is that it is needed to stimulate capital accumulation and risk taking. In the next chapter, we deal at some length with the question of how taxation affects saving and risk taking. For now, we merely note that it is not clear that special treatment for capital gains does increase saving and risk taking. If the goal is to stimulate these activities, there are probably more efficient ways to do so.

Some promote preferential treatment of capital gains because it helps counterbalance inflation's tendency to increase the effective rate at which capital gains are taxed. As we see later, under existing tax rules, inflation does produce an especially heavy burden on capital income, but arbitrarily taxing capital gains at a different rate may not be the best way to deal with this problem.

Finally, we stress that a full picture of the tax treatment of capital income requires taking into account that much of this income is generated by corporations, and corporations are subject to a separate tax system of their own. The overall tax rate on capital income thus depends on the personal and corporate rates. We discuss the effect of the corporation tax on the return to capital in Chapter 24.

Employer Contributions to Benefit Plans

Employers' contributions to their employees' retirement funds, within clearly specified limits, are not subject to tax.[19] Neither does the government tax the interest that accrues on the pension contributions over time. Only when the pension is paid out at retirement are the principal and interest subject to taxation.

As already argued, pensions represent additions to potential consumption and, hence, should be counted as income according to the Haig–Simons criterion. Similarly, the interest on pension funds should be taxable as it accrues. However, the inclusion of such items in the tax base appears to be politically infeasible.

Gifts and Inheritances

Although gifts and inheritances represent increases in the beneficiaries' potential consumption, these items are not subject to the income tax. Separate tax systems cover gifts and estates in most of the industrialized world. However, Canada is one of two countries (Australia is the other) in the industrialized

---

[19] The total allowable employer + employee contribution is $13,500 in 1997. It had been scheduled to rise to $15,500, but is now frozen for several years to help reduce the federal deficit.

world without this form of taxation. Canada's previous use of gift and estate taxes is discussed in Chapter 23.

DEDUCTIONS AND TAX CREDITS

In terms of Figure 20.1, we have now discussed issues associated with Step 1, the identification of total income. Applying existing tax rates to total income would be inappropriate for two reasons:

- expenses associated with earning this income need to be deducted to reflect "net" income available to be taxed, and
- adjustments are required to recognize costs of subsistence, and other nondiscretionary expenses. (How best to identify those expenditures that are not discretionary will always be controversial.)

In addition to these reasons, the government may choose to encourage individuals to allocate their income for specific purposes. Deductions or tax credits may be used to stimulate private saving for retirement, increased spending on education, and donations to charities.

In the case of deductions, an amount is subtracted from total income in order to reach taxable income—the deduction reduces taxable income. We then apply the tax rates to taxable income to obtain the tax payable. In the case of tax credits, the amount of the credit is subtracted from taxes that would otherwise be payable—the credit directly reduces taxes payable.

Deductions

Deductibility and relative prices. Before cataloguing deductible expenditures, let us consider the relationship between deductibility of expenditures on an item and its relative price. Suppose that expenditures on commodity Z are tax deductible. The price of Z is $10 per unit. Suppose further that Cleopatra's marginal tax rate is 40 percent. Then, whenever Cleopatra purchases a unit of Z, it only costs her $6. Why? Because expenditures on Z are deductible, purchasing a unit lowers Cleopatra's taxable income by $10. Given a 40 percent marginal tax rate, $10 less of taxable income saves Cleopatra $4 in taxes. Hence, her effective price of a unit of Z is $10 minus $4, or $6.

More generally, if the price of Z is P_Z and the individual's marginal tax rate is t, allowing deduction of expenses on Z lowers Z's effective price from P_Z to $(1 - t)P_Z$. This analysis brings out two important facts:

- Because deductibility changes the relative price of the commodity involved, in general, we expect the quantity demanded to change.

- The higher the individual's value of *t*, the greater the value to the individual of a given dollar amount of deductions and the lower the effective price of the good.[20]

Expenses in earning income. Most deductions are for expenses incurred in order to earn taxable income. One such expense is for child care. The need for "paid" child care has risen as increasing numbers of women have entered the work force. A second adult would, in many cases, be unable to seek paid employment in the absence of child care. As business expenses can be deducted in reporting business income, child care expenses are permitted (up to $7,800 for a child under age 7 and $4,680 for a child at least 7 but not yet 17 and no more than two-thirds of the earned income of the parent with the lower income). Allowing for a deduction of child care expenses better reflects the *net* addition to taxable income. Where there are two parents, the deduction is made by the one with the lower income.

Union dues or professional dues may also be a required expense if income is to be earned. Thus, they are deductible in calculating taxable income. Other expenses that employees may have to incur include the costs of transportation, meals, and lodging, where the employee is not reimbursed by the employer. The taxpayer must be able to prove to Revenue Canada's satisfaction that the expenditures have been made. A deduction is also provided for moving expenses where the move is required to earn wages, salary, or self-employment income. Common to these deductions is that each is an expense that must be incurred to earn the taxable income. Rules apply in each of these cases in order to avoid unreasonable deductions.

Individuals may borrow money to make income-earning investments. This income may take the form of interest, dividends, capital gains, or business profits. Reasonable expenses incurred in earning this investment income, such as interest on borrowed funds and other carrying charges, are deductible. Where an interest expense exceeds the income from an investment, this expense is generally deductible against other taxable income. Taxable income is the amount after interest and other expenses, or the net income that the investment contributes.

---

[20] Note that these observations apply more generally to expenditures on any items that are excluded from the tax base, not just deductions. For example, the value of excluding fringe benefits such as employer-provided group life insurance or dental care increases with the marginal tax rate, other things being the same.

Some interest expenses are clearly not related to earning taxable income, and are not deductible.[21] These include:

- interest paid on consumer debt such as credit card charges or other loans for purposes of private consumption, and
- interest on mortgages for owner-occupied homes, since the imputed income from home-ownership is not included in taxable income.

Do these rules make sense in terms of the Haig–Simons criterion? For a business investment, it is clear that interest should be deductible. It is a cost of doing business, and hence should not be subject to income tax. In the case of expenditures on consumption goods and services, it seems reasonable to argue that interest on consumer loans should be regarded merely as a higher price one pays to obtain a commodity sooner than would otherwise be possible. And where consumer durables are concerned, since imputed income from these goods is excluded (as with a house), it would be inappropriate to deduct interest.

Note that the deductibility of interest together with the exemption of certain types of capital income from taxation can lead to lucrative opportunities for smart investors. Assume that Caesar, who has a 40 percent tax rate, can borrow all the money he wants from the bank at a rate of 10 percent. Assuming that Caesar satisfies the criteria for deductibility of interest, for every dollar of interest paid, his tax bill is reduced by 40 cents. Hence, Caesar's effective borrowing rate is only about 6 percent. Suppose that the rate of return that Caesar realizes on a tax-exempt investment is 7.5 percent.[22] Then Caesar can borrow from the bank at 6 percent and make an investment at 7.5 percent. Caesar should continue to borrow as long as this opportunity exists. The process of taking advantage of such opportunities is referred to as **tax arbitrage**.

Opportunities for tax arbitrage are limited by the number of tax-free income opportunities, and because in real-world capital markets people cannot bor-

---

[21] Interest deductibility is an area in which Canadian tax law has differed sharply from that in the United States. Mortgage interest for the purchase of up to two residences is deductible in the United States up to a limit of $1 million. Also deductible is interest on a home equity loan—a loan for which the home serves as collateral and whose proceeds can be used to finance any purchase. For example, one can obtain a home equity loan and use the money to buy a car. In effect, then, the law allows home-owners to deduct interest on consumer loans, but denies this privilege to renters. However, deductible interest on home equity loans is limited to $100,000. Since the 1986 tax reform in the United States interest on consumer debt is not generally deductible in calculating taxable income.

[22] Prior to 1995, the $100,000 lifetime capital gain exemption provided a limited opportunity. In this case, if an investment paid no dividends with the total return in capital gains due to the reinvestment of earnings, the taxpayer would earn tax-exempt income, but would be able to deduct the interest on the loan.

row arbitrarily large sums of money. Still, opportunities for gain are present. Tax authorities are vigilant on this issue, and interest on loans that are for investments in tax-deferred plans such as RRSPs is not deductible. Given that money can be used for many different purposes, how can it be proved that a given amount of borrowing is for one investment rather than another? This simple example illustrates some important general lessons:

- Interest deductibility in conjunction with preferential treatment of certain capital income can create major money-making opportunities.
- High-income individuals are more likely than their low-income counterparts to benefit from these opportunities. This is because they tend to face higher tax rates and to have better access to borrowing.
- The tax authorities can certainly declare various tax arbitrage schemes to be illegal, but it is hard to enforce these rules. Moreover, clever lawyers and accountants are always on the lookout for new tax arbitrage opportunities. Many inefficient investments are made, and a lot of resources are spent on tax avoidance and tax administration.

Employee savings for retirement and other purposes. *Registered Pension Plans (RPPs).* Employees may contribute to Registered Pension Plans (RPPs), matching the contributions of their employers, or on some other basis. The total allowable nontaxable contribution by an employer and employee to a "money purchase plan" RPP is $13,500 per taxpayer in 1997. The larger the contribution by the employer, the smaller the tax-deductible amount that the employee is free to contribute. In 1994, RPP deductions allowed to employees totalled $6.9 billion. These funds, and the investment income earned by these funds, are not taxable until paid out as pensions.

Registered Retirement Savings Plans (RRSPs). Under certain circumstances, workers can engage in tax-favoured saving for their retirement. Using a Registered Retirement Savings Plan (RRSP), an individual can, in 1997, deposit up to $13,500. If the employee is part of a pension plan, the allowable contribution is reduced based on the pension benefits in the employer's pension plan that are accruing to the employee during the year. The objective is to encourage employee saving (RRSPs plus RPPs) toward retirement, at least to a certain level. The money contributed to an RRSP is deductible from total income. Just as in an employer-managed pension fund, the interest that accrues is untaxed. Tax is due only when the money is withdrawn or is paid out as part of a retirement plan or annuity. RRSP contributions were $19.3 billion in 1994.

RRSPs were introduced partly to give more people the option to accumulate retirement wealth in tax-favoured funds. Part of the motivation was also to stimulate saving. However, it is not clear how aggregate saving is affected. People may merely shuffle around their portfolios, reducing their holdings of some assets and depositing them into retirement accounts. Much of this does occur, and results remain unclear on the extent to which RRSPs have contributed to a higher level of private or total (public + private) saving in Canada.[23] In any case, it is clear that the existence of plans for the preferential treatment of retirement saving represents another important departure from the H-S criterion.

Registered Home-ownership Savings Plans (RHOSPs). Prior to 1985, taxpayers who did not yet own a home were allowed to deduct up to $1,000 a year, to a maximum of $10,000, to contribute to an account to be used for a first home purchase. Income earned in the account was not taxable, and the funds when withdrawn to purchase a home were not taxable. RHOSPs helped to bring home-ownership within the range of more Canadians in a time of high interest rates and accompanying mortgage payments. Although the 1985 budget abolished RHOSPs, a provision introduced in 1992 allows first-time home-buyers to withdraw $20,000 from RRSP accounts in order to buy a home. The $20,000 must be repaid in equal instalments over fifteen years. This provision creates an additional incentive for saving in a particular form, and also reduces the cost of home-ownership relative to other forms of consumption for which RRSPs are not available.

Registered Education Savings Plans (RESPs). RESPs encourage Canadians to save for education. Although contributions to RESPs are *not* deductible in calculating taxable income, the income earned on RESP accounts is not taxed as it accrues, and is taxable in the hands of the beneficiaries rather than those of the contributor. The benefit of an RESP is that it defers tax on the earnings of the account, and it taxes the earnings at the (probably) lower tax rate applying to the student beneficiary rather than that applying to the contributor.

Alimony. The last deduction included under Step 2 in Figure 20.1 is that for alimony payments. The deduction is permitted where the payments are made under court order or written agreement and are for the maintenance of the taxpayer's spouse, former spouse, and children. The Income Tax Act requires that these payments be included in the income of the recipient for tax purposes.[24]

---

[23] See Jump (1982) and Carroll and Summers (1987) for earlier assessments of the effects of RRSPs on private savings in Canada, and Ingerman and Rowley (1993) for more recent analysis. Many studies have attempted to estimate the effects of tax-preferred savings plans on private savings in the United States. See McCarthy and Pham (1995) for a recent review.
[24] The Federal Court of Appeal ruled (in *Thibaudeau v. The Queen*, 1994) that maintenance payments for the benefit of children were not taxable to the recipient. Revenue Canada appealed this to the Supreme Court and in the interim indicated that it would continue to include such payments in the taxable income of the recipient.

Although opinions will differ, there is a certain logic in viewing the payor as a conduit for this income, and including it in the income of the payee.

Tax Credits

Tax credits and relative prices. Tax credits, like deductions, alter relative prices. But their effects differ. As noted, the higher an individual's marginal tax rate, the greater the value of a deduction of a given dollar amount. In contrast, a tax credit is a subtraction from tax liability (not taxable income), and hence its value is independent of the *individual's* marginal tax rate. A tax credit of $100 reduces tax liability by $100 whether an individual's tax rate is 30 percent or 50 percent. In contrast, a deduction of $200 is worth $100 in tax savings to one with a 50 percent marginal tax rate and $60 to one with a 30 percent tax rate. The credit may also be set to equal x percent of the expenditure on a commodity, x being the same for all taxpayers. In such a case the price of commodity Z is reduced from P_Z to $(1–t)P_Z$, or $0.5P_Z$ if t is set at 50 percent. If there is a 50 percent tax credit for research and development (R&D) spending, $1,000 on R&D costs the taxpayer only $500.

Several types of tax credits are used in Canada. One distinction is whether a tax credit is refundable or nonrefundable. *Refundable* means that if a tax credit exceeds tax that is otherwise payable, the government makes a payment to the taxpayer, creating a negative tax. In the case of *nonrefundable* credits, when a tax credit exceeds the tax otherwise owed, the government does *not* make a payment to the taxpayer. The current GST credits and former child tax credits are examples of refundable credits. The tax credit for medical expenses is nonrefundable.

Another distinction is whether the tax credit is a fixed amount or is affected by a taxpayer's circumstances or behaviour. Tax credits that replaced the basic personal exemption and the exemptions for dependents are fixed amounts. They do not vary with the level of income or level of expenditure. The credit provided for medical expenses in excess of 3 percent of net income is unlimited, but since it is nonrefundable it cannot exceed taxes that would otherwise be due. The credit for charitable donations varies depending on the total amount of donations—17 percent of those below $200 and 29 percent of those above. The credits in any year do not apply on donations in excess of 75 percent of net income.

Taxpayer and spouse. Nonrefundable tax credits recognize the need for a minimal level of income before an individual is self-supporting or able to provide a minimal level of food, housing, and other services for any dependents, including him- or herself. The credit for an individual in 1996 was

$1,098.[25] Additional credits of $915 are provided for a spouse,[26] $522 if over age 65, $720 for a disability, and $400 for a dependent who is infirm. For a married taxpayer over 65, with a disability, the total nonrefundable credit would be $3,255. At 17 percent, taxable income would have to reach $19,147 before the nonrefundable credit is exhausted. A tax payable of $0.17 \times \$19,147 = \$3,255$, and is offset by the credit of $3,255.

CPP, QPP, and UI. Nonrefundable credits are provided for nondiscretionary payments (payroll taxes) that taxpayers make for the Canada Pension Plan, Quebec Pension Plan, and Unemployment Insurance. These required payments are set by statute and reduce funds available for taxes or other purposes. An argument could be made to treat these payments as deductions, since they could be considered an expense of earning income. Instead, the government has chosen to grant a tax credit, equal to 17 percent of the contributions made, thus ensuring that equal payments for these purposes result in the same reduction in taxes whether the taxpayer is in a 30 or 50 percent tax bracket.

Medical expenses. A nonrefundable tax credit is provided for medical expenses in excess of 3 percent of net income.[27] The reason for the tax credit for medical expenses is that large medical expenses may be nondiscretionary and reduce an individual's ability to pay. It is hard to say to what extent health care expenditures are under an individual's control. A person with serious medical and dental problems may have limited choice. Nonetheless, taxpayers can and do choose among a range of medical and dental services that may not be covered by a health care system. Canadians may also claim medical expenses incurred outside of Canada; this may involve choices regarding the level of care, tests undergone, experts consulted, and elective surgery. Moreover, it may be possible for individuals to substitute preventive health care (good diet, exercise, etc.) for formal medical services.

By providing a tax credit for some medical expenses, the tax system provides a kind of social health care insurance. The terms of this "policy" are that the individual has a deductible equal to 3.0 percent of his or her net income, and after that the government pays a share equal to the federal plus provincial lowest marginal tax rate (26.5 percent in Ontario in 1996). This is in addition to

---

[25] Tax would be owed when taxable income exceeded $6,456, causing the tax rate (17 percent) times taxable income to exceed the credit. Note that $0.17 \times \$6,456 = \$1,098$.

[26] In 1996, for every dollar of income over $538 earned by a spouse, the spousal credit is reduced by 17 cents. Thus, the credit for a spouse disappeared when the income of the spouse reached $5,918.

[27] Taxable income equals net income less certain special deductions; for most taxpayers net income equals taxable income.

the Canada Health Plan and must be considered in light of the pros and cons of providing social health insurance discussed in Chapter 15.

Charitable contributions and education. Nonrefundable credits are used to encourage private spending on charities and education. The federal credit provided for education is 17 percent of qualifying expenditures. That for charitable gifts totalling $200 or less is 17 percent, and for the annual amount in excess of $200 the federal credit is 29 percent regardless of the income level of the donor. Once the $200 threshold is passed, an individual receives a 29-cent federal tax credit for each $1 given to qualifying charities. This credit also reduces the provincial tax. Where the provincial tax is calculated as 60 percent of the federal tax, provincial taxes are reduced by 17.4 cents for every $1 given, and the total tax saving is 46.4 cents. The net cost to the taxpayer for each dollar given is 53.6 cents.

Individuals receive a tax credit for contributions made to religious, charitable, educational, scientific, or literary organizations. Beginning in 1997 a tax credit will be given for charitable donations up to 75 percent of net income in a given year, and excess donations can be carried forward for up to five years. In 1994, individuals reported charitable deductions of $3.4 billion (Revenue Canada, 1996).

Some argue that charitable donations constitute a reduction in taxable capacity and, hence, should be excluded from taxable income. However, as long as the contributions are made voluntarily, this argument is unconvincing. If people don't receive as much satisfaction from charity as from their own consumption, why make the donations in the first place? Probably the best way to understand the presence of the credit is as an attempt by the government to encourage charitable giving. Setting the federal credit at 29 percent, rather than at 17 percent (as applying to qualifying education and medical expenses), indicates such encouragement.

Has the credit succeeded in doing so? The credit provision changes an individual's "price" for a dollar's worth of charity in excess of $200 from $1 to $(1 − t)$, where t is the federal tax rate of 29 percent plus the provincial rate. (If the provincial tax is 60 percent of the federal tax, t is $0.29 + 0.6 \times 0.29 = 0.464$.) The effectiveness of the credit in encouraging giving therefore depends on the price elasticity of demand for charitable contributions. If the price elasticity is zero, charitable giving is unaffected. The credit is just a bonus for those who would give anyway. If the price elasticity exceeds zero, then giving is encouraged.

Several attempts have been made to estimate the elasticity of charitable giving with respect to its after-tax price. Typically, a regression is estimated in which the dependent variable is the amount of charitable donations, and the explanatory variables are: (1) the "price" of charitable donations (one minus the marginal tax rate); (2) income; and (3) personal characteristics of individuals that might influence their decisions to give, such as age and marital status. Whereas several U.S. studies have found the price elasticity of demand for donations substantially greater than one,[28] estimates for Canada indicate that the price elasticity for charitable donations may be less that unity.[29] The implications of this result are striking. Consider a province where the combined federal plus provincial credit is at a rate of 46 percent. The credit for charitable donations lowers the price of giving from $1 to 54 cents, a reduction of 46 percent. If the elasticity is less than one, the taxpayer increases charitable giving by less than 46 percent. Hence, charitable organizations gain less than the tax authorities lose.

There is disagreement with respect to the precise value of the elasticity, and lack of agreement on the extent to which measures such as the tax credit stimulate contributions. Whether the government should be subsidizing gifts to private charities also can be questioned. Proponents believe that in the absence of such a subsidy, many institutions now funded privately would be forced to seek more government support. Equally important, the current decentralized system is more likely to stimulate a variety of activities, encourage policy innovations, and promote a pluralistic society.

Child Tax Benefits

The tax credits discussed above include a tax credit for the taxpayer and another for the spouse, but *no* credit for children that may be in the family. Although such a credit existed prior to 1993, **child tax benefits** have since been implemented in place of child tax credits and family allowances. Child tax benefits are discussed after a brief review of alternatives previously used.

Since its inception, various provisions in the Income Tax Act have recognized there is a cost of providing for children. These are summarized in Table 20.3. Methods have included exemptions, nonrefundable tax credits, and refundable tax credits. The Income Tax Act in 1918 had provided a $200 exemption for each child, meaning that an additional $200 was exempt, or free, from tax, before any tax liability was incurred. Nonrefundable credits were introduced in 1942 and exemptions reintroduced in 1947. Refundable credits for dependent children were enacted in 1979. Except in those cases where income is

---

[28] Clotfelter (1985) reviews a number of these studies. See also Joulfaian (1991).
[29] Hood, Martin, and Osberg (1977).

Table 20.3

Changes in Tax Provisions for Children

YEAR	CHANGE
1918:	An exemption was provided for each dependent child.
1942:	Nonrefundable tax credits for children replaced exemptions.
1945:	The Family Allowance (FA) program began, and there was a claw-back of FA benefits based on income.
1947:	Exemptions for dependent children replaced nonrefundable tax credits, and claw-back of FA was dropped.
1974:	Exemptions were indexed for inflation, and FA became taxable to the parent who claimed the child exemption.
1979:	Refundable (disappearing) child tax credits were introduced, and a child exemption continued.
1986:	Refundable sales tax credit was introduced with benefits for dependent children.
1988:	Nonrefundable credits for dependent children replaced exemptions.

SOURCE: Jonathan R. Kesselman, "The Child Tax Benefit: Simple, Fair, Responsive?" *Canadian Public Policy* 19, no. 2 (June 1993): 109.

below the taxable threshold, all of these measures lower the tax liability of families with children relative to those without. In cases where no tax would be due in any case, only the refundable tax credit improves the lot of those with children.

Canada, prior to 1993, also provided Family Allowance payments to families with children. These payments were sometimes free of tax, and sometimes taxed at the marginal rate of the spouse with the highest income. These payments were also, at times, subject to "claw-backs"—for every dollar that a parent's income exceeded a certain level, the Family Allowance payment was reduced by a fraction of a dollar; as income rose it would eventually disappear completely.

The variation over the years in the income tax adjustments for children reflects a lack of consensus on the best way to structure the income tax to reflect the family situation. Prior to 1993, a nonrefundable child tax credit of $601 was provided for each eligible child plus $213 for each child under 7 years of age at the end of the year. The $213 credit for those under age 7 was to be reduced by an amount equal to 25 percent of child care expenses that were deducted by the taxpayer. Where more than $852 was deducted for child care, the child tax credit would be $601 for those under age 7 as well as for those under 18.

These nonrefundable credits were taxed back in 1992 at a 5 percent rate on the total net income of both spouses in excess of $25,921.[30]

The "child tax benefit" replaced the refundable tax credits and the family allowance payments in 1993. The annual basic benefit in 1996 was $1,020 per child under age 18 for the first and second child in a family, and $1,095 for the third and each additional child.[31] The benefit is taxed back (on combined net income of parents over $25,921) at 5 percent where there are two or more children and 2.5 percent if there is only one child. There is an additional earned income supplement (never greater than $500) for families with incomes below $25,921. The benefits are paid monthly.

The child tax benefit is not really part of the income tax since there is no additional calculation on a tax return filed by many taxpayers. However, information from tax returns is used to determine child tax benefits to be paid to a family. The tax return for 1996 will determine the level of the child tax benefit for the period January to June of 1998, and the 1997 tax return will determine the benefits to be paid for July to December of 1998.

Kesselman (1993) points out that with the move to the child tax benefit program in 1993, those with high incomes are not provided with any recognition of the cost of raising children. A taxpayer earning $100,000 and having three children would receive no child tax benefit, and would pay the same income tax as a childless taxpayer earning $100,000. It is consistent with a view that, at least for high-income households, "the presence of children is irrelevant to a household's ability to pay taxes—in effect, that the costs of raising children are simply consumer outlays like the childless family's choice to purchase a fancy boat" (Kesselman, 1993: 117). This is a change from our past, is unusual among developed countries, and is at odds with the view that raising children involves certain nondiscretionary expenses and affects the ability to pay taxes, whatever the level of income.[32] However, it is not clear why expenses involving children should be considered nondiscretionary in the first place. Given the

---

[30] If a family had two children, both under 7, and no child care expenses, the total credit would have been $1,628. If this is taxed back at a 5 percent rate, the credit disappears at a net income level of $58,481.

[31] Federal legislation permits provinces to vary the payments to some extent. Alberta and Quebec have both modified the payments based on age, and Quebec has further modified payments based on family size.

[32] In the past it has been more generally accepted that the income tax should recognize the impact of children on "ability to pay," whether through a deduction or a credit. It is now common to hear the argument that parents have children voluntarily, and that expenditures on children should be viewed no differently than other consumption expenditures (see Davies, 1992).

wide availability of contraceptive methods, many would argue that raising children is undertaken as the result of conscious choice. If one couple wishes to spend its money on European vacations while another chooses to raise a family, why should the tax system reward the latter?[33] On the other hand, the religions of certain people rule out effective birth-control methods, and for them, children are not a choice as the term is conventionally defined.

Tax Credits versus Deductions

Some argue that deductions and exemptions should be converted into credits. Prior to 1988, taxpayers were permitted additional deductions to recognize some of the basic costs of providing for oneself, for one's spouse, for one's children, and for other dependents. These deductions were referred to as the "personal exemption" and "exemptions for spouse and dependents." An additional deduction, known as the "age exemption," was provided for those who were 65 or older on December 31.

These exemptions, like other deductions, reduced taxable income, thus decreasing the base to which the tax rate would be applied. The personal exemption for 1987 was set at $4,220, with an additional age exemption of $2,640 for those over 65. The spousal exemption was $3,700, and that for dependents was $560 for those under 18 and $1,200 for those over 18. An additional exemption of $1,450 was permitted for a child over 18 with a mental or physical disability.

The effect of the exemptions on taxes due, like other deductions, depended on the tax rate of the taxpayer. If your marginal tax rate was 50 percent, the $4,220 personal exemption reduced taxes by $2,110; if 20 percent, by $844. Since the exemptions led to larger reductions for those with higher incomes, they lessened the progressivity of the tax system.

The 1987 tax reform replaced the personal, marital, age, and disability exemptions with tax credits, effective in 1988. This was a substantial change in Canadian tax policy. Deductions for the taxpayer, spouse, dependents, age, pension income, disabilities, medical expenses, charitable donations, and Canada Pension Plan and Unemployment Insurance premiums were converted to credits. Table 20.4 summarizes the anticipated effect of these changes on

---

[33] If there are positive externalities involved in raising children, then a subsidy might be appropriate (see Chapter 8). Some would argue that because the world is overcrowded, additional children create negative externalities and, hence, should be taxed. In China, families with more than one child forfeit certain government benefits. In effect, this is a tax on children.

Table 20.4

1987 Tax Reform: The Effect of Shifting from Exemptions and Deductions to Credits

EXEMPTION OR CREDIT ALLOWED	DEDUCTION ALLOWED	VALUE OF DEDUCTION 17% RATE	VALUE OF DEDUCTION 29% RATE	VALUE OF TAX CREDIT
Basic	$4,250	725	1,240	1,020
Married	3,740	635	1,085	850
Age >64	2,670	455	775	550
Disability	2,920	495	845	550
Dependent <18	388	65	115	65
>17	1,000	170	290	nil
Charitable Donation:				
first $250		42	73	42
Excess (assume $1,000)		170	290	290
Medical Expenses over 3% of net income (assume $1,000)		170	290	170
CPP/UI premium by employee (assume $1,000)		170	290	170

SOURCE: Department of Finance, *Tax Reform 1987: Income Tax Reform* (Ottawa: June 18, 1987), p. 71. Reproduced with permission of the Minister of Public Works and Government Services Canada, 1997.

federal taxes payable in 1988 for two taxpayers—one subject to a 17 percent marginal tax rate and the other to a 29 percent marginal tax rate. The basic exemption, which would have been $4,250 with no change in tax policy, reduced taxes by $1,240 for the individual subject to a 29 percent marginal rate, and by $725 for the individual subject to a 17 percent tax rate. In contrast, the basic credit of $1,020 is independent of an individual's income level and marginal tax rate. The same is true for the other deductions that have been converted to tax credits. Charitable donations of $1,250, if deductible, would result in a tax saving of $212 for individuals subject to the lower marginal rate (17 percent) and savings of $362 for those subject to a higher rate (29 percent). With credits instead, the $1,250 in qualifying donations results in tax savings of $332 for each individual, regardless of income level.

Proponents of credits argue that they are fairer than deductions. Under a regime of tax deductions, a poor person (with a low marginal tax rate) benefits less than a rich person (with a high marginal tax rate) even if they make

identical contributions to their RRSPs. With a credit, the dollar benefit is the same. When the shift was made from personal exemptions to tax credits in 1988 the Department of Finance (1987: 19) argued:

> The conversion of exemptions to credits is a key element in achieving a fairer income tax system. A tax credit deducted from an individual's tax liability is the clearest and most direct form of tax relief, since all taxpayers who qualify receive the same tax reduction regardless of their income. In contrast, a tax exemption or deduction is subtracted from the income on which taxes are calculated. Its value therefore depends on a taxpayer's marginal rate of tax and is greater for those in higher-income brackets.

This is to oversimplify the situation. Adjustments can be made to tax rates that will offset any loss in progressivity that is due to the use of exemptions instead of credits. Moreover, the choice between deductions and credits should depend at least in part on the purpose of the exclusion. If the motivation is to correct for the fact that a given expenditure reduces ability to pay, a deduction seems appropriate. Such deductions might include the expense to feed, clothe, and house children, or for unexpected medical expenses. If the purpose is mainly to encourage certain behaviour, it is not at all clear whether credits or deductions are superior.[34]

A credit reduces the effective price of the favoured good by the same percentage for all individuals; a deduction decreases the price by different percentages for different people. If people differ with respect to their elasticities of demand, it may make sense to present them with different effective prices. For example, it is ineffective to give any subsidy to someone whose elasticity of demand for the favoured good is zero. The subsidy is "wasted" because it encourages no new demand. In this context it is interesting to note that Clotfelter and Steuerle (1981) estimated that the greater a household's income, the higher the price elasticity of demand for charitable donations. On the average, a given percentage decrease in price stimulates more charitable giving by a high-income than by a low-income household.

Impact on the Tax Base and Taxes Payable

To what extent does the presence of deductions and exemptions influence the size of the tax base? To what extent do tax credits reduce the tax that would otherwise be payable. The effect of both is significant. Deductions move us from total income to taxable income. The total income on all tax returns in

---

[34] See Cloutier and Fortin (1989).

1994, as shown in Table 20.5, was about $546 billion. Deductions reduced this by about $103 billion, leaving about $443 billion in taxable income. With an average tax rate of about 20 percent for provinces and the federal government combined, deductions reduced tax revenues by about $20 billion, over $12 billion being due to the federal government. Similarly, credits reduced taxes that would otherwise be payable. The total value of nonrefundable cred-

Table 20.5

Summary Information from Individual Income Tax Returns, 1994 (in millions of dollars)

A. SOURCE OF INCOME

Employment income	$344,572
Income from OAS, CPP, QPP, and pensions	55,224
Unemployment Insurance benefits	14,388
Dividends, interest, rent, annuity income, RRSP, capital gains, and other investment income	80,013
Business and professional income	24,836
Other income	27,815
Total Income Assessed = $546,849	

B. DEDUCTIONS

RPP contributions	6,941
RRSP contributions	19,285
Capital gains deduction	41,907
Other deductions	35,100
Total deductions	103,233
Taxable Income Assessed = $444,405*	

C. NONREFUNDABLE TAX CREDITS

Personal, aged, and spousal amounts	26,048
CPP, QPP, and UI contributions	2,424
Medical expenses	333
Donations and gifts	586
Other credits	1,868
Total Nonrefundable Tax Credits = $31,259	

D. TAXES PAYABLE

Net Federal Tax	61,295
Net Provincial Tax	27,208
Total Tax Payable = $88,504	

* $444,405 is the Revenue Canada figure, although $546,849 – $103,233 is equal to $443,616.

SOURCE: Revenue Canada, *Tax Statistics on Individuals, 1996 Edition* (Ottawa: 1996), p. 54. Reproduced with permission of the Minister of Supply and Services Canada, 1997.

its used to reduce taxes payable was about $31.3 billion in 1994. Deductions and credits play a large and important role in our income tax system.

Tax Expenditures

Failure to include a particular item in the tax base results in a loss to federal and provincial treasuries. Suppose that as a consequence of not taxing item Z, governments lose $1 billion. Compare this to a situation in which the government simply hands over $1 billion of general revenues to those who purchase item Z. In a sense, these activities are equivalent as both subsidize purchases of Z. It just so happens that one transaction occurs on the expenditure side of the account and the other on the revenue side. The former is a *tax expenditure*, a revenue loss caused by the exclusion of some item from the tax base. Credits have a similar effect. The government can give a tax credit of $1 billion based on a certain level of charitable giving by taxpayers, or as an alternative it can give the $1 billion directly to the charities. But the credit, too, appears on the revenue side of the account and is also a tax expenditure.

The federal government defines a tax expenditure as

> an alternative to direct spending for achieving government policy objectives. They are defined as deviations from a benchmark tax system. Typically, they take the form of income exclusions, deductions, credits, or tax deferrals that are available to select groups of individuals or types of activity.[35]

There is a long list of federal and provincial tax expenditures through the personal income tax. Table 20.6 is a partial list of federal personal income tax expenditures; it includes only those tax expenditures each of which resulted in reduced revenues of $100 million or more.

The items combined total more than $39 billion. In areas such as social services and housing, tax expenditures may be as large as direct federal expenditures. Although summing the items does not allow for interaction between the provisions, or for behavioural responses to policy changes, tax expenditures are also very significant relative to taxes collected and to the size of the government deficit. The federal government's budget deficit was $42 billion in fiscal 1993/94, with total revenues of $129 billion. This, however, does not mean that we would be better off if the tax expenditures in the table had been withdrawn in order to eliminate the deficit. It is, nonetheless, apparent that tax expenditures play an important role in government policy.

---

[35] Department of Finance (1992).

Table 20.6

Federal Personal Income Tax Expenditures, Selected Items, 1993

EXPENDITURE AREA	(MILLIONS OF DOLLARS)
Social Services	
Nontaxation of GIS and spousal allowances	$ 225
Nontaxation of social assistance	705
Nontaxation of WCB benefits	610
Nontaxation of veterans' disability pensions/allowances	146
Age credit	1,370
Pension credit	305
RRSPs: Deduction of contributions	4,490
Nontaxation of investment income	3,325
RPPs: Deduction of contributions	5,205
Nontaxation of investment income	8,610
Nontaxation of premiums for group life insurance	165
Deduction of alimony and maintenance payments	220
Health and Education	
Nontaxation of employer-paid health insurance benefits	1,200
Disability credit	270
Medical expenses credit	260
Tuition fee and education credit	218
Education and tuition fee credit transferred	190
Labour, Manpower, and Immigration	
Northern residents deduction	190
Unemployment Insurance: credit for contributions	1,230
Nontaxation of employer's share	2,510
Trade, Industrial Development, Tourism	
$100,000 lifetime capital gains exemption	1,170
Partial inclusion of capital gains	1,185
Deduction of limited partnership losses	215
$500,000 capital gains exemption for small businesses	1,170
Natural Resources, Agriculture, and Environment	
$500,000 capital gains exemption for farms	405
Recreation, Culture, Housing	
Nontaxation of lottery and gambling earnings	910
Charitable donations credit	880
Nontaxation of capital gains on principal residences and partial inclusion	2,050

Note: The above list includes only those items for which forgone revenues are $100 million or greater. Even here it is less than fully inclusive. The list omits (a) the tax abatement provided to Quebec and the transfer of income tax room to the provinces, (b) the basic credit, married credit, dependent credits, and refundable child tax credits, and (c) the nontaxation of imputed rents from home-ownership. The above list also does not show the partially offsetting taxation of withdrawals from RRSPs and RPPs in 1993, which together generated about $5.9 billion; nor does it reflect the revenue loss to provinces whose tax base is also altered by provisions in the Income Tax Act.

SOURCE: Department of Finance, *Government of Canada Tax Expenditures, 1995* (Ottawa: 1996), pp. 24–29. Reproduced with permission of the Minister of Public Works and Government Services Canada, 1997.

No law requires the Department of Finance to annually publish a comprehensive list of tax expenditures, or to approve such a list as part of the budgetary process. This is in contrast to the approval process for direct expenditures. Following private efforts to measure tax expenditures in Canada,[36] the Department of Finance has published the results of its tax expenditure estimates since late 1979. These lists, and the discussion of tax expenditures in the 1981 and 1987 tax reform documents, have raised public consciousness of the symmetry between a direct subsidy for an activity via an expenditure and an implicit subsidy through the tax system. No longer are the preferences in our tax system, and the forgone revenues, as well hidden to policy makers or the public as they once were.

The notion of a tax expenditure list and a tax expenditure budget has, however, been subject to several criticisms. First, a serious technical problem arises in the way the computations are made. It is assumed that in the absence of a deduction for a given item, all the expenditures currently made on it would flow into taxable income—for example, that people would work as hard and spend the same amount on home-ownership even if imputed rents were taxed along with all capital gains on homes. Given that people are quite likely to adjust their behaviour in response to changes in the tax system, this is not a good assumption, so the tax expenditure estimates may be quite far off the mark.

Second, the tax expenditure budget is simply a list of items that either reduce the tax base by exemptions and deductions, or lower taxes payable through credits. To consider these items as forgone or "lost" revenues, we must have some criterion for deciding what the tax base ought to be in the first place, and what, if any, credits are an inherent part of the tax system.[37] As we have seen, no rigorous set of principles exists for determining what belongs in income. Nor has there been much consistency over time in protecting a minimal amount of income for a taxpayer and his or her dependents through the use of exemptions or credits. One person's loophole may be regarded by another as an appropriate adjustment of the tax base. Hence, considerable arbitrariness is inevitably involved in deciding what to include in a tax expenditure list or budget.

---

[36] Smith (1979).

[37] In the fall of 1988 a conference was held at Queen's University to discuss the tax expenditure concept, including the appropriate benchmark when determining provisions that result in tax expenditures. One issue is whether consumption or income is the appropriate benchmark base. Major tax expenditures under the "income" tax in Table 20.6 are due to deductions for contributions to RRSPs and RPPs, and to the deferral of tax on income earned in these funds. If "consumption" were the benchmark base, these would not be tax expenditures. See Bruce (1992).

Finally, the concept of tax expenditures has been attacked on philosophical grounds. It is argued that the tax expenditure concept implies that the forgone revenues belong to the government. This is at odds with a view that government is "of the people" in a democracy, and property is privately held except where the polity supports the transfer of resources, through taxes or by other means, to the government.

Defenders of the tax expenditure concept have argued that the concept does not really carry these ideological implications. It is rather an attempt to force recognition of the fact that the tax system is a major method for subsidizing various activities. Moreover, even though the estimates are not exact they can still be useful for assessing the implications of tax policy. Explicit recognition of tax expenditures

- contributes to the reassessment of policies on a regular basis,
- permits a comparison of direct and indirect means of obtaining a given government objective, and
- allows, in some cases, for the use of benefit–cost analysis in the evaluation of tax expenditures, as in the evaluation of direct expenditures.

Feldstein (1980) has pointed out that, under certain conditions, a tax expenditure may be a more effective way for the government to stimulate a given activity than is a direct payment. Assume the government wants to stimulate the activities of charitable organizations. One possible method is a tax expenditure. When the price elasticity of demand for charitable donations exceeds 1, each dollar forgone by Revenue Canada generates more than a dollar in charitable giving. In this case, the government would have to spend more than the estimated revenue loss to provide the equivalent total expenditure on charity.

Of course, we do not expect every dollar of public spending to replace exactly a dollar of private spending. Nor can we assume the price elasticity of demand for each preferred item exceeds unity. But this simple example illustrates the basic point: In general, whether a tax expenditure or a direct subsidy is more effective depends on the amount of crowding out that occurs, and on how responsive the demand for the preferred item is with respect to its after-tax price. The issue must be examined on a case-by-case basis.[38]

---

[38] Tax expenditures can be made through the corporate income tax, sales taxes, and property taxes, as well as through the personal income tax. It is important that provincial and local authorities, too, are aware of revenues forgone through special provisions in their laws, as well as revenues forgone due to provincial reliance on tax bases defined by the federal government. Some provincial governments, including Saskatchewan and British Columbia, have developed tax expenditure lists.

The Simplicity Issue

The federal personal income tax has been railed at for its complexity and the compliance burden it has placed on taxpayers. Reference is frequently made to the growing length of the Income Tax Act and the inability of intelligent men and women to make sense of it. With some justification, it has been referred to as "the accountants and lawyers full employment act."

One of five objectives in the 1987 tax reform was that the tax system "be simpler to understand and comply with." The basic rate structure was simplified, with tax brackets reduced from thirteen to ten by the 1981 reforms and then to three in 1988.[39] The tax base was broadened (tax expenditures reduced) in order to treat income from different sources, and in the hands of different people, in a similar fashion. The general capital gains exemption was reduced from $500,000 to $100,000, and then eliminated altogether. With three-fourths of capital gains now included in taxable income, the incentive to realize income in the form of capital gains has been reduced. RHOSP plans have been terminated. No longer is $1,000 in investment income tax free. Investments in films and in multiple unit residential buildings (MURBs) are now less generously treated, and provisions that allowed income to be averaged over several years were repealed.

The 1987 tax reform replaced the personal, spousal, dependent, age, and disability exemptions with tax credits. Credits also replaced deductions that had previously provided for pension income, tuition fees, medical expenses, charitable contributions, and CPP/QPP and UI premiums. The value of the credit was stated either as a specific amount (for example, a $1,020 credit in place of the basic personal exemption), or as a set percentage of the expenditure, regardless of the income level of the taxpayer. Prior to this change, each deduction or exemption varied in its value depending on which of ten marginal tax rates applied to the taxpayer.

The law remains complex and will remain so. With the reduction or elimination of preferences, the conversion of exemptions and deductions to credits, and the simplification of the rate structure, taxpayers may feel the complexity of the law now contributes more to fairness and less to the special treatment of some taxpayers. However, simple rules are often inadequate when situations differ greatly in a complex world. Although it is unlikely that the income tax

---

[39] The federal rate structure remains far more complex that the basic rates of 0, 17, 26, and 29 suggest. This is due to a surtax, payroll tax rates that apply over certain ranges of earned income, and to "claw-back" arrangements that reduce transfer payments as income rises. These result in marginal rates on income that substantially exceed the basic rates.

act in Canada, or any other industrialized country, will be other than complex, there will always be room for improvement.

RATE STRUCTURE

After calculating total income, allowed deductions, and taxable income, we have arrived at the third step in Figure 20.1—the application of tax rates to taxable income, and the calculation of income tax payable *before* tax credits. A bracket system is used to define tax rates. The taxable income scale is divided into segments, and the law specifies the marginal tax rate that applies to income in that segment.

Rates and Brackets

Statutory income tax rates changed dramatically over time. When the federal income tax was introduced in 1917, a "normal" tax rate was applied at a 4 percent rate on income over $1,500 for single individuals and over $3,000 for all others. An additional "supertax" was applied, ranging from 2 percent on income from $6,000 to $10,000 up to an additional 25 percent on income over $100,000. Thus, rates ranged from a low of zero to 29 (4+25) percent over eight brackets, including the first $1,500 or $3,000 subject to a zero rate.

With World War II came the need for higher rates, rates that continued after the war. Table 20.7 shows combined federal and provincial marginal rates on selected levels of nominal income for various years from 1917 to 1996.[40] Substantial compression of marginal rates has occurred, compacting from 15 to 84 percent in 1949 to 26 to 46 percent in 1996. The eight brackets in 1917, which had increased to fifteen by 1949, were reduced to ten in the 1981 reform and further to three brackets with the 1987 tax reform. Rates in Table 20.7 for 1996 are the sum of the federal rates of 17, 26, and 29 percent plus the provincial rates, which are expressed as a percentage of the basic federal tax— assumed to be 52 percent in 1996.[41] The first dollar that is taxed is now subject to a much higher tax rate than was true prior to 1988, and the top marginal rate now affects a much larger share of the population than in earlier years. In 1996 the top marginal rate is applicable on income over $59,180 (1996 dollars). This contrasts with top marginal rates that did not become effective until incomes hit $2.9 million (1996$) in 1949 and $240,000 (1996$) in 1972.

---

[40] Table 20.7 does not show *all* of the rates or brackets for years other than 1917 and 1949. It shows only how rates changed over the years for a select number of nominal income levels.

[41] Provincial rates vary, with Ontario at 56 percent, British Columbia at 52 percent, and Alberta at 45.5 percent in 1996. The fourth rate in 1996 is due to the additional federal surtax when federal tax exceeds $12,500.

Table 20.7

Combined Federal and Provincial* Income Tax Marginal Rates for Selected Years and Selected (Nominal) Income Levels, 1917 to 1996

TAXABLE INCOME	1917	1949	1972	1986	1987	1996**
$ 1	0	15	21.68	8.82	9.00	26.35
1,001	0	17	24.23	8.82	9.00	26.35
3,001	4	19	26.78	24.99	25.50	26.35
5,001	4	22	29.33	26.46	25.50	26.35
7,001	6	26	31.88	26.46	27.00	26.35
9,001	6	30	34.43	27.93	28.50	26.35
11,001	9	35	39.53	27.93	28.50	26.35
15,001	9	45	44.63	45.60	30.00	26.35
25,001	12	50	49.73	53.38	37.50	26.35
40,001	14	59	54.83	53.38	45.00	40.30
60,001	19	64	59.93	53.38	51.00	44.95
90,001	19	69	59.93	53.38	51.00	46.40
125,001	29	74	59.93	53.38	51.00	46.40
225,001	29	79	59.93	53.38	51.00	46.40
400,001	29	84	59.93	53.38	51.00	46.40

* The provincial rates are assumed to be 30.5 of the basic federal tax in 1972, 47.0 percent in 1986 and 1987, and 52.0 percent in 1996.

** Due to the refundable Goods and Services Tax credits and child tax benefits, these rates at the lower income levels are not comparable to earlier years.

SOURCE: Canadian Tax Foundation, *The National Finances 1985–86* (Toronto: Canadian Tax Foundation, 1986), p. 101, Table 7.5, and Karin Treff and David Perry, *Finances of the Nation, 1996* (Toronto: Canadian Tax Foundation, 1997), p. 3:7, Table 3.5; Statutes of Canada, 12 Parliament, 7 Session, *The Income War Tax Act*, September 20, 1917.

Factors Affecting Marginal Rates

Unfortunately, these statutory marginal tax rates seldom correspond to the actual marginal tax rates. There are three main reasons for this:

- federal and provincial surtaxes,
- payroll taxes, and
- claw-backs for the child tax benefit and GST credit, UI benefits, and OAS payments.

Surtaxes. Table 20.8 indicates surtaxes applied in 1996. The federal government levied a general 3 percent surtax on basic federal tax and an additional 5 percent (for a total of 8 percent) on basic federal tax in excess of $12,500. This raised the federal marginal rate by 2.32 percentage points, to

Table 20.8

Federal and Provincial Tax Rates, and Surtaxes, 1996

I. Rates of Federal Income Tax

TAXABLE INCOME	TAX RATE
$29,590 or less	17%
$29,591 to 59,179	26%
$59,180 and over	29%
Federal surtax:	3 percent in general plus 5 percent (for a total of 8 percent) on basic federal tax in excess of $12,500 (raises marginal rates to 17.51, 26.78, 29.87, and 31.32 percent)

II. Provincial Income Tax Rates and Surtaxes

PROVINCE	PIT AS % OF BASIC FEDERAL TAX	FLAT TAX, % OF NET INCOME	SURTAX, % OF PROVINCIAL TAX PAYABLE*
Newfoundland	69.0	—	10 on that payable over $7,900
PEI	59.5	—	10 on that payable over $12,500
Nova Scotia	59.5	—	10 on that payable over $10,000
New Brunswick	64.0	—	8 on that payable over $13,500
Quebec	na	na	na
Ontario	56.0	—	20 on that payable between $5,310 and $7,635 33 on that payable over $7,635
Manitoba	52.0	2.0	2 on net income over $30,000
Saskatchewan	50.0	2.0	10 on sum of basic provincial tax and flat tax over $4,000
Alberta	45.5	0.5**	8 on that payable over $3,500
British Columbia	52.0	—	30 on that payable between $5,300 and $8,915 51.5 on that over $8,915
NWT	45.0	—	—
Yukon	50.0	—	5 on that payable over $6,000

* The base differs in Manitoba and Saskatchewan.
** As a percentage of taxable income.

SOURCE: Karin Treff and David Perry, *Finances of the Nation, 1996* (Toronto: Canadian Tax Foundation, 1997), pp. 3:11–12, Tables 3.8 and 3.9.

31.32 percent on those with higher incomes. Provincial surtaxes were as high as 33 percent of the provincial tax payable in Ontario, and British Columbia applied a 51.5 percent surtax to provincial tax payable over $8,915. The 33 percent surtax added over 5 percentage points to marginal rates on higher incomes (in the range of $70,000 and up), and the 51.5 percent surtax in

British Columbia added 7.8 percentage points to the marginal rate on income over $80,000. Adding the surtaxes to the basic rates raises top marginal rates to well over 50 percent in all provinces except Alberta.

Payroll taxes. Payroll taxes, discussed in Part 5, significantly raise the effective marginal rates on wages and salaries over a range of incomes. Canada Pension Plan (CPP) premiums, a form of payroll tax, are collected at a rate of 2.8 percent from employees (also 2.8 percent from the employer) and 5.6 percent from those who are self-employed. These rates apply over income ranging from $3,500 to $35,400, raising marginal tax rates on earned income by as much as 5.6 percentage points.

Unemployment Insurance (UI) premiums in 1996 were paid by each employee at a 2.95 percent rate on the insurable earnings of up to $43,940—an annual maximum tax of $1,150.76. Employers contribute an additional 4.13 percent. Thus, the total tax is 7.08 percent, although the payslip taken home reflects only the 2.95 percent deducted from gross earnings. For much of earnings below $40,000, the combined effect of CPP and UI premiums substantially raises the effective marginal tax rate on income from wages—by as much as 12.7 percent in 1996.[42]

Claw-backs. Some benefits to taxpayers are cut back once income reaches certain levels. This is true for the child tax benefit and for the GST credit. The child tax benefit payment ($1,020 for each child plus $213 for each child under the age of 7) is reduced by 5 percent (2.5 percent in the case of a single child) of the amount that the parents' income exceeds $25,921 in 1996. For a family with two older children, the additional 5 percent rate applies over a range of income from $25,921 to $66,721. Similarly, the GST refundable credit, which was set at $199 each for a taxpayer and spouse, and $105 for each eligible child, is reduced by 5 percent for income over $25,921. For a family with two adults and two children, total GST credit of $608, the credit disappears (along with the extra marginal rate) when income reaches about $38,000. These two claw-backs raise the effective marginal rate above the statutory rates by 10 percentage points over a range of relatively low incomes.

The claw-back of UI benefits applies at relatively high income levels. UI benefits are reduced by 30 percent of the amount that a recipient's net income exceeds 150 percent of maximum insurable earnings (1.5 × $43,940), or $65,910 in 1996. Thus, when the income of a UI recipient exceeds this

---

[42] See the discussion of payroll tax incidence in Chapter 17. The economic incidence of payroll taxes is, over the longer run, little affected by whether the tax is collected from the employee or the employer.

amount, marginal rates normally in the 50 percent range may top 80 percent until UI benefits are fully clawed back.

The OAS payments in 1996 provided $395 per month to those over 65. Benefits are withheld when annual income is over $53,215, at a rate of 15 percent of net income over this amount. This is effectively an additional tax rate, which applies until the entire amount has been clawed back at an income level of $83,275. This creates an income range for the elderly, where marginal rates may exceed 65 percent on income between $63,000 and $83,000.

The foregoing makes clear that the simple federal rate structure of the 1987 tax reform is anything but simple when combined with provincial rates, surtaxes, payroll tax rates, and claw-backs, all of which affect the amount a taxpayer takes home from an additional dollar of gross earnings. The lines in Table 20.9 show the federal rate structure (with surtaxes), plus the Ontario

Table 20.9

Factors Affecting Marginal Tax Rates: An Example in 1994*

INCOME LEVEL	TAX PROVISION	CHANGE IN MARGINAL TAX RATE	MARGINAL TAX RATE
$ 0	Start of UI premiums	+3.07	3.07
3,400	Start of CPP premiums	+2.60	5.67
12,454	Start of 1st bracket plus surtaxes—Fed. + Ontario	+25.88**	31.55
25,921	Start of GST claw-back	+5.00	36.55
29,590	Start of 2nd bracket plus surtaxes—Fed. + Ontario	+14.24	50.79
33,881	End of GST claw-back	−5.00	45.79
34,400	Maximum for CPP premiums	−2.16**	43.63
40,560	Maximum for UI premiums	−2.55**	41.08
46,710	Start of Ontario 20% surtax	+3.02	44.10
59,180	Start of 3rd bracket plus surtaxes—Fed. + Ontario	+4.83	48.93
62,873	Start of Ontario 30% surtax	+2.03	53.98
66,262	Start of Federal 5% surtax	+1.45	55.43

* This for a married couple without dependents. Applicable credits include those for self, spouse, and maximum UI and CPP contributions.

** These are adjusted to reflect that a tax credit is provided for the UI and CPP premiums, thus reducing their contribution to the overall marginal rate once a positive income tax rate begins to be applied. When these taxes hit their ceiling and no longer apply to additional income, they also cease to add to the tax credit.

Figure 20.2

Marginal Tax Rates, 1994

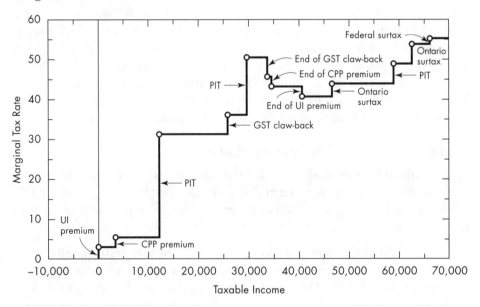

SOURCE: Based on Table 20.9.

rate structure (with surtaxes), plus CPP and UI payroll taxes, plus GST claw-backs. Even without the further complications of claw-backs for child tax benefits, UI benefits, and OAS payments, Table 20.9 and Figure 20.2 adequately demonstrate the complexity of existing marginal tax rates.[43] While the table provides an indication of the situation in Ontario in 1994, it is illustrative of the complexity that currently exists in the rate structure in all provinces.

The Alternative Minimum Tax

Under most income tax laws it is possible for some individuals with high incomes to pay little or no tax. This occurs for reasons that include the form of income received and deductions allowed. Where an individual qualifies for large dividend tax credits, investment and other tax credits, and/or has large deductions due to accelerated depreciation or to contributions to deferred savings plans, taxes in a given year may appear low relative to taxes paid by those receiving income in other forms or not qualifying for similar deductions. The result may be a high income and little tax.

---

[43] For a fuller treatment of the complexity of marginal rates due to factors discussed here, see Howard, Ruggeri, and Van Wart (1995).

The Alternative Minimum Tax (AMT) took effect in 1986 and is payable if it exceeds taxes calculated in the normal way. The AMT tax base includes all of capital gains rather than only three-quarters, and does not allow for various tax incentives or for deductions for contributions to RPPs, RRSPs, and deferred profit sharing plans. There is provision for a $40,000 exemption, which ensures that the AMT only affects those with capital gains and dividend income, tax incentives, and deductions that are high relative to the norm. The AMT is essentially a shadow tax system with its own rules for computing the tax base. However, it applies the normal tax rates to the AMT base, and provincial taxes are calculated as a percentage of the federal tax as in other cases.

Effective versus Statutory Rates

Now is a good time to recall the distinction between statutory and effective tax rates. In this section, we have been discussing the former, the legal rates established by the law. In general, these differ from effective tax rates for at least three reasons:

- Because the tax system treats certain types of income preferentially, taxable income may be considerably lower than some more comprehensive measures of income. The fact that tax rates rise rapidly with taxable income does not by itself tell us much about how taxes vary with comprehensive income.
- Even in the absence of loopholes, the link between statutory and effective tax rates is weak. As was emphasized in Chapter 17, taxes can be shifted, so there is no reason to believe that income taxes will really be borne by the people who pay the money to the government. The economic incidence of the income tax is determined by market responses when the tax is levied, and the true pattern of the burden is not known.
- The tax system imposes decreases in utility that exceed revenue collections. Excess burdens arise because taxes distort behaviour away from patterns that otherwise would have occurred (see Chapter 18). Similarly, the costs of compliance with the Income Tax Act, in taxpayers' own time as well as explicit payments to accountants and lawyers, must be considered.

In this connection, note that contrary to the impression sometimes received in popular discussions, the provision of an item such as tax-free dental care paid for by an employer does not, in general, allow the taxpayer to escape entirely the burden of taxation. Consider again Caesar, whose marginal tax rate is 50 percent. The cost to the employer of providing dental care is $500. Caesar may value the service at $300, more than the after-tax $250 that he would receive if the employer increased wages by $500 instead of providing dental care.

Caesar accepts the dental care, but the tax system nevertheless makes him worse off, because in its absence he would have much preferred the $500 in the form of wages rather than dental care.

Similarly, where tax incentives or preferences encourage certain types of investments, there is a general tendency for the rate of return on tax-preferenced items to fall by an amount that reflects the tax advantage. Because of this tendency, which results from normal market forces, the effective tax rate on capital income for those making such investments, generally high-income individuals, is higher than their tax payments would suggest.

Thus, statutory rates alone probably tell us little about the progressiveness of the current system. Conceivably, a statute with lower marginal tax rates but a broader base would lead to a system with incidence as progressive as that of the current system, and perhaps even more so. At the same time, a system with lower marginal tax rates would reduce excess burden and perhaps lower tax evasion. Such considerations have prompted a number of proposals to restructure the income tax dramatically. One plan that has received a lot of attention is the **flat tax**. A flat tax has two attributes:

- It applies the same rate of tax to everyone and to each component of the tax base.
- It allows computation of the tax base with no deductions from total income except personal exemptions and strictly defined business expenses.[44]

Assuming that a certain amount of tax revenue must be collected, under a flat tax the key trade-off is between the size of the personal exemption and the marginal tax rate. A higher exemption may be desirable to secure relief for those at the bottom of the income schedule and to increase progressiveness (with respect to average tax rates). But a higher exemption means that a higher marginal tax rate must be applied to maintain revenues. A tax rate of roughly 25 percent together with a personal exemption of $12,000, plus additional spousal and dependent exemptions of lesser amounts, could have generated revenues equivalent to those raised by the federal and provincial personal income tax in 1992.[45]

---

[44] In essence, then, a flat tax is just a linear income tax, as defined in Chapter 19.

[45] The federal Reform and Progressive Conservative parties were both urging the adoption of a flat rate in mid-1995. See "Floating the Flat-Tax Balloon over a Tax-Weary Canada," *The Financial Post*, July 1–3, 1995, pp. 1–2.

Proponents of the flat tax claim that lowering marginal tax rates would reduce both the excess burden of the tax system and the incentive to cheat. Moreover, the simplicity gained would cut down on administrative costs and improve taxpayer morale. And all of this could be achieved without a serious cost in equity because, as just noted, the flat tax can be made quite progressive by suitable choice of the exemption level.[46]

Opponents of the flat tax believe that it would redistribute the tax burden from the rich to the middle class, and there is some evidence supporting this. However, it is hard to evaluate this claim because of the usual difficulties involved in doing tax incidence analysis (Chapter 17). One way to think of the tax reforms of 1981 and 1987 is as a movement in the direction of a flat tax— the federal statutory maximum rate was lowered from 43 percent in 1981 to 34 percent in 1982, and to 29 percent in 1988, and the base was broadened by disallowing some deductions and including more investment income— interest, dividends, and capital gains—and the value of some previously untaxed fringe benefits. Whether or not there will be further movement toward a flat tax remains to be seen. There is some evidence that concern over income concentration and tax equity is rising, leading to less interest in tax reform that may shift the burden from those with high incomes to the middle class. In any case, the discussion of federal and provincial surtaxes makes it apparent that both levels of government have dramatically altered the simple rate structure since 1987.

The Final Calculation

Applying the marginal tax rates to taxable income, we calculate tax that is due before credits. This brings us to Step 4 in Figure 20.1, which provides for the subtraction of tax credits from the federal income tax otherwise payable when tax rates are applied to taxable income. These include credits calculated as 17 percent of amounts provided for a taxpayer, taxpayer's spouse, disabilities, and infirm dependents, and 17 percent of qualifying UI, CPP and pension contributions, $1,000 in pension income, and qualifying tuition fees and medical expenses. It allows a credit for 17 percent for the first $200 in charitable donations, and 29 percent for that in excess of $200. Subtracting these and a limited number of other credits from the product of the tax rates and taxable income yields **federal tax payable**. Provincial rates are then applied to the basic federal tax to calculate provincial tax payable (Step 5).

---

[46] Smith (1984 and 1986) provides earlier estimates of the effects of moving from a progressive-rate structure to a flat-rate income tax in Canada. These two studies examine, in a static framework, redistribution of the tax burden that would have accompanied a move to a flat tax in 1980 and 1984, assuming a specified level of exempt income.

CHOICE OF TAX UNIT

We have discussed at length problems that arise in defining income for taxation purposes. Yet, even very careful definitions of income give little guidance with respect to choosing who should be taxed on the income. Should each person be taxed separately on his or her own income? Or should individuals who live together in a family unit be taxed on their joint incomes? The choice of the proper taxable unit is an extremely difficult one. Many alternative approaches are available, and although no general consensus has emerged, a recent review concludes that "during the 1970s and the early 1980s, there was an almost one-way move from joint to individual taxation."[47] We now discuss some of the difficult issues involved in the choice of taxable unit.[48]

Background

To begin, it is useful to consider the following three principles:

1. The income tax should embody increasing marginal tax rates.
2. Families with equal incomes should, other things being the same (including family size), pay equal taxes.
3. Two individuals' tax burdens should not change when they marry; the tax system should be **marriage neutral**.

Although a certain amount of controversy surrounds the second and third principles, it is probably fair to say they reflect a broad consensus as to desirable features of a tax system. While agreement on the first principle is weaker, increasing marginal tax rates seem to have wide political support.

Despite the appeal of these principles, a problem arises when it comes to implementing them: In general, no tax system can adhere to all three simultaneously. This point is made most easily with an arithmetic example. Consider the following simple progressive tax schedule: a taxable unit pays in tax 10 percent of all income up to $6,000, and 50 percent of all income in excess of $6,000. The first two columns of Table 20.10 show the incomes and tax liabilities of four individuals, Lucy, Ricky, Fred, and Ethel. (For example, Ricky's tax liability is $12,100 [= .10 × $6,000 + .50 × $23,000].) Now assume that romances develop—Lucy marries Ricky, and Ethel marries Fred. In the absence of joint filing, the tax liability of each individual is unchanged. However, two

---

[47] Messere (1995: 518).
[48] For further details, see Davies (1992), and "Comments" by Neil Brooks and B. Fortin in Richard M. Bird and Jack M. Mintz, eds., *Taxation to 2000 and Beyond* (Toronto: Canadian Tax Foundation, 1992).

Table 20.10

Tax Liabilities under a Hypothetical Tax System

	INDIVIDUAL INCOME	INDIVIDUAL TAX	FAMILY TAX WITH INDIVIDUAL FILING	JOINT INCOME	JOINT TAX
Lucy	$ 1,000	$ 100	$12,200	$30,000	$12,600
Ricky	29,000	12,100			
Ethel	15,000	5,100	$10,200	$30,000	$12,600
Fred	15,000	5,100			

families with the same income ($30,000) will be paying different amounts of tax. (The Lucy–Rickys pay $12,200, while the Ethel–Freds pay only $10,200, as noted in the third column.) Suppose instead that the law views the family as the taxable unit, so that the tax schedule applies to joint income. In this case, the two families pay equal amounts of tax, but now tax burdens have been changed by marriage. Of course, the actual change in the tax burden depends on the difference between the tax schedules applied to individual and joint returns. This example has assumed for simplicity that the schedule remains unchanged. But it does make the main point: Given increasing marginal tax rates, we cannot have both principles 2 and 3.[49]

What choice has Canada made? The tax unit has been the individual throughout the history of the Canadian personal income tax. Nonetheless, it has been strongly argued that this is wrong-headed and that the family should be the taxable unit. An economist surveying the scene is likely to ask, "What is most efficient?" and "What is most equitable?" We discuss the choice of tax unit with these two questions in mind.

Family. The *Report* of the Royal Commission on Taxation (1966: 122–23) strongly urged that the family be the taxable unit for Canada's personal income tax:

> The family is ... the basic economic unit in society.... Taxation of the individual in ... disregard of his inevitably close financial and economic ties

---

[49] It may be apparent to the reader that a flat-rate tax with a single rate is marriage neutral, and will treat two couples the same regardless of the distribution of income between the two partners (assuming income in all cases is above the taxable threshold). Income-spitting problems are also minimized with a single rate since the applicable rate is more likely to be the same regardless of who reports the income.

with the other members of the basic social unit of which he is ordinarily a member, the family, is in our view [a] striking instance of [a] lack of a comprehensive and rational pattern in ... [a] tax system.

The commission noted that the incomes of spouses and children all contribute to the well-being of a family, and to its ability to pay taxes. With progressive tax rates based on ability to pay, it is reasonable to recognize increased ability to pay. Equity, in the eyes of the commission, is achieved only if family units with the same income pay the same tax—something that will not occur with the individual as the taxable unit.

The commission also noted that enforcement problems arise with individuals as the taxable unit. With progressive tax rates, the incentive for **income splitting** may be great. This is most likely to occur with nonlabour income (dividends, interest, profits). Family members with high levels of taxable income have an incentive to shift income-generating assets to a spouse or to children with lower tax rates. Although laws may limit a taxpayer's income-splitting ability, the laws become more complex and splitting still occurs as substantial transfers are made over time. However, given current high rates of divorce, turning property over to a spouse just for tax purposes may be a risky strategy, and there is no strong evidence that such transfers would occur in massive amounts. With the family as the tax unit, there are no tax implications in the transfer of assets between spouses, or to children so long as they remain within the family unit.

The argument for the family as a unit weakens on efficiency grounds. Aggregation of the income from family members means that the additional dollar earned by a spouse or children, who individually may have little income, may be subject to high marginal tax rates if another family member has high income.[50] The effect on the labour supply may be substantial. Since married women may have more elastic labour supply schedules than their husbands (as we will note in Chapter 21), efficient taxation requires taxing wives at a relatively lower rate. This may also hold true for others in the family unit. Under a family unit all family members face identical marginal tax rates on their last dollars of income. Hence, the family as the taxable unit is inefficient.

There is also the question of whether a wife and husband, both of whom hold full-time jobs, such as Fred–Ethel, should pay income taxes equal to those of another couple, such as Lucy–Ricky, where one spouse working outside the

---

[50] This could not occur, so long as income is above the tax-free threshold, if there were but a single rate.

home earns as much as the combined earnings of the first couple. This occurs with the family as the taxable unit, but ignores the fact that the second couple is likely to benefit more from imputed income associated with care of the home and children, more leisure, and possibly lower transportation and other work-related expenses.

Individual. Taxation of individuals avoids the inefficiency that accompanies high marginal rates on the income of secondary earners in the family unit. Adopting the family as the taxable unit would also not be a simple matter. For example, Bittker (1975: 1398) observed:

> If married couples are taxed on their consolidated income, for example, should the same principle extend to a child who supports an aged parent, two sisters who share an apartment, or a divorced parent who lives with an adolescent child? Should a relationship established by blood or marriage be demanded, to the exclusion, for example, of unmarried persons who live together, homosexual companions, and communes?

In addition to the complexities associated with adopting the family as the taxable unit, other reasons exist for choosing the individual.

There has, perhaps, never been reason to believe that full sharing of income existed within family units. A husband or wife may know relatively little of the other's income, and subjecting the earnings of one spouse to a high tax rate because the other spouse earns much more, as occurs with aggregated incomes, is seen as unfair. There has also been an increasing wish to recognize the earnings of women as theirs to use and control, recognizing that laws in the past have sometimes limited ownership rights available to women.

The earlier example of Lucy–Ricky and Ethel–Fred shows the "marriage penalty" that accompanies the use of the family as the unit of taxation. Both couples experience higher taxes on a joint basis than on an individual basis, but the difference is much greater for one couple than for the other. Continuing to tax them on a individual basis is the only way to remain neutral on the question of marriage and avoid either a marriage "penalty" or "reward" for one or the other.

With increasing numbers of two-income families, even two-city commuting families, families without children, and with high divorce rates, arguments for the individual as the tax unit have strengthened in the past several decades. The individual is expected to continue as the tax unit in Canada. This means that Canada's income tax law will continue to violate principle 2—equal taxes on

families with equal incomes. Principle 3—no change in tax burdens when marriage occurs—will be maintained for working couples.[51] No tax system can satisfy all three criteria, and Canadian society has (for the time) made its choice. Nonetheless, the choice of taxable unit will continue to be influenced by sociological, administrative, and political, as well as economic considerations.

TAXES AND INFLATION

The tax law establishes set amounts to which the 17 percent rate is applied to determine allowable tax credits. It also establishes minimum and maximum dollar amounts for each tax bracket, and thresholds at which claw-backs of tax benefits and credits, OAS payments, and UI benefits begin to apply. With inflation, the real value of these set amounts is maintained only if the amounts are adjusted upward by the rate of inflation. For example, a basic personal allowance needs to be increased from $6,000 to $6,120 in a year in which inflation is at a rate of 2 percent. Where such adjustments are automatically made as prices rise, the tax system is said to be **indexed for inflation**. The purpose is to remove automatically the influence of inflation from real tax liabilities. This section discusses motivations for tax indexing, and whether the Canadian system of indexing is an adequate response to the problems posed by inflation.

How Inflation Can Affect Taxes

Economists customarily distinguish between "anticipated" and "unanticipated" inflation. The latter is generally viewed as being worse for efficiency, because it does not allow people to adjust their behaviour optimally to price-level changes. However, with an unindexed income tax system, even perfectly anticipated inflation causes distortions.

The most popularly understood distortion is the phenomenon known as **bracket creep**. Suppose that an individual's earnings and the price level both increase at the same rate over time. Then that person's real income (the amount of actual purchasing power) is unchanged. However, an unindexed tax system is based on the individual's nominal income—the number of dollars received. As nominal income increases, the individual is pushed into tax brackets with higher marginal tax rates. Hence, the proportion of income that is taxed increases despite the fact that real income stays the same. Even individuals who

---

[51] The situation is not quite this simple. Child tax benefit payments and GST credits are both affected by the combined incomes of spouses. Thus, a GST credit or child tax benefit that is available to a single parent is subject to claw-back when the parent marries if the couple's combined incomes exceed the threshold amount—$25,921 in 1996.

are not pushed into a higher bracket find more of their income taxed at the highest rate to which they are subject. Inflation brings about an automatic increase in real tax burdens without any legislative action.

Another effect of inflation occurs when personal and other allowances are set in nominal terms. In an unindexed system, increases in the price level decrease their real value. Again, the effective tax rate increases as a consequence of inflation.

It turns out, however, that even with a simple proportional income tax without exemptions or deductions, inflation would distort tax burdens. To be sure, under such a system, general inflation would not affect the real tax burden on wage and salary incomes. If a worker's earnings during a year doubled, so would his or her taxes, and there would be no real effects. But inflation would change the real tax burden on capital income.

Suppose Calpurnia buys an asset for $5,000. Three years later, she sells it for $10,000. Suppose further that during the three years the general price level doubled. In real terms, selling the asset nets Calpurnia zero. However, capital gains liabilities are based on the difference between the nominal selling and buying prices. Hence, Calpurnia incurs a tax liability on three-quarters of the illusory capital gain of $5,000. In short, because the inflationary component of capital gains is subject to tax, the real tax burden depends on the inflation rate.

Those who receive taxable interest income are similarly affected. Suppose that the nominal interest rate (the rate observed in the market) is 16 percent. Suppose further that the anticipated rate of inflation is 12 percent. Then for someone who lends at the 16 percent nominal rate, the real interest rate is only 4 percent, because that is the percentage by which the lender's real purchasing power is increased. However, taxes are levied on nominal, not real, interest payments. Hence, tax must be paid on receipts that represent no gain in real income.

Let us consider this argument algebraically. Call the nominal interest rate i. Then the after-tax nominal return to lending for an individual with a marginal tax rate of t is $(1 - t)i$. To find the real after-tax rate of return, we must subtract the expected rate of inflation, π. Hence, the real after-tax rate of return r, is

$$r = (1 - t)i - \pi. \tag{20.1}$$

Suppose $t = .50$, $i = 10$ percent, and $\pi = 4$ percent. Then although the nominal interest rate is 10 percent, the real after-tax return is only 1 percent.

Now suppose that any increase in the expected rate of inflation increases the nominal interest rate by the same amount; if inflation increases by four points, the nominal interest rate increases by four points.[52] It might be expected that the two increases would cancel out, leaving the real after-tax rate of return unchanged at 1 percent. But Equation (20.1) contradicts this prediction. If π goes from 4 percent to 8 percent and i goes from 10 percent to 14 percent, then with t equal to 0.50, r decreases to –1 percent. Inflation, even though it is perfectly anticipated, is not "neutral." This is a direct consequence of the fact that nominal rather than real interest payments are taxed.

So far we have been considering the issue from the point of view of lenders. Things are just the opposite for borrowers. In the absence of the tax system, the real rate paid by borrowers is the nominal rate minus the anticipated inflation rate. However, assuming the taxpayer satisfies certain criteria, the tax law allows deductibility of nominal interest payments from taxable income. Thus, debtors can subtract from taxable income payments that represent no decrease in their real incomes. The tax burden on borrowers is *decreased* by inflation.

Coping with the Tax/Inflation Problem

During the 1950s and 1960s nominal tax rates and tax brackets were unchanged. Although annual inflation during this period was generally less than 4 percent, the consumer price index (CPI) rose by 72 percent over the twenty-two years from 1949 to 1971, and bracket creep led to increased tax rates on individuals with unchanged levels of real income. However, real incomes also rose rapidly during this period, and Canadians paid the higher taxes that were the result of bracket creep plus higher real incomes. Personal income taxes rose from 16 percent of government revenue in 1949 to 30 percent in 1970, an enormous increase. This rapid change was one factor that led to the overall review of the tax system by the Royal Commission on Taxation in the 1960s.[53]

Inflation accelerated in the early 1970s, reaching 8 percent in 1973. Lenin is alleged to have said, "The way to crush the bourgeoisie is to grind them

---

[52] It is not clear that this proposition holds exactly, but it is a useful approximation for our purposes. See Tanzi (1980).

[53] Nonetheless, at a time of modest inflation in the mid-1960s, the commission concluded: "Because it is not possible to make provision for complete recognition of declines in purchasing power brought about by inflation, we have concluded that it should not be the function of the tax system to attempt to relieve only some segments of the population from the effects of inflation. The tax system should therefore, in our opinion, continue to be based on current dollars and not on constant dollars." Royal Commission on Taxation (1966: 349).

between the millstones of taxation and inflation." Although the interaction of taxes and inflation in Canada had not created quite such drastic effects, there was growing concern over the serious distortions caused by inflation. People became acutely aware of the fact that inflation leads to unlegislated increases in the real income tax burden. Table 20.11 shows that a family of four with real income of $42,600 (1994 dollars) paid 12.7 percent of personal income in 1954 and 17.7 percent in 1970, a 30 percent increase during a period when statutory rates and brackets did not change. Increases were proportionately larger for those with lower incomes. The government, in response, partially indexed the personal income tax system. Adjustments in 1974 were made to personal, marital, dependent, age, and disability exemptions; tax-free earnings of dependents were also indexed, as were tax bracket limits. The adjustment for 1974 was based on the change in the average CPI for October 1, 1972, through September 30, 1973, relative to the previous twelve-month period, with similar adjustments for subsequent years. These changes had a major impact on taxes otherwise payable.[54]

Indexing was neither comprehensive nor permanent. No adjustment was made to interest payments, interest receipts, capital gains, or other costs of, or returns to, capital. This is due in part to the administrative complexity such a

Table 20.11

Personal Income Tax Average Tax Rates on Constant Real Family Income for a Family of Four, 1954, 1970, and 1994

REAL GROSS INCOME ($1994) (IN $000)	1954	1970	1994
$ 18.2	3.4	6.3	−10.2
30.4	9.7	13.7	7.9
42.6	12.7	17.7	19.2
60.8	16.2	22.1	27.1
91.2	21.7	29.3	33.6
121.6	27.0	33.8	36.5

SOURCE: George Vukelich, "The Effect of Inflation on Real Tax Rates," *Canadian Tax Journal* 20, no. 4 (July–August 1972), Gregory Jarvis and Roger S. Smith, "Real Income and Average Tax Rates: An Extension for the 1970–75 Period," *Canadian Tax Journal* 25, no. 2 (March–April 1977), and calculations based on 1994 income tax regulations.

---

[54] For an explanation of the rationale behind, and the effects of, indexing when introduced in 1974, see Allen, Dodge, and Poddar (1974).

statute would entail. For example, as suggested earlier, increases in inflation generate real gains for debtors, because the real value of the amounts they have to repay decreases. In a fully indexed system, such capital gains would have to be measured and taxed, a task that would certainly be complex. Thus, significant distortions continued to be created by taxes levied on the nominal returns on capital assets.

Full indexing of exemptions and brackets was maintained from 1974 to 1983. Adjustments in 1984 and 1985 were limited by legislation to 6 percent and 5 percent, consistent with government wage and price policies; and for 1986 and thereafter adjustments have been limited to the amount by which inflation exceeds 3 percent per annum. Facing sizable deficits, the government was reluctant to return to full indexing. This sharply reduced the size of adjustments from 1988 to 1992, and eliminated adjustments after 1992 when the annual rate of inflation fell below 3 percent. Table 20.12 shows the levels for personal and dependent allowances, and the levels at which claw-backs begin for 1989 and for 1995. Indexing that occurred from 1989 to 1995 was about a third of that which would have occurred if full adjustments had been made. The final column shows the approximate amounts that would have existed in 1995 had indexing fully reflected changes in the CPI since 1989. A 17 percent credit for $7,300 rather than the allowed $6,456 would have resulted in federal tax savings of $150, plus another $75 in provincial taxes. In addition, the application of a 26 percent tax rate, rather than a 17 percent tax rate, on income between $29,590 and $33,458 adds $350 to federal taxes and another $175 to provincial taxes.[55] Inflation imposes an additional tax even in the low-inflation post-1995 period, and indexing is an issue that continues to deserve attention.

Should indexing be maintained or enhanced? Some opponents of indexing argue that a system of periodic ad hoc adjustments is a good thing because it allows legislators to examine and revise other aspects of the Income Tax Act that may need changing.[56] Others argue that indexing of the personal income

---

[55] Perry (1985a) anticipated and estimated the much higher taxes Canadians would pay in 1995 due to the move to partial indexing in 1984 and beyond.

[56] We have been dealing with this debate from a microeconomic standpoint. People also disagree about the macroeconomic consequences of indexing. Opponents argue that it would remove an important tool for conducting macroeconomic policy. For example, if more fiscal restraint is needed during an inflationary period, this is automatically generated by increases in tax revenues. In contrast, voting tax increases and/or expenditure cuts takes time. On the other hand, indexing proponents argue that the automatic rise in federal revenues may simply encourage legislators to spend more, and hence have no stabilizing effect. Indeed, they argue that a non-indexed system creates incentives for legislators to pursue inflationary policies, because these policies tend to increase the real quantity of resources available to the public sector.

Table 20.12

Amounts Used to Calculate Tax Credits under the Personal Income Tax

	1989	1995	1995 (FULLY INDEXED)
Basic personal amount	$ 6,066	$ 6,456	$ 7,300
Married amount	5,055	5,380	6,083
Equivalent-to-spouse amount	5,055	5,380	6,083
Net income threshold for married or equivalent amount	506	538	609
Age 65 or over in the year	3,272	3,482	3,938
Disability amount	3,272	4,233	3,938
Dependents reaching age 19 in the year: disabled	1,487	1,583	1,790
Net income threshold for dependents 19 and over	2,528	2,690	3,042
Basic amount for Child tax benefit and GST credit claw-backs	24,355	25,921	29,311
OAS claw-back	50,000	53,215	60,175
UI claw-back	47,190	60,840	56,793
Top of 17% bracket	27,802	29,590	33,460
Top of 26% bracket	55,604	59,180	66,919

SOURCE: R.D. Hogg and M.G. Mallin, *Preparing Your Income Tax Returns* (North York: CCH Canadian Ltd., 1995), p. xii, and calculations by the author. Reproduced with permission.

tax, as it slows growth in income tax revenues, will lead to greater reliance on less equitable forms of taxation. Proponents of indexing argue that reducing opportunities for revising the tax act may itself be a benefit, because it is desirable to have a stable and predictable tax law. Moreover, fewer opportunities to change the law also mean fewer chances for legislative mischief. Certainly the most important argument of those who favour indexing is that it eliminates unlegislated increases in real tax rates. They believe that allowing the real tax schedule to be changed systematically by a nonlegislative process is antithetical to democratic values. The amounts of money involved are substantial; one estimate is that the indexing from 1974 to 1984 resulted in federal and provincial revenues in 1984 that were $19.5 billion, or 40 percent, less than they would have been without indexing.[57]

---

[57] This was not a surprise. See Perry (1985b), and Hull and Leonard (1974).

Proponents of indexing also note that its repeal would have a disproportion-ately large effect on the tax liabilities of low-income families. With the value of personal allowances unadjusted, families previously free from tax move into the ranks of the taxable as nominal incomes increase while real incomes remain unchanged. The claw-back on child tax benefits and GST credits also occurs at lower levels of real income, unless these amounts are fully indexed.

TREATMENT OF INTERNATIONAL INCOME

We now turn to the tax treatment of individual income that is earned abroad. Such income is potentially of interest to the tax authorities of the citizen's home and host governments. Canadian law recognizes the principle that the host country has the primary right to tax income earned within its borders. Taxation in Canada is based on residency, and if an individual is a resident of Canada, income earned abroad is also subject to Canadian tax.[58] To avoid double taxation of foreign-source income, Canada taxes income earned abroad, but allows a credit for tax paid to foreign governments.[59] Suppose that Smith's Canadian tax liability on her income earned in Germany is $7,000, and she had paid $5,500 in German income taxes. Then Smith, a Canadian resi-dent, can take a $5,500 credit on her Canadian tax return, so she need pay only $1,500 to Revenue Canada. A Canadian resident's total tax liability, then, is based on global income.

Since the Canadian system is a residence-based system, Canadian citizens who have established residence outside of Canada are not subject to tax on income earned outside of Canada, and need not submit Canadian tax returns. This contrasts with the U.S. system; U.S. citizens, wherever they reside, are tax-able on their global income, with credits permitted for taxes paid to foreign governments.

Territorial versus global systems. Most countries, like Canada, adhere to a territorial system—a citizen earning income abroad and residing outside of Canada need pay tax only to the host government. In contrast, the philo-sophical premise of the U.S. system is that equity in taxation is defined on a citizenship basis.[60] If you are a U.S. citizen, the total amount of tax you pay

---

[58] Whether or not one is considered a "resident" of Canada depends on a number of fac-tors, including length of time in Canada in a year, ownership of property, maintenance of bank accounts, membership in organizations, and the maintenance of a home. Generally if one spends 183 days or more in Canada in a year, one is deemed a resident; however, it is possible to be deemed a resident even if in the country for less than 183 days.
[59] The credit cannot exceed what the Canadian tax on the foreign income would have been.
[60] For further details, see Ault and Bradford (1990).

should be roughly independent of whether you earn your income at home or abroad. We refer to this as a global system. Which system is better? It is hard to build a case for the superiority of one system over the other on either equity or efficiency grounds. The following paragraphs expand on the problem.

Equity. John, a Canadian citizen, and Sam, a U.S. citizen, both live and work in Hong Kong and have identical incomes. Because Canada has a territorial system, John pays tax only to Hong Kong. Sam, on the other hand, also owes money to the United States (provided that his U.S. tax bill is higher than his Hong Kong tax payment). Thus, Sam pays more tax than John, even though they have the same income and live in the same place. Although the Canadian territorial system produces equal treatment for residents of Hong Kong regardless of their nationality, it can lead to substantially different taxes on Canadian citizens with the same income but who choose to live in different countries, whether for tax or other reasons. Should horizontal equity be defined on the basis of nationality or residence? Each principle has some merit, but in general, no system of international tax coordination can satisfy both.

Efficiency. The global system may distort international production decisions. Suppose that American firms operating abroad have to pay the U.S. income tax for their American employees. Canadian firms, which operate under the territorial system, have no analogous obligation. Other things being the same, then, the U.S. companies may end up paying more for their labour, and hence be at a cost disadvantage.[61] Canadian firms could conceivably win more contracts than the American firms, even if they are technologically equivalent.

On the other hand, a territorial system can produce a different distortion—in people's locational decisions. Canadian citizens may find their decision to work abroad influenced by the fact that their tax liability depends on where they live. Under the U.S. global regime, you cannot escape your country's tax collector unless you change citizenship. Hence, there is less incentive to relocate just for tax purposes.

Thus, the global system may distort production decisions, and the territorial system residential decisions. It is hard to know which distortion creates a larger efficiency cost. From an enforcement perspective, it is likely that the Canadian approach is the more practical.

---

[61] This assumes: (a) the incidence of the U.S. tax falls on employers rather than employees, and (b) American companies cannot respond simply by hiring Canadian or other non-U.S. workers. The validity of assumption (a) depends on the elasticity of supply of U.S. workers to U.S. firms abroad. To the extent the supply curve is not horizontal, employees bear part of the tax. See Chapter 17.

POLITICS AND TAX REFORM

Our discussion of the income tax has revealed a number of features that are hard to justify on the basis of either efficiency or equity. A natural question is why it is so difficult to make improvements in the tax system. One reason is that, in many cases, even fairly disinterested experts disagree about what direction reform should take. For example, we noted earlier that despite a consensus among economists that differentially taxing various types of capital income is undesirable, there is disagreement about how this should be remedied. What one person views as a reform can be perceived by another as an undesirable change. This is reflected in changes in the treatment of capital gains over the past twenty-five years.

Another difficulty is that attempts to change specific provisions encounter fierce political opposition from those whom the changes will hurt. In Chapter 11 we discussed some theories suggesting that in the presence of special interest groups, the political process can lead to expenditure patterns that are suboptimal from society's point of view. The same theories might explain the difficulties involved in attempts to improve the tax system. Organized lobbies are not the only impediments to reform. In many cases, once a tax provision is introduced, ordinary people modify their behaviour on its basis and are likely to lose a lot if it is changed. For example, many families have purchased larger houses than they otherwise would have because imputed income from home-ownership and capital gains on a principal residence are not taxed. Presumably, if these provisions were eliminated, housing values would fall. Home-owners would not take this lying down. Similarly, home-owners, particularly those in retirement, can be expected to object if less reliance on income taxes leads to more reliance on property taxes. Some notions of horizontal equity suggest it is unfair to change provisions that have caused people to make decisions that are costly to reverse (see Chapter 19).

Some have argued that attempts to make broad changes in the tax system are likely to be more successful than attempts to modify specific provisions on a piecemeal basis. If everyone's ox is being gored, people are less apt to fight for their particular loopholes. The experience with the 1987 tax reform lends some support to this viewpoint. Accept a major set of changes, or no changes at all.

What are the prospects for further improvements in the tax system? It is hard to be optimistic. Since the 1987 tax reform, revenue needs have prodded both the federal and provincial governments to raise tax rates through surtaxes. Limited indexing of personal allowances and claw-back thresholds have also led to higher average tax rates for many Canadians. As stressed earlier, higher marginal tax rates increase the value to taxpayers of various exclusions from the tax base. Hence, it will be more worthwhile for special interest groups to devote resources to obtaining tax breaks for their members. While discussion of base broadening and a flat-rate tax continue, the impact of this discussion is not evident in the changes implemented since 1988.

SUMMARY

- Computation of individual income tax liability has four major steps: measuring total income, converting total income to taxable income, calculating tax before allowable tax credits, and deducting tax credits to obtain taxes payable.

- A traditional benchmark measure of income is the Haig–Simons definition: Income during a given period is the net change in the individual's power to consume.

- Implementation of the Haig–Simons criterion is confounded by several difficulties: (1) Income must be measured net of the expenses of earning it. (2) Unrealized capital gains are not easily gauged. (3) The imputed income from durable goods is not directly observable. (4) It is difficult to measure the value of in-kind receipts.

- Critics of the Haig–Simons criterion argue that it does not necessarily guarantee either fair or efficient outcomes.

- The Canadian income tax base excludes: (1) imputed income from home-ownership and other forms of imputed income, (2) employer contributions to pension, medical, and dental plans, (3) gifts and inheritances, (4) lottery winnings, and (5) one-quarter of realized capital gains.

- Deductions reduce taxable income, and are allowed for expenses incurred in earning taxable income, to encourage retirement savings, and to recognize alimony payments.

- Three basic marginal tax rates are applied by the federal government to personal income—17, 26, and 29 percent.

- Adjustments in the form of tax credits, calculated as 17 percent of set allowances, are provided for the taxpayer and his or her dependents. These credits are subtracted from federal taxes otherwise payable.

- Tax credits are provided for charitable donations, medical expenses in excess of 3 percent of net income, certain education and tuition expenses, and required UI, CPP, and QPP premiums.

- Deductions and credits both change after-tax relative prices, and this affects economic behaviour.

- Tax expenditures are the revenues forgone due to preferential tax treatment. In some instances, a tax expenditure may be the most effective way to stimulate a particular private activity.

- Because of surtaxes, payroll taxes, and claw-backs, the effective marginal rates are usually much higher, with a more complex structure, than the three basic rates of 17, 26, and 29 percent established by the 1987 tax reform. Provincial rates and surtaxes further complicate applicable marginal rates.

- No system of personal income taxation can simultaneously achieve increasing marginal tax rates, marriage neutrality, and equal taxes for families with equal incomes. The Canadian tax system has steadfastly adhered to marriage neutrality, with the individual as the taxable unit upon which the personal income tax is based.

- Bracket widths, personal and dependent allowances, and tax-free earnings of dependents are partially indexed against inflation. The decision to limit indexing from 1986 onward to the excess of inflation over 3 percent has resulted in a substantial increase in personal income taxes on constant levels of real income.

- Canada follows a territorial, or residence-based, system with respect to the tax treatment of income earned in other countries. Canadian residents are taxed on their global incomes, but Canadian citizens who reside outside of Canada are taxed only on income earned in Canada. This contrasts with the U.S. system, which taxes global income of U.S. citizens wherever they reside. In both cases, tax credits are provided for taxes paid to the country in which income arises.

- Income tax systems are the primary revenue source for provinces and for the federal government; growth in income tax revenues has been particularly rapid for the provinces in the past two decades. Provincial personal income taxes account for 40 percent of personal income tax collections, and this tax source accounts for 34 percent of total government revenues in Canada.

DISCUSSION QUESTIONS

1. The tax credit for charitable donations rises from 17 percent on the first $200 to 29 percent on donations over $200. Why would the heads of organizations dependent on charitable contributions think it important that the credit be at a rate of 29 percent?

*2. Jones, who has a personal income tax rate of 50 percent, holds an oil stock that appreciates in value by 10 percent each year. He bought the stock one year ago. Jones's stockbroker now wants him to switch the oil stock for a

---

*Difficult.

gold stock that is equally risky. Jones has decided that if he holds on to the oil stock, he will keep it only one more year and then sell it. If he sells the oil stock now, he will invest all the (after-tax) proceeds of the sale in the gold stock and then sell the gold stock one year from now. What is the minimum rate of return the gold stock must pay for Jones to make the switch? Relate your answer to the tax on capital gains and to the lock-in effect.

3. According to well-placed sources, in 1994 the Department of Finance was considering a change in the tax treatment of employer-provided dental care plans. Under the policy being considered, the value of the dental care plans would be included in workers' taxable incomes. Evaluate this proposal from the standpoint of the Haig–Simons criterion. How do you think it would alter the composition of compensation packages?

4. The purpose of this problem is to consider how effective marginal tax rates are affected by various claw-backs, payroll taxes, and surtaxes.

   a. Consider a family of four (two children, age 10 and 12, and one male wage earner) whose net income places it in the range of the GST and child tax benefit claw-backs—net income = $26,000, and whose taxable income places it in the 17 percent federal tax bracket. (Ignore provincial taxes.)

      i.   Suppose the taxpayer's income increases by $2,500. Given a 17 percent tax rate, by how much does his tax liability increase, given the GST and child tax benefit claw-backs?
      ii. Now consider the government's 3 percent surtax on basic federal tax. How does this alter the marginal tax rate on the additional $2,500?
      iii. The earned income of the taxpayer is subject to both CPP and UI premiums. How do these payroll taxes alter the effective marginal tax rate that applies to the additional $2,500?
      iv. Combine your answers from parts (i), (ii), and (iii) to find the effective marginal tax rate. (Divide the change in tax liability by the $2,500 change in income.)

   b. Now consider a different family (same composition with a single wage earner) with $75,000 in salary income. Suppose this taxpayer receives another $2,500 in before-tax salary income.

      i.   Assuming a 29 percent federal marginal tax rate, what is the change in tax liability, including the federal surtax (again ignoring provincial taxes)?
      ii. How will GST and child tax benefit claw-backs, and the UI and CPP payroll taxes, affect the marginal rate on the additional $2,500?

5. Suppose that a taxpayer has a marginal personal income tax rate (including provincial taxes) of 50 percent. The nominal interest rate is 12 percent, and the expected inflation rate is 5 percent.

    a. What is the real after-tax rate of interest?

    b. Suppose that the expected inflation rate increases by 3 percentage points to 8 percent, and the nominal interest rate increases by the same amount. What happens to the real after-tax rate of return?

  *c. If the inflation rate increases as in part (b), by how much would the nominal interest rate have to increase to keep the real after-tax interest rate at the same level as in part (a)? Can you generalize your answer using an algebraic formula?

REFERENCES

Allen, J.R., D.A. Dodge, and S.N. Poddar. "Indexing the Personal Income Tax: A Federal Perspective." *Canadian Tax Journal* 22, no. 4 (July–August 1974).

Auerbach, Alan J. "Retrospective Capital Gains Taxation." *American Economic Review* 81, no. 1 (March 1991): 167–78.

Ault, Hugh J., and David Bradford. "Taxing International Income: An Analysis of the U.S. System and Its Economic Premises," in *Taxation in the Global Economy*, ed. Assaf Razin and Joel Slemrod. Chicago: University of Chicago Press, 1990, pp. 11–54.

Auten, Gerald E., and Joseph J. Cordes. "The Current Status of Capital Gains Taxation." *Journal of Economic Perspectives* (Winter 1991).

Bird, Richard M. "The Tax Kaleidoscope: Perspectives on Tax Reform in Canada." *Canadian Tax Journal* 18, no. 5 (September–October 1970).

Bittker, Boris. "Federal Income Taxation and the Family." *Stanford Law Review* 27 (July 1975): 1392–463.

Bruce, Neil, ed. *Tax Expenditures and Government Policy*. Kingston: John Deutsch Institute, 1992.

Carroll, Chris, and Lawrence H. Summers. "Why Have Private Saving Rates in the United States and Canada Diverged?" *Journal of Monetary Economics* 20 (September 1987).

Chandler, William. "The Value of Household Work in Canada." *Canadian Economic Observer* (April 1994).

Clotfelter, Charles T. *Federal Tax Policy and Charitable Giving*. Chicago: University of Chicago Press, 1985.

Clotfelter, Charles T., and C. Eugene Steuerle. "Charitable Contributions," in *How Taxes Affect Economic Behavior*, ed. Henry J. Aaron and Joseph A. Pechman. Washington, DC: Brookings Institution, 1981.

---

*Difficult.

Cloutier, A. Pierre, and Bernard Fortin. "Converting Exemptions and Deductions into Credits: An Economic Assessment," in *The Economic Impacts of Tax Reform*, ed. Jack Mintz and John Whalley. Toronto: Canadian Tax Foundation, 1989.

Davies, James B. "The Tax Treatment of the Family," in *Taxation to 2000 and Beyond*, ed. Richard M. Bird and Jack M. Mintz. Toronto: Canadian Tax Foundation, 1992.

Department of Finance. *Government of Canada Personal Income Tax Expenditures*. Ottawa: December 1992.

Department of Finance. *Tax Reform 1987: Income Tax Reform*. Ottawa: June 18, 1987.

Feldstein, Martin S. "A Contribution to the Theory of Tax Expenditures: The Case of Charitable Giving," in *The Economics of Taxation*, ed. Henry J. Aaron and Michael J. Boskin. Washington, DC: Brookings Institution, 1980.

Feldstein, Martin S. "On the Theory of Tax Reform." *Journal of Public Economics* 6 (1976): 77–104.

George, Henry. *Progress and Poverty*. New York: Doubleday, 1914, Book VII.

Hood, R.D., S.A. Martin, and L.S. Osberg. "Economic Determinants of Individual Charitable Donations in Canada." *Canadian Journal of Economics* 10 (November 1977).

Howard, R., G.C. Ruggeri, and D. Van Wart. "Federal Tax Changes and Marginal Tax Rates, 1986 and 1993." *Canadian Tax Journal* 43, no. 4 (1995): 906–22.

Hull, Brian, and Lawrence Leonard. "Indexing the Personal Income Tax: An Ontario Perspective." *Canadian Tax Journal* 22, no. 4 (July–August 1974).

Ingerman, S., and R. Rowley. "Tax Expenditures for Retirement Savings: An Appraisal." *McGill Working Papers in Economics*. Montreal: November 1993.

Jarvis, Gregory, and Roger S. Smith. "Real Income and Average Tax Rates: An Extension for the 1970–75 Period." *Canadian Tax Journal* 25, no. 2 (March–April 1977).

Joulfaian, David. "Charitable Bequests and Estate Taxes." *National Tax Journal* 44, no. 2 (June 1991): 169–80.

Jump, Gregory V. "Tax Incentives to Promote Personal Saving: Recent Canadian Experience," in *Saving and Government Policy*, Conference Series No. 25. Boston: Federal Reserve Bank of Boston, 1982.

Kesselman, Jonathan R. "The Child Tax Benefit: Simple, Fair, Responsive?" *Canadian Public Policy* 19, no. 2 (June 1993).

McCarthy, Jonathan, and Han N. Pham. "The Impact of Individual Retirement Accounts on Savings." *Current Issues* 1, no. 6. New York: Federal Reserve Bank of New York, September 1995.

Messere, Ken. "Taxation in Ten Industrialized Countries Over the Last Decade: An Overview." *Tax Notes International*, August 21, 1995.

Perry, D.B. "Comparison of Full and Partial Indexing of the Personal Income Tax System." *Canadian Tax Journal* 33, no. 3 (May–June 1985a).

Perry, D.B. "The Cost of Indexing the Federal Income Tax System." *Canadian Tax Journal* 33, no. 2 (March–April 1985b).

Revenue Canada. *Tax Statistics on Individuals, 1996 Edition.* Ottawa: Revenue Canada, 1996.

Royal Commission on Taxation. *Report*, vol. III. Ottawa: Queen's Printer, 1966.

Simons, Henry C. *Personal Income Taxation.* Chicago: University of Chicago Press, 1938.

Smith, Roger S. "Flat Rate Tax Potential: A Preliminary Comparison of Three Countries." *Canadian Tax Journal* 34, no. 4 (July–August 1986): 835–52.

Smith, Roger S. "Base Broadening and Rate Changes: A Look at the Canadian Federal Income Tax." *Canadian Tax Journal* 32, no. 2 (March–April 1984).

Smith, Roger S. *Tax Expenditures: An Examination of Tax Incentives and Tax Preferences in the Canadian Federal Income Tax System.* Toronto: Canadian Tax Foundation, 1979.

Sunley, Emil M., Jr. "Summary of Conference Discussion," in *Comprehensive Income Taxation*, ed. Joseph A. Pechman. Washington, DC: Brookings Institution, 1977.

Tanzi, Vito. "Inflationary Expectations, Economic Activity, Taxes, and Interest Rates." *American Economic Review* 70, no. 1 (March 1980): 12–21.

Vukelich, George. "The Effect of Inflation on Real Tax Rates." *Canadian Tax Journal* 20, no. 4 (July–August 1972).

Chapter 21

Personal Taxation and Behaviour

Neither will it be that a people overlaid with taxes should ever become valiant and martial.

—Francis Bacon (1561–1626)

The theory of taxation makes clear that ultimately the effects of taxes depend on how they affect behaviour. The impact of taxes on behaviour is a matter of intense debate, both among academics and politicians. Some argue that taxes have very little effect: "Disincentives, like the weather, are much talked about, but relatively few people do anything about them" (Break, 1957: 549). Others suggest that high marginal tax rates lead to "worsening work attitudes, high absenteeism rates, reluctance to work overtime and to assume risks, and the lowest personal saving rate[s]" (Roberts, 1981: 26).

As shown in Chapter 20, the income tax affects incentives for myriad decisions—everything from the purchase of housing to the amount of charitable donations. We choose to focus on four particularly important topics that have been studied intensively—the effects of taxation on labour supply, saving, housing consumption, and portfolio decisions.

LABOUR SUPPLY

In 1994, about 13 million Canadians worked an average of almost thirty-five hours[1] per week and received total compensation of roughly $410 bil-

---

[1] Actual hours worked averaged 42.4 hours per week for those with full-time jobs, and 15.8 hours per week for those with part-time jobs. *Canadian Economic Observer, Historical Statistical Supplement 1994/95*, pp. 8–9, 28, and *Historical Labour Force Statistics, 1994*, pp. 55–56.

lion, approximately 77 percent of national income. How labour supply is determined and whether taxes affect it are the issues to which we now turn.

Theoretical Considerations

Hercules is deciding how much of his time to devote each week to work and how much to leisure. In Chapter 12 on welfare spending, we showed how this choice can be analyzed graphically. To review the main points in that discussion:

1. The number of hours available for market work and nonmarket uses ("leisure") is referred to as the time endowment. In Figure 21.1, it is distance OT on the horizontal axis. Assuming that all time not spent on leisure is devoted to market work, any point on the horizontal axis simultaneously indicates hours of leisure and hours of work.

2. The budget constraint in this diagram shows the combinations of leisure and income available to an individual given his or her wage rate. If Hercules's wage rate is w per hour, then his budget constraint is a straight line whose slope in absolute value is w. In Figure 21.1, this is represented by line TD.

3. The particular point on the budget constraint that is chosen depends on the individual's tastes. Assume that preferences for leisure and income can be represented by normal, convex-to-the-origin indifference curves. Three such curves are labeled *i*, *ii*, and *iii* in Figure 21.1. Utility is maximized at

Figure 21.1

Utility-Maximizing Choice of Leisure and Income

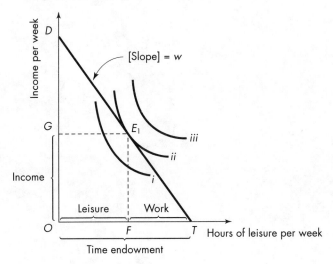

point E_1, where Hercules devotes OF hours to leisure, works FT hours, and earns income OG.

We are now in a position to analyze the effects of taxation. Suppose that the government levies a tax on earnings at rate t. The tax reduces the reward for working an hour from $\$w$ to $\$(1 - t)w$. When Hercules consumes an hour of leisure, he now gives up only $\$(1 - t)w$, not $\$w$. In effect, the tax reduces the opportunity cost of an hour of leisure. This observation is represented in Figure 21.2. The budget constraint facing Hercules is no longer TD. Rather, it is the flatter line, TH, whose slope in absolute value is $(1 - t)w$. Because of the tax, the original income–leisure choice, E_1, is no longer attainable. Hercules must choose a point somewhere along the after-tax budget constraint TH. In Figure 21.2, this is E_2, where Hercules consumes OI hours of leisure, works IT hours, and has an after-tax income of OG'. The tax lowers Hercules's labour supply from FT hours to IT hours.

Can we therefore conclude that a "rational" individual always reduces labour supply in response to a proportional tax? To answer this question, consider Theseus, who faces exactly the same before- and after-tax budget constraints as Hercules, and who chooses to work the same number of hours (FT) before imposition of the tax. As indicated in Figure 21.3, when Theseus is taxed, he *increases* his hours of work from FT to JT. There is nothing "irrational" about

Figure 21.2

Proportional Income Tax Decreasing Hours of Labour Supplied

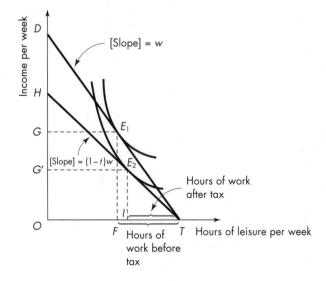

Figure 21.3

Proportional Income Tax Increasing Hours of Labour Supplied

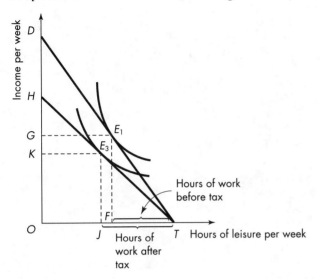

this. Depending on a person's tastes, it is possible to want to work more, less, or the same amount after a tax is imposed.

The source of the ambiguity is the conflict between two effects generated by the tax, the *substitution effect* and the *income effect*. When the tax reduces the take-home wage, the opportunity cost of leisure goes down, and there is a tendency to substitute leisure for work. This is the substitution effect, and it tends to decrease labour supply. At the same time, for any number of hours worked, the tax reduces the individual's income. Assuming that leisure is a normal good, for any number of hours worked, this loss in income leads to a reduction in consumption of leisure, other things being the same. But a decrease in leisure means an increase in work. The income effect therefore tends to induce an individual to work more. Thus, the two effects work in opposite directions. It is simply impossible to know on the basis of theory alone whether the income effect or substitution effect dominates. For Hercules, shown in Figure 21.2, the substitution effect dominates. For Theseus, shown in Figure 21.3, the income effect is more important.

The analysis of a progressive tax system is very similar to that of a proportional tax. Suppose that Hercules is now confronted with increasing marginal tax rates: t_1 on his first $5,000 of earnings, t_2 on his second $5,000 of earnings, and t_3 on all income above $10,000. As before, prior to the tax the budget line is *TD*, which is depicted in Figure 21.4. After tax, the budget con-

Figure 21.4

Leisure–Income Choice under a Progressive Income Tax

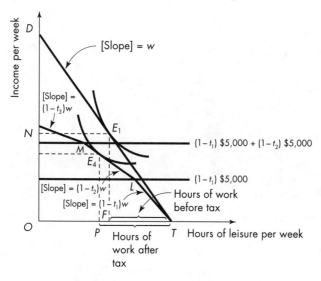

straint is the kinked line *TLMN*. Up to $5,000 of before-tax income, the opportunity cost of an hour of leisure is $(1 - t_1)w$, which is the slope (in absolute value) of segment *TL*. At point *L*, Hercules's income is $(1 - t_1) \times$ $5,000. On segment *ML* the absolute value of the slope is $(1 - t_2)w$. *ML* is flatter than *TL* because t_2 is greater than t_1. At point *M*, after-tax income is $(1 - t_1) \times $5,000 + (1 - t_2) \times $5,000$; this is after-tax income at point *L* plus the increment to income after receiving an additional $5,000 that is taxed at rate t_2. Finally, on segment *MN* the slope is $(1 - t_3)w$, which is even flatter. Depending on his preferences, Hercules can end up anywhere on *TLMN*. In Figure 21.4, he maximizes utility at E_4 where he works *PT* hours.[2]

Empirical Findings

The theory just discussed suggests that an individual's labour supply decision depends on: (a) variables that affect the position of the budget constraint, especially the after-tax wage[3]; and (b) variables that affect the individual's

---

[2] An issue that has received substantial attention is the effect on hours of work of replacing a proportional tax with a progressive tax that yields the same tax revenue. Hemming (1980) shows that the outcome depends on the shape of the indifference curves and exactly how progressivity is defined.

[3] Another important determinant of the budget constraint is nonlabour income: dividends, interest, transfer payments, and so forth. Nonlabour income causes a parallel shift in the budget constraint; there is a constant addition to income at every level of hours worked.

indifference curves for leisure and income, such as age, sex, and marital status. Econometricians have estimated regression equations in which they seek to explain annual hours of work as a function of such variables.[4] Although considerable differences in estimates arise due to inevitable differences in samples, time periods, and statistical techniques, it would be fair to say that the following two important general tendencies have been observed:

1. For males between the ages of roughly 25 to 60, the effect of changes in the net wage on hours of work is small in absolute value and is often statistically insignificant. Most elasticity estimates fall in the range between –0.2 and 0.2 (Hum and Simpson, 1991: 19).

2. Although estimated labour supply elasticities for women vary widely, the hours of work and labour force participation decisions of married women in Canada appear somewhat more sensitive to changes in the net wage. Estimates for elasticities of hours worked with respect to the net wage are generally between –0.2 and 0.5.[5]

Some Caveats

The theoretical and empirical results just described are certainly more useful than the uninformed guesses often heard in political debates. Nevertheless, we should be aware of some important qualifications.

Demand-side considerations. The preceding analyses ignore effects that changes in the supply of labour might have on the demand side of the market. Suppose that taxes on married women were lowered in such a way that their net wages increased by 10 percent. With a labour supply elasticity of 0.5, their hours of work would increase by 5 percent. If firms could absorb all of these hours at the new net wage, that would be the end of the story. More typically, as more hours of work are offered, there is a tendency to bid down the *before*-tax wage. This mitigates the original increase in the *after*-tax wage, so that the final increase in hours of work would be less than originally guessed.

---

[4] See Chapter 3 for an explanation of regression analysis.
[5] See Hum and Simpson (1991: 19–23). They find that "the majority of the Canadian results … seem at odds with the U.S. results that female labour supply is more sensitive to wage rate variation. The results for most of the studies suggest labour supply behaviour for adult females that is not very different from that of U.S adult males" (p. 24) (where there is little effect). Note that these estimates include both substitution and income effects. That is, they are uncompensated responses. Phipps (1993), on reviewing the evidence, concluded that the labour supply behaviour of both men and women is highly inelastic, although "there appears to be more evidence of backward-bending labour-supply curves for women" (p. 38).

The situation becomes even more complicated when we realize major changes in work decisions could influence consumption patterns in other markets. The resulting relative price changes might feed back on labour market decisions. For example, if married women increased their hours of work, the demand for child care would probably increase. To the extent this raised the price of child care, it might discourage some mothers of small children from working, at least in the short run. Clearly, tracing through these general equilibrium implications is a complicated business. Most investigators are willing to assume that the first-round effects are a reasonable approximation to the final result.

Individual versus group effects. Our focus has been on how much an individual will work under alternative tax regimes. It is difficult to use such results to predict how the total hours of work supplied by a group of workers will change. When the tax schedule changes, incentives change differently for different people. For example, in a move from a proportional to a progressive tax, low-income workers may find themselves facing lower marginal tax rates while just the opposite may be true for those with high incomes. It is quite possible, then, that the labour supplies of the two groups could move in opposite directions, making the overall outcome difficult to predict.[6]

Other dimensions of labour supply. The number of hours worked annually is an important and interesting indicator of labour supply. But the effective amount of labour supplied by an individual depends on more than the number of hours elapsed at the workplace. A highly educated, healthy, well-motivated worker presumably is more productive than a counterpart who lacks these qualities. Some have expressed fears that taxes induce people to invest too little in the acquisition of skills. Economic theory yields surprising insights into how taxes might affect the accumulation of *human capital*—investments that people make in themselves to increase their productivity.

Consider Hera, who is contemplating entering an on-the-job training program. Suppose that over her lifetime, the program increases Hera's earnings by an amount whose present value is B. However, participation in the program reduces the amount of time currently available to Hera for income-producing activity, and hence costs her some amount, C, in forgone wages. If she is sensible, Hera enters the program only if the benefits exceed the costs:

$$B - C > 0 \qquad\qquad (21.1)$$

---

[6] See Musgrave (1959: 243–46) for a more detailed discussion of group effects.

Now suppose that Hera's earnings are subjected to a proportional tax at rate t. The tax takes away some of the higher wages earned by virtue of participation in the training program. One might guess that the tax therefore lowers the likelihood that she will participate. This reasoning is misleading. To see why, assume for the moment that after the tax Hera continues to work the same number of hours as she did before.[7] The tax does indeed reduce the benefits of the training program from B to $(1 - t)B$. But at the same time, it reduces the costs. Recall that the costs of the program are the forgone wages. Because these wages would have been subject to tax, Hera gives up not C, but only $(1 - t)C$. The decision to enter the program is based on whether after-tax benefits exceed after-tax costs:

$$(1 - t)B - (1 - t)C = (1 - t)(B - C) > 0. \qquad (21.2)$$

A glance at Equation (21.2) indicates that it is exactly equivalent to (21.1). Any combination of benefits and costs that was acceptable before the earnings tax is acceptable afterward. In this model, a proportional earnings tax reduces benefits and cost in the same proportion and therefore has no effect on human capital investment.

This unambiguous result is a consequence of the assumption that labour supply is constant after the tax is imposed. Suppose instead that as a result of the earnings tax, Hera increases her supply of labour. (The income effect predominates.) In this case, the tax leads to an increase in human capital accumulation. In effect, the after-tax labour supply is the utilization rate of the human capital investment. The more hours a person works, the greater the payoff to an increase in the wage rate from a given human capital investment. Therefore, if the tax induces more work, it makes human capital investments more attractive, other things being the same. Conversely, if the substitution effect predominates so that labour supply decreases, human capital accumulation is discouraged by the tax.

A problem with this simple model is that it ignores the important fact that the returns to a human capital investment usually cannot be known with certainty. Moreover, some types of human capital investment involve costs other than forgone earnings. University tuition is an obvious example. Finally, when the tax system is progressive, the benefits and costs of human capital investments may be taxed at different rates. However, when such factors are considered, the basic result is confirmed—from a theoretical point of view, the effect of

---

[7] In terms of our earlier discussion, the income and substitution effects just offset each other.

earnings taxation on human capital accumulation is ambiguous. Unfortunately, little empirical work on this important question is available.

The compensation package. The standard theory of labour supply assumes that the hourly wage is the only reward for working. In reality, employers often offer employees a compensation *package* that includes not only wages, but also health benefits for dental and eye care, group life insurance, pensions, and "perks" such as access to a company car and in-house sports facilities. As we noted in the last chapter, the nonwage component of compensation may not be subject to taxation. When marginal tax rates fall, the relative attractiveness of such untaxed forms of income declines, and vice versa. Hence, changes in taxes affect the composition of the compensation package.[8]

The expenditure side. The standard analysis of labour supply and taxation ignores the disposition of the tax receipts. However, at least some of the revenues are used to purchase public goods, the availability of which can affect work decisions. If the tax money is used to provide recreational facilities such as national parks, we expect the demand for leisure to increase, *ceteris paribus*. On the other hand, expenditure on child care facilities for working parents might increase labour supply. Ideally, we should examine the labour supply consequences of the entire budget, not just the tax side. In practice, empirical investigators have not learned much about how public expenditures affect work decisions. This is because of the difficulties involved in determining how individuals value public good consumption, a problem that we have already discussed in several different contexts.

Labour Supply and Tax Revenues

So far, our emphasis has been on finding the amount of labour supply associated with any given tax regime. We now explore the related issue of how tax collections vary with the tax rate.

Consider the supply curve of labour S_L depicted in Figure 21.5. It shows the optimal amount of work for each after-tax wage, other things being the same.[9] As it is drawn, hours of work increase with the net wage—the substitution effect dominates. The following argument could be repeated using a labour supply curve for which the income effect is dominant.

---

[8] In an econometric analysis of fringe benefits received by U.S. academics, Hamermesh and Woodbury (1990) found that a 1 percent increase in the value of fringe benefits resulting from higher tax rates induces an increase in fringe benefits of about 2 percent.
[9] The labour supply curve (or equivalently, the leisure demand curve) can be derived from the individual's indifference map.

Figure 21.5

Tax Rates, Hours of Work, and Tax Revenue

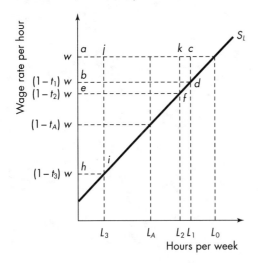

The before-tax wage, w, is associated with L_0 hours of work. Obviously, since the tax rate is zero, no revenue is collected. Now suppose a proportional tax at rate t_1 is imposed. The net wage is $(1 - t_1)w$, and labour supply is L_1 hours. Tax collections are equal to the tax per hour worked (ab) times the number of hours worked (ac), or rectangle, $abdc$. Similar reasoning indicates that if the tax rate were raised to t_2, tax revenues would be $eakf$. Area $eakf$ exceeds $abdc$—a higher tax rate leads to greater revenue collections. Does this mean that the government can always collect more revenue by increasing the tax rate? No. For example, at tax rate t_3, revenues $haji$ are less than those at the lower rate t_2. Although the tax collected per hour is very high at t_3, the number of hours has decreased so much that the product of the tax rate and hours is fairly low. Indeed, as the tax rate approaches 100 percent, people stop working altogether and tax revenues fall to zero.

All of this is summarized compactly in Figure 21.6, which shows the tax rate on the horizontal axis and tax revenue on the vertical. At very low tax rates, revenue collections are low. As tax rates increase, revenues increase, reaching a maximum at rate t_A. For rates exceeding t_A, revenues begin to fall, eventually diminishing to zero. Note that it would be absurd for the government to choose any tax rate exceeding t_A, because tax rates could be reduced without the government suffering any revenue loss.

Figure 21.6

Tax Rates versus Tax Revenue

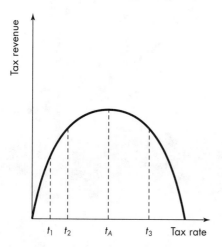

Hard as it may be to believe, Figure 21.6 has been the centre of a major political controversy that, although centred in the United States, affected policy in Canada. This was largely due to the well-publicized assertion by economist Arthur B. Laffer that the United States has operated to the right of t_A (see Laffer, 1979). In the popular press, the tax rate–tax revenue relationship is known as the **Laffer curve**. The notion that tax rate reductions would create no revenue losses became an important tenet of the supply-side economics espoused by the Reagan administration in the United States; it continues to be a potent force in policy debates and was one of the factors contributing to reductions in marginal tax rates in the 1980s in Canada as well as in the United States.

The popular debate surrounding the Laffer curve has been confused and confusing.[10] A few points are worth making:

- The shape of a Laffer curve is determined by the elasticity of labour with respect to the net wage. For any change in the tax rate, there is a corresponding percentage change in the net wage. Whether tax revenues rise or fall is determined by whether changes in hours worked offset the change in the tax rate. This is precisely the issue of the elasticity of labour supply investigated by public finance economists.

---

[10] For a good summary, see Fullerton (1982).

- Some critics of supply-side economics argue that the very idea that tax rate reductions can lead to increased revenue is absurd. However, the discussion surrounding Figure 21.6 suggests that, in principle, lower tax rates can indeed lead to higher revenue collections.

- It is therefore an empirical question whether or not the economy is actually operating to the right of t_A. A careful study of this issue suggests that given all plausible estimates of the elasticity of labour supply, the economy is not operating in this range (see Fullerton, 1982).[11] Tax rate reductions are unlikely to be self-financing in the sense of unleashing so much labour supply that tax revenues do not fall.

- Changes in labour supply are not the only way in which increased tax rates can affect tax revenues. As noted above, people can substitute non-taxable forms of income for wages when tax rates go up, so that even with a fixed supply of labour, tax revenues can fall. Tax rates may also affect willingness to acquire new skills, to assume more responsibility, to work with greater intensity, to move, to travel, or to undertake other activities that enhance productivity. On the basis of an examination of tax return data, Feldstein (1995) argues that the taxable incomes of the rich fall substantially when their tax rates go up.[12] While this claim is controversial, it does suggest that special care is needed when projecting the revenue effects of tax changes.

- One way to substitute nontaxable for taxable income is to shift from the formal to the informal, or underground, economy. Although debate continues, there is evidence that indicates a positive linkage between tax rates in Canada (and elsewhere) and growth in the underground economy (Spiro, 1994).

- Even if tax revenues fail to increase when tax rates fall, it does not mean that tax-rate reduction is necessarily undesirable. As emphasized in previous chapters, determination of the optimal tax system depends on a wide array of social and economic considerations. Those who believe that the government sector is too large should presumably be quite happy to see tax revenues reduced. As should be clear from the theory of optimal income taxation, the fact that revenues are maximized at rate

---

[11] Fullerton's estimates suggested that for tax rate decreases to result in higher revenues, the marginal tax rate would have to be around 50 percent and the labour supply elasticity around 1.0. Although marginal tax rates exceed 50 percent for many Canadians, labour supply elasticities are well below 1.0. See Browning (1989), however, for an analysis suggesting that t_A may not lie too far above current marginal tax rates.

[12] Feldstein (1995) emphasizes that "variations in labour supply are not the same as variations in taxable labour income. High marginal tax rates encourage individuals to take their compensation for labour services in forms that are untaxed or subject to lower effective tax rates" (pp. 553–54).

t_A tells us nothing about whether it is the most desirable tax rate from either an equity or an efficiency perspective.

Overview

In the analysis of taxes and labour supply, economic theory tells us which variables to examine, but provides no firm answers. Econometric work indicates that for prime age males, hours of work are not much affected by taxes. For married women, on the other hand, taxes may be more likely to reduce labour force participation rates and hours of work. An important qualification is that the effect of taxes on other dimensions of labour supply, such as education and job-training decisions or the willingness to assume more on-the-job responsibility and risk, is not well understood.

Some individuals have suggested that if tax rates were cut, such large amounts of labour supply would be unleashed that Revenue Canada would suffer no revenue loss. On the basis of what is known about labour supply, such an effect is unlikely. However, the notion that tax cuts might be self-financing is more plausible (although not proven) when one considers other ways in which taxpayers can substitute nontaxable for taxable forms of income.

SAVING

A second type of behaviour that may be affected by taxation is saving. Most modern theoretical and empirical work on saving decisions is based on the **life-cycle model** that says individuals' consumption and saving decisions during a given year are the result of a planning process that considers their lifetime economic circumstances (Modigliani, 1986). That is, the amount you save each year depends not only on your income that year, but also on the income that you expect in the future and the income you have had in the past. This section uses a life-cycle model to explore the impact of taxes on saving decisions.

Consider Scrooge, who expects to live two periods: "now" (period 0) and the "future" (period 1). Scrooge has an income of I_0 dollars now and knows that his income will be I_1 dollars in the future. (Think of "now" as "working years," when I_0 is labour earnings; and the "future" as retirement years, when I_1 is fixed pension income.) His problem is to decide how much to consume in each period. When Scrooge decides how much to consume, he simultaneously decides how much to save or borrow. If his consumption this period exceeds his current income, he must borrow. If his consumption is less than current income, he saves. We now show how the saving and borrowing decisions are made, and how they are affected by the introduction of a tax.

The first step is to depict the possible combinations of present and future consumption available to Scrooge—his budget constraint. In Figure 21.7, the amount of current consumption, c_0, is measured on the horizontal axis, and the amount of future consumption, c_1, is measured on the vertical axis. One option available to Scrooge is to consume all his income just as it comes in—to consume I_0 in the present and I_1 in the future. This bundle, called the **endowment point**, is denoted by A in Figure 21.7. At the endowment point, Scrooge neither saves nor borrows.

Another option is to save out of current income to be able to consume more in the future. Suppose that Scrooge decides to save S dollars this period. If he invests his savings in an asset with a rate of return of r, he can increase his future consumption by $(1 + r)S$—the principal S plus the interest rS. By decreasing present consumption by S, Scrooge can increase his future consumption by $(1 + r)S$. Graphically, this possibility is represented by moving S dollars to the left of the endowment point A, and $(1 + r)S$ dollars above it—point D in Figure 21.7.

Alternatively, Scrooge can consume more than I_0 in the present if he can borrow against his future income. Assume that Scrooge can borrow money at the same rate of interest, r, at which he can lend. If he borrows B dollars to add to his present consumption, by how much must he reduce his future con-

Figure 21.7

Budget Constraint for Present and Future Consumption

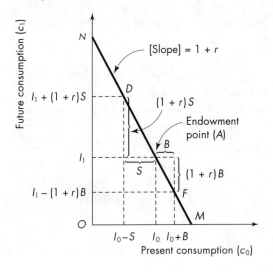

sumption? When the future arrives, Scrooge must pay back B plus interest of rB. Hence, Scrooge can increase present consumption by B only if he is willing to reduce future consumption by $B + rB = (1 + r)B$. Graphically, this process involves moving B dollars to the right of the endowment point, and then $(1 + r)B$ dollars below it—point F in Figure 21.7.

By repeating this process for various values of S and B, we can determine how much future consumption is feasible given any amount of current consumption. In the process of doing so, we trace out budget line MN, which passes through the endowment point A, and has a slope in absolute value of $1 + r$. As always, the slope of a budget line represents the opportunity cost of one good in terms of the other. Its slope of $1 + r$ indicates that the cost of \$1 of consumption in the present is $1 + r$ dollars of forgone consumption in the future.[13] Because MN shows the trade-off between consumption across periods, it is referred to as the **intertemporal budget constraint**.

To determine which point along MN is actually chosen, we introduce Scrooge's preferences for future as opposed to present consumption. It is assumed that these preferences can be represented by conventionally shaped indifference curves. In Figure 21.8 we reproduce Scrooge's budget constraint, MN, and superimpose a few indifference curves labelled *i*, *ii*, and *iii*. Under the reasonable assumption that more consumption is preferred to less consumption, curves further to the northeast represent higher levels of utility.

Subject to budget constraint MN, the point at which Scrooge maximizes utility is E_1. At this point, Scrooge consumes c^*_0 in the present and c^*_1 in the future. With this information, it is easy to find how much Scrooge saves. Because present income, I_0, exceeds present consumption, c^*_0, then by definition the difference, $I_0 - c^*_0$, is saving.

Of course, this does not prove that it is always rational to save. If the highest feasible indifference curve had been tangent to the budget line below point A, present consumption would have exceeded I_0, and Scrooge would have borrowed. Although the following analysis of taxation assumes Scrooge is a saver, the same techniques can be applied if he is a borrower.

---

[13] Budget line MN has a convenient algebraic representation. The fundamental constraint facing Scrooge is that the present value of his consumption equals the present value of his income. The present value of his consumption is $c_0 + c_1/(1 + r)$, while the present value of his income stream is $I_0 + I_1/(1 + r)$. Thus, his selection of c_0 and c_1 must satisfy $c_0 + c_1/(1 + r) = I_0 + I_1/(1 + r)$. The reader can verify that viewed as a function of c_0 and c_1, this is a straight line whose slope is $-(1 + r)$ and that passes through the point (I_0, I_1).

Figure 21.8

Utility Maximizing Choice of Present and Future Consumption

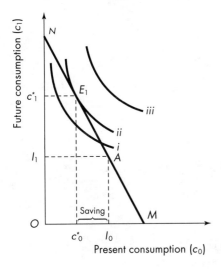

We now consider how the amount of saving changes when a proportional tax on interest income is introduced.[14] In this context, it is important to specify whether payments of interest by borrowers are deductible from taxable income. While interest payments for consumption expenditures are generally not deductible, it may, in some cases, be possible to structure a transaction so that interest is effectively deductible. (See the previous chapter for details.) We therefore analyze the effect on saving both with and without deductibility.

Case I: Deductible interest payments. How does the budget line in Figure 21.8 change when interest is subject to a proportional tax at rate t, and interest payments by borrowers are deductible? Figure 21.9 reproduces the before-tax constraint MN from Figure 21.7. The first thing to note is that the after-tax budget constraint must also pass through the endowment point (I_0, I_1), because interest tax or no interest tax, Scrooge always has the option of neither borrowing nor lending.

The next relevant observation is that the tax reduces the rate of interest received by savers from r to $(1 - t)r$. Therefore, the opportunity cost of consuming a dollar in the present is only $[1 + (1 - t)r]$ dollars in the future. At the

---

[14] We could consider an income tax with a base of both labour and capital income, but this would complicate matters without adding any important insights.

Figure 21.9

Interest Taxed and Interest Payments Deductible: Saving Decreases

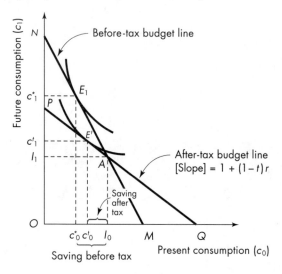

same time, for each dollar of interest Scrooge pays, he can deduct $1 from taxable income. This is worth t to him in lower taxes. Hence, the effective rate that has to be paid for borrowing is $(1 - t)r$. Therefore, the cost of increasing current consumption by one dollar, in terms of future consumption, is only [1 + $(1 - t)r$] dollars. Together, these facts imply that the after-tax budget line has a slope (in absolute value) of [1 + $(1 - t)r$].

The budget line that passes through (I_0, I_1) and has a slope of [1 + $(1 - t)r$] is drawn as PQ in Figure 21.9. As long as the tax rate is positive, it is necessarily flatter than the pretax budget line MAN.

To complete the analysis, we draw in indifference curves. The new optimum is at E^t, where present consumption is c^t_0, and future consumption is c^t_1. As before, saving is the difference between present consumption and present income, distance $c^t_0 I_0$. Note that $c^t_0 I_0$ is less than $c^*_0 I_0$, the amount that was saved before the tax was imposed. Imposition of the interest tax thus lowers saving by an amount equal to distance $c^*_0 c^t_0$.

However, saving does not always fall. For a counterexample, consider Figure 21.10. The before- and after-tax budget lines are identical to their counterparts in Figure 21.9, as is the before-tax equilibrium at point E_1. But the tangency of an indifference curve to the after-tax budget line occurs at point $\tilde{E}$, to the left

Figure 21.10

Interest Taxed and Interest Payments Deductible: Saving Increases

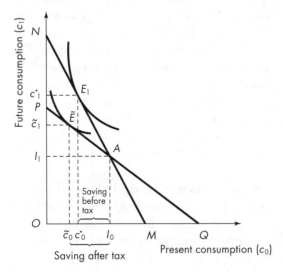

of E_1. Consumption in the present is $\tilde{c}_0$, and in the future, $\tilde{c}_1$. In this case, a tax on interest actually increases saving, from $c^*_0 I_0$ to $\tilde{c}_0 I_0$. Thus, depending on the individual's preferences, taxing interest can either increase or decrease saving.

The source of this ambiguity is the conflict between two different effects. On one hand, taxing interest reduces the opportunity cost of present consumption, which tends to increase c_0 and lower saving. This is the substitution effect, which comes about because the tax changes the price of c_0 in terms of c_1. On the other hand, the fact that interest is being taxed makes it harder to achieve any future consumption goal. This is the income effect, which arises because the tax lowers real income. If present consumption and present saving are normal goods, a decrease in income lowers both. Just as in the case of labour supply, whether the substitution or income effect dominates cannot be known on the basis of theory alone.

If the notion that a rational person might actually increase saving in response to an increased tax on interest seems bizarre, consider the extreme case of a "target saver," whose only goal is to have a given amount of consumption in the future—no more and no less. (Perhaps the person wants to save just enough to pay his or her children's future college tuition.) If the tax rate goes up, then the only way for this person to reach his or her target is to increase saving, and vice versa. Thus, for the target saver, saving and the after-tax interest rate move in opposite directions.

Case II: Nondeductible interest payments. We now consider how the budget constraint changes when interest is taxed at rate t, but borrowers cannot deduct interest payments from taxable income. Figure 21.11 reproduces again the before-tax budget constraint NM from Figure 21.7. As was true for Case I, the after-tax budget constraint must include the endowment point (I_0, I_1). Now, starting at the endowment point, suppose Scrooge decides to save \$1, that is, move \$1 to the left of point A. Because interest is taxed, this allows him to increase his consumption next period by $[1 + (1 - t)r]$ dollars. To the left of point A, then, the opportunity cost of increasing present consumption by \$1 is $[1 + (1 - t)r]$ dollars of future consumption. Therefore, the absolute value of the slope of the budget constraint to the left of point A is $[1 + (1 - t)r]$. This coincides with segment PA of the after-tax budget constraint in Figure 21.9.

Now suppose that starting at the endowment point, Scrooge decides to borrow \$1, that is, move \$1 to the right of point A. Because interest is nondeductible, the tax system does not affect the cost of borrowing. Thus, the cost to Scrooge of borrowing the \$1 now is $(1 + r)$ dollars of future consumption, just as it was before the interest tax. Hence, to the right of point A the opportunity cost of increasing present consumption by a dollar is $(1 + r)$ dollars. This coincides with segment AM of the before-tax budget constraint NM.

Putting all this together, we see that when interest receipts are taxable but interest payments are nondeductible, the intertemporal budget constraint has

Figure 21.11

Interest Taxed and Interest Payments Nondeductible

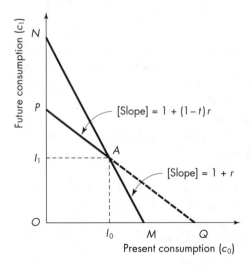

a kink at the endowment point. To the left of the endowment point, the absolute value of the slope is $[1 + (1 - t)r]$; to the right, it is $(1 + r)$. What is the impact on saving? If Scrooge was a borrower before the tax was imposed, the system has no effect on him. That is, if Scrooge maximized utility along segment *AM* before the tax was imposed, he continues to do so after. On the other hand, if Scrooge was a saver before the tax, his choice between present and future consumption must change, because points on segment *NA* are no longer available to him. However, just as in the discussion surrounding Figures 21.9 and 21.10, we cannot predict a priori whether Scrooge will save more or less. It depends on the relative strengths of the income and substitution effects.

Some additional considerations. This simple two-period model ignores some important real-world complications:

- The analysis, as usual, is couched in *real* terms—it is the real net rate of return that governs behaviour. As was emphasized in Chapter 20, care must be taken to correct the *nominal* rates of return observed in the market for inflation.
- In the model there is one vehicle for saving, and the returns to saving are taxed at a single rate. In reality, there are numerous assets, each with its own before-tax rate of return. Moreover, as observed in the last chapter, the returns to different assets are taxed at different rates. It is therefore an oversimplification to speak of how changes in the after-tax rate of return influence saving.
- The model focuses only on private saving. For many purposes, the important variable is *social saving*, defined as the sum of government and private saving. For example, if the government were to save a sufficiently high proportion of tax receipts from an interest tax, social saving could go up even if private saving decreased.
- Some investigators have questioned the validity of the life-cycle model itself. The life-cycle hypothesis posits that people are forward looking; critics argue that a more realistic assumption is that people are myopic. The life-cycle model also assumes that people can borrow and lend freely at the going rate of interest; critics point out that many people are not able to borrow. Of course, neither the proponents of the life-cycle view nor its detractors need be 100 percent correct. At any given time, some families' saving behaviour may be explained by the model, while others' saving behaviour may be myopic or constrained.

Clearly, controversies surround the life-cycle hypothesis. Nevertheless, at this time, most economists are willing to accept it as a good approximation to reality. In any case, the basic result of our theoretical analysis still holds: the effect of taxation on saving cannot be predicted without empirical work.

Econometric Studies of Saving

Several econometric studies have estimated the effect of taxation on saving. In a typical study, the quantity of saving is the left-hand variable and the explanatory variables are the rate of return to saving, disposable income, and other variables that might plausibly affect saving. If the coefficient on the rate of return is positive, the conclusion is that increases in taxes (which decrease the rate of return) depress saving and vice versa.

In an early study, Boskin (1978) claimed that the real after-tax rate of return has an important effect on the amount of saving, finding an elasticity of saving with respect to the net real interest rate between 0.2 and 0.4. This suggests that lowering the tax rate on capital income would induce substantial amounts of saving. However, this finding is controversial. One reason is that computing real market returns requires subtracting the "*expected* inflation rate" from the observed market rate, and researchers, using alternative methods for computing expected inflation rates, have found that the real net rate of return does not have much of an impact on saving (see Bovenberg, 1989).

Beach, Boadway, and Bruce (1988: 34) found that Canadian estimates for Boskin-type equations "do not produce large and significant interest-rate effects on the consumption-savings decision," as for the United States. Although they found an average interest elasticity of savings over all ages of about 0.5 in Canada, they also found that the interest elasticities of savings varied significantly by age cohort (positive for younger cohorts and negative for older cohorts), and depend on the after-tax real interest rate itself. Thus, the issue is a complex one, with interest elasticity changing with demography, the real interest rate, and other factors.

In sum, as McLure (1980: 318) noted some years ago: "Determining the effect interest rates have on saving is no mean trick. It involves considerable conceptual and econometric difficulties that still defy the best efforts of bright and dedicated economists." For Canada as well as for the United States, the conclusion by Hausman and Poterba (1987) that the effect on saving of changes in the after-tax rate of return is about zero seems reasonable. That is, for the population as a whole, the income and substitution effects more or less cancel each other out.

RRSPs, RPPs, and Saving

As noted in the previous chapter, taxpayers are allowed each year to save, up to $13,500 in 1996 (and subsequent years) in tax-deductible retirement savings plans (RRSPs) and pension plans (RPPs). Because the amounts contributed to

these plans are tax deductible, and the interest earnings are not taxed until paid out, these are an attractive form of saving for qualified taxpayers. RRSPs and RPPs have been popular; $26.2 billion was claimed in contributions to RRSPs and RPPs in 1994 (Revenue Canada, *Tax Statistics on Individuals*, 1996).

There have been frequent proposals to increase annual limits on RRSP contributions as a way to increase private saving. The 1987 tax reform proposed an increase from $7,500 in 1987 to $15,500 in 1991 (now frozen at $13,500 through 2003 due to the revenue needs of the government). The central question in debates over proposals to raise the limits is whether RRSPs stimulate new saving. To think about this issue, note the three sources from which RRSPs could be funded. First, households could cut back on their consumption, putting the new saving into an RRSP. Second, they could put into RRSPs money that would otherwise have been saved in some other form; such asset transfers clearly are not new saving. Third, part of the money used to fund an RRSP could come from the tax savings generated by the RRSP itself.[15]

In earlier work on the effect of a $1,000 investment income exclusion as well as RRSPs, Jump (1982) concluded that the effect of these incentives was not at the margin for most people, and that the RRSP deduction would not affect taxpayers who were already saving an amount in excess of the contribution limit. They would simply reallocate their saving. This would result in a fall in government revenues, and possibly a fall in total (private + government) saving. In contrast, Carroll and Summers (1987) concluded that sheltered savings plans such as RRSPs contributed significantly to higher private saving rates in Canada in the 1970s. Beach, Boadway, and Bruce (1988) also found that tax sheltering of savings by RRSPs and other means, by keeping the after-tax real interest rate on savings in Canada at a higher level, may have kept Canada's private savings rate from falling in the 1970s, as had occurred in the United States.[16]

---

[15] Note that if the government borrowed to make up for the decrease in tax revenue, then even if households saved the entire tax cut there would be no net increase in the level of social saving.

[16] Individual Retirement Accounts (IRAs) are the U.S. policy tool that is similar to Canada's RRSPs. In a careful econometric study, Gale and Scholz (1993) estimated that if the $2,000 IRA limit had been raised, only about 2 percent of the additional IRA contributions would have represented new saving; that is, most of the new contributions would have been asset transfers. A brief summary of results of several U.S. studies is included in McCarthy and Pham (1995). Their conclusion that "recent economic research suggests that the effect of the IRA accounts on savings is in fact quite small" (p. 1) is similar to that of Slemrod and Bakija (1996). Sabelhaus (1997), in a recent study, examines factors affecting private saving in Canada and finds that RRSP policies have had limited influence on the level of private saving. For an alternative view of the impact of IRAs in the United States, see Venti and Wise (1992).

Taxes and the Capital Shortage

As a political issue, the taxation of capital income receives at least as much public discussion as the taxation of wages. Part of the debate has centred on the proposition that, by discouraging saving, the tax system contributed to a decline in investment, and in the capital stock of the country. This, in turn, contributes to slower productivity growth than otherwise. This perception is enhanced by the recent high rates of saving, investment, and productivity growth in East Asia, in particular, relative to North America. This leads to a claim that a reduction of taxes on capital is needed to end the so-called productivity crisis.

A major problem with this line of reasoning is that, as we have just shown, it is not at all obvious that taxation has reduced the supply of saving. Let us assume, for the sake of argument, that saving has indeed declined as a consequence of taxes. Nevertheless, as long as the capital market is competitive, a decrease in saving does not create a gap between the demand for investment funds and their supply. Indeed, in a small open economy, we can expect investment opportunities to attract savings from other countries. Where the gap is less than completely filled by foreign saving, the interest rate adjusts to bring quantities supplied and demanded into equality. The new equilibrium may or may not involve a lower rate of investment, and a lower level of productivity growth, depending on the inflow of savings from other countries.

But to look only at these issues is unfair. Taxation of any factor may reduce the equilibrium quantity. Just as in any other case, the important efficiency question is whether taxation of capital income has led to large excess burdens compared to other ways of raising tax revenues. We defer to Chapter 22 a discussion of whether economic efficiency would be enhanced if taxes on capital were eliminated. In the meantime, we note that there is no reason a high rate of investment alone is a desirable objective. In a utilitarian framework, at least, capital accumulation is a means of enhancing individual welfare, not an end in itself.

Finally, we emphasize that the entire argument that saving incentives can help increase the capital stock rests on the premise that investment in the economy depends on its own rate of saving: all national saving is channelled into national investment. This is true in an economy that is closed to international trade. In an open economy, however, domestic saving can be invested abroad. This means that tax policy designed to stimulate saving may not lead to more domestic investment. To the extent that saving flows freely across national boundaries to whatever investment opportunities seem most attractive, the ability of tax policy to stimulate investment through saving is greatly diminished.

How open is the Canadian economy? Feldstein and Horioka (1980) found that countries with high domestic saving tend to have high domestic investment, and vice versa, but this linkage has weakened somewhat over the past two decades.[17] The evidence suggests that saving may not flow into and out of the economy as freely as one would expect in a completely integrated world capital market.[18] As long as saving and investment are correlated, tax policy that affects saving can generally be expected to affect investment. The size of the effect, however, is considerably smaller than one would find in a completely closed economy.

HOUSING DECISIONS

When people talk of a capital shortage, they are usually concerned with the amount of capital available to businesses for producing goods. Such capital is only part of the nation's stock. Some capital, such as schools, hospitals, and roads, is government-owned infrastructure. Some capital, such as pollution abatement equipment, is used by business, but not for increasing output as conventionally measured. Other capital is in the hands of households, with owner-occupied housing being the prime example.[19] Even a tax act that has little impact on the overall level of saving can have significant effects on the allocation of saving across these different types of investment. As we see in this section, the Canadian income tax system favours investment in housing.

Income for owner-occupied housing is not subjected to taxes that apply to income from other investments. Neither imputed rent nor capital gains from a primary residence are taxed in Canada. Consider Macbeth who has an amount, K, in assets. He is choosing between (a) buying a home for an amount equal to K, or (b) continuing to rent and investing K in alternative income-earning assets.

If he buys his own house, Macbeth and his wife derive services from it that have a market value that is equal to its rental value, R. (In order to keep things simple, we assume that R is net of property taxes and maintenance expenses.) Of course, they do not receive this income in dollars—the income is in kind. However, under a comprehensive income tax system, the form in which the

---

[17] Feldstein (1994: 8) found that "the estimated saving retention coefficient has declined from more than 0.8 in the 1960s to about 0.6 in the 1980s but remains very much greater than the value of approximately zero that would be implied by a completely integrated market."

[18] For example, see Frankel (1992).

[19] Owner-occupied capital as a share of total capital in Canada rose from 17.8 percent in 1961 to 27.1 percent in 1989 (Poterba, 1992: 283).

income is received is irrelevant, and the imputed rent from owner-occupied housing is part of taxable income. Moreover, any increase in the market value of the house, C, is income, and should be taxed as a capital gain as with any other asset. (Decreases in house value lower income.) The return that Macbeth receives on his owner-occupied home is $(R + C)/K$, and this return is not reduced by the income tax.

If Macbeth invests in an alternative asset that yields taxable income, the return will be $[(1 - t)(R' + C')/K]$. R' and C' represent the flow of money income from the asset and capital gain (or loss), respectively. The before-tax return on other investments must be $1/(1 - t)$ times that on housing in order to yield the same after-tax return. If Macbeth's tax rate is 40 percent, the return on the alternative investment must be 16.67 percent if the return on his housing investment is 10 percent.

An investment in owner-occupied housing is attractive, due to the exemption of imputed rent and capital gains, even though the before-tax return on housing is substantially below that on other forms of capital. In this way, investment is diverted into housing when it could be more productively used in other areas. The precise size of the increase in demand for owner-occupied housing is difficult to determine, as the demand for housing is influenced by many factors. Owner-occupied housing in the United States, where mortgage interest payments and property taxes can be deducted in calculating taxable income, has received even more favourable treatment than in Canada. Yet owner-occupancy rates and the ratio of owner-occupied capital to total capital stock are about the same in the United States as in Canada.[20]

Exemption of imputed income and nontaxation of capital gains on principal residences have been sizable benefits to home-owners. Federal personal income tax revenues forgone due to the capital gain exemption were estimated to be $4.7 billion in 1989. Revenue forgone due to exemption of imputed rent, although not estimated, is likely of a similar magnitude. This compares with federal personal income taxes of $48 billion in 1989. Provinces, through their provincial income taxes, forgo half again as much. The implicit subsidy affects not only how much housing people purchase, but also whether they become owners or renters in the first place. In fact, owner-occupancy rates

---

[20] The owner-occupancy rate in 1986 was 62.1 percent in Canada and 63.7 percent in the United States (Smith, 1993: 36). Owner-occupied capital in the United States accounted for 27.0 percent of total capital in 1989 compared to the previously mentioned 27.1 percent in Canada (Poterba, 1992: 283).

have not changed dramatically in Canada over the fifty years, equalling 56.6, 65.2, 66.0, 60.3, 62.1, and 62.6, in each of the census years from 1941 through 1991.[21]

Another benefit to home-owners is an interest-free loan that first-time buyers have access to from their RRSP accounts. A provision introduced in 1992 allowed a taxpayer to withdraw up to $20,000 tax-free from his or her RRSP for the purchase of a home. Although the funds must be paid back to the RRSP account over a fifteen-year period, no interest is to be paid on them. The availability of these funds to purchase a house, but not for other purposes, contributes further to the use of capital to purchase housing rather than other consumption goods or capital assets.

So far we have discussed only tax policies affecting owner-occupied housing and ignored rental housing. Historically, however, the Canadian system has provided generous subsidies to the owners of rental housing. (These included accelerated depreciation and the right to create losses that could be offset against other income, discussed in Chapter 24.) These provisions reduced the cost of renting to individuals, although one cannot know by how much without information on the relevant supply and demand elasticities.[22]

---

[21] Evidence concerning the effect of housing incentives is stronger in the United States than in Canada. The share of owner-occupiers in the United States rose from 43.6 percent in 1940 to 63.7 percent by 1986. Smith, Rosen, and Fallis (1988), in a review of the literature, found that "although the research on income tax incentives has taken numerous approaches, these studies have reached remarkably similar conclusions. They have concluded that tax preferences have strongly favored and encouraged homeownership, have transferred resources to more heavily subsidized owner-occupiers from generally less subsidized renters, have raised the gross price of homeownership housing services but lowered the net after-tax price, and have directed resources in favor of housing and away from other capital uses. Empirical estimates (for the United States) suggest that personal income tax benefits for homeownership increased the proportion of homeowners by approximately 4 percentage points (or 7 percent) and that approximately one quarter of the increase in homeownership since the Second World War can be attributed to these tax factors" (p. 55).

[22] Some provisions favourable to real estate in Canada were eliminated in the 1980s. Prior to 1985, Registered Home-ownership Savings Plans (RHOSPs) permitted first-time home-buyers to make a tax-deductible contribution of $1,000 a year, to a limit of $10,000, with the interest earned in the account tax exempt. The proceeds could be withdrawn, tax free, from the RHOSP account when applied to the purchase of a first home. Poterba (1992) estimated that "for a household participating in this program and purchasing a median-priced house in 1980, the subsidy would have amounted to 7–9 percent of the house value" (p. 277). Reforms in 1981 and 1987 limited the extent to which losses on rental property that were due to capital cost allowances could be deducted against other sources of income. This made investment in rental properties by high-income individuals less attractive.

Proposals for Change

In Chapter 8 under "Positive Externalities," we discussed the pros and cons of providing a subsidy for owner-occupied housing. The point made there was that from an externality point of view, the subsidy does not have much merit. Further, the subsidy's value increases with income—since both the rate of home-ownership and marginal tax rates rise with income. Hence, one can hardly claim that it equalizes the income distribution. In light of these facts, a number of proposals have been made to reform the tax treatment of housing. Probably the most radical change would be to include net imputed rent in taxable income. Such a move would create an administrative challenge since authorities would have to determine the potential market rental value of each house, allowing for appropriate costs to arrive at "net" rent. Nevertheless, imputed rental income is taxed in European countries such as the Netherlands, Switzerland, Sweden, and Denmark.[23] It is, however, highly unlikely that taxing imputed rent would be politically feasible. Home-owners are more likely to perceive their houses as endless drains on their financial resources than as revenue producers. It would not be easy to convince home-owners—who comprise more than half the electorate—that taxation of imputed rental income is a good idea.

Finally, we note that much of the debate over the tax treatment of housing implicitly assumes that full taxation of imputed rent would be the most efficient solution. Recall from the theory of optimal taxation (Chapter 19) that if lump-sum taxes are excluded, the efficiency-maximizing set of tax rates is generally a function of the elasticities of demand and supply for all commodities. Only in very special cases do we expect efficiency to require equal rates for all sources of income. We must also recognize the favourable treatment of investment in other sectors and regions under the income tax. On the other hand, it is highly improbable that the efficient tax rate on imputed rental income is zero. Determining the appropriate rate is an important topic for further research.

PORTFOLIO COMPOSITION

Taxes may affect not only the total amount of wealth that people accumulate, but the assets in which that wealth is held as well.[24] Some argue that lowering taxes would encourage people to hold riskier assets. Superficially, this proposition seems plausible. Why take a chance on a risky investment if your gains

---

[23] See Andersson (1990). Similar problems have been dealt with by local tax authorities who levy taxes based on the value of real property. See Chapter 23.
[24] This should be apparent from the previous section. Housing is the most important single element in the portfolios of most Canadians.

are going to be grabbed by the tax collector? However, the problem is considerably more complicated than this line of argument suggests.

Most modern theoretical work on the relationship between taxes and portfolio composition is based on the path-breaking analysis of Tobin (1958). In Tobin's model, individuals make their decisions about whether to invest in an asset on the basis of two characteristics—the expected return on the asset, and how risky that return is. Other things being the same, investors prefer assets that are expected to yield high returns. At the same time, investors are assumed to dislike risk; other things being the same, investors prefer safer assets.

Suppose there are two assets. The first is perfectly safe, but it yields a zero rate of return. (Imagine holding money in a world with no inflation.) The second is a bond that *on average* yields a positive rate of return, but it is risky—there is some chance that the price will go down, so the investor incurs a loss.

Note that the investor can adjust the return and risk on the entire portfolio by holding different combinations of the two assets. In one extreme case he or she could hold only the safe asset—there is no return, but no risk. On the other hand, the investor could hold only the risky asset—his or her expected return rises, but so does the risk involved. The typical investor holds a combination of both the risky and safe assets to suit tastes concerning risk and return.

Now assume a proportional tax is levied on the return to capital assets. Assume also the tax allows for **full loss offset**—individuals can deduct all losses from taxable income. Because the safe asset has a yield of zero, the tax has no effect on its rate of return—the return is still zero. In contrast, the risky asset has a positive expected rate of return, which is lowered by the presence of the tax. It seems that the tax reduces the attractiveness of the risky asset compared to the safe asset.

However, at the same time that the tax lowers the return to the risky asset, *it lowers its riskiness as well*. Why? In effect, introduction of the tax turns the government into the investor's silent partner. If the investor wins (in the sense of receiving a positive return), the government shares in the gain. But because of the loss-offset provision, if the individual loses, the government also shares in the loss. Suppose, for example, that an individual loses $100 on an investment. If the tax rate is 50 percent, the ability to subtract the $100 from taxable income lowers the tax bill by $50. Even though the investment lost $100, the investor loses only $50. In short, introduction of the tax tightens the dispersion of returns—the highs are less high and the lows are less low—and, hence, reduces the risk. Thus, although the tax makes the risky asset *less* attractive by reducing its expected return, it simultaneously makes it *more* attractive by decreasing its risk. If the second effect dominates, taxation can on balance make the risky asset more desirable.

An important assumption behind this discussion is the existence of a perfectly riskless asset. This is not a very realistic assumption. In a world where no one is sure exactly what the inflation rate will be, even the return on money is risky. But the basic reasoning still holds. Because taxes decrease risk as well as returns, the effect of taxes on portfolio choice is ambiguous. (See Feldstein, 1969, for a demonstration.)

Resolving this ambiguity econometrically is very difficult. A major problem is that it is hard to obtain reliable information on just which assets people hold. Individuals may not accurately report their holdings to survey takers because they are not exactly sure of the true values at any point in time. Alternatively, people might purposely misrepresent their asset positions because of fears that the information will be reported to the tax authorities. In one study using a fairly reliable data set, Hubbard (1985) found that, other things being the same, people in higher tax brackets hold a higher proportion of their portfolios in common stock, which is quite risky, than in relatively safe assets such as money and bonds. This finding lends at least tentative support to the notion that taxation *increases* risk taking. But the issue is far from being resolved.

A NOTE ON POLITICS AND ELASTICITIES

Despite much investigation, the effect of income taxation on several important kinds of behaviour is not known for sure. Different "experts" are therefore likely to give policy makers different pieces of advice. In this situation, it is almost inevitable that policy makers will adopt those behavioural assumptions that enhance the perceived feasibility of their goals. Although it is dangerous to generalize, liberals tend to believe that behaviour is not very responsive to the tax system, while conservatives take the opposite view. Liberals prefer low elasticities because they can raise large amounts of money for public sector activity without having to worry too much about charges that they are "killing the goose that laid the golden egg." In contrast, conservatives like to assume high elasticities because this limits the volume of taxes that can be collected before serious efficiency costs are imposed on the economy. Thus, when journalists, politicians, and economists make assertions about how taxes affect incentives, it is prudent to evaluate their claims in light of what their hidden agendas might be.

SUMMARY

- The Canadian personal income tax affects many economic decisions, including labour supply, saving, residential housing consumption, and portfolio choice.

- For labour supply, saving, and choice of portfolio, the *direction* of the effect of taxation is theoretically ambiguous. Further, in each area, the size of tax-induced behavioural changes may be determined only by empirical investigation. For these reasons, the effect of taxation is among the most contentious of all areas of public policy.

- Econometric studies of labour supply indicate prime age males vary their hours only slightly in response to tax changes, while hours of married women are more sensitive to variations in the after-tax wage rate.

- Earnings taxes can increase, decrease, or leave unchanged the amount of human capital investments. The outcome depends in part on how taxes affect hours of work.

- The effect of tax rates on tax revenues depends on the responsiveness of labour supply to changes in tax rates and on the extent of substitution between taxable and nontaxable forms of compensation.

- The effect of taxes on saving may be analyzed using the life-cycle model, which assumes that people's annual consumption and saving decisions are influenced by their lifetime resources. Taxing interest income lowers the opportunity cost of present consumption and thereby creates incentives to lower saving. However, this substitution effect may be offset by the fact that the tax reduces total lifetime resources, which tends to reduce present consumption, that is, increase saving. The net effect on saving is an empirical question.

- Econometric studies of saving behaviour have foundered on both conceptual and practical difficulties. As a result, there is no firm consensus of opinion on the effects of taxation on saving.

- The personal income tax excludes the imputed rent (and capital gains) from owner-occupied housing from taxation. *Ceteris paribus*, this increases both the percentage of those choosing to own their homes and the quantity of owner-occupied housing. Proposals to modify the tax treatment of housing include making imputed rent part of taxable income.

- The theoretical effects of taxation on portfolio composition are ambiguous. Taxes reduce the expected return on a risky asset, but also lessen its riskiness. The net effect of these conflicting tendencies has not been empirically resolved.

DISCUSSION QUESTIONS

1. The Reform Party promotes a shift to a "flat-rate" tax, which reduces the top marginal tax rate applied to high-income individuals. Former Tory leader Jean Charest proposed a similar change (*The Financial Post*, July 1–3, 1995, pp. 1–2). Part of the rationale is to give highly productive Canadians renewed incentives for work. Use the graphical model of leisure–income decisions to analyze the effect of a lower marginal tax rate on a high-income individual.

2. Suppose that individuals view their loss of income from income taxes as offset by the benefits of public services purchased with the revenues. How are their labour supply decisions affected? (Hint: Decompose the change in hours worked into income and substitution effects.)

3. Brian Mulroney's 1987 tax reform included a substantial gradual increase in the limit, from $7,500 to $15,500, for contributions to Registered Retirement Savings Plans (RRSPs). The limit is now frozen at $13,500, but is still much higher than in 1987. The interest earned on RRSPs is not subject to income tax until it is withdrawn. Sketch the intertemporal budget constraint associated with an RRSP. Will RRSPs increase private saving? What about social saving (the sum of private and public saving)?

4. Discuss: "When after-tax rewards are reduced, productivity and risk taking diminish" (Kudlow, 1993: A16).

REFERENCES

Andersson, Krister. "Investment in Housing in the United States: A Portfolio Approach." Working Paper. Washington, DC: International Monetary Fund, 1990.

Beach, Charles M., Robin W. Boadway, and Neil Bruce. *Taxation and Savings in Canada.* Ottawa: Economic Council of Canada, 1988.

Boskin, Michael J. "Taxation, Saving, and the Rate of Interest." *Journal of Political Economy* 86, no. 2 (April 1978): S3–S28.

Bovenberg, A. Lans. "Tax Policy and National Saving in the United States." *National Tax Journal* 42 (June 1989): 123–38.

Break, George F. "Income Taxes and Incentives to Work." *American Economic Review* 47 (1957): 529–49.

Browning, Edgar K. "Elasticities, Tax Rates, and Tax Revenues." *National Tax Journal* (March 1989): 45–58.

Carroll, Chris, and Lawrence H. Summers. "Why Have Private Saving Rates in the United States and Canada Diverged?" *Journal of Monetary Economics* 20 (September 1987).

Feldstein, Martin S. "The Effect of Tax Rates on Taxable Income: A Panel Study of the 1986 Tax Reform Act." *Journal of Political Economy* 103 (June 1995): 551–72.

Feldstein, Martin S. "Tax Policy and International Capital Flows." National Bureau of Economic Research, Working Paper No. 4851. Cambridge: September 1994.

Feldstein, Martin S. "The Effects of Taxation on Risk-Taking." *Journal of Political Economy* 77 (1969): 755–64.

Feldstein, Martin S., and C. Horioka. "Domestic Saving and International Capital Flows." *Economic Journal* 90 (June 1980): 314–29.

Frankel, Jeffrey A. "Measuring International Capital Mobility: A Review." *American Economic Review* 82 (May 1992): 197–202.

Fullerton, Don. "On the Possibility of an Inverse Relationship between Tax Rates and Government Revenues." *Journal of Public Economics* 19, no. 1 (October 1982): 3–22.

Gale, W.G., and J.K. Scholz. "IRAs and Household Saving." Mimeograph. Madison: University of Wisconsin, 1993.

Hamermesh, D., and S. Woodbury. "Taxes, Fringe Benefits, and Faculty." Working Paper 3455. Cambridge, MA: National Bureau of Economic Research, 1990.

Hausman, Jerry A., and James M. Poterba. "Household Behavior and the Tax Reform Act of 1986." *Journal of Economic Perspectives* 1 (1987).

Hemming, Richard. "Income Tax Progressivity and Labour Supply." *Journal of Public Economics* 14, no. 1 (August 1980): 95–100.

Hubbard, R. Glenn. "Personal Taxation, Pension Wealth, and Portfolio Composition." *Review of Economics and Statistics* 67, no. 1 (February 1985): 53–60.

Hum, Derek, and Wayne Simpson. *Income Maintenance, Work Effort, and the Canadian Mincome Experiment.* Ottawa: Economic Council of Canada, 1991.

Jump, Gregory V. "Tax Incentives to Promote Personal Saving: Recent Canadian Experience," in *Saving and Government Policy.* Conference Series No. 25. Boston: Federal Reserve Bank of Boston, 1982, pp. 6–64.

Kudlow, Lawrence A. "The Deficit Obsession." *The Wall Street Journal,* January 25, 1993, p. A16.

Laffer, Arthur B. "Statement Prepared for the Joint Economic Committee, May 20," reprinted in *The Economics of the Tax Revolt: A Reader,* ed. Arthur B. Laffer and Jan P. Seymour. New York: Harcourt Brace Jovanovich, 1979, pp. 75–79.

McCarthy, Jonathan, and Han N. Pham. "The Impact of Individual Retirement Accounts on Savings." Federal Reserve Bank of New York. *Current Issues in Economics and Finance* 1 (September 1995).

McLure, Charles E., Jr. "Taxes, Saving, and Welfare: Theory and Evidence." *National Tax Journal* 33, no. 3 (September 1980).

Modigliani, Franco. "Life Cycle, Individual Thrift, and the Wealth of Nations." *American Economic Review* 76, no. 3 (June 1986): 297–313.

Musgrave, Richard A. *The Theory of Public Finance*. New York: McGraw-Hill, 1959.

Phipps, Shelley A. "Does Unemployment Insurance Increase Unemployment?" *Canadian Business Economics* 1, no. 3 (Spring 1993): 37–50.

Poterba, James M. "Taxation and Housing Markets," in *Canada-U.S. Tax Comparisons*, ed. John B. Shoven and John Whalley. Chicago: University of Chicago Press, 1992, pp. 275–94.

Roberts, Paul C. "The Keynesian Attack on Mr. Reagan's Plan." *The Wall Street Journal*, March 19, 1981, p. 26.

Sabelhaus, John. "Public Policy and Saving in the United States and Canada." *Canadian Journal of Economics* 30, no. 2 (May 1997): 253–75.

Slemrod, Joel, and Jon Bakija. *Taxing Ourselves: A Citizen's Guide to the Great Debate Over Tax Reform*. Cambridge, MA: MIT Press, 1996.

Smith, Lawrence B., Kenneth T. Rosen, and George Fallis. "Recent Developments in Economic Models of Housing Markets." *Journal of Economic Literature* 26 (March 1988).

Smith, Roger S. *Personal Wealth Taxation: Canadian Tax Policy in a Historical and International Setting*. Toronto: Canadian Tax Foundation, 1993.

Spiro, Peter S. "Estimating the Underground Economy: A Critical Evaluation of the Monetary Approach." *Canadian Tax Journal* 42, no. 4 (1994): 1059–81.

Tobin, James. "Liquity Preference as Attitude toward Risk." *Review of Economic Studies* 25 (February 1958): 65–86.

Venti, Steven F., and David A. Wise. "Government Policy and Personal Retirement Saving," in *Tax Policy and the Economy*, ed. James M. Poterba. Cambridge, MA: MIT Press, 1992.

Chapter 22

Consumption Taxation

But when the impositions are laid upon those things which men consume, every man payeth equally for what he useth: nor is the common wealth defrauded by the luxurious waste of private men.

–Thomas Hobbes

Most of our attention in this part of the book has been devoted to various kinds of income taxes. As noted in Chapter 20, the base of an income tax is potential consumption. This chapter discusses taxes that are imposed on actual consumption. There is no reason to believe that "actual" or "potential" consumption is inherently the fairer tax base. The following chapter will consider taxes on wealth, whose base is accumulated saving, that is, the accumulated difference between potential and actual consumption.

OVERVIEW

In Canada today, the most important consumption taxes are those levied on the purchases of a wide variety of goods and services. These, referred to as **general,** or **broad-based, sales taxes,** are generally in a form that imposes the same tax rate on all final purchases. The two forms of such taxes in Canada, one used by the federal government and the other by provincial governments, are the federal Goods and Services Tax (GST) and the provincial retail sales taxes (RSTs). Although both of these taxes exempt a variety of goods and services, the GST has the broader base as it taxes some goods and many services that are exempt under provincial retail sales taxes.

Selective sales taxes, also referred to as **excise taxes,** or **differential commodity taxes,** are levied at different rates on the purchase of different commodities by both the federal government and the provinces. **Customs duties** are a form of selective sales tax levied on different commodities at different rates at the time the goods are imported into the country, and can be used only by the federal government.

Sales taxes generally take one of two forms. A **unit tax** is a given amount for each unit purchased. For example, most provinces levy a tax on motor fuel that is a certain number of cents per litre; a typical rate is around 15 cents. In contrast, an **ad valorem** tax is computed as a percentage of the value of the purchase. For example, the federal excise tax rate on jewellery is 10 percent.

Consolidated revenues. Table 22.1 summarizes the role of consumption taxes in the Canadian revenue structure. Consumption taxes are important to both the federal and provincial levels of government, although they declined from about 30 percent of government revenues in 1965/66 to about 20 percent in 1995/96. This decline was largely due to rapid growth in income tax revenues rather than to any decrease in consumption taxes. As a share of GDP, consumption taxes fell somewhat over this period, from 8.6 percent to 8.2 percent. *General* sales taxes have become more important over the past three decades, up from 55 to 68 percent of consumption taxes, while *selective* sales taxes have declined as a share of consumption taxes. The growth in general sales tax revenues is due to a need for greater revenue, and to equity, efficiency, and administrative concerns related to heavier use of selective sales taxes.

Federal revenues. You will recall that consumption taxes—in the form of customs duties and excise taxes—accounted for *all* federal tax revenues from the time of Confederation until World War I. The income tax was enacted in 1917. Although consumption taxes accounted for 23 percent of federal revenues in 1995/96, income taxes are now by far the most important source of federal revenues.

The mix of federal consumption tax revenues has also changed over time. Customs and excise duties play a smaller role than initially, while the federal general sales tax and taxes on motor fuels have grown in importance. Federal taxes on motor fuels, introduced at the time of the energy crisis in the 1970s, accounted for 13 percent of federal consumption taxes in 1995/96. The general sales tax accounted for 67 percent of federal consumption tax revenues in 1994/95, and taxes on tobacco products and alcoholic beverages for 9 percent.

Table 22.1

Consumption Tax Revenues by Source and Level of Government, 1965/66, 1975/76, and 1995/96

	1965/66 ($ MIL)	SHARE (%)	1975/76 ($ MIL)	SHARE (%)	1995/96 ($ MIL)	SHARE (%)
A. Federal Government Consumption Tax Revenues						
Consumption taxes	$3,343	100.0	$7,107	100.0	$33,266	100.0
General sales tax	1,917	57.3	3,515	49.5	22,130	66.5
Motive fuel tax	–	–	425	6.0	4,180	12.6
Alcoholic beverages & tobacco taxes	688	20.6	1,195	16.8	2,892	8.7
Customs duties	686	20.5	1,887	26.6	3,270	9.8
Other	52	1.6	85	1.2	794	2.4
Federal consumption taxes as share of total federal revenue	37.1%		22.0%		22.9%	
B. Provincial Government Consumption Tax Revenues*						
Consumption taxes	$1,607	100.0	$5,840	100.0	$29,469*	100.0*
General sales tax	813	50.6	3,664	62.7	21,145	71.8
Motive fuel tax	680	42.3	1,518	26.0	6,198	21.0
Alcoholic beverages & tobacco taxes	54	3.4	281	4.8	1,835	6.2
Other	60	3.7	376	6.4	291	1.0
Provincial consumption taxes as share of total provincial revenue	31.2%		24.6%		18.5%	
C. Consolidated Federal, Provincial, and Local Government Consumption Tax Revenues*						
Consumption taxes	$4,957	100.0	$12,969	100.0	$61,467*	100.0*
General sales tax	2,733	55.1	7,189	55.4	42,146	68.4
Motive fuel tax	680	13.7	1,943	15.0	10,017	16.3
Alcoholic beverages & tobacco taxes	742	15.0	1,476	11.3	4,766	7.7
Customs duties	686	13.8	1,887	14.6	3,575	5.8
Other	116	2.3	474	3.7	962	1.6
Consumption taxes —as share of total revenue	29.7%		20.7%		20.3%	
—as share of GDP	8.6%		7.6%		8.2%	

*The final two columns in sections (B) and (C) provide the consolidated data for 1994/95 rather than 1995/96.

SOURCE: Statistics Canada, *Public Sector Finances 1995–1996*, Cat. no. 68-212-XPB (Ottawa: March 1996), and *Public Finance Historical Data 1965/66–1991/92*, Cat. no. 68-512 occasional (Ottawa: March 1992).

Provincial revenues. General sales taxes have also contributed to provincial revenue growth. Provincial retail sales taxes were 72 percent of provincial consumption taxes in 1995/96, up from 51 percent in 1965/66. This increase was offset by a fall in the selective sales tax on motor fuels from 42 percent to 21 percent of provincial consumption tax revenues. As at the federal level, consumption taxes have declined as a share of total provincial own-source revenues, falling from 31.2 percent in 1965/66 to 18.5 percent by 1995/96.

REASONS FOR CONSUMPTION TAXES

The need for revenues continues to be the primary reason for using consumption taxes. This was true prior to Confederation when public revenues were needed to support the construction of canals, bridges, roads, and other public activity, and it continues to be true. But why consumption taxes rather than other forms of taxation?

Administrative Considerations

A main attraction of consumption taxes has always been ease of administration. Early in Canada's history customs duties could be collected at the time goods were imported into the country, and excise duties could be collected at the time of import or from the few producers of the commodities subjected to these duties. As consumption taxes were expanded to include taxes on motor fuels and broad-based federal and provincial sales taxes, administrative ease continued to be an important factor.

The federal broad-based sales tax, introduced in 1924 and levied on manufactured goods, was collected from relatively few taxpayers. Provincial retail sales taxes, generally collected from sellers at the retail level, require tax authorities to deal with a much larger number of taxpayers, but far fewer than for a personal income tax. Relative to an income tax, there are fewer individuals whose behaviour has to be monitored by the tax authorities. This is not to say that administration of a sales tax is without complications. Many difficulties arise because it is unclear whether a given transaction creates a tax liability. Whether at the federal or provincial level, lines have been drawn between taxable and exempt goods. For provincial sales taxes this may involve a distinction between children's clothing and other clothing, prescription drugs and other medications, or restaurant meals above or below a specified threshold. The federal Goods and Services Tax, which replaced the federal sales tax in 1991, has confronted similar problems, with a parliamentary committee noting that "under the current legislation, a single plain croissant is not taxed;

a single chocolate-filled croissant is taxed; however, a package containing six or more chocolate croissants is not taxed."[1]

The point is that defining the base for a sales tax involves arbitrary distinctions, as was true in the case of the personal and corporate income taxes. Moreover, just as is true for other taxes, tax evasion can be a real problem. As noted in Chapter 19, by early 1994 federal and provincial taxes on cigarettes had reached a level that resulted in cigarette smuggling across the U.S. border that was costing millions of dollars in lost tax revenues each month. And there is evidence that the federal GST caused many workers, particularly in the service sector, to shift to the underground economy in order to evade taxes.[2]

Nevertheless, consumption taxes are probably easier to administer than income taxes. Taxes on consumption are therefore an attractive option in less-developed countries, where individual record-keeping is not widespread, and where the resources available for tax administration are quite limited. In countries with high literacy and good record-keeping, these administrative arguments are less compelling. Are there any other justifications?

Optimal Tax Considerations

What role is there for differential taxes on various commodities given that an income tax is already in place? A natural framework for examining this question is the theory of optimal taxation. Atkinson and Stiglitz (1980) showed that if the income tax schedule is chosen optimally, then under fairly reasonable conditions social welfare cannot be improved by levying differential commodity taxes.[3] However, if for some reason the income tax is not optimal, differential commodity taxes can improve welfare. For example, if society has egalitarian goals, social welfare can be improved by taxing luxury goods at relatively high rates. The 10 percent federal excise tax on jewellery may be one example, and the $100 per unit federal tax on automobile air conditioners another.

A related question is how the rates should be set, given that it has been decided to have differential commodity taxes. Obviously, the answer depends on the government's objectives. According to optimal tax theory, if the goal is to col-

---

[1] House of Commons (1994: 16).
[2] See Spiro (1993 and 1994), and Smith (1993).
[3] Suppose the utility function of each individual is a function of his or her consumption of leisure and a set of other commodities. Then as long as the marginal rate of substitution between any two commodities is independent of the amount of leisure, differential commodity taxation cannot improve social welfare in the presence of an optimal earnings tax.

lect a given amount of revenue as efficiently as possible, tax rates should be set so that the compensated demand for each commodity is reduced in the same proportion (see Chapter 19). When the demand for each good depends only on its own price, this is equivalent to the rule that tax rates be inversely related to compensated price elasticities of demand. Goods with inelastic demand are taxed at relatively high rates and vice versa. Efficiency does not require a general sales tax with the same tax rate for each commodity.

If the government cares about equity as well as efficiency, optimal tax theory requires departures from the inverse elasticity rule. As noted in Chapter 19, if price-inelastic commodities make up a high proportion of the budgets of the poor, we expect governments with egalitarian objectives to tax such goods lightly or not at all. This may help explain why the provinces and the federal government exempt food from their general sales taxes.

Within the conventional welfare economics framework, another justification for a sales tax is the presence of externalities. If consumption of a commodity generates costs not included in its price, then in general efficiency requires a tax on the use of that good (see Chapter 8). The high tax rates (Table 22.2) on

Table 22.2

Federal and Provincial Cigarette Taxes, 1996 (per carton of 200 cigarettes)*

PROVINCE	FEDERAL TAXES	PROVINCIAL TAXES	TOTAL
Newfoundland	$10.86	$20.56	$31.42
PEI	8.86	11.35	20.21
Nova Scotia	8.86	6.60	15.46
New Brunswick	8.86	6.60	15.46
Quebec	6.46	3.76	10.22
Ontario	6.86	3.40	10.26
Manitoba	10.86	16.00	26.86
Saskatchewan	10.86	16.00	26.86
Alberta	10.86	14.00	24.86
British Columbia	10.86	22.00	32.86
NWT	10.86	24.80	35.66
Yukon	10.86	16.40	27.26

*These taxes reflect the rate changes made in early 1994 and subsequently to deal with the smuggling problem that was centred in Quebec and Ontario; they also show a sensitivity to potential interprovincial smuggling between the Maritime provinces and Quebec.

SOURCE: Karin Treff and David Perry, *Finances of the Nation, 1996* (Toronto: Canadian Tax Foundation, 1997), p. 5:11, Table 5.6.

tobacco—provincial plus federal rates in 1996 ranged from a low of $10.22 in Quebec to a high of $35.66 in the Northwest Territories per carton of 200 cigarettes (from $1.28 to $4.46 per pack of twenty-five)—are sometimes rationalized in this way. Smokers impose higher costs on our public health care system, so a tax on tobacco may enhance efficiency by equalizing the private and the total social cost of smoking.[4]

In some cases, sales taxes can be viewed as substitutes for user fees. With current technology, it is infeasible to charge motorists a fee for every kilometre driven, even though the process of driving creates costs in terms of road damage, congestion, and so on. Because the amount of road use is related to gasoline consumption, road use can be taxed indirectly by putting a tax on gasoline. Of course, the correspondence is far from perfect: some cars are more fuel efficient than others, and some do more damage than others. Still, some positive user fee may be more efficient than none at all.

Other Considerations

Several rationalizations for differential commodity taxation lie outside the framework of conventional economics. Certain excises can be regarded as taxes on "sin." A particular commodity, such as tobacco or alcohol, is deemed to be bad per se, and its consumption is therefore discouraged by the state. Such commodities are just the opposite of "merit goods" (see Chapter 4), which are viewed as being good per se. In both cases, the government is essentially imposing its preferences on those of the citizenry.

Some argue that politicians are attracted to sales taxes because they are included in the final price of the commodity and so are relatively easy to hide.[5] However, it is hard to determine whether citizens really are less sensitive to sales taxes than to other types of taxes. In an analysis of the effects of fiscal variables on the outcome of provincial elections, Landon and Ryan (1996) found that sales tax increases have a substantial negative effect on a provincial government's probability of re-election.

---

[4] An offsetting effect of smoking is the reduction in expenditures for health and other care in old age for smokers who die younger than nonsmokers. Smokers also create a second-hand smoke problem, but this externality is best handled through zoning—creating non-smoking areas in restaurants and office buildings, because a tax on tobacco does not affect the location of cigarette consumption.

[5] The move to a GST was, among other things, a conscious effort to make the federal sales tax more visible. Resistance to the GST has, in part, been attributed to the move from the "invisible" FST to the much more visible GST. We return to this.

Efficiency and Distributional Implications

From an efficiency point of view, the fundamental question is whether actual sales tax rates are set to minimize excess burden. As pointed out in Chapter 18, when a group of commodities is being taxed, the overall excess burden depends not only on the elasticities of each good, but also on the degree to which the goods are complementary and substitutable. At this time, values of all the relevant elasticities are not known with any degree of certainty. Therefore, no definitive judgment as to the efficiency of the existing pattern of sales taxes is available.

As noted earlier, setting all rates equal is almost certainly not efficient. Recall, from Chapter 18, that the Corlett–Hague rule states that higher tax rates should be imposed on goods that are more complementary with leisure. A uniform sales tax rate on all commodities is only optimal in the unlikely case that all goods are equally good substitutes or complements with leisure. On the other hand, given that the information required to determine fully efficient taxes is not presently available (and perhaps never will be), uniform tax rates may not be a bad approach, and differential sales tax rates often result in high administrative and compliance costs. Furthermore, departures from uniformity open the door to tax rate differentiation based on political rather than equity or efficiency considerations.

The conventional view of the distributional effects of general sales taxes is that they are regressive. This is because higher-income people spend a smaller proportion of their income. Where consumption equals 70 percent of the income of a high-income individual, a 10 percent consumption tax equals 7 percent of income; a person with low income who draws down saving to consume 110 percent of annual income pays a consumption tax equal to 11 percent of income. A recent study estimates that the consumption taxes in 1988 consistently fell as income rose, from 14.0 percent of income for the lowest decile of taxpayers to 5.9 percent for the highest decile.[6]

There are two problems with this line of reasoning. First, it looks at the tax as a proportion of annual income. In the absence of severe credit market restrictions, lifetime income is more relevant, and there is reasonably strong evidence that the proportion of lifetime income devoted to consumption is about the

---

[6] The assumption this result is based on is that "commodity taxes are borne by consumers except for the share of such taxes on government purchases which is borne by personal income taxpayers and the share on purchases of capital goods and exports, the common portion of which is borne by consumers and the differential portion of which is borne by labour" (Vermaeten, Gillespie, and Vermaeten, 1995: 323).

same at all levels.[7] Indeed, computations by Davies, St-Hilaire, and Whalley (1984) suggest general sales taxes may be roughly proportional when measured with respect to lifetime (rather than annual) income.[8] Second, and perhaps more fundamentally, the conventional view totally ignores the theory of tax incidence. Implicitly (or explicitly), it is assumed that the taxes on a good are borne entirely by the consumers of that good. As emphasized in Chapter 17, however, a commodity tax generally is shifted in a complicated fashion that depends on the supply and demand responses when the tax is imposed. The effect of sales taxes on the distribution of income is still an open question.

The incidence of sales taxes, whether general or selective, depends crucially on which goods are taxed at low rates or exempted altogether, and on refundable sales tax credits provided through the income tax system or by some other means. By exempting those goods consumed intensively by the poor, the after-tax income distribution can be made more equal, other things being the same. But problems can arise with attempts to achieve equality in this way. Even if it is true that food expenditures on average play an especially important role in the budgets of the poor, there are still many upper-income families whose food consumption is proportionately very high. Moreover, exempting certain commodities creates administrative complexities, because it is not always clear whether certain goods belong in the favoured category. Just recall the treatment of croissants under the GST described earlier.

An alternative way to improve the distributional effects of consumption taxes is to use a refundable sales tax credit. As Michael Wilson, Minister of Finance, argued when the GST was proposed in 1987:

> A better way to make sales tax fair is to offset the effects of the total tax paid by lower-income families with a refundable sales tax credit. By making the credit refundable, all low-income Canadians receive the credit, even if they do not pay income tax. What is required to qualify is to file a tax return, as most Canadians already do. By phasing the credit out for households with income above a threshold level, the benefits are appropriately targeted to lower-income families. By prepayment of this credit, those in need will receive a payment before they have to purchase goods and services and pay the sales tax.[9]

---

[7] See Friedman (1957).

[8] More recent evidence has reinforced this point. Metcalf (1993) found the general sales taxes used by U.S. states may be somewhat progressive when measured with respect to lifetime income.

[9] Department of Finance (1987: 64).

The refundable credit that accompanied the GST has, even if unnoticed, been sufficient to compensate for any additional regressivity contributed by the GST.[10] It has also added complexity to an already complex tax system (a) by requiring additional tax returns to be filed, (b) by complicating computations by phasing out the credit as income rises, and (c) by implementing a system of prepayments so that those in need do not incur the GST tax payments before they receive the refundable credits. Nonetheless, the credit seems to work well and may be seen as one step toward a more effective integration of the tax and welfare systems in Canada.[11]

The main consumption taxes used in Canada are the federal Goods and Services Tax, provincial retail sales taxes, and the excise taxes and duties used by both levels of government. We now discuss each of these in turn.

CANADA'S VALUE-ADDED TAX: THE GST

Typically, goods are produced in several stages. Consider a simple model of bread production. The farmer grows wheat and sells it to a miller who turns it into flour. The miller sells the flour to a baker who transforms it into bread. The bread is purchased by a grocer who sells it to consumers. A hypothetical numerical example is provided in Table 22.3. Column 1 shows the purchases made by the producer at each stage of production, and column 2 shows the sales value at each stage. For example, the miller pays $400 to the farmer for wheat, and sells the processed wheat to the baker for $700. The *value added* at each stage of production is the difference between the firm's sales and the purchased material inputs used in production. The baker paid $700 for the wheat and sold the bread for $950, so the baker's value added is $250. The value added at each stage of production is computed by subtracting purchases from sales, shown in column 3.[12]

A **value-added tax** (VAT) is a percentage tax on value added applied at each stage of production. For example, if the rate of the VAT is 10 percent, the grocer would pay $5, which is 10 percent of $50. Column 4 shows the amount of VAT liability at each stage of production. The total revenue created by the VAT is found by summing the amounts paid at each stage, and equals $100.

---

[10] See Bird (1994: 4).

[11] For discussion of the distributional effects of zero-rating certain items and providing refundable credits as part of a value-added tax system, see Metcalf (1994).

[12] By definition, value added must equal the sum of factor payments made by the producer: wages, interest, rent, and economic profits.

Table 22.3

Implementation of a Value-Added Tax (VAT)

PRODUCER	PURCHASES	SALES	VALUE ADDED	VAT AT 10 PERCENT RATE
Farmer	$ 0	$ 400	$ 400	$ 40
Miller	400	700	300	30
Baker	700	950	250	25
Grocer	950	1,000	50	5
Total	$2,050	$3,050	$1,000	$100

The identical result could have been generated by levying a 10 percent tax at the retail level, that is, by a tax of 10 percent on the value of sales made to consumers by the grocer. In essence, then, a VAT is just an alternative method for collecting a sales tax,[13] and this is the method chosen by the federal government when it introduced the GST. In contrast to "single-stage" provincial sales taxes, this is a "multi-stage" sales tax. The provincial taxes are collected at the retail level while the GST is collected at each stage, including the retail stage, as value is added. One advantage of the multi-stage tax is that with a portion of the tax collected at each stage, the incentive to evade the tax on the final sale is much reduced in many cases.

Implementation Issues

More that eighty countries have introduced value-added taxes since 1960, including Japan, New Zealand, and the major countries of Europe. Only the United States and Australia, of the industrialized world, have not implemented such a tax. With good reason, the VAT has been referred to as "the fastest rising star on the fiscal horizon."[14]

Certain administrative decisions have a major impact on a VAT's ultimate economic effects. First, it must be decided how purchases of investment assets by firms will be treated in the computation of value added. There are three possibilities:

1. The purchase of an investment good is treated like any other material input. Its full value is subtracted from sales in the computation, despite the

---

[13] In this example, net income is $1,000, the same as value added. Hence, the VAT is equivalent to a proportional income tax. As we see later, this is not always true.
[14] See Bird (1994: 2).

fact that it is durable. This is referred to as a **consumption-type VAT** because the tax base excludes investment and involves only consumption.

2. Each period, firms may deduct only the amount by which investment goods depreciate. The tax base is thus total income net of depreciation, which is why this is characterized as a **net income–type VAT**.

3. Firms are allowed no deductions for investment and depreciation. This is called a **gross income–type VAT**.

Thus, by making different provisions with respect to the treatment of investment goods, a VAT can be transformed into three distinct taxes, each of which has different efficiency and distributional effects. A VAT does not necessarily have to be a tax on consumption, but in Canada, as in most of Europe, VATs are of the consumption type.

Second, a procedure for collection must be devised. The Canadian GST adopted the method long used in Europe—the **invoice-credit method**, which can be illustrated in the hypothetical example in Table 22.3. Each firm is liable for tax on the basis of its total sales, but it can claim the taxes already paid by its suppliers as a credit against this liability. For example, the baker is liable for taxes on his $950 in sales, giving him a tax obligation of $95 (= .10 × $950). However, he can claim a credit of $70 (the sum of taxes paid by the farmer and the miller), leaving him a net obligation of $25. The catch is that the credit is allowed only if supported by invoices provided by the baker and the miller. This system provides an incentive for the producers to police themselves against tax evasion. Whatever taxes the farmer and miller evade must be paid by the baker, so the baker will only do business with firms that provide proper invoices. The invoice-credit method cannot eliminate evasion completely. For example, producers can collude to falsify invoices. Nevertheless, there appears to be some evidence that multi-stage collection has cut down on fraud.[15]

Finally, a rate structure must be established. In our simple example, all commodities are taxed at the same rate. Under the GST, commodities are taxed differentially. Basic food, prescription drugs, and medical devices are not taxed at all; and some services, such as child care and dental care, receive preferen-

---

[15] For a discussion of the various problems confronted in the administration of value-added taxes, see Tait (1988: ch. 14). According to Tait: "All commentators describe the theoretical self-checking mechanism of VAT and all go on to elaborate on how this does not work" (p. 304). Tax authorities do not have the resources required to cross-match sales with invoices, and computers have not provided the solution. False invoices are also a potentially serious problem.

tial treatment, presumably because of equity considerations. For reasons of administrative feasibility, firms with gross annual sales below $30,000 are exempted from the GST. Similarly, banking and finance institutions escape taxation because they tend to provide services in kind; therefore, it is difficult to compute value added. The consumption of services generated by owner-occupied housing is exempt from tax for the same reasons that it is usually exempted from income taxation (see Chapter 20). Non-uniform taxation increases administrative complexity, especially when firms produce multiple outputs, some of which are taxable and some of which are not. But the system can and does work, in Canada as in many other countries.

Problems with the GST: A Brief Review

The Liberal government was elected in 1994 on a platform that included a commitment to repeal the GST. The government was unable to honour this commitment, even though the GST was "broadly and deeply resented by Canadians," because none of the alternative taxes is particularly attractive. Understanding the reasons for Canada's adoption of a VAT (the GST), the problems associated with the GST, and changes that will improve the GST can all contribute to a better tax system. We turn to these issues.

The federal sales tax. The Goods and Services Tax (GST) replaced the federal sales tax (FST) in 1991.[16] One problem with the FST was that it was imposed on a narrow tax base—manufactured goods, which included only a third of total consumption. The narrow base required a higher tax rate to raise needed revenues, and the higher rate has a larger effect on the price of manufactured goods relative to untaxed goods and services. A broader base and lower rates would result in fewer distortions in the individual's consumption decisions.

The taxation of manufactured goods under the FST also resulted in a large share of FST revenues being collected on the *inputs* to production processes, rather than only at the time of final consumption. Taxed inputs were often used in the production of manufactured goods, resulting in a tax being imposed on a tax. This is referred to as *tax cascading*, and one result was that the tax component in the final price of different manufactured goods varied. Tax cascading also meant that the FST added to the cost of goods produced for export, reducing Canada's competitiveness. Although exports could be

---

[16] The FST was generally referred to as the Manufacturers' Sales Tax (MST) prior to the 1987 tax reform. The FST and MST are one and the same; students who examine earlier literature will find frequent reference to the MST.

exempted from the FST at point of export, it was not possible to adjust export prices to eliminate the effect of the higher price caused by the FST included on the inputs.

Effective tax rates on goods also differed because the FST excluded costs incurred beyond the manufacturing stage. Mark-ups subsequent to manufacturing varied from good to good, and led to different effective rates on manufactured goods. This contrasts with the result of a broad-based sales tax applied at a uniform rate on the pretax price of a good at the final point of sale.

Finally, the FST was complex to administer, even though it was applied to relatively few taxpayers compared to the GST. A line had to be drawn between the manufacturing stage and later stages, which included, inter alia, advertising, marketing, transportation, retail and wholesale activities. Lines between the activities are particularly difficult to draw in vertically integrated organizations, and the division of activity sometimes differed for domestic and imported goods, to the disadvantage of domestic producers. This resulted in complex regulations and arbitrary decisions.

The GST. The Goods and Services Tax was designed to address many of the problems of the FST. The base was broadened to include services; and the tax base was extended to include marketing and distribution activities through the wholesale and retail levels. The GST nearly doubled the tax base of the FST, even with food excluded from the tax, and allowed the rate of the federal government's broad-based sales tax to be lowered from 13.5 percent in 1990 to 7.0 percent in 1991 while maintaining revenues. Increased uniformity of effective tax rates and lower rates on final goods and services reduced distortions and lowered excess burdens.[17] The invoice-credit system allowed taxpayers to claim a credit for taxes paid at earlier stages in the production process, and to pay a tax only on the value they added. This avoided the problem of tax cascading, permitted a refund of taxes at point of export, and improved Canada's competitiveness. Nonetheless, the GST has been subjected to intense criticism.

GST problems. Some of the problems that accompanied the introduction of the GST were due to the situation at time of introduction. Although the 1987 tax reform package included the GST, the tax was implemented in the second

---

[17] Estimates of the expected efficiency gain differed greatly. The Department of Finance estimated that replacing the FST with the GST would cause GDP to be $9 billion, or 1.5 percent, higher. Hamilton and Whalley estimated the efficiency gain from this change to be 0.31 percent of GDP, or one-fifth as large. See Department of Finance (1989), and Hamilton and Whalley (1989).

phase of the reform process in January 1991. Canada was in the middle of a recession in 1991, and the timing was unfortunate. This was also a time when the popularity of the federal government was at a low level.

The GST added a significant new tax plus tax compliance costs to small businesses in the service sector, a large and politically mobilized group that was hard hit by the recession. Some reaction was to be expected. Services are also an area of activity where (a) home production can often be readily substituted for market production, and (b) much of the value is contributed in the form of labour in the final stage of production. These characteristics make tax avoidance and evasion activity more prevalent in the service industries, even in the best of circumstances. And this was also a time of increasing awareness that some taxpayers were avoiding or evading taxes by participating in the underground economy.[18]

The service sector is dominated by small businesses, and the evidence is clear that incremental costs of complying with a new tax are likely to be particularly burdensome on small businesses. Small businesses are less likely to have record-keeping systems, or in-house expertise, that facilitate ready response to new demands by tax authorities. Additional costs are spread over a small sales base, and recovering costs has a larger effect on prices, reducing competitiveness. Compliance costs expressed as a percentage of taxable sales, or as a percentage of revenues collected, are much higher than for large businesses.[19]

Another problem for the GST was that the United States was (and is) without a national sales tax. Some U.S border states (New Hampshire and Montana) have no sales tax, and others (New York and Michigan at 4 percent) had sales taxes that were quite low. Combined federal and provincial sales taxes were 13.5 percent in Quebec, 15 percent in Ontario, and 14 percent in British Columbia in 1996. In addition to problems inherent in assessing the GST on goods brought in by shoppers, services purchased abroad by Canadians, such as car repairs, cosmetic surgery, and legal and financial services, were unlikely

---

[18] There is evidence that the strength of a taxpayer's commitment to comply with tax laws is influenced by whether the taxpayer believes that others are complying. This is one reason why it is in the government's interest to publicize evidence of compliance and downplay evidence of noncompliance, whenever possible.

[19] Compliance costs for businesses with annual sales of $100,000 or less were estimated at 16.97 percent of taxes collected, and for businesses with sales over $1 million at 2.65 percent of taxes collected (House of Commons, 1994: 17). Sandford et al. (1989: 116) have estimated compliance costs for the VAT in the United Kingdom in 1986–87, finding that these costs, expressed as a percentage of taxable sales, varied from a high of 1.94 percent for taxpayers with sales of less than £20,500 per annum to .003 percent for those with sales in excess of £10 million per annum.

to be visible to Canadian tax authorities. European countries introducing VATs had not shared borders with a dominant trading partner where the consumption tax situation differed so greatly. The cross-border tax differences, coupled with a relatively high exchange rate, a Canadian dollar worth US$0.87 in 1991, contributed to tax avoidance by means of cross-border shopping.

The GST was highly visible to consumers, replacing a tax, the FST, which had been invisible. Visibility, coupled with the taxation of many goods and services that had not been subject to the FST, made the GST look like a new tax rather than a replacement tax. Small businesses and service providers were joined by many consumers in objecting to the GST. As is generally the case with tax changes, those benefiting from the change, in this case manufacturers, were much less vocal.

The 1987 tax reform package, of which the imposition of the GST in 1991 was a part, coupled a significant decrease in personal income taxes with an increase in consumption taxes. One intended result was some reallocation of tax burdens from those with the lowest and highest incomes to those in the middle. The 1970s and 1980s had been a period when middle-class before-tax incomes had been stagnant and after-tax incomes had been falling. This was not a climate in which the middle class, a large segment of the taxpaying population, was likely to welcome any shift in the burden to them.

Other problems with the GST might have been avoided if the government had more effectively resisted arguments for preferential treatment. The original GST proposal included food within the tax base. This changed. Had it not, our croissant example (and many others) would not exist. Similarly, the integration of provincial sales taxes with the GST was a clearly stated objective. This would achieve a uniform sales-tax base across Canada, but permit the combined federal and provincial rate to vary from province to province depending on the rates chosen by provinces. Such integration would increase understanding and minimize administrative and compliance costs. The federal government was unable to achieve integration before the GST was enacted in 1991. GST administration was also complicated by the federal commitment to ensure, through partial rebates, that the federal sales-tax burden on municipalities, schools, hospitals, and the nonprofit sectors would be no greater than before the GST.

Zero-rated (tax-free) and tax-exempt items. Zero-rated and tax-exempt items complicate the administration of a value-added tax such as the GST, and also make the tax more difficult to understand. There is an important difference between zero-rated and tax-exempt items, which we now explain. Zero-rated items include basic groceries, prescription drugs, medical devices, and exports.

For these items, the seller does not pay the GST on the value added at this stage of production and can claim a tax credit for taxes paid at earlier stages. In Table 22.4A we consider how groceries, a zero-rated item, are treated under the GST. The tax is collected from the farmer, miller, and baker—a total of $95 to that point. Since food from the grocer is a tax-free item, the grocer pays no GST on the $50 of value added, *and* in addition is able to claim a credit for the $95 of GST paid at earlier stages. The result is that the final price of the food is free of GST.

Tax-exempt items include residential rents, most health and dental services, day care services, municipal transit, most educational services, and many financial

Table 22.4

Value-Added Tax with Zero-Rated and Tax-Exempt Items

A. Value-Added Tax with Groceries Zero-Rated

PRODUCER	VALUE ADDED	TOTAL TAX	CREDIT ALLOWED	TAX DUE
Farmer	$ 400	$ 40	$ 0	$ 40
Miller	300	70	40	30
Baker	250	95	70	25
Grocer	50		95	−95
Total	$1,000			$ 00

B. Value-Added Tax with Groceries Tax-Exempt

PRODUCER	VALUE ADDED	TOTAL TAX	CREDIT ALLOWED	TAX DUE
Farmer	$ 400	$ 40	$ 0	$ 40
Miller	300	70	40	30
Baker	250	95	70	25
Grocer	50		–	–
Total	$1,000			$ 95

C. Value-Added Tax with Milled Flour Tax-Exempt

PRODUCER	VALUE ADDED	TOTAL TAX	CREDIT ALLOWED	TAX DUE
Farmer	$ 400	$ 40	$ 0	$ 40
Miller	300	40	0	–
Baker	250	95	0	95
Grocer	50	100	95	5
Total	$1,000			$140

services.[20] If food were instead a tax-exempt item, as in Table 22.4B, the grocer would not pay the $5 tax on the $50 of value added at this stage, but would *not* be able to claim a tax credit for the $95 in GST paid at earlier stages. Thus, the final price of the groceries would include the $95 in GST previously paid. If all of the value added were in the final stage of production (i.e., the grocer produces the wheat, mills the flour, bakes and sells the bread), zero-rated and tax-exempt treatment would be the same. Thus, the importance of tax-exempt treatment depends on where value is added. Moreover, the exemption of goods at an intermediate stage of production may have the perverse effect of increasing the tax component in the price of the final good. This is because the credit given for value added at earlier stages is lost. Table 22.4C provides such an example. In this case the flour sold by the miller is exempt. The miller does not pay the GST, nor is he able to take a tax credit for the $40 in GST paid by the farmer. Thus, under the credit-invoice system the baker owes 10 percent of the total value added, or $95, and may be able to take no credit against this since the invoice from the miller, due to his exemption, may include no GST information. The GST in this case totals $140 by the time the groceries are sold; since the chain of credits was interrupted, the credit of $40 paid by the farmer is lost. From the foregoing it may be apparent that asking small retailers to differentiate between zero-rated and taxable goods and services complicates compliance by taxpayers, and that exemptions add further complications.

Improving the GST. A value-added tax, such as the GST, can be an effective part of Canada's tax system. A number of steps would improve the tax and would likely reduce resistance to it. The Standing Committee on Finance recognized that "in designing a replacement for the GST it is necessary to try to preserve some of the most beneficial aspects of an invoice-credit VAT," and recommended "replacing the GST with a federal–provincial, integrated, value-added tax."[21] This is what the GST was originally intended to be. Although Quebec has integrated its provincial sales tax with the GST to a large extent, and Newfoundland, Nova Scotia, and New Brunswick reached an agreement in early 1996 to do so, the integration of other RSTs with the GST will not be easy. Other provinces have been reluctant to give up their autonomy. The challenge is to find a solution that responds to the need for provincial and federal autonomy while achieving efficiencies by broadening the consumption tax base and reducing compliance and administration costs. The federal government

---

[20] The resale of homes is not subject to the GST. New homes receive special treatment. Those that cost more than $450,000 pay the full 7 percent. Those below $350,000 receive a 2.5 percent rebate, resulting in a 4.5 percent tax rate, and for new homes between $350,000 and $450,000, the rebate is gradually phased out. The 4.5 percent rate approximated the amount of FST that had previously been in the price of new homes.
[21] House of Commons (1994: 39–40).

also needs to work with provinces to eliminate the complex system of rebates, which ensures that the municipalities, universities, schools, and hospitals (the MUSH sector) pay no more in federal sales taxes than before the GST.

Other improvements would include basic groceries within the tax base, and simplify tax compliance for the many small businesses that have confronted in the GST a major sales tax for the first time. Requiring GST returns only once a year for small businesses, constructing the returns so that they draw on information required for income tax purposes, and combining federal and provincial sales tax administration so as to require only one tax return would increase acceptability.[22] A more controversial change may be the move to hide the tax. Surveys indicate that consumers prefer *tax-inclusive pricing*, where advertised and publicized prices include the GST. Whereas the former FST was well hidden in advertised prices, the GST requires that the tax be made visible either by adding the tax at the cash register and/or by clearly identifying the tax on cash register receipts. Economists commonly argue for the visibility of taxes, ensuring that taxpayers within a democracy are aware of taxes they are paying. Resistance to the GST would likely have been lessened if it had replaced a more visible tax, or had been equally well hidden. The extent to which the GST should be hidden will continue to be debated.

There is an additional argument that has been employed against VATs in other countries, and might be used against the GST. This is that its introduction will contribute to further expansion of the public sector at the expense of the private sector. The narrow base of the FST limited the effectiveness of raising rates further—significant additional distortions would generate limited new revenues. With the much broader tax base of the GST, higher rates lead to smaller distortions in choices and larger increases in revenues. Each percentage point increase in the GST in 1995 would raise about $2.5 billion. Indeed, in virtually all countries with a VAT, the rate has increased over time, as has the share of gross domestic product devoted to taxes.[23] In a world where political institutions accurately reflect the wishes of the citizenry, this observation may not be troubling. But for those who believe that at least to some extent the inter-

---

[22] Requiring small businesses to pay their GST only once a year will increase funds available to them during the year by the amount of GST collected. For example, if an average of $10,000 in GST is held by a business during a year, at an interest rate of 8 percent this is worth $800 to the business and helps to reduce the net cost of complying with the GST. See Sandford et al. (1989: ch. 8).

[23] For example, when Denmark introduced a VAT of 10 percent in 1967, total tax revenues as a percent of gross domestic product were 36.1 percent. By 1978, the VAT rate was 22 percent, and the ratio of taxes to gross domestic product was 43.6 percent (Aaron, 1981: 14). Of course, this does not prove that the VAT was responsible for a larger government sector (see Stockfisch, 1985).

ests of the government differ from those of the public (see Chapter 11), the revenue potential of a VAT, such as the GST, may be frightening. Some fear that the VAT might be used to sneak by an increase in the size of the government sector. Indeed, the House of Commons Standing Committee on Finance (1994: 42) urges that "all shelf, sticker, advertised or publicized prices ... be shown only as a combined total of the sale price and the applicable VAT." Hiding the tax, and making the GST more acceptable in that way, is likely to ease the process of future tax-rate increases and public sector expansion.

PROVINCIAL RETAIL SALES TAXES

Provincial retail sales taxes (RSTs) are the second form of general, or broad-based, sales tax widely used in Canada. Nine of Canada's ten provinces have an RST. The RST is a single-stage tax that is collected by retailers at the point of sale. A consumption-type of VAT, such as the GST, and a retail sales tax can be designed to be equivalent. For example, a 10 percent RST on the $1,000 sale by the grocer in Table 22.3 has the same effect and raises the same revenue as the 10 percent VAT. A main difference is that the VAT is collected in smaller amounts for several taxpayers, while the RST results in a larger amount collected from a single taxpayer. This difference has several implications. One is that the paper trail left by the VAT's invoice-credit system, and the assistance it provides to tax authorities, does not exist with the RST. A second is that the exemption of smaller retailers (and hence their value added) under a VAT leads to the loss of much less revenue than if small retailers are exempt from the RST, since under the RST the tax applying to the value added at previous stages of production is also lost. A third is that a VAT, since it is collected at each stage of production, must be collected from many more taxpayers.

The primary advantages of an RST over a VAT are that it is far more familiar to Canadian taxpayers, is easier to understand, and has fewer points of collection. A VAT, on the other hand, is better able to avoid tax cascading and the taxation of goods used as inputs in the production of other goods.

Provincial revenue needs created by the Great Depression led to the introduction of provincial retail sales taxes, first in Alberta in 1936 and then in Saskatchewan in 1937. Alberta, although first in, was first out, repealing its tax in 1937; Alberta remains the only province without a retail sales tax. By 1950, Quebec, Newfoundland, Nova Scotia, and British Columbia had enacted retail sales taxes, and by 1967 the four remaining provinces all had RSTs.

Rates and revenues. Tax rates have steadily risen since the first RSTs were introduced at a 2 percent rate. Rates and revenues differ substantially from province to province. As Table 22.5 shows, aside from Alberta, which has no RST, 1996 rates ranged from 12 percent in Newfoundland to 6.5 in Quebec. Per capita revenues were $970 in Newfoundland and $623 in Manitoba. Recall from Table 22.1 that RSTs accounted for 72 percent of provincial consumption taxes. RSTs have been a very important tax policy tool for provinces.

Tax base. Tax bases also differ from province to province. All provinces exempt most food from the tax base, but there is substantial variation in the treatment of prepared meals. Children's clothing is also exempt, but the treatment of other clothing varies among provinces. Although there is no basis in economic theory for the exemption of services that account for a large and growing share of consumption, most services are exempted from provincial RSTs. One result is that the tax base for the federal GST is broader than that for provincial RSTs. Services that are usually in the RST base include telephones, cable television, temporary accommodations, and dry cleaning; there is substantial variation in the treatment of maintenance, repair, and other services. Whereas the exemption of services undoubtedly reduces administration and compliance costs, the narrowness of the RST tax bases leads to significant distortions that favour the choice of exempt services over taxed goods. RSTs, like the former FST, continue to fall on many goods that are used as inputs in the production of other goods, resulting in tax cascading and higher effective tax rates on the final goods.

EXCISE TAXES AND CUSTOMS DUTIES

Customs duties, those taxes levied on goods at the time of import or export, are the sole purview of the federal government. As noted in Chapter 2, the Constitution Act of 1867 prohibited provinces from the use of taxes on international or interprovincial trade. At the time of Confederation, customs duties raised $9 million and accounted for 75 percent of federal government revenues. In 1994/95 they were expected to generate $3.39 billion, 2.5 percent of federal revenue, on $250 billion of imported goods and services. These revenues have decreased steadily as international negotiations through the General Agreement on Tariffs and Trade (GATT) and bilateral agreements such as the North American Free Trade Agreement (NAFTA) have lowered tariff barriers. While most raw materials are free of tax, import duties on manufactured goods depend in part on whether similar goods are produced in Canada, with higher taxes applied to imported goods that compete with Canadian goods. Choice is intentionally distorted, with these distortions decreasing as tariff rates are lowered.

Excise taxes continue as an important revenue source. The major excise taxes imposed by the provincial and federal governments in 1996 are listed in Table

Table 22.5

Provincial Consumption Tax Rates (1996) and Revenues from Provincial Consumption Taxes (1995/96)

PROVINCE	RST RATE (%)	PER CAPITA* RST REVENUE ($)	TAX ON CIGARETTES (¢/CIG)	TAX ON UNLEADED GASOLINE (¢/LITRE)	TOTAL CONSUMPTION TAX REVENUE ($MIL)	PER CAPITA CONSUMPTION TAX REVENUE ($)	SHARE OF OWN-SOURCE REVENUE (%)
Nfld.	12	$970	10.3	16.5	$ 764.1	$1,306	36.0
PEI	10	904	5.7	12.0	170.6	1,283	33.0
N.S.	11	802	3.3	13.5	1,011.5	1,089	34.2
N.B.	11	943	3.3	10.7	914.3	1,211	29.2
Quebec	6.5	800	1.9	15.2	7,507.2	1,041	21.3
Ontario	8	846	1.7	14.7	11,972.9	1,112	27.9
Manitoba	7	623	8.0	11.5	1,081.3	964	21.8
Sask.	9	735	8.0	15.0	1,222.3	1,210	25.4
Alberta	–	–	7.0	9.0	906.0	338	6.5
B.C.	7	847	11.0	10.0	4,406.1	1,241	20.0
NWT	–	–	12.4	9.6	29.0	460	10.1
Yukon	–	–	8.2	6.2	14.9	497	11.5

*Based on 1993 population figures.

SOURCE: Karin Treff and David Perry, *Finances of the Nation, 1996* (Toronto: Canadian Tax Foundation, 1997), ch. 5; Statistics Canada, *Public Sector Finances 1995–1996*, Cat. no. 68-212-XPB (Ottawa: March 1996).

22.5 and Table 22.6. Excise taxes on motor fuels, at about $0.20 per litre, were expected to raise $10 billion in 1994/95, with other excise taxes contributing $4.8 billion. This, at $500 per capita or $1,000 for a married couple, is substantial. Tax authorities are able to collect the bulk of these tax revenues from the relatively few producers of motor fuels, alcoholic beverages, and tobacco

Table 22.6

Rates for Federal Excise Taxes and Duties, 1996

A. Federal Excise Taxes

Gasoline	10.0¢/litre
Diesel and aviation fuel	4.0¢/litre
Cigarettes*	13.388¢/5 cigarettes
Manufactured tobacco	$10.648/kg
Cigars	3.9¢ or 50%
Tobacco sticks	1.065¢/stick
Wines	
Alcohol, 1.2% or less	2.05¢/litre
Alcohol, 1.2% to 7%	24.59¢/litre
Alcohol, over 7%	51.22¢/litre
Automobile air conditioners	$100/unit
Jewellery	10%
Watches, clocks	10%

B. Federal Excise Duties (in addition to the federal excise taxes)

Distilled spirits	$11.066/litre of alcohol
Mixed beverages up to 7% alcohol	24.59¢/litre
Beer	
Up to 1.2% alcohol	$2.591/hectolitre
1.2% to 2.5% alcohol	$13.9909/hectolitre
Over 2.5% alcohol	$27.985/hectolitre
Cigarettes	
Up to 1,361 grams per 100	$27.475/1,000
Over 1,361 grams per 100	$29.374/1,000
Cigars	$14.786/1,000
Manufactured tobacco	$18.333/kg
Raw leaf tobacco	$1.572/kg
Tobacco sticks	$18.333/1,000

*The federal government entered into agreements with several provinces to cut cigarette taxes in 1994 in order to address a serious smuggling problem. This resulted in the variation in federal excise taxes on cigarettes found in Table 22.2. The rate given here is that which applied outside of PEI, Nova Scotia, New Brunswick, Quebec, and Ontario.

SOURCE: Karin Treff and David Perry, *Finances of the Nation, 1996* (Toronto: Canadian Tax Foundation, 1997), p. 5:10, Tables 5.4 and 5.5.

products, or at time of import. Although excise taxes are generally among the easiest and most cost-effective to administer, the explosion in cigarette smuggling in 1993 and 1994 made clear that there are limits on the use of excise taxes as a source of revenue.[24]

PERSONAL CONSUMPTION TAX

A major objection to both retail sales taxes and value-added taxes, such as the GST, and many excise taxes is that they do not allow personal circumstances to be considered when determining tax liabilities. In particular, differentiating among people on the basis of ability to pay is difficult.

In contrast, a personal tax based on total consumption expenditures during a given period allows the tax authorities to take individual characteristics into account in determining tax liability. Under a **personal consumption tax** (also referred to as a **personal expenditure tax**), each household files a return reporting its consumption expenditures during the year. Table 22.7 outlines how this might be done. Unlike an income tax, the base of a consumption tax excludes unconsumed additions to wealth—saving. Whereas under a personal income tax the tax base is defined as:

$$income = consumption + change\ in\ net\ wealth,$$

under a personal consumption tax the tax base is:

$$consumption = income - change\ in\ net\ wealth.$$

Moreover, just as under the personal income tax, various exemptions and deductions can be taken to allow for special circumstances such as extraordinary medical expenses. Each individual's tax bill is then determined by applying a rate schedule to the adjusted amount of consumption. The rate schedule can be as progressive as policy makers desire.

Some argue that if the income tax were replaced by a consumption tax, efficiency, equity, and administrative simplicity would be enhanced. Indeed, it is argued that we are well on our way to a consumption tax, and that "a con-

---

[24] Revenues from excise taxes on tobacco and alcoholic beverages rose from $5.04 billion in 1988/89 to $7.36 billion in 1991/92, an increase of 46 percent over three years. Higher taxes resulted in a rampant increase in tax evasion through smuggling. To reduce the incentive to evade these taxes, rates were lowered sharply in early 1994 in Quebec, Ontario, and the Maritime provinces, and revenues in 1994/95 were expected to be $4.77 billion, somewhat below the 1988/89 level.

Table 22.7

Calculating a Personal Consumption Tax

Include:
- wages, salaries, interest, dividends, rent, profits, royalties, transfer payments, and other income (excluding capital gains)
- proceeds from the sale of real and financial assets
- proceeds from borrowing
- gifts and bequests
- withdrawals from savings accounts and other investments

Deduct:
- cost of real and financial assets purchased
- capital contributed to partnerships or proprietorships
- repayment of interest and principal on borrowed funds
- deposits into savings accounts and other investments
- other permitted deductions, such as extraordinary medical expenses, as might also be provided under an income tax

Equals:
- tax base

Tax base × applicable tax rates = tax liability

---

sumption tax can essentially be achieved by extending the RPP and RRSP provisions which currently exist in the present system."[25] The defenders of the income tax have argued that the case for expenditure taxation is seriously flawed. We now discuss the controversy.[26]

Efficiency Issues

The efficiency implications of personal consumption versus income taxation can be examined using the life-cycle model of consumption and saving introduced in Chapter 21. In that model, the individual's labour supply in each period is fixed. The two commodities she purchases are present consumption, c_0, and future consumption, c_1. If r is the interest rate, every additional dollar of consumption today means that the individual's future consumption is reduced by $(1 + r)$. Hence, the relative price of c_0—its opportunity cost—is $(1 + r)$.

Consider now the case of Juliet, on whom a 30 percent income tax is levied. Assuming that the tax allows for the deductibility of interest payments, how

---

[25] Beach, Boadway, and Bruce (1988: 106).
[26] For a good discussion of the pros and cons, see Minarik (1980).

does this affect the relative price of c_0?[27] If Juliet saves a dollar and it earns a return of r, the government taxes away 30 percent of the return, leaving her only $.70 \times r$. If she borrows a dollar, the interest payments are deductible, so the cost of borrowing is reduced to $.70 \times r$. In short, as a consequence of the income tax, the relative price of present consumption falls from $(1 + r)$ to $(1 + .70r)$. A wedge is inserted between the amount a borrower pays and a lender receives. As we showed in Chapter 18, the presence of such a tax wedge creates an excess burden. We conclude that an income tax generates an excess burden.

Now consider a consumption tax that raises the same amount of revenue as the income tax. The key thing to note in this context is that the consumption tax leaves unchanged the market rate of return available to Juliet. This is because the receipt of interest income by itself does not create a tax liability—only consuming it does. Hence, after the consumption tax, the relative price of c_0 is still $(1 + r)$. Unlike the income tax, there seems to be no tax wedge, and hence no excess burden. Apparently, consumption taxation is superior to income taxation on efficiency grounds.

Is this result general, or is it a consequence of some special assumptions? Recall that in Chapter 18 a similar argument was used to "prove" that taxes at equal rates on all commodities are always more efficient than differential rates on different commodities. We showed there the fallacy in that argument. Once it is recognized that even an equiproportional tax distorts the choice between leisure and each of the taxed commodities, it is no longer clear that taxing all commodities at the same rate is efficient. The same consideration applies here. The argument in the preceding paragraphs was built on the *assumption* that the supply of labour is fixed. Once the possibility is raised that labour-supply decisions are choices, it is no longer true that the consumption tax is *necessarily* more efficient than an income tax.

True, unlike the income tax, the consumption tax leaves unchanged the rate at which Juliet can trade off consumption between the two periods. However, in general, the consumption tax *does* distort the rate at which she can trade off leisure against consumption. Suppose Juliet's wage rate is w. Before the consumption tax, she can trade off one hour of leisure for w dollars' worth of consumption. If consumption is taxed at rate t_c, however, surrendering one hour of leisure allows her only $w/(1 + t_c)$ dollars' worth of consumption. Thus, the consumption tax distorts the decision between leisure and consumption. In short, as long as labour supply is a matter of choice, both income and con-

---

[27] As stressed in Chapters 20 and 21, not all taxpayers can deduct payments of interest. As an exercise, discuss how the following analysis is modified when interest is not deductible.

sumption taxes distort some decisions. Therefore, both systems induce an efficiency cost, and only empirical work can determine which tax's cost is smaller.

Several studies have suggested that given what is known about labour supply and saving behaviour, a consumption tax creates a smaller excess burden than an income tax, even when labour-supply distortions created by both taxes are taken into account. For example, the Economic Council of Canada (1987: 15) concluded that a move to a form of personal consumption tax from the personal income tax would, at a minimum, lead to "an early increase of 1 percent in the annual income of the average Canadian," and given the expected impact the change would have on savings and investment, the Council suggested that such a change would increase living standards by 7 percent over a longer period.[28] However, such results are quite sensitive to assumptions about the responsiveness of consumption to changes in the interest rate. As we saw in Chapter 21, this is notoriously hard to measure. As research on saving behaviour progresses, our understanding of the efficiency aspects of income versus consumption taxation will improve.

Equity Issues

Progressiveness. Earlier we noted the widespread assumption that sales taxes are regressive. Whatever the merits of this view, there is an unfortunate tendency to assume that it applies to any tax with consumption as a base. This is simply wrong. Given that the base of the tax being considered here is *personal* consumption expenditures, the structure can be made as progressive as desired.

Nonetheless, a shift from a personal income tax to a personal consumption tax involves a move away from the taxation of income from capital to the taxation of income from labour (a tax on consumption can be shown to be the equivalent of a tax on wages if net bequests are zero).[29] With income from capital concentrated in the hands of those with higher incomes, such a shift requires a transition period with rate and base changes that limit windfall gains to owners of capital.[30]

Ability to pay. Those who favour the income base argue that *actual* consumption is merely one component of *potential* consumption. It is the power

---

[28] See Economic Council of Canada (1987).

[29] See Stiglitz (1986: 362).

[30] In considering a shift to a personal consumption tax in the United States, Minarik (1985: 95) comments that "the American public might well reject a system that eliminated taxation of income from property and put the entire tax burden on labour.... A personal expenditure tax would ... be the sharpest reversal from the tax principles that the public has come to hold—taxation according to ability to pay, measured by total income."

to consume, not necessarily its exercise, that is relevant. They point out that under a consumption tax, it would be possible for a miserly millionaire to have a smaller tax liability than a much poorer person. A possible response is that it is fairer to tax an individual according to what he or she "takes out" of the economic system, in the form of consumption, than what he or she "contributes" to society, as measured by income. As Thomas Hobbes said in the seventeenth century:

> For what reason is there, that he which laboureth much, and sparing the fruit of his labour, consumeth little, should be more charged, than he that liveth idly, getteth little, and spendeth all he gets; seeing the one hath no more protection from the commonwealth than the other. (1651/1963: 303)

From this point of view, if the miserly millionaire chooses not to consume very much, that is all to the good, because the resources he or she saves become available to society for capital accumulation.

A related question is whether or not an income tax results in double taxation of interest income. Some argue that an income tax is unfair because it taxes capital income twice: once when the original income is earned, and again when the investment produces a return. However, the logic of income taxation impels that the return to saving be taxed. Whether or not this is fair depends, as usual, on value judgments. The debate is likely to continue.

Annual versus lifetime equity. Events that influence a person's economic position for only a very short time do not provide an adequate basis for determining ability to pay. Indeed, some have argued that ideally tax liabilities should be related to lifetime income. Proponents of consumption taxation point out that an annual income tax leads to tax burdens that can differ quite substantially even for people who have the same lifetime wealth.

To see why, consider Mr. Grasshopper and Ms. Ant, both of whom live for two periods. In the present, they have identical fixed labour incomes of I_0, and in the future, they both have labour incomes of zero. (The assumption of zero second-period income is made solely for convenience.) Grasshopper chooses to consume heavily early in life because he is not very concerned about his retirement years. Ant chooses to consume most of her wealth later in life, because she wants a lavish retirement.

Define Ant's present consumption in the presence of a proportional income tax as c_0^A, and Grasshopper's as c_0^G. By assumption, $c_0^G > c_0^A$. Ant's future income before tax is the interest she earns on her savings: $r(I_0 - c_0^A)$. Similarly,

Grasshopper's future income before tax is $r(I_0 - c_0{}^G)$. Now, if the proportional income tax rate is t, in the present Ant and Grasshopper have identical tax liabilities of tI_0. However, in the future, Ant's tax liability is $tr(I_0 - c_0{}^A)$, while Grasshopper's is $tr(I_0 - c_0{}^G)$. Because $c_0{}^G > c_0{}^A$, Ant's future tax liability is higher. Solely because Ant has a greater taste for saving than Grasshopper, her lifetime tax burden (the discounted sum of her tax burdens in the two periods) is greater than Grasshopper's.

In contrast, under a proportional consumption tax, lifetime tax burdens are *independent* of tastes for saving, other things being the same.[31] To prove this, all we need to do is write down the equation for each taxpayer's budget constraint. Because all of Ant's noncapital income (I_0) comes in the present, its present value is simply I_0. Now, the present value of lifetime consumption must equal the present value of lifetime income. Hence, Ant's consumption pattern must satisfy the relation

$$I_0 = c_0{}^A + [c_1{}^A/(1 + r)]. \tag{22.1}$$

Similarly, Grasshopper is constrained by

$$I_0 = c_0{}^G + [c_1{}^G/(1 + r)]. \tag{22.2}$$

Equations (22.1) and (22.2) say simply that the lifetime value of income must equal the lifetime value of consumption.

If the proportional consumption tax rate is t_c, Ant's tax liability in the first period is $t_c c_0{}^A$; her tax liability in the second period is $t_c c_1{}^A$; and the present value of her lifetime consumption tax liability, $R_c{}^A$, is

$$R_c{}^A = t_c c_0{}^A + [t_c c_1{}^A/(1 + r)]. \tag{22.3}$$

Similarly, Grasshopper's lifetime tax liability is

$$R_c{}^G = t_c c_0{}^G + [t_c c_1{}^G/(1 + r)]. \tag{22.4}$$

By comparing Equations (22.3) and (22.1), we see that Ant's lifetime tax liability is equal to $t_c I_0$. [Just multiply Equation (22.1) through by t_c.] Similar comparison of Equations (22.2) and (22.4) indicates that Grasshopper's life-

---

[31] However, when marginal tax rates depend on the level of consumption, this may not be the case.

time tax liability is also t_cI_0. We conclude that under a proportional consumption tax, two people with identical lifetime incomes always pay identical lifetime taxes (where lifetime is interpreted in the present value sense). This stands in stark contrast to a proportional income tax, where the pattern of lifetime consumption influences lifetime tax burdens.

A related argument in favour of the consumption tax centres on the fact that income tends to fluctuate more than consumption. In years when income is unusually low, individuals may draw on their savings or borrow to smooth out fluctuations in their consumption levels. Annual consumption is likely to be a better reflection of lifetime circumstances than is annual income.[32]

Opponents of consumption taxation would question whether a lifetime point of view is really appropriate. There is too much uncertainty in both the political and economic environments for a lifetime perspective to be very realistic. Moreover, the consumption smoothing described in the lifetime arguments requires that individuals be able to save and borrow freely at the going rate of interest. Given that individuals often face constraints on the amounts they can borrow, it is not clear how relevant the lifetime arguments are. Although a considerable body of empirical work suggests the life-cycle model is a good representation for most households (see King, 1993), this argument still deserves some consideration. Opponents also note that a shift to a personal consumption tax from a personal income tax would lower taxes when income is high relative to consumption, and raise taxes when income is low relative to consumption. Thus, the switch to a consumption tax would increase taxes in tough times, increasing hardship, and lower them in good times.

Administrative Issues

In discussions of personal consumption taxation, administrative issues are of more than usual interest. This is because such a tax system has never been implemented successfully.[33] Indeed, for many years, a consumption tax has been viewed mostly as an intellectual curiosity rather than a realistic policy option. But recently, growing numbers of economists and lawyers have suggested that a consumption tax is feasible and not as different from the current income tax system as one might think.[34]

---

[32] A tax on consumption is a tax on lifetime income if the tax return in the year of death includes all bequests as part of consumption in the final year. In this case, all income over a lifetime is consumed.

[33] India and Sri Lanka were the only two countries to adopt a consumption tax, and both nations soon abandoned it.

[34] See, for example, Economic Council of Canada (1987); Beach, Boadway, and Bruce (1988: ch. 10); Bradford (1986: chs. 5 and 14); Kay and King (1990: chs. 6 and 7).

If the only way to compute annual consumption were to add up all expenditures made over the course of a year, taxpayers would have to keep records and receipts for every purchase. This would be administratively infeasible. All taxpayers cannot be expected to maintain complete balance sheets.

An alternative is to measure consumption on a cash flow basis, meaning that it would be calculated simply as the difference between all cash receipts and saving. To keep track of saving, qualified accounts would be established at savings banks, security brokerage houses, and other types of financial institutions. Funds that were certified by these institutions as having been deposited in qualified accounts would be exempt from tax. Most of the record-keeping responsibility would be met by these institutions and would not involve more paperwork than exists already. As long as capital gains and interest from such accounts were retained, they would not be taxed. For some taxpayers, such qualified accounts already exist in the forms of Registered Retirement Savings Plans (RRSPs) and Registered Pension Plans (RPPs) (see Chapter 20). One way to look at a consumption tax is simply as an expansion of the opportunities to invest in such accounts.

A potentially important administrative problem concerns the valuation of the consumption benefits produced by durable goods. The purchase of a durable is an act of saving and hence would be deductible under a consumption tax. Over time, the durable generates consumption benefits subject to tax. But here the usual problems of imputing consumption streams arise. How do we measure the annual flow of benefits produced by a house or a car?

Proponents of a consumption tax argue that this problem is avoidable if a **tax prepayment approach** for durables is used. When the original durable investment is made, it is taxed as if it were consumption. There is no attempt later to tax the returns generated by the investment. Thus, imputation problems are avoided. But does prepayment yield the appropriate amount of tax? In present value terms, tax prepayment does indeed yield the right amount as long as the tax rate is fixed. To see why, suppose that the durable lasts for T years and produces expected consumption benefits of c_1 in year 1, c_2 in year 2, and so forth. In equilibrium, the price of the durable, V, just equals the present value of the stream of consumption the durable generates:

$$V = c_1/(1 + r) + c_2/(1 + r)^2 + ... + c_T/(1 + r)^T \qquad (22.5)$$

where r is the interest rate. Now, if consumption is taxed at rate t_c, revenue collections under the tax prepayment approach are $t_c V$. On the other hand, if consumption is taxed when it occurs, the present value of the tax proceeds (R_c) is

$$R_c = t_c c_1/(1 + r) + t_c c_2/(1 + r)^2 + \ldots + t_c c_T/(1 + r)^T. \qquad (22.6)$$

Examining Equations (22.5) and (22.6) together, we note that R_c is exactly equal to $t_c V$. Hence, the same amount of tax is collected in present value terms.

Advantages of a consumption tax. Although many people have become convinced that consumption taxation is practical, many others believe it would be an administrative nightmare. We now catalogue some advantages and disadvantages of consumption taxation relative to income taxation and also note a few problems that are common to both.

No need to measure capital gains and depreciation. Some of the most vexing problems in administering an income tax arise from difficulties in measuring additions to wealth. For example, it requires calculation of capital gains and losses even on those assets not sold during the year, a task so difficult that it is not even attempted under the current system. Similarly, for those who have income produced by capital equipment, additions to wealth must be lowered by the amount the equipment depreciates during the year. As we note in Chapter 24, very little is known about actual depreciation patterns. One result of our inability to accurately measure depreciation is the variation in effective tax rates on income arising from different investments. Although the total level of investment may be little affected by our choice between an income or consumption tax, the income tax may lead to a very inefficient allocation of capital. Andrews (1983: 282) views the inability of real-world income tax systems to measure and tax additions to wealth as their fatal flaw: "A comprehensive income tax ideal with an immediate concession that taxation is not to be based on actual value is like a blueprint for constructing a building in which part of the foundation is required to be located in quicksand. If the terrain cannot be changed, the blueprint had better be amended." Under a consumption tax, all such problems disappear because additions to wealth per se are no longer part of the tax base.

Fewer problems with inflation. In the presence of a non-indexed income tax, inflation creates important distortions. Some of these are a consequence of a progressive rate structure, but some would occur even if the tax were proportional. These distortions occur because computing capital income requires the use of figures from years that have different price levels. For example, if an asset is sold, calculation of the capital gain or loss requires subtracting the value in the year of purchase from its value in the current year. In general, part of the change in value is due to inflation, so individuals are taxed on gains that do not reflect increases in real income, and the lock-in effect may be signifi-

cant.[35] With a consumption tax, the sale of an asset results in no change in the tax base if the proceeds of the sale are reinvested in the same year.

As noted in Chapter 20, setting up an appropriate scheme for fully indexing income generated by investments is very complicated and has not been attempted in Canada. In contrast, under a consumption tax, calculation of the tax base involves only current-year transactions. Therefore, any distortions associated with inflation are likely to be much less of a problem.

No need for separate corporation tax. Some argue that implementation of a consumption tax would allow removal of the corporation income tax, at least in theory. We will see in Chapter 24 that one of the main justifications of the corporation tax is to get at income that people accumulate in corporations. If accumulation per se were no longer part of the personal income tax base, this would not be necessary. Elimination of the corporation tax would probably enhance efficiency. However, to receive part of the profit generated by foreign-owned companies operating in Canada, withholding on income arising in Canada would continue to be necessary.

Advocates of the consumption tax often point out that adoption would not be as radical a move as first appearances might suggest. In some respects, the present system *already* looks very much like a consumption tax:

1. For some taxpayers, income is exempt from taxation when it is saved in certain forms such as RRSPs and RPPs.
2. Unrealized capital gains on financial assets are untaxed, as are virtually all capital gains on housing.
3. Accelerated depreciation reduces the amount of investment purchases included in the tax base.

In light of these considerations, characterizing the status quo as an income tax is a serious misnomer; it is more a hybrid between income and consumption taxation.

Disadvantages of a consumption tax. Critics of personal consumption taxation have noted a number of disadvantages.

---

[35] Suppose, for example, that Smith buys an asset for $100. After a year, the asset is worth $200, but the price level has also doubled. In real terms, there has been no increase in income, yet Smith nevertheless has incurred a tax liability.

Administrative problems. Opponents of consumption taxation believe that it would lead to increased monitoring and accounting costs. They argue that even if the cash flow method were adopted, people would have to keep more records with respect to their asset positions. The tax prepayment approach, which is central to the taxation of durables under a consumption tax, has also been criticized. Equation (22.5) indicates the relation between the expected benefits of an investment and its cost. But these returns cannot be known with certainty. If the stream of c's turns out to be higher than expected, the tax prepayment plan would result in a tax liability that is lower than it would be otherwise. Similarly, if the c's are lower, tax prepayment results in higher liabilities. Critics argue that taxes should be based on outcomes, not expectations, so that the tax prepayment approach is fundamentally unfair.

Transitional problems. Critics also argue that despite already existing elements of consumption taxation in the present system, the switch to a consumption tax would be a major one and would be accompanied by enormous transitional problems. During the transition, people would have incentives to conceal their assets and to liquidate them later without reporting the proceeds. Moreover, during the transition, the elderly generation would be hurt by moving to a consumption tax. During their working years, they accumulated wealth to consume during retirement. The interest, dividends, and realized capital gains that they received along the way were subject to the personal income tax. A reasonable expectation for such people is that when they reach retirement, their consumption would not be subject to new taxes. If a personal consumption tax were suddenly introduced, however, these expectations would be disappointed. Clearly, equity—not to mention political feasibility—requires some method for compensating the elderly during the transition. This problem arises in any major tax reform—people who have made commitments on the basis of the existing system are likely to be hurt when it changes. Fairness would seem to require that the elderly be compensated for the losses they would incur during the transition. Those advocating the consumption tax have proposed a number of rules for alleviating transitional problems (see Sarkar and Zodrow, 1993).

Gifts and bequests. The discussion surrounding Equations (22.1) through (22.4) demonstrated that in a simple life-cycle model, a proportional consumption tax is equivalent to a tax on lifetime income. Contrary to the assumptions of the life-cycle model, some people set aside part of their lifetime income for gifts and bequests. How should such transfers be treated under a consumption tax? One view is that there is no need to tax gifts and bequests until they are consumed by their recipients. On the other hand, others argue that gifts and bequests should be treated as consumption on the part of the donor. Hence, gifts and bequests should be taxed at the time the transfer is made. Proponents of this view point out that it would not be politically viable to institute a tax system that allowed substantial amounts of wealth to accumulate free of tax, and then failed to tax it on transfer. However, as explained later, major conceptual and practical problems are involved in taxing transfers of wealth.

Problems with both systems. Even the most enthusiastic proponents of the consumption tax recognize that its adoption would not usher in an era of tax nirvana. Several of the most intractable problems inherent in the income tax system would also plague any consumption tax. These include, but are not limited to:

1. Distinguishing consumption commodities from commodities used in production. (Should a desk purchased for use at home be considered consumption or a business expense?)
2. Defining consumption itself. (Are health care expenditures part of consumption, or should they be deductible?)
3. Choosing the unit of taxation and determining an appropriate rate structure.
4. Valuing fringe benefits of various occupations. (If a job gives a person access to the company swimming pool, should the consumption benefits be taxed? If so, how can they be valued?)
5. Determining a method for averaging across time if the schedule has increasing marginal tax rates.
6. Valuing, for tax purposes, production that occurs in the home.
7. Minimizing tax-created incentives to participate in the underground economy.

Finally, we emphasize that it is not quite fair to compare an ideal consumption tax to the actual income tax. Historically, special interests have persuaded politicians to tax certain types of income preferentially. Adoption of a consumption tax could hardly be expected to eliminate political corruption of the tax structure. One pessimistic observer has suggested, "I find the choice between the consumption base and the income base an almost sterile debate; we do not tax all income now, and were we to adopt a consumption tax system, we would end up exempting as much consumption from the tax base as we do income now."[36] It is hard to predict whether a real-world consumption tax would be better than the current system.

---

[36] Emil Sunley, quoted in Makin (1985: 20).

SUMMARY

- Sales taxes may be levied per unit or as a percentage of purchase value (ad valorem), on all (general sales tax) or specific (excise tax) purchases. General sales and excise taxes are important revenue sources for both the federal and the provincial governments.

- A major attraction of general sales taxes and selective sales taxes is that they are relatively easy to administer. Some sales taxes, such as the excise taxes on tobacco products, alcoholic beverages, and motor fuels, can be justified as correctives for externalities or as substitutes for user fees.

- Taxes on consumption, both general sales taxes and selective taxes, are typically viewed as regressive. However, this view is based on calculations involving annual rather than lifetime income, and assumes that the incidence of the tax lies with the purchaser.

- The Goods and Services Tax (GST) is a value-added tax (VAT). This multi-stage tax, although levied on a similar tax base, differs from a single-stage retail sales tax (RST), which is collected only upon the sale of the final good to the consumer. A VAT is levied on the difference between sales revenue and cost of purchased commodity inputs at all stages of production. Depending on the treatment of capital inputs, a VAT may be equivalent to a tax on consumption, net income, or gross income. The GST treats investment goods like any other material goods, permitting their full value to be subtracted from sales in the tax computation, and is therefore a consumption-type VAT.

- The base of a personal consumption tax is found by subtracting additions to wealth from income: consumption = income – change in net wealth.

- Proponents of the personal consumption tax argue that it eliminates double taxation of interest income, promotes lifetime equity, taxes individuals on the basis of the amount of economic resources they use, may be adjusted to achieve any desired level of progressiveness, and is administratively superior to an income tax.

- Opponents of the personal consumption tax point out difficult transition problems, argue that income better measures ability to pay, feel that it is administratively burdensome, and argue that in the absence of appropriate taxes on gifts and bequests, it would lead to an excessive concentration of wealth.

- Canada's income tax system includes preferential treatment of some forms of savings—for example, RRSP and RPP contributions. Thus, the current income tax system is a hybrid system that includes characteristics of both a personal income tax and a personal consumption tax.

DISCUSSION QUESTIONS

1. "Because the tax base includes the purchase of necessities, both general sales taxes and personal consumption taxes are regressive." Discuss.

2. Discuss carefully the following quotation: "It is reasonable to assume ... that business can pass along the full value of the [value-added] tax to final consumers. But if [it is assumed that] businesses have the power to raise prices a dollar for each dollar they pay in value-added taxes, then it should also [be] assume[d] businesses can similarly raise prices against every dollar they now pay in payroll and corporate income taxes" (Cockburn and Pollin, 1992: A15).

3. Measuring income on an accrual basis creates serious problems for an income tax system. Explain the nature of these problems and how a shift to a personal consumption tax would help to eliminate the problems.

4. Consider the following statement: "I am in favour of a personal consumption tax, but only if bequests and gifts are included in the tax base. It is only in this way that a personal consumption tax becomes equivalent to a tax on lifetime income." Explain the logic behind the statement.

REFERENCES

Aaron, Henry J. "Introduction and Summary," in *The Value-Added Tax: Lessons from Europe*, ed. Henry J. Aaron. Washington, DC: Brookings Institution, 1981, pp. 1–18.

Andrews, William D. "The Achilles' Heel of the Comprehensive Income Tax," in *New Directions in Federal Tax Policy for the 1980s*, ed. Charles E. Walker and Mark A. Bloomfield. Cambridge, MA: Ballinger, 1983, pp. 278–84.

Atkinson, A.B., and J.E. Stiglitz. *Lectures on Public Economics*. New York: McGraw-Hill, 1980.

Beach, Charles M., Robin W. Boadway, and Neil Bruce. *Taxation and Savings in Canada*. Ottawa: Economic Council of Canada, 1988.

Bird, Richard M. *Where Do We Go From Here? Alternatives to the GST*. Toronto: KPMG Centre for Government, April 1994.

Bradford, David F. *Untangling the Income Tax*. Cambridge: Harvard University Press, 1986.

Cockburn, Alexander, and Robert Pollin. "Why the Left Should Support the Flat Tax." *The Wall Street Journal*, April 2, 1992, p. A15.

Davies, J., F. St-Hilaire, and J. Whalley. "Some Calculations of Lifetime Tax Incidence." *American Economic Review 74*, no. 4 (September 1984).

Department of Finance. *Goods and Services Tax: An Overview*. Ottawa: August 1989.

Department of Finance, The Honourable Michael H. Wilson. *The White Paper: Tax Reform 1987*. Ottawa: June 18, 1987.

Economic Council of Canada. *Road Map for Tax Reform: The Taxation of Savings and Investment*. Ottawa: 1987.

Friedman, Milton. *A Theory of the Consumption Function*. Princeton, NJ: Princeton University Press, 1957.

Hamilton, Bob, and John Whalley. "Efficiency and Distributional Effects of the Tax Reform Package," in *The Economic Impacts of Tax Reform*, ed. Jack Mintz and John Whalley. Toronto: Canadian Tax Foundation, 1989.

Hobbes, Thomas. *Leviathan*. New York: Meridian Books, 1963 (1651).

House of Commons, Standing Committee on Finance. *Replacing the GST: Options for Canada*. Ottawa: June 1994.

Kay, J.A., and M.A. King. *The British Tax System*. Oxford: Oxford University Press, 1990.

King, Robert G. "Will the New Keynesian Macroeconomics Resurrect the IS-LM Model?" *Journal of Economic Perspectives* 7 (Winter 1993): 67–82.

Landon, Stuart, and David L. Ryan. "The Political Costs of Taxes and Government Spending." Working Paper, Department of Economics, University of Alberta. Edmonton: 1996.

Makin, John H. *Real Tax Reform—Replacing the Income Tax*. Washington, DC: American Enterprise Institute for Public Policy Research, 1985.

Metcalf, Gilbert E. "Life Cycle Versus Annual Perspectives on the Incidence of a Value Added Tax," in *Tax Policy and the Economy, Volume 8*, ed. J. Poterba. Cambridge: MIT Press, 1994.

Metcalf, Gilbert E. "The Life-Cycle Incidence of State and Local Taxes: Measuring Changes during the 1980s." Working Paper 4252. Cambridge, MA: National Bureau of Economic Research, January 1993.

Minarik, Joseph J. *Making Tax Choices*. Washington, DC: The Urban Institute, 1985.

Minarik, Joseph J. "Conference Discussion," in *What Should Be Taxed: Income or Expenditure?* ed. J.A. Pechman. Washington, DC: Brookings Institution, 1980.

Sandford, C., M. Godwin, and P. Hardwick. *Administrative and Compliance Costs of Taxation*. Perrymead: Fiscal Publications, 1989.

Sarkar, Shounak, and George R. Zodrow. "Transitional Issues in Moving to a Direct Consumption Tax." *National Tax Journal* 46, no. 3 (September 1993): 359–76.

Smith, Roger S. "Comments on Canada's Underground Economy." *Information Bulletin No. 18*. Western Centre for Economic Research, University of Alberta. Edmonton: December 1993.

Spiro, Peter. "Estimating the Underground Economy: A Critical Evaluation of the Monetary Approach." *Canadian Tax Journal* 42, no. 4 (1994).

Spiro, Peter. "Evidence of a Post-GST Increase in the Underground Economy." *Canadian Tax Journal* 41, no. 2 (1993).

Stiglitz, J.E. *Economics of the Public Sector*. New York: W.W. Norton, 1986.

Stockfisch, J.A. "Value-Added Taxes and the Size of Government: Some Evidence." *National Tax Journal* 38, no. 4 (December 1985): 547–52.

Tait, Alan A. *Value Added Tax: International Practice and Problems*. Washington, DC: International Monetary Fund, 1988.

Vermaeten, A., W.I. Gillespie, and F. Vermaeten. "Who Paid the Taxes in Canada, 1951–1988." *Canadian Public Policy* 21, no. 3 (September 1995).

Chapter 23

Taxes on Wealth and Property

'What I, therefore, propose, as the simple yet sovereign remedy, which will raise wages, increase the earnings of capital, extirpate pauperism, abolish poverty, give remunerative employment to whoever wishes it, afford free scope to human powers, lessen crime, elevate morals, and taste, and intelligence, purify government and carry civilization to yet nobler heights, is— to expropriate rent by taxation.

–Henry George[1]

The taxes we have discussed so far are levied on items such as income, consumption, and sales. In the jargon of economics, these are known as **flow variables** because they are associated with a time dimension. For instance, income is a flow, because the concept is meaningful only when put in the context of some time interval. If you say, "My income is $10,000," it means nothing unless one knows whether it is over a week, month, or year. A **stock variable**, on the other hand, has no time dimension. It is a quantity at a point in time, not a rate per unit of time. Wealth is a stock, because it refers to the value of the assets an individual has accumulated as of a given time. This section discusses some taxes that are levied on some form of wealth.

WEALTH TAXES

There are many types of wealth taxes. The tax in Canada that most closely resembles a tax on *personal* wealth is the tax on owner-occupied homes,

---

[1] Henry George, *Progress and Poverty* (New York: The Modern Library, originally published in 1879), pp. 405–6.

which is a major tax revenue source for local governments. Other forms of taxation on wealth in Canada are the taxes levied on business properties by provincial and local governments and the taxes on "paid-up" capital[2] of corporations now used by the federal government and all provincial governments. With none of these taxes, however, is the amount of revenue collected closely related to personal circumstances of individual taxpayers. In the case of property taxes on home-owners, the tax does not reflect the equity of the home-owner—that is, the value of the house net of the mortgage. Instead, it is based on the gross value of the real estate. The net wealth of a taxpayer with a $100,000 home and $75,000 mortgage may be $25,000, but the tax due is still based on the $100,000 value. Similarly, taxes on paid-up capital of corporations and on business property do not reflect individual circumstances, and the incidence of such taxes is far from certain.

Some forms of wealth taxation used in other countries are more closely related to personal circumstances, and allow for an adjustment for liabilities. An example is an *annual tax on the net wealth* of the individual taxpayer. "Net wealth" for such a tax is normally the market value of the nonhuman capital owned by the taxpayer net of his or her liabilities. An *inheritance tax* and *gift tax* can also be adjusted to reflect individual circumstances—the wealth or income of the recipient, or the total amounts received as bequests or gifts. An *estate tax* based on the net value of an estate at the time of death reflects individual wealth at a point in time, although it may be a poor reflection of the taxpaying ability of heirs. Net wealth taxes (NWTs) and death (inheritance and estate) taxes are to some degree adjusted to personal circumstances.

Some wealth taxes, such as the estate tax levied at time of death, are applied once in a generation. Other taxes are applied annually; these include taxes on immovable property in Canada, and annual net wealth taxes elsewhere. Still others are applied periodically, such as gift taxes, which are levied whenever gifts occur. A once-a-generation tax, such as an estate tax, may be levied at relatively high rates (often over 50 percent), while annual net wealth taxes and taxes on immovable properties are generally applied at rates ranging from well below 1 percent to less than 5 percent.

With increased movement of capital and labour across national borders there has been growing reluctance to tax factors of production that are particularly

---

[2] The definition of paid-up capital varies somewhat in federal and provincial statutes. Paid-up capital generally includes the amount received by corporations on stock that has been issued after deducting discounts given and including premiums received. It also includes items such as government grants, retained earnings, all long- and short-term loans from banks and other financial institutions, and all loans from other corporations or shareholders.

mobile. Policy makers have become less willing to rely on taxes that fall on capital such as those on corporate income, capital gains, business properties, personal net wealth, or the transfer of wealth. Evidence of rapid growth in countries with a high rate of private saving—Japan, Taiwan, Korea—has also led to a desire for policies that are believed to encourage saving and the accumulation of capital. Although the evidence is mixed on how the after-tax rate of return affects private saving, in the absence of conclusive evidence countries attempt to encourage saving by reducing taxes on the return to some forms of saving. Thus, a wish to increase private saving as well as the concern over factor mobility has decreased the emphasis placed on taxes that fall on wealth, relative to other taxes, over the past twenty-five years.[3] Establishing and maintaining records of property ownership (e.g., art, coin, and stamp collections), and valuing such property, is accompanied by a substantial set of administrative problems.

Even with the difficulties associated with implementation of such taxes, proponents continue to argue for increased taxation of personal wealth. Why? We saw in Chapter 10 that the distribution of (annual) income in Canada is quite unequal. Evidence suggests that the distribution of wealth may be even more unequal. Statistics Canada estimated that the top 10 percent of wealth holders owned 51.3 percent of wealth in Canada in 1984 (see Table 23.1), and the top 1 percent may own around 25 percent of total wealth. With the rise in value of North American common stocks, the concentration may increase significantly by 1997 (see Wolff, 1995). Hence, proponents of taxes on personal wealth argue that taxes on personal net wealth and wealth transfer taxes are needed to improve wealth distribution (see Davies, 1982, 1991). They also argue that such taxes relate closely to "ability to pay," increase the progressivity of the tax system, fill holes in the income tax system, and generally make the tax system more efficient. Each of these arguments is explored in some depth in recent Canadian fiscal literature.[4]

The role of several different forms of taxes on wealth and property in the tax systems of various industrialized countries is illustrated in Table 23.2. Countries that rely more heavily on taxes on wealth and property are those that draw substantial revenues from taxes on immovable property owned by individuals and businesses. The United States, the United Kingdom, and

---

[3] According to Bird and Mintz (1992: 9), such "considerations suggest that governments will resort increasingly to taxes on immobile factors of production, such as natural resources, land, and less skilled labor."

[4] For a detailed discussion of the literature on net wealth taxes and wealth transfer taxes, and the history of wealth transfer taxes in Canada, see Smith (1993). A lengthy bibliography is included.

Table 23.1

Distribution of Wealth* in Canada in 1984 by Wealth Decile and
by Income Decile (Families and Unattached Individuals)

| | WEALTH DISTRIBUTION BASED ON | |
| | INCOME DECILE | WEALTH DECILE |
DECILE	(PERCENT)	
1 (lowest)	2.5	−0.4
2	3.5	0.1
3	5.5	0.6
4	6.9	1.8
5	7.8	3.6
6	8.6	5.7
7	9.2	8.2
8	11.1	11.6
9	14.7	17.5
10 (highest)	30.1	51.3
Total	100.0	100.0

*Wealth in the survey included: bonds, stocks and shares, deposits, owner-occupied homes, cars, and net investments in personal businesses. It excluded equity in private pension funds, insurance policies, the value of collectibles, and the value of consumer durables other than motor vehicles. It also excluded the value of public pensions, human capital, and other public services and goods such as medical care.

SOURCE: G. Oja, *Changes in the Distribution of Wealth in Canada, 1970–1984*, Statistics Canada Cat. no. 13-588 (Ottawa: May 1987), p. 25; Statistics Canada, *The Distribution of Wealth in Canada, 1984* (Ottawa: Supply and Services, 1986), p. 31.

Canada stand out in this regard, although Japan, Australia, and New Zealand also have quite significant taxes on immovable property. Other taxes on wealth raise substantially less revenues than do property taxes, although Switzerland appears to draw significant revenues from net wealth taxes, and Japan relies relatively heavily on wealth transfer taxes.

The remainder of this chapter focuses on the use and the effects of taxes on real property. Although taxes on net wealth are used in many industrialized countries, such taxes have not been used in Canada. Wealth transfer taxes, which were used in Canada from 1894 to 1985, are no longer used; Canada and Australia were the only industrialized countries not using wealth transfer taxes in 1993. In contrast, due to cutbacks in transfers to local governments from the federal and provincial governments, the role of real property taxes has been growing.

Table 23.2

Revenues from Net Wealth Taxes, Wealth Transfer Taxes, Taxes on Immovable Property, and Total Taxes on Property as a Percent of Total Taxes, Selected Countries, 1993

COUNTRY	RECURRENT TAXES ON IMMOVABLE PROPERTY	NET WEALTH TAXES*	ESTATE, INHERITANCE, & GIFT TAXES	TOTAL TAXES ON PROPERTY***
	(PERCENT OF TOTAL TAX REVENUES)			
CANADA	9.72	–**	–	11.12
Australia	5.55	–	–	10.43
Austria	0.64	0.34	0.14	2.60
Belgium	0.03	–	0.73	2.56
Denmark	2.45	0.19	0.56	4.15
Finland	1.02	0.10	0.42	2.79
France	2.58	0.23	0.90	5.18
Germany	0.95	0.24	0.25	2.72
Ireland	2.44	–	0.43	4.17
Italy	1.93	0.15	0.12	4.96
Japan	6.96	–	2.15	11.09
Netherlands	1.60	0.57	0.54	3.74
New Zealand	5.36	–	0.11	5.94
Norway	0.80	1.04	0.20	2.58
Sweden	2.06	0.34	0.13	3.18
Switzerland	0.46	2.28	0.83	7.26
U.K.	9.43	–	0.60	10.80
U.S.	10.24	–	0.94	11.31
Unweighted avg.	3.57	0.30	0.50	5.92

*These refer only to taxes on "individual" net wealth.

**– indicates that no revenues are reported for such a tax.

***Taxes included are those on immovable property, net wealth taxes on individuals and on corporations, estate taxes, gift taxes, and inheritance taxes, taxes on financial and capital transactions, nonrecurrent taxes on property such as betterment levies, and recurrent taxes on properties such as jewellery or cattle.

SOURCE: Organization for Economic Cooperation and Development, *Revenue Statistics of OECD Member Countries, 1965–1994* (Paris: OECD, 1995).

PROPERTY TAXES

A tax on real property is the major form of wealth taxation in Canada. This tax is the major source of tax revenues for local governments in Canada, the United States, the United Kingdom, Australia, and New Zealand (Table 23.2). The property tax in Canada is predominantly a local tax, but in British

Columbia, Prince Edward Island, and New Brunswick the provincial governments account for more than half of taxes on real property (Table 23.3). Real property taxes in all of these countries raise much more revenue than the alternative forms of wealth taxes used in other countries. Thus, although the property tax base in Canada does not in most cases accurately reflect personal net wealth, Canadians may feel that wealth in Canada is taxed relatively heavily.

In 1933, the property tax accounted for 33 percent of tax revenues raised by all levels of government (Table 23.4). By the mid-1980s, property taxes had fallen to 7 percent of total tax revenues. The rapid growth of federal and provincial income tax and sales tax revenues since the 1930s sharply reduced the *relative* importance of property taxes as a revenue source. Nonetheless, property taxes constantly increased in real per capita terms over this period, an increase that has been particularly sharp in recent years. Real per capita revenue stood at $722 (1986 dollars) in 1994, up 42 percent from 1985, increasing property taxes to 8.6 percent of total government revenues. Of the over $26 billion raised by property taxes that year, $3.7 billion contributed to provincial revenues (about 2 percent of their tax revenues) and $22.4 billion to local revenues, accounting for over 80 percent of local tax revenue. There is no federal property tax. Although it is not as important as many other taxes

Table 23.3

Provincial and Local Property Taxes as a Share of Property Tax Revenues, 1968 and 1994

	1968		1994	
PROVINCE	LOCAL	PROVINCIAL	LOCAL	PROVINCIAL
Newfoundland	100.0	0.0	100.0	0.0
PEI	100.0	0.0	32.7	67.3
Nova Scotia	99.5	0.5	100.0	0.0
New Brunswick	30.6	69.4	49.8	50.2
Quebec	100.0	0.0	100.0	0.0
Ontario	99.8	0.2	99.9	0.1
Manitoba	100.0	0.0	79.6	20.4
Saskatchewan	100.0	0.0	99.9	0.1
Alberta	100.0	0.0	53.8	46.2
British Columbia	96.8	3.2	44.8	55.2
Yukon and NWT	69.8	30.2	83.7	16.3
All Canada	98.7	1.3	85.9	14.1

SOURCE: Harry M. Kitchen, *Property Taxation in Canada*, Canadian Tax Paper no. 92 (Toronto: Canadian Tax Foundation, 1992), p. 9, table 1.7; Statistics Canada, *Public Sector Finance, 1995–1996*, Cat. no. 68-212-XPB (Ottawa: March 1996).

Table 23.4

Real Property Taxes in Canada, 1933–1994

PROPERTY TAXES AS A SHARE OF

YEAR	GOVERNMENT REVENUE	GDP	PERSONAL INCOME	PER CAPITA
		(PERCENTAGE)		(1986$)
1933	33.0	6.3	8.3	$228
1945	8.8	2.4	3.1	174
1955	10.8	2.6	3.6	226
1965	11.3	3.1	4.3	343
1975	7.9	2.8	3.5	427
1985	7.0	2.7	3.2	507
1994	8.6	3.5	4.0	722

SOURCE: M.C. Urquhart and K.A.H. Buckley, *Historical Statistics of Canada,* 2nd ed. (Ottawa: 1983); Statistics Canada, *Public Sector Finance, 1995–1996,* Cat. no. 68-212-XPB (Ottawa: March 1996), and *Public Finance Historical Data, 1965/66–1991/92,* Cat. no. 68-512 (Ottawa: March 1992).

when viewed from a national perspective, the property tax plays a key role in local public finances.

How is the tax liability on a given piece of property determined? An individual's property tax liability is the product of the tax rate and the property's **assessed value**—the value the jurisdiction assigns to the property. In most cases, jurisdictions attempt to make assessed values correspond to market values. However, if a piece of property has not been sold recently, the tax collector does not know its market value and must therefore make an estimate, perhaps based on the market values of comparable properties that have been sold recently.

Market and assessed values diverge to an extent that depends on the accuracy of the jurisdiction's estimating procedure. The ratio of the assessed value to market value is called the **assessment ratio.** If all properties have the same statutory rate and the same assessment ratio, their effective tax rates are the same. Suppose, however, that assessment ratios differ across properties. Ophelia and Hamlet both own properties worth $100,000. Ophelia's property is assessed at $100,000 and Hamlet's at $80,000. Clearly, even if they face the same statutory rate (say 2 percent), Ophelia's effective rate of 2 percent (= $2,000/$100,000) is higher than Hamlet's 1.6 percent (= $1,600/$100,000). In fact, many communities do a poor job of assessing values so that properties with the same statutory rate differ drastically with respect to effective rates.

It is not unusual for assessment ratios to differ systematically for different types of property. The 1988 data for Toronto and North York in Table 23.5 are illustrative. For residential properties, the assessment ratio is lowest for single and double family dwellings and highest for properties with more than six units. Business properties are assessed at higher ratios than are single and double family dwellings, and the assessment ratio for manufacturing and industrial property is substantially above that for professional and commercial property.

To understand how the actual system of property taxes works, at the outset one must realize that property tax systems in Canada differ from province to province, and even within provinces there may be significant differences.[5] No jurisdiction includes a comprehensive measure of wealth in its tax base, but there are major differences with respect to just what types of property are excludable and what rates are applied. Churches, educational properties, hospitals, and cemeteries are generally among properties that are exempt, but there are some differences among provinces. Charitable organizations are also often exempt. Some communities tax new business plants preferentially, presumably to attract more commercial activity. Few areas tax personal wealth other than homes, so items such as cars, jewels, and stocks and bonds are exempt.

Typically, structures and the land on which they are built are subject to tax. But, as Table 23.6 demonstrates, the effective rates differ substantially across

Table 23.5

Assessed Values as a Percent of Market Values, Selected Property Classes in Toronto and North York, 1988

	TORONTO	NORTH YORK
Residential Dwellings		
1–2 units	3.1	4.1
3–6 units	3.9	7.5
>6 units	12.0	14.2
Commercial and		
Professional property	6.8	7.7
Industrial and		
Manufacturing property	13.0	10.2

SOURCE: Harry M. Kitchen, *Property Taxation in Canada*, Canadian Tax Paper no. 92 (Toronto: Canadian Tax Foundation, 1992), p. 25, table 2.3.

---

[5] Including counties, municipalities, townships and towns, school districts, and special districts, there are over 83,000 local governments. About 80 percent of them have the power to levy property taxes.

jurisdictions for both residential and nonresidential properties. Differences in bases and rates contribute to substantial variation in the real per capita revenues from property taxes across Canada (see Table 23.7).

Thus, although we continue to describe the subject matter of this section as "the" property tax, it should now be clear that there is no such thing. The fact that there are many different property taxes is crucial to assessing the economic effects of the system as a whole. There is considerable controversy as to who ultimately bears the burden of the property tax. We discuss three different views and then try to reconcile them.

Incidence and Efficiency Effects: Traditional View— Property Tax as an Excise Tax

The traditional view is that the property tax is an excise tax that falls on land and structures. Incidence of the tax is determined by the shapes of the relevant

Table 23.6

Residential and Nonresidential Effective Property Tax Rates in 1980, Selected Cities

MUNICIPALITY	EFFECTIVE NONRESIDENTIAL RATE	EFFECTIVE RESIDENTIAL RATE
Victoria	2.20	1.88
Vancouver	1.81	2.44
Edmonton	1.66	0.87
Calgary	1.87	1.01
Saskatoon	1.28	1.58
Regina	1.68	1.27
Winnipeg	2.32	1.78
Guelph	1.71	1.30
Hamilton	2.54	1.81
Kingston	2.22	1.59
Waterloo	2.18	1.15
London	2.04	1.85
Ottawa	1.16	1.52
Thunder Bay	2.03	1.20
Toronto	1.76	2.37
Windsor	2.10	1.98

SOURCE: Wayne R. Thirsk, "Political Sensitivity Versus Economic Sensibility: A Tale of Two Property Taxes," in Wayne R. Thirsk and John Whalley, eds., *Tax Policy Options in the 1980s*, Canadian Tax Paper no. 66 (Toronto: Canadian Tax Foundation, 1982), at 388, table 1.

Table 23.7

Real Per Capita Property Taxes by Province, 1970–1994

YEAR	CANADA	MARITIMES	QUE.	ONT.	MAN.	SASK.	ALTA.	B.C.
			(1980 DOLLARS)					
1970	383	163	323	469	364	412	379	464
1975	361	171	304	402	431	354	359	512
1980	380	178	310	440	442	390	389	497
1985	400	174	314	462	493	442	455	488
1994	506	222	330	586	462	419	494	516
Percent increase since 1970	32	36	2	25	27	2	30	11

SOURCE: Roger S. Smith, "Why the Canadian Property Tax(payer) Is Not Revolting," *Canadian Tax Journal* 38, no. 2 (March/April 1990): 304, table 1; Statistics Canada, *Public Sector Finance, 1995–1996*, Cat. no. 68-212-XPB (Ottawa: March 1996).

supply and demand schedules in the manner explained in Chapter 17. The shapes of the schedules are different for land and structures.

Land. As long as the amount of land cannot be varied, by definition its supply curve is perfectly vertical. A factor with such a supply curve bears the entire burden of a tax levied on it. Intuitively, because its quantity is fixed, land cannot "escape" the tax. This is illustrated in Figure 23.1. $S_{\mathscr{L}}$ is the supply of land. Before the tax, the demand curve is $D_{\mathscr{L}}$, and the equilibrium rental value of land is $P_0^{\mathscr{L}}$. The imposition of an ad valorem tax on land pivots the demand curve. The after-tax demand curve is $D'_{\mathscr{L}}$. The rent received by suppliers of land (landowners) is found at the intersection of the supply curve with $D'_{\mathscr{L}}$ and is given by $P_n^{\mathscr{L}}$. The rent paid by the users of land is found by adding the tax per acre of land to $P_n^{\mathscr{L}}$, giving $P_g^{\mathscr{L}}$. As expected, the rent paid by the users of the land is unchanged ($P_0^{\mathscr{L}} = P_g^{\mathscr{L}}$); the rent received by landowners falls by the full amount of the tax. Landowners bear the entire burden of the tax.

As discussed in Chapter 17, under certain circumstances the tax is *capitalized* into the value of the land. Prospective purchasers of the land take into account the fact that if they buy the land, they also buy a future stream of tax liabilities. This lowers the amount they are willing to pay for the land. Therefore, the person who bears the full burden of the tax is the landlord at the time the tax is levied. To be sure, future landlords make payments to the tax authorities, but such payments are not really a burden because they just balance the lower price paid at purchase. Capitalization complicates attempts to assess the

Figure 23.1

Incidence of a Tax on Land

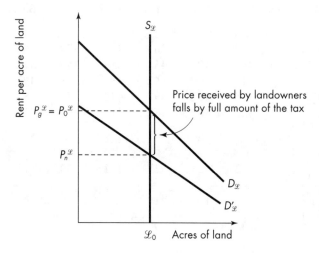

incidence of the land tax. Knowing the identities of current owners is not sufficient; we must know who the landlords *were* at the time the tax was imposed.

To the extent that land is *not* fixed in supply, the preceding analysis requires modification. For example, the supply of urban land can be extended at the fringes of urban areas that are adjacent to farmland. Similarly, the amount of land can be increased if landfills or reclamation of wasteland is feasible. In such cases, the tax on land is borne both by landlords and the users of land, in proportions that depend on the elasticities of demand and supply. But it is usually assumed that a vertical supply curve for land is a good approximation of reality.

Structures. To understand the traditional view of the tax on structures, we begin by considering the national market for capital. Capital can be used for many purposes: construction of structures, equipment for manufacturing, public sector projects like dams, and so forth. At any given time, capital has some price that rations the capital among alternative uses. According to the traditional view, in the long run, the construction industry can obtain all the capital it demands at the market price. Thus, the supply curve of structures is perfectly horizontal—a higher price is not required to obtain more of them.

The market for structures under these conditions is depicted in Figure 23.2. Before the tax, the demand for structures by tenants is D_B, and the supply curve, S_B, is horizontal at the going price, P_0^B. At price P_0^B the quantity exchanged is B_0. On imposition of the tax, the demand curve pivots to D'_B, just as the demand for land pivoted in Figure 23.1. But the outcome is totally different. The price received by the suppliers of structures, P_n^B, is the same as the price before the tax was imposed ($P_n^B = P_0^B$). Demanders of structures pay a price, P_g^B, which exceeds the original price, P_0^B, by precisely the amount of the tax. Hence, the burden is shifted entirely to tenants. This result, of course, is a consequence of the assumption that the supply curve is horizontal. Intuitively, the horizontal supply curve means capital will not stay in the housing sector if it does not receive a return of at least P_0^B. But if the price received by the suppliers of capital cannot be lowered, the tax must be borne entirely by tenants.

The traditional view is based on the assumption that imposing a property tax on structures does not affect the position of the demand curve for land. In other words, the traditional view of the property tax ignores the interaction between the demand for land and rate of return on capital (structures). If the demand for land increases because builders substitute land for structures when the price of structures increases, then the rental price of land will increase, and landowners will bear less than the full burden of the property tax on land. On the other hand, if the demand curve for land shifts to the left because of the reduced demand for housing and other services in the community that has imposed the higher property tax, then the rental price of land will go down, the owners of land will bear more than the burden of the property tax on land, and tenants will bear less than the burden on structures.

Figure 23.2

Incidence of a Tax on Structures

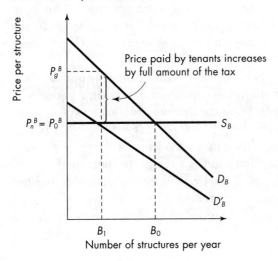

Summary of the traditional view. The part of the tax on land is borne by landowners (or at least the landowners at the time the tax is levied); the tax on structures is passed on to tenants. Therefore, the land part of the property tax is borne by people in proportion to the amount of rental income they receive, and the structures part of the tax is borne by people in proportion to the amount of housing they consume.

Implications for progressiveness. With these observations in mind, we can assess the distributional implications of the traditional view of the property tax. The effect of the land part of the tax on progressiveness hinges on whether or not the share of income from land ownership tends to rise with income. There is fairly widespread agreement that it does, so this part of the tax is progressive.

Similarly, the progressiveness of the tax on structures depends critically on whether the proportion of income devoted to housing rises or falls as income increases. If it falls, then the structures part of the tax tends to be regressive and vice versa.

An enormous amount of econometric work has been done to estimate how housing expenditures actually do respond to changes in income. The ability to reach a consensus has been impeded by disagreement over which concept of income to use. Some investigators use *yearly* income. They tend to find that the proportion of income devoted to housing falls as income increases, suggesting that the tax is regressive. Other investigators believe that some measure of *normal* or *permanent* income is more relevant to understanding housing decisions. According to this view, the fact that a family's annual income in a given year happens to be higher or lower than its normal income should not have much of an impact on that year's housing consumption. Housing decisions are made in the context of the family's long-run prospects, not yearly variations.

Of course, those who believe that permanent income is the appropriate variable must find some way to estimate it. One approach is to define permanent income as the average of several years' annual incomes. Housing expenditures turn out to be more responsive to changes in permanent income than to changes in annual income. Indeed, although the evidence is mixed, it appears reasonable to say that housing consumption is roughly proportional to permanent income. Hence, the structures part of the tax is probably neither regressive nor progressive. Unfortunately, analyses based on annual income, which suggest the tax is regressive, have tended to have the greater influence on public discussion of the tax.

Incidence and Efficiency Effects: New View— Property Tax as a Capital Tax

The traditional view uses a standard partial equilibrium framework. As we noted in Chapter 17, although partial equilibrium analysis is often useful, it may produce misleading results for taxes that are large relative to the economy. The new view of the property tax proposed by Mieszkowski (1972) takes a general equilibrium perspective and leads to some surprising conclusions.

According to the new view, it is best to think of the property tax as a general wealth tax with some assets taxed below the average rate and some taxed above. Both the average level of the tax and the deviations from that average have to be analyzed.

General tax effect. Assume for the moment that the property tax can be approximated as a uniform tax on all capital. Then the property tax is just a general factor tax on capital. Now assume further that the supply of capital to the economy is fixed. As shown in Chapter 17, when a factor is fixed in supply, it bears the full burden of a general tax levied on it. Hence, the property tax falls entirely on owners of capital. And since the proportion of income from capital tends to rise with income, a tax on capital tends to be progressive. Thus, the property tax is progressive, a conclusion that turns the traditional view exactly on its head!

Table 23.8 illustrates the difference in results when incidence estimates are based on the traditional view (columns (c) and (d)), and when incidence is based on the "general tax effect" of the new view (column (a)), and on lifetime income combined with the new view (column (b)). Where the property tax on land is borne by owners of land and that on residential structures by homeowners and renters, the incidence is consistently regressive, as in columns (c) and (d). In contrast, where property taxes are borne by recipients of investment income, the property tax becomes significantly progressive at higher income levels (column (a)). And when the new view is combined with "lifetime" as opposed to "annual" incidence, the incidence of the property tax appears moderately progressive.

Excise tax effects. As noted earlier, the property tax is emphatically not a uniform tax. Rates vary according to the type of property and the jurisdiction in which it is located. Some rates are higher than average, and some are lower. Hence, the property tax is a set of excise taxes on capital. According to the new view, capital tends to migrate from areas where it faces a high tax rate to those where the rate is low. In a process reminiscent of the Harberger model presented

Table 23.8

Estimates of Property Tax Incidence: Annual Incidence versus Lifetime Incidence

DECILE	NEW VIEW (1971–DAVIES ET AL.)		TRADITIONAL VIEW**	
			(1969– VERMAETEN ET AL.)	(1988– VERMAETEN ET AL.)
	ANNUAL	LIFETIME*		
	(A)	(B)	(C)	(D)
1 (low)	1.1	2.4	8.5	8.0
2	1.5	3.1	5.8	6.5
3	1.8	2.8	5.7	5.7
4	1.7	3.3	5.3	5.1
5	1.3	3.2	4.5	4.8
6	1.5	3.6	4.4	4.2
7	1.3	3.6	4.1	3.8
8	1.9	4.5	4.1	3.6
9	2.9	3.7	3.7	3.3
10 (high)	10.6	5.6	3.6	3.0
All	4.5	3.9	4.1	3.8

*Deciles for lifetime incidence are ranked by lifetime resources, and the property tax is calculated as a share of resources available over lifetimes. Here it is assumed that property taxes are borne by recipients of investment income.

**Property taxes are expressed as a share of "broad income," which includes employment and investment income, nontaxed income such as capital gains on residences, retirement savings earnings, and inheritances, and government transfer payments. The share of property taxes on land is assumed to be borne by owners and the share on residential structures by home-owners and renters. The tax on business structures is borne by consumers.

SOURCE: J. Davies, France St-Hilaire, and J. Whalley, "Some Calculations of Lifetime Tax Incidence," *American Economic Review* 74, no. 4 (September 1984): 633–49; A. Vermaeten, W.I. Gillespie, and F. Vermaeten, "Who Paid the Taxes in Canada, 1951–1988?" *Canadian Public Policy* 21, no. 3 (September 1995).

in Chapter 17, as capital migrates into low-tax-rate areas, its before-tax rate of return there is bid down. At the same time, the before-tax rate of return in high-tax areas increases as capital leaves. The process continues until after-tax rates of return are equal throughout the economy. In general, as capital moves, returns to other factors of production also change. The impact on the other factors depends in part on their mobility. Land, which is perfectly immobile, cannot shift the tax. (In this conclusion, at least, the new and old views agree.) Similarly, the least-mobile types of capital are most likely to bear the tax.

As is usually the case in general equilibrium models, the ultimate incidence depends on how production is organized, the structure of consumer demand, and the extent to which various factors are mobile.

Long-run effects. In our discussion of the general tax effect of the property tax, we assumed the amount of capital available to the economy is fixed. However, in the long run, the supply of capital may depend on the tax rate. If the property tax decreases the supply of capital, the productivity of labour, and hence the real wage, falls. If the tax increases capital accumulation, just the opposite occurs.

Summary of the new view. The property tax is a general tax on capital with some types of capital taxed at rates above the average, others below. The general effect of the tax is to lower the return to capital, which tends to be progressive in its impact on the income distribution. The differentials in tax rates create excise effects, which tend to hurt immobile factors in highly taxed jurisdictions. The adjustment process set in motion by these excise effects is very complicated, and not much is known about their effects on progressiveness. Neither can much be said concerning the importance of long-term effects created by changes in the size of the capital stock. If the excise and long-run effects do not counter the general effect too strongly, the overall impact of the property tax is progressive.

Incidence and Efficiency Effects: Property Tax as a User Fee

The discussion so far has ignored the fact that property taxes are often used by communities to purchase public services such as education and police protection. In light of this reality, it may be appropriate to view the property tax as just the cost of purchasing public services. Each individual buys the amount he or she desires by selecting the community in which to live based on the package of local public services (quantity) and the property taxes (price) (see the discussion of the Tiebout model in Chapter 6). Thus, the property tax is really not a tax at all; it is more like a user fee for public services.[6] This view has two important implications:

---

[6] This view appears to exist in New Zealand where the central government's sales tax (GST) is levied on the property tax bills paid by New Zealanders to their local governments. Where property taxes are, in effect, a fee for local services, this is necessary to ensure that services provided by the public sector are not favoured relative to goods and services provided by the private sector. The fees paid for public services must also be taxed if relative prices are to remain unchanged. It is difficult to imagine Canadians accepting that the GST should be levied on the property taxes paid to local and provincial governments.

1. The notion of the *incidence of the property tax* is meaningless because the levy is not a tax in the normal sense of the word.
2. The property tax creates no excess burden. As Hamilton (1975: 13) points out, "If consumers treat the local property tax as a price for public services, then this price should not distort the housing market any more than the price of eggs should distort the housing market."

As noted earlier, the link between property taxes and services received is often tenuous, so we should not take the notion of the property tax as a user fee too literally. Nevertheless, this line of reasoning has interesting implications. For example, if people care about the public services they receive, we expect that the depressing effects of high property taxes on housing values may be counteracted by the public services financed by these taxes. In an important paper, Oates (1969) constructed an econometric model of property value determination. In his model, the value of homes in a community depends positively on the quality of public services in the community and negatively on the tax rate, other things being the same. Of course, across communities, factors that influence house prices do differ. These include physical characteristics of the houses, such as number of rooms, and characteristics of the communities themselves, such as distance from an urban centre. These factors must be considered when trying to sort out the effects of property taxes and local public goods on property values. Oates used multiple regression analysis to do so.

Oates's regression results suggest that increases in the property tax rate decrease housing values, while increases in per pupil expenditures increase housing values. Moreover, the parameter values implied that the increase in property values created by expanding school expenditures approximately offset the decrease generated by the property taxes raised to finance them. These results need to be interpreted with caution. For one thing, expenditure per pupil may not be an adequate measure of local public services. Localities provide many public services other than education, such as police protection, parks, and libraries. Furthermore, even if education were the only local public good, expenditure per pupil might not be a good measure of educational quality. It is possible, for example, that expenditures in a given community are high because the community has to pay a lot for its teachers, its schools are not administered efficiently, or its students are particularly difficult to educate.

Subsequent to Oates's study, a number of other investigators have examined the relationships among property values, property taxes, and local public goods using data from different geographical areas and employing different sets of explanatory variables. Although the results are a bit mixed, Oates's general conclusion seems to be valid—property taxes and the value of local public services are capitalized into housing prices.[7] Thus, if two communities have the same level of public services, but the first has higher taxes than the second (perhaps because its cost of providing the services is greater), we expect the first to have lower property values, other things being the same. More generally, these results imply that to understand how well off members of a community are, we cannot look at property tax rates in isolation. Government services and property values must also be considered.

Reconciling the Three Views

It is a mistake to regard the three views of the property tax as mutually exclusive alternatives. Each may be valid in different contexts. If, for example, we want to find the consequences of eliminating all property taxes and replacing them with a national sales tax, the "new view" is appropriate because a change that affects all communities requires a general equilibrium framework. On the other hand, if a given community is considering lowering its property tax rate and making up the revenue loss from a local sales tax, the "traditional view" offers the most insight. This is because a single community is so small relative to the economy that its supply of capital is essentially perfectly horizontal, and Figure 23.2 applies. Finally, when taxes and benefits are jointly changed and there is sufficient mobility for people to pick and choose communities, the "user fee view" is useful.

The Future of the Property Tax

In the past twenty years, governments in the United States and the United Kingdom have acted to sharply reduce reliance on property taxes for the financing of local governments. In 1978, California voters put a 1 percent ceiling on the property tax rate that any locality could impose, limited the assessed value of property to its 1975 value,[8] and forbade state and local governments from imposing any additional property taxes without approval by a two-thirds' majority local vote. Property taxes were reduced in thirty-seven U.S. states in 1978 and 1979 alone, and the move against property taxes has continued. Although subsequently repealed, Prime Minister Margaret Thatcher replaced taxes on residential properties with a poll, or head, tax as the primary way to finance local services.

In Canada, provincial action to improve property tax administration and limited growth in Canada's property tax revenues in the 1970s and 1980s may

---

[7] For further discussion, see Mieszkowski and Zodrow (1989) and Gyourko and Tracy (1991).
[8] For property transferred after 1975, the assessed value was defined as the market value at which the transaction took place.

have resulted in more modest opposition to this form of taxation.[9] None-theless, with increased reliance on property taxes to offset reduced grants from higher levels of government, resistance to property taxes is growing in Canada. The particularly rapid growth in property taxes in Ontario is likely to continue, and pressure for property tax reform may spread from Ontario to other provinces.

There are several reasons why property taxes will continue to be an appropriate target for criticism by those who seek fair and efficient taxes:

1. As noted earlier, because housing market transactions typically occur infrequently, the property tax must be levied on an estimated value. To the extent that this valuation is done incompetently, or political forces prevent valuations based on current market values, the tax is perceived as unfair.

2. The property tax is highly visible. Under the federal and provincial income and payroll taxes, payments are withheld from workers' paycheques, and the employer sends the proceeds to the government. In contrast, the property tax is often paid directly by the taxpayer. Moreover, the payments are often made on a quarterly or an annual basis, so each payment comes as a large shock.

3. The property tax is perceived as being regressive. This perception is partly a consequence of the fact that the "traditional view" of the property tax continues to dominate public debate. It is reinforced by the fact that some property owners, particularly the elderly, do not have enough cash to make property tax payments and may therefore be forced into selling their homes. All provinces have responded to this phenomenon with one or more programs. Five provinces allow some portion of property taxes to be credited against personal income taxes payable, with the value of the credit declining as taxable income increases. Other relief includes a partial exemption from property taxes for those with incomes below a certain level, grants that fully or partially offset property taxes, and the deferral of property taxes (with a lien against a property) until the time when the property is transferred.

4. Taxpayers may dislike other taxes as much as the property tax, but they feel powerless to do anything about the others. It is relatively easy to take aim at the property tax, where it is levied locally. In contrast, mounting a drive against, say, the federal income tax is more difficult, if for no other reason than a national campaign would be necessary and hence involve large coordination costs.

---

[9] See Smith (1990).

In light of objections to the property tax, it is natural to ask whether there are any ways to improve it. A very modest proposal is to improve assessment procedures. The use of computers and modern valuation techniques can make assessments more frequent and uniform. Where effective tax rates differ within a jurisdiction, uniform tax rates would probably enhance efficiency. The equity issues are more complicated. On one hand, it seems a violation of horizontal equity for two people with identical properties to pay different taxes on them. However, the phenomenon of capitalization requires that we distinguish carefully between the owners at the time the tax is levied and the current owners. A property with an unduly high tax rate can be expected to sell for a lower price, other things being the same. Thus, a high tax rate does not necessarily make an individual who buys the property after the tax is imposed worse off. Indeed, equalizing assessment ratios could generate a whole new set of horizontal inequities.

A more ambitious reform of the property tax would be to convert it into a tax on personal net wealth. An advantage of such a system over a property tax is that by allowing for deduction of liabilities, it provides a better index of ability to pay. Moreover, because it is a personal tax, exemptions can be built into the system and the rates can be varied to attain the desired degree of progressivity. However, administrative problems associated with a net wealth tax are formidable. Difficulties that arise in valuing housing for property tax purposes are likely to pale in comparison to valuing assets such as paintings, antiques, or Persian rugs. Moreover, while a house is difficult to conceal, other types of assets are relatively easy to hide from the tax collector. Note also that because individuals can have assets and liabilities in different jurisdictions, a net wealth tax would undoubtedly have to be administered by the federal government.

In the face of strong criticism, two lines of argument appear foremost in justifying continued reliance on the current system of property taxation as the way to finance local services. The first argument is the local autonomy that is provided by taxes on real property. The second is based on the extent to which the property tax serves as a user fee for locally provided services.

Whatever its flaws, the property tax can be administered locally. Hence, it provides local government with considerable fiscal autonomy. As one observer put it, "Property taxation offers people in different localities an instrument by which they can make local choices significant" (Harris, 1978: 38). According to this view, elimination of the property tax would ultimately destroy the economic independence of local units of government.

Over the past two decades several provincial governments—Manitoba, Alberta, and British Columbia—have increased their involvement in the property tax

field. This has, in some cases, reduced local autonomy as provinces seek to achieve "provincial standards" in areas such as education. This is likely to raise concern over increased concentration of power to set policies and priorities at provincial rather than local levels. Just as provinces have been concerned about undue federal influence through excessive control of revenue sources, local citizens may have similar concern regarding control at the provincial level. Even though localities may have access to other tax bases, the political role of the property tax needs to be taken seriously in any discussion of its reform.

SOME FINAL COMMENTS

Canadians rely heavily on "personal consumption" and "personal income" as tax bases from which to raise substantial government revenue. This is not so for "personal wealth." The property tax applies only to a small share of the wealth of many Canadians. Moreover, to the extent that the property tax is a user fee for local services, it is a payment for services rendered rather than a tax, and in this regard differs from the broad-based personal income and consumption taxes.

We should not expect Canadian policy makers to turn to a personal net wealth tax or wealth transfer taxes as a new or significant revenue source. Interprovincial and international tax competition contributed to the demise of wealth transfer taxes in Canada from 1967 through 1985. Ontario's Fair Tax Commission, reporting in 1993, was unable to recommend the reintroduction of estate or inheritance taxes. There is general agreement that any such tax would need to be nationwide, even if the revenues went to the provinces, in order to avoid interprovincial tax competition. In addition, tax competition with the United States makes it difficult for Canada to employ a significant estate tax while continuing to deem capital gains to be realized at time of death for income tax purposes. Although the United States has an estate tax, it exempts accrued, but unrealized, gains at time of death from its income tax. Nonetheless, estate and inheritance taxes may continue to strike a sympathetic note with many Canadians who seek a "more equal start" for all Canadians, and so long as wealth remains concentrated in the hands of a relatively small minority.

SUMMARY

- Wealth taxes are assessed on a tax base that is a stock of assets instead of a flow such as income or sales.

- Proponents of wealth taxes believe that they help to correct the income tax for unrealized capital gains, reduce the concentration of wealth, and compensate for benefits received by wealth holders. Some also argue that wealth by itself is a good index of ability to pay and should, therefore, be subject to tax.

- Property taxes are an important revenue source for provincial and local governments. There are three, not mutually exclusive, views on the incidence and efficiency effects of the property tax. The "traditional view" is that the property tax is an excise tax on land and structures. The "new view" is that the property tax is a general tax on all capital with rates that vary across jurisdictions and different types of capital. The "user fee view" regards property taxes as payment for local public services.

- The property tax is a very imperfect tax on personal wealth. It is unlikely that it can be extended to become part of an effective tax on personal net wealth, allowing for the full recognition of liabilities as well as assets. Such a change would be administratively complex and may undermine the most appealing aspect of the property tax in the context of a federal system—local administration.

DISCUSSION QUESTIONS

1. As a result of Brian's will, $100,000 is paid to his son John at the time of Brian's death in 1995. The $100,000 is not to be included in the income of John. However, this is not a flaw in the income tax system since the $100,000 was never allowed as a deduction for Brian for income tax purposes while he was alive. Comment.

2. David and Jonathan own identical homes. David has owned his home for many years and paid $100,000 for it. Jonathan purchased his home after a recent property tax increase and paid $80,000. Should the local assessor change the assessed value of Jonathan's home to maintain horizontal equity? (Assume there has been no inflation in housing prices since David purchased his home and that David and Jonathan value equally all public services provided in the local community.) In your answer, carefully define all key concepts.

3. Hamilton, Ontario, has a large amount of industrial property in its tax base. If the demand for goods produced in Hamilton is inelastic, producers are able to export property taxes in the form of higher prices to consumers outside of Hamilton. This may lead to the excessive (and thus inefficient) provision of local public services in Hamilton. Explain. How would you recommend that we address this problem?

4. Opponents argue that taxes on the transfer of wealth will reduce work effort, reduce saving, and reduce the willingness to make risky investments. Whether or not you agree with this assessment, explain why many people, supported by economic theory, think it may not be true.

REFERENCES

Bird, Richard M., and Jack M. Mintz, eds. *Taxation to 2000 and Beyond.* Toronto: Canadian Tax Foundation, 1992.

Davies, James B. "The Distributive Effects of Wealth Taxes." *Canadian Public Policy* 17 (September 1991): 17.

Davies, James B. "The Relative Impact of Inheritance and Other Factors on Economic Inequality." *The Quarterly Journal of Economics* 97 (August 1982).

Davies, James B., France St-Hilaire, and John Whalley. "Some Calculations of Lifetime Tax Incidence." *American Economic Review* 74, no. 4 (September 1984): 633–49.

Gyourko, Joseph, and Joseph Tracy. "The Structure of Local Public Finance and the Quality of Life." *Journal of Political Economy* 99, no. 4 (August 1991): 774–806.

Hamilton, Bruce. "Property Taxes and the Tiebout Hypothesis: Some Empirical Evidence," in *Fiscal Zoning and Land Use Controls: The Economic Issues,* ed. Edwin S. Mills and Wallace E. Oates. Lexington, MA: Lexington Books, 1975, pp. 13–30.

Harris, C. Lowell. "Property Taxation after the California Vote." *Tax Review* 39, no. 8 (August 1978): 35–38.

Kitchen, Harry M. *Property Taxation in Canada.* Toronto: Canadian Tax Foundation, 1992.

Mieszkowski, Peter M. "The Property Tax: An Excise Tax or a Profits Tax?" *Journal of Public Economics* 1 (1972): 73–96.

Mieszkowski, Peter M., and George R. Zodrow. "Taxation and the Tiebout Model." *Journal of Economic Literature* (September 1989): 1098–146.

Oates, Wallace. "The Effects of Property Taxes and Local Spending on Property Values: An Empirical Study of Tax Capitalization and the Tiebout Hypothesis." *Journal of Political Economy* 77 (1969): 957–71.

Smith, Roger S. *Personal Wealth Taxation: Canadian Tax Policy in a Historical and an International Setting.* Toronto: Canadian Tax Foundation, 1993.

Smith, Roger S. "Why the Canadian Property Tax(payer) Is Not Revolting." *Canadian Tax Journal* 38, no. 2 (March–April 1990).

Thirsk, Wayne R. "Political Sensitivity Versus Economic Sensibility: A Tale of Two Property Taxes," in *Tax Policy Options in the 1980s,* ed. Wayne R. Thirsk and John Whalley. Toronto: Canadian Tax Foundation, 1982.

Wolff, Edward N. *Top Heavy: A Study of Increasing Inequality of Wealth in America.* New York: Twentieth Century Fund Press, 1995.

Chapter 24

The Corporation Tax

Variations [in effective tax rates] can result in distortions as business and investment decisions are made on the basis of tax considerations rather than the underlying economic merit.

–Michael H. Wilson, Minister of Finance (June 1987)

INTRODUCTION

*I*n 1993, corporations in Canada had $1.3 trillion in operating revenues, and generated $40 billion in before-tax profits.[1] Federal and provincial corporate income tax revenues were $14.6 billion. Corporations play a major role in the Canadian economy.

A corporation is a form of business organization. It is owned by its stockholders, with ownership usually represented by transferable stock certificates. The stockholders have limited liability for the acts of the corporation. This means that their liability to the creditors of the corporation is limited to the amount they have invested in the corporation.

Corporations are independent legal entities and as such are often referred to as artificial legal persons. A corporation may make contracts, hold property, incur debt, sue, and be sued. And just like any other person, a corporation must pay tax on its income. This chapter explains the structure of the

---

[1] Statistics Canada, *Parliamentary Report of the Minister of Industry under the Corporations and Labour Unions Returns Act: Part I—Corporations* (Ottawa: April 1995), and *National Income and Expenditure Accounts, Quarterly Estimates*, Third Quarter 1994, Cat. no. 13-001 (Ottawa: January 1995).

federal and provincial corporation income taxes and analyzes their effects on the allocation of resources.

The relative importance of corporation income taxes has fallen in recent decades. As shown in Table 24.1, corporate income taxes as a share of all government revenue fell from 16.5 percent in 1955 to 6.0 percent in 1994. One study (Douglas, 1990) found that over three-quarters of the decline in corporate income tax revenues from 1960 to 1985 was due largely to a fall in the profitability of corporations, although there had been some decline in the average tax rate. The 1987 reforms, by broadening the tax base and reducing investment tax credits, raised average tax rates (while lowering marginal rates) in an attempt to increase taxes on the corporate sector. Nonetheless, Table 24.1 shows that corporate tax revenues continued to decline as a share of tax revenues, and on a per capita basis, until the economy began to recover in 1992.

Although corporate income taxes have declined as a share of total revenues, they continue to be important in the formulation of tax policy. The theory of excess burden suggests that a tax may create efficiency costs far out of proportion to the revenues yielded. There is some evidence that the corporation tax is an example of this important phenomenon.

Table 24.1

Corporate Income Taxes in Canada, 1945 to 1994

YEAR	FEDERAL REVENUE	PROVINCIAL REVENUE (MILLIONS)	FEDERAL + PROVINCIAL	AS A PERCENT OF GOVERNMENT REVENUE (%)	PER CAPITA ($1986)
1945	$ 645	$ –	$ 645	17.8	$ –
1955	1,081	54	1,135	16.5	335
1965	1,759	523	2,282	13.7	451
1975	5,748	2,091	7,921	12.6	772
1985	9,210	4,033	13,243	7.3	532
1990	11,726	5,457	17,183	6.2	517
1991	9,359	4,987	14,347	5.2	404
1992	8,278	4,497	12,775	4.5	349
1994	11,604	6,576	18,180	6.0	496

SOURCE: M.C. Urquhart and K.A.H. Buckley, *Historical Statistics of Canada*, 2nd ed. (Ottawa: Minister of Supply and Services, 1983), Statistics Canada, *Public Finance Historical Data, 1965/66–1991/92*, Cat. no. 68-512 (March 1992), and *Public Sector Finance, 1995–1996*, Cat. no. 68-212-XPB (March 1996).

WHY TAX CORPORATIONS?

Before undertaking a description and analysis of the tax, we should ask whether it makes sense to have a special tax system for corporations in the first place. To be sure, from a legal point of view, corporations are people. But from an economic standpoint, this notion makes little sense. As we stressed in Chapter 17, only real people can pay a tax. If so, why should corporate activity be subject to a special tax? Is it not sufficient to tax the incomes of the corporation owners via the personal income tax?

A number of justifications for a separate corporation tax have been proposed. First, contrary to the view just stated, corporations—especially very big ones—really are distinct entities. Large corporations have thousands of stockholders, and the managers of such corporations are controlled only very loosely, if at all, by the stockholder/owners. Most economists would certainly agree that there is separation of ownership and control in large corporations, and this creates important problems for understanding just how corporations function. Nevertheless, it does not follow that the corporation should be taxed as a separate entity.

A second justification for corporate taxation is that the corporation receives a number of special privileges from society, the most important of which is limited liability of the stockholders. The corporation tax can be viewed as a user fee for this benefit. However, the tax is so structured that there is no reason to believe that the revenues paid approximate the benefits received.

Third, the corporate tax serves as a withholding tax. With substantial foreign ownership of corporations operating in Canada, if a tax were not levied at the corporate level much income arising in the corporate sector could flow to foreign owners without taxes being paid to Canadian governments. Direct investment in Canada by foreign corporations amounted to $145 billion at the end of 1994 (Statistics Canada, 1995: 45).

Fourth, the corporate income tax serves as a rent-gathering device. Canadian corporations operating in the resource sector, and other corporations given privileges by the state, realize economic rent from their activities. Royalties on resource production and the sale of crown leases for the exploration and development of resources capture only a portion of the economic rent. The corporate income tax permits the provincial and federal governments to share in remaining rents.[2]

---

[2] For a general discussion of federal and provincial natural resource revenues, see Treff and Perry (1997: ch. 7).

A final justification is that the corporation tax protects the integrity of the personal income tax. Suppose that Karl's share of the earnings of a corporation during a given year is $10,000. According to the standard convention for defining income, this $10,000 is income whether the money happens to be retained by the corporation or paid out to Karl. If the $10,000 is paid out, it is taxed in an amount that depends on his personal income tax rate. In the absence of a corporation tax, the $10,000 creates no tax liability if it is retained by the corporation since the personal income tax does not tax capital gains on an accrual basis. Hence, unless corporation income is taxed, Karl can reduce his tax liability by accumulating income within the corporation.[3]

It is certainly true that if corporate income goes untaxed, opportunities for personal tax avoidance are created. But a special tax on corporations is not the only way to include earnings accumulated in corporations. We discuss an alternative method, one partially adopted in Canada and viewed by many economists as superior, in later sections of this chapter.

STRUCTURE

Corporate Income Tax Statutory Rates

In addition to the federal tax, all ten provinces, as well as the Yukon and Northwest Territories, levy a tax on corporate income. Provincial corporate income taxes generated $6.6 billion in 1994, compared to the $11.6 billion from the federal tax. This equalled 5 percent of the revenues raised by the provinces, and less than 9 percent of federal revenues. Provinces raised six times as much through their taxes on personal income, and the federal government raised over five times as much.

Room has been made for provincial taxes on corporate income through a federal–provincial agreement that provides a credit of up to 10 percent of corporate income earned in a province against federal tax that would otherwise be payable. For example, a federal tax that would be at a 38 percent rate is 28 percent if the provincial tax is imposed at a rate of at least 10 percent. General corporate income tax rates of all provinces exceeded 10 percent in 1996.

The federal government collects the provincial corporate income tax on behalf of seven provinces on the understanding that the provincial tax base differs only to a limited degree from the federal tax base. Ontario, Quebec, and

---

[3] Of course, the money will be taxed when it is eventually paid out, but in the meantime, the full $10,000 grows at the before-tax rate of interest. Remember from Chapter 20, taxes deferred are taxes saved.

Alberta administer their own corporate income taxes; these provinces, as a result, have greater freedom to alter their tax base from the federal base, and increased freedom to use the corporate income tax as an economy policy instrument. Such freedom is purchased at the cost of somewhat higher administrative and compliance costs.

All of the complications that arise in analyzing the incidence and efficiency effects of the federal corporation income tax also bedevil attempts to understand the effects of the provincial taxes. Variation in rates across provincial lines gives rise to a set of possibly even more intractable questions (McLure, 1981). When a given province increases its tax on corporate income, how much of the burden would be exported to citizens of other provinces? How is the portion that is not exported shared by the residents of the province?[4] Thus, analyzing a system of varying corporate tax rates requires that the effects of interprovincial mobility be added to the already formidable list of factors that come into play when studying the federal corporation tax. There is much research that needs to be done on this issue.

Table 24.2 provides the combined federal and provincial corporate income tax rates for 1996. The general rate applies to most large corporations, and special rates apply to income from manufacturing and processing, and to the income of small businesses.

The general rate of the corporate income tax in Canada ranged from 38.0 percent to 46.1 percent in 1996. The standard federal rate was 28 percent; however, to this must be added a 4 percent surtax, which resulted in a federal rate of 29.1 percent. General provincial corporate income tax rates ranged from 8.9 to 17 percent in 1996 (Table 24.3). The combined federal–provincial general rate is given in the last column in Table 24.2. Lower rates are applied to the income of small businesses and to income from manufacturing and processing. The federal rate on small business income is 12 percent, while that on income from manufacturing and processing is 21 percent.[5] The federal surtax adds 1.12 percentage points to these rates as well. Provincial small business rates ranged from 5 percent (Newfoundland) to 9.5 percent (Ontario) in 1996, and provincial rates applying to manufacturing and processing income ranged from 5 to 17 percent.

---

[4] Recall from Chapter 17 the general intuitive proposition that immobile factors of production are more likely to end up bearing a tax than mobile factors, other things being the same. This means, for example, that if capital is easier to move to another province than labour, there is a tendency for the incidence of a provincial corporation tax to fall on labour.

[5] The federal and provincial "small business" rate applies to the first $200,000 of income of Canadian-controlled private corporations, and is reduced when taxable capital of a corporation is over $10 million and eliminated if taxable capital exceeds $15 million.

Table 24.2

Combined Federal and Provincial Corporate Income Tax Rates, 1996

PROVINCE	SMALL BUSINESS	MANUFACTURING & PROCESSING (PERCENT)	GENERAL
Newfoundland	18.1	27.1	43.1
PEI	20.6	29.6	44.1
Nova Scotia	18.1	38.1	45.1
New Brunswick	20.1	39.1	46.1
Quebec	18.9	31.0	38.0
Ontario	22.6	35.6	44.6
Manitoba	22.1	39.1	46.1
Saskatchewan*	21.1	39.1	46.1
Alberta	19.1	36.6	44.6
British Columbia	22.1	38.6	45.6
NWT	18.1	36.1	43.1
Yukon	19.1	24.6	44.1

*The rate depends on the share of manufacturing and processing income of a company that is earned in Saskatchewan.

SOURCE: Karin Treff and David Perry, *Finances of the Nation, 1996* (Toronto: Canadian Tax Foundation, 1997), p. 4:7, table 4.3.

The combined federal and provincial rates vary substantially across provinces. This reflects differing policy objectives and strategies among provinces.

As in the case of the personal income tax, knowledge of the rate applied to taxable income by itself gives relatively little information about the effective burden. To compute taxable income, we must know exactly which deductions from before-tax corporate income are allowed. Accordingly, we now discuss the rules for defining taxable corporate income.[6]

Wage Payments Deducted

As we saw in Chapter 20, a fundamental principle in defining personal income is that income should be measured net of the expenses incurred in earning it. The same logic applies to the measurement of corporate income. One important business expense is labour, and wages paid to workers are excluded from taxable income.

[6] Note also that many of these rules apply to noncorporate businesses. As in the case for the personal income tax, there is a corporate alternative minimum tax.

Table 24.3

Provincial Corporate Income Tax Rates, 1996

PROVINCE	GENERAL	MANUFACTURING/ PROCESSING (PERCENT)	SMALL BUSINESS
Newfoundland	14	5.0	5.0
PEI	15	7.5	7.5
Nova Scotia	16	16.0	5.0
New Brunswick	17	17.0	7.0
Quebec	8.9	8.9	5.75
Ontario	15.5	13.5	9.5
Manitoba	17	17.0	9.0
Saskatchewan	17	17.0	8.0
Alberta	15.5	14.5	6.0
British Columbia	16.5	16.5	9.0
NWT	14	14.0	5.0
Yukon	15	2.5	6.0

SOURCE: Karin Treff and David Perry, *Finances of the Nation, 1996* (Toronto: Canadian Tax Foundation, 1997), p. 4:2, table 4.2.

Depreciation Deducted

Suppose that during a given year the XYZ Corporation makes two purchases: (1) $1,000 worth of stationery, which is used up within the year; and (2) a $1,000 drill press, which will last for ten years.[7] Should there be any difference in the tax treatment of these expenditures?

From the accounting view, these are very different items. Because the stationery is entirely consumed within the year of purchase, its entire value is deductible from that year's corporate income. But the drill press is a durable good. When the drill press is purchased, the transaction is merely an exchange of assets—cash is given up in exchange for the drill press. Thus, unlike stationery, a drill press is not entirely consumed during the year. To be sure, during its first year of use some of the machine is used up by wear and tear, which decreases its value. This process is called **economic depreciation**. But at the end of the year the drill press is still worth something to the firm, and in principle could be sold to some other firm at that price.

---

[7] Understanding the impact of depreciation allowances requires the concept of present value.

We conclude that during the first year of the life of the drill press, a consistent definition of income requires that only the economic depreciation experienced that year be subtracted from the firm's before-tax income. Similarly, the economic depreciation of the machine during its second year of use should be deductible from that year's gross income, and so on for as long as the machine is in service.

It is a lot easier to state this principle than to apply it. In practice, the tax authorities do not know exactly how much a given investment asset depreciates each year, or even what the useful life of the machine is. The tax law has rules that indicate for each type of asset what proportion of its acquisition value can be depreciated each year (referred to as the **capital cost allowance**, or **CCA**), and over how many years depreciation can be taken—the **tax life** of the asset. Next, we discuss these rules, which often fail to reflect true economic depreciation.

Calculating the value of depreciation allowances. Assume that the tax life of the $1,000 drill press is ten years, and a firm is allowed to depreciate 1/10th the machine's value each year. How much is this stream of depreciation allowances worth to the XYZ Corporation?

At the end of the first year, XYZ is permitted to subtract 1/10th the acquisition value, or $100, from its taxable income. With a corporation income tax rate of 35 percent, this $100 deduction saves the firm $35. Note, however, that XYZ receives this benefit a year after the machine is purchased. The present value of the $35 is found by dividing it by $(1 + r)$, where r is the opportunity cost of funds to the firm.

At the end of the second year, XYZ is again entitled to subtract $100 from taxable income, which generates a saving of $35 that year. Because this saving comes two years in the future, its present value is $35/(1 + r)^2$. Similarly, the present value of depreciation taken during the third year is $35/(1 + r)^3$, during the fourth year, $35/(1 + r)^4$, and so on. The present value of the entire stream of depreciation allowances is

$$\$35/(1 + r) + \$35/(1 + r)^2 + \$35/(1 + r)^3 + \dots + \$35/(1 + r)^{10}.$$

For example, if r = 10 percent, this expression is equal to $215.10. In effect, then, the depreciation allowances lower the price of the drill press from $1,000 to $784.90 (= $1,000 − $215.10). Intuitively, the effective price is below the acquisition price because the purchase leads to a stream of tax savings in the future.

More generally, suppose that the tax law allows a firm to depreciate a given asset over T years, and the proportion of the asset that can be written off against taxable income in the nth year is $D(n)$. The $D(n)$ terms sum to one, meaning that the tax law eventually allows the entire purchase price of the asset to be written off. (In the preceding example, T was 10, and $D(n)$ was equal to 1/10th every year. There are, however, several depreciation schemes for which $D(n)$ varies across years.) Consider the purchase of an investment asset that costs \$1. The amount that can be depreciated at the end of the first year is $D(1)$ dollars, the value of which to the firm is $\theta \times D(1)$ dollars, where θ is the corporation tax rate. (Because the asset costs \$1, $D(1)$ is a fraction.) Similarly, the value to the firm of the allowances in the second year is $\theta \times D(2)$. The present value of all the tax savings generated by the depreciation allowances from a \$1 purchase, which we denote ψ, is

$$\psi = [\theta \times D(1)]/[1 + r] + [\theta \times D(2)]/[1 + r]^2 + ... + [\theta \times D(T)]/[1 + r]^T \quad (24.1)$$

Because ψ is the tax saving for one dollar of expenditure, it follows that if the acquisition price of an asset is \$$q$, the presence of depreciation allowances lowers the effective price to $(1 - \psi)q$. For example, a value of $\psi = 0.25$ indicates that for each dollar spent on an asset, 25 cents worth of tax savings are produced. Hence, if the machine cost \$1,000 ($q =$ \$1,000) the effective price is only 75 percent of the purchase price, or \$750.

Equation (24.1) suggests that the tax savings from depreciation depend critically on the value of T and the function $D(n)$. In particular, the tax benefits are greater: (1) the shorter the time period over which the machine is written off—the lower is T; and (2) the greater the proportion of the machine's value that is written off at the beginning of its life—the larger the value of $D(n)$ when n is small. Schemes that allow firms to write off assets faster than true economic depreciation are referred to as **accelerated depreciation**. An extreme possibility is to allow the firm to deduct from taxable income the asset's full cost at the time of acquisition. This is referred to as **expensing**, and in this case $\psi = \theta$ in Equation (24.1).

Under current law, every depreciable asset is assigned to one of forty-four classes, with special rules applying in some cases. The rate at which an asset can be written off differs among the classes, but generally the permitted write-off is faster than economic depreciation. This has potential consequences for corporate investment behaviour, which we discuss later. With respect to the rate at which assets can be depreciated, basically two methods are currently relevant.

Declining-balance method. The declining balance method is that which applies in most cases under existing Canadian law. Existing rates are generally between 4 percent and 50 percent when expensing is not permitted. These rates apply to the full cost of the asset in the first year, and to the remaining undepreciated cost in subsequent years. For example, if the applicable rate is 20 percent and the cost of the depreciable asset is $1,000, the deduction permitted is $200 (0.2 × 1,000) in the first year, $160 (0.2 × 800) in the second year, and $128 (0.2 × 640) in the third year, and so on. It should be apparent that this provides for a slower write-off than if a 20 percent rate were applied to the original cost, and the asset were fully written off over five years.[8]

Straight-line method. The straight-line method applies in a few special cases in Canada and is widely used elsewhere in the world. This is the method we have been using for our examples so far. If the tax life of the asset is T years, the firm can write off $1/T$th of the cost each year. Thus, for a $1,000 asset that may be depreciated over five years, $200 is deducted each year.

Other methods. A variety of other methods have been used to permit faster write-offs in Canada or other countries. The **double declining balance method** allows twice the percentage applied under the declining balance method. The write-offs in the example above would be a 40 percent rather than a 20 percent rate, with deductions for the first three years equal to $400, $240, and $144.

Other possible measures may permit a company to deduct a substantial portion of the investment in the first year, and this may or may not reduce deductions in subsequent years. Thus, the total write-off over the life of the asset may, in some cases, exceed 100 percent of the original investment. Even where future deductions are reduced by an increase in the initial deduction, the present value of the earlier tax saving may be substantial.

Depreciation allowances and tax shelters. When tax depreciation is faster than economic depreciation, tax arbitrage opportunities are created. These opportunities are most dramatic in the case of assets that are legally depreciable for tax purposes, but actually appreciate in value over time. Complicated tax-shelter plans involving investments in real estate, cattle, and timber have been based on this principle. Although tax-shelter opportunities were reduced by the tax reforms of the 1980s, their use is still widespread.

A nice example is provided by baseball. If you buy a baseball team, part of the product you receive is the players' contracts. Normally, the amount allocated

---

[8] Since 1981 the government has limited the capital cost allowance to one-half of the normal CCA rate in the year of acquisition. Although this rule applies for most classes of assets, there are some exceptions.

to player contracts is a large proportion of the acquisition cost of the team. These contracts are viewed as a depreciable asset. Since the tax life of contracts is relatively short, the amount allowed as a deduction in the early years generally exceeds the income generated by the team for those years. This produces an accounting loss that can be used to reduce the owners' taxable income from other sources. However, when the team is sold, if it has increased in value, the owner reaps a capital gain. No wonder that an owner once claimed that you can never lose money on a baseball team!

The foregoing represents only a partial list of the many creative ways that depreciation provisions have been used to influence investment decisions by altering after-tax returns to investors.

Investment Tax Credits

Until recently, the Income Tax Act has included sizable **investment tax credits (ITCs)** to encourage new investment and to achieve development objectives in depressed areas of the country. The ITCs permit a firm to subtract some portion of the purchase price of an asset from its tax liability at the time the asset is acquired. If a drill press cost $1,000, and if the XYZ firm is allowed an investment tax credit of 10 percent, the purchase of a drill press lowers XYZ's tax bill by $100. The effective price of the drill press (before depreciation allowances) is thus $900. More generally, if the investment tax credit is k and the acquisition price is q, the effective price of the asset is $(1 - k)q$. In contrast to depreciation allowances, the value to the firm of an ITC does not depend on the corporate income tax rate. This is because the credit is subtracted from tax liability rather than taxable income.

The general ITC was 7 percent in 1987; investment for manufacturing and processing in certain slow-growth areas qualified for a 40 percent ITC, and ITCs were at 20 percent for the Atlantic region as a whole and at 60 percent for Cape Breton. The general ITC was eliminated by 1989; what remains after the 1994 federal budget is a 10 percent federal ITC for investment in the Atlantic provinces and the Gaspé region, and the continuation of a 20 to 35 percent ITC for qualifying expenditures on research and development.[9] As with gophers that keep popping out of holes as part of the carnival game, ITCs are likely to re-emerge as they are a readily understood investment incentive and likely to remain popular among policy makers.

---

[9] Several provinces also provide investment tax credits for certain types of investments, including those for research and development purposes. For more detail, see Treff and Cook (1995: 4:4 and 4:5).

Treatment of Interest

When corporations borrow, interest payments to lenders are excluded from taxable income. Again, the justification is that business costs should be deductible. However, when firms finance their activities by issuing stock, the dividends paid to the stockholders are not deductible from corporate earnings. We discuss the consequences of this asymmetry in the treatment of interest and dividends later. Now we briefly look at the effect of deducting interest on the cost of an investment.

Calculating the value of interest deductions. Assume that a firm borrows $1,000 to invest in a machine that has a ten-year life. The firm pays annual interest of 7.5 percent, or $75, for the duration of the loan, and repays the full $1,000 after ten years. With interest deductible, taxable income is reduced by $75 each year, and if the corporate tax rate is 35 percent this saves $26.25 each year. The present value of this stream of tax savings is:

$$\$26.25/(1 + r) + \$26.25/(1 + r)^2 + ... + \$26.25/(1 + r)^{10}.$$

If r is equal to 10 percent, this expression is worth $161.33, and the cost of the machine is reduced from $1,000 to $838.67. More generally, the present value of the tax saving resulting from the deductibility of interest for each dollar of capital is:

$$\lambda = [\theta \times R]/[1 + r] + [\theta \times R]/[1 + r]^2 + ... + [\theta \times R/[1 + r]^T, \qquad (24.2)$$

where T is the life of the loan, θ is the tax rate, R is the interest deduction resulting from $1 of capital, and r is the discount rate. Effectively, the price of the asset is reduced by λ. If the cost of acquiring an asset was q prior to allowing for deduction of interest, and q were borrowed to make the purchase, it becomes $(1 - \lambda)\$q$ with the deduction. We will use this result later. If equity financing were used, with dividends not deductible, the cost remains at q.

Treatment of Dividends

So far we have been focusing on taxes directly payable by the corporation. For many purposes, however, the important issue is not the corporation's tax liability per se, but rather the total tax rate on income generated in the corporate sector. As noted in Chapter 20, corporate dividends received by individuals are subject to the personal income tax. Understanding how the corporate and personal tax structures interact is important.

Corporate profits may either be retained by the firm or paid to stockholders in the form of dividends. Dividends paid are not deductible from corporation income and hence are subject to the corporation income tax. At the same time, stockholders who receive dividends must pay personal income tax in an amount that depends on their marginal tax rates. Unlike the United States where there is no recognition of the tax paid at the corporate level, Canada's tax system provides some credit for taxes paid at the corporate level. However, for most dividend income the adjustment is only partial, and dividends are therefore taxed twice—once at the corporation level, and again when distributed to the shareholder. Eliminating **double taxation** is a prime objective of many tax reformers, and was foremost in the minds of Canada's Royal Commission on Taxation in the 1960s. Canada, through its dividend tax credit system, has achieved partial integration of the personal and corporate income tax systems.

Canada's dividend tax credit. Canada uses a system of *partial imputation*—part of the income at the corporate level is imputed to shareholders and included in taxable income at the personal level. The shareholders are then given credit for some of the tax paid at the corporate level. This is achieved through the dividend tax credit system, which grosses up the dividend ($100) that the individual receives by an amount that approximates the amount of taxes paid at the corporate level ($25 if the corporate tax rate were 25 percent). The grossed-up amount ($125) is then included in the taxable income of an individual, and the appropriate personal income tax rate (say 40 percent) is applied to determine the individual's tax liability (0.4 × $125 = $50), and a tax credit ($25) is allowed for the grossed-up amount. The result is that the individual pays an additional $25 (or $50 – $25), and the combined corporate and personal income tax collected on the $125 originating in the corporate sector is $50, or 40 percent. This is the applicable marginal tax rate for this individual. The corporate tax served to withhold the first $25, and credit is later given through the personal income tax system for this withholding. The situation is summarized as follows:

a) Taxable corporate income — $125
b) – Corporate tax collected at a 20% tax rate — 25
c) = Corporate income for distribution [(a) – (b)] — 100
d) Paid as dividends to individual = — 100
e) Gross-up of dividends by 25 percent = — 25
f) Taxable individual income [(d) + (e)] — 125
g) Individual tax liability at a 40% tax rate = [0.4 × (f)] — 50
h) – Dividend tax credit [= (e)] — 25
i) Individual tax payable after credit [(g) – (h)] — 25
j) Total tax on $125 originating in a corporation = (b) + (i) — 50

The foregoing example, however, reflects a situation of full integration, and approximates the situation *only* for Canadian small businesses subject to a corporate tax rate of about 20 percent. But even here, integration may be excessive or inadequate. The dividend tax credit is allowed for dividends paid even when the corporation has paid no tax. The result is a total tax that is below that paid on income from other sources, and "overintegration" occurs. Where dividends are paid from past profits, and the permitted credit does not reflect the time value of corporate taxes paid in the past, "underintegration" may occur.

Most dividends are paid by corporations that do not qualify for the small business tax rate. The marginal tax rate in these cases is around 45 percent. The two examples in Table 24.4 demonstrate the degree of integration that occurs for two individuals. Example 1 is for a small business with a 20 percent corporate tax rate. Example 2 is for a large corporation with a 45 percent corporate tax rate. In both cases the dividend tax credit is calculated as 13 1/3 percent of grossed-up taxable income. This reflects the reduction in federal taxes due to the credit. Since provincial individual income taxes are calculated by multiplying the basic federal tax by rates of around 50 percent, the combined reduction due to the credit is 20 percent (13 1/3 + 6 2/3), and is equal to the gross-up of 25 percent.

Three points from Table 24.4 deserve emphasis:

- Canada's system of partial integration approximates a system of full integration only for small businesses, and even then only when dividends flow from income that has been subject to corporate taxes.
- There is a substantial degree of double taxation on dividends paid by corporations subject to tax rates in excess of 20 percent. In Example 2, an individual subject to a personal income tax rate of 25.5 percent pays nearly double that rate, or 48.8 percent, on income originating in the corporate sector. The corporate tax, even after the gross-up and credit system, discriminates heavily against the corporate sector.
- Example 2 indicates that integration is particularly beneficial to those subject to low marginal rates on their personal income, and double taxation has its greatest impact on those with lower personal income. For individual A, the "penalty" of double taxation is 23.29 percentage points (48.79 − 25.5), whereas for individual B it is only 17.67 percentage points (61.17 − 43.5).

Treatment of Retained Earnings

To assess the tax consequences to the stockholder of retained earnings is a bit more complicated. Suppose that XYZ retains $1 of earnings. To the extent

Table 24.4

The Effect of the Dividend Tax Credit

Assumptions:
1. The combined federal and provincial marginal tax rate on corporate income for a small business is 20 percent, and that for a large corporation is 45 percent.
2. Individual A is subject to a combined federal and provincial marginal tax rate on personal income of 25.5 percent, and individual B is subject to a combined federal and provincial marginal rate of 43.5 percent.
3. The provincial personal income tax is calculated by multiplying the federal personal income tax by 0.50.
4. The corporation earns $200 in before-tax profits, all of which are distributed as dividends to shareholders.

The Dividend Tax Credit Provision:
Dividends from taxable Canadian corporations are grossed up by 25 percent before being included in an individual's taxable income. The federal tax is reduced by a credit equal to 13 1/3 percent of the grossed-up dividend income.

Example 1: A small business subject to a 20% corporate tax rate

Corporate income before tax:	$200	
Corporate tax payable @ 20%:	40	
After-tax income available for distribution:	160	

	TO INDIVIDUAL A (25.5% PIT RATE)	TO INDIVIDUAL B (43.5% PIT RATE)
Dividends received	$160	$160
Gross up (25%)	40	40
Taxable income	200	200
a) Federal PIT payable before credit	34 (@ 17%)	58 (@ 29%)
b) Dividend tax credit @ 13 1/3% × taxable income	26.67	26.67
c) Federal PIT payable after credit (a) − (b)	7.33	31.33
d) Provincial PIT @ 50% of federal PIT 0.5 × (c)	3.67	15.67
e) Total federal + provincial PIT (c) + (d)	11.00	47.00
Combined CIT + PIT $40 + (e)	51.00	87.00
Tax rate	25.5%	43.5%

(continued)

Table 24.4

(continued)

Example 2: A large corporation subject to a 45% corporate tax rate

Corporate income before tax: $200
Corporate tax payable @ 45%:   90
After-tax income distributed as dividends: 110

	TO INDIVIDUAL A (25.5% PIT RATE)	TO INDIVIDUAL B (43.5% PIT RATE)
Dividends	$110	$110
Gross up (25%)	27.50	27.50
Taxable income	137.50	137.50
a) Federal PIT payable before credit	23.38 (@ 17%)	39.88 (@ 29%)
b) Dividend tax credit @ 13 1/3% × taxable income	18.33	18.33
c) Federal PIT payable after credit (a) – (b)	5.05	21.55
d) Provincial PIT @ 50% of federal PIT 0.5 × (c)	2.53	10.78
e) Total federal + provincial PIT (c) + (d)	7.58	32.33
Combined CIT + PIT $90 + (e)	97.58	122.33
Tax rate	48.79%	61.17%

that the stock market accurately values firms, the fact that the firm now has one more dollar causes the value of XYZ stock to increase by $1.[10] But as we saw in Chapter 20, income generated by increases in the value of stock—capital gain—is treated preferentially for tax purposes. This is because the gain received by a typical XYZ stockholder is not taxed until it is realized, and even then only three-quarters of the gain is taxable. The tax system thus

---

[10] Bradford (1981) describes conditions under which the increase might not be on a one-for-one basis.

creates incentives for firms to retain earnings rather than pay them out as dividends.[11]

Tax Expenditures under the Corporate Income Tax

As with the personal income tax, "special" provisions that exclude an item from the tax base, permit a deduction in calculating the tax base or tax liability, and create preferential rates result in losses to federal and provincial treasuries. Governments may, and do, use the corporate income tax structure to channel assistance to particular industries. Where the tax structure, rather than direct expenditure, encourages industrial development in a particular region, expenditures on research, or renewal of the manufacturing sector, a tax expenditure occurs, and the structure of the corporate income tax is changed. Table 24.5 includes estimates by the Department of Finance for federal tax expenditures made through the corporate income tax in 1992; it includes only those items where the forgone revenue exceeds $50 million. Additional revenues are forgone by provinces due to these measures.

Effective Tax Rate on Corporate Capital

We began this section by noting the statutory tax rate on capital income in the corporate sector is currently about 45 percent when provincial and federal rates are combined. Clearly, it would be most surprising if this were the effective rate as well. At the corporate level, computing the effective rate requires considering the effects of interest deductibility, depreciation allowances, and inflation. Moreover, as just noted, corporate income in the form of dividends and realized capital gains is also taxed at the personal level. Finally, some corporate income is affected by provincial and local property taxes. Allowing for all these considerations, Daly, Mercier, and Schweitzer (1993: 116) estimated the effective overall *marginal* tax rate on corporate capital income to be 47.7 percent in 1989.

Of course, any such calculation requires assumptions on items such as the appropriate choice of discount rate [r of Equation (24.1)], the expected rate of inflation, the extent of true economic depreciation, and so forth. Moreover, as we see below, the effective burden of the corporate tax depends in part on how

---

[11] Corporate after-tax profits were $46 billion in 1988, at the top of the business cycle. $18.9 billion was paid as dividends and $26.3 billion was retained. At the bottom of the cycle in 1991, when after-tax profits were only $12.5 billion, $12.3 billion was paid in dividends and undistributed profits were at –$0.8 billion. Statistics Canada, *National Income and Expenditure Accounts*.

Table 24.5

Federal Corporate Income Tax Expenditures, Selected Items of $50 Million or More, 1992

ITEM	MILLIONS OF DOLLARS
Low tax rate for small businesses	$ 1,934
Low tax rate for manufacturing and processing	368
Low tax rate for credit unions	60
Deductibility of itemized charitable donations	82
Nontaxation of life insurance companies world income	60
Interest credited to life insurance policies	60
Scientific research and experimental development investment tax credit	597
ITCs claimed in current year, but earned in prior years	211
Partial exclusion of capital gains	436
Fast write-off for Canadian development and exploration expenses	680
Transfer of income tax room to provinces for shared programs	353
Excess of tax depreciation over depreciation for financial statement purposes	752

Note: These items, and the method for calculating the tax expenditures, are explained in the source document: Department of Finance, *Government of Canada Tax Expenditures, 1995* (Ottawa: 1996), pp. 30–33 and Appendix B.

investments are financed—by borrowing, issuing stock, or using internal funds. It is therefore likely that investigators using other assumptions would generate a somewhat different effective tax rate. It is unlikely, however, that alternative methods would much modify the difference between statutory and effective marginal tax rates.

Some effects of inflation. Studies during the 1970s highlighted the impact that inflation has on effective corporate tax rates. Inflation affects taxable income in three important ways, two of which cause an overstatement of taxable income and one of which results in an understatement. The first is the failure to recognize the cost of replacing goods sold from inventories that were acquired at a lower cost. Canadian law requires that accounts be kept on a first-in first-out (FIFO) basis. A good acquired for $100 a year ago is deducted at that cost, even though increases in the general price level have raised its replacement cost to $110. If this good is sold for $150 and inventory is replaced for $110, the taxable profit based on FIFO accounting is $50, whereas the firm has realized real income of only $40. Taxable income is overstated by $10.

Second, depreciation allowances for capital assets are based on historical cost, and not on replacement cost. In a time of inflation, depreciation based on his-

torical cost results in an overstatement of taxable income. Capital equipment with a five-year life and costing $500 would, on a straight-line basis, be depreciated at $100 a year. If, due to a 10 percent rise in the general price level, the replacement cost increases to $550, annual depreciation should be $110. Failure to make this adjustment overstates profits by $10.

Finally, the current system leads to an understatement of taxable income to the extent that deductible interest payments include an element that compensates the lender for the decline in the real value of the debt that occurs as prices rise. Where this occurs, the borrower is in effect deducting part of the repayment of the loan in calculating taxable income. In general, repayment of principle is not deductible.

With inflation at low rates, these factors may have little impact on corporate taxes. However, if price increases are significant and unpredictable, the effects can be great. From 1973 through 1982 the annual change in the consumer price index (CPI) reached a high of 12.4 percent and was never below 7.8 percent. Bossons (1977: 95) found that pretax income for 279 large Canadian companies was reduced by 43 percent in 1975 when adjustments were made for the above three factors. Corporate income taxes, although 44 percent of "reported" pretax income, were 77 percent of "real" pretax income.[12]

The corporate income tax's lack of adjustment for inflation affects some industries much more severely than others. The effect depends on the importance of inventories, capital equipment, and debt finance. Inflation-induced distortions in the early 1970s were particularly severe in capital-intensive sectors such as forest products and chemicals, and much less severe for merchandising businesses. Inflation resulted in a tax on *real* profits that was well in excess of 100 percent for some companies. Thus, the effect of inflation on tax rates may have a major influence on investment decisions in a time of rapid price changes.

INCIDENCE AND EXCESS BURDEN

Understanding tax rules and computing effective tax rates is only the first step in analyzing the corporation tax. We still must determine who ultimately bears the burden of the tax and measure the costs of any inefficiencies it induces. The economic consequences of the corporation tax are among the most controversial subjects in public finance. An important reason for the controversy is disagreement with respect to just what kind of tax it is. We can identify several views.

---

[12] See Bossons (1977). For further discussion of these issues, also see Jenkins (1977).

A Tax on Corporate Capital

Recall from our discussion of the structure of the corporation tax that the firm is not allowed to deduct from taxable income the opportunity cost of capital supplied by shareholders. Since the opportunity cost of capital is included in the tax base, it appears reasonable to view the corporation tax as a tax on capital used in the corporate sector. In the classification scheme developed in Chapter 17 under "General Equilibrium Models," the corporation tax is a partial factor tax. This is the view that predominates in most writing on the subject.

In a general equilibrium model, the tax on corporate capital leads to a migration of capital from the corporate sector until after-tax rates of return are equal throughout the economy. In the process, the rate of return to capital in the noncorporate sector is depressed so that ultimately all owners of capital, not just those in the corporate sector, are affected. The reallocation of capital between the two sectors also affects the return to labour. The extent to which capital and labour bear the ultimate burden of the tax depends on the technologies used in production in each of the sectors, as well as the structure of consumers' demands for corporate and noncorporate goods. Using what he considered to be plausible values for the relevant technological and behavioural parameters, Harberger (1974) concluded capital bears the entire burden of the tax.

Turning now to efficiency aspects of the problem, we discussed computation of the excess burden of a partial factor tax in Chapter 17. By inducing less capital accumulation in the corporate sector than otherwise would have been the case, the corporation tax diverts capital from its most productive uses and creates an excess burden. The increase in excess burden when one more dollar is raised via the corporation tax—the marginal excess burden—may well be in excess of 50 cents.[13]

The Harberger model assumes perfect competition and profit-maximizing behaviour. Without these conditions, a tax on corporate capital may have quite different incidence and efficiency implications. Moreover, the model is static—the total amount of capital to be allocated between the corporate and noncorporate sectors is fixed. Suppose that over time, the tax on corporate

---

[13] Jorgenson and Yun (1991) estimated the excess burden of one more dollar raised by the U.S. corporate income tax at 45 cents. Dahlby (1994) estimated the excess burden of one more dollar raised by the personal income tax in Canada to range from 40 cents in Alberta to 99 cents in Quebec in 1993. Dahlby notes that U.S. studies indicate the cost of an additional dollar from taxing capital income is generally higher than from taxing labour income, and that this "would probably also hold for Canada."

capital changes the total amount of capital available to the economy. If the tax lowers the total amount of capital, the marginal product of labour, and hence the wage rate, falls. Thus, labour bears a greater share of the burden than otherwise would have been the case. If the tax increases the amount of capital, just the opposite results. Hence, even if we accept the view of the corporation tax as a partial factor tax, its efficiency and incidence effects are not at all clear.

A Tax on Economic Profits

An alternative view is that the corporation tax is a tax on economic profits. This view is based on the observation that the tax base is determined by subtracting costs of production from gross corporate income, leaving only "profits." As we explained in Chapter 17, analyzing the incidence of a tax on economic profits is straightforward. As long as a firm maximizes economic profits, a tax on them induces no adjustments in firm behaviour—all decisions regarding prices and production are unchanged. Hence, there is no way to shift the tax, and it is borne by the owners of the firm at the time the tax is levied. Moreover, by virtue of the fact that the tax leaves behaviour unchanged, it generates no misallocation of resources. Hence, the excess burden is zero.

Modelling the corporation tax as a simple tax on economic profits is almost certainly wrong. Recall that the base of a pure profits tax is computed by subtracting from gross earnings the value of *all* inputs *including* the opportunity cost of the inputs supplied by the owners. As noted earlier, no such deduction for the capital supplied by shareholders is allowed, so the base of the tax includes elements other than economic profits.

Nevertheless, there are circumstances under which the corporation tax is *equivalent* to an economic profits tax. Stiglitz (1973) showed that under certain conditions, as long as the corporation is allowed to deduct interest payments made to its creditors, the corporation tax amounts to a tax on economic profits.

To understand the reasoning behind Stiglitz's result, consider a firm that is contemplating the purchase of a machine costing $1. Suppose the before-tax value of the output produced by the machine is known with certainty to be G dollars. To finance the purchase, the firm borrows $1 and must pay an interest charge of r dollars. In the absence of any taxes, the firm buys the machine if the net return (total revenue minus depreciation minus interest) is positive. Algebraically, the firm purchases the machine if

$$G - r > 0. \qquad (24.3)$$

Now assume that a corporation tax with the following features is levied: (1) net income is taxed at rate θ; and (2) net income is computed by subtracting interest costs from total revenue. How does such a tax influence the firm's decision about whether to undertake the project? Clearly, the firm must make its decision on the basis of the *after*-tax profitability of the project. In light of feature 2, the firm's taxable income is $G - r$. Given feature 1, the project therefore creates a tax liability of $\theta(G - r)$, so the after-tax profit on the project is $(1 - \theta)(G - r)$. The firm does the project only if the after-tax profit is positive; that is, if

$$(1 - \theta)(G - r) > 0. \tag{24.4}$$

Now note that any project that passes the after-tax criterion (24.4) also satisfies the before-tax criterion (24.3). [Just divide Equation (24.4) through by $(1 - \theta)$ to get Equation (24.3).] Hence, imposition of the tax leaves the firm's investment decision unchanged—anything it would have done before the tax, it will do after. The owners of the firm continue to behave exactly as they did before the tax; they simply lose some of their profit on the investment to the government. In this sense the tax is equivalent to an economic profits tax. And like an economic profits tax, its incidence is on the owners of the firm, and it creates no excess burden.

This conclusion depends critically on the underlying assumptions, and these can easily be called into question. In particular, the argument assumes that firms finance their additional projects by borrowing. There are several reasons why they might instead raise money by selling shares or using retained earnings. For example, firms may face constraints in the capital market and be unable to borrow all they want. Alternatively, if a firm is uncertain about what the project's return will be, it might be reluctant to finance the project by borrowing. If things go wrong, the greater a firm's debt, the higher the probability of bankruptcy, other things being the same.

Hence, the main contribution of Stiglitz's analysis is not the conclusion that the corporate tax has no excess burden. Rather, the key insight is that the way in which corporations finance their investments has a major influence on how the corporation tax affects the economy.

EFFECTS ON BEHAVIOUR

The corporation tax influences a wide range of corporate decisions. In this section we discuss three important types: (1) the total amount of physical investment (equipment and structures) to make; (2) the types of physical assets to purchase; and (3) the way to finance these investments. In a sense, it is artificial to discuss these decisions separately because presumably the firm makes them simultaneously. However, we discuss them separately for expositional ease.

Total Physical Investment

A firm's net investment during a given period is the increase in physical assets during that time. The main policy question is whether features such as accelerated depreciation and the investment tax credit stimulate investment demand. The question is important. For example, when the Minister of Finance, Paul Martin, reduced regionally based investment tax credits in 1994 he argued that the credits had not been cost effective in encouraging new investment. Yet, when these and other investment tax credits were enacted, ministers of finance argued that the ITCs increase investment substantially. Who was right?

The answer depends in part on your view of how corporations make their investment decisions. Many different models have been proposed, and there is no agreement on which is the best.[14] We discuss three investment models that have received substantial attention.

Accelerator model. Suppose the ratio of capital to output in production is fixed. For example, production of every unit of output requires three units of capital. Then for each unit increase in output, the firm must increase its capital stock—invest—three units of capital. Thus, the main determinant of the amount of investment is changes in the level of output.

This theory, sometimes referred to as the accelerator model, implies that depreciation allowances and ITCs are for the most part irrelevant when it comes to influencing physical investment. It is only the quantity of output that influences the amount of investment, because technology dictates the ratio in which capital and output must be used. In other words, tax benefits for capital (such as ITCs) may make capital cheaper, but in the accelerator model this does not matter, because the demand for capital does not depend on its price.

Neoclassical model. A less extreme view of the investment process is that the ratio of capital to output is not technologically fixed. Rather, the firm can choose among alternative technologies. But how does it choose? According to Jorgenson's (1963) neoclassical model, a key variable is the firm's **user cost of capital**—the cost the firm incurs as a consequence of owning an asset. As we

---

[14] See Chirinko (1993) for a survey of various models.

show later, the user cost of capital includes both the opportunity cost of for-going other investments and direct costs such as depreciation and taxes. The user cost of capital indicates how high a project's rate of return has to be to be profitable. For example, if the user cost of capital on a project is 15 percent, a firm undertakes the project only if its rate of return exceeds 15 percent. The higher the user cost of capital, the lower is the number of profitable projects, and the lower the firm's desired stock of capital. In the neoclassical model, when the cost of capital increases, firms choose less capital-intensive tech-nologies, and vice versa. To the extent that tax policy reduces the cost of cap-ital, it can increase the amount of capital that firms desire and, hence, increase investment.

All of this leaves open two important questions: (1) How do changes in the tax system change the user cost of capital? and (2) Just how sensitive is investment to changes in the user cost of capital? To examine these points, we must first calculate the user cost of capital.

The user cost of capital. Consider the Leona Corporation, a company that operates a chain of hotels. The corporation can lend its money and receive an after-tax rate of return of 10 percent. Because it can always earn 10 percent simply by lending in the capital market, the Leona Corporation will not make any investment in the hotel that yields less than that amount. Assume that the corporation is considering the acquisition of a vacuum cleaner that would experience economic depreciation of 2 percent annually. Ignoring taxes for the moment, the user cost of capital for the vacuum cleaner would be 12 percent, because the vacuum cleaner would have to earn a 12 percent return to earn the Leona Corporation the 10 percent return that it could receive simply by lend-ing its money. Algebraically, if r_t is the after-tax rate of return and δ is the eco-nomic rate of depreciation, the user cost of capital is $(r_t + \delta)$. If the vacuum cleaner cannot earn $(r_t + \delta)$ (or 12 percent) after taxes, there is no reason for the firm to purchase it.

Now assume that the corporate tax rate is 45 percent. Then if the corporation earns \$1, a corporation tax of \$0.45 (= 0.45 × \$1) is due, leaving \$0.55 avail-able to distribute or reinvest. If θ is the corporate tax rate, the after-tax return from \$1 of corporate profits is $(1 - \theta) \times \$1$.

How does the corporate tax affect the cost of capital? We have to find a before-tax return such that, after the corporate tax, the Leona Corporation receives 12 percent. Calling the user cost of capital C, then C must be the solution to the equation $(1 - .45) \times C = 12$ percent, or C = 21.8 percent. Thus, the corpo-ration is unwilling to purchase the vacuum cleaner unless its before-tax return

is 21.8 percent or greater. Using our algebraic notation, the user cost of capital is the value of C that solves the equation $(1 - \theta) \times C = (r_t + \delta)$, or

$$C = (r_t + \delta)/(1 - \theta). \tag{24.5}$$

So far, we have shown how the corporate tax rate increases the user cost of capital. However, certain provisions in the Income Tax Act such as accelerated depreciation and interest deductibility tend to lower the cost of capital. In Equations (24.1) and (24.2), we defined ψ and λ as the present value of depreciation allowances and the interest deductions that flow from a \$1 investment.[15] First, consider depreciation. Suppose that ψ for the vacuum cleaner is 0.25. In effect, then, depreciation allowances reduce the cost of acquiring the vacuum cleaner by one-fourth, and hence lower by one-fourth the before-tax return that the firm has to earn to attain any given after-tax return. In our example, instead of having to earn 21.8 percent, the Leona Corporation now only has to earn 16.4 percent [$= 21.8 \times (1 - 0.25)$]. Algebraically, depreciation allowances lower the cost of capital by a factor of $(1 - \psi)$, and $C = [(r_t + \delta) \times (1 - \psi)]/(1 - \theta)$.

Referring back to Equation (24.1), recall that if the Leona Corporation were able to immediately write off, or **expense**, the investment, then $\psi = \theta$, and the cost of the asset is reduced by θ. In this case, $C = [(r_t + \delta) \times (1 - \theta)]/(1 - \theta)$, which collapses to $r_t + \delta$. The result is that the corporate tax has no effect on the user cost of capital, and is neutral with respect to the investment decision. Where the asset is written off over a longer period, $\psi < \theta$, the user cost of capital is higher, and investment is lower.

Similarly, we showed that an investment tax credit at rate k reduces the cost of a \$1 acquisition to $(1 - k)$ dollars. In the presence of both depreciation allowances and an investment tax credit, the cost of capital is reduced by a factor of $(1 - \psi - k)$.[16] Thus, the expression for C in Equation (24.5) must be multiplied by $(1 - \psi - k)$ to adjust for the presence of accelerated depreciation and investment tax credits:

$$C = [(r_t + \delta) \times (1 - \psi - k)]/(1 - \theta). \tag{24.6}$$

---

[15] Note from Equation (24.2) that ψ depends on the statutory rate θ, and increases as θ increases.

[16] This assumes the basis used to compute depreciation allowances is not reduced when the firm takes the ITC. Generally, an ITC reduces the cost of an asset for depreciation purposes by the amount of the tax credit, k. Where this is true, the cost of capital is $(1 - k) \times (1 - \psi)$.

Equation (24.6) summarizes how the corporate tax system influences the firm's user cost of capital for investments that are financed from retained earnings or by other equity financing. By taxing corporate income, the tax makes the user cost of capital more expensive, other things being the same. However, depreciation allowances and ITCs tend to lower the user cost of capital.

We now refer back to Equation (24.2). Where debt is used to finance an investment, the deductibility of interest payments reduces the user cost of capital. If λ represents the present value of deductible interest for $1 of capital, then the user cost of capital, C, equals $[(r_t + \delta) \times (1 - \lambda - \psi - k)]/(1 - \theta)$, where depreciation and interest are deductible, and where there is also an ITC. The user cost of capital is lower by λ than for equity-financed investments.

The corporate tax, by itself, increases the user cost of capital. Where an equity-financed investment is expensed, the user cost of capital is unchanged and investment decisions are unaffected. The result is similar for expensing of a debt-financed investment so long as interest is not deductible. Depreciation allowances, ITCs, and interest deductibility all lower the user cost of capital. Such provisions may more than offset the increase in the user cost of capital caused by the corporate tax. Where this occurs, the overall effect is the subsidization of investment by the government, or negative tax rates. In sum, changes in tax rates, depreciation allowances, ITCs, and interest deductibility influence θ, ψ, k, and λ, and affect investment decisions through the user cost of capital.[17]

Effect of user cost on investment. After determining how the tax system affects the user cost of capital, the next step is to ascertain how changes in the user cost influence investment. If the accelerator model is correct, even drastic reductions in the user cost have no impact on investment. On the other hand, if investment is responsive to the user cost of capital, depreciation allowances and ITCs can be powerful tools for influencing investment. Jorgenson (1963) estimated a regression equation for the United States in which the right-hand side variables include (among others) the user cost of capital and concluded that the amount of investment is indeed quite sensitive to tax-induced changes in the cost of capital.[18]

---

[17] For a more comprehensive, and somewhat more technical, study of the neoclassical theory of investment, see Boadway (1979: 265–76).

[18] One survey (see Jog and Mintz, 1989: 92) found that: "Empirical studies of the effectiveness of tax incentives have concluded that investment increases on average by about one half-dollar for each dollar [of] forgone tax revenue. The results of these studies range, however, from 10 cents to as high as 80 cents."

Substantial controversy has swirled around the conclusion that accelerated depreciation and investment tax credits are potent inducements to investment. A number of criticisms have been raised. One of the most important is that the user cost of capital approach takes no account of the importance of expectations. Compare scenario 1, in which firms expect the investment tax credit to be raised considerably next year, and scenario 2, in which investors expect it to be reduced. According to Jorgenson's model, the amount of capital that firms desire depends only on the user cost of capital this period. Therefore, the value of C is identical under both scenarios. This result is implausible; if firms expect the investment tax credit to go up next period, it would make sense to defer some investment until then and vice versa. The fact is that we cannot observe individuals' expectations, and as of now there is no really satisfactory way for estimating how expectations affect behaviour. Given that different assumptions concerning expectations formation can have quite different implications for the effectiveness of tax policy, the sensitivity of investment to the user cost of capital is thrown into question.

Other criticisms of the neoclassical model have also been raised. The key point of the critics is that when assumptions are modified in reasonable ways, the implications for tax policy can differ substantially (see Chirinko, 1993). Nevertheless, it is difficult to choose among models based on different assumptions using standard statistical criteria. Apparently, the sheer complexity of the investment process has stymied attempts to reach a consensus with respect to how sensitive investment is to tax incentives. Some years ago Richard Bird (1980: 60) concluded: "It is frustrating to thus conclude that we know so little, and can know so little, about such an important subject as tax incentives for investment, but, on the evidence available, no other conclusion is possible." Although Bird's conclusion may still be appropriate, recent studies using data now available for individual firms come to more positive conclusions concerning the possible impact of tax incentives on investment.[19]

For the depreciation allowances, ITCs, and interest deductibility to have their full impact on the user cost of capital, corporations must have sufficient income or tax liability against which the deductions and credits can be taken. In Equations (24.1) and (24.2), ψ and λ are positive only if there is otherwise taxable income against which to make the deductions. Although these deductions may be carried forward and used to reduce taxable income in the future, the discounted value of tax savings is less than if the savings could be immediately realized. This would only be avoided if the government either allowed

---

[19] See, for example, Cummins and Hassett (1992).

for negative taxes (i.e., paid subsidies where deductions cannot be taken because of limited income) or paid interest to those who must defer their tax reduction because of insufficient income against which to take the deduction.

Canada permits losses to be carried forward for the following seven taxation years, and to be carried back for the three preceding taxation years through refilings. Due to earlier losses and the carry-forward provision, corporations may pay no tax even in a very profitable year.[20] This is often the situation faced by new enterprises with significant start-up expenses and insufficient income against which to take allowable deductions. Where tax savings have to be deferred, the effect of deductions on the user cost of capital, and on investment decisions, is less than otherwise.

Finally, we must remember that Canada is, to a large extent, an open economy. If the tax law makes investment in Canada more attractive to foreigners, saving from abroad can finance investment in this country. The consequence for tax policy toward investment is the flip side of the relationship we saw in Chapter 21 between tax policy and saving: The possibility of domestic saving flowing out of the country makes it harder to stimulate domestic investment indirectly by manipulating saving, but the possibility of attracting foreign capital makes it easier to stimulate investment through direct manipulation of the user cost of capital. Investment in Canada is not determined, alone, by the amount Canadians save.

Cash flow model. If you ask people in business what determines the amount of investment they make, they likely will mention **cash flow**—the difference between revenues and expenditures for inputs. The more money that is on hand, the greater the capacity for investment. In contrast, cash flow is irrelevant in the neoclassical investment model. In that model, if the return on manufacturing a new kind of computer chip exceeds the opportunity cost, the firm will make the chip, whether it has to borrow the money or use internal sources. But if the return on the project is below the opportunity cost, the firm will not make the chip because the borrowing cost will be higher than the return. Further, even if the firm has internal funds on hand, it will not make the chip, because the firm can make more money by lending the funds to someone else than by investing in a substandard project.

---

[20] Due to corporate-loss carry-overs, federal revenues were reduced by $1.07 billion in 1992. Although an estimate is not available, provincial revenues were probably also reduced by well over half a billion dollars. Department of Finance, *Government of Canada Tax Expenditures, 1995* (Ottawa: 1996), p. 32.

A critical assumption behind the neoclassical story is that the cost to the firm of internal and external funds is the same. Many economists believe that this is a bad assumption. To see why, suppose that the managers of the firm have better information about the prospects for the computer chip than the potential lenders do. In particular, the lenders may view the project as being more uncertain than management and so charge a very high interest rate on the loan. Or they might not be willing to lend any money at all. Thus, the cost of internal funds is lower than the cost of external funds, so the amount of investment depends on the flow of these internal funds, the cash flow.

There does indeed seem to be a statistical relationship between cash flow and investment (see Fazzari, Hubbard, and Petersen, 1988). However, the interpretation of this finding is not quite clear: Do firms invest because their cash flow is high, or do successful firms have both high cash flow and investment? In any case, if the cash flow theory is correct, it has major implications for the impact of taxes on investment behaviour. For example, in the neoclassical model, a lump-sum tax on the corporation would have no effect on investment. In contrast, in a cash flow model, investment would fall. Currently, cash flow models are an active subject of research.[21]

Types of Asset

So far our focus has been the total volume of investment spending without much attention to its composition. It is likely, though, that the tax system affects the types of assets purchased by firms, and investment by industry sector. Purchases of assets that receive relatively generous depreciation allowances tend to be encouraged, other things being the same; and investment is likely to flow to those industries that are more lightly taxed. Several studies have examined the effect of taxes on the user cost of capital, calculating the marginal effective tax rate (METR) for different investments. The METR is the tax paid as a proportion of the income generated by the last, or marginal, dollar of capital invested.

McKenzie and Mintz (1992) computed the METR on various assets and industries before and after the 1987 tax reform. Some of their results are reported

---

[21] A Statistics Canada survey of 186 large corporations in 1992 examined the sources of financing capital expenditures in the corporate sector. Although 1992 was at the bottom of an economic cycle and retained earnings were relatively scarce, operating funds were the most important source, accounting for 27 percent of capital expenditures. Funds from the sale of other assets accounted for another 20 percent, with bond and equity issues accounting for 16 and 13 percent, respectively. Statistics Canada, *Quarterly Financial Statistics for Enterprises*, Second Quarter 1994, Cat. no. 61-008 (Ottawa: October 1994).

in Table 24.6. The table indicates that before the 1987 tax reform, buildings were taxed much more heavily than equipment, with the situation reversed after 1987. Corporate tax reforms dramatically reduced the difference between taxes on buildings and equipment from 1985 to 1990. Inventories were taxed much more heavily than either machinery or buildings both before and after the 1987 reform, in part due to FIFO (first in, first out) accounting as previously discussed. Changes in METRs from 1985 to 1990 were caused by, among other things, reducing depreciation allowances for machinery, phasing out earned depletion for resource industries, reducing provisions for the reserves of financial institutions, increasing the share of realized capital gains to be included in taxable income, and reducing the difference in tax rates applied to manufacturing profits versus other profits.

Because the mix of assets differs among industries, we can expect marginal effective tax rates to differ among industries. Here, too, Table 24.6 shows that tax reform significantly altered the relative treatment of industries—the METR

Table 24.6

Marginal Effective Corporate Tax Rates, Corporate Sector, 1980, 1985, and 1990: (a) by Asset Type, and (b) by Industry

INDUSTRY OR ASSET	1980 CANADA	1985 CANADA	1985 U.S.	1990 CANADA	1990 U.S.
Agriculture, Forestry, Fishing	22.1	31.9	31.7	27.6	26.2
Manufacturing	28.0	21.3	28.8	31.1	27.0
Construction	62.3	45.7	34.4	43.4	24.0
Transport & Storage	10.7	25.5	(12.0)	21.7	8.3
Communications	(5.4)	26.2	23.7	17.5	25.2
Public Utilities	1.0	22.8	2.7	19.8	12.5
Wholesale Trade	41.9	31.5	31.4	34.9	24.8
Retail Trade	35.0	28.4	26.0	30.5	21.3
Services	19.0	26.2	13.8	22.9	16.1
Buildings & Structures	5.4	24.7	12.8	21.1	17.6
Machinery and Equipment	14.2	16.2	1.6	25.6	18.9
Inventories	59.0	37.1	38.4	43.2	28.0
Land	(36.0)	29.3	27.7	20.2	19.0
Total	27.7	26.0	18.9	28.9	20.4

Note: Brackets indicate a negative number.

SOURCE: Kenneth J. McKenzie and Jack M. Mintz, "Tax Effects on the Cost of Capital," in John B. Shoven and John Whalley, eds., *Canada-U.S. Tax Comparisons* (Chicago: University of Chicago Press, 1992), p. 203.

on manufacturing rose sharply following the 1987 reforms, and the METRs for the communication and service industries were lower. The tax system has become more nearly neutral between assets and industries since the 1970s, with this process furthered by the 1987 reforms. As a consequence, excess burdens associated with tax-induced distortions in investment patterns are smaller than previously.

Table 24.6 also shows that the more equal treatment among types of assets and industries was accompanied by a slight increase in the overall marginal effective tax rate on income generated by all assets—from 28 percent in 1980 to 29 percent in 1990. Efficiency gains from equalizing tax rates on different assets need to be weighed against efficiency losses from increasing tax rates on capital in general. Table 24.6 shows that the overall Canadian METR and the METRs applying to individual industries remain much above those in the United States. Since Canada remains heavily dependent on foreign capital to finance investment in Canada, this is of particular concern as it may influence investment decisions being made by Canadian companies and by multinational corporations.

As emphasized earlier, computations like those in Table 24.6 require making a number of assumptions. For example, the value of depreciation allowances depends on the discount rate used by firms [see Equation (24.1)], and different values lead to different answers. Hence, it is possible that different investigators might find results somewhat different from those in the table. There is little doubt, however, that the qualitative picture suggested in the table is correct.[22]

Corporate Finance

In addition to "real" decisions concerning physical investment, the owners of a firm must determine how to finance the firm's operations and whether to distribute profits or retain them. We discuss the effects of taxes on these financial decisions in this section.

Why do firms pay dividends?
Profits earned by a corporation may be either distributed to shareholders in the form of dividends or retained by the company. If it is assumed that (1) outcomes of all investments are known in advance with certainty, and (2) there are no taxes, then the owners of a firm are indifferent in choosing between a dollar of dividends and a dollar of retained earnings. Provided that the stock market accurately reflects the firm's value, $1

---

[22] For a further example of METR calculations for different assets and industries in Canada, see Daly, Mercier, and Schweitzer (1993).

of retained earnings increases the value of the firm's stock by $1. This $1 capital gain is as much income as a $1 dividend receipt. Under the previous assumptions, then, stockholders do not care whether profits are distributed.[23]

Of course, in reality, considerable uncertainty surrounds the outcomes of economic decisions, and corporate income is subject to a variety of taxes. As already noted, when dividends are paid out, the shareholder will often incur a tax liability even with the dividend tax credit; retained earnings generate no concurrent tax liability. True, retention creates a capital gain for the stockholder, but no tax is due until the gain is realized.

On the basis of these observations, it appears that paying dividends is often equivalent to giving away money to the tax collector, and we would expect large firms to retain virtually all of their earnings. Surprise! Between 1987 and 1993, about 55 percent of after-tax corporate profits in Canada were paid out as dividends.[24] This phenomenon continues to baffle many students of corporate finance.

One possible explanation is that dividend payments signal the firm's financial strength. If investors perceive firms that regularly pay dividends as "solid," then paying dividends enhances the value of the firms' shares. In the same way, a firm that reduces its dividend payments may be perceived as being in financial straits. However, although it is conceivable that the owners of a firm would be willing to pay some extra taxes to provide a positive signal to potential shareholders, it is hard to imagine that the benefits gained are worth the huge sums sacrificed. After all, there are certainly ways other than dividend policy for potential investors to obtain information about a firm's status.

Another explanation centres on the fact that not all investors have the same marginal tax rate. High-income individuals currently face rates as high as 54 percent, while untaxed institutions (such as pension funds and universities) face a rate of zero. Those with low marginal tax rates would tend to put a relatively high valuation on dividends, and it may be that some firms "specialize" in attracting these investors by paying out dividends. Feldstein and Green (1983) proposed a model with two types of investors, taxable individuals and untaxed institutions. They show that if stock returns are known in advance with certainty, taxable individuals purchase only shares of firms that pay no dividends, while the untaxed institutions invest exclusively in firms that pay

---

[23] For a rigorous discussion of this argument, see Fama and Miller (1972: 80–81).
[24] Statistics Canada, *National Income and Expenditure Accounts, Quarterly Estimates,* Third Quarter 1994, Cat. no. 13-001 (Ottawa: January 1995).

out all dividends. This is referred to as a **clientele effect**, because firms set their financial policies to cater to different clienteles. In the real world, of course, such dramatic segmentation of stockholders is not observed. According to Feldstein and Green, the reason for this is the uncertainty of stock returns. Even if your tax rate on dividends is high, you will not invest exclusively in low-dividend firms, because when there is uncertainty, it is bad policy to put all your eggs in one basket.

The notion that firms specialize in attracting shareholders with particular tax situations has stimulated empirical research. Studies in this area are hindered by the lack of data on just who owns shares in what firms. However, there is some indirect evidence for the existence of clientele effects (see Scholz, 1992).

Effect of taxes on dividend policy. Because the tax system appears to bias firms against paying dividends (although it by no means discourages them completely), the natural question is how corporate financial policy would change if the tax treatment of dividends vis-à-vis retained earnings were modified. Suppose that for whatever reasons, firms want to pay some dividends as well as retain earnings. One factor that determines the desired amount of retained earnings is the opportunity cost in terms of after-tax dividends paid to stockholders. For example, if there were no taxes, the opportunity cost of $1 of retained earnings would be $1 of dividends. On the other hand, if the stockholder faces a 25 percent marginal income tax rate (even after the dividend tax credit), the opportunity cost of retaining a dollar in the firm is only 75 cents of dividends.[25] In effect, then, the current tax system lowers the opportunity cost of retained earnings.

Over the last several decades, a number of shifts in British tax policy have generated dramatic changes in the opportunity cost of retained earnings in dividends. Data from the United Kingdom therefore provide an excellent opportunity for examining the impact of taxes on firm dividend policy. Poterba and Summers (1985) used British data to estimate a regression in which the dependent variable is the proportion of corporate income paid out as dividends, and the independent variables include the opportunity cost of retained earnings. They found that when the opportunity cost of retained earnings increases by 10 percent, dividend payments go up by about 18 percent.

Several studies have found qualitatively similar results for the United States (see U.S. Department of the Treasury, 1992: 117). It appears, then, that the tax

---

[25] A more careful calculation would take into account the effective capital gains tax liability that is eventually generated by the retention. This is ignored for purposes of illustration.

system has substantially increased the amount of earnings retained by corporations. Some argue that this is desirable because increasing retained earnings makes more money available for investment. Now, it is true that retained earnings represent saving. However, it may be that shareholders take corporate saving into consideration when making their personal financial decisions. Specifically, if owners of the firm perceive that the corporation is saving a dollar on their behalf, they may simply reduce their personal saving by that amount. Thus, although the composition of overall saving has changed, its total amount is just the same as before the retention. There is indeed some econometric evidence that personal and corporate saving are somewhat offsetting.[26] This analysis illustrates once again the pitfalls of viewing the corporation as a separate person with an existence apart from the stockholders.

Debt versus equity finance. Another important financial decision for a corporation is how to raise money. The firm has basically two options. It can borrow money (issue debt). However, the firm must pay interest on its debt, and inability to meet the interest payments or repay the principal may have serious consequences. A firm can also issue shares of stock (equity), and stockholders may receive dividends on their shares.

Recall that under the Canadian tax system, corporations are permitted to deduct payments of interest from taxable income, but are not allowed to deduct dividends. The tax law therefore builds in a bias toward debt financing, although Canada's dividend tax credit somewhat reduces this bias.[27] It is difficult to precisely estimate the impact that this bias has had on the debt–equity choice, but there is evidence that the effective tax rates of debt-financed investments may be significantly lower than on equity-financed investments (see Daly et al., 1993: 117). In one U.S. econometric study, Nadeau (1988) estimated that a 1 percent increase in the tax advantage of debt relative to equity leads to a 0.2 percent increase in the fraction of external funds obtained by issuing debt.

---

[26] See Poterba (1991). Also see Smith (1990: 21–22) for a brief literature summary. Evidence indicates that an additional $1 of saving in the corporate sector is not fully offset by a $1 drop in personal saving. Musgrave and Musgrave (1984) concluded that "the savings impact of the corporate tax dollar is … substantially above that of most other taxes. A policy designed to foster growth, therefore calls for restraint in the taxation of business profits" (p. 662). The shift away from taxes on personal income and toward taxes on corporate income in both the Canadian and U.S. tax reforms of the late 1980s is at odds with this counsel.

[27] In the absence of taxation and given complete certainty with respect to investment outcomes, firms are indifferent between debt and equity finance. This is often referred to as the Modigliani–Miller theorem after the authors who first proved it. See Modigliani and Miller (1958). For a careful intuitive exposition, see Fama and Miller (1972).

Indeed, we might wonder why firms do not use debt financing exclusively. Part of the answer lies in the fact that the outcomes of a firm's decisions are uncertain. There is always some possibility of a very bad outcome and therefore a fear of bankruptcy. The more a firm borrows, the higher its debt payments, and the greater the probability of bankruptcy, other things being the same. Indeed, heavy reliance on debt finance has led some major corporations to declare bankruptcy, including Southland Corporation (parent of the 7-Eleven Food Stores), Campeau Corporation (the parent company of several major department stores), and Olympia and York (a major real estate development company). It has been argued that by encouraging the use of debt, the tax system has had the undesirable effect of increasing probabilities of bankruptcy above levels that otherwise would have prevailed.

TAXATION OF MULTINATIONAL CORPORATIONS

Canadian firms do a substantial amount of business abroad. Canadian-held assets due to direct investment in foreign subsidiaries and branches totalled $125.2 billion at the end of 1994. The income, mostly dividends, flowing back to Canada from these direct investments was $3.5 billion in 1994. Canadians held an additional $78 billion in portfolio investments in foreign stocks and bonds, plus another $43 billion in foreign assets held by the government of Canada; these contributed $6.9 billion in interest and dividends to Canadians in 1994.[28] The tax treatment of foreign-source income is of some importance.

"Active business income" versus "passive investment income." The Canadian approach to the taxation of foreign-source income attempts to be neutral with respect to the place of investment while maintaining the integrity of the Canadian tax system. The government wishes to minimize personal or corporate tax avoidance through financial manipulations. However, it does not wish to discourage foreign investment by Canadians and Canadian corporations, and attempts to ensure that investments abroad are not subject to higher taxes than similar investments made at home. Although it is difficult to achieve these objectives, the following policies are designed with them in mind.

- First, the Income Tax Act attempts to prevent Canadian corporations from easily avoiding or postponing Canadian taxes on "passive"[29]

---

[28] Statistics Canada, *Canada's International Investment Position, 1994*, Cat. no. 67-202 annual (Ottawa: March 1995), pp. 17–25, and 45.
[29] "Passive" income is income from sources other than an active business and includes portfolio income in the form of interest, property income, some capital gains, and income that results from non–arm's length transactions.

investment income by diverting this income (FAPI, or Foreign Accrual Property Income) to foreign corporations and trusts. Income from such "passive" investment in foreign assets must be included in the taxable income in the year in which it is earned. Credit, within limits, is given for foreign taxes paid.

- Second, "active" business income of foreign affiliates is generally subject to tax only in the source country. Foreign affiliates, as **incorporated subsidiaries** and separate legal entities, are subject to the laws of the source country. Where there is a tax treaty between Canada and the source country, the active business income of foreign affiliates goes into an "exempt surplus" account. This income is *not* subject to Canadian tax when earned, and is *not* subject to Canadian tax when paid as dividends to Canadian owners. Most dividends now come from countries with which Canada has a tax treaty.

  Where dividends received come from a foreign affiliate in a country with which Canada does not have a tax treaty, the dividends must be included in the taxable income of the Canadian owner. In this case the Canadian company may credit foreign tax paid on the dividend income against Canadian taxes, up to the amount of the Canadian tax that would otherwise be due. Where tax rates in the source country are as high or higher than in Canada, no additional tax is due.

  In sum, dividends from foreign-source active business income are seldom subject to further tax in Canada. However, source countries, under existing tax treaties, usually impose a 5 percent withholding tax on dividends paid to Canadian companies; so there is a cost involved in repatriating earnings (returning the income to Canada).

- Third, income from **branch** operations of Canadian corporations in foreign countries must be included in the taxable income of the Canadian corporations in the year it is earned. Unincorporated branches are used primarily by financial institutions, where incorporated subsidiaries would deprive foreign depositors of the security provided by the Canadian institution. Credit is given for taxes paid to the source country, and the credit cannot exceed the Canadian tax on the foreign income.[30]

This brief discussion does not reflect the difficulties that may exist in distinguishing between the active business income and passive investment income of controlled affiliates, or the continuing opportunities to avoid Canadian taxation through the use of holding companies located in other countries.[31]

---

[30] Where foreign tax exceeds the Canadian tax due, the excess can be carried forward for crediting purposes for seven years.

[31] See Arnold and Harris (1994) for a very useful summary of Canadian taxation of foreign-source income, particularly as it relates to NAFTA.

Income allocation. It is often difficult to know how much of a multinational firm's total income to allocate to its operations in a given country. The procedure now used for allocating income between domestic and foreign operations is the **arm's length system.** Essentially the domestic and foreign operations are treated as separate enterprises doing business independently ("at arm's length"). The taxable profits of each entity are computed as its own sales minus its own costs.

The problem is that certain factors of production are like public goods from the firm's point of view. Suppose, for example, that all research and development (R&D) is done at the firm's head office. The results of R&D are available to all the company's operations and hence serve as an "input" for all of them. But under a strict application of the arm's length system, the operation at headquarters deducts all the R&D expenditures.

This procedure does not make sense, but it is not at all clear how the R&D expenditures should be allocated across operations. For practical purposes, some fairly arbitrary rules may have to be devised. One way would be to allow certain head-office charges to be allocated among operations based on the sales and assets of each operation. Essentially, the greater a given operation's share of total company assets and sales, the greater the proportion of company public goods it can deduct. This is known as the shares allocation approach.

A potential problem arises if different governments have different rules for allocating incomes between home and foreign operations. International tax treaties usually indicate that countries will try to coordinate their rules.

Evaluation

An evaluation of the Canadian tax treatment of multinational firms requires a careful statement of the policy goal. One possible objective is to maximize worldwide income; another is to maximize national income. A system that is optimal given one goal may not be optimal given another.[32]

Maximization of world income. The maximization of world income requires that the before-tax rate of return on the last dollar invested in each country—the marginal rate of return—be the same.[33] To see why, imagine a situation in which marginal returns are not equal. Then it would be possible to increase world income simply by taking capital from a country where its marginal return was low and moving it to one where the marginal return was high.

---

[32] See Hines (1993) for further details.
[33] As usual, we refer here to rates of return after differences in risk are taken into account.

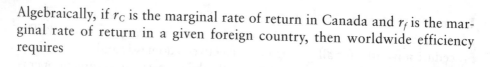

Algebraically, if r_C is the marginal rate of return in Canada and r_f is the marginal rate of return in a given foreign country, then worldwide efficiency requires

$$r_f = r_C. \tag{24.7}$$

What kind of tax system induces profit-maximizing firms to allocate their capital so that the outcome is consistent with Equation (24.7)? The answer hinges on the fact that investors make their decisions on the basis of after-tax returns. They therefore allocate their capital across countries so that the after-tax marginal return in each country is equal. If t_C is the Canadian tax rate and t_f is the foreign tax rate, a firm allocates its capital so that

$$(1 - t_f)r_f = (1 - t_C)r_C. \tag{24.8}$$

Clearly, condition (24.8) is satisfied if and only if t_f equals t_C. Intuitively, if we want capital allocated efficiently from a global point of view, capital must be taxed at the same rate wherever it is located.

The policy implication seems to be that if Canada cares about maximizing world income, it should devise a system that makes its firms' tax liabilities independent of their location. A *full* credit against foreign taxes paid would do the trick. However, as already noted, the Canadian system allows a tax credit *only* up to the amount that Canadian tax on the foreign earnings would have been.

Why is the credit limit present? Our model implicitly assumes the behaviour of foreign governments is independent of Canadian government actions. Suppose Canada announces it will pursue a policy of allowing a full foreign tax credit to its multinational firms. Then foreign governments have an incentive to raise their own tax rates on Canadian corporations virtually without limit. Doing so will not drive out the foreign countries' Canadian firms, because the tax liability for their domestic operations is reduced by a dollar for every dollar foreign taxes are increased.[34] Essentially, the program turns into a transfer from Canada to foreign treasuries. Limiting the credit is an obvious way to prevent this from happening.

---

[34] The amount the foreign government can extract in this way is limited to the firm's tax liability to Canada on its domestic operations. Suppose the firm's tax liability on its Canadian operations is $1,000. If the foreign government levies a tax of $1,000, under a full credit, the firm's Canadian tax liability is zero. If the foreign government raises the tax to $1,001, the firm's domestic tax liability cannot be reduced any further (assuming there is no negative income tax for corporations).

Maximization of national income. At the outset, we noted the importance of defining the objectives of tax policy on foreign-source corporate income. Some have argued that tax policy should maximize not world income, but national income. Some care must be taken in defining national income here. It is the sum of *before*-tax domestically produced income and foreign-source income *after* foreign taxes are paid. This is because taxes paid by Canadian firms to the Canadian government, although not available to the firms themselves, are still part of Canadian income. Thus, domestic income is counted before tax. However, taxes paid to foreign governments are not available to Canadian citizens, so foreign income is counted after tax.

National income maximization requires a different condition than that in Equation (24.7). The difference arises because marginal rates of return must now be measured from the Canadian point of view. According to the Canadian perspective, the marginal rate of return abroad is $(1 - t_f)r_f$—foreign taxes represent a cost from the Canadian point of view and hence are excluded in valuing the rate of return. The marginal return on investments in Canada is measured at the before-tax rate, r_C. Hence, maximization of national income requires

$$(1 - t_f)r_f = r_C. \qquad (24.9)$$

A comparison with Equation (24.7) suggests that under a regime of world income maximization, investments are made abroad until $r_f = r_C$, while if national income maximization is the goal, foreign investment is carried to the point where $r_f = r_C/(1 - t_f)$. In other words, if national income maximization is the goal, the before-tax marginal rate of return on foreign investment is higher than it would be if global income maximization were the goal. [As long as t_f is less than one, $r_C < r_C/(1 - t_f)$.] But under the reasonable assumption that the marginal return to investment decreases with the amount of investment, a higher before-tax rate of return means less investment. In short, from a national point of view, world income maximization results in "too much" investment abroad.

What kind of tax system induces Canadian firms to allocate their capital so that Equation (24.9) is satisfied? Suppose that multinational firms are allowed to *deduct* foreign tax payments from their Canadian taxable income. (For example, a firm with domestic income of $1,000 and foreign taxes of $200 would have a Canadian taxable income of $800.) Given that foreign tax payments are deductible, a firm's overseas return of r_f increases its taxable Canadian income by $r_f(1 - t_f)$. Therefore, after Canadian taxes, the return on the foreign investment is $r_f(1 - t_f)(1 - t_C)$. At the same time, the after-tax return

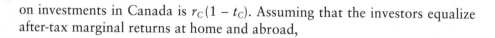

on investments in Canada is $r_C(1 - t_C)$. Assuming that the investors equalize after-tax marginal returns at home and abroad,

$$r_f(1 - t_f)(1 - t_C) = r_C(1 - t_C). \qquad (24.10)$$

Clearly, Equations (24.9) and (24.10) are equivalent. Just divide both sides of Equation (24.10) by $(1 - t_C)$. Because Equation (24.9) is the condition for national income maximization, this implies that deduction of foreign tax payments leads to a pattern of investment that maximizes Canadian income.

Such reasoning may lead to arguments to replace credits for foreign taxes paid with deductions. One important problem with the case for deductions is that the analysis assumes the capital-exporting country can impose the tax rate that maximizes its income, while the capital-importing foreign countries passively keep their own tax rates constant. Feldstein and Hartman (1979) analyzed a model in which the capital-exporting country takes into account the possibility that changes in its tax rate may induce changes in the host countries' tax rates. Suppose, for example, that if Canada lowers its tax rate on capital invested abroad, host governments do the same. In this case, it may be worthwhile for Canada, as a capital-importing country, to tax preferentially income earned abroad. Of course, it is also possible that host governments could choose to raise their tax rates when the Canadian rate goes down. The point is that when interdependent behaviour is allowed, the national income-maximizing tax system generally does not consist of a simple deduction for foreign taxes paid. The effective tax rate on foreign-source income can be either larger or smaller than that associated with deductibility. We conclude that just as in the strictly domestic context, optimal tax theory shows that simple rules of thumb for tax policy do not necessarily achieve a given goal.

In general, the Canadian tax system treats foreign-source income of Canadian corporations, and hence foreign investment, quite favourably. Where foreign tax rates approximate rates in Canada, Canada's policy of exempting foreign-source income from further tax is comparable to giving a credit for the foreign tax. And where taxes are imposed when profits are repatriated, tax credits rather than deductions are permitted. Thus, existing Canadian policy is more in line with maximizing world income rather than national income. Such a policy encourages foreign investment, and better enables Canada to advocate similar policies globally.[35] As a net importer of capital, Canada is likely to be well served by policies that reduce barriers to the international movement of capital.

---

[35] Note that lower tax rates in other countries, such as the United States (as illustrated in Table 24.6), also may encourage Canadians to invest abroad.

CORPORATION TAX REFORM

Toward the beginning of this chapter, we observed that if corporation income were untaxed, individuals would be able to avoid personal income taxation by accumulating income within corporations. Evidently, this would lead to serious equity and efficiency problems. The government's response has been to construct a system that taxes much of corporate income twice: first at the corporate level, where the combined federal and provincial tax rate for large corporations is around 45 percent, and again when dividends are received by individuals and included in their taxable personal income. The dividend tax credit fully alleviates this double taxation only in the case of some small businesses.

The Partnership Method

A number of proposals have been made to integrate personal and corporate income taxes into a single system. The most radical approach is the **partnership method**, sometimes also referred to as **full integration**. Under this approach, all earnings of the corporation during a given year, whether they are distributed or not, are attributed to stockholders just as if the corporation were a partnership. Each shareholder is then liable for personal income tax on his or her share of the earnings. Thus, if Karl owns 2 percent of the shares of Stelco, each year his taxable income includes 2 percent of Stelco's taxable earnings. The corporation tax as a separate entity is eliminated. This was the approach followed in the *Report* of the Royal Commission on Taxation, although it was never enacted.

Partial Imputation

Canada's dividend tax credit, previously discussed, is a **partial imputation** system similar to those used by many countries in the industrialized world. It is "partial" in the sense that only dividend income is attributed or imputed at the personal level. Retained earnings are taxed only at the corporate level. Such a system includes in taxable personal income the dividend, "grossed up" for the corporate tax that has been paid. The personal tax is calculated on the grossed-up amount, and a credit is permitted for the tax paid at the corporate level. In this way, double taxation of corporate income that is paid out as dividends is reduced or eliminated.

As noted earlier, Canada's system of dividend tax credits has serious shortcomings. One that astounds many observers is the granting of credits even when no tax has been paid at the corporate level. A second is the partial nature of the relief provided. Third, examples in Table 24.4 also make clear the unevenness in relief given to different taxpayers.

Other Methods

There exist a number of other ways to reduce the degree of double taxation. These include the **dividend exclusion method**, which exempts dividends from taxation at the level of the individual. Corporate income is taxed but once, at the corporate rate. Hence, the tax paid does not reflect individual circumstances, and a low-income corporate shareholder pays the same tax on dividend income as a high-income shareholder. This is perceived by many to be unfair and, as a result, is seldom used. Alternatively, the **dividend deduction method** allows corporations to deduct dividends in calculating taxable income, just as interest is deductible. The dividends would be taxable to the recipients. In such a case, withholding taxes would have to be used if tax revenues were not to be lost when untaxed corporate profits were paid to foreign shareholders. A few countries use this method. Finally, as a modification of the dividend deduction method, a **split rate** may be used to apply a lower corporate rate (rather than a zero rate) to that part of corporate income distributed as dividends, or a preferential rate may be applied to dividend income under the personal income tax. A number of countries currently apply lower rates to dividend income as a form of relief. Each of these methods eliminates or lessens the double taxation of corporate dividends, but each maintains the corporation tax as a separate entity.[36]

High effective marginal tax rates on income in the corporate sector and the limited relief provided by Canada's dividend tax credit ensure that debate will continue on whether a more complete shift to the "partnership method," or to some other means of lessening distortions created by taxes on capital income, should be adopted.[37] This debate has focused on several issues.

Nature of the Corporation

Those who favour full integration emphasize that a corporation is, in effect, merely a conduit for transmitting earnings to shareholders. It makes more sense to tax the people who receive the income than the institution that happens to pass it along. Those who oppose full integration argue that, in large modern corporations, it is ridiculous to think of the shareholders as partners, and that the corporation is best regarded as a separate entity.

---

[36] A useful survey of methods used by different countries to reduce double taxation of dividends is found in Cnossen (1993).

[37] Jog and Mintz (1989), for example, suggested that "it may be appropriate for Canada to shift from the corporate income tax to the goods and services tax to eliminate the economic distortions that remain(ed) after phase 1 of corporate tax reform" (p. 112).

Administrative Feasibility

Opponents of full integration stress the administrative difficulties that it would create.[38] How are corporate earnings imputed to individuals who hold stock for less than a year? Would shareholders be allowed to deduct the firm's operating losses from their personal taxable income? Proponents of full integration argue that a certain number of fairly arbitrary decisions must be made to administer any complicated tax system. The administrative problems here are no worse than those that have arisen in other parts of the tax laws and can probably be dealt with satisfactorily.

Effects on Efficiency

Those who favour integration point out that the current corporate tax system imposes large excess burdens on the economy, many of which would be eliminated or at least lessened under full integration. The economy would benefit from four types of efficiency gains:

- The misallocation of resources between the corporate and noncorporate sectors would be eliminated.
- To the extent that integration lowered the rate of taxation on the return to capital, tax-induced distortions in savings decisions would be reduced.
- Integration would remove the incentives for "excessive" retained earnings that characterize the current system. Firms with substantial amounts of retained earnings do not have to enter capital markets to finance new projects. Without the discipline that comes from having to convince investors that projects are worthwhile, such firms may invest inefficiently.
- Integration would remove the bias toward debt financing that occurs in the present system because there would be no separate corporate tax base from which to deduct payments of interest. High ratios of debt to equity increase the probability of bankruptcy. This increased risk and the actual bankruptcies that do occur lower welfare without any concomitant gain to society.

Although it is difficult to determine the value of all these efficiency gains, some estimates suggest that they may be quite high.[39]

---

[38] Administrative issues are discussed carefully by the U.S. Department of the Treasury (1992).
[39] For the United States (where no integration currently exists), Fullerton and Rogers (1993: 226) found that the present value of the lifetime efficiency gain from full integration would be more than $10,000 per person.

Opponents of full integration point out that given all the uncertainties concerning the operation of the corporation tax, the supposed efficiency gains may not exist at all. For example, as discussed earlier, to the extent that Stiglitz's view of the tax as equivalent to a levy on pure profits is correct, the tax induces no distortion between the corporate and noncorporate sectors. Similarly, there is no solid evidence that corporations invest internal funds less efficiently than those raised externally.

Effects on Saving

Some argue that full integration would lower the effective tax rate on capital and therefore lead to more saving. As we saw in Chapter 21, this is a non sequitur. From a theoretical point of view, the volume of saving may increase, decrease, or stay the same when the tax rate on capital income decreases. Econometric work has not yet provided a definitive answer.

Effects on the Distribution of Income

If the efficiency arguments in favour of full integration are correct, then in principle, all taxpayers could benefit if it were instituted. Still, people in different groups would be affected differently. For example, those stockholders with relatively high personal income tax rates would tend to gain less from integration than those with low personal income tax rates (see Table 24.4). At the same time, integration would tend to benefit those individuals who receive a relatively large share of their incomes from capital.

Overview

The discussion in this section makes it clear that there is considerable uncertainty surrounding the likely impact of full integration. This simply reflects our imperfect knowledge of the workings of the current system of corporate taxation. There is by no means unanimous agreement that introducing the partnership method would be a good thing. However, on the basis of the existing and admittedly imperfect evidence, many economists have concluded that both efficiency and equity would be enhanced if the personal and corporate taxes were fully integrated.

In addition to full integration, other reforms that would make the corporate income tax more neutral have been promoted. One proposal is for a "cash flow" tax at the corporate level. The base for such a tax would be revenues from the sale of goods and services less operating costs and capital expenditures on physical assets, that is, the cash flow of a firm. Although such a tax has not been used by any country, its advantages remain of interest. Among them are the neutral effect it has on investment spending due to the "expensing" of capital assets, and the reduction of problems associated with measuring economic depreciation and making adjustments for inflation. The interested student is referred to Boadway, Bruce, and Mintz (1987).

SUMMARY

- Corporations are subject to separate federal and provincial income taxes. These taxes account for about 6 percent of all government revenues.

- All provinces and the two territories have their own corporate income taxes. In all but three provinces (Quebec, Ontario, Alberta) these taxes are collected for the provinces by the federal government. The possibilities for tax exporting and interprovincial mobility of factors of production complicate analysis of these taxes.

- Before applying the corporate income tax rate, often around 45 percent, firms may deduct wage payments, interest payments, and depreciation allowances. These are meant to measure the cost of producing revenue. Dividends, the cost of acquiring equity funds, are not deductible.

- Investment tax credits (ITCs) are deducted from the firm's tax bill when particular physical capital assets are purchased. Tax reforms since 1986 have repealed most ITCs. Remaining federal ITCs encourage investment in the Atlantic and Gaspé regions, and investment in scientific research and experimental development (SR&ED). Several provinces use ITCs to encourage specific investments.

- Canada partially integrates its corporate and personal income taxes through a system of dividend tax credits. For certain small businesses the result is relatively complete integration as taxes paid at the corporate level reduce the tax liability on dividends at the individual level. For larger corporations, integration through the dividend tax credit in Canada is far from complete.

- The corporate tax has been viewed either as an economic profits tax or as a partial factor tax. In the former case, the tax is borne entirely by owners of firms, while in the latter the incidence depends on capital mobility between sectors, substitution of factors of production, the structure of consumer demand, and the sensitivity of capital accumulation to the net rate of return.

- The effect of the corporate tax system on physical investment depends on: (1) its effect on the user cost of holding capital goods, and (2) the sensitivity of investment to changes in the user cost. In the accelerator model, investment depends only on output, making the user cost irrelevant. The neoclassical model incorporates both effects.

- In the neoclassical investment model, the user cost of capital is:

$$C = [(r_t + \delta) \times (1 - \psi - \lambda - k)]/(1 - \theta)$$

where C is the user cost, r_t the after-tax interest rate, δ the economic depreciation rate, θ the corporation tax rate, k the ITC, ψ the present value of depreciation allowances per dollar, and λ the present value of deductible interest payments per dollar. Thus, corporate taxation raises the user cost, while ITCs, depreciation allowances, and interest deductibility reduce it.

- Estimates of the effect of the user cost on investment vary greatly. One reason is the critical role played by unobservable changes in expectations.

- Effective tax rates vary between machinery, buildings, and inventory, creating efficiency losses. Reductions in depreciation allowances (CCAs) and ITCs in 1986 and 1987 reduced the differences among tax rates on various assets, but the reforms significantly raised the overall tax rate.

- Due to combined corporate and personal income taxation of dividends, it is somewhat surprising that firms continue to pay out so much in dividends. Dividends may serve as a signal of the firm's financial strength, or be used to cater to particular clienteles.

- Interest deductibility provides a strong incentive for debt finance. However, increasing the proportion of debt may lead to larger bankruptcy costs.

- Most foreign-source income of Canadian subsidiaries is subject to tax only in the source country. Where the Canadian corporate income tax applies, Canadian corporations are allowed tax credits for taxes paid to foreign governments. Complications may arise due to the need to distinguish between passive and active business income, due to the use of holding companies, and due to the need to allocate net income to countries in which a multinational operates.

- One possible corporate tax reform is full integration of the corporate and personal income taxes. Owners of stock would be taxed on their share of corporate income as if they were partners. The corporation tax as a separate entity would cease to exist. Canada's dividend tax credit is a step in this direction, but achieves nothing close to full integration for most income arising in the corporate sector. Other possible reforms include a shift to a "cash flow" tax.

DISCUSSION QUESTIONS

1. Some Canadian political leaders have referred to "those corporate welfare bums" when average tax rates on corporate-source income have been low.

What view of the corporation is implicit in this statement? Contrast this view with the view of conventional economics.

2. Under Canadian law, depreciation allowances are based on the original cost of acquiring the asset. No account is taken for the effects of inflation on the price level over time.

   a. How does inflation affect the real value of depreciation allowances? Organize your answer around Equation (24.1).
   b. When inflation increases, what is the impact on the user cost of capital? Organize your answer around Equation (24.6).
   c. Suggest a policy that could undo the effects on inflation from part (b).

3. Finance Minister Michael Wilson's 1987 tax reform contained several provisions that increased corporate taxes. The White Paper that accompanied the tax reform did not include an analysis of the distributional implications of corporate income tax changes, although it did include analysis regarding the distributional effects of other changes. How would you have distributed an increase in corporate taxes across households? How did the failure to distribute the corporate provisions bias the analysis of the distributional implications, across income classes, of the tax reform as a whole?

4. Canada, through its dividend tax credit, has achieved partial integration of its corporate income tax with its personal income tax. Would a move to more complete integration, or some other means of eliminating "double" taxation of corporate sector income, make sense from the standpoint of the Haig–Simons definition of income? How would you expect a move to full integration to affect the following in Canada: the allocation of capital between the corporate and noncorporate sectors, the share of corporate earnings that is distributed, and the ratio of debt to equity?

REFERENCES

Arnold, Brian J., and Neil H. Harris. "NAFTA and the Taxation of Corporate Investment: A View from within NAFTA." *Tax Law Review* 49, no. 4 (Summer 1994): 560–76 in particular.

Bird, Richard M. *Taxing Corporations.* Montreal: Institute for Research on Public Policy, 1980.

Boadway, Robin W. *Public Sector Economics.* Cambridge: Winthrop, 1979.

Boadway, Robin W., Neil Bruce, and Jack Mintz. *Taxes and Capital Income in Canada: Analysis and Policy.* Toronto: Canadian Tax Foundation, 1987.

Bossons, John. *The Impact of Inflation on Income and Financing of Large Non-Financial Corporations.* Ontario Commission on Inflation Accounting, Supplementary Paper No. 5. Toronto: 1977.

Bradford, David F. "The Incidence and Allocation Effects of a Tax on Corporate Distributions." *Journal of Public Economics* 15, no. 1 (February 1981): 1–22.

Chirinko, Robert S. "Business Fixed Investment Spending: A Critical Survey of Modeling Strategies, Empirical Results, and Policy Implications." *Journal of Economic Literature* 31, no. 4 (December 1993): 1875–911.

Cnossen, Sijbren. "What Kind of Corporation Tax?" *Bulletin for International Fiscal Documentation* 47, no. 1 (January 1993).

Cummins, Jason G., and Keven A. Hassett. "The Effects of Taxation on Investment: New Evidence from Firm Level Panel Data." *National Tax Journal* 45, no. 3 (September 1992): 243–51.

Dahlby, Bev. "The Distortionary Effects of Rising Taxes," in *Deficit Reduction: What Pain, What Gain?* ed. W. Robson and W. Scarth. Toronto: C.D. Howe Institute, 1994.

Daly, Michael J., Pierre Mercier, and Thomas Schweitzer. "Chapter 3: Canada," in *Tax Reform and the Cost of Capital*, ed. D. Jorgenson and R. Landau. Washington, DC: Brookings Institution, 1993.

Douglas, Alan V. "Changes in Corporate Tax Revenue." *Canadian Tax Journal* 38, no. 1 (January/February 1990): 66–81.

Fama, Eugene F., and Merton H. Miller. *The Theory of Finance.* New York: Holt, Rinehart and Winston, 1972.

Fazzari, Steven M., Robert Glenn Hubbard, and Bruce C. Petersen. "Financing Constraints and Corporate Investment." *Brookings Papers on Economic Activity.* Washington, DC: Brookings Institution, 1988, pp. 141–95.

Feldstein, Martin S., and Jerry Green. "Why Do Companies Pay Dividends?" *American Economic Review* 73, no. 1 (March 1983): 17–30.

Feldstein, Martin S., and David Hartman. "The Optimal Taxation of Foreign Source Investment Income." *Quarterly Journal of Economics* 93, no. 4 (November 1979).

Fullerton, Don, and Diane Lim Rogers. *Who Bears the Lifetime Tax Burden?* Washington, DC: Brookings Institution, 1993.

Harberger, Arnold C. "The Incidence of the Corporation Income Tax," in *Taxation and Welfare*, ed. Arnold C. Harberger. Boston: Little, Brown, 1974, pp. 135–62.

Hines, James R. "Review of *U.S. Taxation of International Income: Blueprint for Reform.*" *National Tax Journal* 46, no. 1 (March 1993): 69–71.

Jenkins, Glenn P. *Inflation: Its Financial Impact on Business in Canada.* Ottawa: Economic Council of Canada, 1977.

Jog, Vajay M., and Jack Mintz. "Corporate Tax Reform and Its Economic Impact: An Evaluation of Phase 1 Proposals," in *The Impacts of Tax Reform*, ed. Jack Mintz and John Whalley. Toronto: Canadian Tax Foundation, 1989, pp. 83–124.

Jorgenson, Dale W. "Capital Theory and Investment Behavior." *American Economic Review* 53, no. 2 (May 1963): 247–59.

Jorgenson, Dale W., and Kun-Young Yun. "The Excess Burden of Taxation in the United States." *Journal of Accounting, Auditing and Finance* 6, no. 4 (Fall 1991): 487–508.

McKenzie, Kenneth J., and Jack M. Mintz. "Tax Effects on the Cost of Capital," in *Canada-U.S. Tax Comparisons*, ed. John B. Shoven and John Whalley. Chicago: University of Chicago Press, 1992.

McLure, Charles E., Jr. "The Elusive Incidence of Corporate Income Tax: The State Case." *Public Finance Quarterly* 9, no. 4 (October 1981): 395–413.

Modigliani, F., and M. Miller. "The Cost of Capital, Corporation Finance, and the Theory of Investment." *American Economic Review* 48 (1958): 261–97.

Musgrave, Richard A., and Peggy B. Musgrave. *Public Finance in Theory and Practice*, 4th ed. New York: McGraw-Hill, 1984.

Nadeau, Serge. "A Model to Measure the Effects of Taxes on the Real and Financial Decisions of the Firm." *National Tax Journal* 41, no. 4 (December 1988): 467–81.

Poterba, James M. "Dividends, Capital Gains, and the Corporate Veil: Evidence from Britain, Canada, and the United States," in *National Saving and Economic Performance*, ed. Douglas B. Bernheim and John B. Shoven. Chicago: University of Chicago Press, 1991, pp. 49–71.

Poterba, James M., and Lawrence H. Summers. "The Economic Effects of Dividend Taxation," in *Recent Advances in Corporate Finance*, ed. Edward I. Altman and Marti G. Subrahmanyam. Homewood, IL: Richard D. Irwin, 1985, pp. 227–84.

Scholz, John Karl. "A Direct Examination of the Dividend Clientele Hypothesis." *Journal of Public Economics* 49, no. 3 (December 1992): 261–86.

Smith, Roger S. "Factors Affecting Saving, Policy Tools, and Tax Reform." IMF *Staff Papers* 37, no. 1 (March 1990): 1–70.

Statistics Canada. *Canada's International Investment Position, 1994*. Ottawa: March 1995.

Stiglitz, Joseph E. "Taxation, Corporate Financial Policy, and the Cost of Capital." *Journal of Public Economics* 2 (1973): 1–34.

Treff, Karin, and T. Cook. *Finances of the Nation, 1995*. Toronto: Canadian Tax Foundation, 1995.

Treff, Karin, and David B. Perry. *Finances of the Nation, 1996*. Toronto: Canadian Tax Foundation, 1997.

U.S. Department of the Treasury. *Integration of the Individual and Corporate Tax Systems*. Washington, DC: U.S. Government Printing Office, 1992.

Wilson, Michael H. *Tax Reform 1987: Income Tax Reform*. Ottawa: Department of Finance, June 18, 1987.

Glossary

Ability to Pay Principle
A principle for equitable taxation that maintains the tax burden should be distributed in relation to individuals' ability to pay taxes.

Absolute Tax Incidence
The effect of a tax on the distribution of income when there is no change in either other taxes or government spending.

Accelerated Depreciation
Allowing firms to take depreciation allowances faster than true economic depreciation.

Actuarially Fair Premium
The insurance premium that equals the expected payout for the insurance policy.

Additive Social Welfare Function
An equation defining social welfare as the sum of individuals' utilities.

Ad Valorem Tax
A tax computed as a percentage of the purchase value.

Adverse Selection
The situation that occurs when the people who are most likely to receive benefits from a certain type of insurance are the ones who are most likely to purchase it.

Agenda Manipulation
The process of organizing the order in which votes are taken to assure a favourable outcome.

Alternative Minimum Tax
The tax liability calculated by an alternative set of rules, designed to force individuals with high levels of preference income to incur at least some tax liability.

Altruistic
An individual who feels that he or she is better off when other individuals are better off.

Arm's Length System
A method of calculating taxes for multinational corporations by treating transactions between domestic and foreign operations as if they were separate enterprises.

Arrow–Lind Theorem
The riskiness of a project will decline as the number of individuals who share in the gains and losses increases if the net return from the project is uncorrelated with the returns on other assets.

Arrow's Impossibility Theorem
It is impossible to translate individual preferences into collective preferences without violating at least one of

a specified list of ethically reasonable conditions.

Assessed Value
The value a jurisdiction assigns to a property for tax purposes.

Assessment Ratio
The ratio of a property's assessed value to its market value.

Automatic Stabilizers
Taxes (expenditures) that rise (decline) when the economy is strong and decline (rise) when the economy is weak.

Average Tax Rate
The ratio of the total tax paid to the total tax base.

Balanced-Budget Incidence
The combined distributional effect of levying taxes and the government spending financed by those taxes.

Benefit–Cost Ratio
The ratio of the present value of a stream of benefits to the present value of a stream of costs for a project.

Benefits-Received Principle
Consumers of a publicly provided service should be the ones who pay for it.

Bequest Effect
Individuals save more to counteract the redistribution of income from children to parents implicit in

...e public pension system. The increased saving is used to finance a larger bequest to children.

Block Grant
A grant where few conditions are attached to the use of the funds.

Bracket Creep
When an increase in an individual's nominal income pushes him or her into a higher tax bracket despite the fact that the individual's real income is unchanged. *See also* **Tax Indexing**.

Branch Operation
A part of a Canadian corporation that operates in a foreign country and is *not* established as a separate legal entity through incorporation in the foreign country.

Budget Constraint
The representation of the bundles among which consumers may choose, given their income and the prices they face.

Budget Line
See **Budget Constraint**.

Canada Assistance Plan (CAP)
A federal matching grant to the provinces that funded welfare programs between 1966 and 1996. It was replaced by the CHST grant.

Canada Health and Social Transfer (CHST)
A federal block grant to the provinces that funds spending on welfare, health

care, and postsecondary education.

Canada Pension Plan (CPP)
A contributory pension plan administered by the federal government. Contributions are collected from the employers and employees. The Quebec Pension Plan (QPP) operates in Quebec.

Capital Cost Allowance (CCA)
The term in the Income Tax Act that refers to the depreciation of capital assets allowed for income tax purposes.

Capital Gain (Loss)
An increase (decrease) in the value of an asset.

Capital Intensive
An industry in which the ratio of capital to labour inputs is relatively high.

Capitalization
The process by which a stream of tax liabilities becomes incorporated into the price of an asset.

Cash Flow
The difference between the revenues obtained from the sale of output and assets and the expenditures on the purchase of inputs.

Catastrophic Cap
An upper limit to the amount of an individual's out-of-pocket costs for an illness.

Categorical Grants
Grants for which the donor specifies how the funds can be used.

Centralization Ratio
The proportion of total direct government expendi-

tures made by the central government.

Certainty Equivalent
The value of an uncertain project measured in terms of how much certain income an individual would be willing to give up for the set of uncertain outcomes generated by the project.

Ceteris Paribus
Other things being the same.

Child Tax Benefit
An annual amount paid by the government to parents for each child under the age of 18. The benefit is reduced when the income of parents reaches a certain level and eventually disappears as income rises.

Claw-backs
Provisions in the law that reduce benefits once incomes reach a certain level. The child tax benefit, GST credits, and Employment Insurance benefits are all subject to claw-backs.

Clientele Effect
Firms structure their financial policies to meet different clienteles' needs. Those with low dividend payments attract shareholders with high marginal tax rates, and vice versa.

Club
A voluntary association of people who band together to finance and share some kind of benefit.

Coase Theorem
Provided that transaction costs are negligible, an efficient solution to an externality problem is achieved

as long as someone is assigned property rights, independent of who is assigned those rights.

Coinsurance Rate
The proportion of costs above the deductible for which an insured individual is liable.

Commodity Egalitarianism
The idea that some commodities ought to be made available to everybody.

Compensated Demand Curve
A demand curve that shows how quantity demanded varies with price, holding utility constant.

Compensated Response
How a price change affects quantity demanded when income is simultaneously altered so that the level of utility is unchanged.

Complements
Two goods are complements if an increase in the price of one good leads to decreased consumption of the other good.

Conditional Grants
See Categorical Grants.

Consumer Surplus
The amount by which consumers' willingness to pay for a commodity exceeds the sum they actually have to pay.

Consumption-Type VAT
Capital investments are subtracted from sales in the computation of the value added.

Contract Curve
The locus of all Pareto-efficient points.

Corlett–Hague Rule
Efficient taxation requires taxing commodities that are complementary to leisure at relatively high rates.

Corporation
A state-chartered form of business organization, usually with limited liability for shareholders (owners) and an independent legal status.

Cost-Based Reimbursements
A system under which health care providers report their costs to the government and receive payment in that amount.

Cost–Benefit Analysis
A set of procedures based on welfare economics for guiding public expenditure decisions.

Cost-Effectiveness Analysis
Comparing the cost of the various alternatives that attain similar benefits to determine which one is the cheapest.

Cost-Plus Contract
A contract specifying that a firm is paid a certain fee plus all costs it incurs in completing a project.

Credit Budget
An annual statement that estimates the volume of new direct loans and loan guarantees made by the federal government for the fiscal year.

Crowding Out Hypothesis
Government borrowing decreases private investment by raising the market interest rate.

Customs Duties
Taxes imposed on imported and exported goods and services that may be in addition to all other taxes.

Cycling
When paired majority voting on more than two possibilities goes on indefinitely without a conclusion ever being reached.

Debt
The total amount owed at a given point in time; the sum of all past deficits.

Deductible
The expenses an individual must pay out of pocket before an insurance policy makes any contribution.

Deductions
Certain expenses that may be subtracted from adjusted gross income in the computation of taxable income.

Deficit
The excess of expenditures over revenues during a period of time.

Demand Curve
A graph of the demand schedule.

Demand Schedule
The relation between the price of a good and the quantity demanded, *ceteris paribus*.

Differential Commodity Tax
See Excise Tax.

Differential Tax Incidence
The effect on the income distribution of a change in taxes, with government expenditures held constant.

Diminishing Marginal Rate of Substitution
The marginal rate of substitution falls as we move down along an indifference curve.

Discount Factor
The number by which an amount of future income must be divided to compute its present value. If the interest rate is r and the income is receivable T periods in the future, the discount factor is $(1 + r)^T$.

Discount Rate
The rate of interest used to compute present value.

Discouraged Workers
Individuals who have stopped looking for a job because they think that the probability of finding a job is very low.

District Power Equalization Grant
Grant to local government to raise local revenue to a level that would be achieved if the local property tax base were at a certain hypothetical level.

Dividend Deduction Method
When corporate income distributed as dividends is exempted from taxation at the corporate level in recognition that it is taxed at the individual level. It is a means of reducing "double taxation."

Dividend Exclusion Method
When dividends are exempted from taxation at the individual level in recognition that corporate taxes are applied prior to distribution. It is a means of reducing "double taxation."

Dividend Relief Approach
A method for relieving double taxation under which the corporation deducts dividends paid to the stockholders.

Dividend Tax Credit
The credit allowed to taxpayers receiving taxable dividends in recognition of taxes that may have been paid on income at the corporate level prior to distribution.

Double Declining Balance Method
The depreciation rate is twice the rate applied under the declining balance method.

Double-Peaked Preferences
If, as a voter moves away from his or her most preferred outcome, utility goes down, but then goes back up again.

Double Taxation
Taxing corporate income first at the corporate level, and again when it is distributed to shareholders.

Earnings Test
An individual whose earnings exceed a certain ceiling faces a reduction in concurrent social security benefits.

Econometrics
The statistical tools for analyzing economic data.

Economic Depreciation
The extent to which an asset decreases in value during a period of time.

Economic Incidence
The change in the distribution of real income induced by a tax.

Economic Profit
The return to owners of a firm above the opportunity costs of all the factors used in production. Also called supranormal or excess profit.

Edgeworth Box
A device used to depict the distribution of goods in a two good–two person world.

Efficient
See **Pareto Efficient.**

Effluent Fee
The payment that a firm has to make if it emits a pollutant.

Elasticity of Substitution
A measure of the ease with which one factor of production can be substituted for another.

Empirical Work
Analysis based on observation and experience as opposed to theory.

Employment Rate
The ratio of the total number of employed individuals to the total working-age population.

Endowment Point
The consumption bundle that is available if there are no exchanges with the market.

Entitlement Programs
Programs whose expenditures are determined by the number of people who qualify, rather than preset budget allocations.

Equilibrium
A situation that tends to be maintained unless there is an underlying change in the system.

Equivalent Variation
A change in income that has the same effect on utility as a change in the price of a commodity.

Established Program Financing (EPF)
A federal block grant to the provinces that funded health care and postsecondary education. It was replaced by the CHST grant in 1996.

Ex Ante Redistribution
Occurs when an individual's expected payout from a program does not equal his or her contribution or premium.

Excess Burden
A loss of welfare above and beyond taxes collected. Also called welfare cost or deadweight loss.

Excise Tax
A tax levied on the purchase of a particular commodity.

Exclusionary Zoning Laws
Statutes that prohibit certain uses of land.

Exemption
When calculating taxable income, an amount per family member that can be subtracted from adjusted gross income.

Expected Loss
The probability of a loss times the magnitude of the loss.

Expected Utility
The probability of an outcome times the utility attained with that outcome summed over all possible outcomes. *See* **Expected Utility Model**.

Expected Utility Model
A framework for analyzing decision making under uncertainty. Individuals are assumed to choose the action that maximizes the probability of an outcome times the utility attained with that outcome summed over all possible outcomes.

Expected Wealth
The probability that an individual's wealth level takes on a particular value multiplied by that wealth level and summed over all possible wealth levels.

Expenditure Incidence
The impact of government expenditures on the distribution of real income.

Expenditure Tax
See **Personal Consumption Tax**.

Expensing
Deducting the entire value of an asset in the computation of taxable income.

Experience Rated
A method of determining what unemployment insurance tax rate a firm should pay based on the firm's past layoff experience.

Ex Post Redistribution
An insurance scheme that redistributes wealth from those who do not suffer losses to those that did.

External Debt
The amount a government owes to foreigners.

Externality
An activity of one entity affects the welfare of another entity in a way that is outside the market.

Factors of Production
See **Inputs**.

Federal Government
A public sector with both centralized and decentralized levels of decision making.

Federal Sales Tax (FST)
The federal sales tax imposed on manufactured goods, known also as the Manufacturers' Sales Tax (MST), prior to the enactment of the GST.

Federal Tax Payable
The amount of income tax levied by the federal government on a taxpayer.

Fiscal Federalism
A community of higher order that coordinates its activities with the activities of the rest of society with a view to the common good.

Fiscally Induced Migration
Migration response to differences in net fiscal benefits among regions.

Flat Tax
A tax schedule for which the marginal tax rate is constant throughout the entire range of incomes.

Flow Variable
A variable that is measured over a period of time. *See also* **Stock Variable**.

paper Effect
A dollar received by the community in the form of a grant to its government results in greater public spending than a dollar increase in community income.

Foreign Subsidiary
A company incorporated abroad, but owned by a Canadian corporation.

Foundation Aid
Grant designed to assure a minimum level of expenditure.

Foundation Grant
Provincial per student grants to local jurisdictions that ensure a minimum basic level of expenditure on education and do not vary with local spending.

Free-Rider Problem
The incentive to let other people pay for a public good while you enjoy the benefits.

Full Integration
See **Partnership Method.**

Full Loss Offset
Allowing individuals to deduct from taxable income all losses on capital assets.

Functional Distribution of Income
The way income is distributed among people when they are classified according to the inputs they supply to the production process (for example, landlords, capitalists, labourers).

Functional Finance
Using fiscal policy to keep aggregate demand at the desired level, regardless of the impact on deficits.

General Agreement on Tariffs and Trade (GATT)
A multinational pact that regulates international trade practices. GATT allows a country to grant an export rebate on certain taxes.

General Equilibrium Analysis
The study of how various markets are interrelated.

General Sales Tax
A tax levied at the same rate on the purchase of all commodities. Also referred to as broad-based sales tax.

Generation Skipping
Arranging an estate in such a way that one or more generations avoid paying taxes on it.

Global System
A system under which an individual is taxed on income whether it is earned in the home country or abroad.

Goods and Services Tax (GST)
Canada's value-added tax. *See* **Value-Added Tax.**

Gross Income–Type VAT
No deductions are allowed for capital investments when calculating value added.

Gross Replacement Rate
The proportion of pretax earnings replaced by unemployment insurance.

Guaranteed Income Supplement (GIS)
A negative income tax program for the elderly. Bene-fits are reduced by 50 percent for each dollar of income received by the pensioner.

Haig–Simons (H-S) Definition of Income
Money value of the net increase to an individual's power to consume during a period.

Hicks–Kaldor Criterion
A project should be under-taken if it has a positive net present value, regard-less of the distributional consequences.

Horizontal Equity
People in equal positions should be treated equally.

Horizontal Summation
The process of creating a market demand curve by summing the quantities demanded by each individ-ual at every price.

Impure Public Good
A good that is rival to some extent. *See* **Public Good.**

Imputed Rent
The net monetary value of the services a home-owner receives from a dwelling.

Incentive Contract
A contract specifying that the contracting firm receives a fixed fee plus some fraction of the cost of the project.

Income Allocation Formula
A formula that allocates a firm's income (based on sales and wages) among the provinces in order to deter-mine how much income tax should be paid in each province.

Income Effect
The effect of a price change on the quantity demanded due exclusively to the fact that the consumer's real income has changed.

Income Splitting
Lowering total family income tax payments by assigning ownership of income-producing assets to the members of the family with lowest incomes.

Incorporated Subsidiary
A foreign corporation owned by a Canadian corporation, but established as a separate legal entity in the country in which it is located.

Independence of Irrelevant Alternatives
Society's ranking of two different projects depends only on individual's rankings of the two projects, not on how individuals rank the two projects relative to other alternatives.

Indexed for Inflation
Tax credits and tax brackets are adjusted by the increase in the price level to prevent an increase in the real tax burden.

Indifference Curve
The locus of consumption bundles that yield the same total utility.

Indifference Map
The collection of all indifference curves.

Inferior Good
A good whose demand decreases as income increases.

Inheritance Tax
Tax levied on an individual receiving an inheritance.

In-Kind Transfers
Payments from the government to individuals in the form of commodities or services rather than cash.

Inputs
Factors that are used in the production process.

Internal Debt
The amount that a government owes to its own citizens.

Internal Rate of Return
The discount rate that would make a project's net present value zero.

Intertemporal Budget Constraint
The schedule showing all feasible consumption levels across time.

Inverse Elasticity Rule
For goods that are unrelated in consumption, efficiency requires that tax rates be inversely proportional to elasticities.

Investment Tax Credit (ITC)
A reduction in tax liability equal to some portion of the purchase price of an asset.

Invoice-Credit Method
Each firm is liable for taxes on total sales, but can claim the taxes already paid by suppliers as a credit against this liability, provided this tax payment is verified by invoices from suppliers.

Labour Force
The total number of individuals who are employed or unemployed and willing to work.

Labour Force Participation Rate
The labour force as a percentage of the working-age population.

Labour Intensive
An industry in which the ratio of capital to labour inputs is relatively low.

Laffer Curve
A graph of the tax rate–tax revenue relationship.

Life-Cycle Model
Individuals' consumption and saving behaviour during a given year is the result of a planning process that considers their lifetime economic circumstances.

Lindahl Prices
The tax share an individual must pay per unit of public good.

Linear Income Tax Schedule
See **Flat Tax.**

Loan Guarantee
Promise to repay principal and interest on a loan in case the borrower defaults.

Local Public Good
A public good that benefits only the members of a particular community.

Lock-In Effect
The disincentive to change portfolios that arises because an individual incurs a tax on realized capital gains.

Logrolling
The trading of votes to obtain passage of a package of legislative proposals.

mp-Sum Tax
tax whose value is independent of the individual's behaviour.

Majority Voting Rule
One more than half of the voters must favour a measure for it to be approved.

Marginal
Incremental, additional.

Marginal Cost
The incremental cost of producing one more unit of output.

Marginal Cost of Public Funds (MCF)
The cost to the economy of raising an additional dollar of tax revenue.

Marginal Effective Tax Rate
Tax paid as a proportion of the income generated by the last, or marginal, dollar of capital invested.

Marginal Rate of Substitution
The rate at which an individual is willing to trade one good for another; it is the slope of an indifference curve.

Marginal Rate of Transformation
The rate at which the economy can transform one good into another good; it is the slope of the production possibilities frontier.

Marginal Tax Rate
The proportion of the last dollar of income taxed by the government.

Marriage Neutral
Individuals' tax liabilities are independent of their marital status.

Maximin Criterion
Social welfare depends on the utility of the individual who has the minimum utility in the society.

Maximum Insurance Earnings (MIE)
The maximum annual earnings that can be used to determine a worker's unemployment insurance benefits.

Means-Tested
A spending program whose benefits flow only to those whose financial resources fall below a certain level.

Mechanistic View of Government
Government is a creation of individuals to better achieve their individual goals.

Median Voter
The voter whose preferences lie in the middle of the set of all voters' preferences; half the voters want more of the item selected, and half want less.

Median Voter Theorem
As long as all preferences are single-peaked and several other conditions are satisfied, the outcome of majority voting reflects the preferences of the median voter.

Merit Good
A commodity that ought to be provided even if people do not demand it.

Monopoly
A market with only one seller of a good.

Moral Hazard
Arises in an insurance market when an individual can influence the probability, or the magnitude, of a loss by undertaking an action that the insurance company cannot observe.

Multiple Regression Analysis
An econometric technique for estimating the parameters of an equation involving a dependent variable and more than one explanatory variable.

Natural Monopoly
A situation in which factors inherent to the production process lead to a single firm supplying the entire industry's output.

Negative Income Tax
An income support program that provides a basic level of support and that allows recipients to keep a fraction of their earnings.

Neoclassical Model
A model in which the cost of capital is the primary determinant of the amount of capital investment.

Net Fiscal Benefits
The value of publicly provided services minus their cost to the recipient.

Net Income–Type VAT
The tax base for the VAT is based on net income so that depreciation is excluded from the base.

Net Replacement Rate
The proportion of after-tax income replaced by unemployment insurance.

Net Wage
The wage after taxes.

Net Wealth Tax
A tax based on the difference between the market value of all the taxpayer's assets and liabilities.

Neutral Taxation
Taxing each good at the same rate.

Nominal Amounts
Amounts of money that are valued according to the price levels that exist in the year that the amount is received.

Nominal Income
Income measured in terms of current prices.

Nominal Interest Rate
The interest rate observed in the market.

Normal Good
A good whose demand increases as income increases.

Normative Economics
The study of whether or not the economy produced socially desirable results.

Not in the Labour Force
Individuals who do not have a job and are not looking for a job.

Old Age Security Pension (OAS)
A federal pension for those 65 years and older. There is a claw-back of benefits for high-income recipients.

Organic View of Government
The political philosophy that views society as a natural organism with the government as its heart.

Original Position
An imaginary situation in which people have no knowledge of what their economic status in society will be.

Overlapping Generations Model
A model that takes into account the fact that several different generations may coexist simultaneously.

Parameters
In econometrics, the coefficients of the explanatory variables that define the relationship between a change in an explanatory variable and a change in the dependent variable.

Pareto Efficient
An allocation of resources such that no person can be made better off without making another person worse off.

Pareto Improvement
A reallocation of resources that makes at least one person better off without making anyone else worse off.

Partial Equilibrium Models
Models that study only one market and ignore possible spillover effects in other markets.

Partial Factor Tax
Tax levied on an input in only some of its uses.

Partial Imputation
An income tax measure in which "part" of the income at the corporate level is attributed to the individual shareholder and taxed at the individual's tax rate. Canada's dividend tax credit is such a measure.

Partnership Method
When all earnings of a corporation, whether distributed or not, are attributed to shareholders as would be done in a partnership, and are taxed at the personal income-tax rate of the individual shareholders.

Pay-As-You-Go
A public pension system under which benefits paid to current retirees come from payments made by current workers.

Peak
A point on the graph of an individual's preferences at which all the neighbouring points have lower utility.

Pecuniary Externality
Effects on welfare that are transmitted via the price system.

Percentage Equalization Grant
Provincial grants to local jurisdictions that increase as local spending increases. Such grants, as a share of per student spending on education, may increase as the local tax base decreases.

Perfect Price Discrimination
When a producer charges each person the maximum he or she is willing to pay for the good.

...onal Consumption Tax
A system under which each household's tax base is its consumption expenditures.

Personal Expenditure Tax
See **Personal Consumption Tax.**

Pigouvian Tax
A tax levied on each unit of a polluter's output in an amount equal to the marginal damage that it inflicts at the efficient level of pollution.

Positive Economics
The study of how the economy actually functions (as opposed to how it ought to function).

Potential Pareto Improvement
A reallocation of resources where the gains achieved by those who are made better off exceed the losses sustained by those who are made worse off.

Poverty Gap
The amount of money that would be required to raise the incomes of all poor households to the poverty line, assuming that the transfers would induce no changes in behaviour.

Poverty Line
A fixed level of real income considered enough to provide a minimally adequate standard of living.

Present Value
The value today of a certain amount of money to be paid or received in the future.

Present Value Criteria
Rules for evaluating projects stating that (1) only projects with positive net present value should be carried out; and (2) of two mutually exclusive projects, the preferred project is the one with the higher net present value.

Price Elasticity of Demand
The absolute value of the percentage change in quantity demanded divided by the percentage change in price.

Price Elasticity of Supply
The absolute value of the percentage change in quantity supplied divided by the percentage change in price.

Price Taker
An agent unable to affect the price of a good.

Principal–Agent Problem
When one person (the principal) wants another person (the agent) to perform a task, the principal has to design the agent's incentives so that the principal's expected gain is maximized.

Privatization
The process of changing ownership or control of an enterprise from the public to the private sector.

Production Possibilities Frontier
The set of all the feasible combinations of goods that can be produced with a given quantity of efficiently employed inputs.

Progressive
A tax system under which an individual's average tax rate increases with income.

Proportional
A tax system under which an individual's average tax rate is the same at each level of income.

Public Economics
See **Public Finance.**

Public Finance
The field of economics that analyzes government taxation and spending policies.

Public Good
A good that is not rival in consumption; the fact that one person benefits from this good does not prevent another person from doing the same simultaneously.

Public Sector Economics
See **Public Finance.**

Pure Public Good
See **Public Good.**

Quebec Pension Plan (QPP)
The Quebec equivalent of the Canada Pension Plan.

Ramsey Rule
To minimize total excess burden, tax rates should be set so that the tax-induced percentage reduction in the quantity demanded of each commodity is the same.

Random Error
The term of a regression equation representing the unexplained difference between the dependent variable and its value as predicted by the model.

Rate Schedule
A list of the tax liabilities associated with each level of taxable income.

Real Amounts
Amounts of money adjusted for changes in the general price level.

Real Income
A measure of income taking into account changes in the general price level.

Real Interest Rate
The nominal interest rate corrected for changes in the level of prices by subtracting the expected inflation rate.

Realized Capital Gain
A capital gain resulting from the sale of an asset.

Regional Extended Benefits
A feature of the unemployment insurance program whereby unemployed workers in high-unemployment regions receive benefits for a longer period of time.

Registered Education Savings Plan (RESP)
Plan to encourage saving for education. Contributions are not deductible, but interest on the plan would be taxable to the beneficiary (i.e., student) of the plan at the time of withdrawal. The beneficiary may have a much lower tax rate than the contributor (i.e., parent). Income earned on RESP accounts is not taxed as it accrues.

Registered Home-ownership Savings Plan (RHOSP)
A savings plan (terminated in 1985) that permitted specified amounts (to a maximum of $10,000) if placed in an RHOSP to be deducted in calculating taxable income. Funds, accumulated contributions plus earned interest, could be withdrawn, tax free, from the RHOSP for "first home" purchases.

Registered Pension Plan (RPP)
Pension plans operated by public and private organizations, funded by employers and employee contributions, and benefiting from the deferral of taxes on contributions and the income earned by the plans.

Registered Retirement Savings Plan (RRSP)
Savings plans for employees and the self-employed that permit a specified annual contribution, if placed in an RRSP, to be deducted in calculating taxable income. The tax on the contribution and the interest earned in the RRSP is deferred.

Regression Coefficient
See **Parameters**.

Regression Line
The line that provides the best fit through a scatter of points.

Regressive
A tax system under which an individual's average tax rate decreases with income.

Regulatory Budget
An annual statement of the costs imposed on the economy by government regulations. (Currently, there is no such budget.)

Repatriate
To return the earnings of a subsidiary to its parent company.

Retirement Effect
Public pensions may induce an individual to retire earlier, which means that, *ceteris paribus*, he or she has to save more to finance a longer retirement period.

Risk Averse
An individual who would prefer to receive a given amount of wealth with certainty rather than take a chance on an uncertain opportunity that offers the same expected wealth.

Risk Neutral
An individual who is indifferent between receiving a given amount of wealth with certainty and taking a chance on an uncertain opportunity that offers the same expected wealth.

Risk Pooling
The mechanism whereby risk is reduced when a number of risky projects or risky assets are combined.

Risk Seeker
An individual who would prefer to take a chance on an uncertain opportunity rather than a sure thing that offers the same expected wealth.

Spreading
mechanism whereby risk is reduced when a number of individuals share the gains and losses from a risky project.

Rivalness of Consumption
When one person benefiting from consumption of a specific good prevents another person from doing so simultaneously.

Selective Sales Tax
See **Excise Tax.**

Seniors Benefit
A new income-tested benefit for those 65 years and older that replaces the OAS and GIS programs in 2001.

Shadow Price
The underlying social cost of an input.

Single-Peaked Preferences
Utility consistently falls as a voter moves away from his or her most preferred outcome.

Size Distribution of Income
The way that total income is distributed across income classes.

Slope
The change in the variable measured on the vertical axis divided by the change in the variable measured on the horizontal axis.

Social Insurance
Government programs that replace income losses that are, at least in part, outside personal control.

Social Rate of Discount
The rate at which society is willing to trade off present

consumption for future consumption.

Social Security Wealth
The present value of expected future social security benefits.

Social Welfare Function
A function reflecting society's views on how the utilities of its members affect the well-being of society as a whole.

Split-Rate Method
When a lower corporate income tax rate is applied to the share of corporate income distributed as dividends than to corporate income that is retained. It is a modification of the "dividend deduction method."

Spouse's Allowance (SA)
An income-tested benefit paid to the spouse of an OAS pensioner or to a widow or widower.

Standard Error
A statistical measure of how much an estimated parameter might vary from its true value.

Statistically Significant
When the standard error of a regression coefficient is low in relation to the size of the estimated parameter.

Statutory Incidence
Indicates who is legally responsible for a tax.

Stock Variable
Variable that is measured as of a given point in time. *See also* **Flow Variable.**

Subsidiary
A company owned by one corporation, but chartered

separately from the parent corporation.

Substitutes
Two goods are substitutes if an increase in the price of one good leads to increased consumption of the other good.

Substitution Effect
The tendency of an individual to consume more of one good and less of another because of a change in the two goods' relative prices.

Supply Schedule
The relation between market price of a good and the quantity that producers are willing to supply, *ceteris paribus.*

Taxable Income
The amount of income subject to tax.

Tax Amnesty
Allowing delinquent taxes to be paid without prosecution.

Tax Arbitrage
Producing a risk-free profit by exploiting inconsistencies in the tax act.

Tax Avoidance
Altering behaviour in such a way to reduce your legal tax liability.

Tax Credit
A subtraction from tax liability (as opposed to a subtraction from taxable income).

Tax Effort
The ratio of tax collections to tax capacity.

Tax Evasion
Not paying taxes legally due.

Tax Expenditure
A loss of tax revenue because some item is excluded from the tax base.

Tax Indexing
Automatically adjusting the tax schedule to compensate for inflation so that an individual's real tax burden is independent of inflation.

Tax Life
The number of years an asset can be depreciated.

Tax Prepayment Approach
Under a personal consumption tax, durables are taxed when they are purchased, and future consumption benefits generated by the durable are not taxed.

Tax Shifting
The difference between statutory incidence and economic incidence.

Tax Wedge
The tax-induced difference between the price paid by consumers and the price received by producers.

Territorial System
A system under which an individual earning income in a foreign country owes taxes only to the host government.

Theory of the Second Best
In the presence of existing distortions, policies that in isolation would increase efficiency can decrease it, and vice versa.

Third-Party Payment
Payment for services by someone other than the provider or the consumer.

Time Endowment
The maximum number of hours per year an individual can work.

Time Inconsistency of Optimal Policy
The best fiscal policy, after individuals and firms have made investment decisions and other commitments, may be different from the best policy before those decisions and commitments were made.

Transfer Dependency
Response of migration to regional differences in unemployment benefits leading to a less efficient labour market by inhibiting migration as a result of wage differentials.

Turnover Tax
A tax whose base is the total value of sales at each level of production.

Two-Part Tariff
A system under which a consumer first pays a lump sum for the right to purchase a good and then pays a price for each unit of the good actually purchased.

Uncompensated Response
The total change in quantity in response to a price change, incorporating both the substitution and the income effects.

Underground Economy
Those economic activities that are either illegal, or legal but hidden from tax authorities.

Unearned Income
Income, such as dividends and interest, that is not directly gained through supplying labour.

Unemployed
Individuals who do not have a job, but are available for work and have made an effort to find a job.

Unemployment Rate
The percentage of the labour force that is unemployed.

Unit Tax
A tax levied as a fixed amount per unit of commodity purchased.

Unrealized Capital Gain
A capital gain on an asset not yet sold.

User Cost of Capital
The opportunity cost to a firm of owning a piece of capital.

User Fee
A price paid by users of a government-provided good or service.

Utilitarian Social Welfare Function
An equation stating that social welfare is some function of individuals' utilities.

Utility
The amount of satisfaction a person derives from consuming a particular bundle of commodities.

Utility Definition of Horizontal Equity
A method of classifying people of "equal positions"

rms of their utility

Utility Possibilities Curve
A graph showing the maximum amount of one person's utility given each level of utility attained by the other person.

Value Added
The difference between sales and the cost of purchased material inputs.

Value-Added Tax (VAT)
A percentage tax on value added at each stage of production.

Value of the Marginal Product (VMP)
The value of the additional output obtained by using an additional unit of an input.

Vertical Equity
Distributing tax burdens fairly across people with different abilities to pay.

Vertical Summation
The process of creating an aggregate demand curve for a public good by adding the prices each individual is willing to pay for a given quantity of the good.

Voting Paradox
With majority voting, community preferences can be inconsistent even though each individual's preferences are consistent.

Vouchers
Grants earmarked for particular commodities, such as medical care or education, given to individuals.

Wagner's Law
Government expenditures rise faster than incomes.

Wealth Neutrality
Expenditure on a public good or service in a jurisdiction is not dependent on its level of wealth. If school expenditures are determined by the provincial government they are less likely to vary according to the wealth of a local jurisdiction.

Wealth Substitution Effect
Individuals save less in anticipation of the fact that they will receive public pension benefits after retirement, *ceteris paribus*.

Welfare Economics
The branch of economic theory concerned with the social desirability of alternative economic states.

Workfare
Able-bodied individuals who qualify for income support receive it only if they agree to participate in a work-related activity.

Yearly Maximum Pensionable Earnings (YMPE)
The maximum earnings that are used to compute an individual's CPP contribution and benefit.

Year's Basic Exemption (YBE)
An individual's CPP contributions are based on his or her annual earnings in excess of the YBE.

Index

747

cut here

STUDENT REPLY CARD

In order to improve future editions, we are seeking your comments on *Public Finance in Canada,* First Canadian Edition, by Rosen, Boothe, Dahlby, and Smith. Please answer the following questions and return this form via Business Reply Mail. Your opinions matter. Thank you in advance for sharing them with us!

Name of your college or university: _____

Major program of study: _____

Course title: _____

Were you required to buy this book?   yes _____   no _____

Did you buy this book new or used?   new _____   used _____ ($_____)

Do you plan to keep or sell this book?   keep _____   sell _____

Is the order of topic coverage consistent with what was taught in your course?

cut here

fold here

Are there chapters or sections of this text that were not assigned for your course? Please specify:

Were there topics covered in your course that are not included in this text? Please specify:

What did you like most about this text?

What did you like least?

If you would like to say more, we'd love to hear from you. Please write to us at the address shown on the reverse of this card.

- - - - - - *cut here* - ¬

- - - - - - - - - - - - - *fold here* - - - - - - - - - - - - - - - -

MAIL ⟫ POSTE

Canada Post Corporation
Société canadienne des postes

Postage paid — Port payé
if mailed in Canada — si posté au Canada
Business Reply — Réponse d'affaires

0183560299   01

```
Att.: Senior Sponsoring Editor
College Division
McGRAW-HILL RYERSON LIMITED
300 WATER STREET
WHITBY ON   L1N 9Z9
```

cut here